# VISUALIZING TECHNOLOGY
## Premium Media Site

## Improve your grade with hands-on tools and resources!

- Master *Key Terms* to expand your vocabulary.
- Assess your knowledge with fun *Crossword Puzzles* and *Jeopardy* games.
- Prepare for exams by taking practice quizzes in the *Online Chapter Review*.
- Download *Student Data Files* for the applications projects in each chapter.

And for even more tools, you can access the following Premium Resources using your Access Code.
Register now to get the most out of *Visualizing Technology!*

- *Viz Clips* are short videos that demonstrate key concepts from each chapter.*
- Interactive *IT Simulation*s for each chapter let you work through an activity, covering key topics, in a lab environment.*

*Access code required for these premium resources

## Your Access Code is:

Note: If there is no silver foil covering the access code, it may already have been redeemed, and therefore may no longer be valid.
In that case, you can purchase online access using a major credit card or PayPal account. To do so, go to **www.pearsonhighered.com/geoghan**,
select your book cover, click on "Buy Access" and follow the on-screen instructions.

## To Register:

- To start you will need a valid email address and this access code.
- Go to **www.pearsonhighered.com/geoghan** and scroll to find your text book.
- Once you've selected your text, on the Home Page, click the link to access the Student Premium Content.
- Click the Register button and follow the on-screen instructions.
- After you register, you can sign in any time via the log-in area on the same screen.

## System Requirements

Windows 7 Ultimate Edition; IE 8
Windows Vista Ultimate Edition SP1; IE 8
Windows XP Professional SP3; IE 7
Windows XP Professional SP3; Firefox 3.6.4
Mac OS 10.5.7; Firefox 3.6.4
Mac OS 10.6; Safari 5

## Technical Support

http://247pearsoned.custhelp.com

Complete
# VISUALIZING
# TECHNOLOGY

# Complete

# VISUALIZING TECHNOLOGY

## Second Edition

**Debra Geoghan**
*Bucks County Community College*

PEARSON

Boston   Columbus   Indianapolis   New York   San Francisco
Upper Saddle River   Amsterdam   Cape Town   Dubai   London
Madrid   Milan   Munich   Paris   Montreal   Toronto   Delhi   Mexico City
Sao Paulo   Sydney   Hong Kong   Seoul   Singapore   Taipei   Tokyo

**Editor in Chief:** Michael Payne
**Executive Editor:** Jenifer Niles
**Product Development Manager:** Laura Burgess
**Editorial Project Manager:** Anne Garcia
**Development Editor:** Linda Harrison
**Editorial Assistant:** Andra Skaalrud
**Director of Digital Development:** Taylor Ragan
**Executive Editor, Digital Learning & Assessment:** Paul Gentile
**Digital Editor:** Eric Hakanson
**Production Media Project Manager:** John Cassar
**Director of Marketing:** Maggie Moylan Leen
**Marketing Coordinator:** Susan Osterlitz

**Marketing Assistant:** Darshika Vyas
**Managing Editor:** Camille Trentacoste
**Sr. Production Project Manager/Procurement IT Lead:** Natacha Moore
**Senior Art Director:** Jonathan Boylan
**Cover Art:** © Shutterstock/Lynn Watson, Shutterstock/FikMik, and Fotolia/L_amica
**Cover Design:** Jonathan Boylan
**Composition and Full-Service Project Management:** PreMediaGlobal
**PreMediaGlobal Project Manager:** Kristy Zamagni
**Cover Printer:** Lehigh-Phoenix Color/Hagerstown
**Printer/Binder:** Courier Companies, Inc./Kendallville
**Text Font:** 10/13 Helvetica Neue LT Std Roman

Credits and acknowledgments borrowed from other sources and reproduced, with permission, in this textbook appear in the Rear Matter of this book.

**Library of Congress Cataloging-in-Publication Data**
CIP data on file

ISBN 10:     0-13-311070-2
ISBN 13: 978-0-13-311070-8

# Brief Contents

# Contents

## Chapter 2

# Application Software .............. 46

## Chapter 3

## Chapter 5

## Chapter 7

# The Internet ........................... 270

## Chapter 9

# Networks and Communication.............................356

## Chapter 10

# Security and Privacy ................ 402

## Chapter 11

# Databases ........................... 448

## Chapter 12

# Program Development.......... 496

# What's New in This Edition?

We asked folks like you how we could make this book even better—and we listened. With a brighter, lighter design, better flow, reorganized and updated content, and some cool new features, the second edition of Visualizing Technology is better than ever.

- **Enhanced Design.** Lightened the color palette and improved the flow of text to make reading the book easier

- **Added New and Expanded Topic Coverage.** Everything is current and up to date, plus we added more coverage of hot topics such as tablets, Macs, and cloud computing

- **Reorganized content.** The biggest change we made was moving application software up to chapter 2, so students are introduced to software before hardware

- **Additional Hands-on activities.** You asked and we answered by adding a second hands-on project to each chapter, with Mac specific instructions too!

- **NEW Application projects.** For those classes that cover apps too, we've added two Microsoft Office application projects to the end of each chapter. *One of these exercises is also available in MyITLab as a grader project.*

- **VizClips.** Added short videos that demo key concepts from each chapter.

- **Updated IT Simulations.** These interactive simulations have been updated and enhanced to allow your students to work through an activity covering key topics – one per chapter.

- **Tech Bytes Weekly.** This feature delivers the latest technology news stories for use in your classroom, including discussion topics and activities.

And we kept the things that you loved about this book. A highly visual layout with bite-sized chunks of texts, images used to represent concepts, making them easy to remember, chapters organized as articles with catchy headlines, and coverage of ethics, green computing, and careers in every chapter. And the content is modular, so you can use this book the way you teach your course.

# Changes by Chapter

## Chapter 1  What Is a Computer?

- Moved coverage of bits and bytes to chapter 1
- Updated coverage of types of computers
- Updated coverage of mobile devices and added tablets
- Introduced Alan Turing and the Turing test
- New: How To Use QR codes

## Chapter 2  Application Software

- Repositioned application software chapter from chapter 5 to chapter 2 to enhance the student experience
- Updated content and included more Mac alternatives
- Added coverage of Mobile Apps and App stores
- Upgraded coverage of cloud computing, SaaS, and Cloud Service Providers
- New: How to Edit a Photo with Adobe Photoshop Express Editor Online

## Chapter 3  File Management

- Added Mac coverage (Finder, Spotlight, and Time Machine)
- Introduced Windows 8
- Added a section on mobile devices and file storage
- Added coverage of cloud storage and backups
- New: How to Organize Your Files

## Chapter 4  Hardware

- Updated coverage of hardware
- Added more Mac content
- Upgraded coverage of solid-state drives
- Added coverage of safely removing external and flash drives
- Provided additional coverage of OLED and AMOLED
- Introduced HDMI
- Added coverage of 3D printers
- New: How to Manage Printing on Your Computer

## Chapter 5  System Software

- Introduced Windows 8 and SkyDrive
- Introduced OS X Lion and Mountain Lion
- Provided coverage of mobile operating systems, including Android, iOS, and Windows Mobile
- New: How to Examine and Update Your Printer Driver

## Chapter 6  Multimedia and Digital Devices

- Added coverage of compact system cameras
- Introduced Flickr Commons
- Added more cloud coverage for photos and music
- Enhanced coverage of tablets, e-readers, and mobile apps

- Introduced SIRI
- New: How to Edit a Photo
- New: How to Edit Videos Using the YouTube Editor
- New Find Out More: Gutenberg Project

## Chapter 7  The Internet and World Wide Web

- Updated and enhanced coverage of mobile Internet access
- Updated 3G and 4G information
- Added coverage of Google Scholar
- New: How to Manage Browser Home Page, Favorites, and Search

## Chapter 8  Communicating and Sharing

- Added more coverage of Google +, Skype, Facebook, Mac tools, Twitter, Tumblr, and Pinterest
- Enhanced coverage of massively multiplayer online role-playing games (MMORPG)
- Increased coverage of mobile apps (Instagram)
- Added coverage of SoundCloud
- Provided examples of social media in politics and social movements
- New: How to Create a LinkedIn Profile
- New: How to Create a Blog with Blogger

## Chapter 9  Networks and Communication

- Updated coverage of LAN topologies
- Enhanced coverage of networking
- Added Mac coverage to network figures and instructions
- Introduced 802.11ac
- New: How to Examine Network and Sharing Settings

## Chapter 10  Security and Privacy

- Updated and included social network attacks
- Added coverage of hacktivism and security for mobile apps
- Added information on Mac attacks
- Enhanced coverage of WiFi Protected Setup (WPS) and wireless security
- Upgraded coverage of password managers and biometric scanners
- Enhanced coverage of encryption via BitLocker and File Vault
- Introduced the Cybersecurity Act of 2012
- New: How to Secure a Microsoft Word Document

## Chapter 11  Databases

- Added coverage of Filemaker Pro
- Introduced Blue C.R.U.S.H
- New: How To Create a Form Using Google Docs

## Chapter 12  Program Development

- Added elements to assist students in exploring mobile app development
- New: How To Create a Flowchart

# Visual Walkthrough

## VISUALIZING TECHNOLOGY

- Addresses visual and kinesthetic learners— images help students to learn and retain content while hands-on projects allow students to practice and apply what they learned.

- Easy to read—it has the same amount of text as other concepts books but broken down into smaller chunks of text to aid in comprehension and retention.

- Clear, easy-to-follow organization—each chapter is broken into a series of articles that correspond to chapter objectives.

- Highly visual—students will want to read!

Explanation of the running project for that chapter

## CHAPTER 3
## File Management

**Running Project**

In this chapter, you learn about the importance of file management. Look for instructions as you complete each article. For most, there's a series of questions for you to research or a set of tasks to perform. At the conclusion of this chapter you're asked to submit your responses to the questions raised and the results of the tasks you've performed.

### OBJECTIVES

1. **Create folders to organize files.**

2. **Explain the importance of file extensions.**

3. **Explain the importance of backing up files.**

4. **Demonstrate how to compress files.**

5. **Use advanced search options to locate files.**

6. **Change the default program associated with a file type.**

### IN THIS CHAPTER

The concepts of file management are not unique to computing. We use file cabinets, folders, boxes, drawers, and piles to manage our paper files. These files can be anything from bills to photographs to homework assignments to coupons. In this chapter, we look at managing electronic files.

Visit **pearsonhighered.com/Geoghan** for data files, simulations, VizClips, and additional study materials.

Objectives clearly outlined in chapter opener and restated at the beginning of each article

> Catchy headlines begin each article.

# What's in a Name?

HELLO
my name is

## 2 OBJECTIVE
## Explain the importance of file extensions.

There are two types of files on every computer: the ones that the computer uses to function, such as programs and device drivers, and the ones that are used and created by you, the user, including music, documents, photos, and videos. Let's look at a few of these user files and compare their properties.

### FILE NAMES AND EXTENSIONS

Every file has a **file name** that consists of a name and an extension. The name is useful to the user and describes the contents of the file. When creating your own files, you decide the name. In the example in Figure 3.10, ch03_homework is the name of the file. On early PCs, file names were limited to eight characters with a three-letter extension and were often cryptic. Today, file names on Windows computers can be up to 260 characters long (including the extension and the path to the file) and can include spaces and special characters. The only illegal characters in a file name are the \ / ? : " > < | characters. OS X file names can be up to 255 characters, and the only illegal character is the colon ( : ).

.docx

.mp3

.xlsx

file name
ch_03_homework.docx

ch_03_homework.docx

file extension
.docx

.pdf

**FIGURE 3.10** A file name includes a name and an extension to identify the contents and type of file.

The second part of the file name is the **file extension**. In this example, .docx is the extension. The extension is assigned by the program that's used to create the file. Microsoft Word files have the extension .docx when you save them. Windows maintains an association between a file extension and a program, so double-clicking on a .docx file opens Microsoft Word. The extension helps the operating system determine the type of file. If you change the file extension of a file, you may no longer be able to open it. Figure 3.11 lists some common file types and programs associated with them.

**FIGURE 3.11** Common File Extensions and Default Program Associations

| EXTENSION | TYPE OF FILE | DEFAULT PROGRAM ASSOCIATION (WINDOWS) | DEFAULT PROGRAM ASSOCIATION (OS X) |
|---|---|---|---|
| .docx/.doc | Word document | Microsoft Word | Microsoft Word |
| .rtf | Rich text format | Wordpad or Word | TextEdit |
| .pages | Pages document | | Pages |
| .xlsx/.xls | Excel | Excel | Excel |
| .pptx/.ppt | PowerPoint | PowerPoint | PowerPoint |
| .bmp | bitmap image | Microsoft Paint | Preview |
| .jpeg/.jpg | Image file (Joint Photographic Experts Group) | Windows Photo Viewer or Photo Gallery | Preview |
| .mp3 | audio file | Windows Media Player | iTunes |
| .aac | Audio file (advanced audio coding) | iTunes | iTunes |
| .mov | video file | Apple QuickTime | QuickTime |
| .wmv | Video file | Windows Media Player | |
| .pdf | portable document format | Adobe Acrobat and Reader | Preview |

.bmp

.jpg

### FILE PROPERTIES

Each file includes **file properties**, which provide other information about that file. We can use these properties to organize, sort, and find files more easily. Some file properties, such as type, size, and date, are automatically created along with the file. Others, such as title and authors, can be added or edited by the user.

### Find Out MORE

The characters \ / ? : " > < | can't be used in a file name because they each have a special meaning in Windows. For example, the colon ( : ) is used when you indicate the letter of a drive (such as C: for your hard drive or D: for your DVD drive). Use the Internet to research the remaining illegal characters. What does each of these symbols represent?

> Find Out More—prompts for additional research on a given topic

## HOW SAFE IS MY CREDIT CARD?

E-commerce on the Web requires you to hand over some sensitive information. So, is it OK to shop online? Yes, but just as you wouldn't leave your doors unlocked, you need to be sure that you're shopping wisely. Shop at well-known sites or use third-party payment sites such as Google Checkout and PayPal to protect credit card information. Make sure you're on a secure website when completing transactions. Look at your browser's address bar. If the URL begins with https, then the site is using SSL security. You'll also notice a padlock that indicates a secure site. Clicking on the padlock will open a security report about the website.

The Internet has changed how most companies do business, and the social Web has added a new dimension. Businesses that successfully leverage the power of social media are able to create customers who, in turn, create new customers.

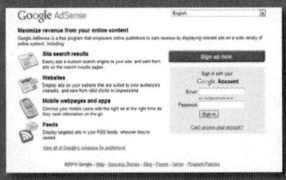

## CAREER SPOTLIGHT

Although most blogs are personal in nature and earn the writer no compensation, some lucky folks are professional bloggers. These bloggers may be paid by a company to blog about a product or provide news or reviews, and their blogs are usually part of a bigger website. Some professional bloggers use their blogs to drive customers to their other products. Successful bloggers monetize the content on their sites in several ways, including placing ads and links to other sites. A professional blog may earn money by using Google AdSense to place ads and links on it. It takes a lot of time and work to write a good blog and even more to make money while doing it.

# GREEN COMPUTING

### RAISING SOCIAL AWARENESS

How much paper mail do you receive every week? And how much of it do you actually read? The cost of a direct-mail campaign is huge, and many people simply toss what they see as junk mail in the trash anyway, so the costs are also large in terms of the environment. SMM isn't just for businesses—it can also be used to raise awareness of important issues.

Not long ago, women all over Facebook posted one-word status updates. White, red, gray, black. What was going on? Women were sharing a message with each other that said: "Some fun is going on. . . . Just write the color of your bra in your status. Just the color; nothing else. It will be neat to see if this will spread the wings of breast cancer awareness. It will be fun to see how long it takes before people wonder why all the girls have a color in their status. . . . Haha." The message quickly spread, and thousands of women (and even some men) responded. The idea was to raise social awareness about breast cancer. Did it work? Well, it certainly didn't do any harm, and the story was also picked up by the news media. So, a simple act of social networking resulted in raising social awareness. The beauty of the idea was that it got women thinking about something we usually prefer not to at no cost to the environment. Facebook has an application called Causes that can be used to raise both awareness and funds for social causes without printing a single piece of paper.

### Running Project

Visit Amazon.com. What are two ways that Amazon uses social media marketing? Can you find any other ways? How is this experience different from shopping in a store?

### 2 Things You Need to Know

● E-commerce is business on the Web.
● Social Media Marketing (SMM) uses social media sites to sell products and services.

### Key Terms

e-commerce

social media marketing (SMM)

Subtopics have same color background as main topics—makes it easy to follow each piece

Students can scan the QR code and go directly to the website suggested for additional information or explanation.

Ethics boxes provide thought-provoking questions about the use of technology.

## SOCIAL BOOKMARKING AND NEWS SITES

**Social bookmarking sites** allow you to save and share your bookmarks or favorites online. Delicious allows you to not only save and share your bookmarks online but to also search the bookmarks of others. It's a great way to quickly find out what other people find interesting and important right now. Figure 8.24 shows the Delicious page with links that I post for my students and readers of this book at **delicious.com/visualizingtechnology**. The links are organized into topics, or tags, to make it easier for you to find links. You can click the *Follow* button if you have a Delicious account, but you don't need an account to view the page.

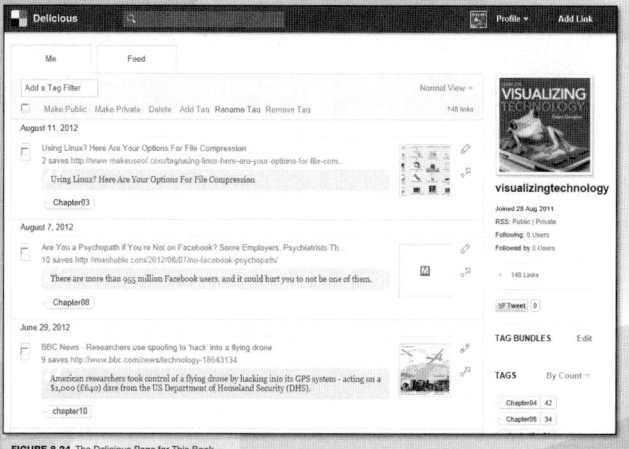

**Delicious**

| Me | Feed |

Add a Tag Filter                                                      Normal View ▾

☐ Make Public  Make Private  Delete  Add Tag  Rename Tag  Remove Tag        148 links

**August 11, 2012**

☐ Using Linux? Here Are Your Options For File Compression
2 saves http://www.makeuseof.com/tag/using-linux-here-are-your-options-for-file-com.

Using Linux? Here Are Your Options For File Compression

Chapter03

**August 7, 2012**

☐ Are You a Psychopath if You're Not on Facebook? Some Employers, Psychiatrists Th...
10 saves http://mashable.com/2012/06/07/no-facebook-psychopath/

There are more than 955 million Facebook users, and it could hurt you to not be one of them.

Chapter08

**June 29, 2012**

☐ BBC News - Researchers use spoofing to 'hack' into a flying drone
9 saves http://www.bbc.com/news/technology-18643134

American researchers took control of a flying drone by hacking into its GPS system - acting on a $1,000 (£640) dare from the US Department of Homeland Security (DHS).

chapter10

**VISUALIZING TECHNOLOGY**

**visualizingtechnology**

Joined 28 Aug 2011
RSS: Public | Private
Following: 0 Users
Followed by 0 Users

• 148 Links

Tweet  0

TAG BUNDLES        Edit

TAGS        By Count ▾

Chapter04  42
Chapter08  34

**FIGURE 8.24** The Delicious Page for This Book

StumbleUpon discovers websites based on your interests. When you sign up, you indicate topics that interest you. Then, as you visit websites, you can click the *StumbleUpon* button to be taken to a similar site. You can click *I like this* to improve the selection of pages you stumble onto. Pinterest is a newer website that is growing in popularity, notably among women. With Pinterest you create virtual cork boards and pin Web pages to them. You can share your boards with others and follow other people to see what they have pinned.

**Social news sites** are different than traditional media news sites in that at least some of the content is submitted by users. It's interactive in a way that traditional media isn't. It's like having millions of friends sharing their finds with you. Content that's submitted more frequently or gets the most votes is promoted to the front page.

Two of the most popular social news sites are reddit and Digg. Digg doesn't publish content but allows the community members to submit content they discover on the Web and puts it in one place for everyone to see and to discuss. Slashdot, which focuses primarily on technology topics, does produce its content but also accepts submissions from its readers. Whatever your interests, there's probably a social news site for you.

Relying on the wisdom of the crowd is much like asking your friends, family, and coworkers for advice. Did you enjoy the movie? Where should I go for the best ice cream? How do you change the oil in your car? Everybody's an expert in something. The Web just makes it easier for us to find and share that expertise with each other. But a word of caution: Like anything else you read on the Web, be critical in your evaluation of the credibility and reliability of its author.

morena,
*murrum
mor•al (
ment of
ethical:
rectnes

## ETHICS

Some people create multiple accounts on social bookmarking and news sites so they can promote their own content. For example, a blogger might create several accounts on Digg and use each one to Digg a blog post, thereby artificially raising its popularity on Digg and driving more traffic to it. This violates the Digg terms of use. But what if the blogger had all his friends and family members create accounts and Digg his post? Is it ethical? Does it violate the terms of use? Is it fair to other bloggers?

### Running Project

Go to the Wikipedia article "Reliability of Wikipedia" at **wikipedia.org/wiki/Reliability_of_Wikipedia**. How does Wikipedia assure that the content is correct? What procedures are in place to remove or correct mistakes? How does Wikipedia compare to other online sources of information?

### 3 Things You Need to Know

● Social media relies on the wisdom of the crowd rather than that of an expert.

● A wiki can be edited by anybody.

● Social bookmarking and news helps users find content that others recommend.

### Key Terms

crowd-sourcing

social bookmarking site

social news site

social review site

wiki

Running Project—Specific instructions are provided for compiling information for the Running Project.

Things You Need to Know—Key takeaway points are provided for each article.

Key Terms—Students are reminded of the key terms they should understand after reading each article.

## LAYER 3: ALARM SYSTEMS

The alarm system on a computer network includes software-based firewalls and antivirus and antimalware software on the individual computers on the network (see Figure 9.26). Your individual computers should be protected by software firewalls such as those included with Windows or OS X. If an intruder somehow breaches your network, software will detect unauthorized actions and prevent them.

**FIGURE 9.26** Each computer on the network should have its own up-to-date security software installed.

## LAYER 4: GUARD DOGS

The network administrator (on a home network, that's you) needs to be diligent in keeping the systems on the network up to date and secure. Windows and OS X can be configured to automatically check for and install updates (see Figure 9.27), but other software applications can also be potential vulnerabilities and should be kept up to date as well. Unpatched systems are easy targets for hackers and can allow them access into your network.

Although you can never be completely secure, it *is* possible to make your home so difficult to break into to that the thief moves on to an easier target. That's also the goal with network security.

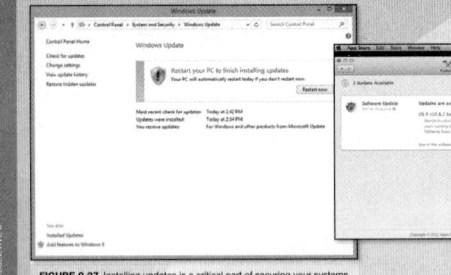

**FIGURE 9.27** Installing updates is a critical part of securing your systems.

### ETHICS

The term **piggybacking** means using an open wireless network to access the Internet without permission. Many times, people intentionally use open wireless access. If an access point is left unsecured, they figure, "Why not?" In some places, it's illegal to use a network without authorization, but many statutes—if they exist at all—are vague. It's difficult to detect someone that's piggybacking. Still, it's unethical to use someone's connection without his or her knowledge.

To make things more confusing, some free hotspots—such as in cafes and hotels—might be accessible beyond the premises. So, a person sitting in a car parked on the street might be able to access the coffee shop hotspot intended for patrons of the shop.

The practice of wardriving is closely related. **Wardriving** means driving around and locating open wireless access points. There are communities on the Internet where wardrivers post maps of the open networks they find, along with free software that makes it easy to locate wireless networks. Wardrivers don't actually access the wireless networks, so the practice isn't illegal—but is it ethical? You decide.

## CAREER SPOTLIGHT

You'll find computer networks in every type of business, and knowing how to access network resources is a critical skill for most employees. A network administrator is the person responsible for managing the hardware and software on a network. The job may also include troubleshooting and security. Although not required, a two- or four-year college degree is helpful in this field, as are certifications. According to Salary.com, the average salary for a person in this field with 2–5 years of experience is about $64,000. As with any technical field, you should expect to continue your training to keep up with the changes in technology. An entry-level person may be called a network technician rather than an administrator.

The importance of networks and connectivity for most businesses requires employees that are experts at making networks secure and reliable. The *Occupational Outlook Handbook* predicts that network-related jobs will grow faster than the average for all occupations over the next decade, so considering a career in this field might be a good choice for you.

### 4 Things You Need to Know

- A firewall examines the data packets as they enter or leave your network.
- Network users should have strong passwords that are hard to crack and be granted access only to what they need.
- Individual computers on the network must be protected with firewalls and antivirus and antimalware software.
- Systems on the network must be kept up to date and secure.

### Key Terms

piggybacking

wardriving

Visual Walkthrough

xxiv

390

391

OBJECTIVE 5

Chapter 9

How To projects—Each chapter provides two step-by-step projects, complete with visual instructions, to complete interesting and useful items.

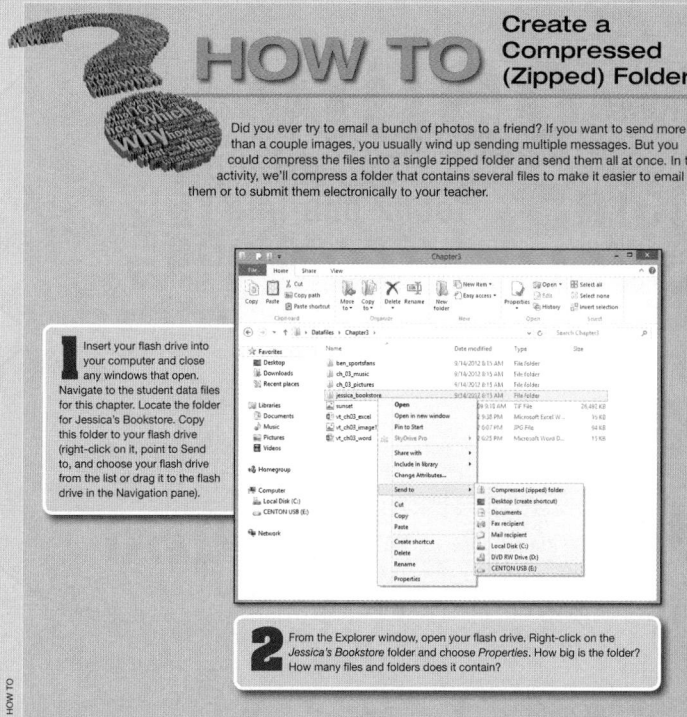

# HOW TO

### Create a Compressed (Zipped) Folder

Did you ever try to email a bunch of photos to a friend? If you want to send more than a couple images, you usually wind up sending multiple messages. But you could compress the files into a single zipped folder and send them all at once. In this activity, we'll compress a folder that contains several files to make it easier to email them or to submit them electronically to your teacher.

**1** Insert your flash drive into your computer and close any windows that open. Navigate to the student data files for this chapter. Locate the folder for Jessica's Bookstore. Copy this folder to your flash drive (right-click on it, point to Send to, and choose your flash drive from the list or drag it to the flash drive in the Navigation pane).

**2** From the Explorer window, open your flash drive. Right-click on the *Jessica's Bookstore* folder and choose *Properties*. How big is the folder? How many files and folders does it contain?

**3** Close the Properties dialog box. Right-click on *Jessica's Bookstore*, point to Send to, and choose *Compressed (zipped) folder* to create a zipped archive.

**4** Right-click on the compressed folder and choose *Properties*. Compare the size to the original folder.

**5** Write up your answers, save the file as **lastname_firstname_ch04_howto2**, and submit it as directed by your instructor.

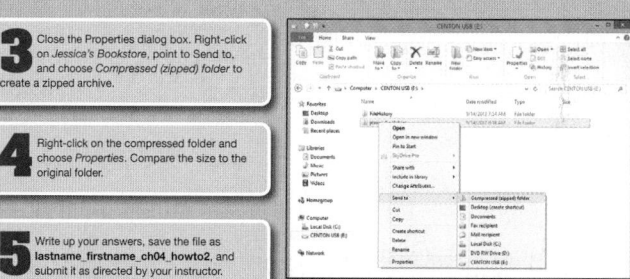

**MAC**

**If you are using a Mac:**
1. Insert your flash drive into your computer. Open Finder and locate the datafiles for this chapter. Copy the folder for Jessica's Bookstore by dragging it to your flash drive.
2. Click the Flash drive in the Sidebar and select the folder in the right pane. From the File menu, select *Get Info*. How big is the folder? How many files and folders does it contain?
3. Close the Info pane. From the File menu, select *Compress "Jessica's Bookstore"* to create a zipped archive.
4. Select the ZIP file and from the File menu, select *Get Info*. Compare the size to the original folder.
5. Write up your answers, save the file as **lastname_firstname_ch04_howto2**, and submit it as directed by your instructor.

Mac coverage—Where appropriate, instructions are included so Mac users can complete the exercises.

The End-of-Chapter content ranges from traditional review exercises to application and hands-on projects that have students working independently, collaboratively, and online.

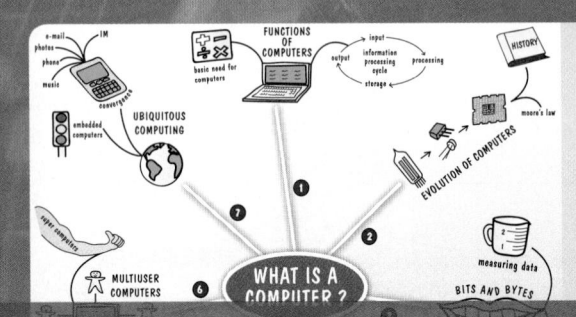

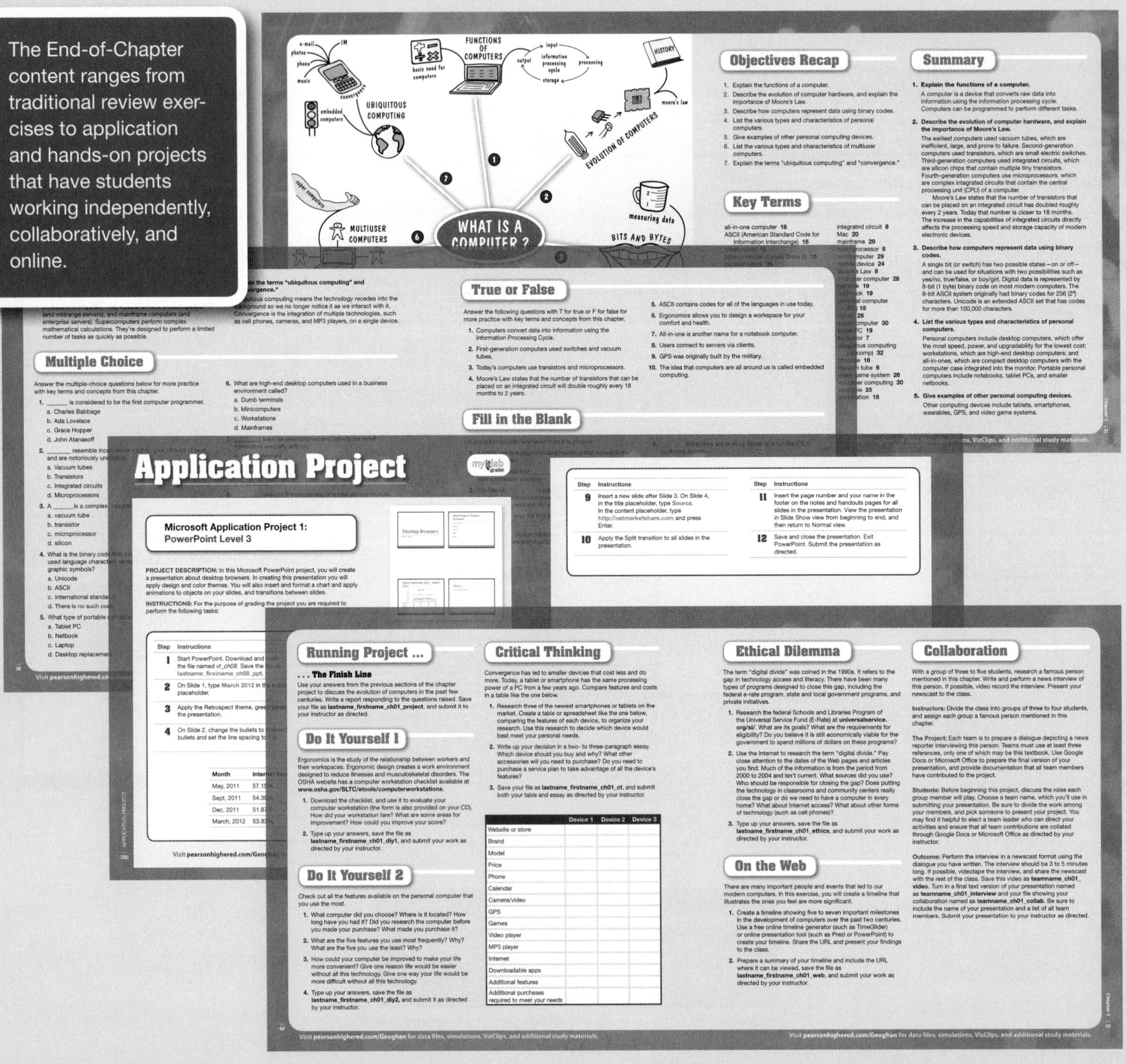

## Objectives Recap

1. Explain the functions of a computer.
2. Describe the evolution of computer hardware, and explain the importance of Moore's Law.
3. Describe how computers represent data using binary codes.
4. List the various types and characteristics of personal computers.
5. Give examples of other personal computing devices.
6. List the various types and characteristics of multiuser computers.
7. Explain the terms "ubiquitous computing" and "convergence."

## Key Terms

| | |
|---|---|
| all-in-one computer 18 | integrated circuit 8 |
| ASCII (American Standard Code for Information Interchange) 16 | Mac 20 |
| | mainframe 29 |
| | microprocessor 8 |
| binary number (or digit) (bit) 2) 16 | minicomputer 28 |
| processing 2b | Moore's Law 8 |
| | netbook computer 28 |
| | netbook 19 |
| | notebook 28 |
| | personal computer 18 |
| | PC 28 |
| | server 19 |
| | supercomputer 7 |
| | ubiquitous computing (ubicomp) 32 |
| | Unicode 16 |
| | vacuum tube 6 |
| | video game system 26 |
| | wearable computing 30 |
| | wearable 25 |
| | workstation 18 |

## Summary

1. **Explain the functions of a computer.**
   A computer is a device that converts raw data into information using the information processing cycle. Computers can be programmed to perform different tasks.

2. **Describe the evolution of computer hardware, and explain the importance of Moore's Law.**
   The earliest computers used vacuum tubes, which are inefficient, large, and prone to failure. Second-generation computers used transistors, which are small electric switches. Third-generation computers used integrated circuits, which are silicon chips that contain multiple tiny transistors. Fourth-generation computers use microprocessors, which are complex integrated circuits that contain the central processing unit (CPU) of a computer.
   Moore's Law states that the number of transistors that can be placed on an integrated circuit has doubled roughly every 2 years. Today that number is closer to 18 months. The increase in the capabilities of integrated circuits directly affects the processing speed and storage capacity of modern electronic devices.

3. **Describe how computers represent data using binary codes.**
   A single bit (or switch) has two possible states—on or off—and can be used for situations with two possibilities such as yes/no, true/false, or boy/girl. Digital data is represented by 8-bit (1 byte) binary code on most modern computers. The 8-bit ASCII system originally had binary codes for 256 ($2^8$) characters. Unicode is an extended ASCII set that has codes for more than 100,000 characters.

4. **List the various types and characteristics of personal computers.**
   Personal computers include desktop computers, which offer the most speed, power, and upgradability for the lowest cost; workstations, which are high-end desktop computers; and all-in-ones, which are compact desktop computers with the computer case integrated into the monitor. Portable personal computers include notebooks, tablet PCs, and smaller netbooks.

5. **Give examples of other personal computing devices.**
   Other computing devices include tablets, smartphones, wearables, GPS, and video game systems.

## True or False

Answer the following questions with T for true or F for false for more practice with key terms and concepts from this chapter.

1. Computers convert data into information using the Information Processing Cycle.
2. First-generation computers used switches and vacuum tubes.
3. Today's computers use transistors and microprocessors.
4. Moore's Law states that the number of transistors that can be placed on an integrated circuit will double roughly every 18 months to 2 years.

5. ASCII contains codes for all of the languages in use today.
6. Ergonomics allows you to design a workspace for your comfort and health.
7. All-in-one is another name for a notebook computer.
8. Users connect to servers via clients.
9. GPS was originally built by the military.
10. The idea that computers are all around us is called embedded computing.

## Multiple Choice

Answer the multiple-choice questions below for more practice with key terms and concepts from this chapter.

1. _____ is considered to be the first computer programmer.
   a. Charles Babbage
   b. Ada Lovelace
   c. Grace Hopper
   d. John Atanasoff

2. _____ resemble ... and are notoriously un...
   a. Vacuum tubes
   b. Transistors
   c. Integrated circuits
   d. Microprocessors

3. A _____ is a complex ...
   a. vacuum tube
   b. transistor
   c. microprocessor
   d. silicon

4. What is the binary code ... used language charac... graphic symbols?
   a. Unicode
   b. ASCII
   c. International standar...
   d. There is no such co...

5. What type of portable ...
   a. Tablet PC
   b. Netbook
   c. Laptop
   d. Desktop replacement

6. What are high-end desktop computers used in a business environment called?
   a. Dumb terminals
   b. Minicomputers
   c. Workstations
   d. Mainframes

## Fill in the Blank

# Application Project

### Microsoft Application Project 1: PowerPoint Level 3

**PROJECT DESCRIPTION:** In this Microsoft PowerPoint project, you will create a presentation about desktop browsers. In creating this presentation you will apply design and color themes. You will also insert and format a chart and apply animations to objects on your slides, and transitions between slides.

**INSTRUCTIONS:** For the purpose of grading the project you are required to perform the following tasks:

| Step | Instructions |
|---|---|
| 1 | Start PowerPoint. Download and ... the file named vf_ch08. Save the ... lastname_firstname_ch08_ppt. |
| 2 | On Slide 1, type March 2012 in the ... placeholder. |
| 3 | Apply the Retrospect theme, gree... the presentation. |
| 4 | On Slide 2, change the bullets to ... bullets and set the line spacing to ... |

| Step | Instructions |
|---|---|
| 9 | Insert a new slide after Slide 3. On Slide 4, in the title placeholder, type Source. In the content placeholder, type http://letmarketshare.com and press Enter. |
| 10 | Apply the Split transition to all slides in the presentation. |
| 11 | Insert the page number and your name in the footer on the notes and handouts pages for all slides in the presentation. View the presentation in Slide Show view from beginning to end, and then return to Normal view. |
| 12 | Save and close the presentation. Exit PowerPoint. Submit the presentation as directed. |

## Running Project ...

**... The Finish Line**

Use your answers from the previous sections of the chapter project to discuss the evolution of computers in the past few centuries. Write a report responding to the questions raised. Save your file as lastname_firstname_ch01_project, and submit it to your instructor as directed.

## Do It Yourself 1

Ergonomics is the study of the relationship between workers and their workspaces. Ergonomic design creates a work environment designed to reduce illnesses and musculoskeletal disorders. The OSHA website has a computer workstation checklist available at www.osha.gov/SLTC/etools/computerworkstations.

1. Download the checklist, and use it to evaluate your computer workstation (the form is also provided on your CD). How did your workstation fare? What are some areas for improvement? How could you improve your score?
2. Type up your answers, save the file as lastname_firstname_ch01_diy1, and submit your work as directed by your instructor.

## Do It Yourself 2

Check out all the features available on the personal computer that you use the most.

1. What computer did you choose? Where is it located? How long have you had it? Did you research the computer before you made your purchase? What made you purchase it?
2. What are the five features you use most frequently? Why? What are the five you use the least? Why?
3. How could your computer be improved to make your life more convenient? Give one reason life would be easier without all this technology. Give one way your life would be more difficult without all this technology.
4. Type up your answers, save the file as lastname_firstname_ch01_diy2, and submit it as directed by your instructor.

## Critical Thinking

Convergence has led to smaller devices that cost less and do more. Today, a tablet or smartphone has the same processing power of a PC from a few years ago. Compare features and costs in a table like the one below.

1. Research three of the newest smartphones or tablets on the market. Create a table or spreadsheet like the one below, comparing the features of each device, to organize your research. Use this research to decide which device would best meet your personal needs.
2. Write up your decision in a two- to three-paragraph essay. Which device should you buy and why? What other accessories will you need to purchase? Do you need to purchase a service plan to take advantage of all the device's features?
3. Save your file as lastname_firstname_ch01_ct, and submit both your table and essay as directed by your instructor.

| | Device 1 | Device 2 | Device 3 |
|---|---|---|---|
| Website or store | | | |
| Brand | | | |
| Model | | | |
| Price | | | |
| Phone | | | |
| Calendar | | | |
| Camera/video | | | |
| GPS | | | |
| Games | | | |
| Video player | | | |
| MP3 player | | | |
| Internet | | | |
| Downloadable apps | | | |
| Additional features | | | |
| Additional purchases required to meet your needs | | | |

## Ethical Dilemma

The term "digital divide" was coined in the 1990s. It refers to the gap in technology access and literacy. There have been many types of programs designed to close this gap, including the federal e-rate program, state and local government programs, and private initiatives.

1. Research the federal Schools and Libraries Program of the Universal Service Fund (E-Rate) at universalservice.org/sl/. What are its goals? What are the requirements for eligibility? Do you believe it is still economically viable for the government to spend millions of dollars on these programs?
2. Use the Internet to research the term "digital divide." Pay close attention to the dates of the Web pages and articles you find. Much of the information is from the period from 2000 to 2004 and isn't current. What sources did you use? Who should be responsible for closing the gap? Does putting the technology in classrooms and community centers really close the gap or do we need to have a computer in every home? What about Internet access? What about other forms of technology (such as cell phones)?
3. Type up your answers, save the file as lastname_firstname_ch01_ethics, and submit your work as directed by your instructor.

## On the Web

There are many important people and events that led to our modern computers. In this exercise, you will create a timeline that illustrates the ones you feel are more significant.

1. Create a timeline showing five to seven important milestones in the development of computers over the past two centuries. Use a free online timeline generator (such as TimeGlider) or online presentation tool (such as Prezi or PowerPoint) to create your timeline. Share the URL and present your findings to the class.
2. Prepare a summary of your timeline and include the URL where it can be viewed, save the file as lastname_firstname_ch01_web, and submit your work as directed by your instructor.

## Collaboration

With a group of three to five students, research a famous person mentioned in this chapter. Write and perform a news interview of this person. If possible, video record the interview. Present your newscast to the class.

**Instructors:** Divide the class into groups of three to four students, and assign each group a famous person mentioned in this chapter.

**The Project:** Each team is to prepare a dialogue depicting a news reporter interviewing this person. Teams must use at least three references, only one of which may be this textbook. Use Google Docs or Microsoft Office to prepare the final version of your presentation, and provide documentation that all team members have contributed to the project.

**Students:** Before beginning this project, discuss the roles each group member will play. Choose a team name, which you'll use in submitting your presentation. Be sure to divide the work among your members, and pick someone to present your project. You may find it helpful to elect a team leader who can direct your activities and ensure that all team contributions are collated through Google Docs or Microsoft Office as directed by your instructor.

**Outcome:** Perform the interview in a newscast format using the dialogue you have written. The interview should be 3 to 5 minutes long. If possible, videotape the interview, and share the newscast with the rest of the class. Save this video as teamname_ch01_video. Turn in a final text version of your presentation named as teamname_ch01_interview and your file showing your collaboration named as teamname_ch01_collab. Be sure to include the name of your presentation and a list of all team members. Submit your presentation to your instructor as directed.

Mind maps are visual outlines of the chapter content, organized by objectives. They help students organize and remember the information they learned.

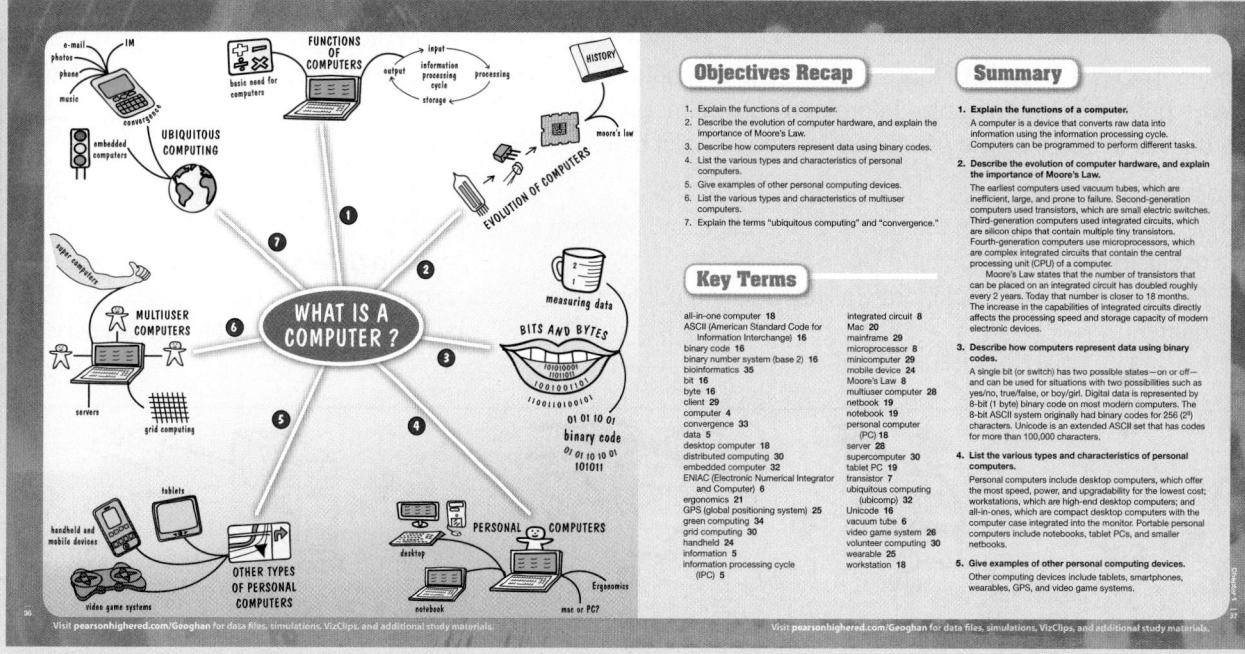

# Instructor Materials

- Annotated Instructor's Edition
  - Chapter tabs with article and special feature summaries, as well as a correlation guide between chapter objectives and end of chapter projects
  - Social Media tabs for each chapter with Facebook, Twitter, Blogger and polleverywhere.com assignments
- Instructor's Resources
  - PowerPoints
  - Audio PowerPoints
  - End-of-Chapter solutions
  - Testbanks
  - Tech Bytes Weekly

...these resources can be found at pearsonhighered.com/geoghan

# Student Materials

- Facebook site for the latest updates in technology
- Companion Website
  - Student data files
  - Online Chapter Review
  - Jeopardy game
  - Crosswords
  - *TechTown*, a computer concepts game
  - VizClips

# Mind Maps

A mind map is a visual tool that's useful for taking notes and studying. It helps you organize information using images and key-words and to see how the pieces are related to each other.

To draw a mind map:

1.  Write the main topic in the center of the page and then put a circle around it.
2.  For each major subtopic, draw a line radiating out from the center.
3.  Draw branches off the subtopics as you dig deeper into the material.
4.  Draw dotted connecting lines between branches that are related.

Use single words and simple phrases, color, and images to help clarify the material.

Mind maps are used throughout this book to outline the basic structure of each chapter, but you can build on those beginning maps to delve deeper into the material. The figure at the top of the next page shows the mind map for Chapter 2. We can build on it by adding more detail to the branches.

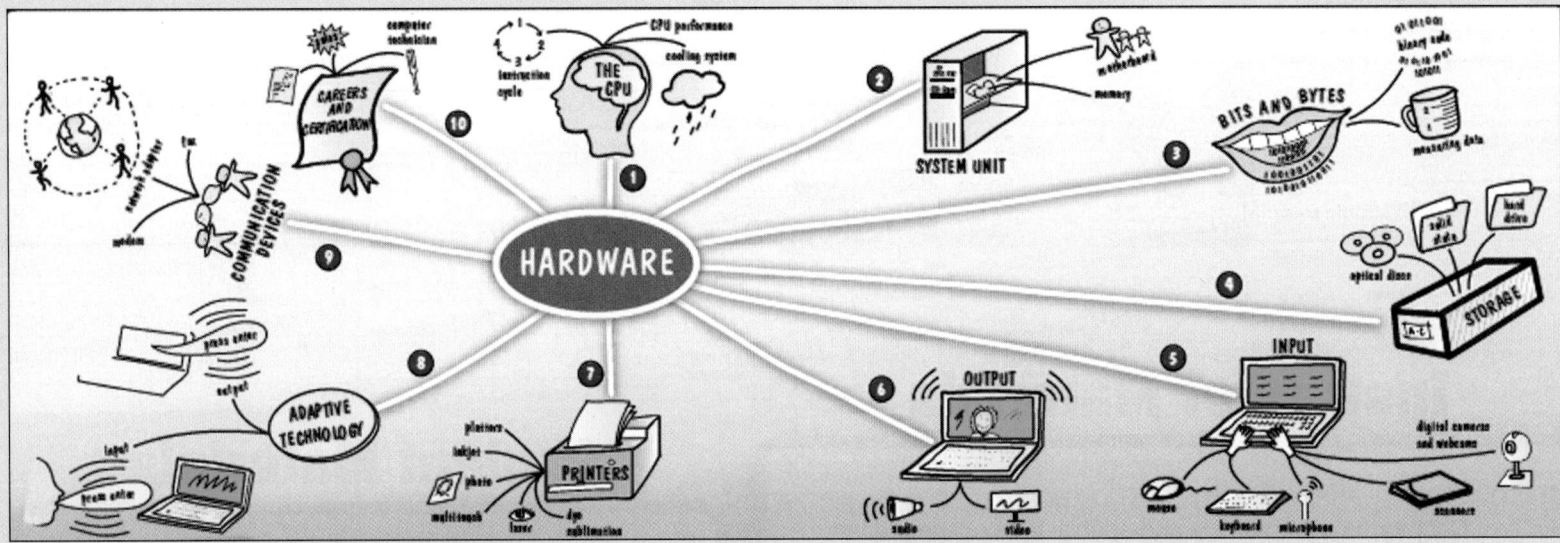

The printer branch is a good place to expand. What topics and concepts would you list on the printer branch? Look at the chapter, and you'll see many choices that you might put here. The next figure shows some ideas you might include on your map of this branch. We could draw a connection between PictBridge on the printer branch and the digital camera on the input branch as well as the solid-state storage (memory card) on the storage branch.

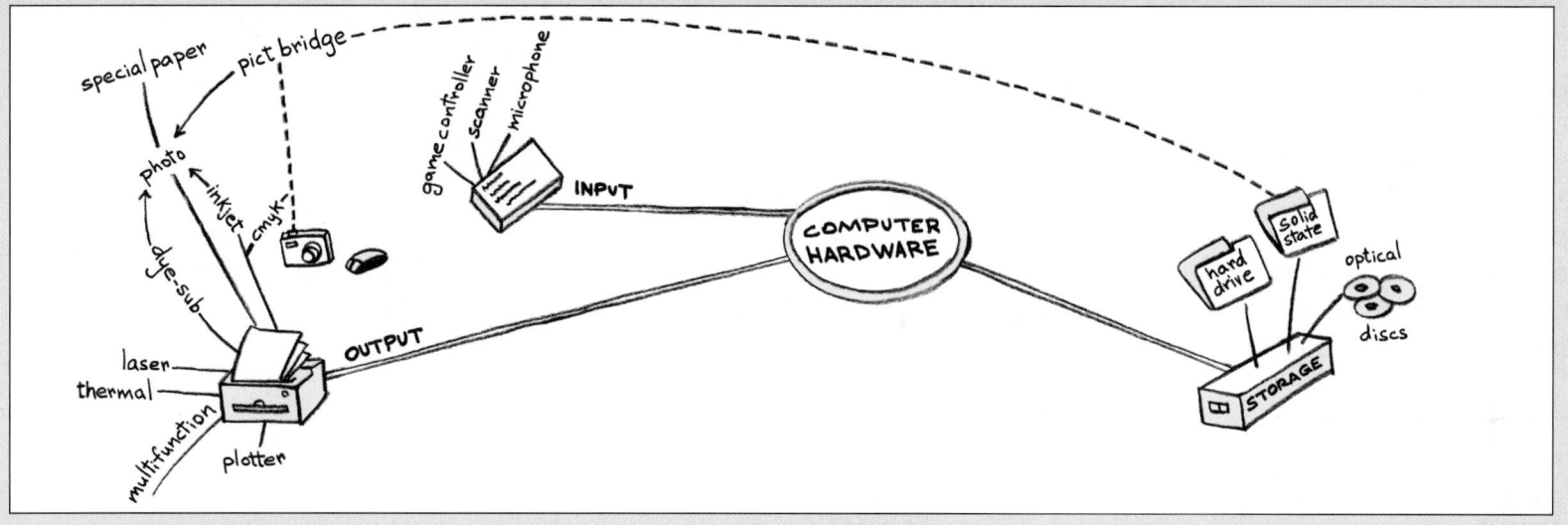

   Because mind maps are used to help you remember and connect information, there's no right or wrong answer. Some people like to hand-draw mind maps; others use software to make maps cleaner. Mind maps help you review material and see connections between the topics. They're one tool you could use to take notes and study.

# About the Author

Debra is currently a professor of computer and information science at Bucks County Community College, teaching computer classes ranging from basic computer literacy to cybercrime, computer forensics, and networking. She has earned certifications from Microsoft, CompTIA, Apple, and others. Deb has taught at the college level since 1996 and also spent 11 years in the high school classroom. She holds a B.S. in Secondary Science Education from Temple University and an M.A. in Computer Science Education from Arcadia University.

Throughout her teaching career Deb has worked with educators to integrate technology across the curriculum. At BCCC she serves on many technology committees, presents technology workshops for BCCC faculty, and runs a summer workshop for K–12 teachers interested in using technology in their classrooms. Deb is an avid user of technology, which has earned her the nickname "gadget lady."

# Dedication

This project would not have been possible without the help and support of many people. I cannot express how grateful I am to all of you. Thank you.

My team at Pearson—Jenifer, Anne, Michael, Linda, and everyone else: you have been amazing, helping to bring my vision to reality and teaching me so much along the way.

My colleagues and students at Bucks County Community College: for your suggestions and encouragement throughout this process. You inspire me every day.

And most importantly—my family. My husband and sons for your patience, help, and love—even when it meant taking a photo "right this minute," or reading a chapter when you wanted to be doing something else, or missing me while I was away. And the rest of my family who agreed to let me use their photos throughout the book. I couldn't have done this without your love and support.

And finally my dad—who taught me to love technology and not be afraid to try new things. I miss you and love you, daddy.

# Reviewers

Special thanks to Lisa Hawkins, Frederick Community College

## Second Edition Advisors:

**Phil Valvalides**   Guilford Technical Community College

**Jim Taggart**   Atlantic Cape Community College

**Svetlana Marzelli**   Atlantic Cape Community College

**Pat Lyon** - Tomball College

**Arta Szathmary**   Bucks County Community College

**June Lane**   Bucks County Community College

**Ralph Hunsberger**   Bucks County Community College

**Sue McCrory**   Missouri State

**Laura White**   University of West Florida

## Second Edition Reviewers:

**Mimi Spain**   Southern Maine Community College

**Kathie O'Brien**   North Idaho College

**Pat Franco**   Los Angeles Valley College

**Claire Amorde**   Florida Institute Of Technology

**Michael Haugrud**   Minnesota State University Moorhead

**Sanjay Adhikari**   Miami Dade College

**Lynne Lyon**   Durham College

**Kate Le Grand**   Broward College

**Carolyn Barren**   Macomb Community College

**Bob Benavedis**   Collins College

**Theresa Hayes**   Broward College

**Mary Fleming**   Ivy Tech Community College

**Penny Cypert**   Tarrant County College

**Bernice Eng**   Brookdale Community College

**Deb Fells**   Mesa Community College

# 1

# What Is a Computer?

Visit **pearsonhighered.com/Geoghan** for data files, simulations, VizClips, and additional study materials.

## Running Project

In this project, you'll explore computers that are used in everyday life. Look for instructions as you complete each article. For most, there's a series of questions for you to research. At the conclusion of the chapter, you're asked to submit your responses to the questions raised.

**OBJECTIVES**

1. **Explain the functions of a computer.**

2. **Describe the evolution of computer hardware, and explain the importance of Moore's Law.**

3. **Describe how computers represent data using binary codes.**

4. **List the various types and characteristics of personal computers.**

5. **Give examples of other personal computing devices.**

6. **List the various types and characteristics of multiuser computers.**

7. **Explain the terms "ubiquitous computing" and "convergence."**

# IN THIS CHAPTER

If you've gone grocery shopping, put gas in your car, watched the weather report on TV, or used a microwave oven today, then you've interacted with a computer. Most of us use computers every day, often without even realizing it. Computers have become so commonplace that we don't even consider them computers. In this chapter, we discuss what a computer is and look at the development of computers in the last few centuries.

# What Does a Computer Do?

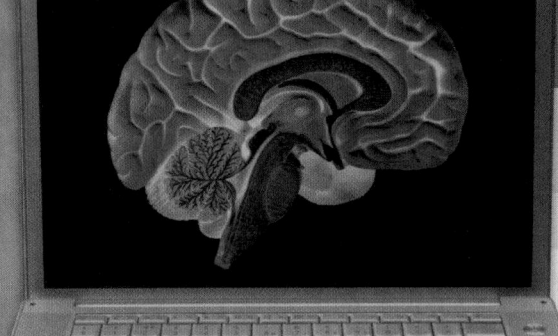

## I OBJECTIVE
## Explain the functions of a computer.

A **computer** is a programmable machine that converts raw data into useful information. A toaster can never be anything more than a toaster—it has one function—but a computer can be a calculator, a media center, a communications center, and so much more. The ability to change its programming is what distinguishes a computer from any other machine.

## NECESSITY IS THE MOTHER OF INVENTION

The original computers were people, not machines, and the mathematical tables they computed tended to be full of errors. The technical and scientific advancements of the Industrial Revolution led to a growing need for this type of hand-calculated information, and the first mechanical computers were developed to automate the tedious work of computing such things as tide charts and navigation tables.

In the early 19th century, mathematician Charles Babbage designed a machine called an Analytical Engine, a mechanical computer that could be programmed using punched cards, which were originally developed by Joseph Marie Jacquard as part of the Jacquard loom to manufacture textiles with complex patterns. Had the Analytical Engine actually been built, it would have been the first mechanical computer, but the technology simply didn't exist at the time to build the machine. In his 1864 book *Passages from the Life of a Philosopher*, Babbage wrote, "The whole of the development and operations of analysis are now capable of being executed by machinery. As soon as an Analytical Engine exists, it will necessarily guide the future course of science." In 2011, a group of researchers at London's Science Museum began a project to build Babbage's computer. The project is expected to take 10 years and cost millions of dollars.

Mathematician Ada Lovelace (see Figure 1.1), a contemporary of Babbage, wrote a program for the Analytical Engine to calculate a series of Bernoulli numbers. Because of her efforts, she is considered by many to be the first computer programmer. Lovelace never tested the program because there were no machines capable of running it; however, when run on a computer today, the program yields the correct mathematical results. In 1979, the Ada computer language was named in her honor.

**FIGURE 1.1**
Augusta Ada King, Countess of Lovelace

In 1936, mathematician Alan Turing wrote a paper, "On Computable Numbers," in which he introduced the concept of machines that could perform mathematical computations (later called Turing machines). In 1950, he developed the Turing test, which tests a machine's ability to display intelligent behavior. Alan Turing is considered by many to be the father of computer science and artificial intelligence.

STORAGE: The raw data is stored temporarily until it can be processed. The processed information is stored for later retrieval.

INPUT: Data is collected from customers who submit a form on a website.

OUTPUT: The processed data—now information—is output as reports and charts that managers can use to help make decisions.

PROCESSING: The data is then manipulated, or processed, so it can be used to evaluate the customer's needs.

FIGURE 1.2 The information processing cycle converts raw data, perhaps collected from a form on a website, into useful information.

# THE INFORMATION PROCESSING CYCLE

Computers convert data into information using the **information processing cycle (IPC)**. The four steps of the IPC are input, processing, storage, and output. Raw **data** is entered into the system during the input stage. The data is processed, or manipulated, to create useful **information**. The information is then stored for later retrieval and is returned to the user in the output stage. An example of how this works is illustrated in Figure 1.2.

As amazing as it may seem, it took nearly a century after Babbage designed his Analytical Engine before the first working mechanical computers were built. From that point, it took only about 40 years to go from those first-generation machines to the current fourth-generation designs. Since the first working computers became a reality, the computer has become an integral part of our modern lives.

## Running Project

Many developments of the Industrial Revolution helped pave the way for modern computers. In this article, we discussed the Jacquard loom. Use the Internet to find out how the following people also contributed: George Boole, Vannevar Bush, Nikola Tesla, and Gottfried Wilhelm Leibniz.

## 3 Things You Need to Know

- Computers are programmable machines.
- The four steps of the information processing cycle are input, processing, storage, and output.
- The IPC converts raw data into useful information.

## Key Terms

computer

data

information

information processing cycle (IPC)

# A Brief History of Computers

## Describe the evolution of computer hardware, and explain the importance of Moore's Law.

In this article, we look at the evolution of computers in the past century—from the first-generation massive machines of the 1930s and 1940s to the modern fourth-generation devices—and how Moore's Law has predicted the exponential growth of technology.

**ENIAC (Electronic Numerical Integrator and Computer)**, built at the University of Pennsylvania from 1943 to 1946, was the first working, digital, general-purpose computer. It used about 18,000 vacuum tubes, weighed almost 30 tons, and occupied about 1,800 square feet. Originally created to calculate artillery firing tables, ENIAC wasn't actually completed until after the war ended. Fortunately, the computer was capable of being reprogrammed to solve a range of other problems, such as atomic energy calculations, weather predictions, and wind-tunnel design. The programming was done by manipulating switches and took six programmers several days to complete (see Figure 1.4).

## HISTORY OF COMPUTERS

Computers have come a long way since Babbage and Lovelace. Between the mid-19th and mid-20th centuries, the Industrial Revolution gave way to the Information Age. Since that time, the pace of technology has grown exponentially—faster than it ever has before.

### FIRST-GENERATION COMPUTERS

During the 1930s and 1940s, several electromechanical and electronic computers were built. These first-generation computers were massive in size and used vacuum tubes and manual switches to process data. **Vacuum tubes**, which resemble incandescent lightbulbs, give off a lot of heat and are notoriously unreliable. Some of the most important first-generation computers include the Z1 and Z3 built in Germany; the Colossus machines in the United Kingdom; and the Atanasoff-Berry Computer (ABC), the Harvard Mark 1, ENIAC, and UNIVAC in the United States (see Figure 1.3).

60       1970       1980       1990       20

**FIGURE 1.3** Important First-generation Computers

| DATE | COMPUTER | ORIGIN | CREATOR | DESCRIPTION |
|---|---|---|---|---|
| 1936–41 | Z1–Z3 | Germany | Konrad Zuse | The Z1 through Z3 were mechanical, programmable computers. Working in isolation in Germany, Konrad Zuse didn't receive the support of the Nazi government, and his computers were destroyed during the war. |
| 1942 | Atanasoff-Berry Computer (ABC) | United States | Professor John Atanasoff and graduate student Clifford Berry at Iowa State College | The ABC was never fully functional, but Atanasoff won a patent dispute against John Mauchly (ENIAC), declaring Atanasoff the inventor of the electronic digital computer. |
| 1944 | Colossus | United Kingdom | Tommy Flowers | Used by code-breakers to translate encrypted German messages, these computers were destroyed after the war and kept secret until the 1970s. |
| 1944 | Harvard Mark 1 | United States | Designed by Howard Aiken and programmed by Grace Hopper at Harvard University | The Mark 1 was used by the U.S. Navy for gunnery and ballistic calculations until 1959. |
| 1946 | ENIAC | United States | Presper Eckert and John Mauchly at the University of Pennsylvania | ENIAC was the first working, digital, general-purpose computer. |
| 1951 | UNIVAC | United States | Eckert/Mauchly | The world's first commercially available computer, UNIVAC was famous for predicting the outcome of the 1952 presidential election. |

**FIGURE 1.4** ENIAC was the first working, digital, general-purpose computer.

## SECOND-GENERATION COMPUTERS

**Transistors**, tiny electronic switches, were invented in 1947 and led to second-generation computers in the 1950s and 1960s. The use of transistors in place of vacuum tubes allowed these newer computers to be more powerful, smaller, and more reliable. Equally important, they could be reprogrammed in far less time. Figure 1.5 illustrates the difference between the size of a vacuum tube and a transistor.

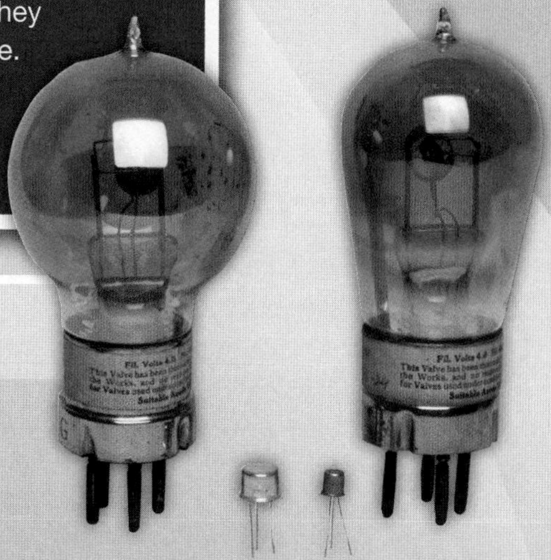

**FIGURE 1.5** The Vacuum Tube and the Transistor

## THIRD-GENERATION COMPUTERS

Developed in the 1960s, **integrated circuits** (see Figure 1.6) are chips that contain large numbers of tiny transistors that are integrated into a semiconducting material called silicon. Third-generation computers used multiple integrated circuits to process data and were even smaller, faster, and more reliable than their predecessors, although there was much overlap between second- and third-generation technologies in the 1960s. The Apollo Guidance Computer, used in the moon landing missions, was originally designed using transistors, but over time, the design was modified to use integrated circuits instead. The 2000 Nobel Prize in physics was awarded for the invention of the integrated circuit.

**FIGURE 1.6** Two Integrated Circuits on a Circuit Board

## FOURTH-GENERATION COMPUTERS

The integrated circuit made the development of the microprocessor possible in the 1970s. A **microprocessor** is a complex integrated circuit that contains the central processing unit (CPU) of a computer. The first microprocessor was developed in 1971 and was as powerful as ENIAC. Today's personal computers use microprocessors and are considered fourth-generation computers. Microprocessors can be found in everything from alarm clocks to automobiles to refrigerators.

## MOORE'S LAW

In 1965, Intel cofounder Gordon Moore observed that the number of transistors that could be placed on an integrated circuit had doubled roughly every 2 years. **Moore's Law** predicted this exponential growth would continue. The current trend is closer to doubling every 18 months and is expected to continue for another 10 to 20 years (see Figure 1.7). The increase in the capabilities of integrated circuits directly affects the processing speed and storage capacity of modern electronic devices.

Moore stated in a 1996 article: "More than anything, once something like this gets established, it becomes more or less a self-fulfilling prophecy. The Semiconductor Industry Association puts out a technology road map, which continues this [generational improvement] every three years. Everyone in the industry recognizes that if you don't stay on essentially that curve they will fall behind. So it sort of drives itself." Thus, Moore's Law really became a technology plan that guides the industry.

# Find Out MORE

Play the integrated circuit game at **www.Nobelprize.org/educational_games/physics/integrated_circuit/about** to learn more about this invention. Who invented the integrated circuit? Where might you still find a vacuum tube today? How did the invention of the transistor affect the radio? What's the significance of the handheld calculator?

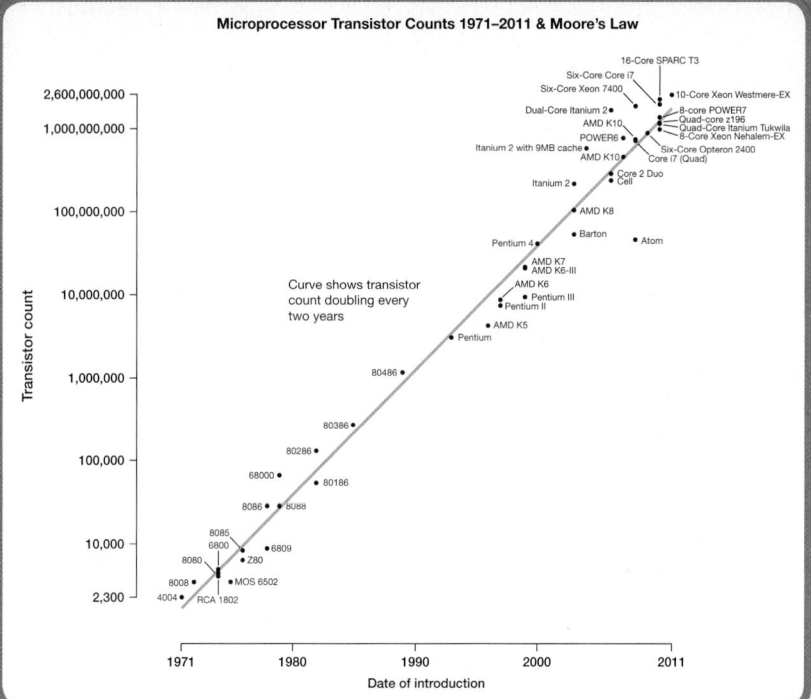

**Microprocessor Transistor Counts 1971–2011 & Moore's Law**

Transistor count

2,600,000,000
1,000,000,000
100,000,000
10,000,000
1,000,000
100,000
10,000
2,300

Date of introduction
1971    1980    1990    2000    2011

16-Core SPARC T3
Six-Core Core i7
Six-Core Xeon 7400
Dual-Core Itanium 2
10-Core Xeon Westmere-EX
8-core POWER7
AMD K10
Quad-core z196
POWER6
Quad-Core Itanium Tukwila
8-Core Xeon Nehalem-EX
Itanium 2 with 9MB cache
AMD K10
Six-Core Opteron 2400
Core i7 (Quad)
Itanium 2
Core 2 Duo
Cell
AMD K8
Pentium 4
Barton
Atom
AMD K7
AMD K6-III
AMD K6
Pentium III
Pentium II
AMD K5
Pentium
80486
80386
80286
68000
80186
8086
8088
8085
6800
6809
8080
Z80
8008
MOS 6502
4004
RCA 1802

Curve shows transistor
count doubling every
two years

**FIGURE 1.7** Moore's Law Graphically Represented

Over the last several decades, the end of Moore's Law has been predicted. Each time, new technological advances have kept it going. Moore himself admits that exponential growth can't continue forever, but there's no denying the impact his law has had on the pace of technology in the last 45 years (see Figure 1.8).

In less than a century, computers have gone from massive, unreliable, and costly machines to being an integral part of almost everything we do. As technology has improved, the size and costs have dropped as the speed, power, and reliability have grown. Today, the chip inside your cell phone has more processing power than that first microprocessor developed in 1971. Technology that was science fiction just a few decades ago is now commonplace.

**Because electricity travels** a shorter distance in a smaller transistor, smaller transistors mean faster chips. It would take you about 25,000 years to turn a light switch on and off 1.5 trillion times, but Intel has developed transistors that can switch on and off that many times each second.

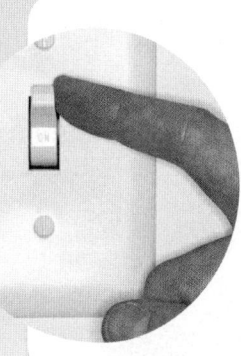

**In 1978, a commercial flight** between New York and Paris cost around $900 and took seven hours. If the principles of Moore's Law had been applied to the airline industry the way they have to the semiconductor industry since 1978, that flight would now cost about a penny and take less than one second.

**FIGURE 1.8** In 2005, to celebrate its 40th anniversary, Intel released some interesting statistics that illustrate Moore's Law.

## Running Project

Use the Internet to look up vacuum tubes and transistors. What are some of the places they're still used today?

## 5 Things You Need to Know

- First-generation computers used vacuum tubes.
- Second-generation computers used transistors.
- Third-generation computers used integrated circuits (chips).
- Fourth-generation computers use microprocessors.
- Moore's Law states that the number of transistors that can be placed on an integrated circuit doubles roughly every 2 years—although today it is closer to every 18 months.

## Key Terms

ENIAC (Electronic Numerical Integrator and Computer)

integrated circuit

microprocessor

Moore's Law

transistor

vacuum tube

# HOW TO
## Use QR Codes

*QR* (or *Quick Response*) *codes* are those funny-looking black-and-white checkered squares that you may have seen in magazines, on store merchandise, and in this text-book. They can contain more information about a product, a link to a website, a coupon, or even serve as a digital business card. In this How To, you learn how to use your mobile device to scan and use QR codes, and how to create one for your own use.

Many smartphones and tablets come with built-in QR code readers. For those that don't, there are many free and paid apps that you can download and install. So, the first step in this exercise is to figure out whether you already have the ability to scan the codes. If you do, you can use your mobile device to scan the QR codes throughout this book. Scan the test QR code at the end of this exercise to test your setup.

Open your word processor and type your name and date in the document. Save the file as **lastname_firstname_ch01_howto1**.

In your document, answer the following questions before you begin.

What type of mobile device do you have? Does it have an app that can be used to scan QR codes installed on it? If so, which one? Have you used this app before? If so, for what?

## ANDROID DEVICES PART A
## INSTALLING GOOGLE GOGGLES

If you have an Android device, check to see if you have Google Goggles installed on your device. If you do, you are all set and can skip to Part B. If not, you'll need to open the Play Store app.

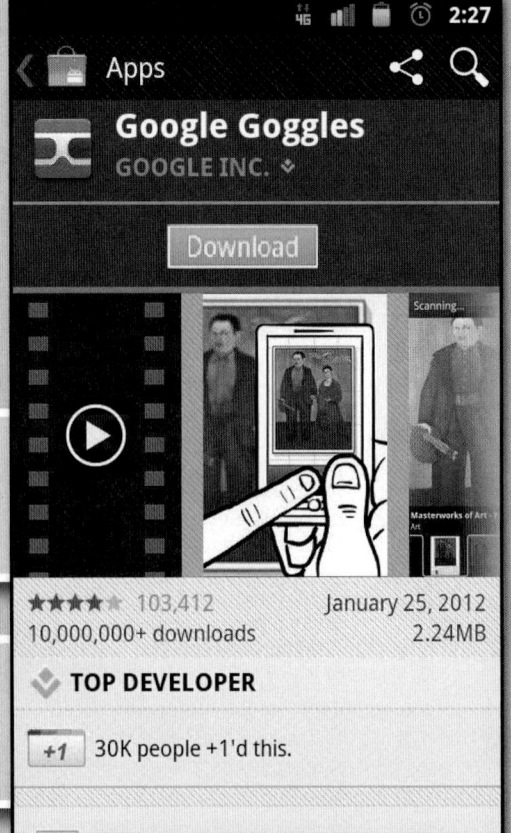

**1** Open the Play Store on your phone. In the Search box, type **Google Goggles.**

**2** Read through the description and reviews. Press *Download* to begin.

**3** Read the information under PERMISSIONS to make sure that you are comfortable with them and then choose *Accept and Download.*

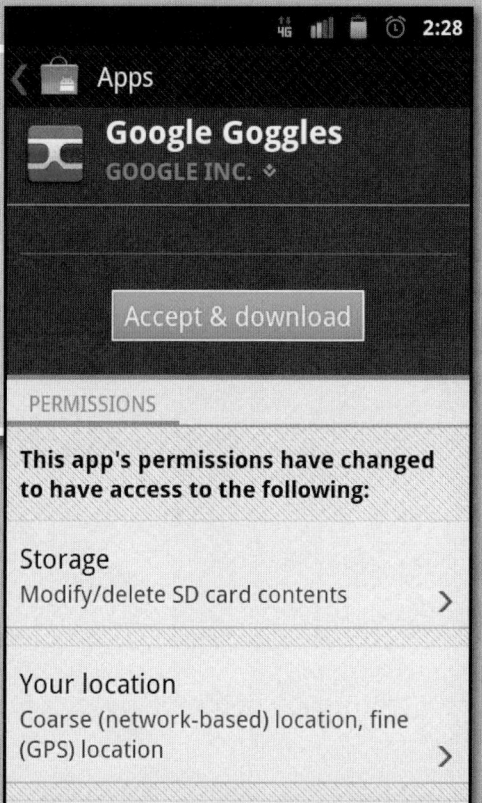

**4** Once the installation is finished, press Open to start the app.

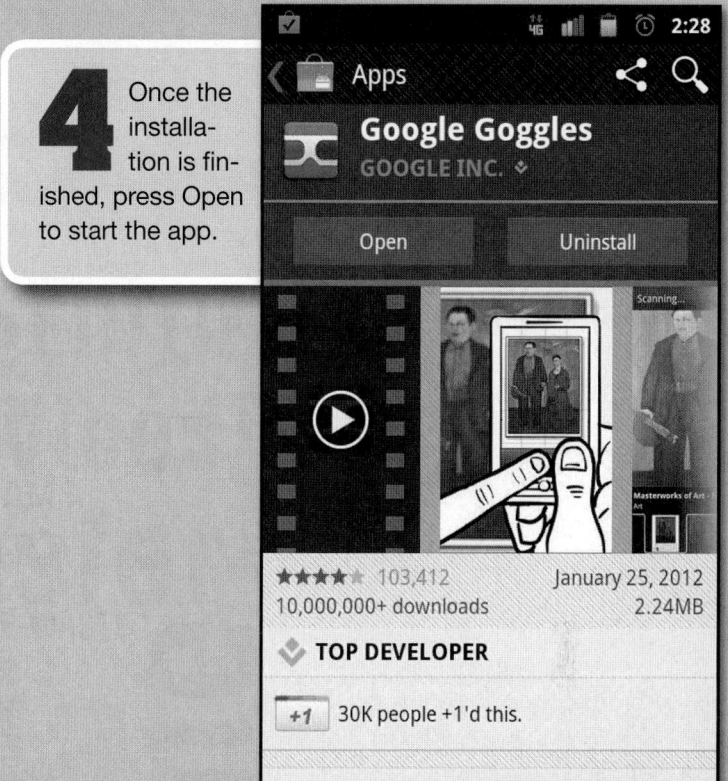

**5** Choose *Learn more* to find out what Goggles can do.

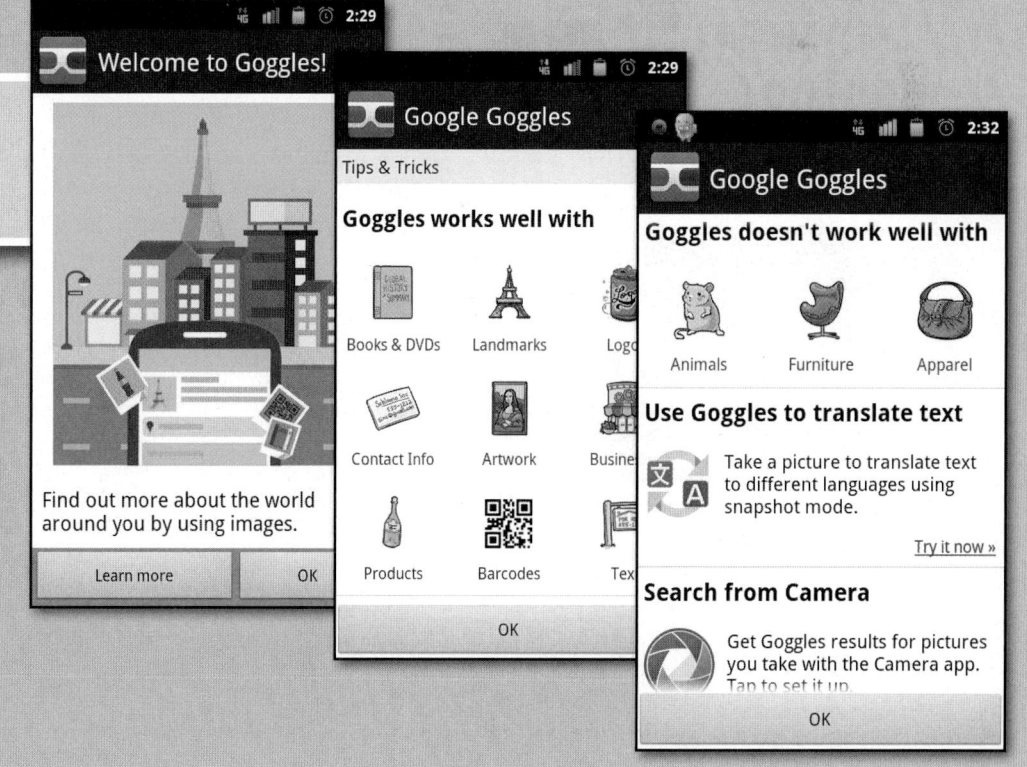

# ANDROID DEVICES PART B
## SCANNING A QR CODE

**6** Test the app using this QR code. Point your phone camera toward the code and press *Snapshot*.

**7** Press the link at the bottom of the result to be taken to the URL.

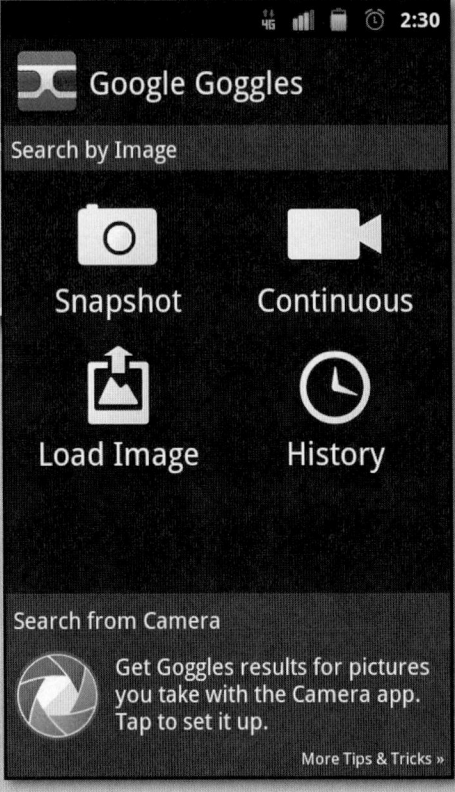

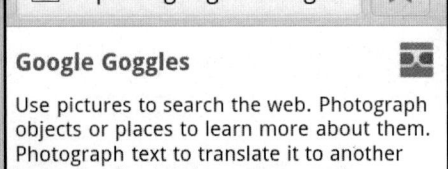

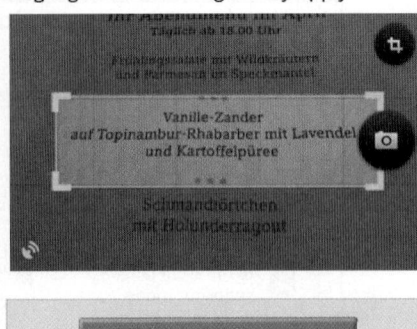

**8** What website did the link take you to? What did you learn from this website? Do you think that scanning the QR code was easier than typing in a URL?

Enter your answers in your document, save the file, and submit it as directed by your instructor.

# APPLE IOS DEVICES PART A
## INSTALLING GOOGLE SEARCH

**1** On your iPad or iPhone, open the App Store and search for Google Search.

**2** Press the *FREE* button and then press *INSTALL APP.*

**3** Enter your Apple ID Password.

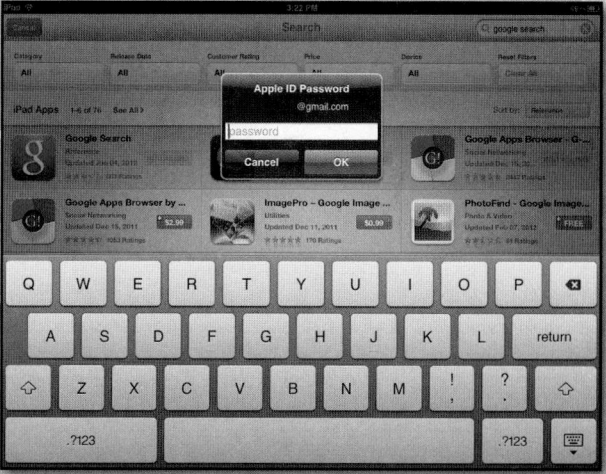

**4** Once the app has installed, open it by pressing the *Google Search* icon.

**5** Click *Goggles*.

**6** Swipe through screens to learn more about the app.

**7** Read and accept mobile terms of service.

**8** Decide whether to enable search History.

# APPLE IOS DEVICES PART B
## SCANNING A QR CODE

**9** Test the app by scanning this QR code. Point your phone camera toward the code, and the app should automatically recognize and scan it.

**10** Press the link at the bottom of the screen to be taken to the URL.

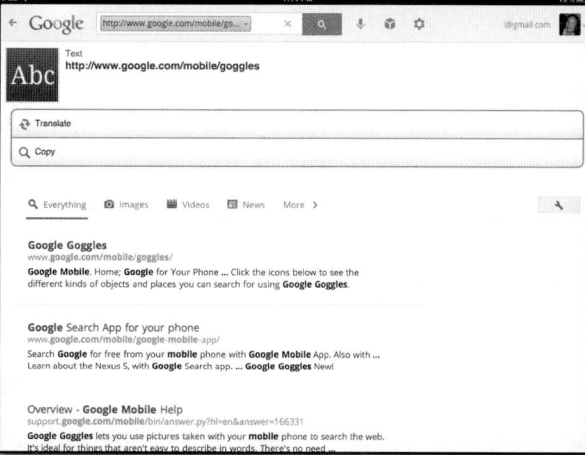

**11** What website did the link take you to? What did you learn from this website? Do you think that scanning the QR code was easier than typing in a URL?

**12** Enter your answers in your document, save the file, and submit it as directed by your instructor.

To learn more about what this app can do, visit **google.com/mobile/goggles.** Google Search is available for many different mobile platforms. To install it on a device not described in this exercise, use your mobile browser to visit **m.google.com/search**.

Can you scan a QR code from a desktop or notebook computer? Yes! There are apps that you can download to these devices. You will need a webcam to scan the codes.

Test that your QR scanner is working correctly by scanning this QR code.

# Bits and Bytes

**VIZ CLIP**

## 3 OBJECTIVE
## Describe how computers represent data using binary code.

Humans have 10 digits (fingers), which is why we find the decimal, or base 10, number system to be natural. (Remember how you used your fingers and toes to do math when you were a kid?) Computers don't have fingers; they have switches and use the **binary number system (base 2)**, which has only two digits (0 and 1).

## BINARY CODE

Computers don't speak English (or Spanish, Chinese, or Greek, for that matter), so how does a computer understand what we enter? On a typewriter, when you press the A key, you get an A, but computers only understand 0s and 1s, so when you press the A key, it must somehow be represented by 0s and 1s. Digital data is represented using a binary code.

    **Binary code** works like a bank of light switches. If you have only a single light switch in a room, there are two possible states—the light can either be on or it can be off. This code can be used for situations with only two possibilities, such as yes/no, true/false, or boy/girl, but it fails when there are more than two choices (yes/no/maybe). Adding another switch, or bit, increases the possible combinations by a factor of two ($2^2$), which equals 4 possibilities (see Figure 1.9). A third bit (switch) gives us $2^3$ or 8 possibilities and so on. A **bit** (short for binary digit) is the smallest unit of digital information. Eight bits equals a **byte**, which gives us $2^8$ or 256 possibilities. A byte is used to represent a single character in modern computer systems. For example, when you press the A key, the binary code 01000001 (which equals 65 in decimal) is sent to the computer.

**FIGURE 1.9** A binary code using 8 switches, or bits, has 256 different possible combinations.

| NUMBER OF BITS (SWITCHES) | POSSIBILITIES | POWER OF TWO |
|---|---|---|
| 1 | 2 | $2^1$ |
| 2 | 4 | $2^2$ |
| 3 | 8 | $2^3$ |
| 4 | 16 | $2^4$ |
| 5 | 32 | $2^5$ |
| 6 | 64 | $2^6$ |
| 7 | 128 | $2^7$ |
| 8 | 256 | $2^8$ |

**ASCII (American Standard Code for Information Interchange)** was originally developed in the 1960s using a 7-bit system that represented 128 characters and included English alphabet symbols (upper- and lowercase), numbers 0 through 9, punctuation, and a few special characters. It was later expanded to an 8-bit extended set with 256 characters. ASCII needed to be adapted to be used for other languages, and many extended sets were developed. The most common extended ASCII set is **Unicode**. It has become the standard on the Internet and includes codes for most of the world's written languages, mathematical systems, and special characters. It has codes for more than 100,000 characters. The first 256 characters are the same in both ASCII and Unicode; however, the characters in the last rows in Figure 1.10 include Latin, Greek, and Cyrillic symbols, which are represented only in Unicode.

| CHARACTER | ASCII | UNICODE |
|---|---|---|
| " | 34 | 34 |
| # | 35 | 35 |
| $ | 36 | 36 |
| 0 | 48 | 48 |
| 1 | 49 | 49 |
| 2 | 50 | 50 |
| A | 65 | 65 |
| B | 66 | 66 |
| C | 67 | 67 |
| a | 97 | 97 |
| b | 98 | 98 |
| c | 99 | 99 |
| ő | | 337 |
| œ | | 339 |
| ŕ | | 341 |
| ə | | 399 |
| ƛ | | 411 |
| α | | 945 |

**FIGURE 1.10** ASCII and Unicode Representations

| Decimal Prefix | Symbol | Decimal Value | |
|---|---|---|---|
| | | Exponential | Numeric |
| kilo | K or k | $10^3$ | 1,000 |
| mega | M | $10^6$ | 1,000,000 |
| giga | G | $10^9$ | 1,000,000,000 |
| tera | T | $10^{12}$ | 1,000,000,000,000 |
| peta | P | $10^{15}$ | 1,000,000,000,000,000 |
| exa | E | $10^{18}$ | 1,000,000,000,000,000,000 |
| zetta | Z | $10^{21}$ | 1,000,000,000,000,000,000,000 |
| yotta | Y | $10^{24}$ | 1,000,000,000,000,000,000,000,000 |

| Binary Prefix | Symbol | Binary Prefix | Decimal Value |
|---|---|---|---|
| kibi | Ki | kibi | 1,024 |
| mebi | Mi | mebi | 1,048,576 |
| gibi | Gi | gibi | 1,073,741,824 |
| tebi | Ti | tebi | 1,099,511,627,776 |
| pebi | Pi | pebi | 1,125,899,906,842,624 |
| exbi | Ei | exbi | 1,152,921,504,606,846,976 |
| zebi | Zi | zebi | 1,180,591,620,717,411,303,424 |
| yobi | Yi | yobi | 1,208,925,819,614,629,174,706,176 |

**FIGURE 1.11** A Comparison of Decimal and Binary Storage Capacity Prefixes

# MEASURING DATA

Today, bits (b) are used to measure data transfer rates (such as your Internet connection), and bytes (B) are used to measure file size and storage capacity. The decimal prefixes of kilo ($10^3$), mega ($10^6$), giga ($10^9$), etc., are added to the base unit to indicate larger values. Binary prefixes kibi ($2^{10}$), mebi ($2^{20}$), and gibi ($2^{30}$), have been adopted, although their use isn't widespread. A megabyte (MB) is equal to 1,000,000 bytes, and a mebibyte (MiB) is equal to 1,048,576 bytes, a slightly larger value. Figure 1.11 compares the two systems.

A megabyte (MB) can hold about 500 pages of plain text, but a single picture taken with a modern digital camera can be several megabytes in size. As the types of files we save have changed from plain text to images, music, and video, the file sizes have become larger, and the need for storage has grown dramatically—but, fundamentally, all files are still just 0s and 1s.

## 4 Things You Need to Know

- Computers use the binary (base 2) number system.
- ASCII and Unicode are binary code character sets.
- A bit is the smallest unit of digital information.
- A byte is equal to 8 bits and represents one character.

## Key Terms

ASCII (American Standard Code for Information Interchange)

binary code

binary number system (base 2)

bit

byte

Unicode

# Let's Get Personal

## 4 OBJECTIVE
### List the various types and characteristics of personal computers.

A personal computer is a small microprocessor-based computer designed to be used by one person at a time. Today, the term **personal computer (PC)** usually refers to a computer running a Windows operating system; however, Macintosh computers and those running Linux operating systems are also personal computers.

**Try the Internet Simulation**

SIMULATION

## DESKTOP COMPUTERS

**Desktop computers** are designed to sit on a user's desk. They range in price from under $300 for basic personal systems to thousands of dollars for cutting-edge machines that can be used for video editing, gaming, and number crunching. Desktop computers offer the most speed, power, and upgradability for the lowest cost. The term **workstation** is used in a business environment to refer to a high-end desktop computer or one that's attached to a network.

**FIGURE 1.12** An all-in-one desktop computer with the components mounted behind the monitor is popular in settings in which desktop space is limited.

An **all-in-one computer** is a compact desktop computer with an integrated monitor (see Figure 1.12). Some systems have a touch-screen monitor and are wall-mountable. All-in-ones save desktop real estate but may be difficult to upgrade because of their small size. They are popular in places where space is at a premium, such as emergency rooms, bank teller windows, and business cubicles.

# NOTEBOOK COMPUTERS

**Notebook**, or laptop, computers are portable personal computers. Today's notebook computers rival desktops in power and storage capacity—but at a price. A notebook can cost about twice as much as a comparable desktop system. However, the cost of all computers has come down dramatically, and notebook computers are becoming more popular as a result. In 2008, sales of notebooks surpassed desktop sales, and by 2015 notebooks are expected to outsell desktops more than 2:1. Once used primarily by business travelers, notebooks are now common on college campuses, in living rooms, and in coffee shops. Modern notebook computers typically come with built-in wireless networking capabilities, webcams, and bright widescreen displays. Desktop replacements are high-end notebooks with large screens and powerful processors.

A **tablet PC** is a type of notebook computer that has a screen that can swivel to fold into what resembles a notepad or tablet. These computers include a special digital pen or stylus that allows the user to write directly on the screen. Tablet PCs are useful for taking notes or drawing diagrams and for making information such as sales catalogs portable. Recent versions of Windows include a feature called Windows Touch, which offers multi-touch capability. Newer all-in-ones and tablets that support multi-touch allow you to interact with your computer using not just one finger but two or even four!

The smallest type of notebook computer is called a **netbook**. These lightweight, inexpensive computers are designed primarily for Internet access. Netbooks have built-in wireless capabilities but have small screens and offer limited computing power and storage. With prices starting under $200, netbooks are a popular option for casual users or for use as a second machine (see Figure 1.13).

**FIGURE 1.13** A large desktop replacement notebook and a tiny netbook are two types of notebook computers.

# MAC OR PC?

You've seen the commercials on TV and perhaps have used different types of computers at work or in school. In the personal computer market, there are two main types of personal computers to choose from: Macs and PCs. So, the question is: What's the difference between the two, and which one should you choose? All the types of hardware discussed in this chapter apply to both types of computers. The primary difference between them is the operating system they run. We'll discuss operating systems in detail in another chapter.

**Mac** computers are built by Apple and run the OS X operating system. Using a program called Boot Camp that's included with OS X, users can also run Windows on a Mac. Macs have a reputation for being secure, stable, and fun. They come with a variety of useful programs already installed and are very user-friendly. Macs are often used in creative businesses, such as advertising and graphic design.

PCs can be built by any number of companies, including Dell, Hewlett-Packard, Acer, and Toshiba. PCs that run some version of the Windows or Linux operating systems constitute over 90 percent of the U.S. market share. Because they're produced by many manufacturers, PCs are available in numerous models, configurations, and price ranges. They also have a vast selection of software available.

The type of computer you choose depends on many factors, including personal preferences, the types of software you need to run, compatibility with school or work computers, and, of course, cost.

Figure 1.14 highlights some of the features of both types of computers.

**FIGURE 1.14** Comparing Mac and PC Computers

## MAC

### ADVANTAGES
- Easy to set up and use
- Great multimedia capabilities
- Secure and stable
- iLife software suite included

## PC

### ADVANTAGES
- Less expensive for similar capabilities
- Can run many versions of Windows and Linux
- More configuration choices
- The preferred platform in most businesses
- Most computer games are only available for Windows PCs

Personal computers, designed to be used by one person at a time, have become so commonplace that even in the tough economy of 2011, it was estimated that U.S. sales topped 370 million units, and roughly 80 percent of U.S. households had at least one personal computer.

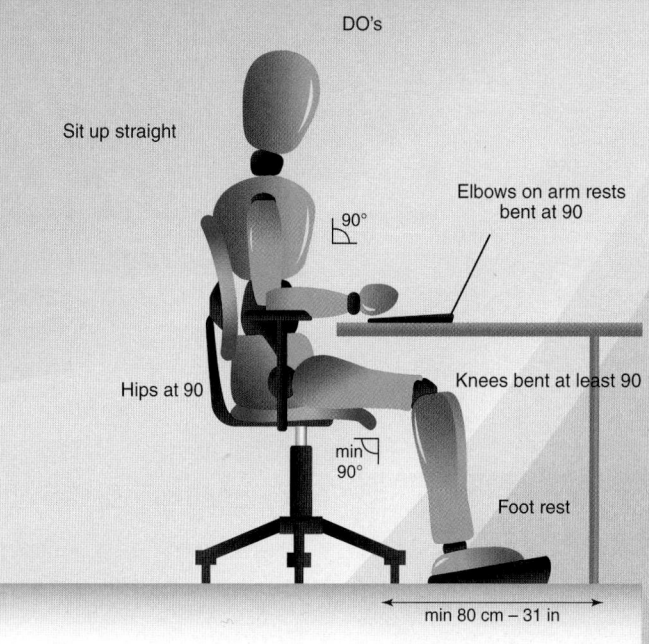

## ERGONOMICS

**Ergonomics** is the study of the relationship between workers and their workspaces. An improperly set up workspace can affect your health, comfort, and productivity. Ergonomic design creates a work environment designed to reduce illnesses and musculoskeletal disorders. The furniture you use, the lighting in the room, and the position of your equipment all affect your work environment.

Your basic goals should be to keep your body in a neutral body position, without twisting or turning to reach or see your screen. You should not need to lean forward, and your feet should be flat on the ground or on a footrest. Your monitor should be at or below eye level so you don't need to tilt your neck to see it, and the lighting shouldn't cause glare on your screen. The keyboard and mouse should be positioned so your arms are in a relaxed position. One important step that many people forget is to take regular breaks to stretch and move around. Whether you're writing a report for school, doing your income taxes, or playing a video game, following ergonomic design principles will help you work more comfortably and reduce strain on your body.

## Running Project

It's hard to imagine a job that doesn't require a working knowledge of personal computers. Look up the term "digital literacy." Use several different websites to get an idea of what this term means. Then, write up a description of digital literacy for the career that you plan to pursue.

## 5 Things You Need to Know

- Desktop computers give you the most bang for your buck.
- All-in-one computers are smaller but less upgradable desktops.
- Notebook computers are portable and have dramatically dropped in price.
- Tablet PCs and netbooks are specialized notebook computers.
- The primary difference between a Mac and a PC is the operating system, not the hardware.

## Key Terms

all-in-one computer

desktop computer

ergonomics

Mac

netbook

notebook

personal computer (PC)

tablet PC

workstation

# HOW TO

## Create Screenshots of your Desktop

Throughout this book, you're asked to provide screenshots of the work you've done. This is quite easy to do and is also useful in other situations. For example, it's very helpful for providing someone else with directions on how to do something or for keeping a record of an error message that appears on your screen.

Recent Windows releases include a nifty little utility called the Snipping Tool.

The Snipping Tool can capture four types of Snips:

- **Free-form Snip:** Allows you to draw the boundaries around an object for a snip
- **Rectangular Snip:** Allows you to draw a rectangle around an object for a snip
- **Window Snip:** Captures a selected window for a snip
- **Full-screen Snip:** Captures the whole screen for a snip

Click and then drag the mouse around the object for a Free-form or Rectangular Snip. Click the object for a Window or Full-screen Snip.

You can save your screenshots, email them, paste them into documents, and even annotate and highlight them using the buttons on the Snipping Tool toolbar.

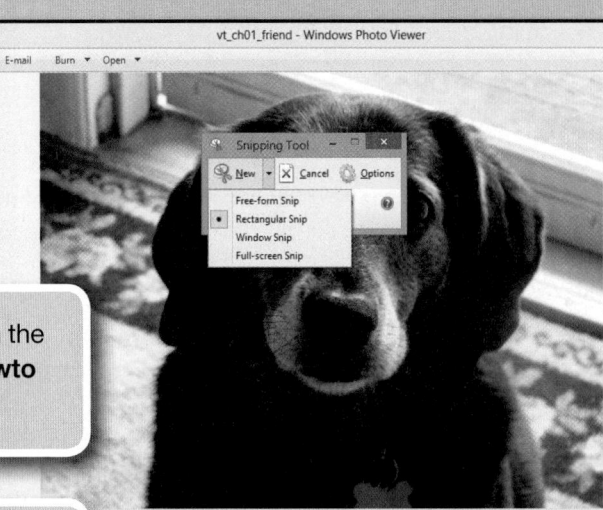

 Open your word processor and type your name and date in the document. Save the file as **lastname_firstname_ch01_howto**

 Locate to the student files for this chapter. Right-click the file *vt_ch01_friend*, point to Open with, and choose Windows Photo Viewer.

 Display the Windows 8 Start screen and type **snip**. From the Start Search results, click the Snipping Tool app.

 In the Snipping Tool window, click the drop-down arrow next to New and select *Free-form snip*.

 Draw a line around the dog's head with the Snipping Tool scissors. Paste the snip into your document and type **Free-form Snip** under it.

Use the same procedure to capture a rectangular snip of the dog's head, paste it into your document, and type **Rectangular Snip** under it.

Use the Snipping Tool to capture a Window Snip and a Full-screen Snip of the dog, pasting and labeling each in your document.

In a paragraph, describe the difference between each of the snips you took. Save the file and submit your file as directed by your instructor.

If you are using a Mac, follow these directions for steps 3–7 instead:

Use the Launchpad to open Grab, located in the Utilities folder. From the Capture menu, choose Selection, Window, or Screen, as appropriate. Follow the on-screen directions to take your capture. Once you have captured each image, use the Edit menu to copy it and paste it into your document.

# Beyond the Desktop

## Give examples of other personal computing devices.

Today, the term "computer" no longer refers only to those desktop devices used for office work. We carry computers with us everywhere we go. In some countries, mobile devices have become the primary computing devices that many people have access to.

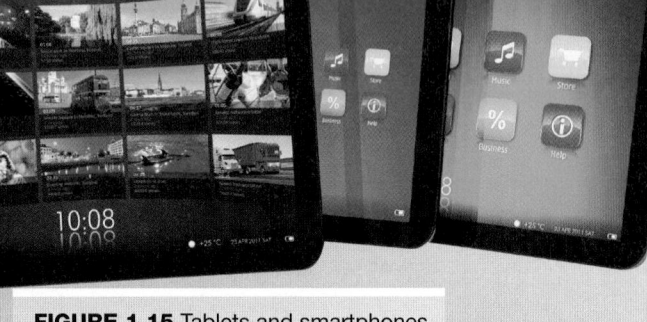

**FIGURE 1.15** Tablets and smartphones are portable handheld computers.

## HANDHELD AND MOBILE DEVICES

Handheld and mobile devices are portable computers used for business and entertainment and come in many different shapes and sizes—from smartphones to heart-rate monitors that you wear on your wrist. Some of these devices serve specialized functions, such as GPS navigation, while others, such as tablets, are more general-purpose devices. These devices have more features and capabilities with every new model introduced, and prices continue to drop.

## SMARTPHONES AND TABLETS

**Mobile devices** such as smartphones and tablets are small computers we carry with us wherever we go (see Figure 1.15). They combine such features as Internet and email access, digital cameras, GPS and mapping tools, the ability to edit documents, and access to thousands of mobile apps. Also referred to as **handhelds**, these devices are useful when carrying a regular notebook computer isn't practical. Once primarily the tool of the business professional, smartphones have become indispensable to the rest of us. Mobile devices are the fastest-growing segment of personal computers, making up over 60 percent of worldwide PC sales in 2011.

**FIGURE 1.16** The Global Positioning System (GPS) is a satellite-based navigation system composed of a network of 24 satellites placed into orbit by the U.S. Department of Defense.

**GPS AND WEARABLES** Commonly found on cell phones and in newer cars, another familiar device is a GPS unit. Originally built by the military, **GPS (global positioning system)** consists of 24 satellites (see Figure 1.16) that transmit signals that can be picked up by a GPS receiver on the ground and used to determine its current location, time, and velocity through triangulation of the signals. Since the mid-1990s, GPS devices have been available for civilian use. There are also scientific applications for GPS technology, such as surveying, map making, self-navigating robots, and clock synchronization. GPS is used in automobiles, airplanes, and boats for navigation and tracking. There are many mobile apps that use GPS for navigation, location services, and just plain fun. For example, some apps will use your location to determine the types of information you should be presented with (such as nearby restaurant or gas station information).

Computers designed to be worn on the body are called **wearables**. These hands-free computers are used for health monitoring, communications, military operations, and entertainment (see Figure 1.17).

**FIGURE 1.17** Modern technology is incorporated into the equipment worn by soldiers.

# Find Out MORE

Geocaching is an electronic scavenger hunt played around the world. Geocachers hide geocaches and post GPS coordinates on the Internet. Other geocachers can then find geocaches using their own GPS devices. The geocaches have logbooks to sign and often small prizes. Geocachers that find a prize leave something else in return, so you never know what you'll find!

Visit **geocaching.com** to find geocaches near you. How many geocaches are there near you? Are they in an urban or rural area? How many are there globally? What is "Cache In Trash Out"? What are Geocoins and Travel Bugs?

On your mobile device, search the app store for GPS. How many hits did you get? What types of apps are listed?

# VIDEO GAME SYSTEMS

A **video game system** is a computer that's designed primarily to play games. The first arcade video games were released in the early 1970s, and video game systems for the home soon followed. Magnavox released its Odyssey game console in 1972. It was programmed to play 12 different games. Atari released a home version of PONG (see Figure 1.18) for the 1975 holiday season, sold exclusively through Sears. For many people, video game consoles were the first computers they had in their homes.

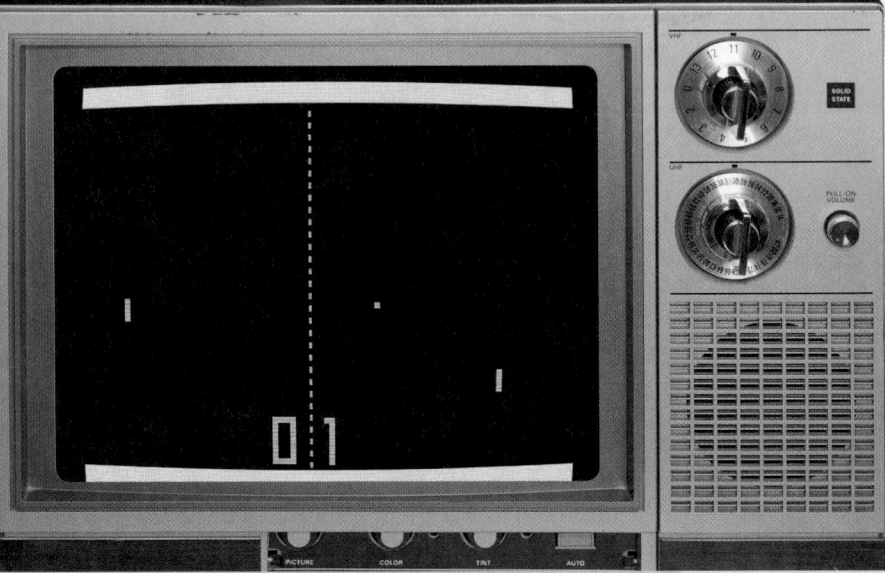

**FIGURE 1.18** Atari released a home version of PONG, an electronic ping-pong game, in 1975. It became one of the hottest gifts of the year.

Today's systems are considered seventh-generation video games and have high-end processing and graphic capabilities, the ability to play movies and music, enable online game play, and even allow users to browse the Internet. Game consoles, such as Microsoft Xbox 360 and Sony Playstation 3, have built-in hard drives, can play DVDs, and offer high-definition resolution. Kinect for Xbox 360 has motion and voice sensors allowing you to play certain games without a controller. Nintendo's Wii is less powerful and less expensive than either the Xbox 360 or the Playstation 3, but it's also more popular. The Wii has unique motion-sensing controllers, giving players new gameplay experiences and interactivity. The Wii has reached out to nontraditional markets, such as senior citizens and suburban moms, by offering such unique games as bowling, tennis, Wii Fit, and Brain Age. All three systems offer some level of backward-compatibility with older systems.

Handheld video games, such as the Nintendo 3DS and DSi and Playstation Portable (PSP) Vita allow you to take your games wherever you go. Newer versions even allow you to view photos and listen to music. You can download and watch movies on the PSP Vita and chat with friends over 3G or WiFi. The 3DS has two built-in cameras for taking pictures as well as built-in photo-editing software. Both systems include Internet capabilities, 3D graphics, and a multicamera system that lets you take 3D photos (Figure 1.19). These devices even allow you to view photos, listen to music, and browse the Web.

**FIGURE 1.19** Kids young and old play video games today.

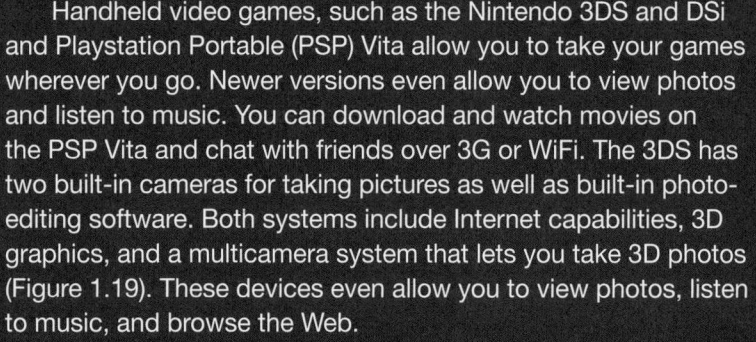

## Running Project

Video game systems aren't just for entertainment anymore. Use the Internet to find out how medical students are using video games to learn to be better doctors. What are some of the medical schools using such systems? How are they used? How do professors and students feel about them?

## 4 Things You Need to Know

● Smartphones and tablets are handheld, mobile computers.

● GPS is a satellite-based navigation system.

● Wearables are computers designed to be worn on the body.

● Today's video game consoles are seventh-generation systems with high-end graphics and processing.

## Key Terms

GPS (global positioning system)

handheld

mobile device

video game system

wearable

# Multiuser Computers

**6** OBJECTIVE
## List the various types and characteristics of multiuser computers.

**Multiuser computers** are systems that allow multiple, simultaneous users to connect to them. The advantages of multiuser systems include centralized resources and security. Multiuser computers are also more powerful than personal computers.

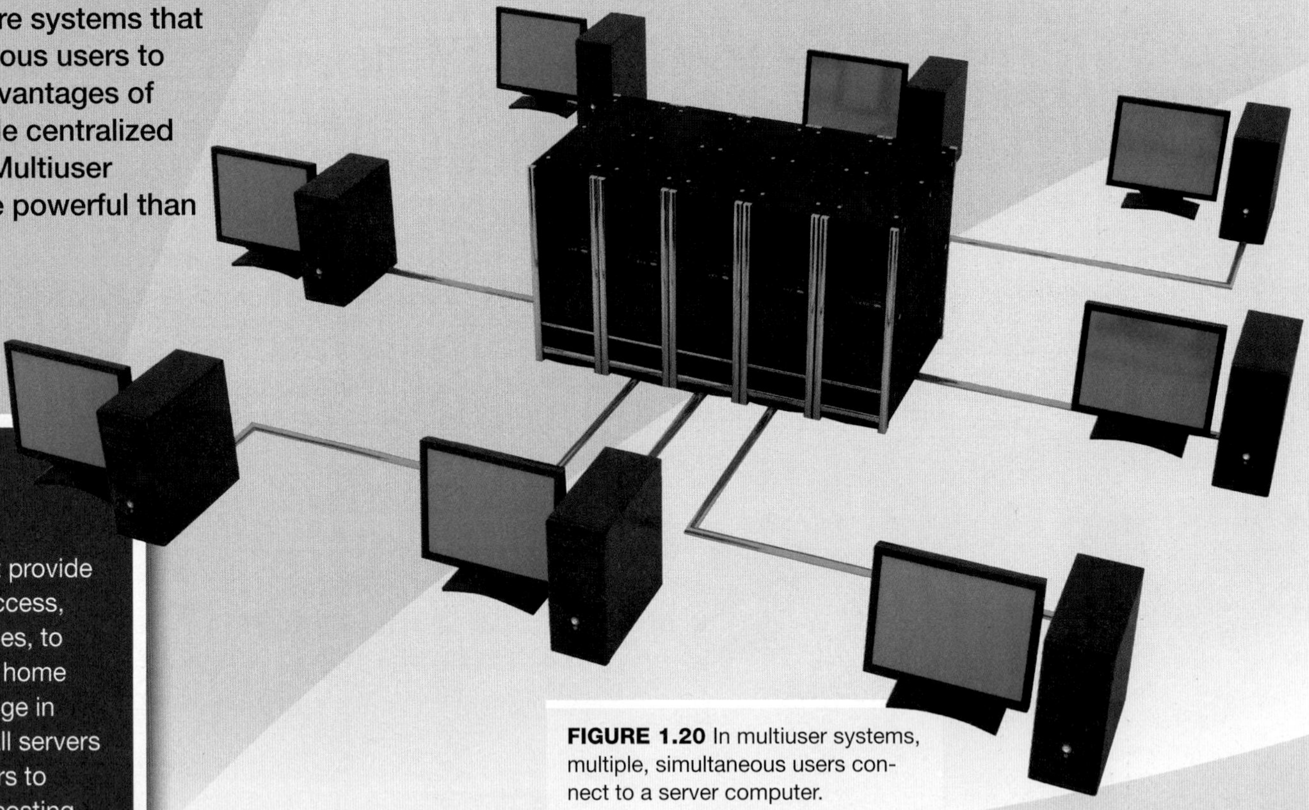

## SERVERS

**Servers** are computers that provide services, such as Internet access, email, or file and print services, to client systems such as your home or office computer. They range in size and cost from very small servers costing a few hundred dollars to massive enterprise servers costing hundreds of thousands of dollars (see Figure 1.20).

**FIGURE 1.20** In multiuser systems, multiple, simultaneous users connect to a server computer.

**FIGURE 1.21** Enterprise servers can allow thousands of simultaneous users and perform millions of transactions every day.

The smallest multiuser computers are called **minicomputers** and support fewer than 200 users. Users connect to minicomputers via dumb terminals, which have no processing capabilities of their own. Today, minicomputers have been replaced by midrange servers that users connect to via personal computers called **clients**. Midrange servers can be used to perform complex calculations, store customer information and transactions, or host an email system for an organization. They can support hundreds of simultaneous users and are scalable, allowing for growth as a company's needs change.

**Mainframes** are large computers that can perform millions of transactions in a day. These are most commonly found in businesses that have massive amounts of data or transactions to process, such as banks and insurance companies. Mainframe computers have largely been replaced by enterprise servers, and the terms are sometimes used synonymously (see Figure 1.21). These systems allow thousands of users to utilize the system concurrently.

# SUPERCOMPUTERS

**Supercomputers** are very expensive computer systems that are used to perform complex mathematical calculations, such as those used in weather forecasting and medical research. Designed to perform a limited number of tasks as quickly as possible, supercomputers can consist of a single computer with multiple processors or a group of computers that work together. The world's top supercomputers can be found at major universities and research institutes around the world. Figure 1.22 provides a sampling from the listing of the top 500 supercomputers, which is located at **top500.org**.

**FIGURE 1.22** Key Supercomputers

| RESEARCH INSTITUTE | LOCATION | USES |
|---|---|---|
| RIKEN Advanced Institute for Computational Science (AICS) (#1- Nov 2011) | Japan **aics.riken.jp/en/** | • Simulation research<br>• Human resource development programs |
| Shanghai Supercomputer Center (#58 - Nov. 2011) | China **ssc.net.cn/** | • Weather forecasts<br>• Oil exploration<br>• Biomedical<br>• Gene research<br>• Aviation and aeronautics |
| NASA/Ames Research Center/NAS (#7- Nov. 2011) | United States **nas.nasa.gov** | • Critical NASA missions<br>• Scientific discoveries for the benefit of humankind |
| Amazon Web Services (#42- Nov. 2011) | United States **aws.amazon .com/ec2/ hpc-applications** | • High Performance Computing (HPC) |

# DISTRIBUTED AND GRID COMPUTING

**Distributed computing** distributes the processing of a task across a group of computers. This can be done on a fairly small scale, using a few computers in one location (known as **grid computing**) or on a much larger scale. Some of these projects rely on **volunteer computing**, using the processing power of hundreds or thousands of personal computers. At **boinc.berkeley .edu**, a volunteer can choose from a variety of projects to join.

SETI@home Multi-Beam

Computing Fast Fourier Transform
Doppler drift rate 11.1521 Hz/sec   Resolution 0.596 Hz
Best Gaussian: power  2.89, fit 1.305, score −1.774

Overall 15.094% done     CPU time: 1 hr 30 min 39.57 sec

Data info
From:   9 hr 55' 46" RA, +22 deg 18' 29" Dec
Recorded on: Wed Nov 23 10:01:02 2011
Recorded at: Arecibo 1.4GHz Array, Beam 5, Pol 1
Base frequency: 1.420429688 GHz

User info
Name: Home
Team:
Total credit: 0.00

Time (sec)

Power

Frequency (Hz)

SETI@home
The Search for Extraterrestrial Intelligence

**FIGURE 1.23** The SETI@home screen gives you a picture of what your computer's doing.

A volunteer interested in astronomy might join SETI@home. One of the first volunteer computing projects, SETI@home has had more than 6 million participants since it was launched in 1999. A volunteer downloads and installs a program that runs as a screensaver when the computer is idle. This allows SETI to utilize the processing abilities of the individual's computer without having to pay for processing time and without compromising the user's ability to complete his or her own projects. The SETI screensaver is actually a complex piece of software that downloads and analyzes radio telescope data to Search for Extraterrestrial Intelligence (see Figure 1.23). The Seti@Home website (**setiathome.ssl.berkeley.edu/**) has an active message board system where volunteers can talk to the scientists and to each other.

Multiuser systems allow users to leverage the power of computers that far exceed what a PC can do. The ability to centrally manage information and security and to distribute the processing across multiple systems has given the scientific and business communities the power to solve many of our most pressing problems in an extremely short amount of time.

## Running Project

Select one supercomputer from the current top 50 list at **top500.org**, and use the Internet to find out more about the type of work it is used for. Write two or three paragraphs highlighting some of its achievements.

## 5 Things You Need to Know

- Servers provide services such as file and print sharing and email to client computers.
- Minicomputers have largely been replaced by midsized servers that can support hundreds of concurrent users.
- Mainframes/enterprise servers can process millions of transactions in a day.
- Supercomputers perform complex mathematical calculations for such things as weather forecasting and medical research.
- Distributed computing distributes processing tasks across multiple computers.

## Key Terms

| | | |
|---|---|---|
| client | mainframe | server |
| distributed computing | minicomputer | supercomputer |
| grid computing | multiuser computer | volunteer computing |

# Computers Are Everywhere
# Ubiquitous Computing

## 7 OBJECTIVE
## Explain the terms "ubiquitous computing" and "convergence."

Computers have become so commonplace that sometimes we don't even recognize the technology as being a computer. **Ubiquitous computing (ubicomp)** means the technology recedes into the background and is sometimes called invisible computing. The technology actually becomes part of our environment. Digital signage has replaced traditional billboards, we can pay for gas with the wave of a credit card, and we can upload pictures to Facebook from our mobile phones. Smart homes—in which the lights, climate, security, and entertainment are automated—are a glimpse into the future of ubiquitous computing.

## EMBEDDED COMPUTERS

**Embedded computers** are present at the gasoline pump, in home appliances, in traffic lights, and at the self-checkout line at the supermarket (see Figure 1.24). Computer chips regulate the flow of gas in your car and the temperature of water in your dishwasher. All serve to make our modern lives easier. These specialized computers have become so common that it would be hard for us to imagine living without them, yet we don't really even think of them as computers.

**FIGURE 1.24** Embedded computers can be found in many objects that we come in contact with every day.

VIZ CLIP

# CONVERGENCE

The **convergence** or integration of technology on multifunction devices, such as smartphones, has accustomed us to carrying technology with us. We no longer need to carry around several different devices because these devices now incorporate cell phones, personal information management tools, email, Web browsing, document editing, MP3 players, cameras, GPS, games, and more (see Figure 1.25). In many parts of the world, there are more mobile phones than people, and this has resulted in the rapid development of technologies such as mobile payment systems. In many cases, mobile phones have replaced personal computers.

As we rely more and more on technology, we come to expect it to just work. We take for granted that the traffic light timing will protect us, the microwave won't burn our food, GPS will guide us to our destination, and the ATM will dispense our funds only to us. Ubiquitous computing is only in its infancy, and we've already made it an integral part of our lives. It will be interesting to see where ubicomp takes us in the not-too-distant future.

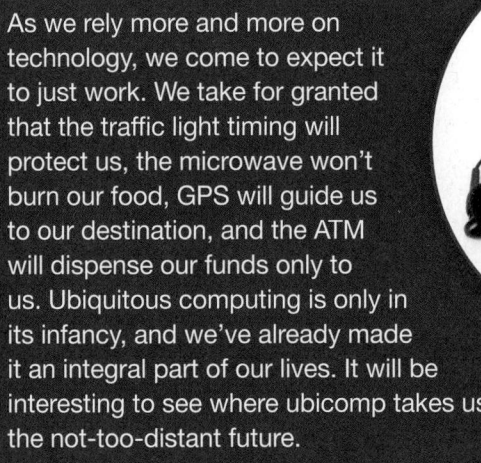

**FIGURE 1.25** The Convergence of Technology on a Smartphone

# GREEN COMPUTING

## SMART HOMES

The efficient and eco-friendly use of computers and other electronics is called **green computing**. Smart homes and smart appliances help save energy and, as a result, are good for both the environment and your pocketbook.

Smart homes use home automation to control lighting, heating and cooling, security, entertainment, and appliances in a home. The system can be programmed to turn various components on and off at set times to maximize energy efficiency. So, the heat can turn up, and the house can be warm right before you get home from work, while not wasting the energy to keep it warm all day while you're away. If you're away on vacation or have to work late, a smart home can be remotely activated by phone or over the Internet. Some utility companies offer lower rates during off-peak hours, so programming your dishwasher and other appliances to run during these times can save you money and help energy utility companies better manage the power grid, potentially reducing the need for new power plants.

Can't make your home a smart home overnight? No worries! There are some small steps you can take without investing in a whole smart home system. Try installing a programmable thermostat, putting lights on timers or motion sensors, and running appliances during off-peak hours.

Smart appliances go one step further. They plug into the smart grid and can actually monitor signals from the power company. When the electric grid system is stressed, appliances can react by cutting back on their power consumption.

# CAREER SPOTLIGHT

**BIOINFORMATICS** Computers have become integral in almost every modern career. Nowhere is this more evident than in the field of biology. **Bioinformatics** is the application of information technology to the field of biology. Computers are used to analyze data, predict how molecules will behave, and maintain and search massive databases of information. The rapid growth of biological information over the past few decades has created a demand for new technologies and people that know how to use them. This field requires at least a four-year degree. If you have a strong interest in science and technology, bioinformatics might be a good career choice for you.

## Running Project

Science fiction meets science fact? Many of our modern devices were envisioned by famous science fiction writers, such as Gene Roddenberry. Use the Internet to research some of the Star Trek technologies that do exist today. Write a paragraph about at least three of them.

## 3 Things You Need to Know

- Ubiquitous computing is technology that's invisible to us.
- Embedded computers are found in everything from traffic lights to dishwashers.
- The convergence of technology allows us to carry a single multi-function device that can do the job of many separate devices.

## Key Terms

bioinformatics

convergence

embedded computer

green computing

ubiquitous computing (ubicomp)

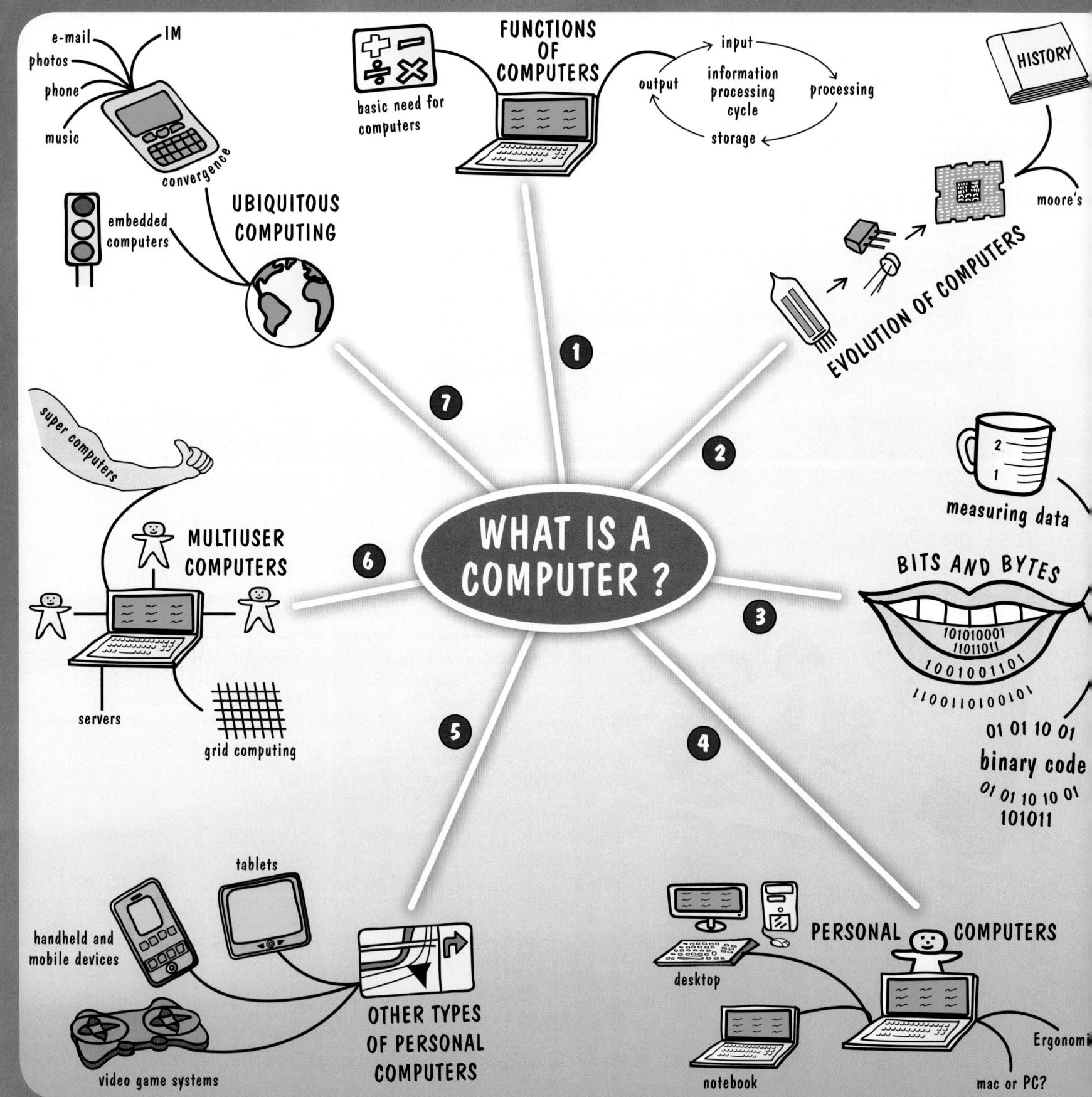

FUNCTIONS OF COMPUTERS

basic need for computers

information processing cycle

input → processing → storage → output

HISTORY

moore's

EVOLUTION OF COMPUTERS

e-mail
IM
photos
phone
music

convergence

embedded computers

UBIQUITOUS COMPUTING

measuring data

BITS AND BYTES

101010001
11011011
1 00100 1101
1100110100101

01 01 10 01

binary code

01 01 10 10 01
101011

super computers

MULTIUSER COMPUTERS

servers

grid computing

WHAT IS A COMPUTER ?

①
②
③
④
⑤
⑥
⑦

tablets

handheld and mobile devices

OTHER TYPES OF PERSONAL COMPUTERS

video game systems

PERSONAL COMPUTERS

desktop

notebook

Ergonomi

mac or PC?

# Objectives Recap

1. Explain the functions of a computer.
2. Describe the evolution of computer hardware, and explain the importance of Moore's Law.
3. Describe how computers represent data using binary codes.
4. List the various types and characteristics of personal computers.
5. Give examples of other personal computing devices.
6. List the various types and characteristics of multiuser computers.
7. Explain the terms "ubiquitous computing" and "convergence."

# Key Terms

all-in-one computer **18**
ASCII (American Standard Code for Information Interchange) **16**
binary code **16**
binary number system (base 2) **16**
bioinformatics **35**
bit **16**
byte **16**
client **29**
computer **4**
convergence **33**
data **5**
desktop computer **18**
distributed computing **30**
embedded computer **32**
ENIAC (Electronic Numerical Integrator and Computer) **6**
ergonomics **21**
GPS (global positioning system) **25**
green computing **34**
grid computing **30**
handheld **24**
information **5**
information processing cycle (IPC) **5**

integrated circuit **8**
Mac **20**
mainframe **29**
microprocessor **8**
minicomputer **29**
mobile device **24**
Moore's Law **8**
multiuser computer **28**
netbook **19**
notebook **19**
personal computer (PC) **18**
server **28**
supercomputer **30**
tablet PC **19**
transistor **7**
ubiquitous computing (ubicomp) **32**
Unicode **16**
vacuum tube **6**
video game system **26**
volunteer computing **30**
wearable **25**
workstation **18**

# Summary

1. **Explain the functions of a computer.**

   A computer is a device that converts raw data into information using the information processing cycle. Computers can be programmed to perform different tasks.

2. **Describe the evolution of computer hardware, and explain the importance of Moore's Law.**

   The earliest computers used vacuum tubes, which are inefficient, large, and prone to failure. Second-generation computers used transistors, which are small electric switches. Third-generation computers used integrated circuits, which are silicon chips that contain multiple tiny transistors. Fourth-generation computers use microprocessors, which are complex integrated circuits that contain the central processing unit (CPU) of a computer.

   Moore's Law states that the number of transistors that can be placed on an integrated circuit has doubled roughly every 2 years. Today that number is closer to 18 months. The increase in the capabilities of integrated circuits directly affects the processing speed and storage capacity of modern electronic devices.

3. **Describe how computers represent data using binary codes.**

   A single bit (or switch) has two possible states—on or off—and can be used for situations with two possibilities such as yes/no, true/false, or boy/girl. Digital data is represented by 8-bit (1 byte) binary code on most modern computers. The 8-bit ASCII system originally had binary codes for 256 ($2^8$) characters. Unicode is an extended ASCII set that has codes for more than 100,000 characters.

4. **List the various types and characteristics of personal computers.**

   Personal computers include desktop computers, which offer the most speed, power, and upgradability for the lowest cost; workstations, which are high-end desktop computers; and all-in-ones, which are compact desktop computers with the computer case integrated into the monitor. Portable personal computers include notebooks, tablet PCs, and smaller netbooks.

5. **Give examples of other personal computing devices.**

   Other computing devices include tablets, smartphones, wearables, GPS, and video game systems.

**6. List the various types and characteristics of multiuser computers.**

Multiuser computers allow multiple simultaneous users to connect to the system. They include servers, minicomputers (and midrange servers), and mainframe computers (and enterprise servers). Supercomputers perform complex mathematical calculations. They're designed to perform a limited number of tasks as quickly as possible.

**7. Explain the terms "ubiquitous computing" and "convergence."**

Ubiquitous computing means the technology recedes into the background so we no longer notice it as we interact with it. Convergence is the integration of multiple technologies, such as cell phones, cameras, and MP3 players, on a single device.

# Multiple Choice

Answer the multiple-choice questions below for more practice with key terms and concepts from this chapter.

1. _____ is considered to be the first computer programmer.
   a. Charles Babbage
   b. Ada Lovelace
   c. Grace Hopper
   d. John Atanasoff

2. _____ resemble incandescent lights, give off a lot of heat, and are notoriously unreliable.
   a. Vacuum tubes
   b. Transistors
   c. Integrated circuits
   d. Microprocessors

3. A _____ is a complex, integrated circuit.
   a. vacuum tube
   b. transistor
   c. microprocessor
   d. silicon

4. What is the binary code that can represent most currently used language characters as well as mathematical and graphic symbols?
   a. Unicode
   b. ASCII
   c. International standards
   d. There is no such code.

5. What type of portable computer is the smallest?
   a. Tablet PC
   b. Netbook
   c. Laptop
   d. Desktop replacement

6. What are high-end desktop computers used in a business environment called?
   a. Dumb terminals
   b. Minicomputers
   c. Workstations
   d. Mainframes

7. _____ such as smartphones and tablets are small computers we carry with us.
   a. Mobile devices
   b. Supercomputers
   c. Enterprise servers
   d. Netbooks

8. _____ share(s) the processing of a task across multiple computer systems.
   a. Distributed computing
   b. Supercomputers
   c. Enterprise servers
   d. Multitasking

9. Computers in traffic lights, at supermarket checkouts, and in appliances are examples of _____ computers.
   a. personal
   b. portable
   c. ubiquitous
   d. embedded

10. A _____ is an example of convergence.
    a. smart home
    b. traffic light
    c. video game console
    d. smartphone

# True or False

Answer the following questions with T for true or F for false for more practice with key terms and concepts from this chapter.

1. Computers convert data into information using the Information Processing Cycle.

2. First-generation computers used switches and vacuum tubes.

3. Today's computers use transistors and microprocessors.

4. Moore's Law states that the number of transistors that can be placed on an integrated circuit will double roughly every 18 months to 2 years.

5. ASCII contains codes for all of the languages in use today.

6. Ergonomics allows you to design a workspace for your comfort and health.

7. All-in-one is another name for a notebook computer.

8. Users connect to servers via clients.

9. GPS was originally built by the military.

10. The idea that computers are all around us is called embedded computing.

# Fill in the Blank

Fill in the blanks with key terms from this chapter.

1. A computer is a programmable machine that converts raw data into useful _____.

2. The development of _____ made the creation of the microprocessor possible.

3. The use of _____ in place of vacuum tubes allowed second-generation computers to be more powerful, smaller, more reliable, and able to be reprogrammed in far less time.

4. _____ was the first working, digital, general-purpose computer.

5. _____ design creates a work environment designed to reduce illnesses and musculoskeletal disorders.

6. _____ computers are built by Apple and run the OS X operating system.

7. A _____ is a hands-free computer designed to be worn on the body.

8. _____ are computers that provide services, such as Internet access, email, or file and print services, to client systems.

9. Very expensive computer systems that are used to perform complex mathematical calculations, such as those used in weather forecasting and medical research, are _____.

10. _____ is technology that is invisible to us.

# Application Project

## Microsoft Office Application Project 1:
### Word Level 1

**PROJECT DESCRIPTION:** In the following Microsoft Word project, you will create a letter telling your new boss about the things you have learned in this class. In the project you will use Word to enter and edit text, format text, insert graphics, check spelling and grammar, and create document footers.

**INSTRUCTIONS:** For the purpose of grading the project you are required to perform the following tasks:

Jerome Clarke
15870 Mulberry Ave
Unit 26
Frederick, MD 21703

September 30, 2012

Clearview Medical Supplies
Ms. Marlene Rollians
275 Regency Sq.
Frederick, MD 21703

Dear Ms. Rollians:

Subject: Eager intern

Thank you so much for giving me the opportunity to work with you as an intern this semester. I have learned a lot about computers in my class at school and I'm eager to share my knowledge with you at *Clearview Medical Supplies*. For example, I have learned about the different types of personal computers and other devices.

Thank you so much for this amazing opportunity. I am eager to get started and believe that I can really help you effectively leverage technology in the office.

Sincerely,

Jerome Clarke, Intern

lastname_firstname_ch01_word

1. Start Word. Download and open the file named *vt_ch01_word.* Save the document as **lastname_firstname_ch01_word**.

2. On the last line of the document, type **Jerome Clarke, Intern** to complete the letter.

3. Select the first four lines of the document containing the name and street address. Apply the No Spacing style.

4. Format the entire document as Arial, 12 pt.

5. In the first paragraph format Clearview Medical Supplies as italic.

6. Place the insertion point before Jerome on the last line of the document. Insert the picture of a QR code, *vt_ch01_image1*.

7. Change the text wrapping style of the picture to Top and Bottom.

8. Use the shortcut menu to correct the misspelling of the word semsester to *semester*.

9. Use the Spelling and Grammar dialog box to correct the misspelling of the word beleive to *believe*.

10. Using the Spelling and Grammar dialog box, accept the suggested correction for the verb form. Ignore all other spelling and grammar suggestions.

11. Insert the file name in the footer of the document using the FileName field.

12. Save and close the document and then exit Word. Submit the document as directed.

**Visit pearsonhighered.com/Geoghan** for data files, simulations, VizClips, and additional study materials.

# Microsoft Office Application Project 2:
## PowerPoint Level 1

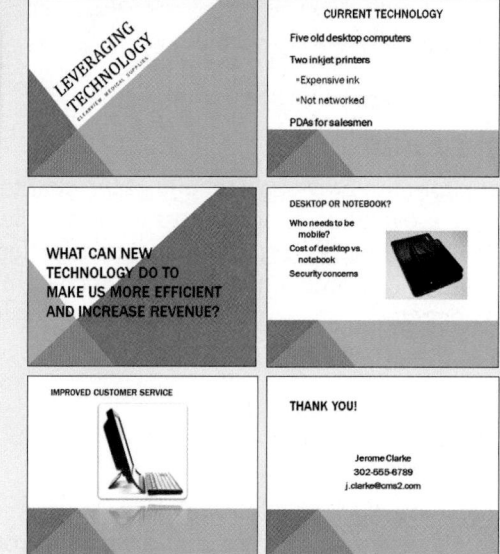

**PROJECT DESCRIPTION:** Your new boss has asked you to help her create a presentation discussing technology needs at Clearview Medical Supplies. In this project, you will use Microsoft PowerPoint to edit and format text and bullets, insert and format pictures, check spelling, add new slides and change slide layout, apply transitions, and add speaker notes.

**INSTRUCTIONS:** For the purpose of grading of the project you are required to perform the following tasks:

**1** Start PowerPoint. Download and open the file named *vt_ch01_ppt* and save it as **lastname_firstname_ch01_ppt**.

**2** On Slide 1, change the subtitle text (Clearview Medical Supply) to **Clearview Medical Supplies**.

**3** On Slide 1, use the shortcut menu to correct the spelling of Technology. Change the font of the title text, Leveraging Technology, to Cambria and change the size to 54.

**4** On Slide 2, center the title, Current Technology. Change the line spacing of the bullets on Slide 2 to 1.5 and the font size to 32.

**5** Insert a new Title and Content slide after Slide 3 and add the following as the title text: **Improved Customer Service.**

**6** On the new Slide 4, in the content placeholder, insert the picture *vt_ch01_image2*.

**7** On Slide 4, apply the Reflected Bevel, White picture style to the picture.

**8** Find and replace the word sales with **revenue**.

**9** Use the Spelling tool to check the spelling in the document. Correct the spelling errors on Slide 2, but ignore all instances of the spelling of Clearview.

**10** Change the layout of Slide 5 to Two Content. In the right placeholder, insert the picture *vt_ch01_eoc_image3*.

**11** Switch to Slide Sorter view and delete Slide 6. Move Slide 5 into the Slide 4 position. Switch back to Normal view.

**12** In the Notes Pane on Slide 2, add the following speaker note and change the Font Size to 16: **Clearview Medical Supplies needs to be a forward-thinking company.**

**13** Apply the Gallery transition with a duration of 01.5 to all of the slides in the presentation.

**14** Insert the page number and enter your name in the footer on the notes and handouts pages for all slides in the presentation. View the presentation in Slide Show view from beginning to end, and then return to Normal view.

**15** Save and close the presentation and then exit PowerPoint. Submit the presentation as directed.

Visit **pearsonhighered.com/Geoghan** for data files, simulations, VizClips, and additional study materials.

Chapter 1 | 41

# Running Project ...

## ... The Finish Line

Use your answers from the previous sections of the chapter project to discuss the evolution of computers in the past few centuries. Write a report responding to the questions raised. Save your file as **lastname_firstname_ch01_project**, and submit it to your instructor as directed.

# Do It Yourself 1

Ergonomics is the study of the relationship between workers and their workspaces. Ergonomic design creates a work environment designed to reduce illnesses and musculoskeletal disorders. The OSHA website has a computer workstation checklist available at **www.osha.gov/SLTC/etools/computerworkstations**.

1. Download the checklist, and use it to evaluate your computer workstation (the form is also provided on your CD). How did your workstation fare? What are some areas for improvement? How could you improve your score?

2. Type up your answers, save the file as **lastname_firstname_ch01_diy1**, and submit your work as directed by your instructor.

# Do It Yourself 2

Check out all the features available on the personal computer that you use the most.

1. What computer did you choose? Where is it located? How long have you had it? Did you research the computer before you made your purchase? What made you purchase it?

2. What are the five features you use most frequently? Why? What are the five you use the least? Why?

3. How could your computer be improved to make your life more convenient? Give one reason life would be easier without all this technology. Give one way your life would be more difficult without all this technology.

4. Type up your answers, save the file as **lastname_firstname_ch01_diy2,** and submit it as directed by your instructor.

# Critical Thinking

Convergence has led to smaller devices that cost less and do more. Today, a tablet or smartphone has the same processing power of a PC from a few years ago. Compare features and costs in a table like the one below.

1. Research three of the newest smartphones or tablets on the market. Create a table or spreadsheet like the one below, comparing the features of each device, to organize your research. Use this research to decide which device would best meet your personal needs.

2. Write up your decision in a two- to three-paragraph essay. Which device should you buy and why? What other accessories will you need to purchase? Do you need to purchase a service plan to take advantage of all the device's features?

3. Save your file as **lastname_firstname_ch01_ct**, and submit both your table and essay as directed by your instructor.

| | Device 1 | Device 2 | Device 3 |
|---|---|---|---|
| Website or store | | | |
| Brand | | | |
| Model | | | |
| Price | | | |
| Phone | | | |
| Calendar | | | |
| Camera/video | | | |
| GPS | | | |
| Games | | | |
| Video player | | | |
| MP3 player | | | |
| Internet | | | |
| Downloadable apps | | | |
| Additional features | | | |
| Additional purchases required to meet your needs | | | |

# Ethical Dilemma

The term "digital divide" was coined in the 1990s. It refers to the gap in technology access and literacy. There have been many types of programs designed to close this gap, including the federal e-rate program, state and local government programs, and private initiatives.

1. Research the federal Schools and Libraries Program of the Universal Service Fund (E-Rate) at **universalservice. org/sl/**. What are its goals? What are the requirements for eligibility? Do you believe it is still economically viable for the government to spend millions of dollars on these programs?

2. Use the Internet to research the term "digital divide." Pay close attention to the dates of the Web pages and articles you find. Much of the information is from the period from 2000 to 2004 and isn't current. What sources did you use? Who should be responsible for closing the gap? Does putting the technology in classrooms and community centers really close the gap or do we need to have a computer in every home? What about Internet access? What about other forms of technology (such as cell phones)?

3. Type up your answers, save the file as **lastname_firstname_ch01_ethics**, and submit your work as directed by your instructor.

# On the Web

There are many important people and events that led to our modern computers. In this exercise, you will create a timeline that illustrates the ones you feel are more significant.

1. Create a timeline showing five to seven important milestones in the development of computers over the past two centuries. Use a free online timeline generator (such as TimeGlider) or online presentation tool (such as Prezi or PowerPoint) to create your timeline. Share the URL and present your findings to the class.

2. Prepare a summary of your timeline and include the URL where it can be viewed, save the file as **lastname_firstname_ch01_web**, and submit your work as directed by your instructor.

# Collaboration

With a group of three to five students, research a famous person mentioned in this chapter. Write and perform a news interview of this person. If possible, video record the interview. Present your newscast to the class.

**Instructors:** Divide the class into groups of three to four students, and assign each group a famous person mentioned in this chapter.

**The Project:** Each team is to prepare a dialogue depicting a news reporter interviewing this person. Teams must use at least three references, only one of which may be this textbook. Use Google Docs or Microsoft Office to prepare the final version of your presentation, and provide documentation that all team members have contributed to the project.

**Students:** Before beginning this project, discuss the roles each group member will play. Choose a team name, which you'll use in submitting your presentation. Be sure to divide the work among your members, and pick someone to present your project. You may find it helpful to elect a team leader who can direct your activities and ensure that all team contributions are collated through Google Docs or Microsoft Office as directed by your instructor.

**Outcome:** Perform the interview in a newscast format using the dialogue you have written. The interview should be 3 to 5 minutes long. If possible, videotape the interview, and share the newscast with the rest of the class. Save this video as **teamname_ch01_ video**. Turn in a final text version of your presentation named as **teamname_ch01_interview** and your file showing your collaboration named as **teamname_ch01_collab**. Be sure to include the name of your presentation and a list of all team members. Submit your presentation to your instructor as directed.

# 2

# Application Software

Visit **pearsonhighered.com/Geoghan** for data files, simulations, VizClips, and additional study materials.

OBJECTIVES

## Running Project

In this chapter, you learn about different kinds of application software and how to obtain it. Look for instructions as you complete each article. For most, there's a series of questions for you to research. At the conclusion of this chapter, you're asked to submit your responses to the questions raised.

**OBJECTIVES**

1. **Identify types and uses of business productivity software.**

2. **Identify types and uses of personal software.**

3. **Assess a computer system for software compatibility.**

4. **Compare various ways of obtaining software.**

5. **Discuss the importance of cloud computing.**

## IN THIS CHAPTER

A computer is a programmable machine that converts raw data into useful information. Programming—in particular, application software—is what makes a computer a flexible and powerful tool. In this chapter, we look at software applications for both business and personal use.

# Making Business Work

## OBJECTIVE
### Identify types and uses of business productivity software.

Companies large and small rely on computers for virtually every aspect of running a business—from billing to inventory to payroll to sales. Most businesses depend on a variety of software applications to complete tasks.

## OFFICE SUITES

The most commonly used application software in business is an **office application suite**, such as Microsoft Office, Apple iWork, or Apache OpenOffice. These suites include several applications that are designed to work together to manage and create different types of documents and include features that allow multiple users to collaborate. In a business environment (and in many schools), Microsoft Office is the standard, but most programs have the ability to save a file in other file types, making them compatible with other products or backward-compatible with older software versions.

## WORD PROCESSING A **word processor** is an application that is used to create, edit, and format text documents; the documents can also contain images. A full-featured word processor, such as Microsoft Word, iWork Pages, or Apache OpenOffice Writer, can create everything from simple memos to large and complex documents.

In Figure 2.1, some of the more common features of a word processor were used to create a document in Word 2010. The page number in the header was automatically generated, and a word processor renumbers the pages of a long document as the content changes. The Title Style was used to format the title of the essay. Styles allow you to apply a predefined set of formatting steps to text. The image is center-aligned on the page, but the rest of the text is left-aligned. The spell-checker put a red squiggly line under the word Geoghan, indicating that the word wasn't found in the spell-check dictionary. It's possible to add words to the dictionary and even to create a custom dictionary that contains words you commonly use that aren't spelled incorrectly, such as your last name or industry-specific terms and brand names.

**Header with automatically generated and formatted page number**

**Page number and word count statistics**

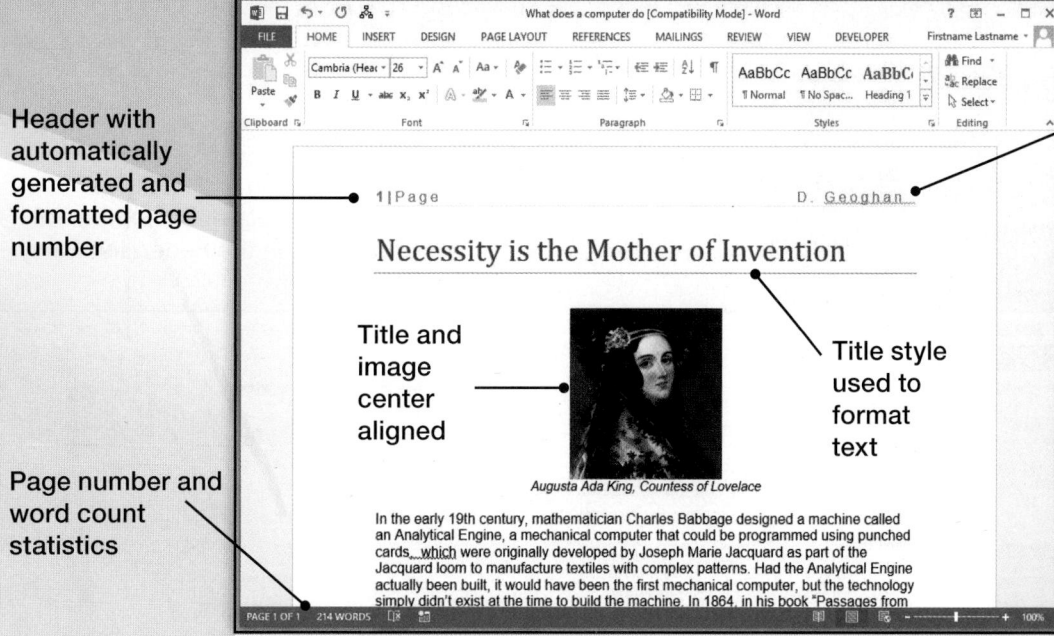

Title and image center aligned

Spelling checker—*Geoghan* is Not in the Microsoft Word Dictionary

Title style used to format text

**FIGURE 2.1** This simple essay uses some Microsoft Word features.

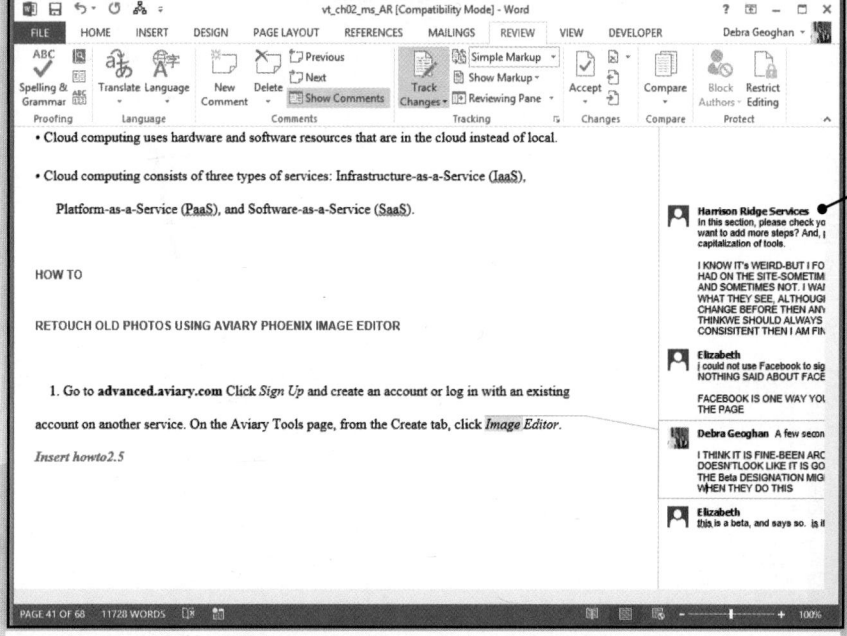

Comments from three different collaborators indicated by different colors

**FIGURE 2.2** Microsoft Word allows multiple reviewers to collaborate on a document.

Standard features of modern word processors include the following:

- **What you see is what you get:** The layout on the computer screen shows the document layout as it would appear when printed.
- **Formatting styles:** Text style, font, color, size, and alignment
- **Spelling (and sometimes grammar) checkers:** Includes the ability to have custom dictionaries
- **Graphics:** The ability to insert and format images
- **Text organization tools:** Tables, bullets, and lists
- **Statistics:** Includes such features as word count
- **Content guides:** Footnotes, indexes, and tables of contents
- **Page layout:** Headers and footers, page numbers, and margins
- **Mail merge:** The ability to generate mail labels or form letters for lists of people

Businesses take advantage of more advanced features—such as track changes, mail merge, and document protection—to create many kinds of business documents. Figure 2.2 shows comments and edits from multiple reviewers working on the same document. This is one way that users can collaborate on a project.

Most businesses rely on word processing for creating all types of documents; however, when calculations are involved, a spreadsheet program is necessary.

**SPREADSHEET SOFTWARE** A **spreadsheet** application, such as Microsoft Excel or iWork Numbers, creates electronic worksheets composed of rows and columns. Spreadsheets are used for applications such as budgeting, grade books, and inventory. They are useful tools for managing business expenses, payroll, and billing, although businesses may use tools that are specifically made for such tasks. Spreadsheets are critical to researchers in the natural and social sciences as a statistical analysis tool.

In a spreadsheet, the intersection of a row and a column is called a **cell**. Cells can contain numbers, text, or formulas. Three-dimensional spreadsheets can have multiple worksheets that are linked together, making them flexible and powerful. Spreadsheet applications have the ability to create charts or graphs to visually represent data. Although there are other spreadsheet programs available, in a business environment, Microsoft Excel is used almost exclusively.

One advantage to using a spreadsheet program is that it can be customized. For example, a teacher might use a spreadsheet so he or she can create formulas and calculations rather than having to adjust his or her grading methods to fit into a commercial grade-book program's format. Another advantage is cost savings. Because most office computers already have a spreadsheet program installed as part of a software suite, there's no need to purchase additional software. Also, users will have some familiarity with the program interface and need less training to use it.

Spreadsheets are also good at organizing data so it can be sorted, filtered, and rearranged, making them useful for things that don't involve calculations at all, such as address lists and schedules. Figure 2.3 shows a spreadsheet created for a U.S. history course that lists all the U.S. presidents and their political parties. As you can see, the number of presidents in each party was calculated, and a pie chart showing that information was generated.

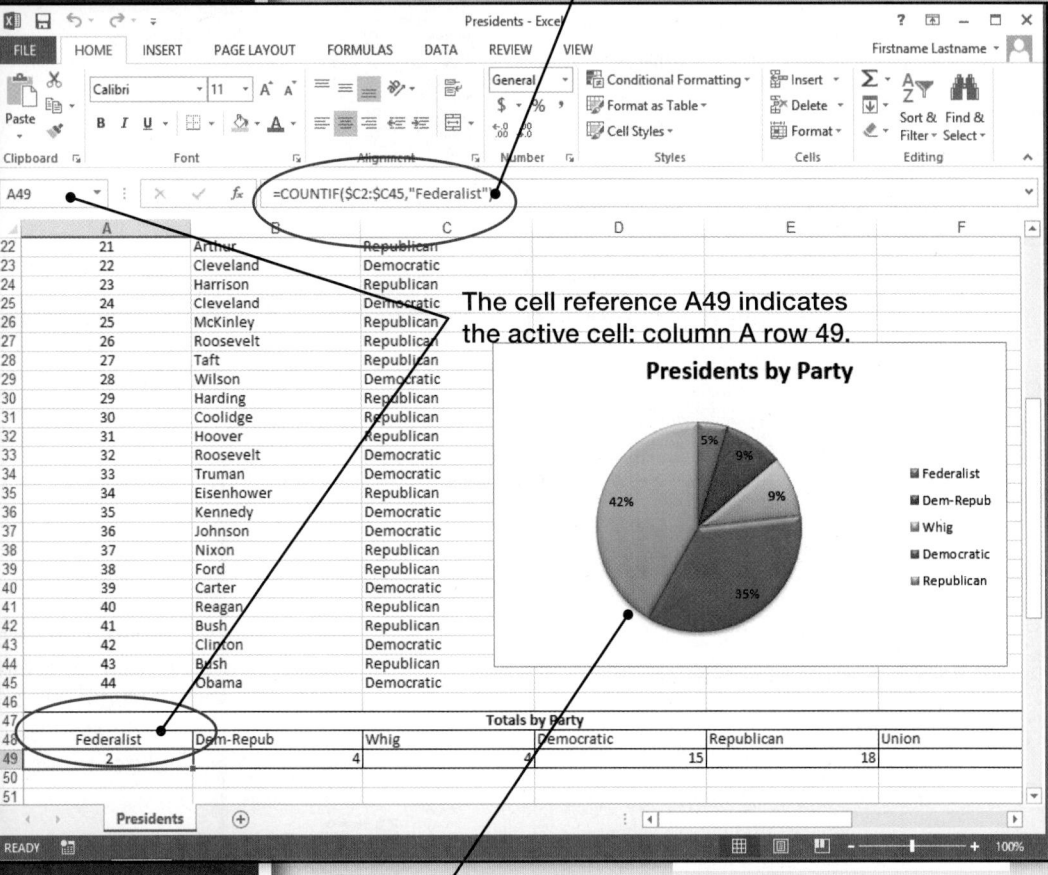

The formula in cell A49 was used to calculate the number of presidents in the Federalist Party.

The cell reference A49 indicates the active cell: column A row 49.

A pie chart was created to visually represent the data.

**FIGURE 2.3** This simple spreadsheet illustrates text, numbers, a formula, and a pie chart.

**PRESENTATION SOFTWARE** A presentation application, such as Microsoft PowerPoint or iWork Keynote, is used to create electronic presentations. If you want to present facts, figures, and ideas and engage your audience at the same time, you need visual aids. With presentation software it's easy to create them. Each slide can contain text, graphics, video, audio, or any combination of these, making your visual aids dynamic and enhancing your presentation. A good speaker creates a presentation that audiences will be interested in and will remember.

Figure 2.4 shows a Keynote presentation on digital cameras. The presentation here is shown in Navigator view, which allows the author to see how the slides look in order and easily change the order by dragging the slides into position. This presentation contains 13 slides—some containing images— and uses a built-in design template with predefined colors, fonts, and layouts. Good design principles for presentations include using easy-to-see color schemes and large font sizes, limiting the amount of text on each slide, limiting the use of slide transitions and animations, and using images to enhance your words.

**FIGURE 2.4** This Keynote presentation contains many commonly used elements.

# DATABASE SOFTWARE

A desktop database program such as Microsoft Access can be used alone or as part of a larger enterprise database system. A **database** is nothing more than a collection of information that is organized in a useful way. Your telephone book or email contact list is a simple database. A library catalog, patient records in a doctor's office, and Internet search engines are all examples of commonly used databases. You can use a desktop database application to create small databases for contact management, inventory management, and employee records.

A database is a collection of records organized into a table. More complex databases typically include multiple tables. A **record** contains information about a single entry in the database (such as a customer or product). Other objects can be generated to organize the data, including forms, reports, and queries.

Let's use a contact list as an example. Each contact has a record. Every record consists of **fields** of information. In this case, each record would contain fields for name, address, email, phone, etc. Figure 2.5 shows a simple contact list database consisting of five records in a table. While a simple database like this could also be created in a spreadsheet, using a database program gives us more options. Forms, such as the one in the figure, can be created for easy data entry. Reports can be generated to display selected information—in this case, a phone list. And most flexible of all, queries can be created to pull out records that meet specific criteria.

Database table

**FIGURE 2.5** Database Tables, Forms, Reports, and Queries

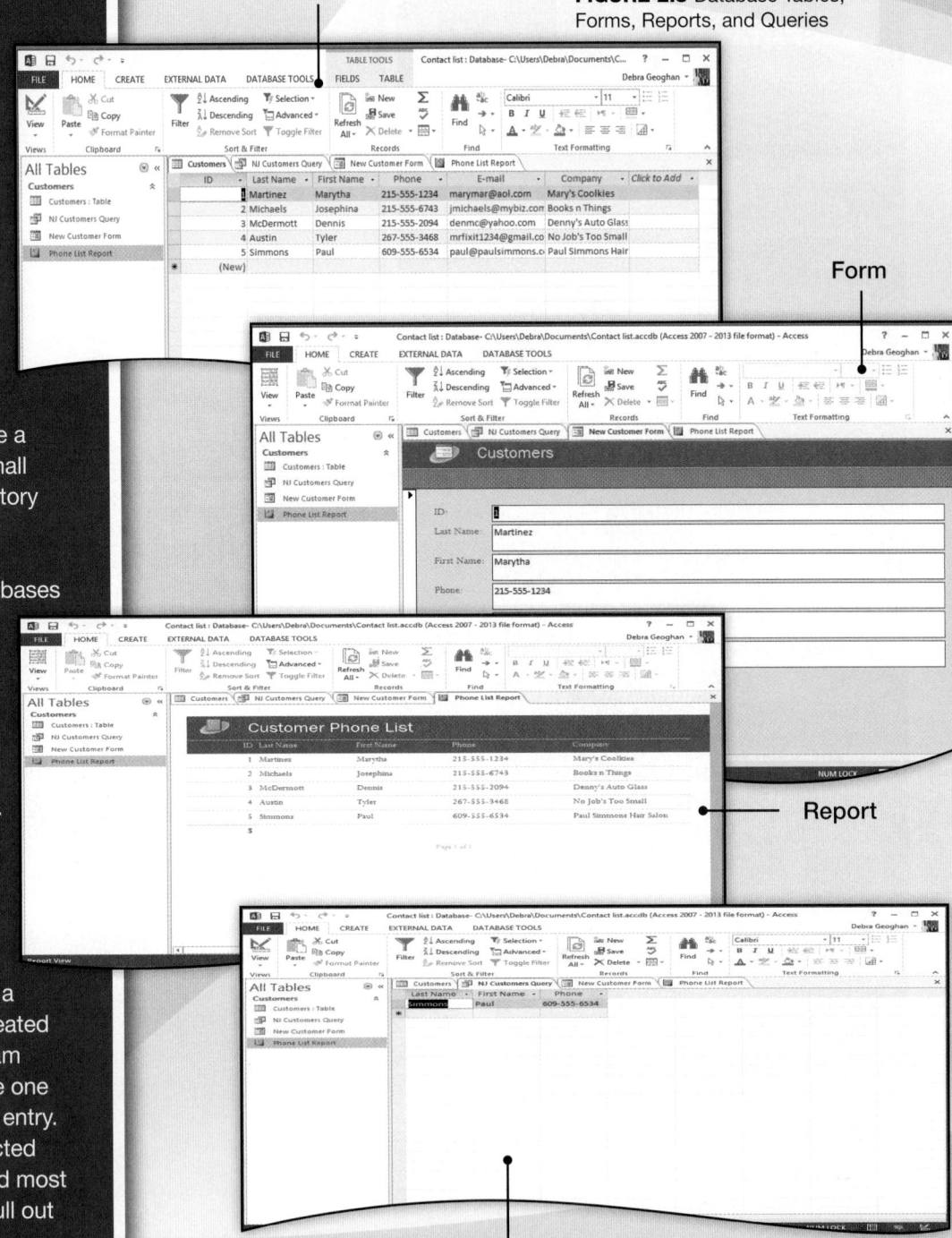

Form

Report

Query result

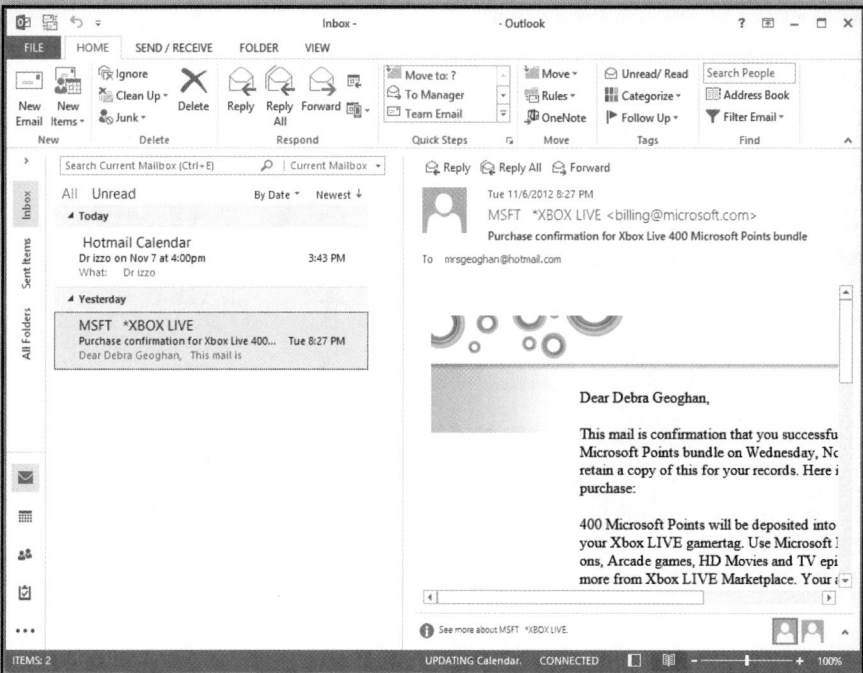

**FIGURE 2.6** Microsoft Outlook PIM manages your email, contacts, calendar, and tasks in one place.

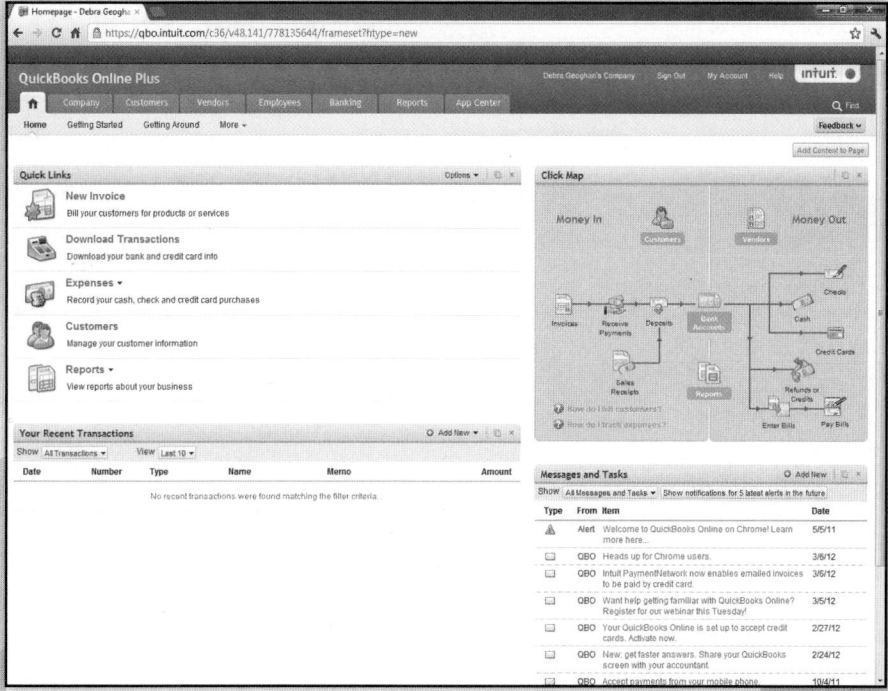

**FIGURE 2.7** The Home Screen of the QuickBooks Online Plus Edition

## PERSONAL INFORMATION MANAGER

A **personal information manager (PIM)** may be a stand-alone program or part of an office suite. The most widely used of these programs is Microsoft Outlook (see Figure 2.6). A PIM manages your email, calendar, contacts, and tasks all in one place. It includes the ability to share calendars and schedule meetings.

# OTHER TYPES OF BUSINESS SOFTWARE

While office suites cover the majority of business documents, other software is often used for more complex and larger scale management and projects. Keeping track of finances, projects, and the sheer number of documents even the smallest business might have can be a daunting task. Specialized software can help make these tasks easier and more efficient.

**FINANCIAL** Even small businesses have to keep track of expenses and taxes. While an Excel spreadsheet system might work for very simple situations, most businesses find the need for basic accounting software such as Intuit QuickBooks (see Figure 2.7) or Sage Peachtree. Accounting software allows you to track your business finances and generate reports and graphs to help you make business decisions. You can use QuickBooks for expense tracking, invoicing, payroll, and inventory management. By organizing all your financial information in one place, it makes it easy to see the big picture and to handle year-end tasks such as income tax returns.

**PROJECT MANAGEMENT** **Project management software**
helps you complete projects, keep within your budget, stay on schedule, and even collaborate with others. The most popular project management program is Microsoft Project, and the leading Web-based application is Basecamp. Both of these tools excel at helping your projects run smoothly. Figure 2.8 shows a workshop planning project in Microsoft Project. The left column contains the tasks and dates for the project, and the right side shows those tasks in a graphic known as a Gantt chart.

There are literally thousands of software applications used in businesses, including many that are created in-house or made for a specific type of business, but the programs discussed in this article are fairly universal. Modern businesses depend on both people and technology to remain competitive.

**Try the Application Software Simulation**

SIMULATION

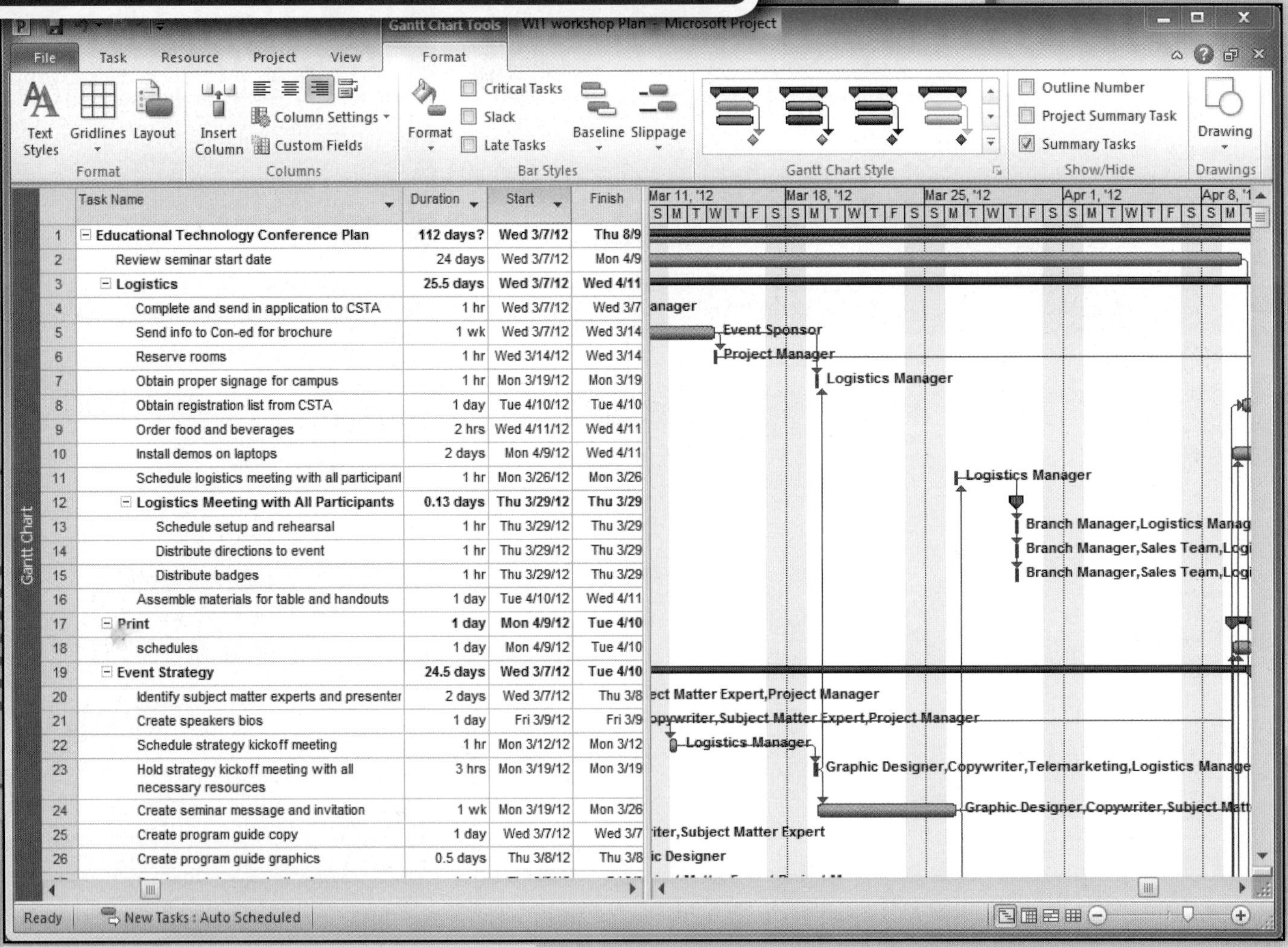

**FIGURE 2.8** Planning a Workshop Using Microsoft Project Software

**DOCUMENT MANAGEMENT** For both practical and often legal reasons, even the smallest business needs document management capabilities—the ability to save, share, search, and audit electronic documents throughout their life cycle. Keeping track of all the documents in a business, ensuring that the right people have access to them, and ensuring that the correct version is available are all part of a **document management system (DMS)** such as Microsoft SharePoint, KnowledgeTree, and Alfresco. One of the keys to using DMS is storage. Instead of keeping files on local drives, the files are stored on a server or on the Web, making them more accessible and secure.

## Running Project

Microsoft Office is a full suite of programs, but not every user needs the whole package. Use the Internet to research the versions of the current release of Microsoft Office that are available. Write a two- to three-paragraph essay comparing the versions. Explain which applications are in each, the costs, the number of licenses available, and any other details you deem important.

## 4 Things You Need to Know

- Office application suites include word processing, spreadsheet, presentation, and database software.
- Personal information manager software manages email, contacts, calendars, and tasks.
- Project management software helps businesses keep projects on schedule.
- Document management systems allow businesses to save, share, search, and audit electronic documents.

## Key Terms

cell

database

document management system

field

office application suite

personal information manager (PIM)

project management software

record

spreadsheet

word processor

# Making it Personal

## Identify types and uses of personal software.

Software is what makes our computers useful. The variety of software available today is vast, but it only takes a couple of programs to make our computers indispensable to us—and even fun to use. In this article, we look at some of the software you might want to install on your own system.

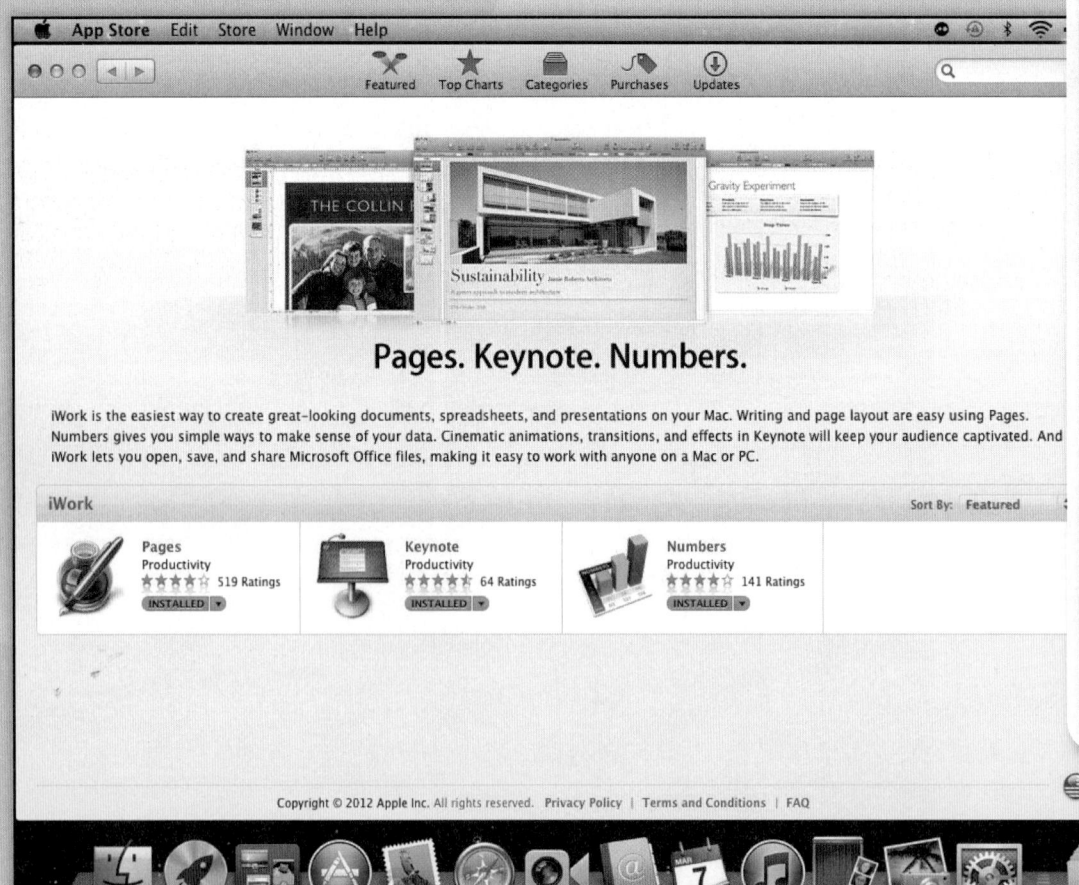

## OFFICE APPLICATIONS

A full office application suite, which typically includes word processing, spreadsheet, database, presentation, and personal information management applications, is usually more than the average home user needs or wants. A basic word processor and perhaps a spreadsheet and presentation program are often included in home or student versions of the software. Microsoft Office comes in several different versions, allowing you to purchase just the applications you actually need. For the Mac, the iWork programs—Pages, Numbers, and Keynote—are now sold as individual apps, so you can purchase only the tools that you need (see Figure 2.9). Nevertheless, commercial software can become expensive. There are many free or low-cost alternatives if you're willing to spend some time finding them and learning how to use them. All of these alternatives have the ability to save files in common file formats, allowing you to move your work between programs and across platforms.

**FIGURE 2.9** The iWork programs can be purchased individually from the Apple App Store.

Apache OpenOffice is a free, open source alternative office program available in Windows, Mac, and Linux versions. **Open source** means that the source code is published and made available to the public, enabling anyone to copy, modify, and redistribute it without paying fees. Some open source websites, Apache OpenOffice, ask for donations to support the development of the product. Apache OpenOffice contains word processor, spreadsheet, presentation, drawing, database, and formula writer applications. It can open and work with documents created in other programs, such as Microsoft Office, and can save files in its own format or common formats such as Microsoft Word or Rich Text Format so you can work with your files in other programs and across platforms. Figure 2.10 shows the welcome screen of Apache OpenOffice 3.

Online alternative office suites are another solution. Some of the most popular are Microsoft Web Apps, Google Docs, and Zoho Docs. All of these free websites offer easy-to-use interfaces, with word processing, spreadsheet, presentation, and communication applications. You access them through a browser and don't need to install anything on your computer. The beauty of these websites is that you can access and edit your files from anywhere (including many mobile devices) and easily collaborate and share with others. Figure 2.11 shows a spreadsheet in Google Docs and in Zoho Docs.

**FIGURE 2.10** The Apache OpenOffice welcome screen allows you to choose an application with which to work.

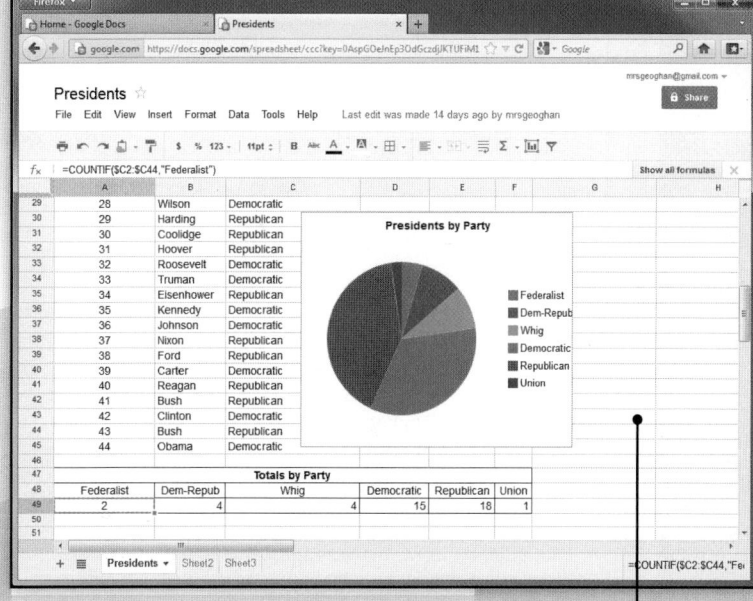

**FIGURE 2.11** A Comparison of a Google Docs Spreadsheet and a Zoho Docs Sheet

Google Docs

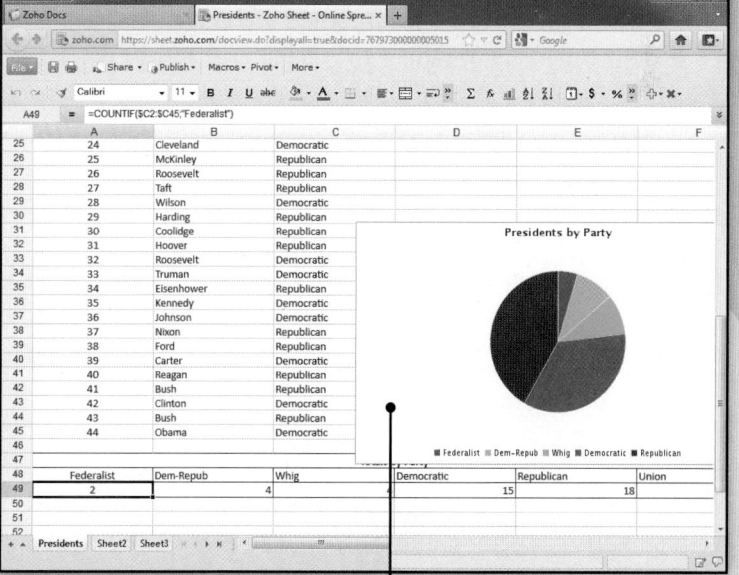

Zoho Docs

Microsoft Office Web Apps include Word, Excel, PowerPoint, and OneNote. Figure 2.12 shows a PowerPoint presentation being edited using the Web App version. The free Web Apps are not full-featured versions.

The market for free and inexpensive application software has grown exponentially as computers have become ubiquitous in our lives. Take the time to decide which options are best for you before spending a lot of money on a complicated software package that you may not even need.

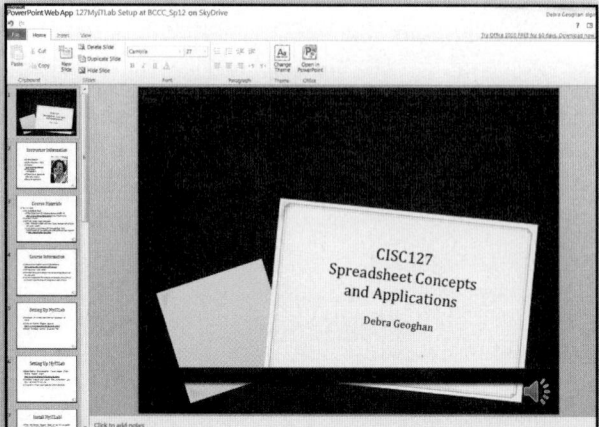

**FIGURE 2.12** The Microsoft PowerPoint Web App

# FINANCE AND TAX PREPARATION SOFTWARE

Personal finance software can help you keep track of your bank accounts, monitor your investments, create and stick to a budget, and file your income taxes. As with office applications, personal finance software ranges from expensive commercial packages to free and online options.

Two of the most popular commercial packages are Intuit Quicken and Moneydance. Both of these programs include advanced features, such as online banking and bill payment, investment portfolio tracking, and budgeting. You can also generate reports, calculate loan interest, and even write checks. When tax time comes around, you can easily gather the information you need from these applications.

If you prefer to use an online application, Mint.com has become a popular choice. Once you enter all your accounts, you can use Mint.com to track your spending. Figure 2.13 shows a Mint account.

Tax preparation software allows you to complete your income tax returns yourself on your computer. This reduces the chance of making errors in your calculations and makes it easy to save—and later retrieve—your returns. You can file your return electronically or print and mail it. Previous years' returns can be imported into a new return, and you can generate year-to-year comparisons. Tax preparation programs walk you through the process step by step and provide you with suggestions and help throughout. The three main tax preparation programs are TurboTax from Intuit, H&R Block At Home, and TaxACT. For simple tax returns, there are free online options. For more complex returns, you can install the full programs on your computer or use online versions. In general, the more complicated your return is, the more expensive the software you need is. If you start a free return and later discover that you need to upgrade to a full version, you can do so without losing any of the information you have already input. Figure 2.14 shows the TurboTax Deluxe edition.

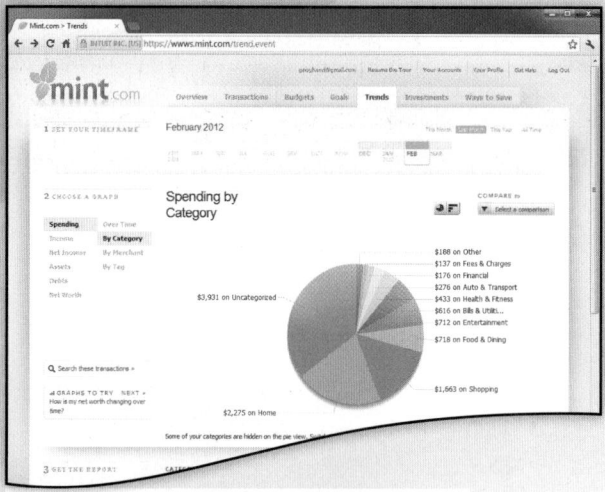

**FIGURE 2.13** Track your budget and spending on Mint.com.

No matter how simple or complex your financial situation, there's a financial software solution that you can use.

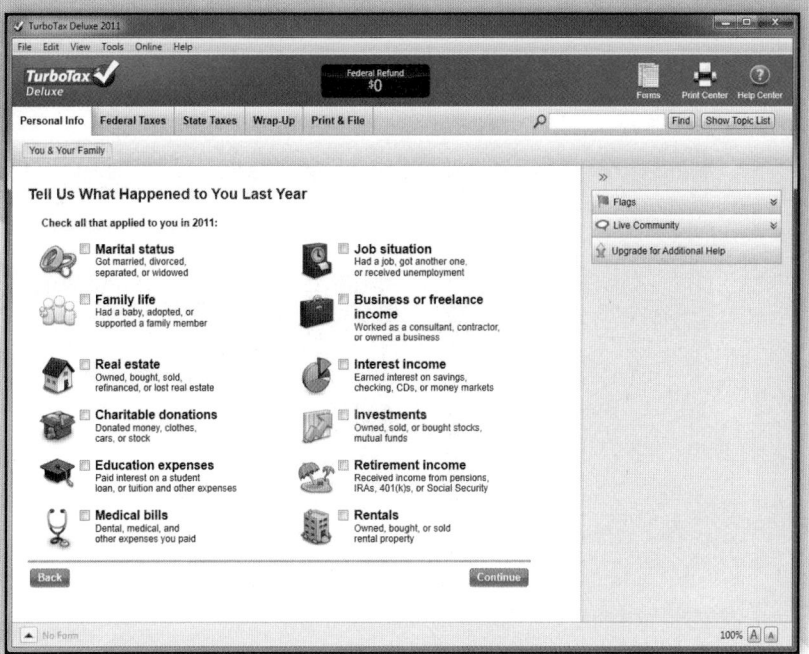

**FIGURE 2.14** TurboTax Deluxe Edition

### ENTERTAINMENT AND MULTIMEDIA SOFTWARE

Office applications and personal finance software aside, entertainment and multimedia software make our computers fun to use. There are thousands of programs available to educate and entertain us.

**MEDIA MANAGEMENT** Media management software is what we use to keep track of and play all the multimedia files on our computers—music, TV shows, and videos. Media player software, such as Windows Media Player, Apple iTunes, and Winamp, are all examples of media management software. With iTunes, you can organize your music and videos and watch TV shows and movies (see Figure 2.15).

**FIGURE 2.15**
You can watch TV programs using iTunes.

## VIDEO AND PHOTO EDITING Video
and photo editing software allows you to create masterpieces from your personal photos and videos. You can spend hundreds of dollars for professional programs, but for most people, free or low-cost alternatives have all the features they need.

Picasa is a free program that you can download from Google. One really cool feature is facial recognition (see Figure 2.16). Picasa learns from the tags you apply to images and makes suggestions when it discovers other images with the same person, making it easy for you to locate pictures of that person later on.

Picasa can also edit your images. You can crop, straighten, adjust contrast and color, and apply various effects, such as sepia or black and white—most of the tasks you'd want to accomplish. In Figure 2.17, the image has been cropped and enhanced. Picasa saves your edits in a separate file, and you can always reset the image to its original state if you change your mind.

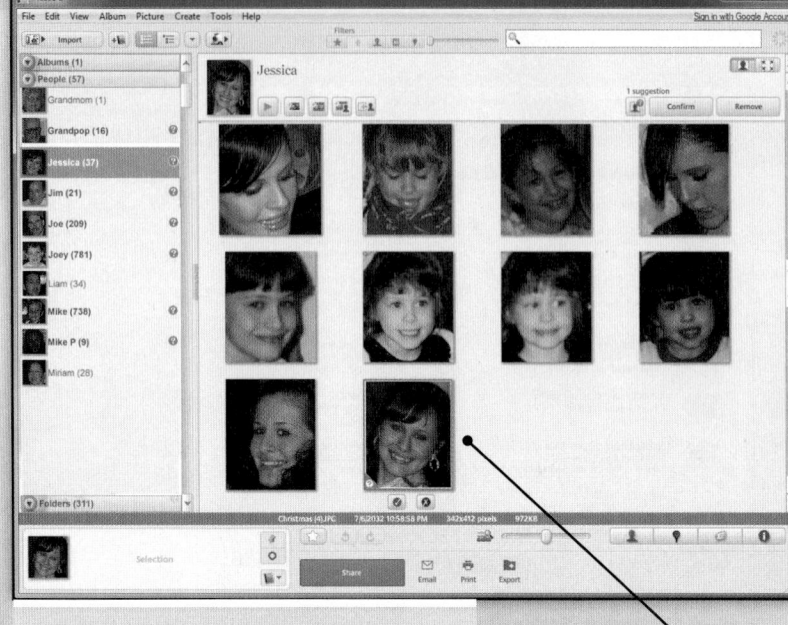

**FIGURE 2.16** Picasa's facial recognition has identified a possible match.

**Picasa suggested an image based on facial recognition.**

**FIGURE 2.17** The original photo has been cropped and brightened up.

**FIGURE 2.18** It's easy to create a collage with just a few mouse clicks in Picasa.

**FIGURE 2.19** Creating a Video with iMovie

You can also create some interesting projects using Picasa, such as a screensaver, a gift CD, a movie, and a collage, such as the example in Figure 2.18. You can upload your images to Picasa Web Albums right from within the program and share the link with others.

Picasa has some limited ability to organize and work with your videos, but you need a video editing program to really edit and create the movies you want. Windows Live Movie Maker is free, and Apple iMovie comes preloaded on Mac computers. If you want something else, several commercial products are available for about $100. Two of the most popular are Sony Vegas Movie Studio and Adobe Premiere Elements. Because video editing requires a lot of system resources, there are few online options available. Figure 2.19 shows a movie created using iMovie.

**GAMES** When you think of someone who plays video games, do you picture a young man shooting aliens? What about the grandmother playing solitaire, or the dad playing online poker, or the preschooler learning colors and shapes? Games and simulations are more than just first-person shooters, and they're played by all sorts of people. Video game sales in 2011 reached $23 billion, with computer games sales accounting for about $500 million of that total. While the average age of a video game player is 32 to 35 years old, 20 percent are over 50. In addition, about 40 percent are female. So much for stereotypes.

Games are one type of software for which you really need to pay attention to the system requirements for installation. They take a lot of processing, memory, and video power to run well (see Figure 2.20), and trying to play a game on an inadequate system will just frustrate you.

**FIGURE 2.20** Skyrim

# EDUCATIONAL AND REFERENCE SOFTWARE

Educational and reference software is a broad category of software. There's software to study, plan, design, and create just about anything you are interested in. Let's look at a few of the most popular offerings.

**TRIP PLANNING** When I was a little girl and the family planned a vacation, we had to go to the store to buy maps, tour books, and yellow highlighters. We would spend hours mapping out our route, planning our stops based on the often outdated information in the tour books, and hoping the food would be decent and the hotel rooms would be clean. Today, we still spend hours researching and planning our trips, but we use online mapping software, such as Microsoft Streets & Trips or Google Maps, read reviews from other travelers, and can easily reroute our trip if the unexpected happens.

**GENEALOGY** There are many genealogy tools on the market today. The most popular is Family Tree Maker (see Figure 2.21), which integrates with Ancestry.com. For Mac users, there is MacFamilyTree. You can create family trees and slideshows of your photos, view timelines and maps, and search through millions of historical records on the Internet.

**HOME AND LANDSCAPE DESIGN** Want to build a deck? Plant a garden? Remodel your kitchen? Rearrange your furniture? Paint the dining room? Home and landscape design software has you covered. Free or retail, online or installed on your system, there are programs to help you design and plan all your home improvement projects.

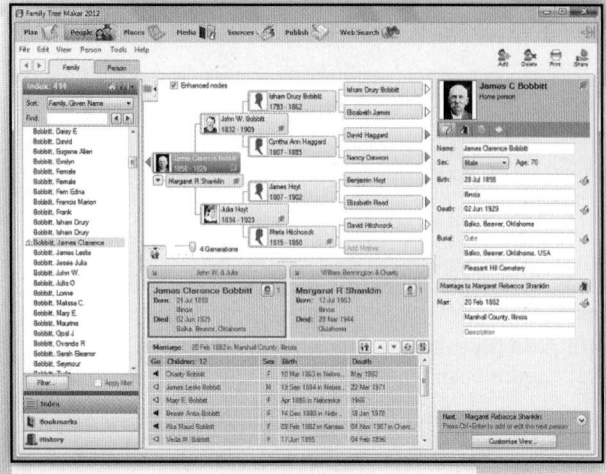

**FIGURE 2.21** Family Tree Maker

**FIGURE 2.22** Colorjive.com lets me "paint" my garage a new color.

# Find Out MORE

One place to learn about free software alternatives is **MakeUseOf. com.** This website is a daily blog that includes a directory of hundreds of useful websites and apps. Go to the Directory (**makeuseof.com/dir**), and select a category that interests you. Select two articles to read, and write a one- to two-paragraph summary of each article. Did you decide to try the application described? Why or why not? If so, did you find it useful? Would you recommend it to a friend?

There are several online apps to compare paint colors. Just upload a picture of your room and experiment with the color choices until you find your favorites. Behr Paint Your Place (behr.com), Sherwin-Williams Color Visualizer (**sherwin-williams.com**), and the Benjamin Moore Personal Color Viewer (**benjaminmoore.com**) all allow you to upload and color your own photos for free and will help you select the colors from their particular paint lines. Colorjive (**colorjive. com**, see Figure 2.22) isn't affiliated with any brand and includes colors across multiple brands. You should use whatever program has the color codes for the brand of paint you plan to buy.

# PORTABLE APPS

We sometimes find ourselves without our own computers—at work, school, travel, or a friend's house. **Portable apps** are programs that you can carry and run from a flash drive. They need no installation, so you can run them on just about any computer system. Your settings and data are on your flash drive—not the host computer—and when you remove your drive, there's no personal information left behind. One place to find portable apps is at **portableapps.com** (see Figure 2.23). The Portable Apps platform is open source, and the apps are free. The same apps you use on your computer—Mozilla Firefox, Apache OpenOffice, email clients, games, utilities, and even operating systems—can be run as portable apps.

No matter what you need or want to do, there is probably at least one program that can do it. Choosing the right option often requires a bit of research and comparison shopping, but when you find the program, you'll expand the usefulness of your computer.

**FIGURE 2.23** The Portable Apps Website

## Running Project

Use the Internet to learn about Apache OpenOffice. Is it available in different versions? What applications are included? Compare it to the Microsoft Office versions you researched in the previous project. Does Apache OpenOffice offer everything that Microsoft Office does? If not, what is missing?

## 4 Things You Need to Know

- Personal productivity software includes office applications as well as financial and reference software.
- Entertainment software includes media management software, photo and video editing software, and games.
- Educational and reference software is available to cover a variety of interests, including trip planning, genealogy, and landscaping.
- Portable apps can be stored on and run from a flash drive.

## Key Terms

open source

portable apps

# HOW TO

## Create a Document Using Wordpad or Textedit

Microsoft Windows includes a word processing application called WordPad. OS X includes TextEdit. These are basic programs that can be used to create simple documents, such as homework assignments, even if you don't have a full word processor, such as Microsoft Word, installed.

To access WordPad, swipe in from the right edge of the screen, and click *Search*. Being to type **wordpad**. In the Search results, click *WordPad*. The File menu contains commands to open, save, print, and email your documents. The right column contains a list of the nine most recent documents, making it easy to reopen them. The Quick Access Toolbar has buttons for Save, Undo, and Redo by default, but you can customize it by clicking the arrow on the right.

The Ribbon has two tabs: Home and View. The Home tab contains the commands for formatting the document and inserting objects; the View tab contains commands to change the way the document displays on your screen. When WordPad opens, it begins with a blank document open. The figure below identifies the parts of the WordPad window.

## LET'S CREATE A SIMPLE DOCUMENT

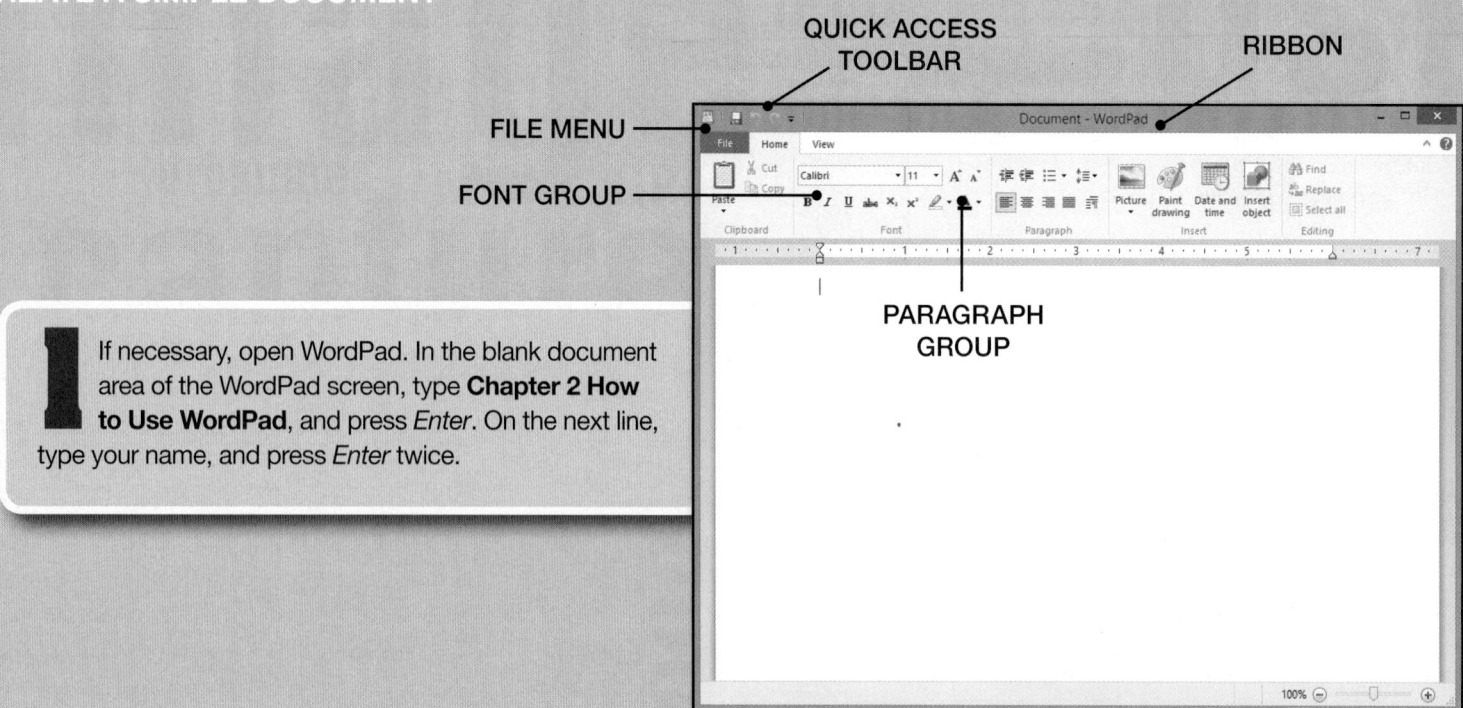

QUICK ACCESS TOOLBAR

RIBBON

FILE MENU

FONT GROUP

PARAGRAPH GROUP

**1** If necessary, open WordPad. In the blank document area of the WordPad screen, type **Chapter 2 How to Use WordPad**, and press *Enter*. On the next line, type your name, and press *Enter* twice.

**2** Type the following paragraph: **WordPad is a basic word processor that is included with Windows. I can use it to type homework assignments and other documents that are compatible with most word processing programs.**

**3** Press *Enter*. Click the *Start a list* button, and type the following three bullet points (press *Enter* after each): **Free, Easy to use, Compatible.** Press *Enter* again to exit the bulleted list.

**4** Click the *Date and Time* button in the Insert group; select a date format that includes the day of the week; and click *OK*.

**5** Drag your mouse to select the paragraph of text, the bulleted list, and the date. In the Font group, click the Font family arrow to change the font from Calibri to Times New Roman. Click the Font size arrow to change the font size to 12.

**6** Select the first two lines and use the buttons on the WordPad Ribbon to format them. In the Paragraph group, click the *Center* button. In the Font group, change the font size from 11 to 14 and click the *B* button to make the text bold. Compare your document to the figure below.

START A LIST
BUTTON

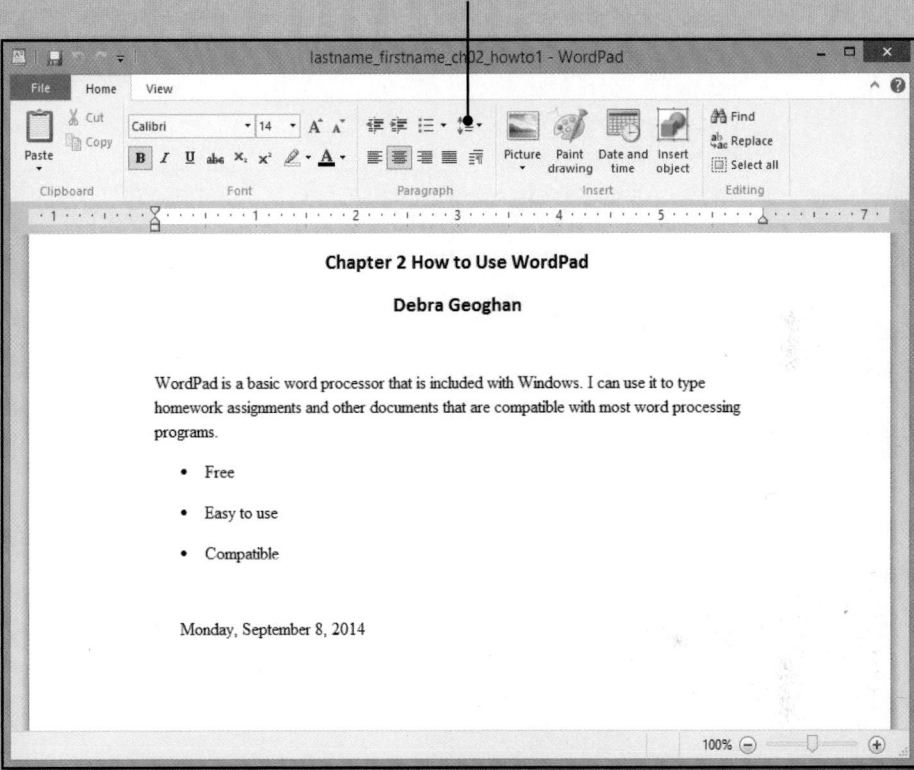

**7** To save the file, click the *WordPad* button, point to Save as, and choose the appropriate format. The default format is Rich Text document, which is compatible with all word processors. If you're required to submit your work in the Microsoft Word format, select Office Open XML document from the list instead.

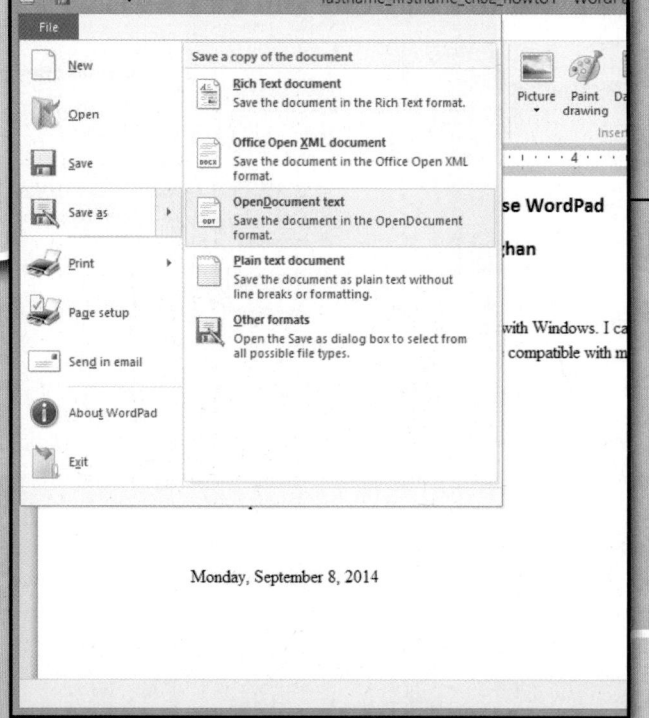

USE OFFICE OPEN XML DOCUMENT TO SAVE YOUR FILE IN MICROSOFT WORD FORMAT.

**8** Navigate to the folder that you created for your Chapter 2 work and save the file as **lastname_firstname_ch02_howto1**. Submit this file as directed by your instructor.

**If you are using a Mac:**

Open *TextEdit* from the Launchpad. TextEdit has a Menu bar with six menu choices. The TextEdit menu includes options to customize the program. The File menu includes such items as Open, Close, Save, and Print. The Edit menu is where you will find options to edit the text in your document such as Cut, Copy, Insert, and the Spelling and Grammar checker. The Format menu has the tools to format the text, tables, lists, etc. and the Window menu allows you to modify how your document displays on your screen.

Follow directions for steps 1–3, replacing WordPad with **TextEdit** in your document. For step 4, type in the date.

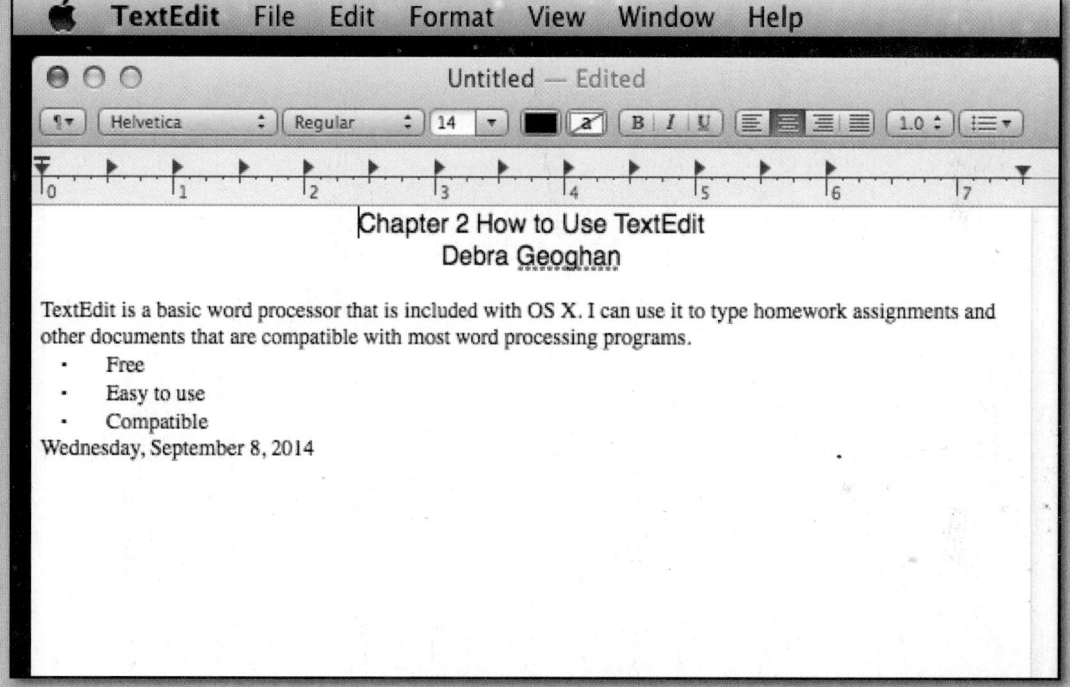

# Will It Run?

## 3 OBJECTIVE
### Assess a computer system for software compatibility.

Your best friend just told you about an awesome new game she bought. Should you run right out and buy it, too? At $60, the game is an investment that warrants at least a little bit of research on your part, as do most software purchases. So, what do you need to know?

## YOUR SYSTEM SPECS

Before you rush out (or go online) to buy software, you need to do a little bit of work. You need to document your system specs so you can compare them to the system requirements of the software. That is the only way you'll know your system can run the program. You can get the information you need with just a few mouse clicks.

Let's start with drives. For most software you buy in a store, you'll need a DVD drive to do the installation. While a few programs will run from a DVD (or flash drive), most programs are installed on your hard drive. The amount of drive space required is listed in the system requirements. You can verify that you have enough free space by simply opening the Computer window by typing **computer** in the Windows 8 Search box. The Windows computer in Figure 2.24 has a DVD drive and 254 GB of free space on the hard drive (C).

To find this information on a Mac, click the Apple menu and then click About This Mac. On the About This Mac screen, click *More Info. . .* and then click the *Storage* tab. The Mac in Figure 2.25 has about 88GB free on the hard drive Macintosh HD. Most of the other information you need to know, such as processor speed, memory, and operating system version, can be found using the other tabs in this window.

On a Windows computer, one of the easiest ways to obtain the other information you need is to open the System Control Panel. To do this, you can right-click on *Computer* in the Explorer window and select *Properties*.

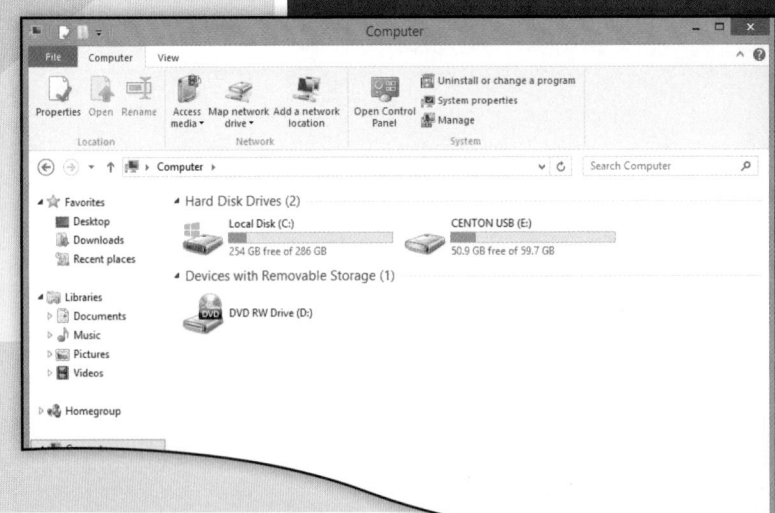

**FIGURE 2.24** Open the Computer window to verify the space available on the drives on your system.

Most of the information you need is found on this page: operating system version, processor type and speed, and amount of memory installed. The **Windows Experience Index** (see Figure 2.26) is a rating system that assesses these traits as well as your video card performance to determine the types of software that your computer can run. When you click on the index, it will show you a list of subscores for the components assessed. Some software packages list Windows Experience Index ratings under system requirements.

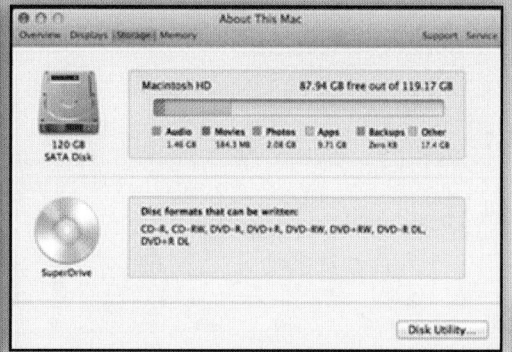

**FIGURE 2.25** Use About This Mac to locate information about your system.

Windows Experience Index and Other System Information

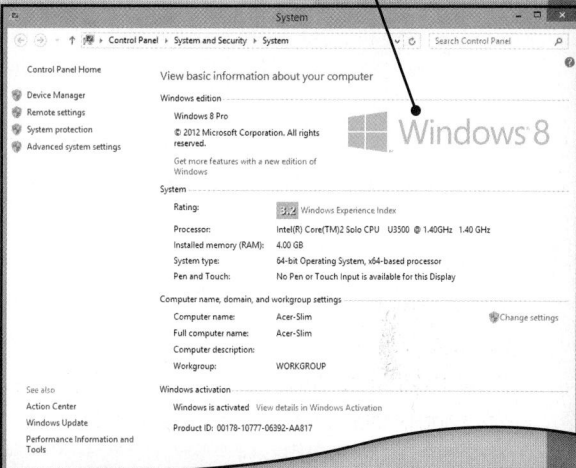

**FIGURE 2.26** You can use the System Control Panel and Windows Experience Index to determine if a computer meets the system requirements for software.

# SYSTEM REQUIREMENTS

**System requirements** for software are usually right on the box or on the publisher's website. These are *minimum requirements* to get the program running, but exceeding the requirements will give you better performance. These requirements list both the hardware and software specifications the computer must meet in order to run the program. Sometimes, you may need to upgrade your system to meet or exceed these requirements. As software becomes more sophisticated, the system requirements go up.

It's important to know what the system requirements are for a program before you buy it so you're not stuck with a purchase that you can't use. Spending a few minutes verifying that your system meets the requirements will help ensure that you can actually use the software you buy or let you know if a system upgrade is necessary.

## Running Project

Research a game that you would like to run on your computer. What are the system requirements for the game? Does your computer meet the minimum requirements to run the game? In what ways does it exceed them?

## 3 Things You Need to Know

- You can find out your system specifications using the Computer window and System Control Panel or the About This Mac window.

- The Windows Experience Index can help you determine the software that your system can run.

- System requirements are the minimum requirements needed to run software and include hardware and software specifications.

## Key Terms

system requirements

Windows Experience Index

# Where to Get It

## 4 OBJECTIVE
## Compare various ways of obtaining software.

There are many different ways to obtain software. You can go out to the store and buy it, order it online and have it shipped to you, or download it from a website or app store. In this article, we look at software licensing and how to obtain software.

## LICENSING

When you purchase and install software on your computer, you do not actually *own* the program. Instead, you license it. The software is owned by the company that created it. There are several different software license types. Carefully read the **EULA (end-user license agreement)**—the agreement between the user and the software publisher—on all software to know your rights before you install it, including the number of computers you can legally install it on, the length of time you have access to it, and any privacy notices (see Figure 2.27). You should also look for important hidden information in the fine print. For example, by clicking I Agree on some EULAs, you allow the installation of additional "features," such as toolbars and spyware on your computer.

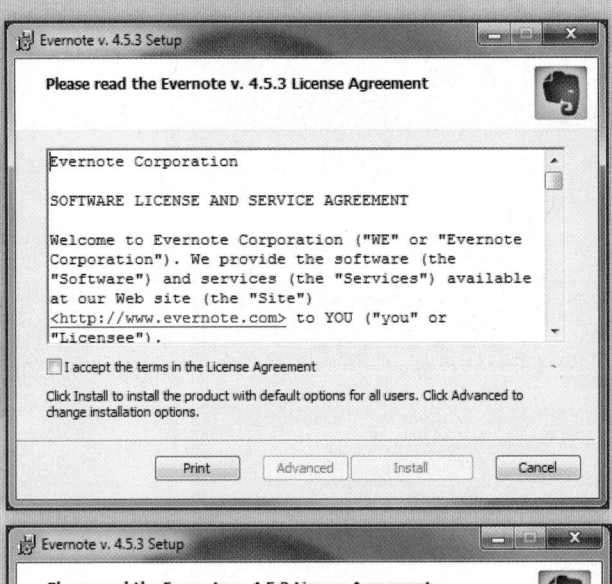

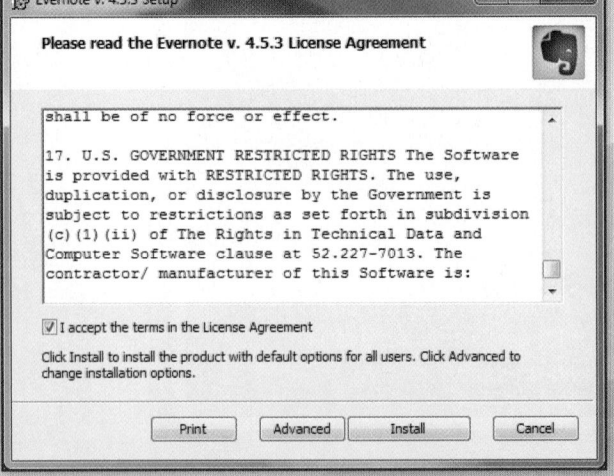

**FIGURE 2.27** Scroll through and read the entire License Agreement before checking the I accept the terms box and installing the software.

The two most common software licenses are the following:

- **Proprietary software license:** Grants a license to use one or more copies of software, but ownership of those copies remains with the software publisher. This is the type of license found on most commercial software and is the most restrictive in terms of your right to distribute and install the software.
- **Open source software license:** Grants ownership of the copy to the end-user. The source code for that software must be made freely available. The end-user has the right to modify and redistribute the software under the same license. Open source software is growing in popularity, and there are more offerings available all the time.

In both cases, there may or may not be a fee for the use of the software. The cost of software is a big factor in choosing which programs to install.

# FREE OR FEE

Not all proprietary software has a fee, and not all open source software is free. The cost of software is determined by the publisher. There are four basic models for software distribution:

- **Retail software:** User pays a fee to use the software for an unlimited period of time. Microsoft Office, Adobe Photoshop, and TurboTax are all examples of retail software.
- **Freeware:** Software can be used at no cost for an unlimited period of time. Some popular freeware includes Apple iTunes, Evernote, and 7-Zip.
- **Shareware:** Software is offered in trial form or for a limited period that allows the user to try it out before purchasing a license. It's sometimes referred to as trialware. This marketing model of selling software has become so popular that you can purchase most retail software this way. You can download a 30- or 60-day free trial of products from Microsoft, Adobe, and many other publishers. New computers often come preloaded with lots of trialware.
- **Donationware:** This software is a form of freeware where the developers accept donations, either for themselves or for a nonprofit organization. OpenOffice.org is an example of donationware.

# Find Out MORE

Visit the Open Source Initiative (**OSI; opensource .org**). Who are they, and what do they do? How do they define open source?

# SOURCES OF SOFTWARE

Software is available in a variety of places. Where you choose to obtain it will depend on the type of software you're looking for and the time frame in which you need it.

**RETAIL BRICK-AND-MORTAR STORES** You can purchase software in specialized computer and electronics stores, office supplies stores, mass merchandise stores, and even drugstores. The price and variety of programs available in these places will vary widely. If you're looking for a popular piece of software, such as game or tax preparation software, then you'll likely find it for a good price. But if you're looking for something less popular, you may have a hard time finding it on the shelf.

**BEST BUY**

**RETAIL WEBSITES** You'll find a much larger selection of software available through online retailers, such as Amazon.com or Buy.com. These sites sell the same software in a box and ship it to you. Some software may also be available for immediate download. Online retailers often have a larger selection of software than retail stores, and prices are comparable.

**PUBLISHER WEBSITES** When you purchase software directly from the software publisher's website, you can immediately download it. The cost can be competitive with retailers, but it pays to shop around.

**SOFTWARE DOWNLOAD WEBSITES** Websites such as cnet.com, tucows.com, and zdnet.com have vast libraries of freeware and shareware to download. For open source software, go to sourceforge.net. An advantage to using sites like these is that they include editor and user reviews to help you choose the program that is right for you. Also, these websites test the programs for malicious intent. The CNET website states: "We will not list software that contains viruses, Trojan horses, malicious adware, spyware, or other potentially harmful components."

The Apple App Store is part of OS X (see Figure 2.28) and gives you access to thousands of programs, both free and paid, right from your Mac desktop. In fact, when Apple released the OS X Lion upgrade, the App Store was the only way you could purchase it.

Software apps for mobile devices should be downloaded from trusted sources. It is safest if you use the recommended app store/marketplace for your device. The apps must pass through rigorous testing to be placed in the market, thus reducing the risk of malicious or harmful code running on your device.

When you download software from a website, it's good practice to back up the downloaded file and license should you ever need to reinstall the program. Wherever you finally decide to purchase software, be sure that you understand the license terms before you click the I Accept button.

**FIGURE 2.28** The Most Popular Downloads from the Apple App Store as of March 2012

## Running Project

Use the Internet to find out what the terms "shrink-wrap license" and "click-wrap license" mean. What are they? How are they alike? Are they legal and binding?

## 3 Things You Need to Know

- When you purchase software, you don't own it but are only licensing it—unless it's open source.
- You should read the EULA (end-user license agreement) to determine the restrictions and potential add-on features related to the software before you install it.
- Not all proprietary software has a fee, and not all open source software is free.

## Key Terms

donationware

EULA (end-user license agreement)

freeware

retail software

shareware

# Your Head in the Cloud

**OBJECTIVE**

## Discuss the importance of cloud computing.

You may have heard the term "cloud computing." The cloud refers to the Internet. In this chapter, we've already discussed some online applications. **Cloud computing** takes the processing and storage off your desktop and business hardware and puts it in the cloud—on the Internet. As the need for storage, security, and collaboration has grown, cloud computing has become an important part of business and personal systems.

## CLOUD COMPUTING

There are three types of services that can be delivered through the cloud: Infrastructure-as-a-Service, Platform-as-a-Service, and Software-as-a-Service. Together, these three services can provide a business with an integrated system for delivering applications and content using the cloud. The companies that deliver these cloud services, such as Amazon, Google, Sun Microsystems, and Salesforce.com, are known as **Cloud Service Providers (CSPs).** Cloud solutions save money in software, hardware, and personnel costs, increase standardization, and increase efficiency and access to technology. The CSPs can build huge datacenters in remote locations near cheap (and green) power supplies, such as hydroelectric plants, which is impractical for most businesses.

### INFRASTRUCTURE-AS-A-SERVICE (IAAS)

Infrastructure costs can be as much as 80 percent of a typical IT budget. **Infrastructure-as-a-Service (IaaS)** means that a company uses servers in the cloud instead of purchasing and maintaining them. This saves costs for hardware, software, and support personnel. Even small companies that don't have the expertise in-house can have sophisticated servers to house large databases, centralized document management, and security, using and paying for just what they need, increasing during surges in demand, such as a holiday or tax season, and decreasing during the lulls. A commonly used IaaS service is off-site backup services. There is some concern about the security of using cloud services for storing sensitive information, although large CSPs have very secure environments.

### PLATFORM-AS-A-SERVICE (PAAS)

**Platform-as-a-Service (PaaS)** provides a programming environment to develop, test, and deploy custom Web applications. This gives businesses the ability to build, deploy, and manage Software-as-a-Service applications. PaaS also makes collaboration easier and requires less programming knowledge. Three popular PaaS programs are AppEngine from Google, Force.com from SalesForce, and Microsoft Azure Services Platform.

## SOFTWARE-AS-A-SERVICE (SAAS)

**Software-as-a-Service (SaaS)** means the delivery of applications over the Internet—or Web apps. This is the most visible to the user. Any time you open your browser to access your email, upload photos, use Facebook, or share a file, you're using SaaS. Figure 2.29 illustrates some common SaaS applications you probably already use.

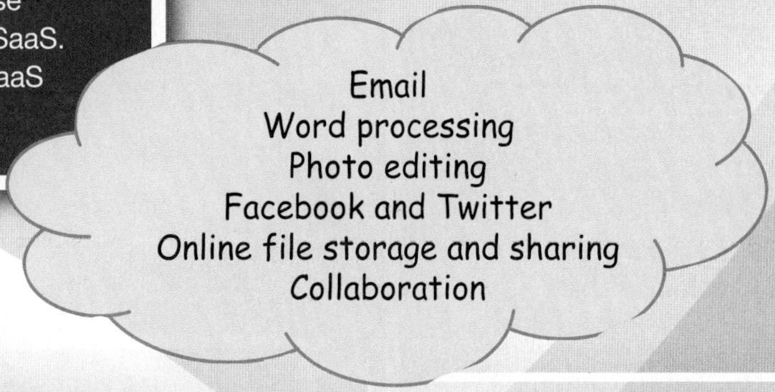

Email
Word processing
Photo editing
Facebook and Twitter
Online file storage and sharing
Collaboration

**FIGURE 2.29** Commonly used SaaS applications

SaaS has several advantages over installing software locally. Because SaaS is delivered on demand, it's available anytime from any computer with Internet access. In addition to the convenience, SaaS also eliminates the need to apply updates to local software installations. You use SaaS whenever you use Web mail. Using Web mail means that you don't download your email messages to your personal computer. They're stored and accessed from a hosted email server, providing backup and security for you, giving you access from anywhere, and eliminating the need to install and configure an email program on your computer.

Microsoft Web Apps, Google Docs, and Zoho Docs are all examples of personal SaaS. For businesses there are more powerful, fee-based tools. Google Apps for Business and Microsoft Office 365 include collaboration tools, email, calendar, and documents. Figure 2.30 compares the cost of using Microsoft Office 2010, Google Apps, or Microsoft Office 365 for a small business with 10 users.

Applying an update to an application on each computer can be a costly, time-consuming process. But with a SaaS solution, the updates happen on the remote system and do not impact the local users. Users will instantly have access to new features as soon as they log in to their account on the SaaS site. No local configuration is needed.

For businesses, using the cloud to deliver apps offers several benefits: a simple and quick way of accessing applications from anywhere, a relatively small cost per user, and the elimination of the need to maintain and support the applications onsite. SaaS may not be a term most people use very often, but the services it provides are used every day by individuals and businesses alike. As cloud computing continues to mature, we'll find more and more of our computing up in the cloud.

**FIGURE 2.30** Small Business Costs

| COST COMPARISON FOR A SMALL BUSINESS | MS OFFICE HOME AND BUSINESS 2010 | GOOGLE APPS FOR BUSINESS | MS OFFICE 365 SMALL BUSINESS PLAN |
|---|---|---|---|
| Initial Cost | $199.95 per license | — | — |
| Price Per User Per Year | — | $50 | $6/month = $72 |
| Annual Cost for 10 Users | $1,999.50 for first year- or $666.50 per year over *3 years, plus support costs | $500 | $720 |
| Support/updates | Local updates must be done on site by users or IT. Microsoft community support | 24/7 phone and email support; self-services online support | Microsoft community support |
| | *New MS Office releases about every 3 years. | | |

# GREEN COMPUTING

## ONLINE AND DOWNLOADED PROGRAMS VS. STORE-BOUGHT SOFTWARE

We've talked about your options for purchasing software from a convenience and cost standpoint, but there are also environmental issues to consider.

When you walk into a store and pick up software in a box or order from an online retailer and have the package shipped to you, there are several environmental impacts. First, there's the packaging material used to ship the product and product packaging. While cardboard and paper are recyclable, the EPA estimates that only about 70 percent of it is actually recycled. The rest of it—and other materials, such as plastic shrink-wrap and packing peanuts—ends up in our landfills. Then, there's the media inside the package. What happens to the CD or DVD when the software is no longer needed? It ends up in the trash—and into the landfill it goes. Finally, the transportation costs of shipping the product to you or to the store—air pollution, fuel consumption, and emission of greenhouse gases—all add up.

All these environmental impacts are eliminated using online applications or purchasing software online and downloading it to your computer. No packaging, no transportation costs, no obsolete media, and the convenience of having the software delivered to you on the spot make these alternatives the better choices for the environment.

## ▶ Running Project

Does your school use cloud computing (also known as above-campus computing)? If so, which services do you access from the cloud (for example, email, apps)? Give two examples of your personal use of cloud computing.

## 3 Things You Need to Know

- The cloud is the Internet.
- Cloud computing uses hardware and software resources that are in the cloud instead of local.
- Cloud computing consists of three types of services: Infrastructure-as-a-Service (IaaS), Platform-as-a-Service (PaaS), and Software-as-a-Service (SaaS).

## Key Terms

cloud computing

cloud service provider (CSP)

Infrastructure-as-a-Service (IaaS)

Platform-as-a-Service (PaaS)

Software-as-a-Service (SaaS)

# HOW TO

## Edit Photos with Photoshop Express Editor Online

**1** Go to **http://www.photoshop.com**. Click *Online Tools* and select *Photoshop Express Editor*.

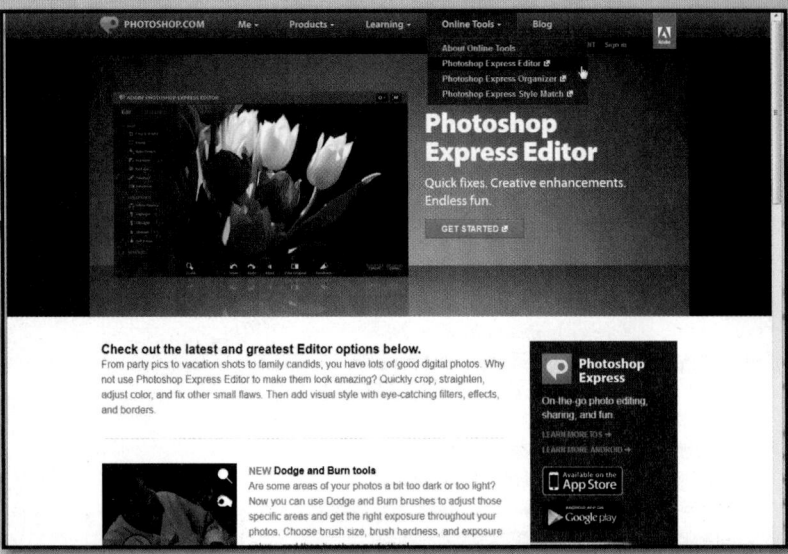

**2** Click *Load an image file*. Browse to the files for this chapter and upload *ch02_image1*.

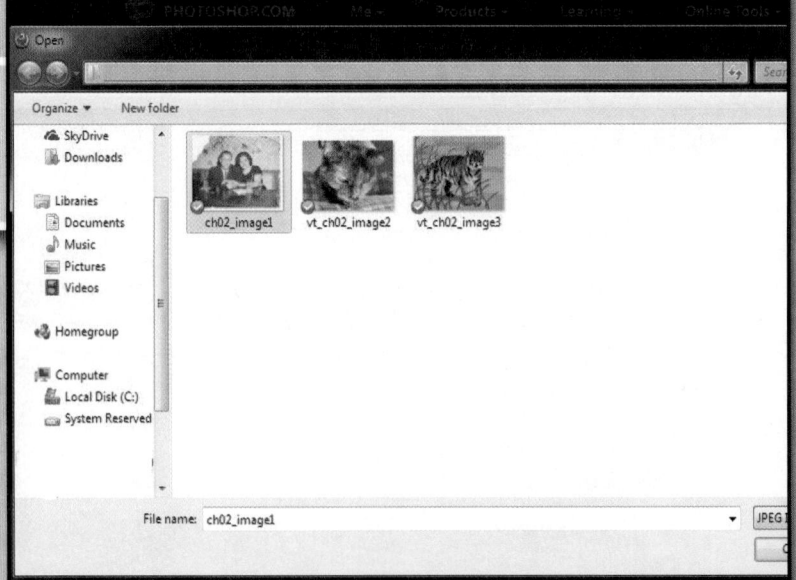

**3** Click the *Touchup Tool*. We will use this tool to erase the gold spots next to the man and the green lines next to the woman.

Move the mouse pointer to the left of the gold spots, click to create a green circle, and then drag the circle over the area to be touched up. If necessary, drag the red circle to a clean area of the image next to the gold spots. This will be the area that will replace the area in the green circle. This process is known as cloning and takes some practice and patience to get right. Keep cloning until you are happy with the result. You can use the Undo button at the bottom of the screen if you need to try again.

**4** Repeat the process to erase the two green lines to the right of the woman; these will be easier to remove. If you want to keep cleaning up the image, try to remove the crease through the middle of the image, across their chests. Work slowly and carefully, resetting the green and red circles frequently to get the lines just right.

**5** From the Basic menu, click *Crop and Rotate*. Drag the shape around the couple, trying to frame them nicely and eliminate as much of the damage and clutter as possible. When you are satisfied with your selection, click the *Decorate* tab.

**6** From the Graphics menu, click *Frames*. Choose an appropriate frame from the options and then click *Add*.

**7** Click *Text* and position it in the bottom right corner of the picture. Click and type **March 1963**. Change the font to Tekton, click the *B* button.

**8** Click the Edit tab and from the Adjustments menu, click *Soft Focus* to soften the image. Click *Done*, and then click *Save to my computer*. Save the file as **lastname_firstname_ch02_howto2**.

**9** Click *Next*, and then click *Done*.

**10** Submit yourfile to your instructors as directed.

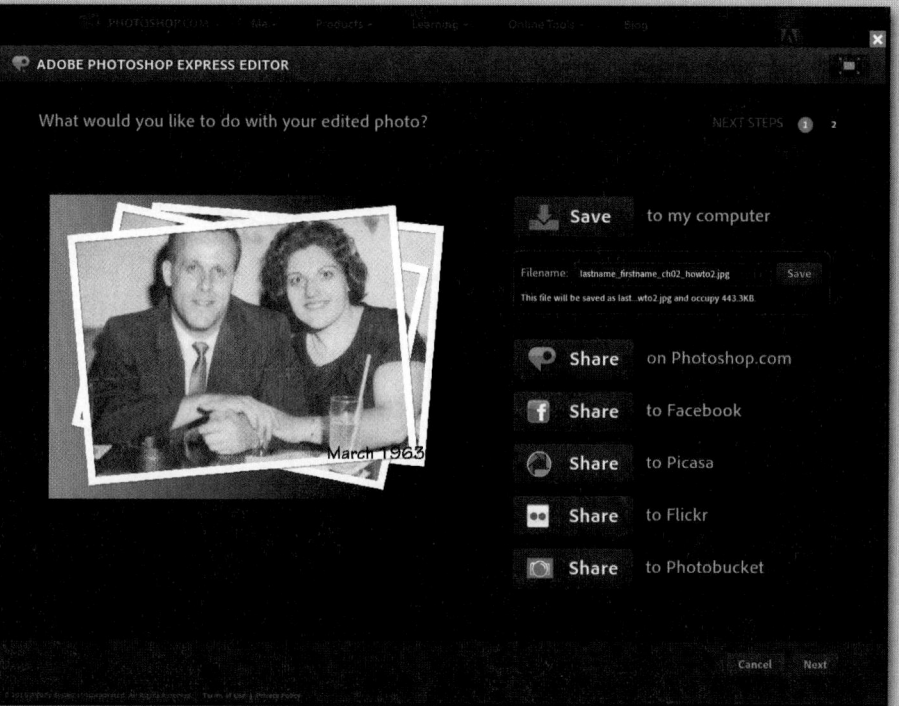

# CAREER SPOTLIGHT

Software trainers—sometimes called corporate trainers—are in demand as companies deploy more software programs. This high-paying career may involve some travel and requires good computer skills, organization, and communication skills. Software trainers usually have at least a bachelor's degree and on-the-job training. Some companies offer train-the-trainer courses that can lead to a certification. You might work for a training company, in the training department of a large company, or as a consultant to many companies.

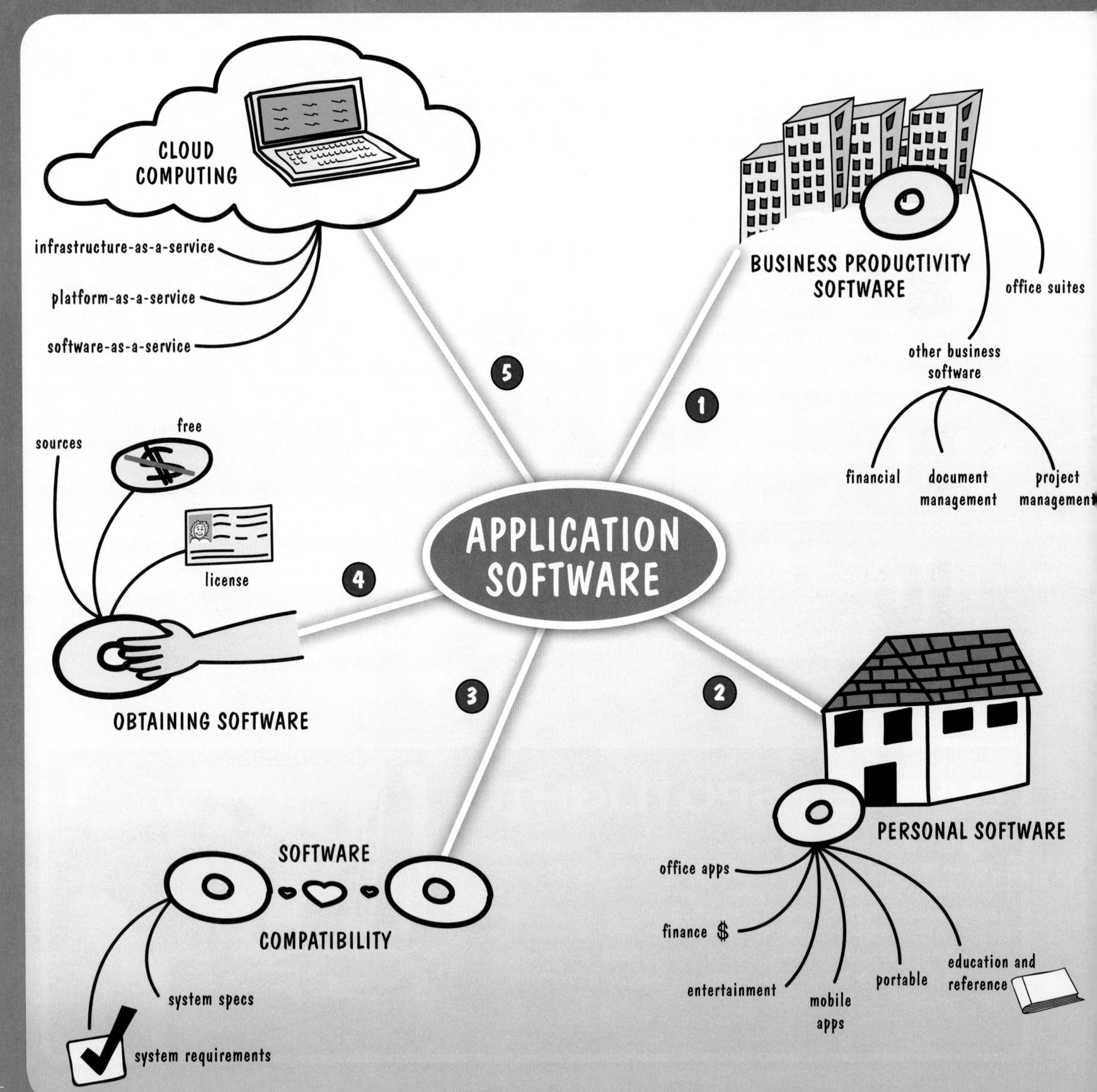

CLOUD COMPUTING

infrastructure-as-a-service

platform-as-a-service

software-as-a-service

BUSINESS PRODUCTIVITY SOFTWARE

office suites

other business software

financial

document management

project management

APPLICATION SOFTWARE

sources

free

license

OBTAINING SOFTWARE

⑤

①

④

③

②

SOFTWARE

COMPATIBILITY

system specs

system requirements

PERSONAL SOFTWARE

office apps

finance $

entertainment

mobile apps

portable

education and reference

# Objectives Recap

1. Identify types and uses of business productivity software.
2. Identify types and uses of personal software.
3. Assess a computer system for software compatibility.
4. Compare various ways of obtaining software.
5. Discuss the importance of cloud computing.

# Key Terms

cell **48**
cloud computing **72**
cloud service provider (CSP) **72**
database **50**
document management
     system **53**
donationware **69**
EULA (end-user license
     agreement) **68**
field **50**
freeware **69**
Infrastructure-as-a-Service
     (IaaS) **72**
office application suite **46**
open source **55**
personal information manager
     (PIM) **51**

Platform-as-a-Service
     (PaaS) **72**
portable apps **61**
project management
     software **52**
record **50**
retail software **69**
shareware **69**
Software-as-a-Service
     (SaaS) **73**
spreadsheet **48**
system requirements **67**
Windows Experience Index **67**
word processor **46**

# Summary

**1. Identify types and uses of business productivity software.**

The most common business software is an office application suite—including a word processor, spreadsheet, presentation program, database, and personal information manager. Other business applications include financial software, document management, and project management software.

**2. Identify types and uses of personal software.**

Personal software includes office applications, especially word processors, spreadsheets, and presentation programs. Other personal applications include entertainment and multimedia software such as media managers, video and photo editing software, and video games. Financial and tax preparation software as well as educational and reference software are also popular. You can run portable apps from a flash drive and take them with you.

**3. Assess a computer system for software compatibility.**

Before purchasing and installing software, you should research the system requirements needed to run the program and compare them to your system specifications using the System Control Panel.

**4. Compare various ways of obtaining software.**

You can obtain software from brick-and-mortar and online stores, publisher websites, and download websites. Download mobile apps only from trusted markets. It's important to read the EULA to understand the restrictions the software license puts on you.

**5. Discuss the importance of cloud computing.**

Cloud computing moves hardware and software into the cloud, or Internet. Cloud computing allows you to access applications and data from any Web-connected computer. Some benefits include lower cost, easier maintenance, security, and collaboration.

# Application Project

## MS Office Application Project 1:
## PowerPoint Level 1

**PROJECT DESCRIPTION:** Your new boss has asked you to create a presentation discussing good PowerPoint design. In this project, you will edit and format text and bullets, insert and format pictures, check spelling, add new slides and change slide layout, apply transitions, and add speaker notes.

**INSTRUCTIONS:** For the purpose of grading of the project you are required to perform the following tasks:

**1** Start PowerPoint. Download and open the file named *vt_ch02_ppt.* Save the file as **lastname_firstname_ch02_ppt**.

**2** On Slide 1, type the subtitle text **Presentations with Style**. Change the font of the title text, *PowerPoint Design,* to Cambria and change the size to 48.

**3** On Slide 2, change the line spacing of the bullets to 1.5 and the font size to 36.

**4** On Slide 3, use the shortcut menu to correct the spelling of Layout. Change the line spacing of the bullets to 1.5 and the font size to 36.

**5** Insert a new Comparison slide after Slide 3 and add the following as the title text: **Images**

**6** On the new Slide 4, in the bottom left content placeholder, insert the picture *vt_ch02_image.* In the content place holder, type **Inserted image**.

**7** On the new Slide 4, in the bottom right content placeholder, insert a clipart image of a cat, or use the provided picture *vt_ch02_image2* In the content place holder, type **ClipArt**.

**8** Format both images to a height of 3". Adjust the location so they are evenly aligned.

**9** Switch to Slide Sorter view and delete Slide 5. Switch back to Normal view.

**10** In the Notes Pane on Slide 2, add the following speaker note and change the Font Size to 16: **Keep your fonts simple and easy to read.**

**11** In the Notes Pane on Slide 3, add the following speaker note and change the Font Size to 16: **Your layout should focus the viewer's attention.**

Visit **pearsonhighered.com/Geoghan** for data files, simulations, VizClips, and additional study materials.

**12** In the Notes Pane on Slide 4, add the following speaker note and change the Font Size to 16: **Images and clipart should enhance what you have to say.**

**13** Apply the Uncover transition with a duration of 01.25 to all of the slides in the presentation.

**14** Insert the page number and then type your name in as the footer on the notes and handouts pages for all slides in the presentation. View the presentation in Slide Show view from beginning to end, and then return to Normal view.

**15** Save and close the presentation and then exit PowerPoint. Submit the presentation as directed.

Visit **pearsonhighered.com/Geoghan** for data files, simulations, VizClips, and additional study materials.

Chapter 2 | 83

# MS Office Application Project 2:
## Excel Level 1

**PROJECT DESCRIPTION:** In this Microsoft Excel project, you will format cells and a worksheet. You will create a formula and insert a header and footer.

**INSTRUCTIONS:** For the purpose of grading the project you are required to perform the following tasks:

### Cost Comparison for a Small Business

| | MS Office Home and Business 2010 | Google Apps for Business | MS Office 365 Small Business plan |
|---|---|---|---|
| Initial Cost- per license | $200 | $ - | $ - |
| Price Per User Per Month | 0 | $ 5 | $ 6 |
| Annual Cost for 10 Users | $1999.50 for first year- or $666.50 per year over *3 years- plus support costs | $ 600 | $ 720 |
| Live Support/updates | Local updates must be done on site- by users or IT. | 24/7 phone and email support | |
| Online support | Microsoft community support | self-service online support | Microsoft community support |

*New MS Office releases about every 3 years.

lastname_firstname_ch02_excel_solution

1. Start Excel. Open the downloaded Excel file named *vt_ch02_excel* and save the file as **lastname_firstname_ch02_excel**.

2. Apply the Facet theme to the workbook.

3. Merge and center the text in cell A1 over columns A:D. Change the cell style to Heading 1.

4. Select the range A2:D2 and set the text to wrap in the cells. Center and middle align the text in the selected range. Change the cell style to Heading 3.

5. In cell C5, create a formula to calculate the annual cost of Google Apps for 10 users. Copy the formula to cell D5.

**6** Select the range C3:D5. Apply the Currency (0) Format to the selected range.

**7** Reduce the number of decimals in cell B3 to 0.

**8** Change the scaling of the Sheet 1 worksheet so the width will fit to one page. Center the worksheet vertically on the page.

**9** Rename the Sheet1 tab as **Comparisons**

**10** Insert a header with the Sheet name in the center cell. Insert a footer with the file name in the left cell.

**11** Save the workbook. Close the workbook and then exit Excel. Submit the workbook as directed.

Visit **pearsonhighered.com/Geoghan** for data files, simulations, VizClips, and additional study materials.

Chapter 2 | 85

# Multiple Choice

Answer the multiple-choice questions below for more practice with key terms and concepts from this chapter.

1. Which application would be the best choice for creating a budget?
   a. Word processor
   b. Spreadsheet
   c. Database
   d. Personal information manager

2. Software that has the source code published and made available to the public—enabling anyone to copy, modify and redistribute it without paying fees—is called _____ software.
   a. freeware
   b. free source
   c. open source
   d. trial version

3. Which part of a database contains information about a single entry—such as a customer or product?
   a. Field
   b. Record
   c. Chart
   d. Table

4. _____ is an online alternative to office application suites.
   a. Google Apps
   b. Mint.com
   c. TextEdit
   d. WordPad

5. _____ software helps you manage email, calendar, and tasks.
   a. Project management
   b. Document management
   c. Personal information management
   d. Word processing

6. Programs that can run from a flash drive are known as _____.
   a. suites
   b. SaaS
   c. portable apps
   d. open source software

7. The Windows Experience Index _____.
   a. evaluates the fun factor of video games
   b. refers to the Windows Media Center
   c. refers to your personal computing experience
   d. evaluates the computer's ability to run software

8. _____ can be used at no cost for an unlimited period of time.
   a. Retail
   b. Freeware
   c. Shareware
   d. Donationware

9. Which acronym refers to the delivery of applications over the Internet—or Web apps?
   a. Waps
   b. IaaS
   c. PaaS
   d. SaaS

10. _____ provides a programming environment to develop, deploy, and manage Web apps.
    a. IaaS
    b. PaaS
    c. SaaS
    d. CSP

# True or False

Answer the following questions with T for true or F for false for more practice with key terms and concepts from this chapter.

1. In a business environment, you'll find Microsoft Excel almost exclusively as the spreadsheet application.

2. A cell is the intersection of a row and a column in a spreadsheet.

3. Apache OpenOffice can't open and work with documents created in Microsoft Office.

4. Documents created with a word processor can also contain images.

5. A document management system manages your email, calendar, contacts, and tasks all in one place. It includes the ability to share calendars and schedule meetings.

6. Most office applications have the ability to save files in common file formats allowing you to move work between programs and across platforms.

7. If your computer doesn't meet the minimum system requirements for a piece of software, it will probably still run on your system.

8. A proprietary software license grants a license to use one or more copies of software, but ownership of those copies remains with the software publisher.

9. It is generally safe to download mobile apps from unknown sources.

10. Web mail is an example of SaaS.

# Fill in the Blank

Fill in the blanks with key terms from this chapter.

1. A(n) _____ is an application that's used to create, edit, and format text documents.

2. A(n) _____ is a collection of records organized in a useful way.

3. A(n) _____ is a program that helps you complete projects, keep within your budget, stay on schedule, and collaborate with others.

4. _____ is used to save, share, search, and audit electronic documents throughout their life cycle.

5. _____ software has its source code published and made available to the public, enabling anyone to copy, modify, and redistribute it.

6. _____ are the minimum hardware and software specifications required to run a software application.

7. _____ is software offered in trial form or for a limited period that allows the user to try it out before purchasing a license.

8. The license agreement between the software user and the software publisher is the _____.

9. A(n)_____ takes the processing and storage off your desktop and business hardware and puts it on the Internet.

10. Part of cloud computing, _____ is the use of Internet-based servers.

# Running Project ...

## ... The Finish Line

Assume that you just got a new computer with no software on it. Use your answers to the previous sections of the project to help you select five pieces of software that you consider indispensable to have. Which programs did you pick and why? If you could only afford to buy one program, which would it be? Which would you likely use a Web-based tool for?

Write a report describing your selections and responding to the questions raised. Save your file as **lastname_firstname_ch02_project** and submit it to your instructor as directed.

# Do It Yourself 1

System requirements for new software often require a computer system with lots of available processing power, storage space, and memory. In this activity, you learn a little bit about your own computer to help you make smart software purchases.

Windows and OS X provide many details about your computer through built-in utilities. For this exercise, you'll use the System Control Panel and Computer window. For a Mac, use the About This Mac window to complete the table.

1. Click the *Start* button and click *Computer*. (If you are using a Mac, open the About This Mac window from the Apple menu.)

2. In the right pane is a listing of all the drives available on your computer. Create a table like the one below to record details about your system—include the name, capacity, and free space for each drive.

| Hard Disk Drives | Devices with Removable Storage | Network Locations | Other Locations |
|---|---|---|---|
| | | | |
| | | | |
| | | | |
| | | | |

3. Right-click on *Computer* in the navigation pane and choose *Properties* to open the System Control Panel. Click on *Windows Experience Index*. What is your lowest subscore? What can you do to improve your system's score?

4. Type up your answers, save the file as **lastname_firstname_ch02_diy1**, and submit the assignment as directed by your instructor.

# Do It Yourself 2

Windows and OS X come with several applications. In this activity, you'll examine these accessories.

1. Click the *Start* button, click *All Programs*, and click *Accessories*. What programs are listed? For a Mac, click the *Launchpad* and look at items listed in the first screen.

2. Use Windows Help and Support to look up Calculator, Math Input Panel, Paint, and Sticky Notes. If you are using a Mac, in the Help Center search for Apps Included with your Mac. Look up Calculator, Solver, Preview, and Stickies. Write a one- to two-paragraph summary of each application.

3. Close the Help window. Save the file as **lastname_firstname_ch02_diy2** and submit it as directed by your instructor.

# Critical Thinking

You're starting a small home business. You want to be sure to keep good records and will need to use finance software to help you. You'll be the only employee of your business, so you need something basic and easy to use. Compare two small business finance programs:

1. Evaluate two programs from current newspaper ads and websites and compare them with respect to your requirements.

2. Use a word processor or spreadsheet to create a table like the one below, comparing the features of each program, to organize your research.

| | Program 1 | Program 2 |
|---|---|---|
| Name of program | | |
| Cost | | |
| Local install or online? | | |
| Important features | | |
| Online ratings (website) | | |
| Support | | |

3. In the same document, write your conclusion in a two- to three-paragraph essay. Which program should you buy and why? Is there anything else (hardware, software, office supplies) that you'll need to purchase to use the program?

4. Save your file as **lastname_firstname_ch02_ct** and submit both your table and essay as directed by your instructor.

# Ethical Dilemma

You decided to buy an expensive video editing program and look online for a good deal. You find a listing from a seller that has good ratings, so you buy the software. When the software arrives, you're disappointed to find that it is a pirated copy and includes a program to generate a license key to unlock the program—a key gen program.

1. You bought the software in good faith and really need it to complete your homework assignment. What do you do? Would you install the software? Why or why not?

2. Is it acceptable to install the software for the assignment and uninstall it when you're finished?

3. Type up your answers, save the file as **lastname_firstname_ch02_ethics**, and submit it as directed by your instructor.

# On the Web

The CNET website provides information to help you evaluate and compare both hardware and software. Visit **reviews.cnet.com/software** and answer the following questions:

1. Click the *Editor's Picks* link. What are the top 5 applications?

2. Select an application category from the menu on the left. Choose one application that looks interesting and you do not already use and read the review. How do the editor's and average user's ratings compare? What are the strengths and weaknesses of the program?

3. Type up your answers, save the file as **lastname_firstname_ ch02_web**, and submit it as directed by your instructor.

# Collaboration

**Instructors:** Divide the class into five groups, and assign each group one software license topic for this project. The topics include freeware, shareware, donationware, open source software, and EULAs.

**The Project:** Each team is to prepare a multimedia presentation for its license type. The presentation should be designed to educate consumers about the license type. Teams must use at least three references, only one of which may be this textbook. Use Google Docs or Microsoft Office to plan the presentation, and provide documentation that all team members have contributed to the project.

**Students:** Before beginning this project, discuss the roles each group member will play. Choose a team name, which you'll use in submitting your presentation. Be sure to divide the work among your members, and pick someone to present your project. You may find it helpful to elect a team leader who can direct your activities and ensure that all team contributions are collated through Google Docs or Microsoft Office as directed by your instructor.

**Outcome:** You're to prepare a multimedia presentation on your assigned topic in PowerPoint or another tool approved by your instructor and present it to your class. The presentation may be no longer than three minutes and should contain five to seven slides. On the first slide, be sure to include the name of your presentation and a listing of all team members. Turn in a final version of your presentation named as teamname_ch02_presentation and your file showing your collaboration named as teamname_ch02_collab. Submit your presentation to your instructor as directed.

# 3

# File Management

Visit **pearsonhighered.com/Geoghan** for data files, simulations, VizClips, and additional study materials.

**OBJECTIVES**

1. **Create folders to organize files.**

2. **Explain the importance of file extensions.**

3. **Explain the importance of backing up files.**

4. **Demonstrate how to compress files.**

5. **Use advanced search options to locate files.**

6. **Change the default program associated with a file type.**

## IN THIS CHAPTER

The concepts of file management are not unique to computing. We use file cabinets, folders, boxes, drawers, and piles to manage our paper files. These files can be anything from bills to photographs to homework assignments to coupons. In this chapter, we look at managing electronic files.

# A Place for Everything

VIZ CLIP

## OBJECTIVE
## Create folders to organize files.

One of the most important things that you need to do when working with computers is called **file management.** This means opening, closing, saving, naming, deleting, and organizing digital files. In this article, we discuss organizing your digital files, creating new folders, and navigating through the folder structure of your computer.

## NAVIGATING YOUR COMPUTER

Before you can create files, you need a place to put them. Let's start with the existing folder structure of your computer and explore how to navigate through it.

### THE WINDOWS USER AND PUBLIC FOLDERS

By default, Windows comes with certain files and folders already created. When a user account is added to a Windows computer, Windows automatically creates a personal user folder for that username and the subfolders inside it (see Figure 3.1). You can access your user folder through the File Explorer or it may appear on the desktop. **Folders** are containers that are used to organize files on your computer. Your user folder is normally only accessible by you. If someone else logs on to the computer using another username, that person won't see your files. Windows also creates **Public folders** that are common to all users and provide an easy way to share files among them. You can also share files across computers that are on a network or in the same homegroup (computers on your home network running Windows 7 or 8).

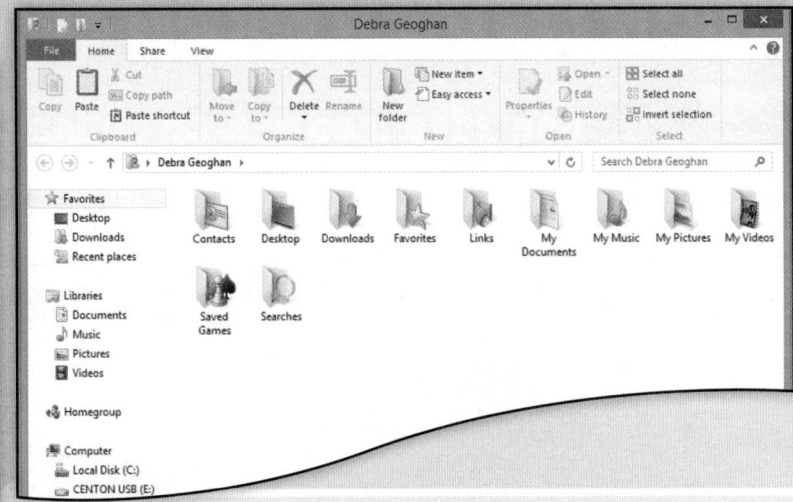

**FIGURE 3.1** The user folder for my account consists of subfolders that I use to organize my files.

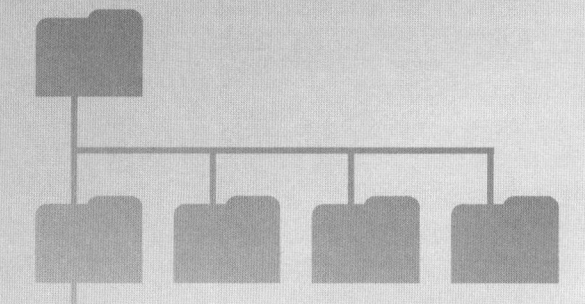

What folders are located under your username? The folder structure created by Windows is a **hierarchy**. There are folders within folders, known as subfolders or children, which allow you to further organize your files. Windows creates a set of folders to help you sort out your files. The My Documents folder is the place to store files such as word processing files, spreadsheets, presentations, and text files. There are also folders set up for pictures, music, and videos. These specialized folders are the best places to save your pictures, music, and videos so they're easy to find. Without this folder structure, all your files would be lumped together, making it much harder to keep track of what you have, similar to dumping all your snapshots into a shoebox. The sequence of folders to a file or folder is known as its **path**.

**WINDOWS LIBRARIES** Windows 7 introduced **libraries** to help you organize your files. There are four libraries: Documents, Music, Pictures, and Videos, and you can create more to suit your needs. Each library includes the matching user subfolder and the corresponding Public folder. This gives you quick access to both your personal files and the public shared files in one place. You can also customize libraries by adding other locations to the list. For example, if you store pictures on an external hard drive, you can add its location to the Picture library by right-clicking on the location (see Figure 3.2).

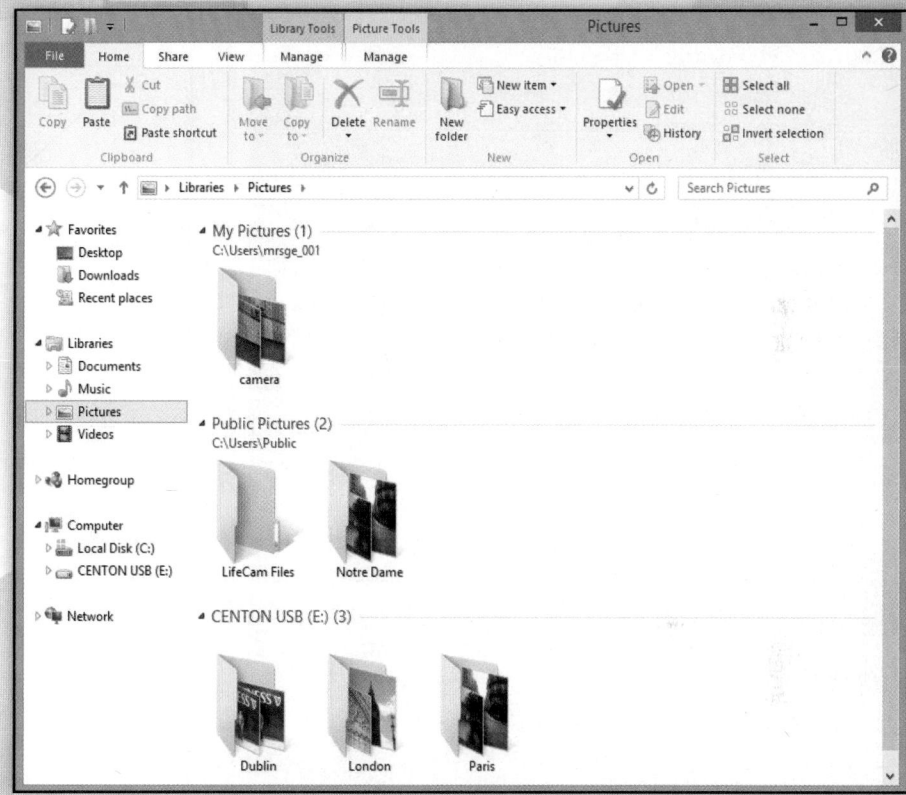

**FIGURE 3.2** Libraries gather files that are located in different locations. In this example, the Pictures folder on the external drive (E:) is added to the Pictures library.

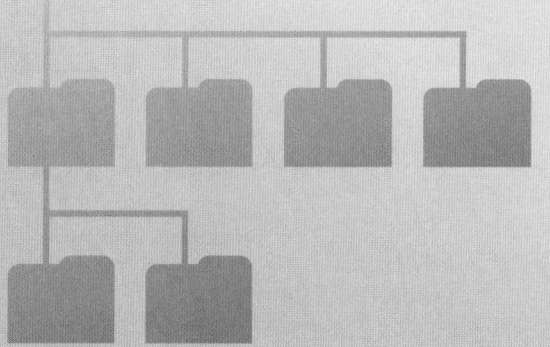

**FILE EXPLORER** The window you use to look at a library or folder is called **File Explorer**. You can open it by clicking the File Explorer icon on the taskbar. You can use Explorer to navigate through the folders and drives on your system and to handle most file management tasks. Figure 3.3 identifies some of the parts of the Explorer window.

File Explorer includes the following items:

- The Search box is used to search for files located in the current Explorer window. Windows searches the files in your current location for the text you type into the Search box. We explore searching in more detail later in this chapter.
- The Ribbon is used to perform common tasks on the items in the file list area. The tabs change depending on the objects displayed.
- The File list area takes up most of the window and displays the contents of the current library or folder displayed in the Explorer window.
- The Address bar contains the path to the current location in the Explorer window and is used to navigate through folders and libraries. You can move down in the folder hierarchy by clicking the arrow after your location. You can move back up in the folder hierarchy by clicking the arrows or links before your location in the Address bar.
- The Navigation pane is used to navigate the folders, libraries, and drives available on a computer. The Navigation pane is divided into several sections:
- Favorites—a list of your favorite/common locations—Libraries, Homegroup, Computer, and Network. Clicking on any of these sections changes the contents in the right pane. Clicking the small triangle before an item in the Navigation pane expands it to display the locations it contains.
- The View tab allows you to change the way the file list objects are displayed in the file list area. For picture files, choosing Large Icons, as in Figure 3.4, displays a small preview, or thumbnail, of the image. Selecting Details from the View tab displays a list of files with some of their properties.

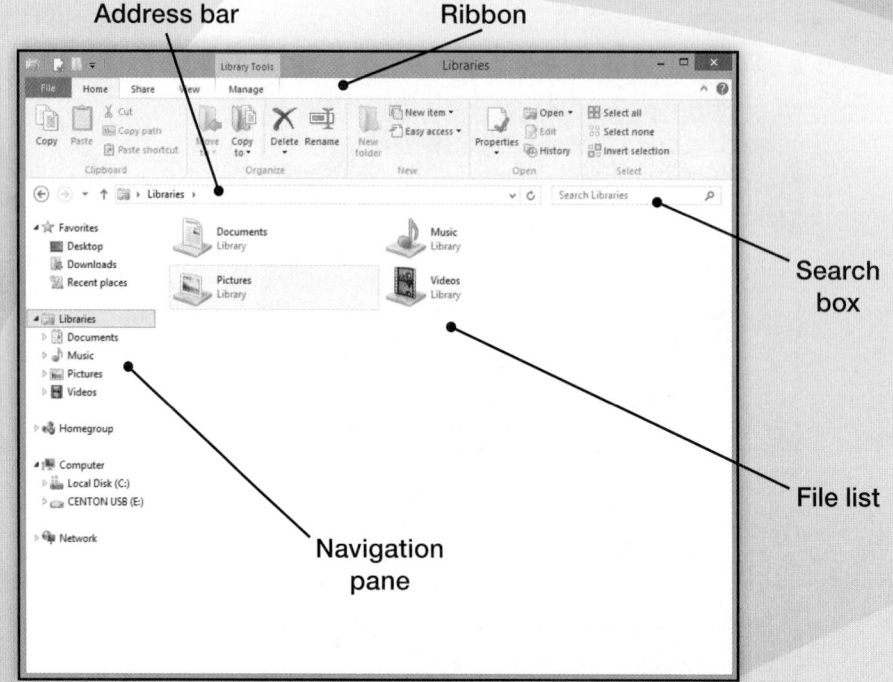

**FIGURE 3.3** The Parts of File Explorer

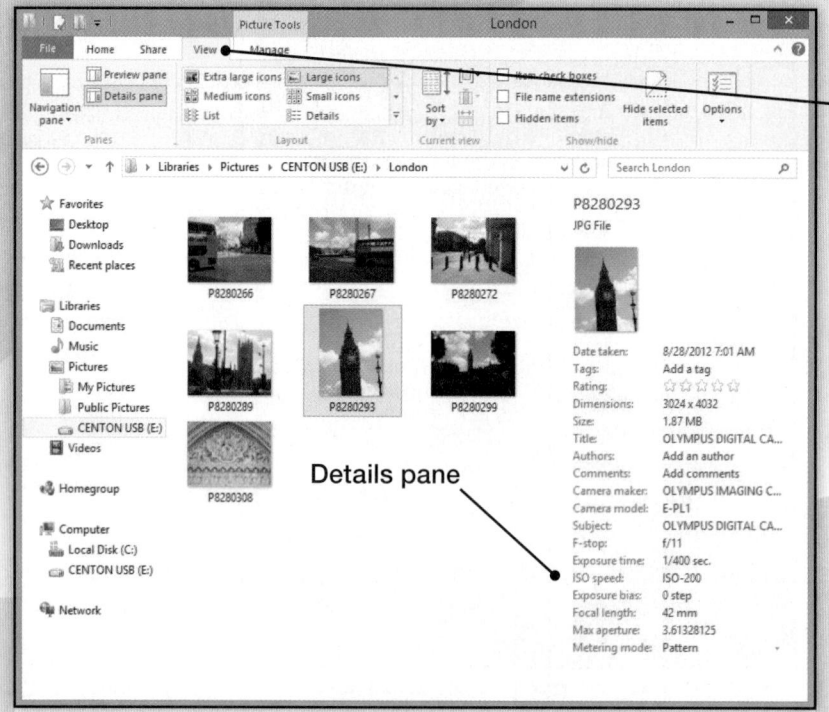

**FIGURE 3.4** The Large Icons view displays small previews of image files.

# MAC OS X FINDER AND FOLDERS

The **Finder** in Mac OS X is used to find and organize files, folders, and apps. It is similar to Windows Explorer. To open the Finder, click the Finder icon on the dock or from the Finder menu bar, click *File,* and select *New Finder Window*. Figure 3.5 identifies some of the parts of the Finder window. OS X creates a Home folder for each user. The Home folder includes subfolders to store Documents, Downloads, Movies, Music, and Pictures.

Elements of the Finder include the following:

- The Sidebar contains icons for things you frequently use such as disks, folders, shared resources, and other devices.
- The Toolbars contain buttons to change the way the Finder behaves.
- The View options on the toolbar change the way Finder displays information.
- The Search field is used to search for files on your Mac.
- The Contents area displays the contents of the currently selected location.

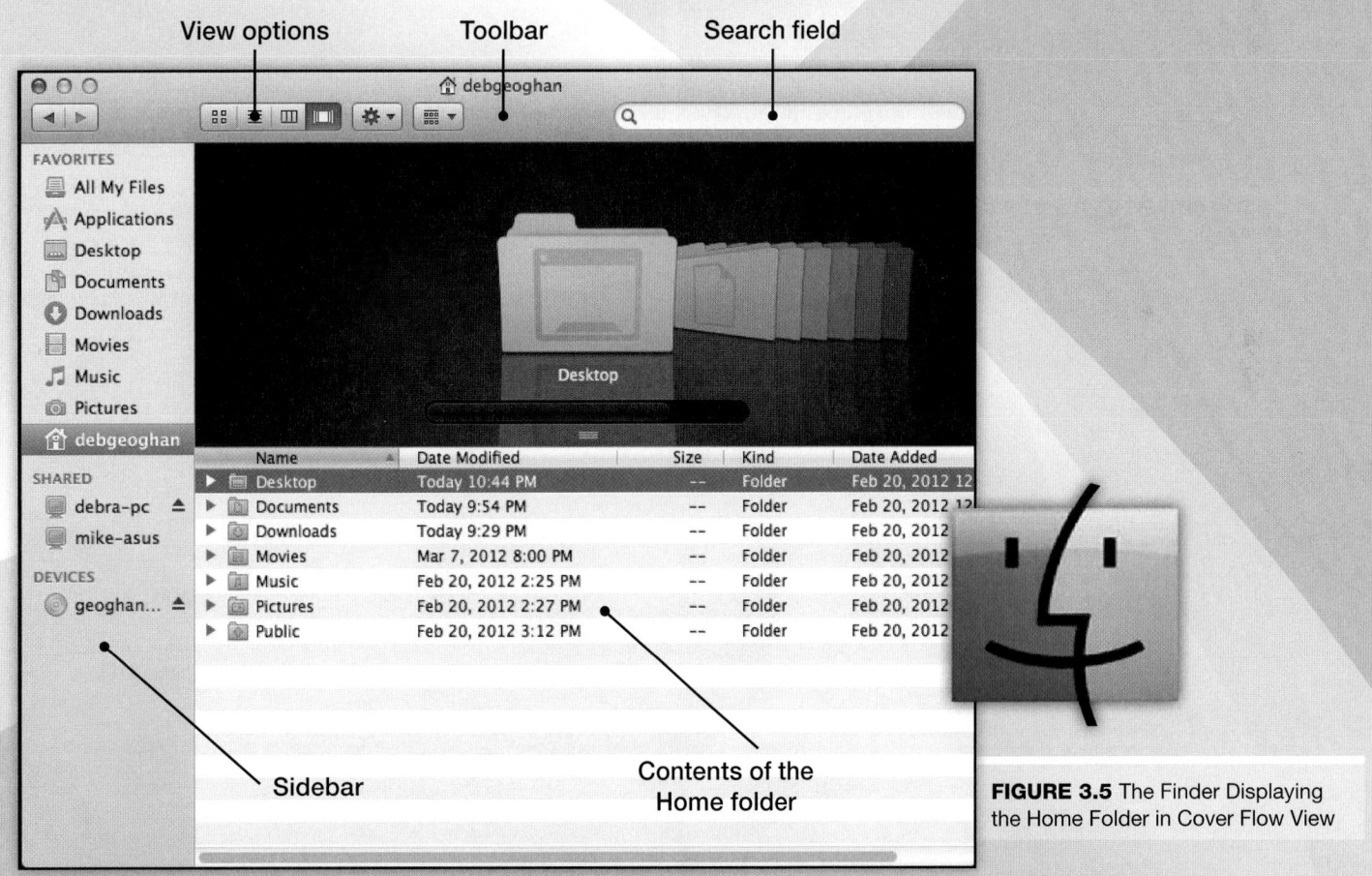

**FIGURE 3.5** The Finder Displaying the Home Folder in Cover Flow View

## MOBILE DEVICES AND FILE STORAGE

Mobile devices are meant to be mobile—fast and light—and don't have a lot of room to store your files. Some allow you to add storage using an SD card, but in general, rely on using cloud to organize and store your files. This has the advantage of making your mobile files accessible on all of your devices, not just the one in your hand. Cloud storage is discussed in the "Back It Up" article later in this chapter.

## CREATING AND USING FOLDERS

You're not limited to using the folder structure that's created by Windows or OS X. You can create your own organizational scheme to fit your needs. This is especially useful when you use flash drives and other locations that aren't part of the user folder hierarchy.

Suppose you print 25–30 photos a month (or 300–360 photos a year). How would you keep track of them? If you put them in a big box, in a few years, you'd have thousands of photos in the box. It would be nearly impossible to keep track of them or find anything unless you organized them into photo albums. The same is true of the files on your computer. Creating folders to organize your files will make storing and finding them easier to do. Figure 3.6 demonstrates how to create a new folder on a flash drive.

1. Insert the flash drive into the computer. Close any windows that open automatically.

Double-click to open your flash drive.

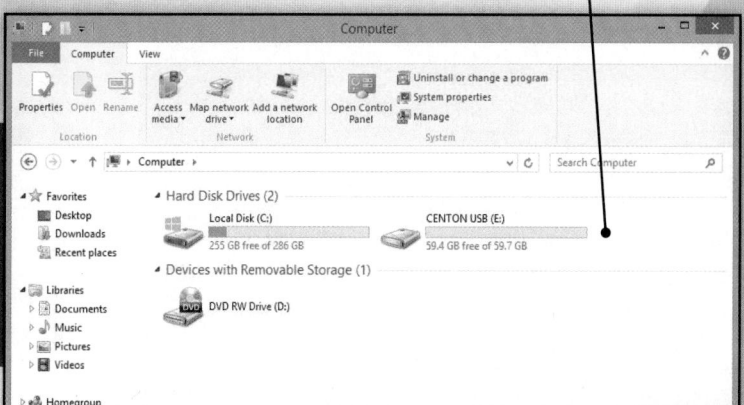

2. Open File Explorer button and click *Computer*. You should see the flash drive listed under *Devices with Removable Storage*. The drive letter will vary depending on the other drives on the system.

3. Double-click the icon for the flash drive to open it. On the toolbar, click *New folder*. (You can also create a folder by right-clicking on a blank area of the window, pointing to New, and choosing *Folder* or by pressing CTRL+Shift+N.)

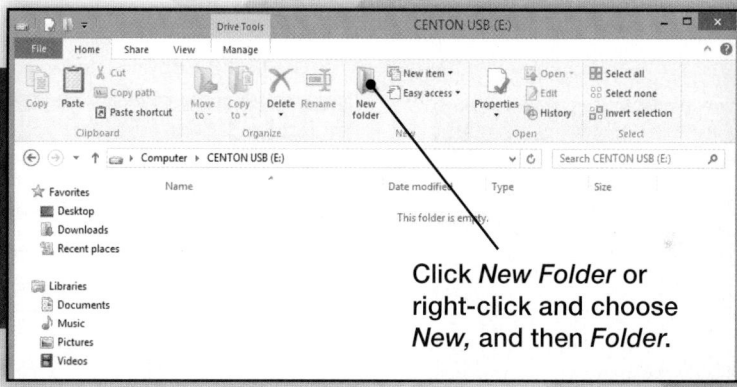

Click *New Folder* or right-click and choose *New,* and then *Folder*.

4. Type a name for the folder and press *Enter*. You have created a new folder to store your files. (When you have finished working with your flash drive, be sure to properly remove it using the Safely Remove Hardware icon.)

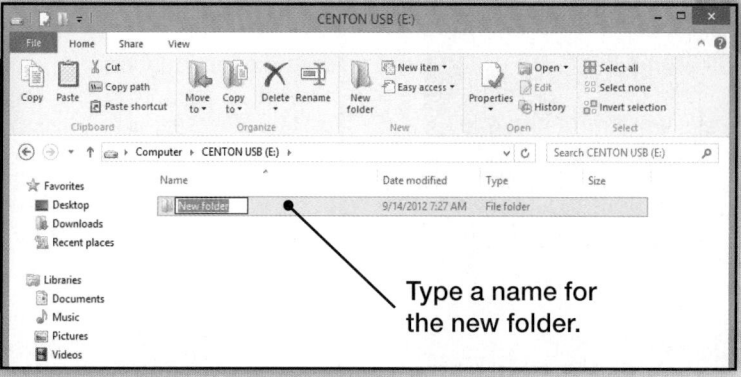

Type a name for the new folder.

**FIGURE 3.6** The Steps to Create a New Folder on a Flash Drive (Windows)

You can create new folders on a Mac using the File menu in the Finder or by pressing shift+command+N (see Figure 3.7).

You can also create a new folder when you save a file. This allows you to organize your files as they're created instead of after the fact. The Save As dialog box that opens when you save a file looks very much like File Explorer and includes the New folder button.

Organizing your files into folders is easy once the folders have been created. You can use File Explorer or Finder to copy and move files to different locations on your computer. When you copy a file, you make a duplicate that can be put in another location, leaving the original file intact. Moving a file changes the location of the file. Both of these tasks can be accomplished in several ways, as explained in Figure 3.8 (Windows Explorer) and Figure 3.9 (Finder).

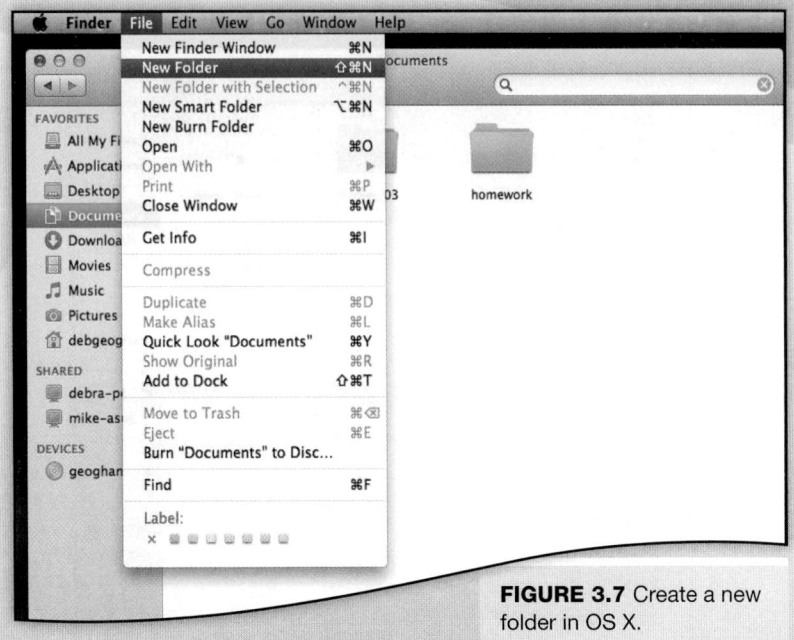

**FIGURE 3.7** Create a new folder in OS X.

To select multiple files to copy or move, hold down the Ctrl key in Windows as you click on each file. If the files are adjacent, in Windows you can click the first file, hold down the Shift key, and click the last file. To select all of the files in a window, press Ctrl+A (command+A). In OS X, use the command or shift key to select multiple files.

Learning to work with folders and libraries will make organizing your files much easier and more efficient. File Explorer and Finder give you the ability to navigate and view your files in several different ways so you can use the methods you find the most useful.

**FIGURE 3.8** Copying and Moving Files Using Windows Explorer

| METHOD | COPY | MOVE |
|---|---|---|
| Mouse click: Click the right mouse button to display the menu. | To copy a file, right-click on the file and click *Copy*.<br><br>Navigate to the destination folder, right-click on it, and choose *Paste*. | To move a file, right-click on the file and click *Cut*.<br><br>Navigate to the destination folder, right-click on it, and choose *Paste*. |
| Mouse drag: Hold down the left mouse button while moving the file to the destination location. | To copy a file to a folder on a different disk, hold down the left mouse button and drag the file to its destination.<br><br>To copy a file to a folder on the same disk, hold down the right mouse button and drag the file to its destination. Release the mouse button and choose *Copy here*. | To move a file to a folder on the same disk, hold down the left mouse button and drag the file to its destination.<br><br>To move a file to a folder on a different disk, hold down the right mouse button and drag the file to its destination. Release the mouse button and choose *Move here*. |
| Keyboard shortcut: Hold down Ctrl while pressing the designated letter. | Select the file to be copied and press Ctrl+C to copy the file.<br><br>Navigate to the destination location and press Ctrl+V to paste the file. | Select the file to be moved and press Ctrl+X to move the file.<br><br>Navigate to the destination location and press Ctrl+V to paste the file. |

**FIGURE 3.9** Copying and Moving Files Using Finder

| METHOD | COPY | MOVE |
|---|---|---|
| Mouse click: Press control and click the mouse button to display the menu. | To copy a file, press control+click, select *Copy*.<br><br>Navigate to the destination folder, press control+click, and choose *Paste Item*. | Follow the steps to copy a file and then drag the original file to the trash. |
| Mouse drag: Hold down the mouse button while moving the file to the destination location. | To copy a file to a folder on a different disk, hold down the mouse button and drag the file to its destination. | To move a file to a folder on the same disk, hold down the mouse button and drag the file to its destination. |
| Keyboard shortcut: Hold down command while pressing the designated letter. | Select the file to be copied and press control+C to copy the file.<br><br>Navigate to the destination location and press control+V to paste the file. | Follow the steps to copy a file and then drag the original file to the trash. |

## Try the File Management Simulation

SIMULATION

## Running Project

Using Windows or OS X help, research the Public folder on your computer. What purpose does it serve? What types of files can be stored in it? Who has access to those files? What restrictions are there on their access?

## 4 Things You Need to Know

● Windows and OS X create a folder hierarchy for storing files.

● Each user has his or her own folder structure for storing documents, pictures, music, videos, and more.

● Libraries gather files that are located in different locations.

● File Explorer and the Finder in OS X are used to navigate through folders and drives.

## Key Terms

File Explorer

file management

Finder

folder

hierarchy

library

path

Public folder

# HOW TO

## Organize Your Files

In this activity you will use File Explorer or Finder to view various file types and folders.

**1** On your flash drive, create a new folder for this class, and create a folder for Chapter 3 inside the class folder (if necessary, refer to Figure 3.6 for help). Use this folder to save your work for this chapter. Open a new document and save it in your Chapter 3 folder as **lastname_firstname_ch03_howto1**. Open File Explorer and navigate to the data files for this chapter. Drag the ch_03_pictures folder to the Pictures library in the Navigation pane. Drag the ch_03_music folder to the Music library.

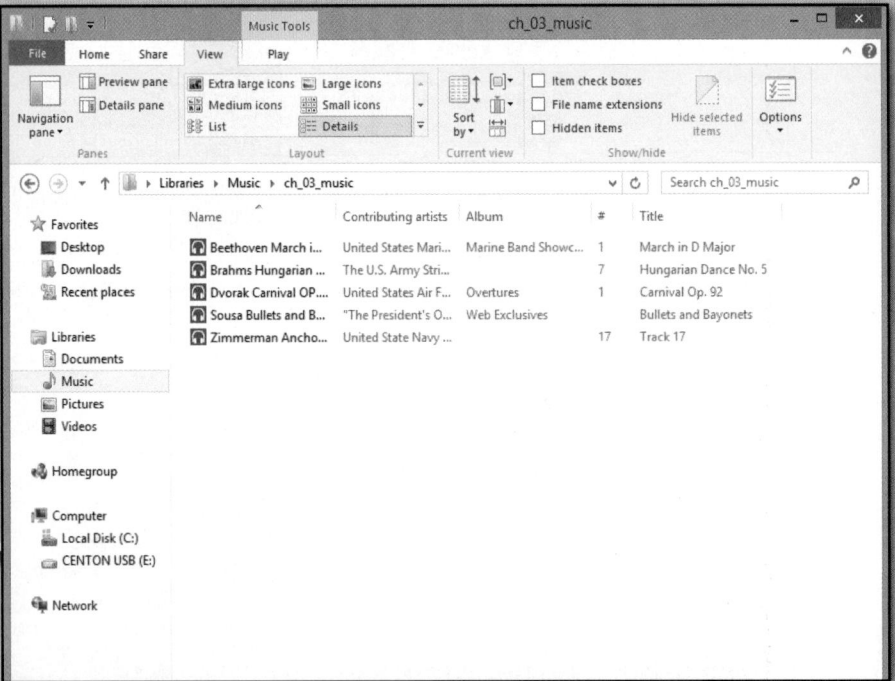

**2** In the Explorer Navigation pane, under Libraries, click *Music*. In the file list on the right, double-click the *ch_03_music* folder. If it has not been customized, the default view is Music Details. Click the View tab, and if necessary, in the Layout group, click Details. What are the headings of the columns in this view? Click the *Title* column heading. What happens to the files in the window? Click the *Name* column heading. What happens? Take a screen shot and paste it into your document.

**3** In the Navigation pane, under Libraries, click *Pictures*. In the file list on the right, double-click the *ch_03_pictures* folder. The default view for this folder is Large Icons. Use the View tab, if necessary, to change the view to Large Icons. How is the view in this folder different from the Music folder? Take a screen shot and paste it into your document.

**4** Click the View tab and in the Panes group, if necessary, select Details Pane. Select one image (but do not open it) and look at the Details pane. What information is found in this pane? Change the rating of the file. What other information can you change? Take a screen shot and paste it into your document.

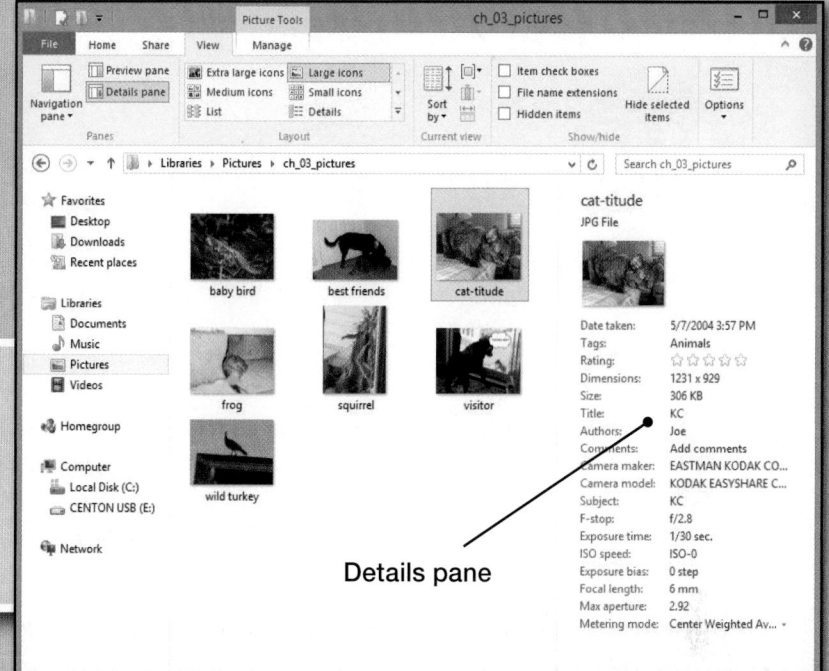

Details pane

**5** On the Address bar, click the arrow to the right of Libraries, and choose *Documents* from the menu. What two locations are included in this view? If necessary, change the view of the Document folder to Details. How is the Details view of this folder different from the Music Details view? Click the *Title* column heading. Click *Organize*, point to Layout, and choose *Preview pane*. Scroll down and select various files from this folder. What file types display their contents in the Preview pane? Take a screen shot and paste it into your document. Type up your answers, including the appropriate screen shots, save your file, and submit as directed by your instructor.

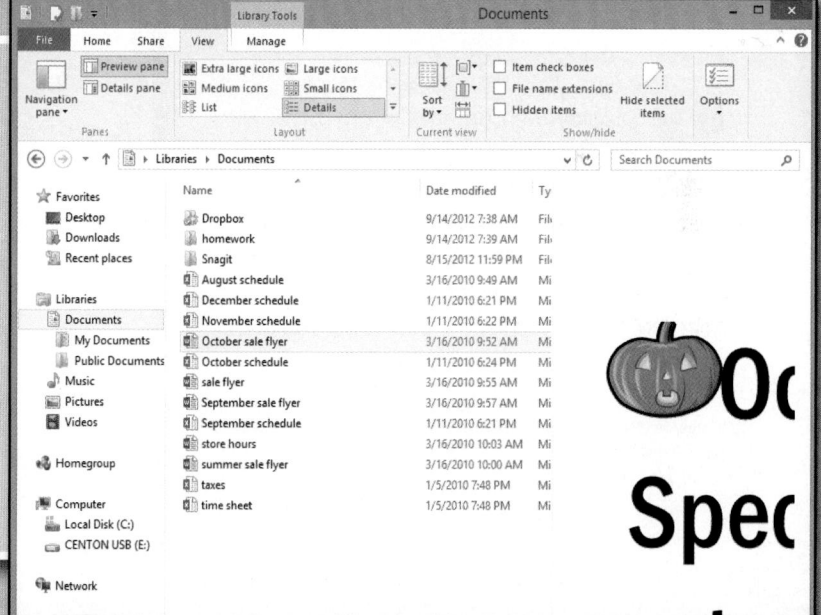

**If you are using a Mac:**

**1** Open Finder. If the Music and Pictures folders are not visible in the Sidebar, open Finder preferences and click the *Sidebar* tab to display them. Navigate to the data files for this chapter. Drag the ch_03_pictures folder to Pictures and drag the ch_03_ music folder to Music in the sidebar.

**2** Display the contents of ch_03_music in List view using the button on the toolbar or the View menu. What are the headings of the columns in this view? Click the *Name* column heading. What happens to the files in the window? Click the *Name* column heading. What happens? Take a screen shot and paste it into your document.

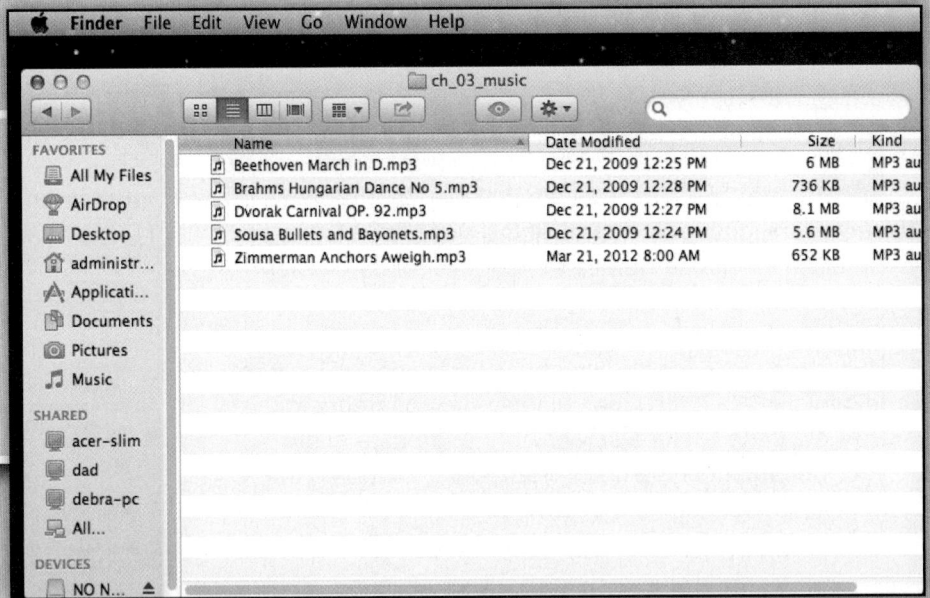

**3** Display the contents of the ch_03_
pictures folder in Cover Flow view.
How is the view in this folder different
from the Music folder? Take a screen shot and
paste it into your document.

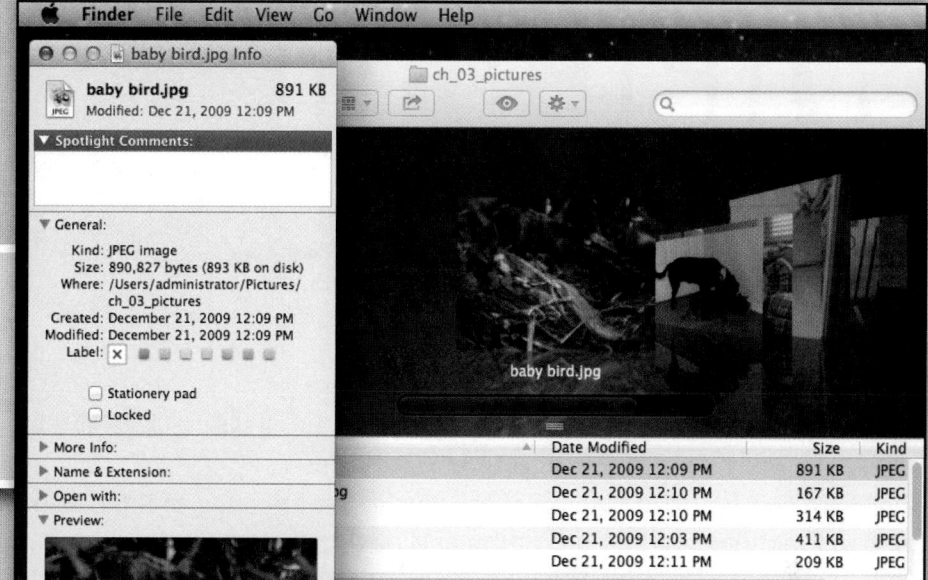

**4** Select one image (but do not open it). Select *Get Info* from
the File menu. What information is found in this pane?
What information can you change? Take a screen shot and
paste it into your document.

**5** Display the documents in Column view.
How is the Column view of this folder
different from List view? Select various
files from this folder. What file types display their
contents in the Preview pane? Take a screen shot
and paste it into your document. Type up your
answers, including the appropriate screen shots,
save your file, and submit as directed by your
instructor.

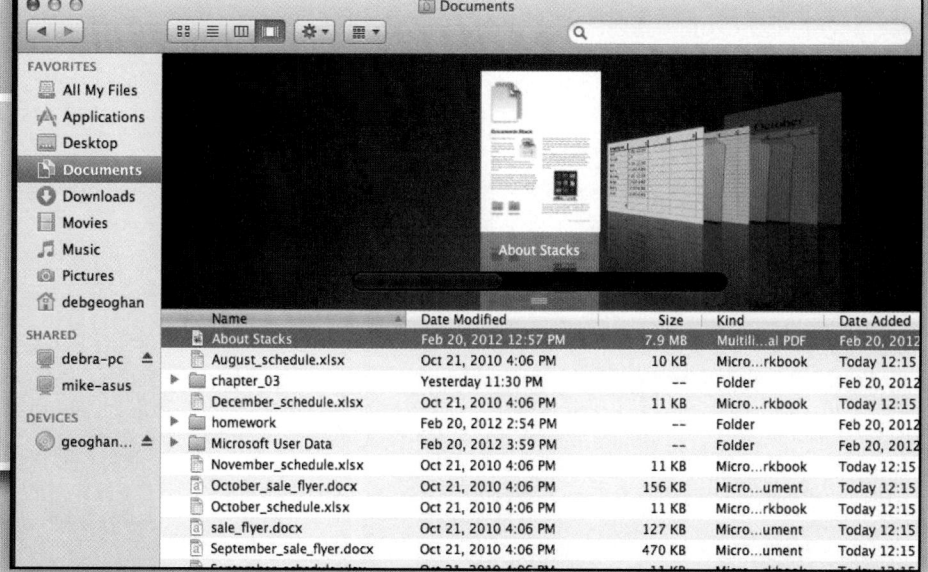

# What's in a Name?

HELLO
my name is

OBJECTIVE

## Explain the importance of file extensions.

There are two types of files on every computer: the ones that the computer uses to function, such as programs and device drivers, and the ones that are used and created by you, the user, including music, documents, photos, and videos. Let's look at a few of these user files and compare their properties.

.docx

.mp3

## FILE NAMES AND EXTENSIONS

Every file has a **file name** that consists of a name and an extension. The name is useful to the user and describes the contents of the file. When creating your own files, you decide the name. In the example in Figure 3.10, ch03_homework is the name of the file. On early PCs, file names were limited to eight characters with a three-letter extension and were often cryptic. Today, file names on Windows computers can be up to 260 characters long (including the extension and the path to the file) and can include spaces and special characters. The only illegal characters in a file name are the \ / ? : * " > < | characters. OS X file names can be up to 255 characters, and the only illegal character is the colon ( : ).

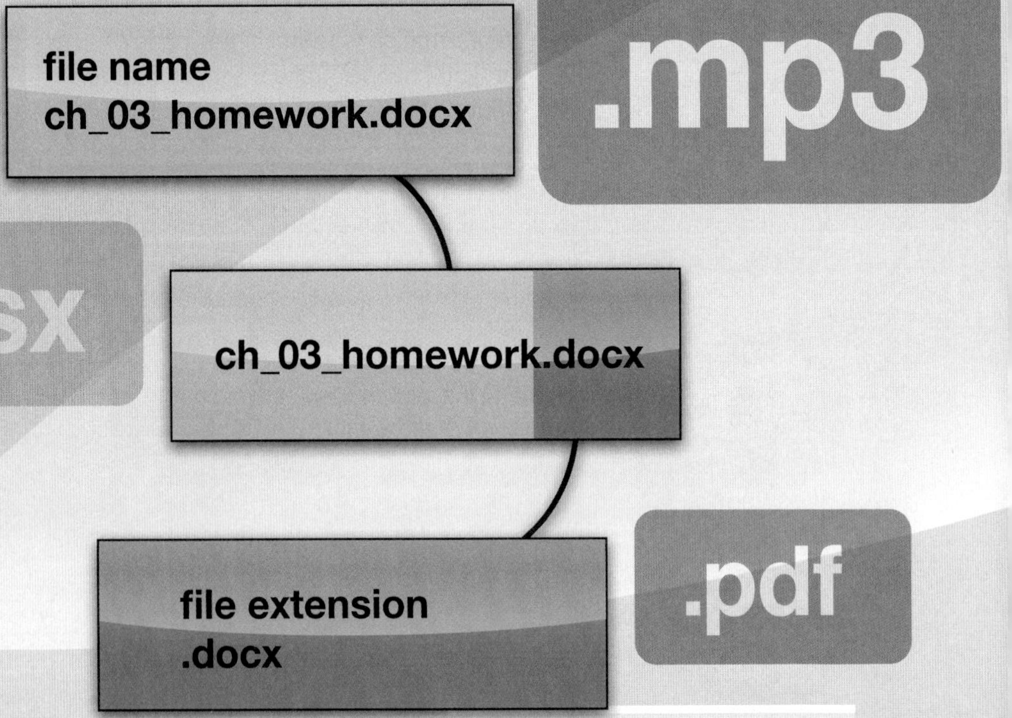

file name
ch_03_homework.docx

.xlsx

ch_03_homework.docx

file extension
.docx

.pdf

**FIGURE 3.10** A file name includes a name and an extension to identify the contents and type of file.

The second part of the file name is the **file extension**. In this example, .docx is the extension. The extension is assigned by the program that's used to create the file. Microsoft Word files have the extension .docx when you save them. Windows maintains an association between a file extension and a program, so double-clicking on a .docx file opens Microsoft Word. The extension helps the operating system determine the type of file. If you change the file extension of a file, you may no longer be able to open it. Figure 3.11 lists some common file types and programs associated with them.

**FIGURE 3.11** Common File Extensions and Default Program Associations

| EXTENSION | TYPE OF FILE | DEFAULT PROGRAM ASSOCIATION (WINDOWS) | DEFAULT PROGRAM ASSOCIATION (OS X) |
|---|---|---|---|
| .docx/.doc | Word document | Microsoft Word | Microsoft Word |
| .rtf | Rich text format | Wordpad or Word | TextEdit |
| .pages | Pages document | | Pages |
| .xlsx/.xls | Excel | Excel | Excel |
| .pptx/.ppt | PowerPoint | PowerPoint | PowerPoint |
| .bmp | bitmap image | Microsoft Paint | Preview |
| .jpeg/.jpg | Image file (Joint Photographic Experts Group) | Windows Photo Viewer or Photo Gallery | Preview |
| .mp3 | audio file | Windows Media Player | iTunes |
| .aac | Audio file (advanced audio coding) | iTunes | iTunes |
| .mov | video file | Apple QuickTime | QuickTime |
| .wmv | Video file | Windows Media Player | |
| .pdf | portable document format | Adobe Acrobat and Reader | Preview |

# FILE PROPERTIES

Each file includes **file properties**, which provide other information about that file. We can use these properties to organize, sort, and find files more easily. Some file properties, such as type, size, and date, are automatically created along with the file. Others, such as title and authors, can be added or edited by the user.

## Find Out MORE

The characters \ / ? : * " > < | can't be used in a file name because they each have a special meaning in Windows. For example, the colon ( : ) is used when you indicate the letter of a drive (such as C: for your hard drive or D: for your DVD drive). Use the Internet to research the remaining illegal characters. What does each of these symbols represent?

Figure 3.12 shows the properties of a file in the Details pane of File Explorer. The Details pane at the bottom of the Explorer window gives you a preview of the file. You can modify some of these properties, such as Title and Authors, right in the Details pane.

When the files are displayed in Details view, as they are in this figure, you can use the column headings to sort files by their properties. For example, clicking on the Name column heading lists the files in alphabetical order. The properties that display in this view depend on the type of files in the folder.

You can view more information about a file by right-clicking the file in File Explorer and choosing *Properties* from the context menu. This opens the Properties dialog box for the file. The four tabs of the Properties dialog box contain a lot of information, but you'll probably find the General and Details tabs to be the most useful. The General tab makes it easy to change the name of a file. The Details tab lists information about the content of the file, such as word count. Figure 3.13 shows these two tabs for the same file. Notice that the Details tab contains too much information to display on the page. You'll need to scroll down to see the rest of it. The type of information that's displayed depends on the type of file you're viewing.

Turn on the Details pane.

Use the View tab to change the Explorer window to Details view and display the columns.

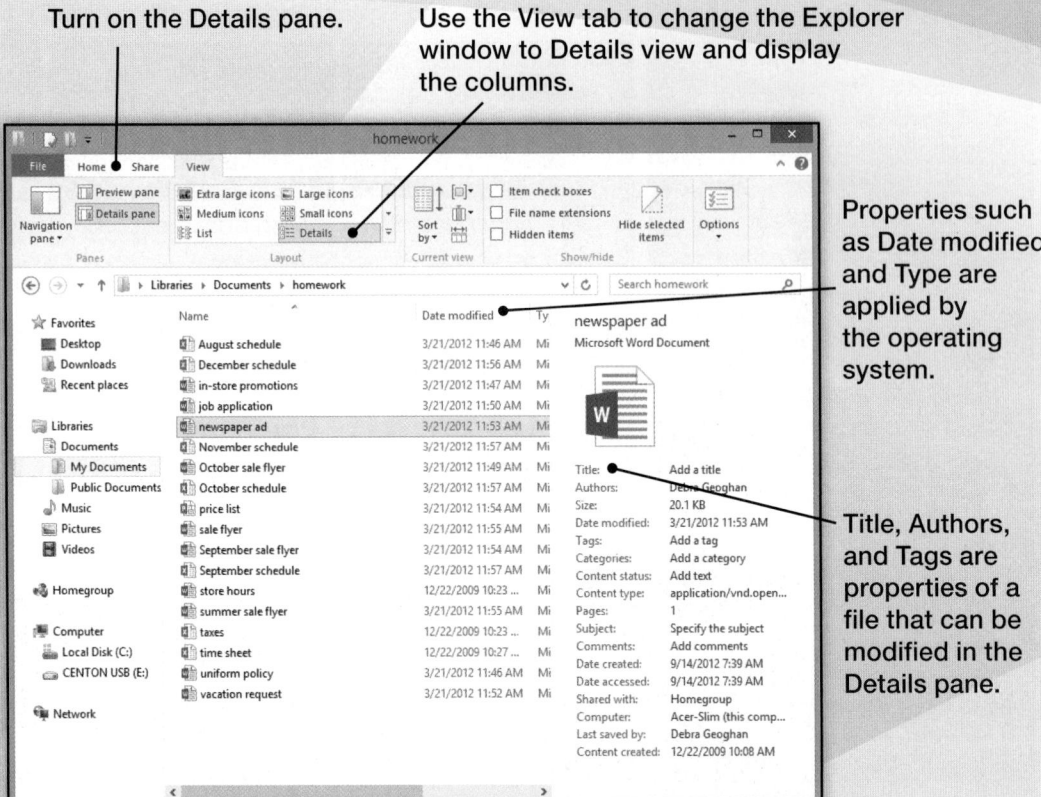

Properties such as Date modified and Type are applied by the operating system.

Title, Authors, and Tags are properties of a file that can be modified in the Details pane.

**FIGURE 3.12** File Explorer allows you to view and modify some file properties.

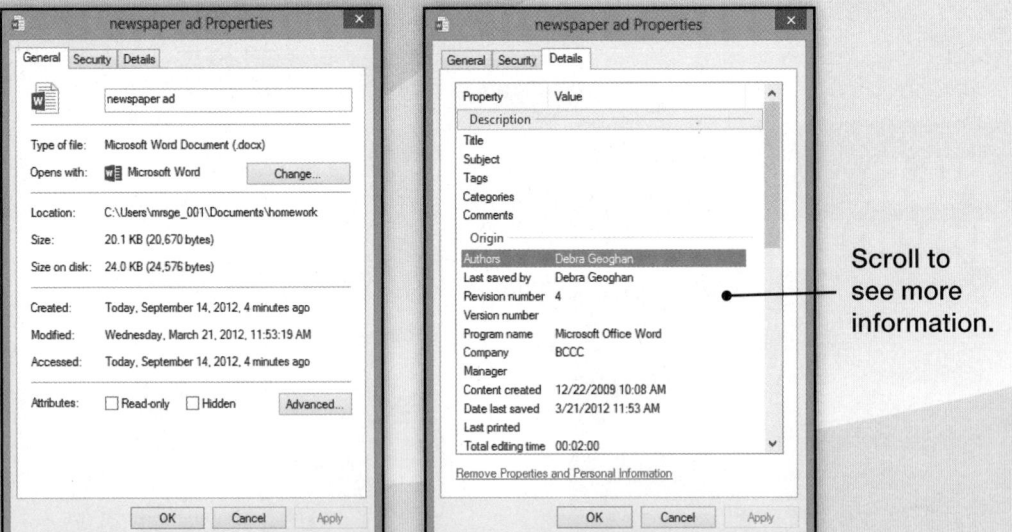

Scroll to see more information.

**FIGURE 3.13** Right-clicking on a file in File Explorer allows you to open the Properties dialog box for the file. The four tabs on this sheet contain more information about the file.

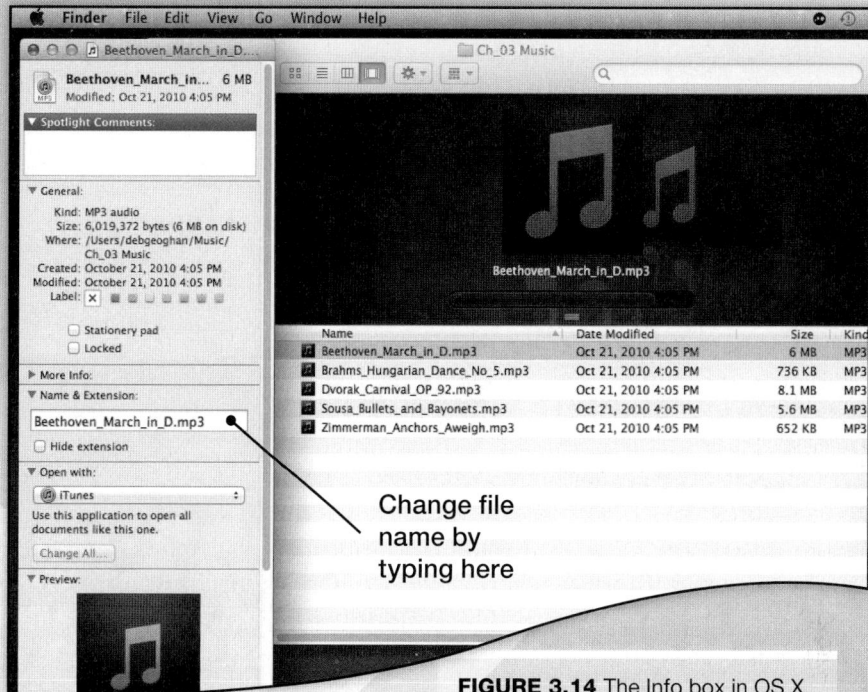

Change file name by typing here

FIGURE 3.14 The Info box in OS X displays file properties.

You can view and modify file properties in OS X, too. In the Finder, select the file and choose *Get Info* from the File menu. This will open the Info pane for the file where you can view and change some of the file properties such as the file name, sharing permissions, and Spotlight Comments (see Figure 3.14).

File names and other properties give us more information about files, making them more useful and easier to manage and locate. They also save us time and give us more control over our computer systems.

## Running Project

In this article, we discussed how to add properties to a file, but how would you remove them? Which properties can you remove? Use Windows Help and Support or the Internet to find the answers.

## 4 Things You Need to Know

- Windows file names can be up to 260 characters long, including the path. OS X file names can be up to 255 characters long.

- Windows file names can't include \ / ? : * " > < | and OS X file names can't include the colon.

- File extensions indicate the type of file.

- File properties, such as size, type, date, and author, can be used to sort and search for files.

## Key Terms

file extension

file name

file property

# Back It Up

## Explain the importance of backing up files.

It's something most people don't think about until it's too late—losing files on a computer system that wasn't backed up. One simple step to take is to periodically **back up** or copy your files to another drive, a DVD, or a flash drive. Of course, this requires you to remember to do it. In this article, we look at how easy it is to automatically back up your files for protection.

## WINDOWS BACKUP

Windows 8 makes this easier with a new utility called File History, which creates copies of your files on an external or network drive (see Figure 3.15).

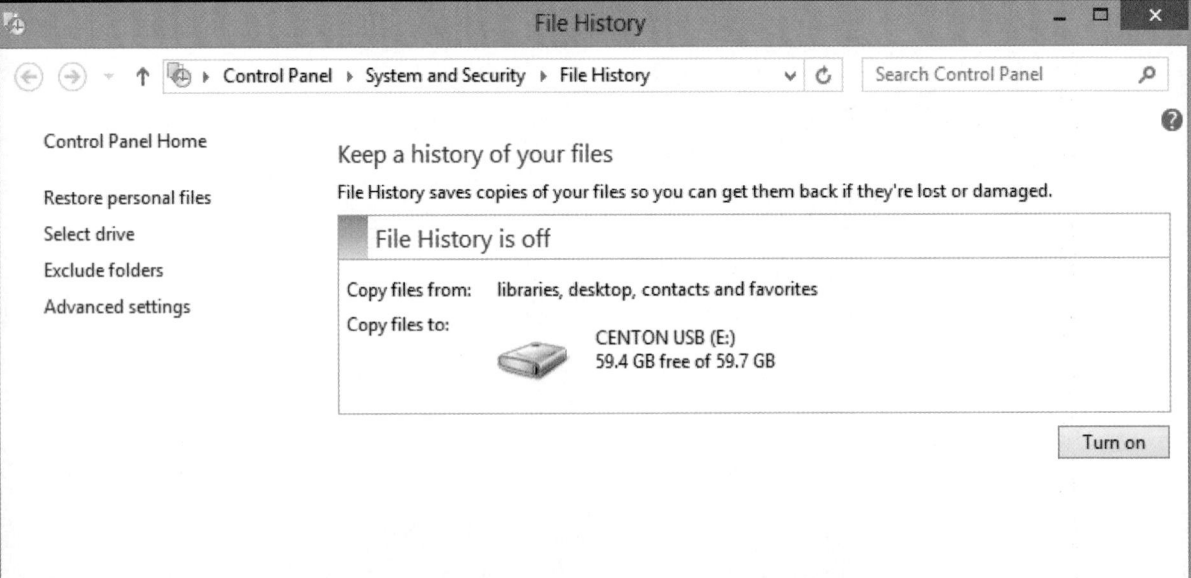

FIGURE 3.15 The Windows Action Center warns you if you've not set up a backup for your system.

File History is not turned on by default. To keep backup copies of your files, you should turn it on. You can access File History from the System and Security Control Panel. To use File History, you must have an external drive or network location accessible for the copies to be stored. In Figure 3.16, the files are being copied to a USB flash drive.

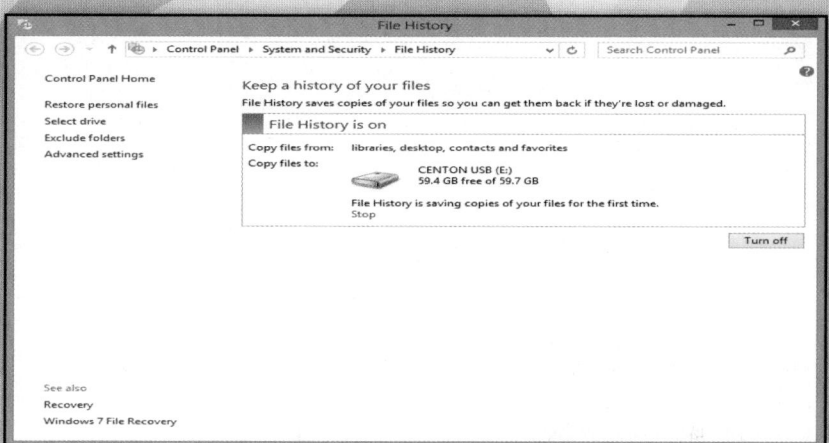

**FIGURE 3.16** Determine what information to include in the backup. Once you click the Save settings and exit button, the backup will automatically run on a regular schedule.

# OS X TIME MACHINE

Macs come with a backup utility called Time Machine. You can open Time Machine (see Figure 3.17) from the Launchpad to configure it. Alternatively, you can connect a new disk, such as an external hard drive, to your Mac, and Time Machine will ask you if you want to use the disk to back up your files. Time Machine keeps three types of backups: hourly backups for the previous 24 hours, daily backups for the previous month, and weekly backups for all previous months. The oldest backups are deleted as the disk fills up. Time Machine backs up everything on your computer: your personal files, as well as system files, applications, and settings.

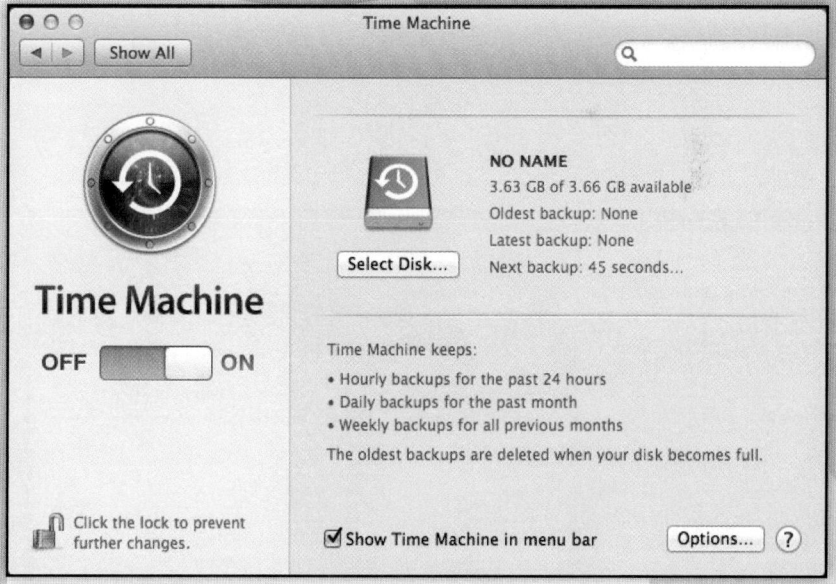

**FIGURE 3.17** Time Machine backs up everything on a Mac.

# OTHER BACKUP SOFTWARE

External hard drives are an inexpensive place to back up your files. Many of these drives include a backup program that you can use for automatic or one-touch backups of your system. For example, Seagate FreeAgent external drives include Seagate Manager software, and Western Digital's Passport drives include WD SmartWare software. You can purchase a large-capacity external hard drive for less than $100.

Another alternative is commercial software. There are dozens of programs on the market, including many that are free or cost less than $50. DVD-burning software, such as Roxio Creator and Nero BackItUp & Burn, also include backup features.

# BACKUP TO THE CLOUD

The use of Internet or cloud backup services is becoming increasingly popular. Many sites offer free personal storage of 1 or 2 GB or unlimited storage for about $5–10 per month. Business solutions can cost thousands of dollars, depending on the amount of storage needed.

Using an online or cloud backup service has the advantage of keeping your backups at another location—but easily accessible—thus protecting your assets from fire, flood, or damage to your main location. Cloud backups are accessible from any computer with an Internet connection, so you can access your backed-up files even if you're not using the same device. Companies such as Mozy (see Figure 3.18) and Carbonite offer free or low-cost plans for home users that include desktop software to automatically back up your files.

Professional backup companies make setup easy, and their services are very safe and reliable. Once the initial setup is complete, the backup process is automatic, and your backed-up files are then accessible from any Internet-connected computer. As with any service, you should do your homework before trusting online backup services with your files.

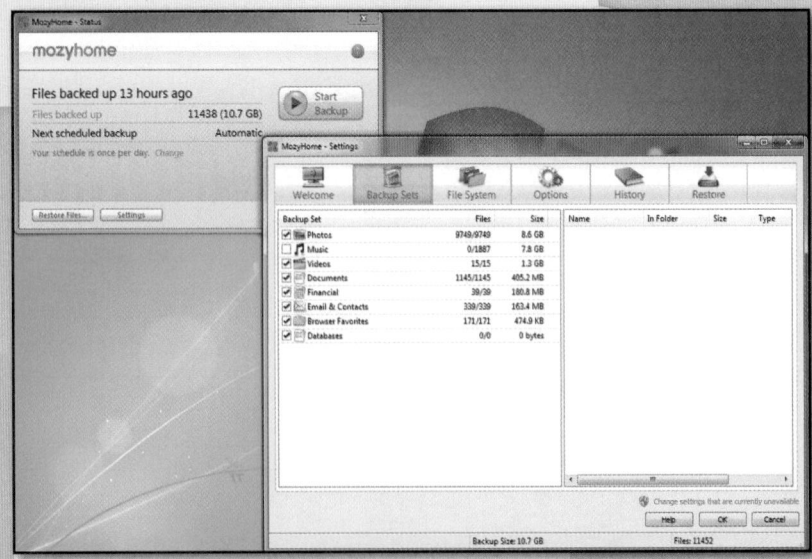

**FIGURE 3.18** Mozy backs up my files once per day.

# CLOUD STORAGE

While some people don't differentiate, there is a difference between cloud backups and cloud storage. Cloud storage is a way to store working files in a convenient place. While this also serves to back them up, cloud storage is generally more limited than a backup in what and how much you can store.

OS X and iOS devices include iCloud. iCloud can be set to automatically sync your personal files to the cloud (see Figure 3.19). It comes with 5 GB of free storage, and there is even a Windows version, so you can share your files between all of your devices. Some of your files can be accessed from the iCloud website (see Figure 3.20)— but notably missing are your photos. iCloud uploads and stores the last 30 days of your photos and pushes them to your iOS devices and computers; however, they are not accessible on the iCloud website. Because the storage is only 5GB and the types of files that are included are limited, iCloud is not a full-featured backup program. Still, you may find it is enough for you.

**FIGURE 3.19** iCloud can automatically back up your files and sync them with other devices.

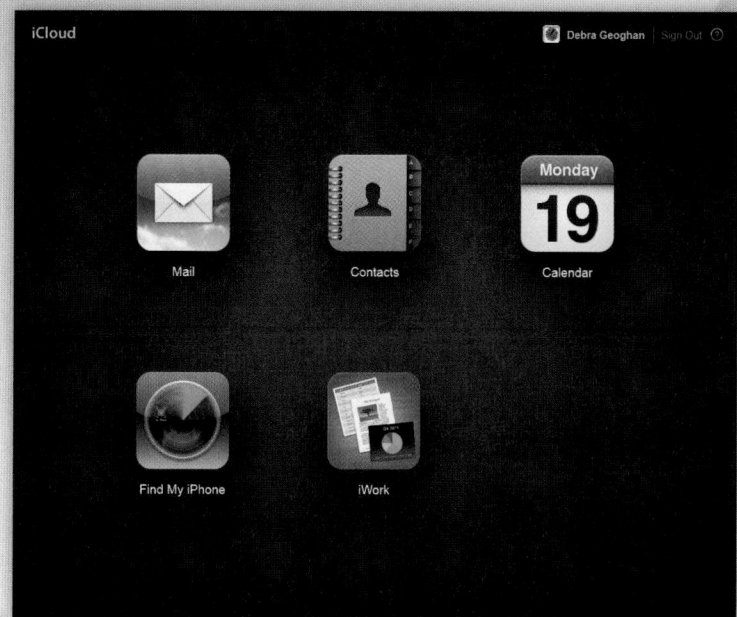

**FIGURE 3.20** Files Accessible from the iCloud Website

Another alternative is Microsoft Skydrive (see Figure 3.21). This free service gives you 7 GB of storage for your files. You can save directly to Skydrive from Microsoft Office applications. Windows computers can connect to Skydrive using the Skydrive app. There are also apps for OS X, Windows Phone, iOS, and Android. With Skydrive, you can store files, photos, and favorites in the cloud and access them from any Internet connected device, and you can easily share them with others. Skydrive also has the advantage of integrated Web Apps allowing you to create and edit Microsoft Office documents.

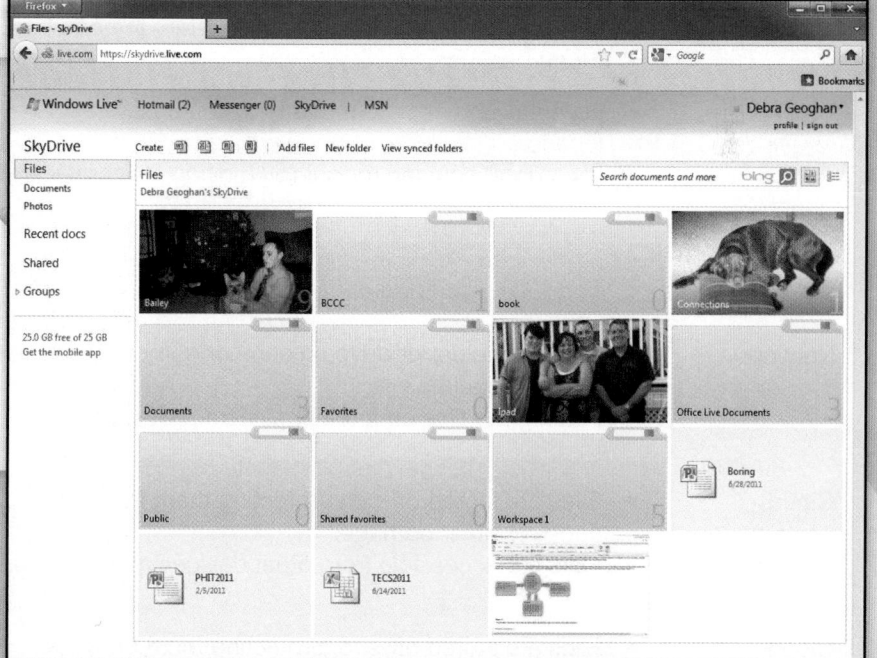

**FIGURE 3.21** Skydrive

**FIGURE 3.22** Comparing Backup Storage Types

| STORAGE TYPE | PROS | CONS |
|---|---|---|
| Internal hard drive | • The price per GB is relatively low.<br>• The speed of transfer is fastest.<br>• The drive is secure inside the system unit. | • You need to open the system unit to install it.<br>• Because it's in same physical location as the original files, backing up to the internal hard drive doesn't keep files safe from fire, flood, or other damage. |
| External hard drive | • The price per GB is relatively low.<br>• The speed of transfer is fast.<br>• The drive is easy to move and secure in another location. | • If the external hard drive is stored in another location, it must be transported back to the system location to perform a backup.<br>• If the backup storage device is left in same physical location as the original files, the files aren't safe from fire, flood, or other damage. |
| Optical drive (CD/DVD/Blu-ray) | • Media (discs) are inexpensive and easy to purchase.<br>• Media is easy to move to store in another location.<br>• Using new discs for each backup means the discs don't have to be returned to the system to complete future backups. | • Disc capacity is small compared to hard drives and may require several (or many) discs to complete a backup. |
| Flash drive | • It's small and easy to move and store in another location.<br>• It's a good solution for quickly moving files between systems. | • The capacity is still small compared to hard drives.<br>• If it's stored in another location, the flash drive must be transported back to the system to complete a backup.<br>• If the flash drive is left in the same physical location as the original files, the files aren't safe from fire, flood, or other damage. |
| Network | • A shared folder or drive on another computer can be used for backup.<br>• Placing the files on another system protects them. | • Using a network as a backup location requires some advanced setup of the network.<br>• The network location must be available when the backup runs. |
| Cloud backup | • Files are stored off-site protecting them from fire, flood, or other damage.<br>• Files are accessible from other devices and location. | • This can be expensive.<br>• Cloud backup requires an active Internet connection.<br>• Restoring files can be time consuming. |
| Cloud Storage | • Files are stored off-site, protecting them from fire, flood, or other damage.<br>• Files are accessible from other devices and location. | • Storage capacity and types of files allowed may be limited. |

Some mobile devices include apps that automatically upload photos to websites such as Flickr, Photobucket, Instagram, or Facebook. Because many people rely on the camera in their mobile devices for capturing life's important (and not so important) moments, as well as storing all of their contacts and calendars, it is wise to regularly back up these devices as well.

Figure 3.22 compares various types of backup solutions. However you choose to back up your files, you can rest easy knowing that your files are safe and that if the inevitable hard drive failure strikes, you won't lose your important work and precious photos.

## Running Project

Research two online backup sites and investigate their cost, reliability, storage size, and features. Write a brief report to convince your boss of the importance of backing up files and how backups should be handled. Should the company use online storage? Explain your thoughts. In the report, be sure to describe the type and size of the business you're working for.

## Key Term

back up

## 4 Things You Need to Know

- You should use a backup program to regularly back up your important files.
- Keep your backup files in a different physical location than your working files.
- Back up (verb) is the process of creating a backup (noun).
- Cloud backup services are free or inexpensive for personal use.

# Shrink It

## Demonstrate how to compress files.

Some of the files we use today can be quite large, especially media files, such as photos, music, and videos. File **compression** is the process of making files smaller to conserve disk space and make them easier to transfer.

## TYPES OF FILE COMPRESSION

There are two types of file compression: lossless and lossy. The type of compression depends on the type of file you're trying to compress.

**Lossless compression** takes advantage of the fact that files contain a lot of redundant information. This is especially true of files that contain text and numbers. With lossless compression, the compressed file can be decompressed with no loss of data. A lossless compression **algorithm** (procedure for solving a problem) looks for the redundancy in the file and creates an encoded file using that information to remove the redundant information. When the file is decompressed, all the information from the original file is restored. Lossless compression is used in ZIP files.

A **lossy compression** algorithm is often used on image, audio, and video files. These files contain more information than humans can typically discern, and that extra information can be removed from the file. An image file taken with a digital camera on its highest setting can yield a file of 5 to 10 MB in size (or more), while the normal quality setting yields a file of 1 to 2 MB. If the file is going to be used to create a large high-quality print or for medical images where every detail is critical, then the high-quality information is important. Most people, however, couldn't tell the difference between the two when viewing them on a computer screen. The high-quality setting results in an uncompressed BMP or TIF file. An image taken at the lower quality setting results in a JPG file—a BMP file with lossy compression. It's possible to compress a BMP or TIF file after it's been taken, but it's not possible to decompress a JPG file because the information has been removed from the file.

Another type of file that is commonly compressed is video. Video files can be very large, making them difficult to transfer, or upload/download to/from a website. YouTube accepts many video formats for upload, such as MPEG4, 3GPP, MOV, AVI, and WMV, but these files are then processed and converted to other (compressed) formats such as Flash for viewing.

# WORKING WITH FILE COMPRESSION

Windows includes the ability to compress and decompress files using the ZIP format. This is a common format that's used to send files by email or download them from the Internet. A ZIP file, known as an archive, can contain multiple files zipped together. The files in the archive may be compressed using different algorithms and can be browsed and extracted from the archive. This makes transferring multiple files easier.

To zip files using Windows, you simply right-click on the file or folder that you want to zip, point to Send to, and choose *Compressed (zipped) folder* (see Figure 3.23). To compress using a Mac, choose *Compress* from the File menu in Finder. In this example, the Chapter 3 folder was compressed from 3.50 MB down to 1615 KB (1.615 MB). This ZIP file can more easily be sent as an email attachment or uploaded to the Web and takes up less than half the space on a disk.

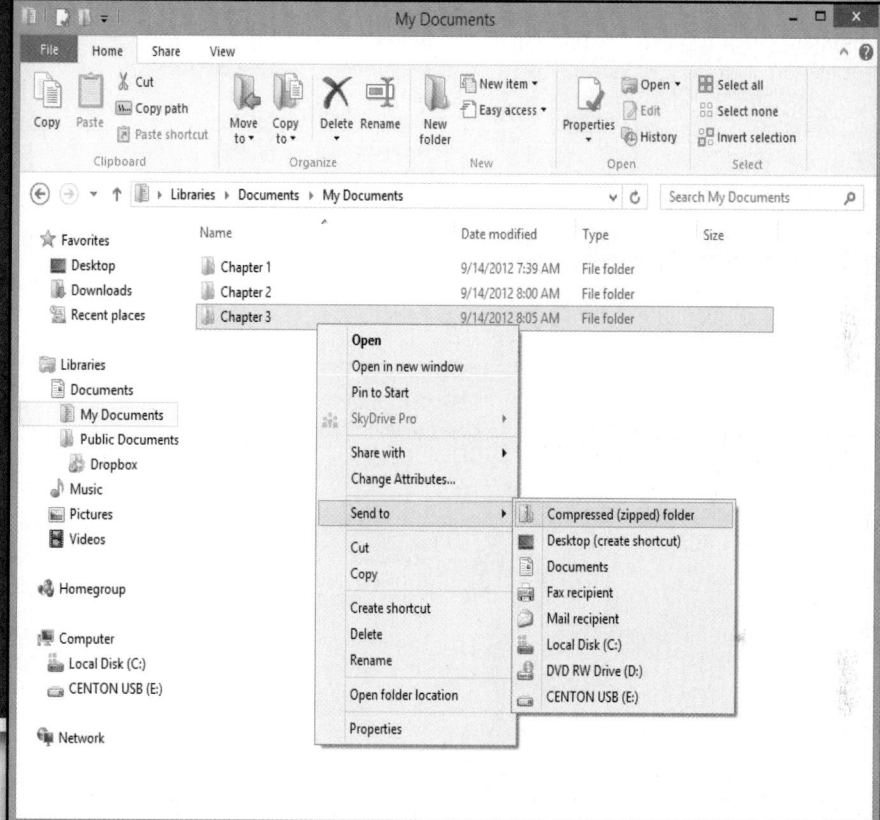

**FIGURE 3.23** The Chapter 3 folder (3.50 MB) is compressed. The resulting ZIP file is 1615 KB or 1.6 MB.

Windows can open and browse the files in a ZIP archive. Figure 3.24 shows the Chapter 3.zip file and the compression ratio for each file inside it. Because each file contains different types and amounts of information, the compression ratio varies.

Windows can browse and use files inside a zipped folder, but sometimes, you need to decompress or extract the files. In Windows, click the *Extract all* button (see Figure 3.25), or right-click on the ZIP file and choose *Extract All*. If you are using a Mac, just double-click the ZIP file to unzip it.

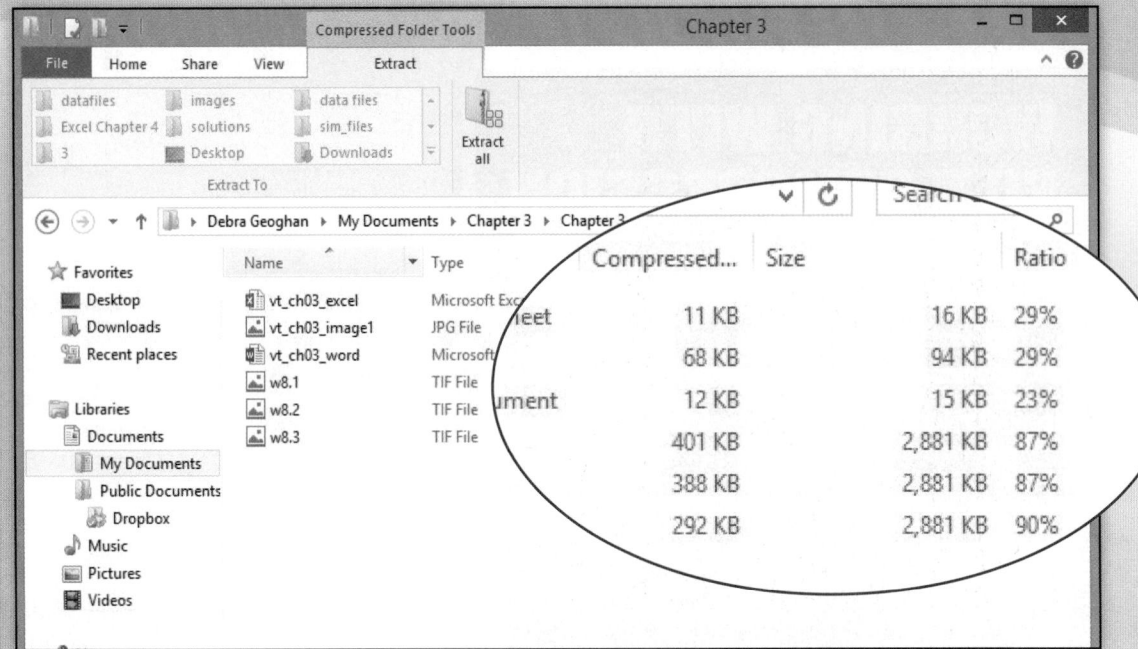

**FIGURE 3.24** A look inside a ZIP file using File Explorer shows the compression ratios for each file.

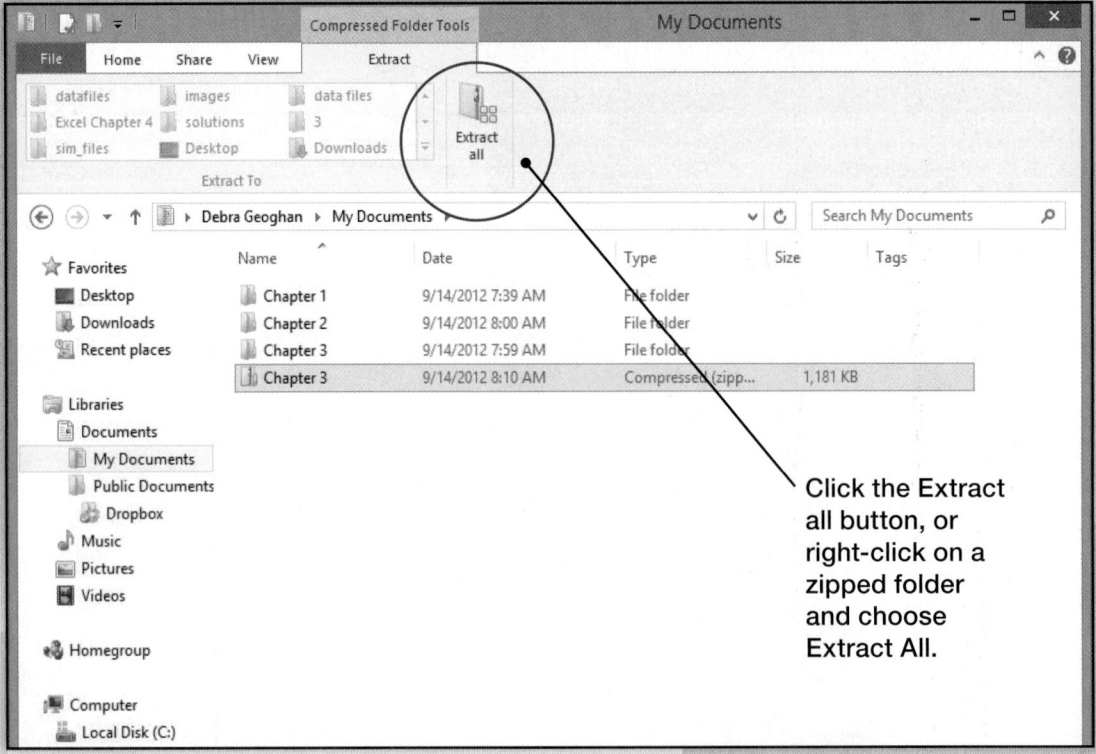

Click the Extract all button, or right-click on a zipped folder and choose Extract All.

**FIGURE 3.25** Extracting Files from a ZIP Archive in Windows

There are other programs that you can use to compress and decompress ZIP files, and there are other compressed formats, such as TAR and RAR, that Windows can't create or open. Some of the more popular programs available are 7-Zip (free), WinRAR, WinZip, and StuffIt.

File compression has become increasingly common as the size of files we use has increased, along with our need to transfer files by email or to websites. Working with compression using Windows or another program is a fairly easy and important skill to have, notably when it comes to submitting your homework for this class.

## Running Project

An MP3 file is a compressed audio file that uses a lossy compression algorithm. Many audiophiles say that they can hear a noticeable difference in the quality of the sound. Use the Internet to research ways to improve the quality of MP3 files.

## 4 Things You Need to Know

- File compression saves disk space and makes transferring files easier.
- A file compressed with lossless compression can be decompressed back to the original file.
- A file compressed with lossy compression can't be decompressed because information has been removed from the file.
- Windows and OS X have the ability to create and extract ZIP archives.

## Key Terms

| | |
|---|---|
| algorithm | lossless compression |
| compression | lossy compression |

# HOW TO

## Create a Compressed (Zipped) Folder

Did you ever try to email a bunch of photos to a friend? If you want to send more than a couple images, you usually wind up sending multiple messages. But you could compress the files into a single zipped folder and send them all at once. In this activity, we'll compress a folder that contains several files to make it easier to email them or to submit them electronically to your teacher.

**1** Insert your flash drive into your computer and close any windows that open. Navigate to the student data files for this chapter. Locate the folder for Jessica's Bookstore. Copy this folder to your flash drive (right-click on it, point to Send to, and choose your flash drive from the list or drag it to the flash drive in the Navigation pane).

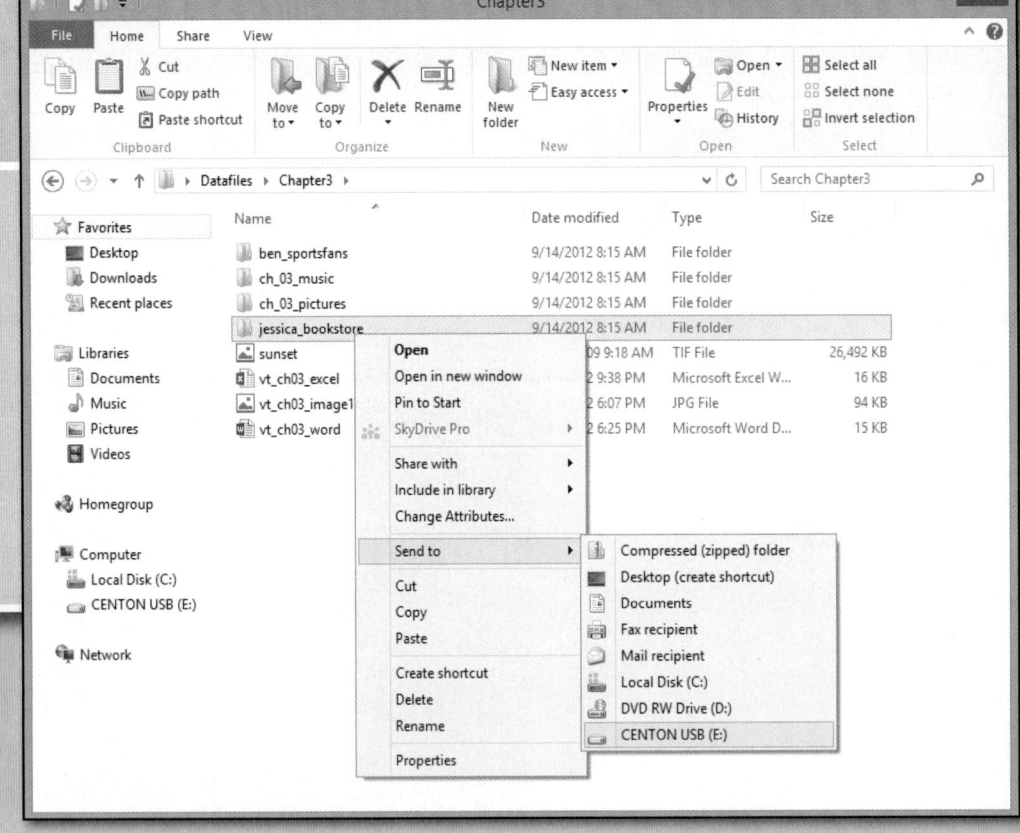

**2** From the Explorer window, open your flash drive. Right-click on the *Jessica's Bookstore* folder and choose *Properties*. How big is the folder? How many files and folders does it contain?

**3** Close the Properties dialog box. Right-click on *Jessica's Bookstore*, point to Send to, and choose *Compressed (zipped) folder* to create a zipped archive.

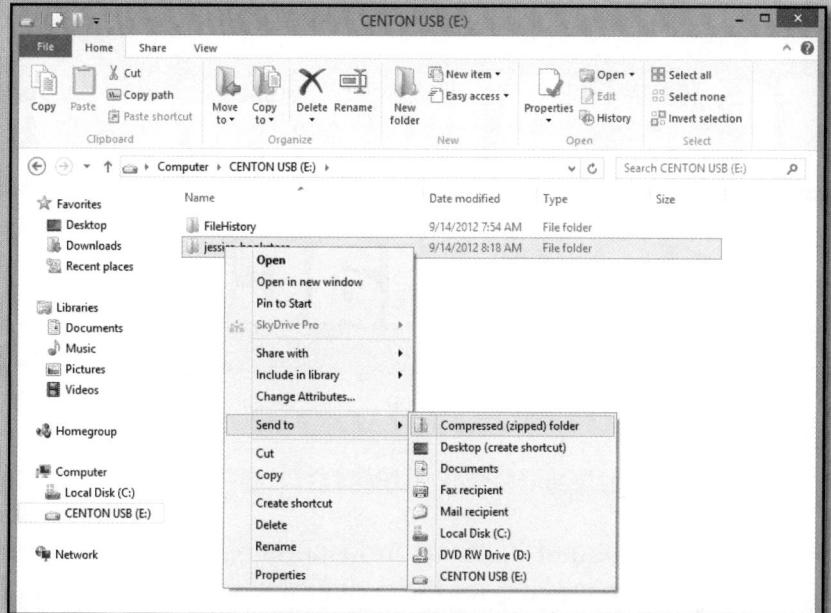

**4** Right-click on the compressed folder and choose *Properties*. Compare the size to the original folder.

**5** Write up your answers, save the file as **lastname_firstname_ch04_howto2**, and submit it as directed by your instructor.

**If you are using a Mac:**

1. Insert your flash drive into your computer. Open Finder and locate the datafiles for this chapter. Copy the folder for Jessica's Bookstore by dragging it to your flash drive.

2. Click the Flash drive in the Sidebar and select the folder in the right pane. From the File menu, select *Get Info*. How big is the folder? How many files and folders does it contain?

3. Close the Info pane. From the File menu, select *Compress "Jessica's Bookstore"* to create a zipped archive.

4. Select the ZIP file and from the File menu, select *Get Info*. Compare the size to the original folder.

5. Write up your answers, save the file as **lastname_firstname_ch04_howto2**, and submit it as directed by your instructor.

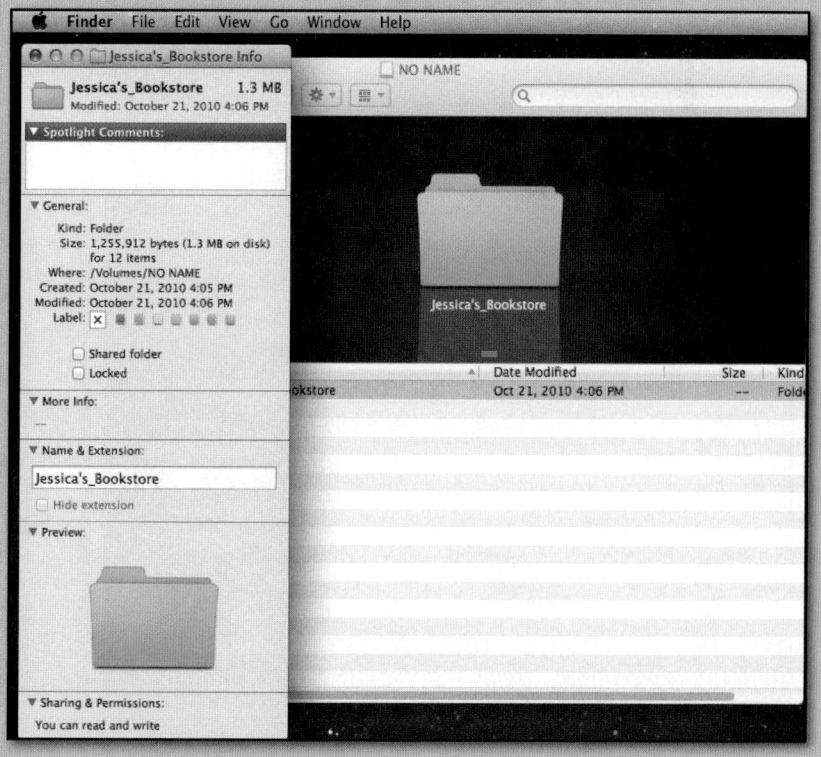

# It's Always in the Last Place You Look

## 5 OBJECTIVE
### Use advanced search options to locate files.

An average computer contains thousands of files, and finding what you need among them can be like looking for the proverbial needle in a haystack. If you follow the principles of good file management, create folders, and save your files in an organized way, then you'll have a much easier time keeping track of your materials. In this article, we look at how using search options can help you find what you're looking for.

## USING WINDOWS TO SEARCH FOR FILES

We know that our files contain properties that we can use to help organize and find them. Using the Windows Search feature can help us do just that. Notice that there's a search box in almost every place you go in Windows. It's in the Start menu, the Help and Support window, every Control Panel window (such as the Default Programs control panel), and every Explorer window. When you begin to type something in the search box, Windows immediately begins searching for you.

When you begin looking for a file, you typically open File Explorer or the Start screen and begin to type something in the Search box. Windows maintains an index that contains information about the files located on your computer. The index contains information about files stored in libraries as well as emails, but it doesn't contain information about program and system files. This index makes searching for files very fast. You can include unindexed locations in your search, but it causes the search to be slower.

In Figure 3.26, the search began as soon as I typed the letter "f" in the Search box. The search results include files in the current location and the folders below it in the hierarchy. Notice in the Search Results that Windows found the letter "f" in file names and in the contents and other properties of the file, such as tags and author. The search results can be further refined by typing more letters or by adding a search filter, such as Type or Name. You can also save a search to be repeated later. If you don't find what you're looking for from your initial search, adjust your criteria. One way to do that is to expand the search to include other locations by clicking on the appropriate location at the bottom of the Search Results page.

In addition to the Search box in Explorer, in Windows 8 you can just start typing from the Start screen or click the Search charm to search Apps, Settings, and Files (see Figure 3.27).

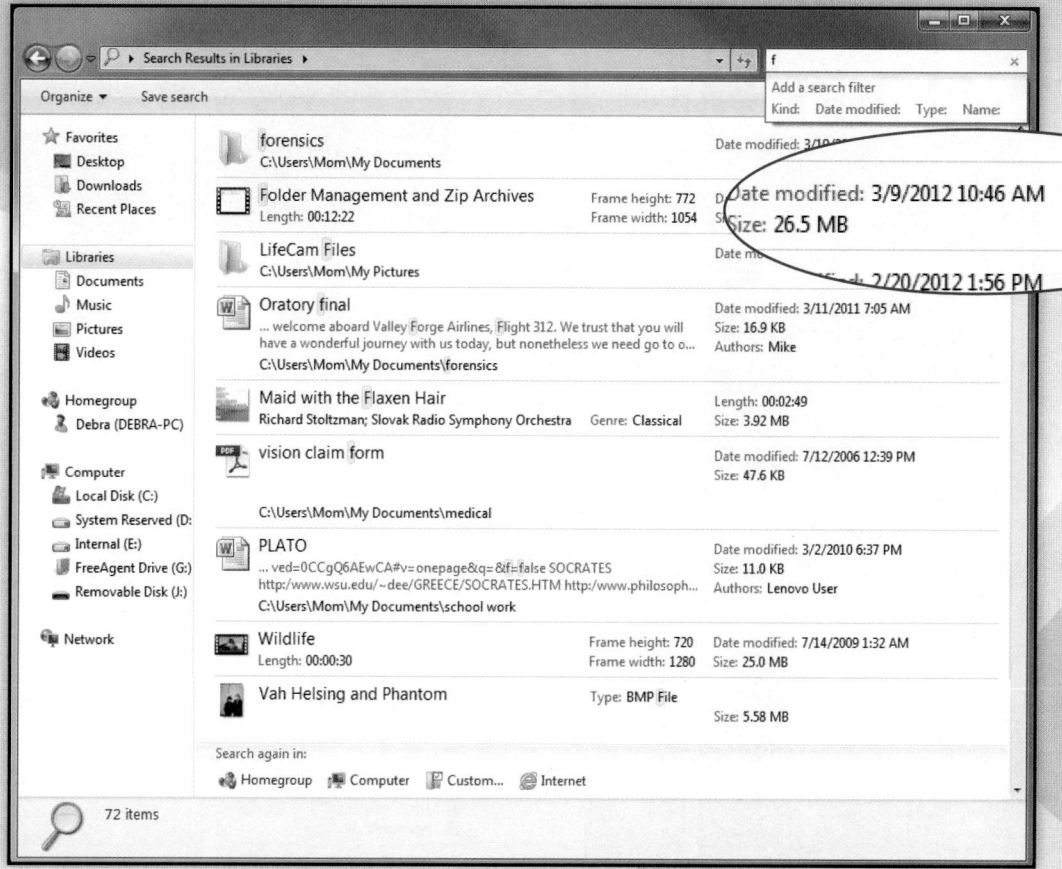

**FIGURE 3.26** The Search Results in File Explorer show the "f" found in file names, content, and other file properties.

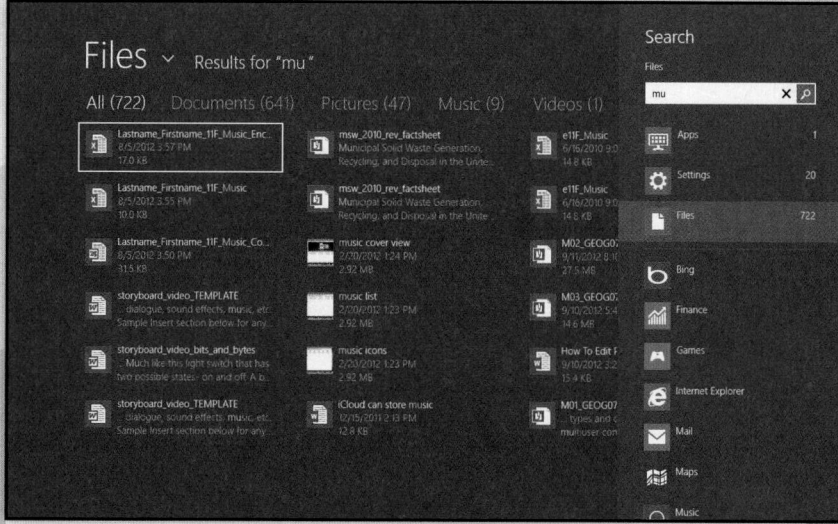

**FIGURE 3.27** Windows 8 Search locates programs (apps) and settings as well as files.

# SEARCHING IN MAC OS X

You can use the search field in Finder to search for files and folders (see Figure 3.28), and the Help Center also has a built-in search; but the most powerful search tool in OS X is called Spotlight. You can access Spotlight by clicking the magnifying glass on the upper right-hand side of your screen. Spotlight searches applications, files and folders, contacts, and other objects on your computer (see Figure 3.29). Spotlight can even provide a definition and do simple math calculations.

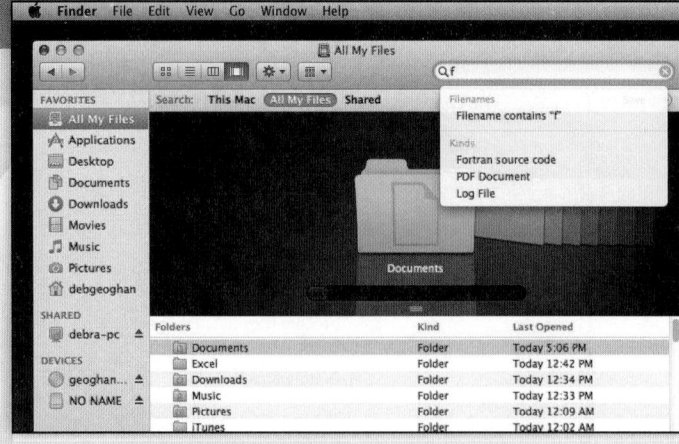

**FIGURE 3.28** Searching for Files and Folders through Finder

# USING BOOLEAN LOGIC TO REFINE SEARCHES

You can further refine your searches by using Boolean filters. George Boole was a 19th century mathematician that we can thank for creating this system. While it can seem complex, there are three **Boolean operators** that define the relationships among words or groups of words: AND, OR, and NOT. Notice that they're written in uppercase. You can use these operators to create search filters or queries in most searches, including databases and Web searches. Figure 3.30 illustrates the effect of Boolean filters on the search using the terms John and Kennedy:

- **AND:** Search results must include both words: John AND Kennedy. This filter excludes files that don't include both terms.
- **OR:** Search results must include either word: John OR Kennedy. This filter includes all files that contain either or both terms.
- **NOT:** Search results must include the first term and must not include the second term: John NOT Kennedy. This filter excludes files that include the term Kennedy.

Using the Search feature of Windows or OS X can make locating a file or program quick and easy, saving you both time and aggravation. The combination of good file management and good searching skills will serve you well.

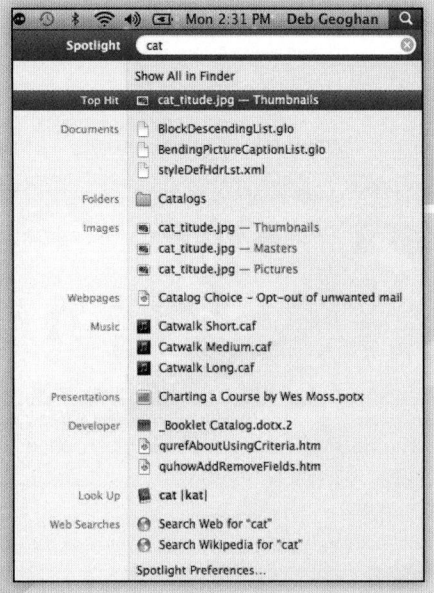

**FIGURE 3.29** OS X Spotlight searches for many types of objects on your computer.

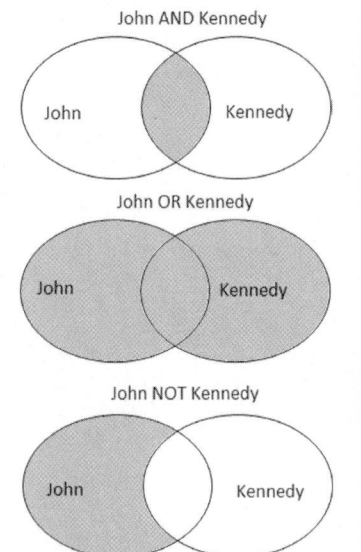

**FIGURE 3.30** Boolean operators can be used to filter search results. The blue areas represent the search results for each Boolean filter.

# GREEN COMPUTING

## THE PAPERLESS OFFICE

The promise of the paperless office hasn't quite become a reality. In fact, we're buried under more paper today than ever. According to the U.S. Environmental Protection Agency (EPA), in 2010, paper and paperboard made up 28.5% of our municipal solid waste generated.

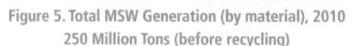

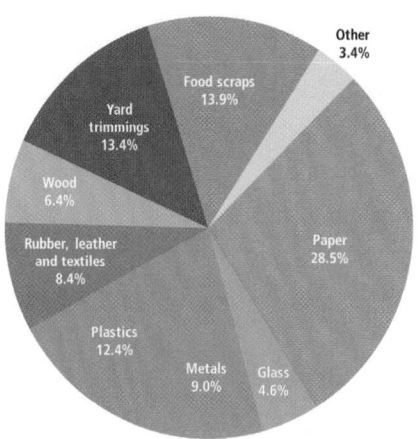

Figure 5. Total MSW Generation (by material), 2010
250 Million Tons (before recycling)

Other 3.4%
Food scraps 13.9%
Yard trimmings 13.4%
Wood 6.4%
Rubber, leather and textiles 8.4%
Plastics 12.4%
Metals 9.0%
Glass 4.6%
Paper 28.5%

Source: www.epa.gov/epawaste/nonhaz/municipal/pubs/msw_2010_rev_factsheet.pdf

The process of making paper uses water and energy in addition to trees, and results in greenhouse emissions and air and water pollution. Reduce your paper usage to help the environment.

The prospect of going paperless has advantages for the environment and for your bottom line. So, how do you achieve it? The reality is you probably can't go totally paperless, but here are a few ways to reduce your paper usage:

1. Send emails and make phone calls instead of sending greeting cards and letters.
2. Pay your bills online and opt for paperless billing from your billers and banks.
3. Don't print out electronic documents unless absolutely necessary.
4. Read magazines and books in electronic formats.
5. Opt out of receiving junk mail at the DMA website (**www.dmachoice.org**) and catalogs at Catalog Choice (**www.catalogchoice.org**).

## Running Project

Use Windows Help and Support or the Internet to research natural language search. What is it and how does it change the way you can search your computer?

## 4 Things You Need to Know

- There's a Search box in the Start menu, most windows, control panels, and help screens.
- Windows maintains an index that contains information about the files located on your computer.
- The search tool on a Mac is called Spotlight.
- The Boolean operators AND, OR, and NOT can be used to create search filters.

## Key Term

Boolean operators

# That's Not the Program I Want to Open This File Type

## Change the default program associated with a file type.

Your operating system maintains a list of file extensions and associated **default programs** that enable it to automatically open the correct program when you click on a file. This is fine for file types that are specific to one program—such as .docx for Microsoft Word and .mov for Apple QuickTime (refer back to Figure 3.11 for some more examples). However, it can be a problem with more generic file types that can be opened with several different programs. For example, take the file extension .mp3. By default, Windows associates MP3 files with Windows Media Player, but if you install another program that can play music files, such as Apple iTunes or Winamp, the association may be changed. In this article, we look at how to manage default programs and file type associations in Windows and OS X.

In Windows you can manage these settings via the Default Programs control panel (see Figure 3.31). To access it, click the *Start* button and click *Default Programs*.

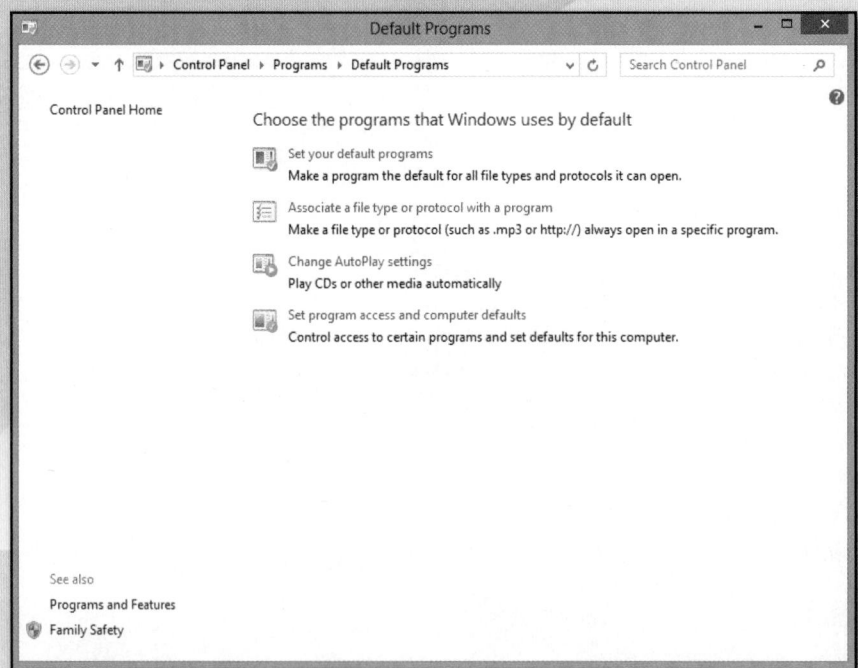

**FIGURE 3.31** The Default Programs control panel has options to work with programs or file types.

1. Select the program from the list to view information about the file types the program can open.

2. Select the first option to set all the defaults, or the second option to select defaults individually.

# SETTING PROGRAM DEFAULTS

In the Default Programs control panel, click the *Set your default programs* option to work with the programs on your computer. This opens the Set Default Programs window (see Figure 3.32). This window allows you to view and modify the file types the program opens by default.

To restore all the program's defaults at once, click *Set this program as default* or click *Choose defaults for this program* to modify them individually. This allows you to specify which file types should be automatically opened by this program.

If you select the *Choose defaults for this program* option, a new window opens and allows you to pick items individually. For example, Windows Photo Viewer is capable of viewing many types of image files, such as JPG and GIF files. If you installed Picasa on your computer, however, the default association for GIF files might change to Picasa Photo Viewer. You can use this dialog box to change the association back to Windows Photo Viewer.

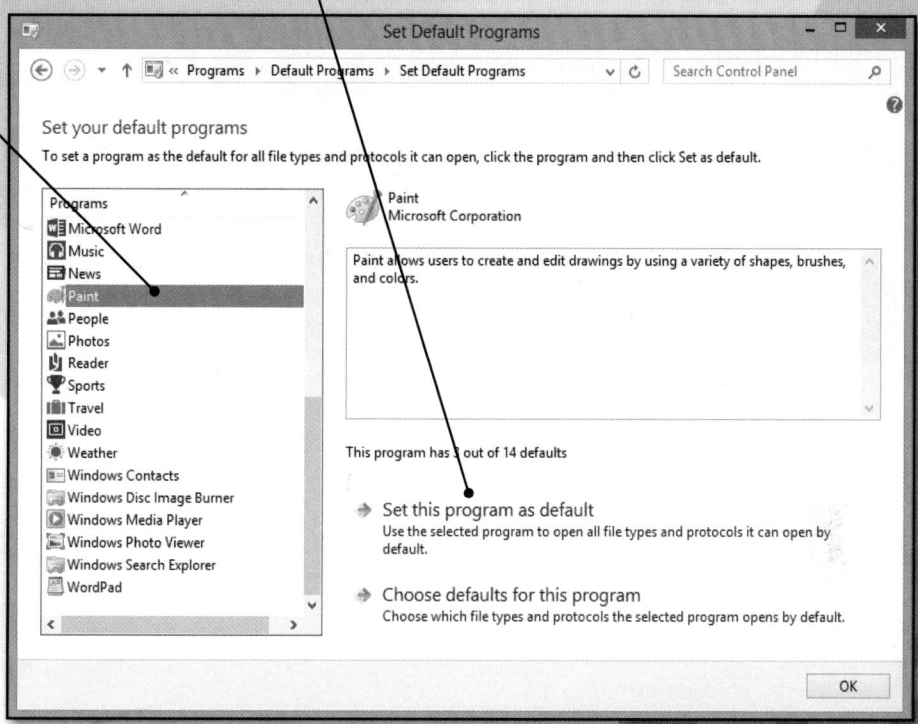

**FIGURE 3.32** The Set Default Programs Window for Paint

# MANAGING FILE TYPE ASSOCIATIONS

To manage file type associations directly, in the Default Programs control panel, click *Associate a file type or protocol with a program*. This opens the window shown in Figure 3.33. This example shows the process for associating .bmp files, which are currently associated with Photos, with Windows Photo Viewer.

**1.** Click the file extension that you wish to modify, and then click the Change program button.

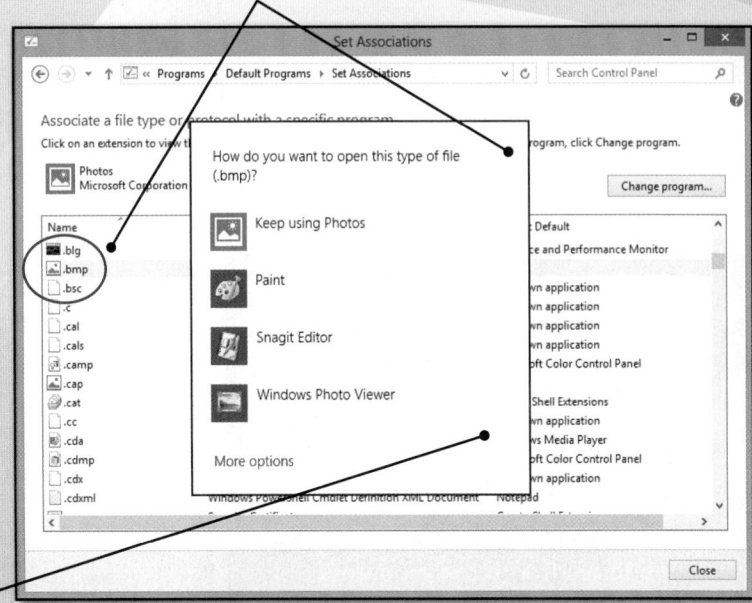

**2.** Select the program that you want to use to open the file type, or click the Browse button to locate it, and then click OK.

**FIGURE 3.33** The Set Default Programs for Windows Live Photo Gallery

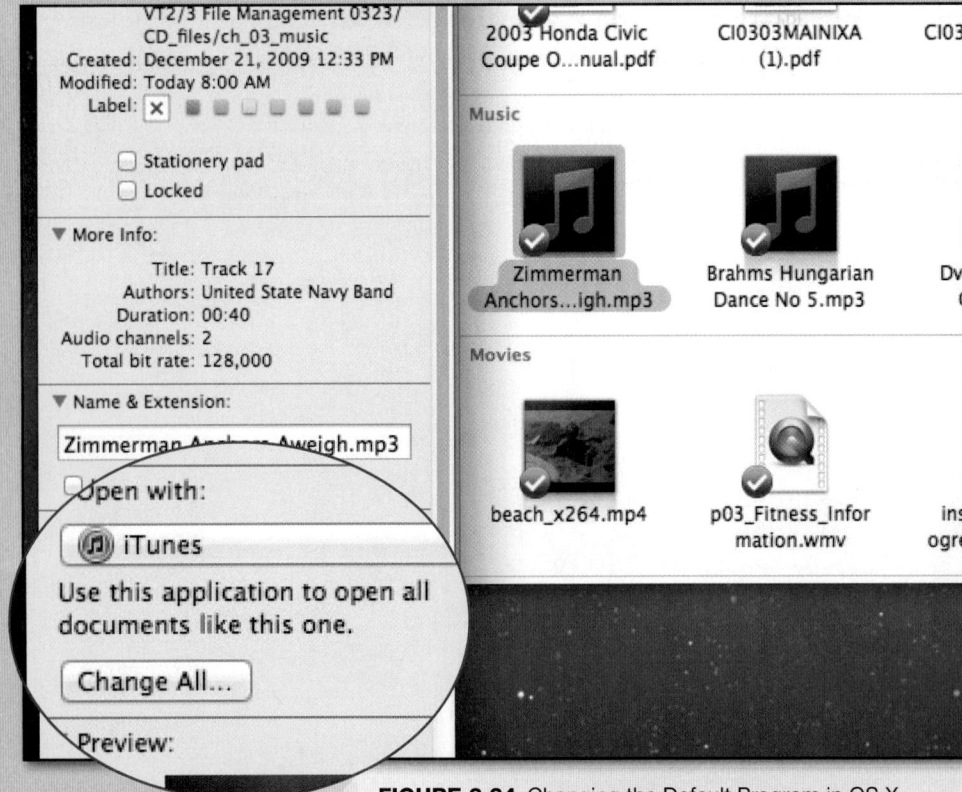

**FIGURE 3.34** Changing the Default Program in OS X

To change the program that opens a file in OS X, use the Finder. The process is very easy. Open Finder and select the file. From the File menu, select *Get Info*. In the Info pane, click *Open with* and choose the proper application from the list. To make sure that every file of that type uses the new application, click the *Change All* button (see Figure 3.34).

Understanding file type associations will help you avoid frustration when an association is incorrect and allow you to configure your programs the way that works best for you.

# CAREER SPOTLIGHT

It's hard to imagine a career today that doesn't require you to have some file-management skills. Any work that deals with documents—from traditional office work to doctor's offices, flower shops, contractors, and teachers—has files that need to be managed. Many industries, such as healthcare, finance, and government agencies, have document management regulations that require individuals with excellent file-management skills to complete.

The U.S. National Archives and Records Administration (NARA) offers a certification track for federal employees. To receive the Certification of Federal Records Management, you must complete five Knowledge Area courses and exams. The organization offers an overview course in records management that's optional. Required courses include Creating and Maintaining Agency Business Information; Records Scheduling; Records Schedule Implementation; Asset and Risk Management; and Records Management Program Development. The NARA certification focuses on federal record management and regulations.

## Running Project

Use the Default Programs control panel or Finder on your computer to complete this section of the project. What program is currently associated with MP3 files? What other files types can this program open by default? What other programs are installed on your computer that can open MP3 files by default?

## 2 Things You Need to Know

● Your operating system maintains a list of file extensions and associated default programs.

● You can use the Default Programs control panel or Finder to change these associations.

## Key Term

default program

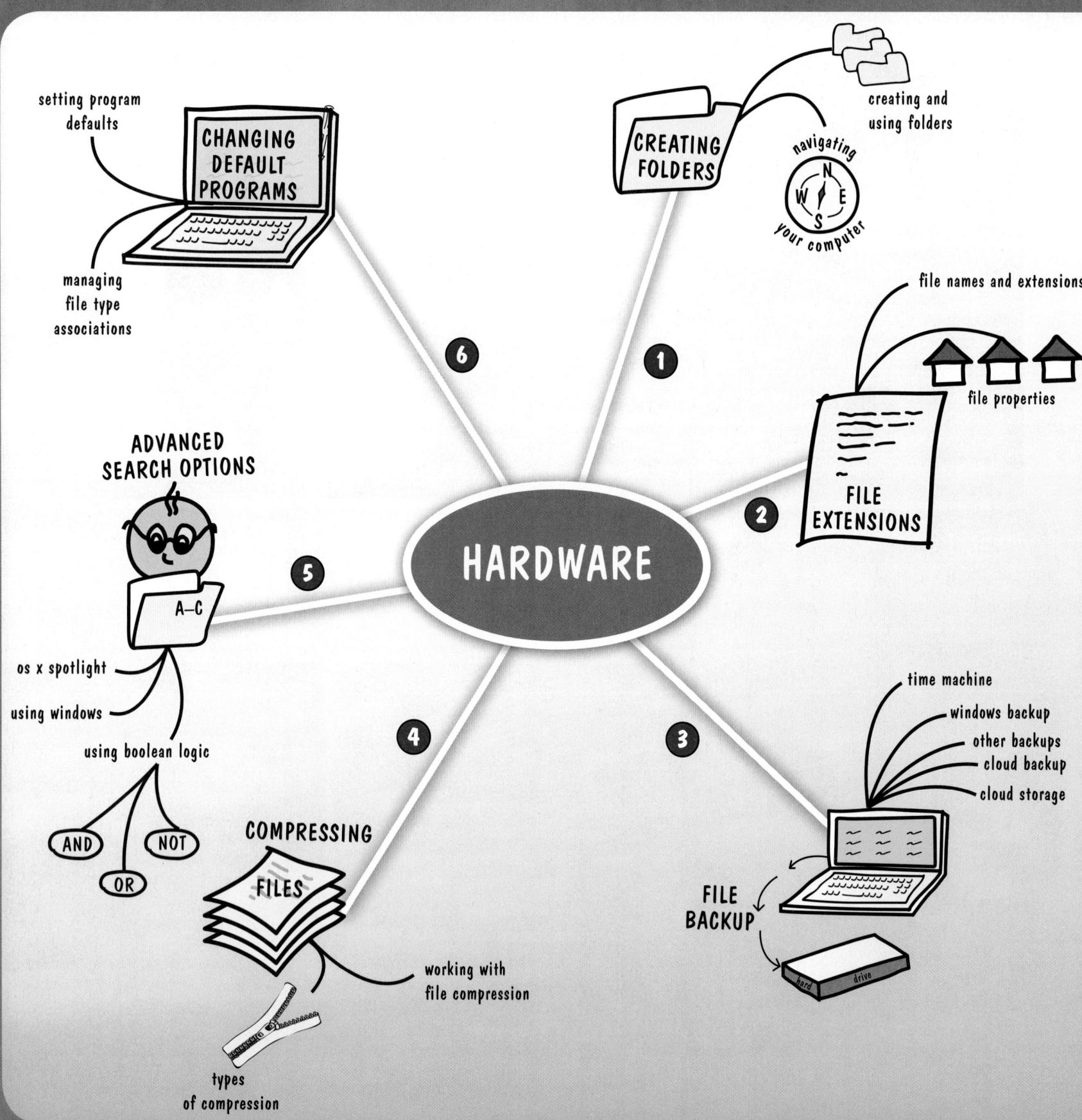

setting program defaults

CHANGING DEFAULT PROGRAMS

managing file type associations

CREATING FOLDERS

creating and using folders

navigating your computer

file names and extensions

file properties

ADVANCED SEARCH OPTIONS

A–C

os x spotlight

using windows

using boolean logic

AND    NOT

OR

HARDWARE

FILE EXTENSIONS

time machine

windows backup

other backups

cloud backup

cloud storage

FILE BACKUP

hard drive

COMPRESSING FILES

working with file compression

types of compression

1  2  3  4  5  6

# Objectives Recap

1. Create folders to organize files.
2. Explain the importance of file extensions.
3. Explain the importance of backing up files.
4. Demonstrate how to compress files.
5. Use advanced search options to locate files.
6. Change the default program associated with a file type.

# Key Terms

algorithm **114**
back up **108**
Boolean operators **122**
compression **114**
default program **124**
File Explorer **94**
file extension **105**
file management **92**
file name **104**

file property **105**
Finder **95**
folder **92**
hierarchy **93**
library **93**
lossless compression **114**
lossy compression **114**
path **93**
Public folder **92**

# Summary

**1. Create folders to organize files.**

Windows and OS X create a user folder hierarchy for you to use to store your files. You can create new folders in this hierarchy and in other locations, such as a flash drive, to organize and store your files. Windows Libraries are used to gather several locations together and make locating files easier. Windows Explorer and Mac Finder are tools you can use to work with these folders and libraries.

**2. Explain the importance of file extensions.**

A file name consists of two parts: the name that's used by people to describe the contents of the file and the extension that's used by the operating system to identify the type of file and determine which program should be used to open it.

**3. Explain the importance of backing up files.**

Scheduling a regular, automatic backup of important files ensures that you won't lose your files if something happens to your computer. For the greatest protection, keep the backup files in a different physical location.

**4. Demonstrate how to compress files.**

Files can be compressed using several methods. The easiest method on a Windows computer is to right-click on a file or folder, point to Send to, and choose *Compressed (zipped) folder.* In OS X, the Compress option is in the Finder File menu.

**5. Use advanced search options to locate files.**

Windows creates an index of common files found on your computer that's used when you use the Search box in the Start menu or in an Explorer window. The search tool in OS X is called Spotlight. In either search tool, you can add filters, such as Type and Author, to your search as well as use Boolean operators (AND, OR, or NOT) to further refine it.

**6. Change the default program associated with a file type.**

Windows provides a Default Programs control panel that can be used to modify the programs associated with specific file types. This tool allows you to control which program to open automatically when you click on a file. The Info pane in OS X contains the Open with option.

# Application Projects

## Microsoft Office Application Project 1:
### Word Level 1

**PROJECT DESCRIPTION:** In the following Microsoft Word project, you will create a report about the importance of file management. In the project you will enter and edit text, format text, insert graphics, check spelling and grammar, and create document footers.

**INSTRUCTIONS:** For the purpose of grading the project you are required to perform the following tasks:

### File Management Primer

Have you ever saved a file on your computer and then lost it? Is your email Inbox full? Is your desktop covered with icons and files? Have you downloaded a file from the Internet or email and been unable to locate it? *All of these are symptoms of poor file management.* Poor file management causes frustration, inefficiency, lost productivity, and duplication of effort. So, it is critical to practice good file management—and it's easy too.

First, get to know your folder hierarchy. Both Windows and OS X create your user folder for you—with folders for documents, pictures, music, videos, and downloads. This is a great start. It gives you logical places to put things. But if you have a lot of files or want to save them on other disks or in another structure, you'll need to do more.

Second, learn to navigate your file system. On a Windows computer, learn to use **Explorer**. On a Mac, get friendly with **Finder**. These tools are your best friends when it comes to finding and organizing your files.

Third, organize your files into folders. Create the folders that make sense to you. Consider creating folders for each class you take, or each project you work on.

Finally, remember to use your new organization scheme. Save you files in the right place, and you will always be able to find them!

PS- I mentioned email in the first paragraph. Well guess what, same rules apply. Create folders or labels in your email program to organize your email messages—and file or delete them as soon as you have finished with them. Nothing is more satisfying at the end of the day than an empty Inbox!

lastname_firstname_ch03_word-2

---

**1** Start Word. Download and open the file named *vt_ch03_word*. Save the file as **lastname_firstname_ch03_word**.

**2** Select the first line of the document and apply the Title style.

**3** Format the rest of the document as Times New Roman, 12 pt.

**4** In the first body paragraph format *All of these are symptoms of poor file management.* as italic.

**5** In the third body paragraph, format *Explorer* and *Finder* as bold.

**6** Place the insertion point at the end of the third body paragraph (begins with Second), and then press *Enter*. Insert the picture of Explorer *vt_ch03_image1*.

**7** Resize the image to a height of 2.8" and center it.

**8** Use the Spelling and Grammar checker to correct the misspelling of the word *lables* to *labels* and correct the misspelling of the word *delte* to *delete*.

**9** Using the Spelling and Grammar dialog box, accept the suggested correction for the Word Choice error *n*. Ignore all other spelling and grammar suggestions.

**10** Insert the file name in the footer of the document using the FileName field.

**11** Save the document. Close the document and then exit Word. Submit the document as directed.

**Visit pearsonhighered.com/Geoghan** for data files, simulations, VizClips, and additional study materials.

# Microsoft Office Application Project 2: Excel Level 1

**PROJECT DESCRIPTION:** In this Microsoft Excel project, you will format cells and a worksheet. You will create a formula and insert a header and footer.

**INSTRUCTIONS:** For the purpose of grading the project you are required to perform the following tasks:

**1** Start Excel. Open the downloaded Excel file named *vt_ch03_excel*. Save the file as **lastname_firstname_ch03_excel**.

**2** Increase the width of columns B, C, and D to 15. Select the text in the range B4:D4 and set the text to wrap. Center and middle align the text in the selected range. Change the cell style to Heading 4.

**3** Merge and center the text in cell A1 over columns A:D. Change the cell style to Heading 3. Merge and center the text in cell A2 over columns A:D. Change the cell style to Heading 3.

**4** Change the cell style in cell A18 to Heading 4. Format D5:D23 as percentage, 1 decimal place.

**5** Delete rows 7 and 10.

**6** Change the cell style of the range A15:D15 to Total. Change the cell style of the range A20:D20 to Total.

**7** In cell B21, create a formula to calculate the total municipal solid waste, by adding the values for total materials in products and total other wastes. Copy the formula to cell C21.

**8** In cell D21, create a formula to calculate the percentage of municipal waste that is recovered by dividing the weight recovered by the weight generated.

**9** Rename the Sheet1 tab as 2010.

**10** Insert a header with the Sheet name in the center cell. Insert a footer with the file name in the left cell. Center the worksheet vertically on the page.

**11** Save the workbook. Close the workbook and then exit Excel. Submit the workbook as directed.

**Visit pearsonhighered.com/Geoghan** for data files, simulations, VizClips, and additional study materials.

Chapter 3 | 131

# Multiple Choice

Answer the multiple-choice questions below for more practice with key terms and concepts from this chapter.

1. An easy way to share files with other users is to put them
   a. on the desktop.
   b. in a library.
   c. in a Public folder.
   d. in your user folder.

2. In a hierarchy, a folder within a folder is called a _____.
   a. Home folder
   b. subfolder
   c. archive
   d. library

3. Which part of an Explorer window contains buttons for common tasks?
   a. Toolbar
   b. Address bar
   c. Views button
   d. Details pane

4. Which of the following contains an illegal character and, therefore, isn't a legal file name?
   a. hello.goodbye.hello.txt
   b. make_my_day.bmp
   c. homework 11-04-12.docx
   d. homework :ch_03.xlsx

5. Which storage location has the largest capacity?
   a. Tape drive
   b. Optical drive
   c. Internal hard drive
   d. Flash drive

6. Cloud backup services
   a. are very expensive for the average user.
   b. are for large businesses only.
   c. are complicated and unreliable.
   d. can automatically back up your files.

7. Which type of image uses lossy compression to reduce file size?
   a. JPG
   b. BMP
   c. TIF
   d. ZIP

8. Which Boolean operator can be used to exclude certain words from the search results?
   a. AND
   b. OR
   c. NOT
   d. EXCLUDE

9. Which tool can be used to search for both files and applications on a Mac?
   a. Toolbar
   b. Spotlight
   c. Coverflow
   d. Explorer

10. What is the default file extension of Word files?
    a. .doc
    b. .docx
    c. .rtf
    d. .txt

# True or False

Answer the following questions with T for true or F for false for more practice with key terms and concepts from this chapter.

1. You must create your user folder.

2. Libraries give you quick access to both user folders and public folders.

3. The folder structure created by Windows is a hierarchy.

4. Windows Explorer is a tool used to navigate the Internet.

5. You can't change the properties of a file.

6. If you change the file extension of a file, you may be unable to open it.

7. The Finder is a tool used in Windows to find files.

8. A file compressed with a lossless compression algorithm can't be decompressed to its original form.

9. Searching from the Windows Start menu yields the same results as searching from Windows Explorer.

10. The default program that opens a file can be easily changed.

# Fill in the Blank

Fill in the blanks with key terms from this chapter.

1. The processes of opening, closing, saving, naming, deleting, and organizing digital files are collectively called _____.

2. The _____ is the sequence of folders to a file or folder.

3. The user folder structure of subfolders within folders is organized in a(n) _____.

4. Windows 7 introduced the _____, which is used to gather files from several locations.

5. The tool you use to work with files and folders on a Mac computer is called _____.

6. You should regularly _____ your files for ease of recovering files in case of computer damage.

7. _____ uses a compression algorithm that looks for the redundancy in a file and creates an encoded file by removing the redundant information.

8. Windows maintains a(n) _____ of common files on your computer to speed up searching.

9. The _____ AND, OR, and NOT are used to create search filters.

10. The _____ at the end of a file name is used by the operating system to determine which program to use to open it.

# Running Project ...

## ... The Finish Line

Using your answers to the previous projects' questions, write a report describing the importance of file management. Explain how to organize, protect, and manage the files you save on your computer. Save your file as **lastname_firstname_ch03_project**, and submit it to your instructor as directed.

# Do It Yourself 1

In this activity you will set up folders you can use to store the work you complete in this class. This activity assumes you're using a USB flash drive to save your work for this class. If you're storing your files on your own computer, you can store them in the user's My Documents folder. If you didn't complete the steps in the Running Project to create a class folder and a Chapter 3 folder, do so now.

1. As you complete more work for this course, you may find it useful to organize your files by creating folders for each chapter. Navigate to the folder that you created for this class using Windows Explorer or Finder. Create new folders for each chapter. Take a screenshot of the window showing these folders.

2. Open your word processor, and type your name and date in the document. Paste the screen shot into this document. Write a brief note to a friend explaining how to create a folder and why it is useful.

3. In your word processor, click *File* and click *Save As*. When the Save As dialog box opens, in the left pane, click *Computer* and click your flash drive. Open the class folder and the Chapter 3 folder. In the File name text field, type the file name **lastname_firstname_ch03_diy1** and click *Save*. Close your word processor. Submit the file as directed by your instructor.

# Do It Yourself 2

Lossy compression is used when a BMP or TIF file is converted into a JPG file. Most people can't tell the difference between the two when viewing them on the computer screen. To complete this exercise, you need to have a photo editing program such as Windows Live Photo Gallery installed on your Windows computer. If you have a Mac, you can use Preview to complete this exercise. You can also use a different program, such as Paint, iPhoto, or Picasa.

Using File Explorer or Finder, navigate to the data files folder for this chapter. Locate the sunset image file. This is a TIF file taken with the camera's highest setting. Drag this file to your Pictures folder. Open the Pictures folder and locate the sunset file. Select the file, and look at the properties in the Details pane of the window (on a Mac, choose *Get Info* from the File menu).

1. How big is the image file? What are the dimensions of the image? What is the file type?

2. Click the *More Options* arrow next to the Preview button on the toolbar, and choose *Windows Live Photo Gallery*. Click *Fix* on the toolbar to open the editing window for the image. Click *File* and click *Make a copy*. (Mac users—double-click the file to open Preview. From the File menu choose *Export*.)

3. Change the file type in the Save As (Export As) dialog box to JPG, and save the file with the suggested name. Navigate to the location where you saved (exported) the image, and select the new .jpg version of the file. Look in the Details pane (open Get Info), and notice the new file size, dimensions, and file type. How much was the file compressed by converting it from a TIF to a JPG? Open the image files and look at them carefully. Compare both files. Can you tell the difference? If so, what differences do you notice? Is the JPG file acceptable for viewing on the screen or is the image quality too poor?

4. Type up your answers, save the file as **lastname_firstname_ch03_diy2**, and submit the file as directed by your instructor.

# Critical Thinking

Your boss Ben owns a sporting goods store. He's overwhelmed by all the information he has to keep track of. He has hired you to help him get organized. All his files are stored on one flash drive, and he needs you to sort them out for him.

1. Locate the data files for this course. Copy the folder ben_sportsfans onto your flash drive. Examine the file names to determine the contents of each.

2. Use a word processor or spreadsheet to create a table like the one that follows. Create columns with appropriate categories to organize the files on the disc (such as flyers, payroll, and so on). In each column, list the files that belong in each category.

3. In the same document, write a two- to three-paragraph essay for Ben explaining why he should organize his files in this way and what other ways he could organize the files.

4. Use File Explorer or Finder to create a folder that represents each category. Move the files into the appropriate folders. Take screen shots that show the contents of each folder you create and paste these into your document.

5. Save your file as **lastname_firstname_ch03_ct**, and submit it as directed by your instructor.

| Flyers | Category 2 | Category 3 |
|--------|------------|------------|
| sale flyer | | |
| | | |
| | | |
| | | |

# Ethical Dilemma

The Public folders are accessible by all users of a computer system and provide an easy way to share files among them.

1. You log in to the computer in the lab at school and notice that another student has stored his or her homework assignments in the Public folder. It's the same class that you're taking, so the work could help you. What is the ethical thing to do? If the work was for a different course, what would you do?

2. Type up your answers, save the file as **lastname_firstname_ch03_ethics,** and submit it as directed by your instructor.

# On the Web

1. Use the Internet to search for jobs that have file management listed as a required skill. Use at least two websites. What websites did you use? How many jobs were listed with your criteria? What were some of the industries that require this skill?

2. Type up your answers, save the file as **lastname_firstname_ch03_web,** and submit it as directed by your instructor.

# Collaboration

**Instructors:** Divide the class into five groups, and assign each group one topic for this project. The topics include WMA and MP3; TIF and JPG; MP4 and WMV; AAC and MP3; and MOV and AVI.

**The Project:** Each team is to prepare a presentation comparing its file types. The presentation should explain both the pros and cons of each file type and include examples of when it's appropriate to use them. Teams must use at least three references, only one of which may be the textbook. Use Google Docs or Microsoft Office to plan the presentation, and provide documentation that all team members have contributed to the project.

**Students:** Before beginning this project, discuss the roles each group member will play. Choose a team name, which you'll use in submitting your presentation. Be sure to divide the work among your members, and pick someone to present your project. You may find it helpful to elect a team leader who can direct your activities and ensure that all team contributions are collated through Google Docs or Microsoft Office as directed by your instructor.

**Outcome:** You're to prepare a multimedia presentation on your assigned topic in PowerPoint (or another tool, if approved by your instructor) and present it to your class. The presentation may be no longer than 3 minutes and should contain 5 to 7 slides. On the first slide, be sure to include the name of your presentation and a list of all team members. Turn in a final version of your presentation named as **teamname_ch03_presentation** and your file showing your collaboration named as **teamname_ch03_collab**. Submit your presentation to your instructor as directed.

# 4

# Hardware

Visit **pearsonhighered.com/Geoghan** for data files, simulations, VizClips, and additional study materials.

## Running Project

In this chapter, you'll explore the key hardware components of the computer and put them together to create a computer that fits your needs. Look for instructions as you complete each article. For most, there's a series of questions for you to research. At the conclusion of the chapter, you're asked to submit your responses to the questions raised and present and justify your selections.

1. **Explain the function of the CPU.**

2. **Identify the parts of a system unit and motherboard.**

3. **Compare different types of storage devices.**

4. **List different input devices and their uses.**

5. **List different video and audio output devices and their uses.**

6. **Compare the features of different types of printers.**

7. **Explain and provide examples of the concept of adaptive technology.**

8. **Discuss the different communication devices that can be used.**

# IN THIS CHAPTER

**Hardware** refers to the physical components of a computer. Computers perform four tasks: input, processing, output, and storage. The computer itself consists of the components that process data. The components that serve the input, output, and storage functions are called **peripheral devices**. Peripherals can be external devices or they can be integrated into the system unit.

# The CPU: The Brains of the Operation

VIZ CLIP

## OBJECTIVE

### 1 Explain the function of the CPU.

The brain of a computer is called the **CPU (central processing unit)**, or **processor**, and is housed inside the system unit on the motherboard (see Figure 4.1). The CPU consists of two parts: the arithmetic logic unit and the control unit.

The **arithmetic logic unit (ALU)** performs arithmetic (addition and subtraction) and logic (AND, OR, and NOT) calculations. The **control unit** manages the movement of data through the CPU. Together, these units perform three main functions: executing program instructions, performing calculations, and making decisions.

**FIGURE 4.1** The central processing unit fits into the motherboard inside the system unit.

## CPU FUNCTIONS

- Execute program instructions (control unit)
- Perform calculations (ALU)
- Make decisions (control unit)

## INSTRUCTION CYCLE

To perform the three functions, the CPU utilizes the **instruction cycle**, which is also known as the "fetch-and-execute cycle" or the "machine cycle." Here's how it works (see Figure 4.2).

- **Fetch:** The instruction is retrieved from the main memory.
- **Decode:** The control unit translates the instruction into a computer command.
- **Execute:** The ALU processes the command.
- **Store:** The results are written back to the memory (stored).

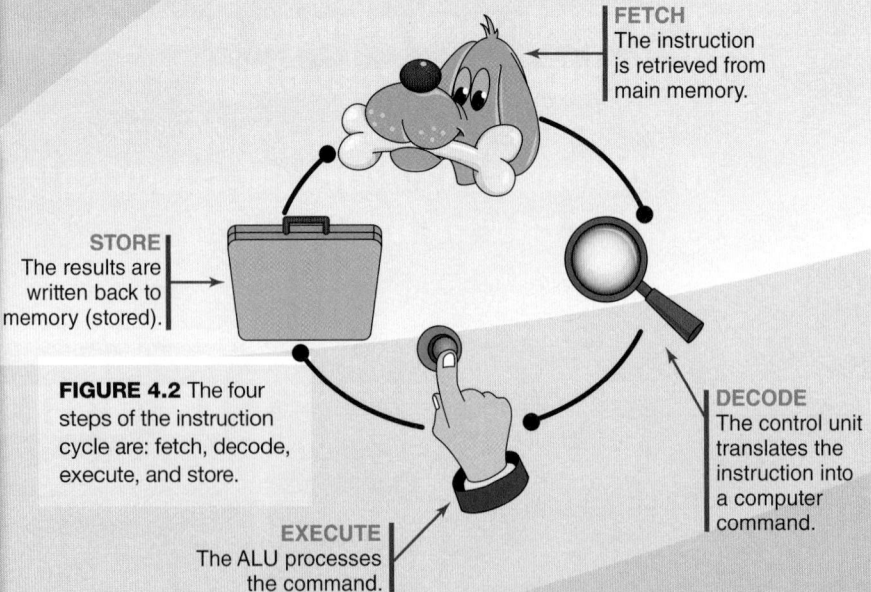

**FETCH** The instruction is retrieved from main memory.

**STORE** The results are written back to memory (stored).

**DECODE** The control unit translates the instruction into a computer command.

**EXECUTE** The ALU processes the command.

**FIGURE 4.2** The four steps of the instruction cycle are: fetch, decode, execute, and store.

# Find Out MORE

One way to improve processor performance is to overclock the processor. This means forcing it to run at speeds higher than it was designed to perform at. How is this possible? Is it legal? Why might you consider overclocking your CPU? What are the risks? Where did you find this information?

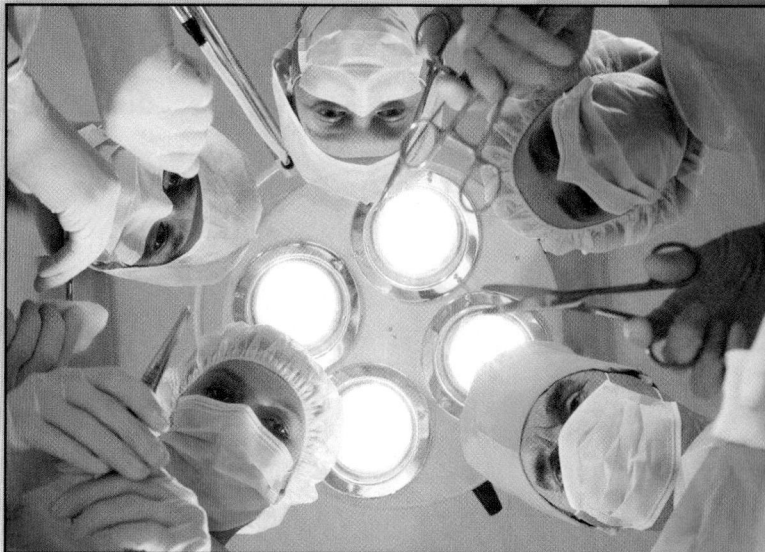

FIGURE 4.4 Parallel processing is like a surgical team, with each member performing a part of the operation.

## CPU PERFORMANCE

The instruction cycle happens so quickly that you don't realize what's happening. In fact, the processor executes billions of cycles each second. When you evaluate processors for performance, one of the variables you look at is **clock speed**, which is the speed at which the processer executes the cycles. Today, that speed is measured in **gigahertz (GHz)**—billions of cycles per second. A 3 GHz processor has 3 billion data cycles per second.

So far, we've looked at how a processor executes one instruction at a time. Modern computers are capable of processing multiple instructions simultaneously, which increases the efficiency of the processor and the performance of the computer.

**PIPELINING Pipelining** is used by a single processor. As soon as the first instruction has moved from the fetch to the decode stage, the processor fetches the next instruction. The process is much like an assembly line in a factory (see Figure 4.3).

**PARALLEL PROCESSING Parallel processing** uses multiple processors, or multi-core processors, to divide up the work (see Figure 4.4). It can dramatically increase computer performance when running processor-intensive programs, such as system scans or multiple simultaneous programs. Each processor may also use pipelining to further boost the processing efficiency of the system.

FIGURE 4.3 Commands are fed to the processor as the previous command completes a phase—like the stations on this assembly line.

Parallel processing is most effective when software developers write programs that can take advantage of multiple processors. Modern operating systems, such as Microsoft Windows, MAC OS X, and Linux, were all developed with parallel processing in mind.

Multiple processors are typically found in servers, which may have anywhere from two to several hundred processors (see Figure 4.5). Supercomputers are considered "massively multiprocessor" computers and may have thousands of processors, just as the massively multiplayer online game *World of Warcraft* has thousands of players.

A **multi-core processor** consists of two or more processors that are integrated on a single chip. Multi-core processing increases the processing speed over single-core processors and reduces energy consumption over multiple separate processors. Today, dual-core, quad-core, and even six-core processors are found on most personal computers. Video cards have their own processor called a GPU (graphics processing unit), which can contain multiple cores.

# COOLING SYSTEM: AIR CONDITIONING FOR THE PROCESSOR

Working quickly and using multiple processors or processing paths generates a great deal of heat. Excessive heat can damage a processor or cause it to fail, so modern computers provide cooling systems for the CPU.

To keep the processor from overheating, a heat sink and cooling fan are generally installed above the processor to dissipate the heat the processor produces. The heat sink is composed of metal or ceramic and draws heat away from the processor. The cooling fan simply moves the heat away (see Figure 4.6). A system unit has one or more case fans to keep the entire system cool.

**FIGURE 4.5** Multiple Processors on a Server Motherboard

**FIGURE 4.6** A copper heat sink and a small fan are installed above the CPU to keep it cool.

**FIGURE 4.7** In this high-performance system, tubes from the liquid cooling system can be seen inside the case.

When using a notebook computer, you should place it on a hard surface, making sure not to block the air vents. You shouldn't use a notebook on your lap, where it can actually cause skin damage to you and overheat your computer. You can also purchase a USB-powered cooler for notebooks that run hot.

Some computers have a liquid cooling system that works like a car radiator by circulating liquid through tubes in the system, carrying heat away from the processor. The advantage to liquid cooling is that it's more efficient and quieter than a fan. The biggest disadvantage is that the liquid cooling system takes up much more space in the system unit (see Figure 4.7).

The ability to process instructions is what makes a computer different from a toaster. The CPU is what makes this possible. Without the CPU, a computer is nothing more than a big nightlight.

## Running Project

Use the Internet to research current processors. What is the fastest processor available today for desktop computers? What about notebooks? Netbooks? What are the two main manufacturers of processors today?

## 4 Things You Need to Know

- The CPU consists of the arithmetic logic unit (ALU) and the control unit.
- The four steps of the instruction cycle are fetch, decode, execute, and store.
- Modern processors use pipelining and parallel processing to improve performance.
- A multi-core processor consists of more than one processor on a single chip.

## Key Terms

arithmetic logic unit (ALU)

clock speed

control unit

CPU (central processing unit)

gigahertz (GHz)

hardware

instruction cycle

multi-core processor

parallel processing

peripheral device

pipelining

processor

# Getting to Know Your System Unit and Motherboard

VIZ CLIP

## 2 OBJECTIVE
## Identify the parts of a system unit and motherboard.

The **system unit** is the case that encloses and protects the power supply, motherboard, processor (CPU), and memory of a computer. It also has drive bays to hold the storage devices and openings for peripheral devices to connect to expansion cards on the motherboard (see Figure 4.8). All-in-one systems and notebook computers may also have the keyboard and monitor integrated into the system unit. The system unit is what holds everything together.

## THE MOTHERBOARD

The main circuit board of your computer is the **motherboard** (see Figure 4.9). In addition to housing the processor (CPU), it contains drive controllers and interfaces, expansion slots, data buses, ports and connectors, BIOS, and memory. A motherboard may also include integrated peripherals, such as video, sound, and network adapters. The motherboard provides the way for devices to attach to your computer.

Drive bays

Power supply

Processor and cooling fan

Expansion cards

**FIGURE 4.8** In this typical desktop system unit with the cover removed, the processor is hidden under the cooling fan. The motherboard is mostly obscured by the other components.

Expansion slots

Memory slots

**FIGURE 4.9** A Motherboard with Expansion Slots and Memory Slots

**EXPANSION CARDS** Also called "adapter cards," **expansion cards** plug directly into expansion slots on the motherboard and allow you to connect additional peripheral devices to a computer. Video cards, sound cards, network cards, TV tuners, and modems are common expansion cards (see Figure 4.11). Most expansion cards plug into a **PCI (peripheral component interconnect)** slot on the motherboard. Video cards and some other devices use the faster **PCI express (PCIe)** slots. Systems manufactured before 2009 used an **AGP (accelerated graphics port)** for video.

**DRIVE CONTROLLERS AND INTERFACES** A **drive controller** on the motherboard provides a drive interface, which connects disk drives to the processor. **SATA (serial ATA)** has become the standard internal drive interface, but the **EIDE (enhanced integrated drive electronics)** interface is still found on older computers. SATA is up to three times faster than EIDE and has smaller, thinner cables that take up less room and allow for better airflow inside the system unit (see Figure 4.10).

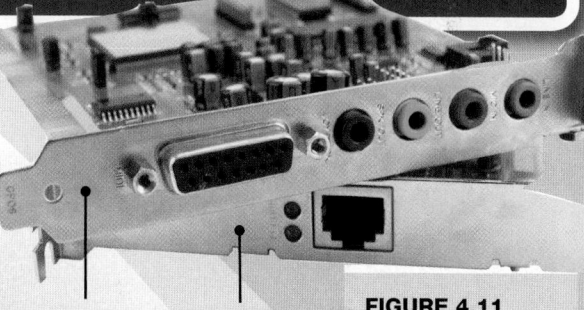

Sound card      Network card

**FIGURE 4.11** Examples of Common Expansion Cards: Sound Card and Network Card

**FIGURE 4.10** A SATA cable (top) takes up less room in the system unit than an EIDE cable (bottom).

**DATA BUSES** Information flows between the components of the computer over wires on the motherboard called **data buses**. Local buses connect the internal devices on the motherboard, while external buses connect the peripheral devices to the CPU and memory of the computer. The speed of the data bus is an important factor in the performance of the system.

## PORTS AND CONNECTORS

**Ports** are used to connect peripheral devices to the motherboard (see Figure 4.12). The most common types of ports found today are USB and FireWire. **Serial and parallel ports** are legacy ports that aren't typically found on modern computers. **PS/2 ports**, which used to connect a keyboard and mouse, have also been widely replaced by USB. Bluetooth is a technology designed to connect peripherals wirelessly.

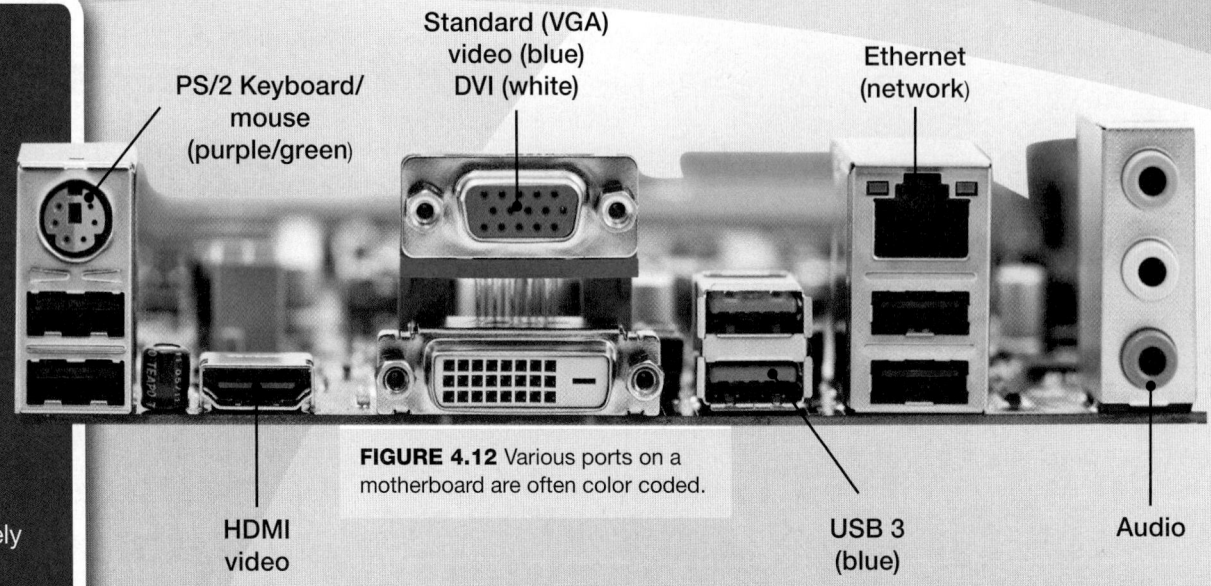

PS/2 Keyboard/
mouse
(purple/green)

Standard (VGA)
video (blue)
DVI (white)

Ethernet
(network)

**FIGURE 4.12** Various ports on a motherboard are often color coded.

HDMI
video

USB 3
(blue)

Audio

**USB (Universal Serial Bus)** is a standard port type that is used to connect many kinds of devices, including printers, mice, keyboards, digital cameras, cell phones, and external drives. Up to 127 devices can share a single USB port by using a **USB hub** (see Figure 4.13). Most desktop computers today have six to twelve USB ports and notebooks have two to four USB ports that provide enough connections for all the peripheral devices you might have. USB also provides power to some devices, which allows this type of connection to be used to charge a media player or cell phone and power devices such as webcams. Another advantage of USB devices is that they are **hot-swappable**, meaning they can be plugged and unplugged without turning off the computer.

USB 1.0 was introduced in 1996 and was replaced by USB 2.0 (2000), which is called Hi-Speed USB and is 40 times faster than its predecessor. The USB 3.0 (SuperSpeed) standard, released in 2008, is about 10 times faster. This additional speed is particularly valuable for hard drives and digital video applications.

**FIGURE 4.13** Multiple USB cables connected through a hub can share a single USB port on your computer.

There are several types of USB connectors. The standard connection to the computer or hub is called USB-A. USB-B and various mini, micro, and proprietary formats are used to connect to USB devices (see Figure 4.14).

**FireWire**, also known as **IEEE 1394**, was originally released by Apple in 1995. FireWire is hot-swappable and can connect up to 63 devices per port. It also allows for peer-to-peer communication between devices, such as two video cameras, without the use of a computer. The original FireWire 400 is roughly equal to USB 2.0 in speed, and FireWire 800 is twice as fast. Today, FireWire is primarily used to connect high-end digital camcorders, which benefit from its superior speed. There are three types of FireWire connectors: 4-circuit and 6-circuit alpha connectors used in FireWire 400 (see Figure 4.15) and a 9-circuit beta connector used in FireWire 800. Both the 6-circuit and 9-circuit connector can supply power to some devices.

**FIGURE 4.14** USB connectors: Type A (top) connects to a computer or hub, and type B (bottom) connects to a USB device, such as a printer or external drive.

**Bluetooth** is a short-range wireless technology that's used to connect many types of peripheral devices. It's commonly used to connect cell phones, mice, keyboards, and printers to personal computers. Bluetooth is also used in game consoles, such as the Nintendo Wii and Sony PlayStation 3 to connect game controllers. A computer must have an adapter to communicate with Bluetooth-enabled devices.

Several other ports may be found on a computer, such as Ethernet ports to connect to a network, audio ports for speakers and microphones, and video ports to connect monitors and projectors. These are covered in more detail later in this chapter.

**FIGURE 4.15** FireWire 400 Connectors: 4-Circuit (or 4-Pin) Connector (left) and 6-Circuit (or 6-Pin) Connector (right)

**BIOS** The **BIOS (basic input output system)** is a program stored on a chip on the motherboard that's used to start up the computer. The BIOS chip is **ROM (read-only memory)**, a nonvolatile form of memory that does not need power to keep its data. The BIOS uses settings that are stored on the **CMOS (complementary metal oxide semiconductor)** chip, which is also on the motherboard. CMOS is volatile memory and uses a small battery to provide it with power to keep the data in memory even when the computer is turned off.

# MEMORY

**Memory** is temporary storage that's used by the computer to hold instructions and data. It's sometimes referred to as primary storage. In this section, we look at two types of memory used by a computer: random access memory and cache memory.

**RANDOM ACCESS MEMORY** The operating systems, programs, and data the computer is currently using are stored in **RAM (random access memory)**. You can think of it as your workspace. A computer that doesn't have enough RAM will be very slow and difficult to use. This type of memory is volatile memory, meaning that any information left in memory is lost when the power is turned off. For this reason, any unsaved work is lost when you close a program or turn off your computer.

Memory boards are small circuit boards that contain memory chips. Most desktop memory uses a DIMM (dual in-line memory module), and notebooks use the SODIMM (small outline dual in-line memory module) configuration (see Figure 4.16). There are several types of RAM available today. Older computers used SDRAM (synchronous dynamic random access memory), or DDR (double data rate) and DDR2 SDRAM. Newer computers use DDR3. Each type of memory is faster and more efficient than its predecessor.

RAM is fairly easy to install, and adding more memory to a computer is an inexpensive way to increase its performance. Installing additional RAM in an older computer can significantly extend its useful life.

**FIGURE 4.16** A desktop DIMM is about twice the physical size of a notebook SODIMM.

**CACHE MEMORY** Most computers have a small amount of very fast memory that's used to store frequently accessed information close to the processor. This type of memory is called **cache memory**. Because it's located so close to the processor, it speeds up the time it takes to access the data and improves the processor performance. Level 1 (L1) cache is actually built into the processor, and Level 2 (L2) cache is on a separate chip and takes slightly longer to access. Modern processors may actually have L2 cache built in and have a Level 3 (L3) cache on the motherboard. Each progressive level of cache is farther from the CPU and takes longer to access.

Although it's commonly referred to as the CPU, the system unit is so much more. The system unit is the case that holds the components inside your system, including the CPU and the motherboard. The motherboard provides the ports and connectors for devices to attach to the system. Together, they allow you to build a system that's powerful and versatile in a relatively small package.

## Running Project

Use the Internet to research RAM. What's the fastest RAM available today for desktop computers? What about notebooks? Look at computer ads on some current retail websites. What is the average amount of RAM in desktop computers? In notebooks? What type of RAM is found in the most expensive systems?

## 5 Things You Need to Know

- The motherboard is the main circuit board in a computer.
- A motherboard provides the way for devices to attach to a computer.
- Information flows between the components of a computer over data buses.
- The BIOS is a program stored on a chip on the motherboard that's used to start up the computer.
- RAM is volatile memory that holds the operating systems, programs, and data the computer is currently using.

## Key Terms

AGP (accelerated graphics port)

BIOS (basic input output system)

Bluetooth

cache memory

CMOS (complementary metal oxide semiconductor)

data bus

drive controller

EIDE (enhanced integrated drive electronics)

expansion card

FireWire

hot-swappable

IEEE 1394

memory

motherboard

PCI (peripheral component interconnect)

PCI express (PCIe)

port

PS/2 port

RAM (random access memory)

ROM (read-only memory)

SATA (serial ATA)

serial and parallel ports

system unit

USB (Universal Serial Bus)

USB hub

# A Place for Everything

OBJECTIVE
## Compare different types of storage devices.

There are two ways to think about the storage of data: how it's physically stored on disks and how we organize the files we store. In this article, we'll look at physical storage devices.

## OPTICAL DISCS

**Optical discs** are a form of removable storage and include CDs, DVDs, and Blu-ray discs. The spelling *d-i-s-c* refers to optical discs, and *d-i-s-k* refers to magnetic disks. Data is stored on these discs using a laser to either melt the disc material or change the color of embedded dye. A laser can read the variations as binary data (see Figure 4.17).

**FIGURE 4.17** The data on an optical disc is read by a laser.

Optical disc drives are mounted in the system unit in external drive bays, which enables you to access them to insert or eject discs. They can also be peripheral devices connected by USB or FireWire. Optical discs can take several forms: read-only (ROM), recordable (+R/–R), or rewritable (+RW/–RW). The type of disc you should purchase depends on the type of drive you have. This is usually labeled on the front of the drive, as seen in Figure 4.18.

**FIGURE 4.18** The type of disc supported is labeled on the front of the disc drive.

**CD** A **CD (compact disc)** is the oldest type of optical disc in use today and has a storage capacity of about 700 MB. CDs are still used to distribute software and music and to store photos and data, but they have, for the most part, been replaced by larger capacity DVDs to distribute movies and some software.

**DVD** A **digital video disc** or **digital versatile disc**, more commonly known as a **DVD**, has the same dimensions as a CD but stores more than six times as much data. Single-layer (SL) DVDs can hold about 4.7 GB of information. Double-layer (DL) DVDs have a second layer to store data and can hold about 8.5 GB.

**BLU-RAY** A **Blu-ray disc** (BD) is an optical disc with about five times the capacity of a DVD, which it was designed to replace. The single-layer disc capacity is 25 GB, and double-layer disc capacity is 50 GB. Today, Blu-ray is mainly used for high-definition video and data storage. BD-R discs are recordable, and BD-RE discs can be erased and re-recorded multiple times. Figure 4.19 provides a comparison of the storage capacities of the various optical media.

**FIGURE 4.19** Comparison of the Capacities of Optical Disc Formats

| OPTICAL DISC | CAPACITY | NUMBER OF 3.5 MB PHOTOS | VIDEO | HIGH-DEFINITION VIDEO |
|---|---|---|---|---|
| CD-ROM | 700 MB | 200 | 35 minutes | — |
| DVD single layer | 4.7 GB | 1,343 | 2 hours | — |
| DVD dual layer | 8.5 GB | 2,429 | 4 hours | — |
| Blu-ray single layer | 25 GB | 7,143 | — | 4.5 hours |
| Blu-ray dual layer | 50 GB | 14,286 | — | 9 hours |

# SOLID-STATE STORAGE

Unlike optical (and magnetic) storage, **solid-state storage** is nonmechanical. The data is stored using **flash memory** on a chip. Because there are no moving parts, **solid-state drives (SSD)** are quiet and durable. SSDs are often used in small electronic devices, such as media players, as well as in notebooks and netbooks. Solid-state drives can use the same controllers as hard drives and can be either internal or external. Because SSDs are significantly more expensive than similar capacity hard drives, they are used primarily where speed and durability are necessary.

**FLASH DRIVES** Sometimes called *key drives*, *thumb drives*, *pen drives*, or *jump drives*, **flash drives** are small, portable, solid-state drives that can hold up to 128 GB of information. They have become the standard for transporting data. Flash drives connect to a computer by a USB port and come in a variety of shapes and sizes, including pens, watches, toys, and Swiss Army knives (see Figure 4.20). Flash drives are also used as the internal storage in tablets and mobile devices.

**FIGURE 4.20** Zip Zip's Memory Bricks connect together when not in use as a flash drive. You can also get a Swiss Flash USB knife with an integrated flash drive.

**MEMORY CARDS** You can expand the storage of digital cameras, video games, and other devices with **memory cards**. The type of memory card you use is dependent upon the device. The most common formats include Secure Digital (SD), CompactFlash (CF), Memory Stick (MS), and xD-Picture Card (xD). Figure 4.21 provides a comparison of these formats.

Card readers are used to transfer data, such as photos and music, between a card and a computer or printer. Personal computers and photo printers may have built-in card readers, but you can use USB card readers on computers that don't have them (see Figure 4.22).

**FIGURE 4.21** Comparison of Flash Memory Card Formats

| TYPE OF MEMORY CARD | CAPACITY | DETAILS |
|---|---|---|
| Secure Digital (SD)/SDHC (SD High Capacity)/ SDXC (Extended Capacity) | The most common format, SD cards come in capacities up to 4 GB. SDHC cards can be from 4–32 GB in size. SDXC cards range from 32 GB up to 2 TB, although current models are 64–128 GB. | Micro and mini SD cards are small cards and are typically used in cell phones. |
| CompactFlash (CF) | CompactFlash has capacities of up to 100 GB and is used by many high-end digital cameras, from Nikon, Canon, Sony, and Olympus. | CF+ is a magnetic form of CompactFlash used in microdrives (tiny, 1-inch hard drives). |
| Memory Stick (MS) | Memory sticks are more expensive and have a smaller capacity (currently up to 32 GB) than other formats. | Memory sticks are a proprietary format developed by Sony for use with their digital cameras. |
| xD-Picture Card (xD) | Picture cards have capacities up to 2 GB. | xD cards are a proprietary format of Olympus and Fujifilm that's used by most Olympus digital cameras. |

**FIGURE 4.22** A photo printer with a built-in card reader and a USB card reader with slots for several different memory card formats are tools to transfer files from device to device.

# HARD DRIVES

**Hard drives** are the main mass-storage devices in a computer. They are sometimes called "hard disks" or "hard disk drives." Hard drives are a form of nonvolatile storage; when the computer is powered off, the data isn't lost. The primary hard drive holds the operating system, programs, and data files. Hard drives are measured in hundreds of gigabytes and even terabytes and can hold hundreds of thousands of files.

Hard drives can be either internal or external. Internal drives are located inside the system unit in an internal drive bay and are not accessible from the outside. External drives may be attached as a peripheral device using a USB or FireWire connection. The advantages of external drives are that they can be installed without opening the system unit and can be easily moved to another computer.

Hard drives store data magnetically on metal platters. The platters are stacked, and read/write heads move across the surface of the platters, reading data and writing it to memory (see Figure 4.23). The drives spin at up to 15,000 revolutions per minute, allowing for very fast data transfer.

Removable drives that connect to your computer via USB, such as flash drives or external hard drives, need special steps to be disconnected from a Windows computer. It is important to be sure that Windows has finished writing to the drive before unplugging it. In the notification area of the taskbar, there is an application to *Safely Remove Hardware and Eject Media*. Clicking this icon gives you a list of connected devices, and you can choose which one to remove or eject (see Figure 4.24). Once Windows has finished with the device, you will get a message that tells you when it is safe to remove the device.

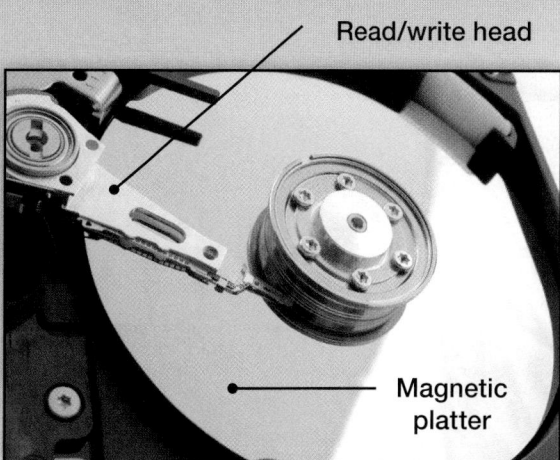

**Read/write head**

**Magnetic platter**

**FIGURE 4.23** The read/write head is visible above the disk surface in this view of the inside of a hard drive.

The capacity of storage has grown dramatically over the past few years, as the operating systems and software we use have gotten more sophisticated and the files we save have become larger and more numerous. A decade ago, a floppy disk could hold 1.4 MB of information—roughly 750 pages of text. Today, the 1 TB hard drive in your personal computer can store about 500,000,000 pages of text, 180 hours of high-definition video, or more than 280,000 high-quality photos. That is a lot of photo albums!

**FIGURE 4.24** Safely Removing a Flash Drive from a Windows Computer

## Running Project

Look at computer ads on some current retail websites. What is the average size of a hard drive in desktop computers? In notebooks? Netbooks? What type of optical disc drive is found in most desktops? Notebooks? Netbooks? What type and capacity of storage is found in most tablets? Think about your needs. What type(s) of storage do you need and how much? Can you easily add more storage later?

## 3 Things You Need to Know

- Lasers read the data on optical discs (CDs, DVDs, Blu-rays).
- Hard drives store data magnetically on metal platters.
- Solid-state storage stores data on a chip.

## Key Terms

Blu-ray disc (BD)

CD (compact disc)

DVD (digital video disc; digital versatile disc)

flash drive

flash memory

hard drive

memory card

optical disc

solid-state drive (SSD)

solid-state storage

# What Goes In...

## 4 OBJECTIVE
## List different input devices and their uses.

An **input device** is a device that's used to get data into the computer system so it can be processed. There are many types of input devices, but the most common are keyboards and mice. Input devices allow us to interact with technology in many different ways, from playing a guitar in a video game to typing out an email to checking for the best price on an item using our cell phones. In this article, we'll look at some of the many input devices you can use.

Try the
Hardware
Simulation

SIMULATION

## KEYBOARDS

The first thing that comes to mind when we discuss input devices is the **keyboard**. As basic as that seems, there are many different types of keyboards available. The most common type of keyboard is the standard QWERTY format, so called because Q-W-E-R-T-Y are the first alphabetic keys on the keyboard. The QWERTY design was originally developed by Christopher Sholes in 1874 to reduce the number of key jams, which can occur when keys that are next to each other on the keyboard are pressed quickly and interfere with each other on a mechanical typewriter. While it may reduce the interference, it's an inefficient typing layout that's no longer needed because

computer keyboards aren't mechanical. We have become so accustomed to the QWERTY layout that many cell phones now feature a QWERTY keyboard for faster texting (see Figure 4.25).

In addition to the alphabet and number keys, most standard keyboards have specialized keys (see Figure 4.26). Some keys, such as Esc and the Function keys, have specific actions associated with them. Other keys, such as Ctrl, Alt, and Shift, are modifiers and are pressed in conjunction with other keys. Toggle keys, such as Caps Lock and Num Lock, turn a feature on or off when pressed. Full-sized keyboards contain 101 or 104 keys, but notebook computer keyboards are smaller and may not include a separate numeric keypad.

**FIGURE 4.25** QWERTY keyboards are found on handheld devices such as this smartphone.

| KEY | TYPE | ACTION |
| --- | --- | --- |
| Esc | | Cancel |
| Caps Lock | Toggle | Turns capitalization on/off |
| Shift | Modifier—pressed with at least one other key | Activates uppercase or alternate-key assignment |
| Ctrl (Windows)/Command (Mac) | Modifier—pressed with at least one other key | Modifies the behavior of a key press |
| Alt (Windows)/Option (Mac) | Modifier—pressed with at least one other key | Modifies the behavior of a key press |
| Windows logo | | Opens the Start menu |

**FIGURE 4.26** Special Keys on a Keyboard

# Find Out MORE

There are many standard keystroke combinations that can be used to perform common tasks. For example: Ctrl/Command+X cuts a selected item, Ctrl/Command+C copies a selected item, and Ctrl/Command+V pastes the copied or cut item. Research useful keystroke shortcuts that can be used with your favorite program and present them in a table. Which program did you research? Where did you find your information? Are there any keystroke shortcuts you already use? Is there a way to create your own keystroke shortcuts in this program? If so, what additional tasks would you create them for?

Keyboards can also have alternate layouts or be customized for a particular application. The Dvorak Simplified Keyboard was designed to put the most commonly used letters where they're more easily accessed to increase efficiency and reduce fatigue (see Figure 4.27). Most modern operating systems include support for the Dvorak layout, but it's not been widely adopted.

Ergonomic keyboards are full-sized keyboards that have a curved shape and are designed to position the wrists in a more natural position to reduce strain (see Figure 4.28). They may look funny, but many people that spend a lot of time on the computer rely on them to prevent injuries.

Another alternative keyboard is a **keypad**, a small keyboard that doesn't contain all the alphabet keys. This type of input device is typically found in Point-of-Sale (POS) terminals (see Figure 4.29). People who enter a lot of numbers, such as teachers, accountants, and telemarketers, might find it useful to attach a USB keypad to a notebook computer. Many computer gamers find a dedicated game keypad makes game play easier and more fun.

## QWERTY Keyboard

## DVORAK Keyboard

**FIGURE 4.27** The QWERTY Keyboard Layout (top) and the Dvorak Keyboard Layout (bottom)

# CAREER SPOTLIGHT

Computer sales is a good career choice for a person who has good communication skills and technical skills. Salespeople must be able to help customers find the right computer based on their needs and explain the features of a system in laypeople's terms. Many companies offer employee on-the-job training in this field, but a background in computers, including the A+ certification, is helpful.

If you like helping people, have strong communication skills, and are good with computers, a computer technician position might be a good career for you. Companies, such as Geek Squad, send technicians out to homes and businesses to troubleshoot and repair computer systems. This is hands-on work that may involve travel and working nights and weekends. A+ certification is usually the minimum requirement at the entry-level positions in this field. Much of the training in this field takes place on the job.

Even if you're not looking for a technical career, understanding how computer hardware works and being able to make decisions about the hardware purchases you might make will help you be a better consumer and enable you to succeed in many different careers. For example, an office worker might need to make decisions about the type of printer to buy or a teacher might need help choosing the type of projector to install in a classroom. There are very few careers today that don't involve the use of some computer technology.

**FIGURE 4.28** The curved shape of an ergonomic keyboard reduces wrist strain.

**FIGURE 4.29** Keypads typically contain numbers and are used in such applications as Point-of-Sale (POS) terminals and as peripherals for personal computers. The model above is designed like a telephone keypad to speed up dialing phone numbers.

# THE MOUSE AND OTHER POINTING DEVICES

Pointing devices, such as mice and touchpads (see Figure 4.30), are input devices that allow a user to interact with objects by moving a pointer, also called a cursor, on the computer screen. Many different versions of each of these devices are available. They allow us to point and click instead of typing in text commands.

**MOUSE** A **mouse** may include one or more buttons and a scroll wheel and works by moving across a smooth surface to signal movement of the pointer. Older mechanical mice had a ball that rolled across the surface. The ball tended to get dirty, which caused the mouse to become difficult to use. Modern optical mice detect motion by bouncing light from a red LED (light-emitting diode) off the surface below it. Because they have fewer moving parts, optical mice are less prone to failure than mechanical mice.

**TOUCHPAD** Most notebook computers include a built-in **touchpad** instead of a mouse. With this device, motion is detected by moving your finger across the touch-sensitive surface. Touchpads also have buttons that function like mouse buttons and special areas that enable you to quickly scroll through documents, Web pages, and images.

**TOUCH INPUT** Tablets, graphic design tablets (see Figure 4.31), cell phones, handheld game consoles and other devices have **touchscreens** that can accept input from a finger or stylus. A **stylus** is a special pen-like input tool. Touchscreens that are resistive sense pressure and can be used with a finger or an ordinary stylus. A resistive screen could be used by someone wearing gloves. A capacitive screen senses the conductive properties of an object such as your finger or a specially designed conductive stylus. Interactive whiteboards are large interactive displays used in classrooms and businesses. They have touch-sensitive surfaces and allow the user to control the computer from the screen as well as capture what's written on the screen with special pens.

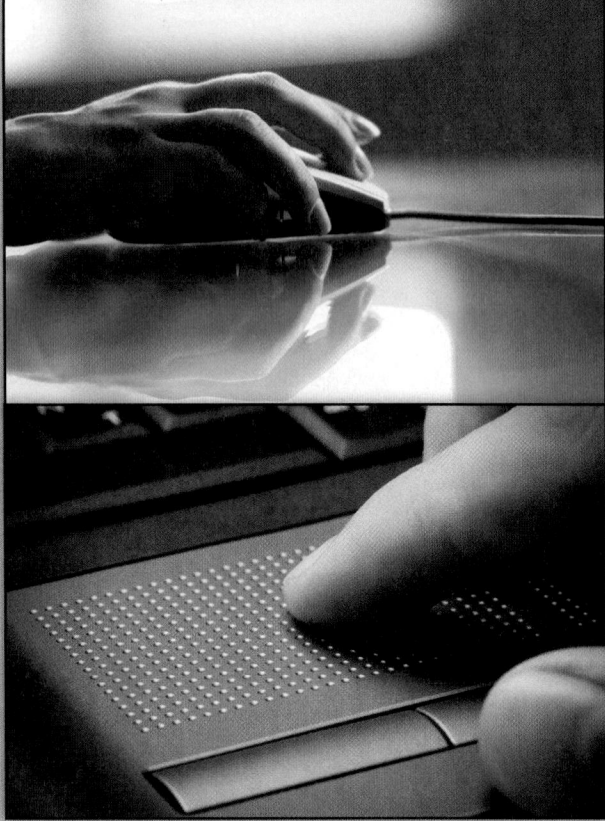

**FIGURE 4.30** A mouse and touchpad are common pointing devices found on personal computers.

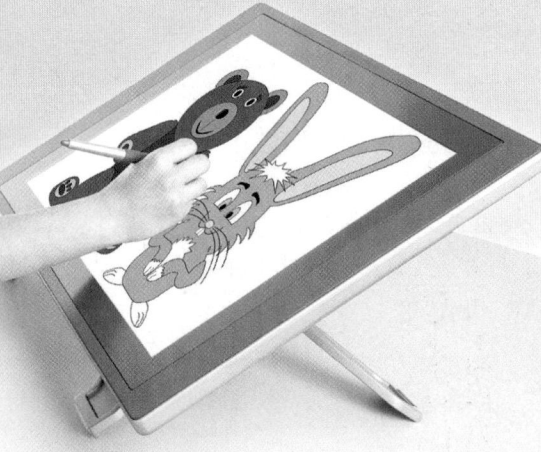

**FIGURE 4.31** A graphic design tablet with a stylus is a specialized input device used in graphic arts, CAD (computer-aided design), and other applications.

# DIGITAL CAMERAS AND WEBCAMS

Digital cameras can capture still images or video. The cameras can be built in or directly connected to a computer by USB or FireWire cable or the files can be transferred to the computer via a removable flash card. **Webcams** are specialized video cameras that provide visual input for online communication, such as Web conferencing or chatting, as seen in Figure 4.32.

**FIGURE 4.32** A boy and his grandfather talk over the Internet using the webcam built into this monitor.

# SCANNERS

Scanners have many uses, from archiving old documents to checking out customers in grocery stores to organizing libraries to assisting law enforcement. The use of **scanners** increases the speed and accuracy of data entry and converts information into a digital format that can be saved, copied, and manipulated.

**OPTICAL SCANNERS** You can convert a photo or document into a digital file with an optical scanner. Flatbed scanners are the most common type of optical scanner used in homes and offices. You simply place the document or photo you wish to scan on a glass screen, and the scanner head moves underneath the glass to convert the image to a digital file. Business card readers and photo scanners typically have a sheet-feed format that moves the page to be scanned and keeps the scanner head stationary. Handheld scanners such as bar code readers are small and portable (see Figure 4.33). You see these in supermarket checkout lines, library circulation desks, and shipping operations.

QR (Quick Response) **code readers** and bar code readers on cell phones have turned shopping in stores into an interactive activity. Many retail stores include a QR code on the merchandise tag that the shopper can scan to learn more about the item (see Figure 4.34). Using bar code scanners, shoppers can scan an item in a mall and quickly determine the store or website with the lowest price. Website analytics can track Web pages accessed from QR codes, providing useful information to the retailer about its shoppers.

**FIGURE 4.33** A bar code reader quickly scans the label on this carton, saving time and reducing data entry errors.

**FIGURE 4.34** A QR code on store merchandise allows a shopper to get more details about the item.

**RFID SCANNERS AND MAGNETIC STRIP READERS** An RFID scanner can read the information in an **RFID tag**, which contains a tiny antenna for receiving and sending a radio-frequency signal. RFID (radio frequency identification) is used in inventory tracking, electronic toll collection, and contactless credit card transactions, such as Exxon Mobil Speedpass and MasterCard PayPass. It's also the technology used in passports. There have been some security and privacy concerns over the United States' decision to use RFID passports.

Another type of scanner that's used frequently is a magnetic strip reader. Such scanners can read information encoded in the magnetic strip on plastic cards, such as drivers' licenses, gift cards, library cards, credit cards, and even hotel door keys (see Figure 4.35).

**BIOMETRIC SCANNERS** Used in banks to identify patrons, in theme parks to assure that tickets aren't transferred to other guests, and in corporate security systems, **biometric scanners** measure human characteristics such as fingerprints and eye retinas. Some notebook computers even use a fingerprint scanner to ensure that the person trying to access the computer is an authorized user (see Figure 4.36).

**MICROPHONES AND GAME CONTROLLERS** Other common input devices include microphones, game controllers, and joysticks. **Microphones** convert sound into digital signals and are used simply to chat in real time or as part of voice-recognition applications used in video games and for dictating text. They are often integrated into notebook computers and headsets or can be connected via USB or to the microphone port on a sound card.

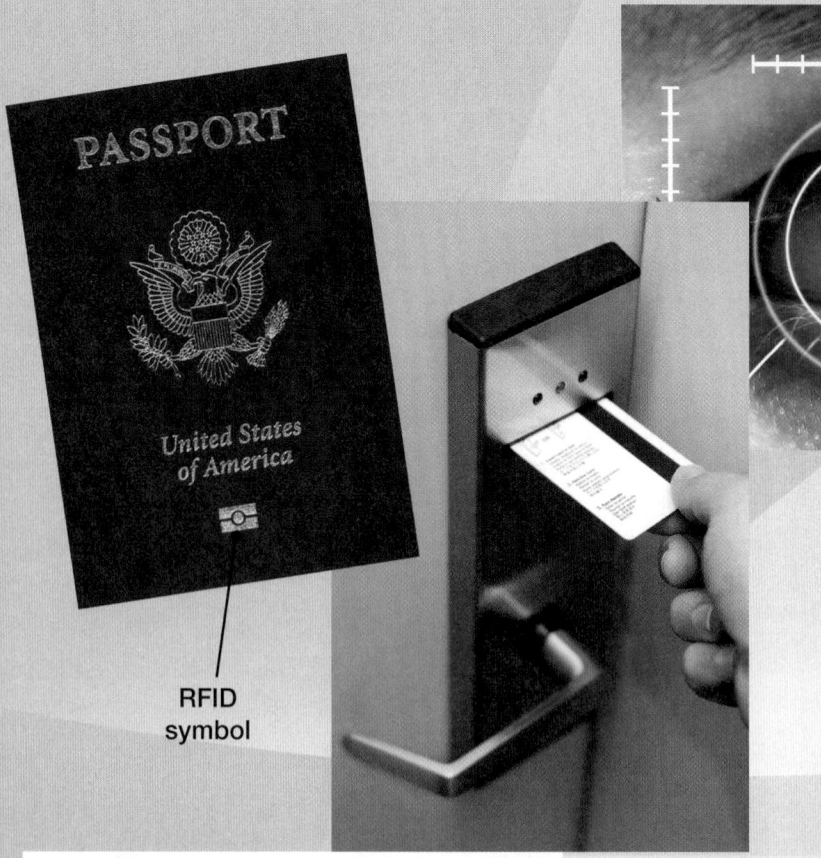

RFID symbol

**FIGURE 4.36** A fingerprint scanner built into a notebook computer can be used for added security.

**FIGURE 4.35** An RFID chip is embedded in this U.S. passport. On the right, a magnetic strip reader reads the information on the magnetic strip on the back of the card to open an electronic door lock.

**Game controllers** provide a way to interact with video games. Special game controllers include steering wheels, tennis rackets, guns, musical instruments, and pressure-sensitive mats. These controllers make the gameplay more realistic (see Figure 4.37). A **joystick**, which is mounted on a base, consists of a stick, buttons, and sometimes a trigger. Typically used as a game controller, especially in flight-simulator games, a joystick also may be used for such tasks as controlling robotic machinery in a factory.

**FIGURE 4.37** Game controllers can be shaped like different objects to make gameplay more realistic—and more fun.

## Running Project

A mouse or touchpad and keyboard are standard input devices. Think about how you might use your computer in the future. What other input devices might you need? Pick at least one additional input device, and research current models and costs. Which model would you choose and why?

## 4 Things You Need to Know

- The mouse and keyboard are the most common input devices.
- Digital cameras and webcams input images and video.
- Scanners convert information into a digital format.
- Microphones are audio input devices.

Input devices come in all shapes and sizes and allow you to interact with computer systems in many different ways. The type of input device you use depends on many factors, including the type of data to be input, the type of computer the input device is connected to, and the application you're using. Whether you're narrating a PowerPoint presentation, drawing a picture, or writing an email, input devices are how you get the data into the computer system so it can be processed.

## Key Terms

biometric scanner

game controller

input device

joystick

keyboard

keypad

microphone

mouse

QR code reader

RFID tag

scanner

stylus

touchpad

touchscreen

webcam

# ...Must Come Out

## List different video and audio output devices and their uses.

Information is returned to the user through **output devices**. The most common output devices provide video or paper document output. Other devices provide audio output or other types of hard copy, such as X-rays and maps. This article focuses on video and audio output. Printers are discussed in the next article.

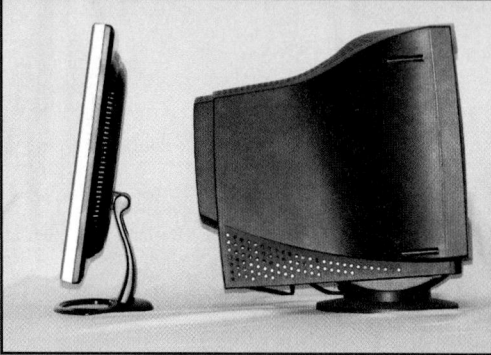

**FIGURE 4.38** An LCD monitor is much thinner than a CRT monitor of the same screen size.

## VIDEO OUTPUT DEVICES

What you see on your computer screen is video output. There are a variety of video output devices that provide visual output to the user. The most popular types of monitors and projectors come in many different sizes, technologies, and price ranges.

**MONITORS** Similar to television screens, **monitors** work by lighting up **pixels** (short for picture elements) on the screen. Each pixel contains three colors: red, green, and blue (RGB). From that base, all colors can be created by varying the intensities of the three colors. Display **resolution** indicates the number of horizontal pixels by vertical pixels, for example 1280×1024 or 1920×1080. The higher the resolution, the sharper the image is. The size of a monitor is measured diagonally across the screen.

Older **CRT monitors** and televisions use a cathode ray tube to excite phosphor particles coating the glass TV screen to light up the pixels. CRT monitors are big and use a lot of energy. As a result, they've been replaced by

smaller and more energy-efficient flat-panel monitors (see Figure 4.38). CRT monitors are considered **legacy technology**, which is old technology that's still used alongside its more modern replacement, typically because it still works and is cost-effective.

Most modern desktop and notebook computers have flat-panel monitors, which create bright, crisp images without using traditional picture tubes. Instead, such displays use LCD or plasma panels.

**LCD (liquid crystal display)** panels are found on most desktop and notebook computers. They consist of two layers of glass that are glued together with a layer of liquid crystals between them. When electricity is passed through the individual crystals, it causes them to pass or block light to create an image. LCDs do not give off any light, so they need to be backlit by a light source, typically CCFLs (cold cathode fluorescent lamps). Some LCD monitors are backlit by LEDs. The LED versions are generally thinner and more energy efficient, but they're also more expensive.

Available in larger screen sizes that you wouldn't use with a desktop computer, plasma screen monitors are typically included in media center systems or are used in conference rooms. **Plasma monitors** work by passing an electric current through gas sealed in thousands of cells inside the screen. The current excites the gas, which in turn excites the phosphors that coat the screen to pass light through an image.

Choosing between an LCD and plasma screen monitor depends on many factors, including size and cost. Figure 4.39 provides a comparison of the advantages and disadvantages of LCD and plasma flat-panel monitors.

The newest technology in monitors is **OLED (organic light-emitting diode)**. These monitors are composed of extremely thin panels of organic molecules sandwiched between two electrodes. The prototypes of these monitors are less than 1 inch thick and are even bendable. OLEDs use very little energy and are expected to be at least 10 times more energy efficient than today's LCDs, but OLED monitors are just beginning to become available and cost many times more than LCD or plasmas. OLED has a way to go before prices drop enough to make them practical for most consumers. AMOLED (active matrix OLED) screens can be found in some mobile devices. AMOLED screens are sharper and have a wider viewing angle than LCDs. They are ideal for watching video and sports.

**FIGURE 4.39** The Advantages and Disadvantages of Flat-Panel Monitor Formats

| DISPLAY TYPE/SIZE | ADVANTAGES | DISADVANTAGES |
|---|---|---|
| LCD Size: 13" to 65" and larger | • Panels weigh less than plasma<br>• Use less energy than CRTs or plasmas<br>• Better in bright-light situations | • Picture is slightly less natural than top plasmas<br>• More expensive than comparable plasmas<br>• Screens larger than 52" are very expensive |
| Plasma Size: 32" to 61" | • The screen's phosphor coating creates lifelike color and truer blacks that are closest to conventional tube TVs. | • Not available in sizes smaller than 32"<br>• Heavy and fragile, plasmas are difficult to install |

# PROJECTORS

When making a presentation or sharing media with a group in such places as classrooms, businesses, and home theaters, **projectors** are more practical than monitors because they produce larger output. They can be classified as video projectors, which are typically used in home media centers to display movies on a wall or screen, and data projectors, which are designed for presentations in a business or classroom setting. The two main types of projectors used today are DLP and LCD projectors.

**DLP (digital light-processing) projectors** have hundreds of thousands of tiny swiveling mirrors that are used to create an image. They produce high-contrast images with deep blacks but are limited by having weaker reds and yellows. The most portable projectors on the market today are DLP projectors, which weigh less than 3 pounds. DLPs also are very popular home theater projectors because of the higher contrast and deeper blacks that they produce.

**LCD projectors** pass light through a prism, which divides the light into three beams—red, green, and blue—which are then passed through an LCD screen. These projectors display richer colors but produce poorer contrast and washed-out blacks. LCDs tend to have sharper images than DLPs and are better in bright rooms, making them ideal for presentations in conferences and classrooms.

Each technology has distinct advantages and disadvantages. The choice between them depends on many factors, including the primary use, the room the projector is in, whether it needs to be portable, and cost. Figure 4.40 compares some features of DLP and LCD projectors.

**VIDEO CARDS** The data signal and connection for a monitor or projector are provided by the **video card**, also called a "graphic accelerator" or "display adapter." Modern video cards contain their own memory (VRAM or video RAM) and processor (GPU or graphics processing unit) in order to produce the best and fastest images. A DVI (digital visual interface) port is the standard video port found on video cards, although some cards also have an HDMI port, S-Video port, and a VGA port. The DVI port provides a digital connection for flat-panel displays, data projectors, TVs, and DVD players. HDMI is a digital port that can transmit both audio and video signals. It is the standard connection for high-definition TVs, video game consoles, and other media devices. S-Video (super video) is an analog port used to connect a computer to a television, while a VGA (video graphics array) port is a legacy analog port used by CRT monitors and projectors (see Figure 4.41). A video card may also include input ports to connect a TV tuner or another video device to the system.

**AUDIO OUTPUT DEVICES** Audio output can be anything from your favorite song to sound effects in a video game to an email alert chime. The sound can be heard through speakers or headphones.

**SPEAKERS** Speakers convert digital signals from a computer or media player into sound. They may be integrated into notebook computers and monitors or connected via USB or to the speaker ports on a sound card. Typical desktop speaker systems include two or three speakers, but speaker systems designed for gaming or home theater uses include as many as eight speakers and can cost hundreds of dollars.

**FIGURE 4.40** A Comparison of DLP and LCD Projectors

| PROJECTOR TYPE | ADVANTAGES | DISADVANTAGES |
|---|---|---|
| DLP projectors | • Smoother video<br>• Smaller and lighter<br>• Truer blacks<br>• Higher contrast | • Some noise created by moving parts<br>• Weaker reds and yellows<br>• Need more lumens than LCD |
| LCD projectors | • Richer color for better results in bright rooms<br>• More energy efficient<br>• Gives off less heat<br>• Quieter | • More visible pixels<br>• Larger and heavier<br>• Poorer contrast<br>• Washed-out blacks |

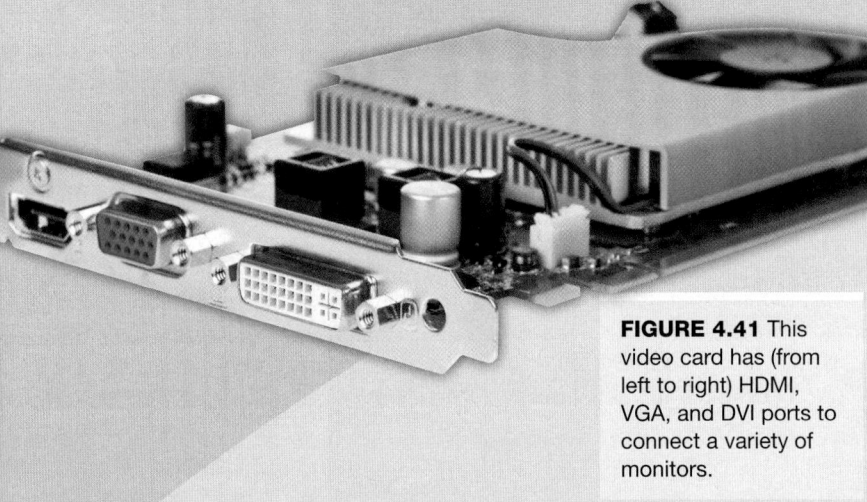

**FIGURE 4.41** This video card has (from left to right) HDMI, VGA, and DVI ports to connect a variety of monitors.

**HEADPHONES** Like speakers, **headphones** convert digital signals into sound. They come in several different sizes and styles, ranging from tiny earbuds that fit inside your ear to full-size headphones that completely cover your outer ear. High-quality headphones can cost hundreds of dollars and incorporate up to eight speakers in the design. Noise-cancelling headphones reduce the effect of ambient noise and are especially useful in noisy environments, such as in airplanes. Headphones can plug into the headphone or speaker port of a computer, the headphone port on a speaker, or USB ports and can connect wirelessly via Bluetooth. Headphones that also include a microphone are called "headsets."

**SOUND CARDS** A **sound card** provides audio connections for both input devices (microphones and synthesizers) and output devices (speakers and headphones), as shown in Figure 4.42. Sound cards can be integrated into the motherboard (onboard) or connected through expansion cards or external USB or FireWire ports. High-end sound cards support surround sound, have connections for up to eight speakers, and include a digital optical port for connecting to a home entertainment system.

Computer output comes in two basic forms: tangible and intangible. In this article, we looked at intangible outputs: video and audio. The output devices in this section allow us to listen to Beethoven or Lady Gaga and to view a Picasso painting or watch some idiot fall off his skateboard on YouTube. Video and audio output has changed computers from simply being calculators of data to being an integral part of our education and entertainment experiences.

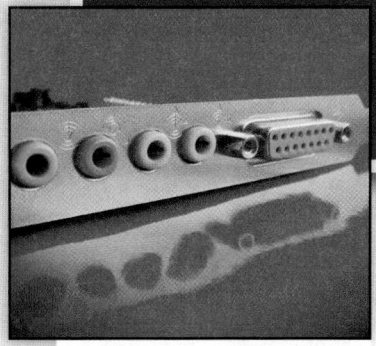

**FIGURE 4.42** A basic sound card is illustrated with color-coded connections: line-in (blue), microphone (pink), speakers or headphone (green), MIDI (Musical Instrument Digital Interface; gold).

## Running Project

If you were going to purchase a new desktop computer today, one decision you would have to make is what type and size of monitor to get. Think about the room you would put the system in and what you might use it for. Would you be watching movies on the screen? Is the room really bright? Does the screen need to be large enough for several people to view at once? Using the answers to these questions, determine the type and size of monitor you would need. Use the Internet to compare several models, and select the one that best fits your needs.

## 6 Things You Need to Know

- Most personal and notebook computers have LCD monitors.
- Large plasma monitors are found in media centers and conference rooms.
- Resolution is the number of horizontal pixels by the number of vertical pixels on a screen.
- The two types of video projectors are DLP and LCD.
- Video cards connect monitors and projectors to your computer.
- Speakers and headphones are audio output devices that connect to a sound card.

## Key Terms

CRT monitor

DLP (digital light-processing projector)

headphones

LCD (liquid crystal display)

LCD projector

legacy technology

monitor

OLED (organic light-emitting diode)

output device

pixel

plasma monitor

projector

resolution

sound card

speakers

video card

# Pick a Printer

## 6 OBJECTIVE
## Compare the features of different types of printers.

Hard copies (printouts) of documents and photos are produced by printers. There are many different types of printers that generate everything from photos to blueprints to ID cards. In this article, we'll look at some of the most common types of printers used in homes and businesses.

## INKJET PRINTERS

The most common personal printers are **inkjet printers**. They work by spraying droplets of ink onto paper. Some printers use one ink cartridge; others may use two, three, four, or even more. The standard ink colors are cyan, magenta, yellow, and key (black), abbreviated as **CMYK**. Printers mix these colors to form every color (see Figure 4.43). Inkjets are inexpensive to purchase, but the cost of ink can quickly add up. When purchasing a printer, you should factor in the cost of ink, which is responsible for a large portion of the cost per page.

**FIGURE 4.43** CMYK (cyan, magenta, yellow, key [black]) are the colors used by inkjet and dye-sublimation printers.

## PHOTO PRINTERS

A **photo printer** is designed to print high-quality photos on special photo paper. Photo printers can be inkjet printers that use special ink cartridges or dye-sublimation printers, which produce lab-quality prints.

Some photo printers connect directly to a PictBridge-enabled digital camera or read data from a memory card. **PictBridge** is an industry standard that allows a camera to connect directly to a printer, usually by a USB connection or special dock, as seen in Figure 4.44. Many newer cameras and cell phones connect to printers through WiFi or Bluetooth.

**FIGURE 4.44** You can print directly from a PictBridge-enabled camera or cell phone connected by a USB cable to a compatible printer.

**FIGURE 4.45** A thermal printer uses special thermal paper to print receipts that you might get at a gas pump.

# DYE-SUBLIMATION PRINTERS

**Dye-sublimation printers** (or dye-sub printers) use heat to turn solid dye into a gas that's then transferred to special paper. The dye comes on a three- or four-color ribbon that prints a single color at a time. After all colors have been printed, the print is then coated with a clear protective layer to produce a high-quality photo that lasts longer than those printed on an inkjet printer. Dye-subs aren't general-purpose printers. They're limited to printing photos and some specialty items, such as ID badges and medical scans.

# THERMAL PRINTERS

The receipts you receive from gas pumps, ATMs, and many cash registers are printed by **thermal printers**. They create an image by heating specially coated heat-sensitive paper, which changes color where the heat is applied. These receipts will fade over time. If you'll need the receipt later, you should scan it for long-term access. Thermal printers can print in one or two colors and can also be used to print bar codes, postage, and labels (see Figure 4.45).

# LASER PRINTERS

The most common type of printers found in schools and businesses are **laser printers**. Laser printers produce the sharpest text at a much lower cost per page than inkjet printers. Although they initially cost more that inkjets, the lower cost per page makes them less expensive for high-volume printing. Laser printers use a laser beam to draw an image on a drum. The image is electrostatically charged and attracts a dry ink called toner (see Figure 4.46). The drum is then rolled over paper, and the toner is deposited on the paper. Finally, the paper is heated and pressure is applied, bonding the ink to it.

# MULTIFUNCTION DEVICES

Also known as "all-in-one printers," **multifunction devices** have built-in scanners and sometimes have fax capabilities. They can also be used as copy machines and eliminate the need for several different devices, saving both space and money. The disadvantage to using an all-in-one device is that if it needs to be repaired, all of its functions are unavailable.

# PLOTTERS AND 3D PRINTERS

To produce very large printouts, such as blueprints, posters, and maps, **plotters** use one or more pens to draw an image on a roll of paper. Large inkjet and laser printers have mostly replaced pen plotters (see Figure 4.47). 3D printers can create objects such as prototypes and models. A digital image is created by scanning an object or designed using computer software. The 3D printer creates the model by building layers of material such as paper, polymers, resin, or even metal. 3D printing has many interesting uses such as dental and medical imaging, paleontology, architecture, and even creating sculpture and jewelry.

**FIGURE 4.46** Static electricity causes this balloon to attract this little guy's hair, much like toner is attracted to the drum in a laser printer.

**FIGURE 4.47** A plotter can create much larger printouts than a typical desktop printer can.

Printers produce tangible output. The type of printer you choose depends on many things, including the type and size of output you need, cost, and size. Businesses might have several different types of printers on hand to meet all their needs. For a home user, a multifunction device might be the best choice. As the technology grows and the costs decrease, home users have the ability to have high-quality prints at home.

## Running Project

What type of printer will you need? Think about the types of documents you'll print. Will you need to print mostly text? Do you print a lot of photos? Do you want to be able to connect your camera or memory card directly to the printer? Do you want to be able to scan and fax? Will your printouts get wet? Do they need to last a long time? Using the answers to these questions, decide which type of printer is right for you. Use the Internet to compare several models, and select the one that best fits your needs.

## 4 Things You Need to Know

- The most common personal printer is an inkjet.
- The most common office printer is a laser.
- Dye-subs, thermal printers, and plotters are specialized printers.
- PictBridge is a standard that lets you connect a digital camera directly to a printer.

## Key Terms

CMYK

dye-sublimation printer

inkjet printer

laser printer

multifunction device

photo printer

PictBridge

plotter

thermal printer

# HOW TO

## Manage Printing on Your Computer

There are many different types of printers that you may use. Windows and Mac OS X allow you to set up multiple printers on your computer so you can choose the appropriate printer for the task. So, for example, you can print photos to an inkjet printer but send a research paper to a laser printer.

In this exercise, you will look at the printers that you have access to through your computer and determine which one is set up as your default printer.

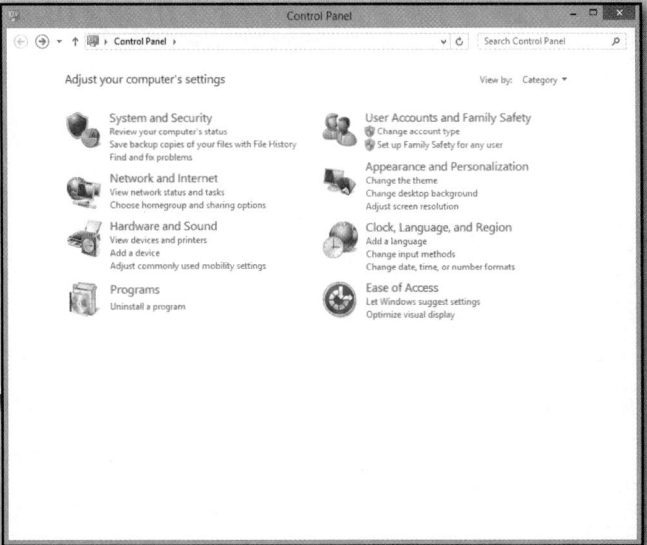

**1** Open your word processor and type your name and date in the document. Save the file as **lastname_firstname_ch04_howto1**. From the Windows Start screen, type **control**. From the search results, click *Control Panel*. Under Hardware and Sound click *View devices* and *printers*.

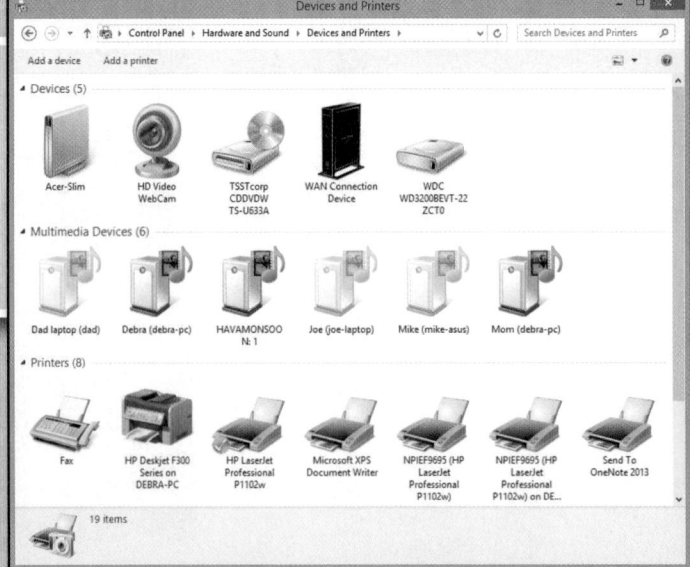

**2** How many objects are listed under Devices? What type of devices do you have? If you are not sure what the device is, click once to select it and then look in the status bar at the bottom of the window. Take a screen shot of the Devices and Printers window and paste it into your document.

**3** How many printers and fax devices are listed? Which one is set as your default device (hint: look for the green check)? Right-click on the default printer and look at the menu choices.

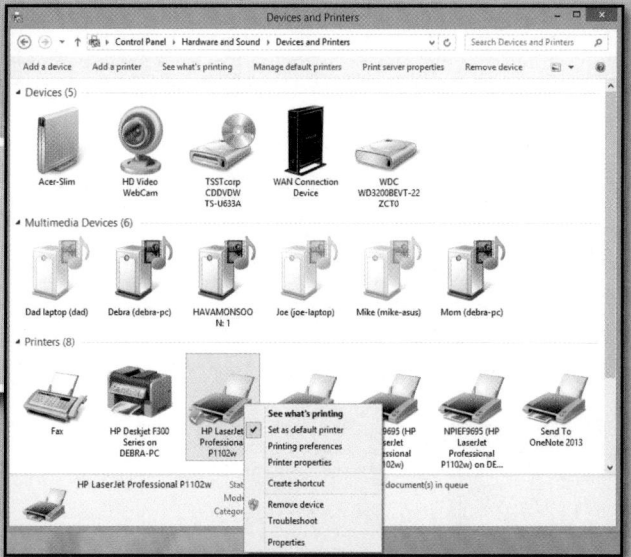

**4** Click *Printing preferences*. Your screen will vary depending upon the printer manufacturer. Look around and note the settings that you can modify. Take a screen shot of the Printing preferences window. Is this a physical printer or does it print to a document or file?

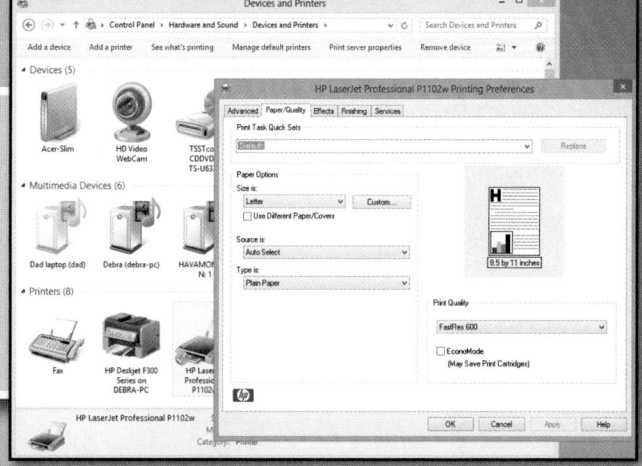

**5** Close the Printing preferences window to return to the Devices and Printers window. Choose a different printer to set as your default printer. Right-click on the new printer and click *Set as default printer*.

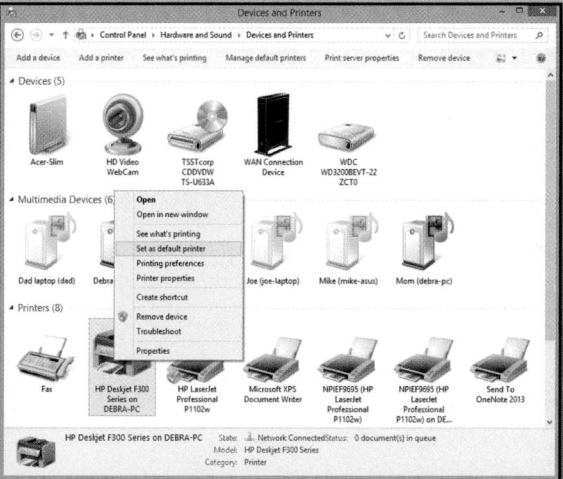

**6** Take a screen shot showing the new default printer.

**7** Use Windows Help and Support to search for default printer. Click *Change your default printer* in the results. What is the purpose of a default printer? Close the Help window.

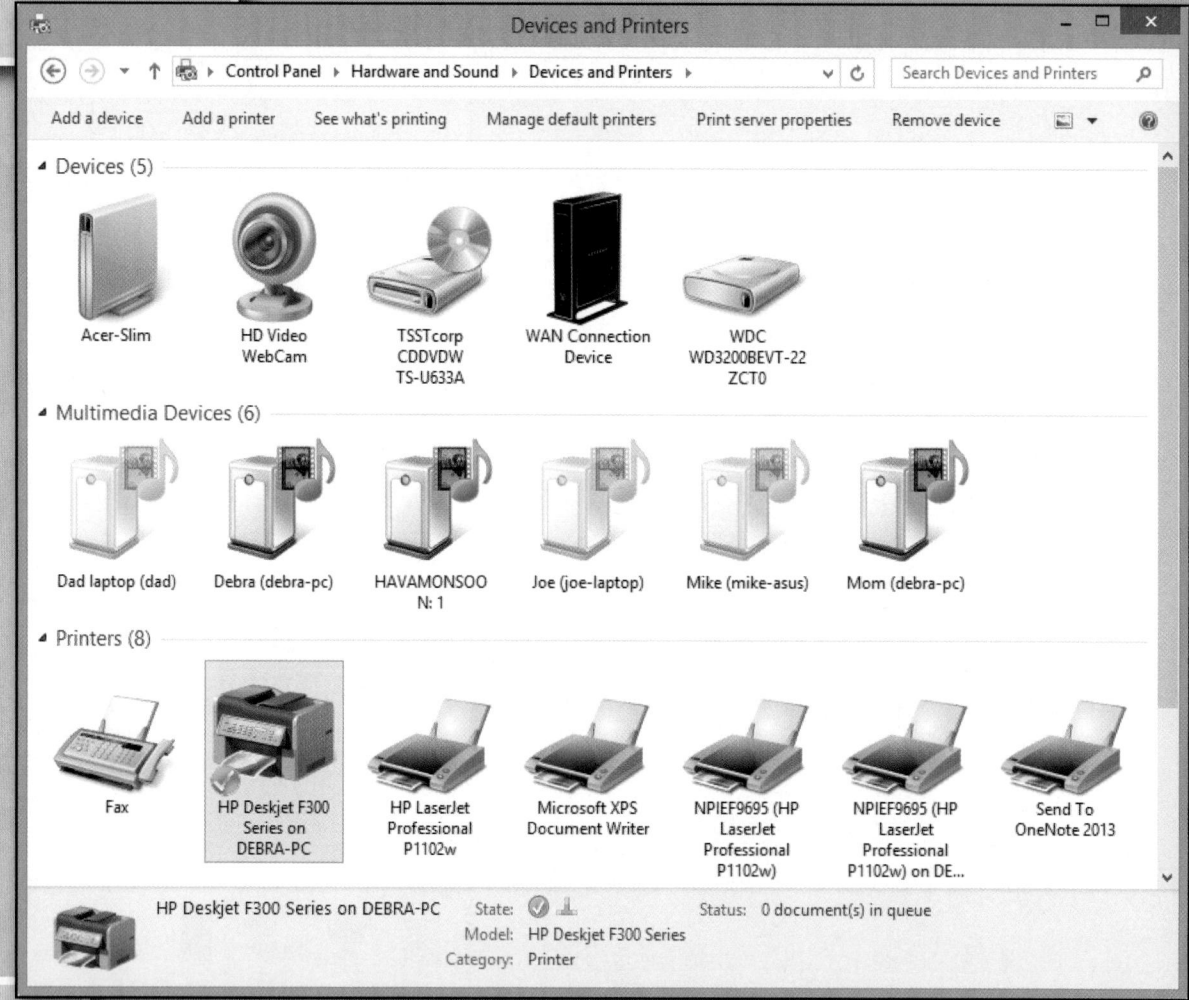

**8** Change your default printer back to the original printer.

**If you have a Mac:**

For step 2, open System Preferences from the dock or Apple menu and use the items in the Hardware row.

For step 3–5, open Print & Scan. For step 7 use the Internet to find the answer.

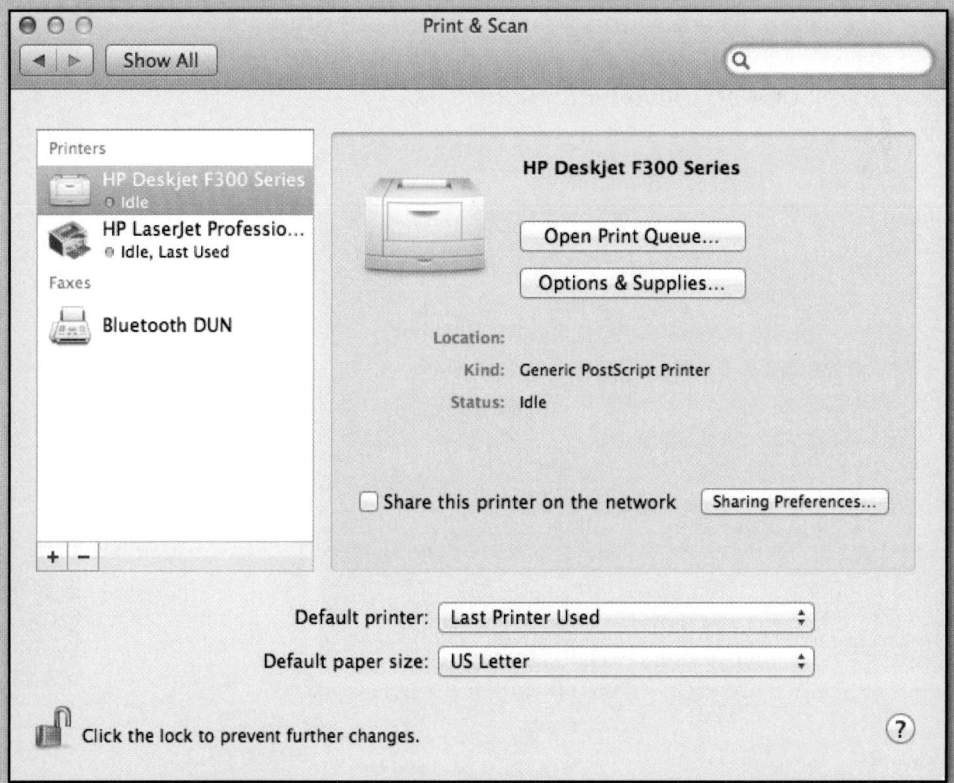

# Adaptation: Making Technology Work for You

## Explain and provide examples of the concept of adaptive technology.

The Americans with Disabilities Act of 1990 (ADA) requires employers with 15 or more employees "to make a reasonable accommodation to the known disability of a qualified applicant or employee if it would not impose an 'undue hardship' on the operation of the employer's business. Reasonable accommodations are adjustments or modifications provided by an employer to enable people with disabilities to enjoy equal employment opportunities." As a result of the ADA, many hardware and software vendors have developed adaptive technology.

**Adaptive technology**, also called "assistive technology," is used by individuals with disabilities to interact with technology (see Figure 4.48). It includes both hardware and software, and in many cases, everyday input and output devices can be adapted to the user. For example, a computer monitor screen image can be enlarged for a visually impaired user, and a hearing impaired user might have lights flash when an audio signal would normally be heard. Modern operating systems include accessibility settings that you can easily change.

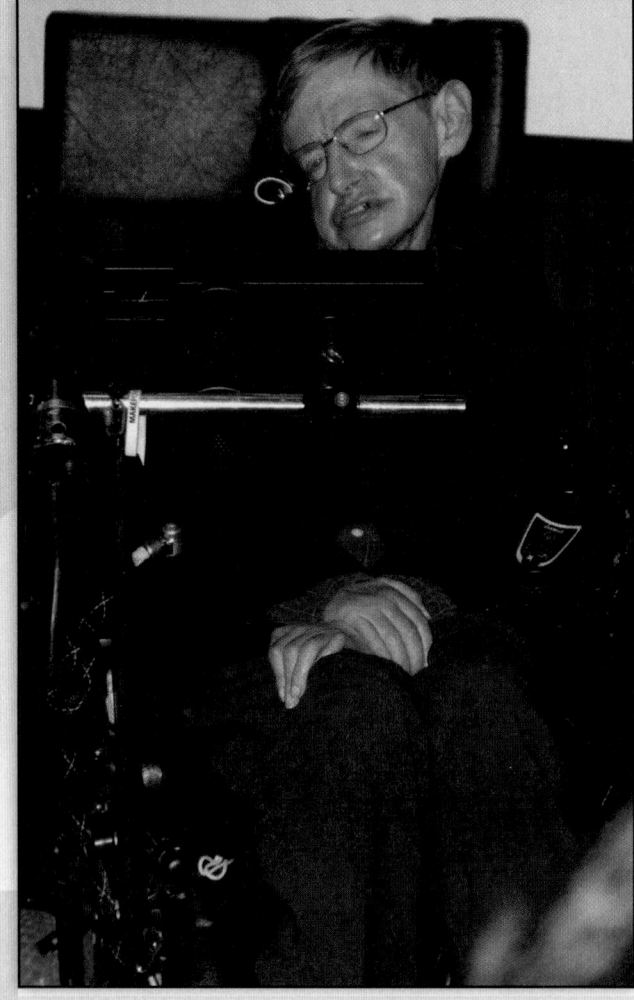

**FIGURE 4.48** Many talented professionals, including physicist Stephen Hawking, use adaptive technology.

# ADAPTIVE INPUT DEVICES

Alternate input devices include Braille-writing devices, eye-driven keyboards, and keyboards that have locator dots on commonly used keys or large-print key labels. On-screen keyboards can be typed on using a pointing device or a touchscreen. Such devices are being used in many public locations, such as libraries, schools, and polling places (see Figure 4.49). Trackballs, head wands, mouth sticks, and joysticks are all alternatives to the standard mouse.

Voice-recognition software allows a user to verbally control a computer and dictate text. Dragon NaturallySpeaking and MacSpeech Dictate are two of the most popular voice-recognition programs, and Windows and OS X include built-in speech recognition. Software settings, such as Sticky Keys and Mouse Keys on a Windows computer, adapt a standard keyboard for users with limited fine-motor control and allow the user to use arrow keys on the keyboard to move the pointer. OS X includes similar accessibility features that can be used to control the computer.

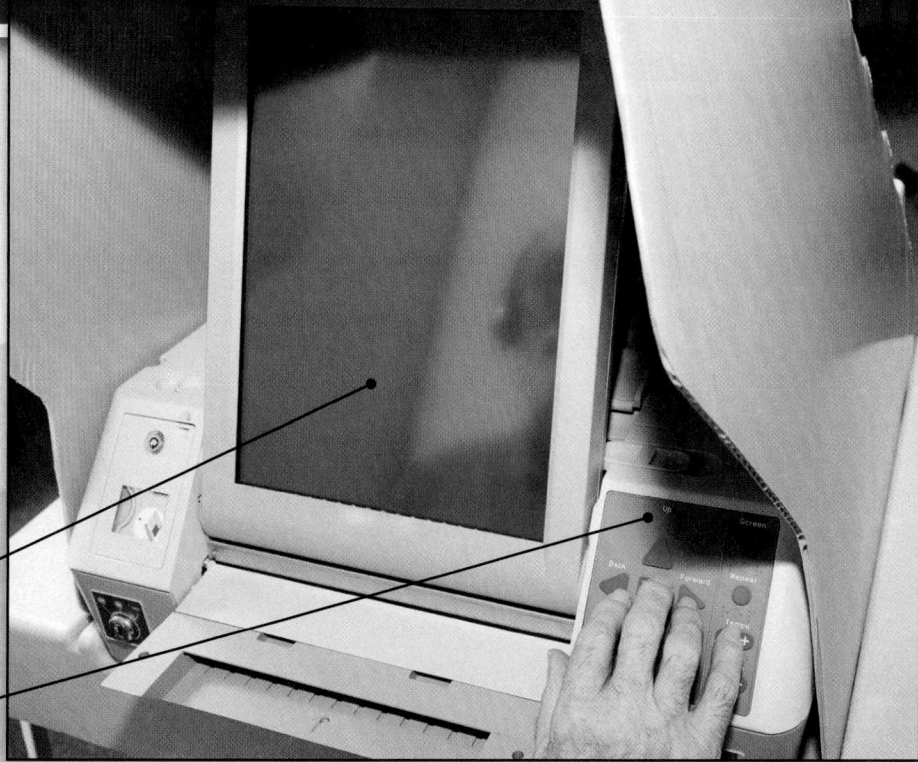

Touchscreen

Braille Keyboard

**FIGURE 4.49** Introduced in 2008, this touch-screen voting machine is wheelchair-accessible and equipped for visual, auditory, and other disabilities.

# ADAPTIVE OUTPUT DEVICES

Standard monitors can be adapted by magnifying the screen (see Figure 4.50) and adjusting color and contrast settings. Speech synthesis screen-reader software and audio alerts aid visually and learning disabled users, while closed captions and visual notifications, such as flashing lights, aid those with auditory disabilities. Braille embossers are special printers that translate text to Braille. They're impact printers that create dots in special heavy paper that can be read by touch by visually impaired users.

While adaptive technology can make technology more accessible for individuals with disabilities, it also benefits those without disabilities. Enlarging the screen, touch-sensitive surfaces, easy-to-read buttons, and other accommodations make accessing technology easier for everybody. Businesses benefit by gaining the skills and talents of disabled employees.

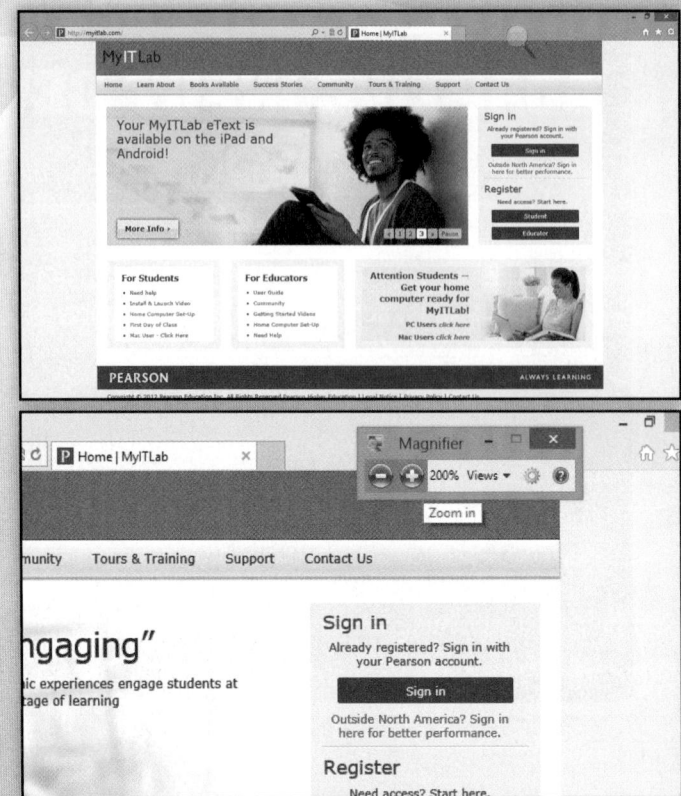

**FIGURE 4.50** Windows includes Magnifier, a screen magnification program that can be used to enlarge portions of the screen, as it has in this web page.

# GREEN COMPUTING

## SHOP SMART

The efficient and eco-friendly use of computers and other electronics is called green computing. Green computing is good for the environment, but it also saves money, making it a win-win proposition.

Choose Energy Star–rated devices. Energy Star (**www.energystar.gov**) is a rating system that's awarded to devices that use an average of 20–30% less energy than comparable devices. Saving energy saves money and reduces greenhouse gas emissions that contribute to global warming.

The Green Electronics Council has a program called EPEAT (Electronic Product Environmental Assessment Tool; **www.epeat.net**) that can help you choose systems with environmentally friendly designs. The assessment is based on industry standards and ranks the devices as bronze, silver, or gold depending on the number of environmental performance criteria they meet.

## ETHICS

The Americans with Disabilities Act (see **www.ada.gov**) requires businesses with 15 or more employees to provide reasonable accommodation for all employees who have—or who have a record of having—a disability. A disability is any condition that limits one or more major life activities. Are there questionable conditions that fall into that category? As an employer, how would you address such a condition?

Should small businesses be required to provide adaptive technology to all employees, regardless of cost? Should they have to provide the technology the employee wants? Or can they choose other methods of addressing the issue of concern? What if the disability becomes so great that it causes the business financial hardship? Is the business then legally required to provide accommodation? What is the moral responsibility?

## Running Project

Are there any adaptive technology devices that you would include to meet the needs of any of the users of this computer?

## 3 Things You Need to Know

- Adaptive technology helps individuals with disabilities to interact with technology.
- The Americans with Disabilities Act (ADA) requires employers to make reasonable accommodations for disabled employees.
- Adaptive technology includes both hardware and software.

## Key Term

adaptive technology

# Communicate, Communicate, Communicate

## 8 OBJECTIVE
## Discuss the different communication devices that can be used.

**Communication devices** serve as both input and output devices and allow you to connect to other devices on a network or to the Internet. These include network adapters, modems, and fax devices.

**FIGURE 4.51** A wireless adapter connects this notebook to a hot spot at an airport (top). A blue Ethernet cable can plug into the onboard network adapter on this notebook computer (bottom).

## NETWORK ADAPTERS

Used to establish a connection with a network, **network adapters** may be onboard expansion cards or USB devices and may be wired or wireless. Wired cards are sometimes referred to as Ethernet cards and have a port that resembles a telephone jack, while wireless cards are used to connect to WiFi networks at home and in hot spots in airports and cafes, as shown in Figure 4.51.

## MODEMS

**Modems** are used to connect a computer to a telephone line and are most often used for dial-up Internet access. Modem is short for *modulator-demodulator*. A modem modulates digital data into an analog signal that can be transmitted over a phone line and, on the receiving end, demodulates the analog signal back into a digital data.

We use the terms "analog" and "digital" devices throughout this book. The difference is in the way the data is encoded and transmitted (see Figure 4.52). Analog input devices convert data signals into continuous electronic waves or pulses, while analog output devices, such as telephones, televisions, and CRT monitors, translate the electronic pulses back into audio and video signals. In digital devices, the audio or video data is represented by a series of 0s and 1s. Digital signals can carry more data and are less prone to interference than analog signals.

Some modems also include the capability to send and receive faxes. With fax software and a fax modem, a computer can be used as a fax machine. A cable modem is a special type of modem that connects to the cable system instead of a telephone line to provide fast Internet access. DSL (digital subscriber line) modems, which are used to provide broadband services, aren't really modems at all because the DSL line is already digital and there's no need to modulate the signal to analog.

# Find Out MORE

In 2009, broadcast television was converted to digital TV (DTV). Older televisions now require a DTV converter box to convert the digital TV signal into an analog signal the TV can display. Why was the switch made? Was is strictly an economic decision or does it benefit society in some ways? What are the advantages of DTV over analog TV? Try checking **www.dtv.gov** for answers.

## FAX DEVICES

A fax device can be a stand-alone fax machine, part of a multifunction device, or built into a modem. A fax device (or facsimile) works by scanning a document and converting it into a digital format that can then be transmitted over telephone lines to a receiving fax device, which then outputs the document.

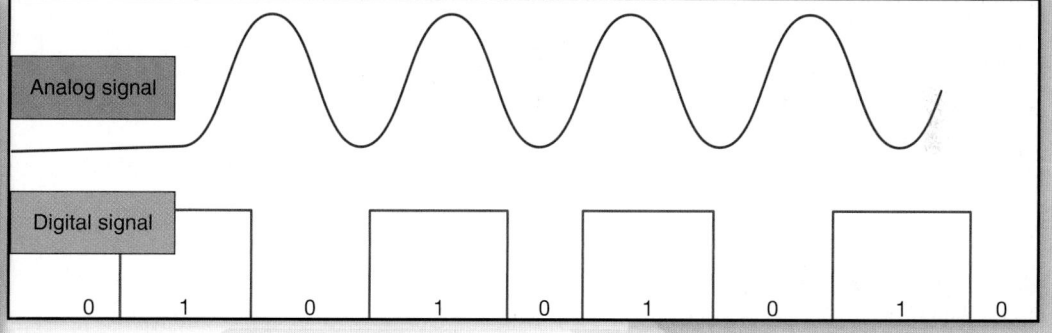

**FIGURE 4.52** An analog signal is a continuous wave, while a digital signal is an on/off transmission.

Communication devices allow us to connect our computers to other devices in our own homes and to the world, enabling us to access resources that just a few short years ago were unimaginable.

## Running Project

Think about the location for this computer. What type of communications devices do you need to connect this system to the Internet? Will it connect to a network? Is it wired or wireless? Do you need fax capabilities?

## Key Terms

communication device

modem

network adapter

## 3 Things You Need to Know

● Network adapters connect a computer to a network.
● A modem is used for dial-up Internet access.
● Digital signals carry more data and are less prone to interference than analog signals.

# HOW TO

## Assess Your Computer Hardware

Computer performance is affected by many things. In this tutorial, you'll learn a little bit about your own computer and how you might improve its performance by upgrading hardware components.

The Windows operating system can provide many details about your computer's hardware through a variety of built-in utilities. For this exercise, you'll use the System Control Panel and Computer window.

**1** Open your word processor and type your name and date in the document. Save the file as **lastname_firstname_ch04_howto2**

**2** From the Windows desktop, open the File Explorer. In the Navigation pane right-click *Computer* and choose *Properties*.

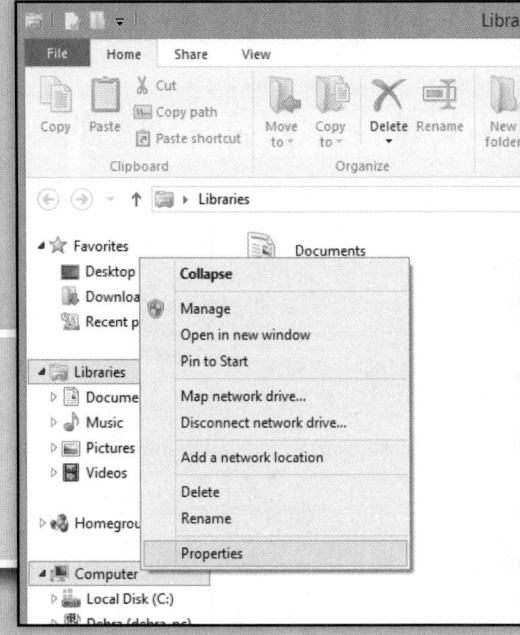

**3** In the middle of the screen, under System, is the information about your processor and memory. What type of processor do you have? Is it multi-core? What is its clock speed? How much RAM do you have?

**4** Click the *Windows Experience Index*. (Note: If you are using a notebook computer, you can't run this when you are on battery power.) What are the scores for your processor and memory? What is your lowest subscore? What can you do to improve your system's score?

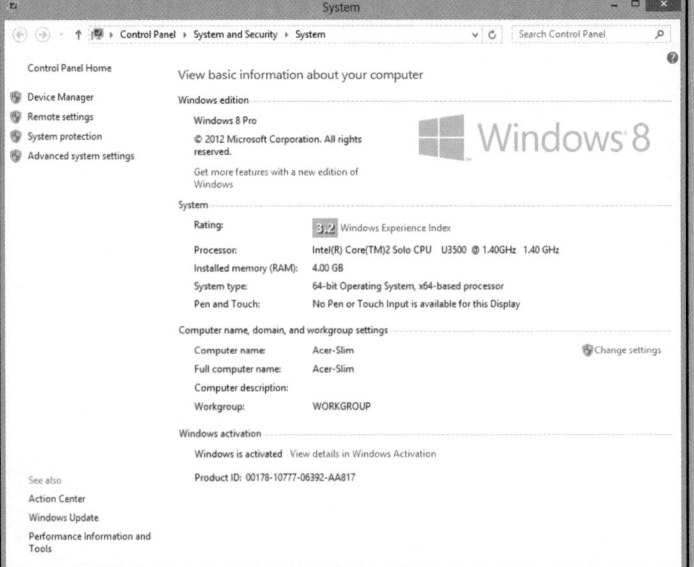

**5** Close the Control Panel and return to the Explorer window. Click *Computer*. List all hard disk drives and devices with removable storage that are displayed. Include any additional information, such as size and free space, for each.

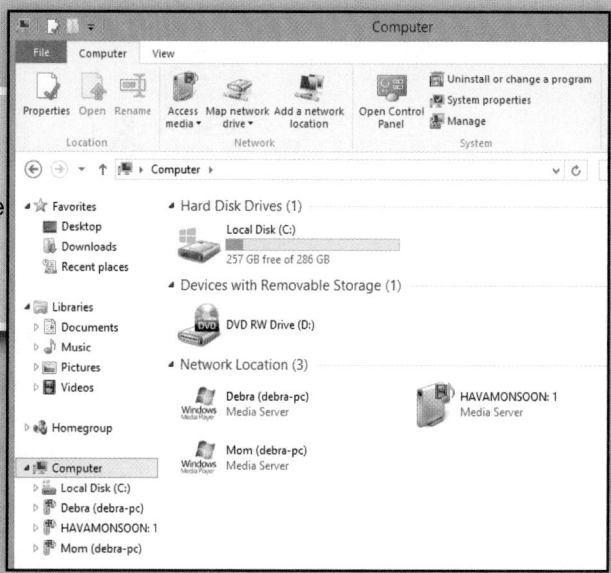

**6** Type up your answers, save the file, and submit it as directed by your instructor.

### If you are using a Mac:

For steps 2–5: Click the *Apple Menu* and then click *About This Mac*. This screen gives you basic information. Click the *More Info* button to open the System Profiler for more details.

For step 6: Exit the System Profiler. At the desktop, click *Help*. Search for "mouse." How can you change the way your mouse works? Use Help to search for keyboard shortcuts. How can you change modifier keys?

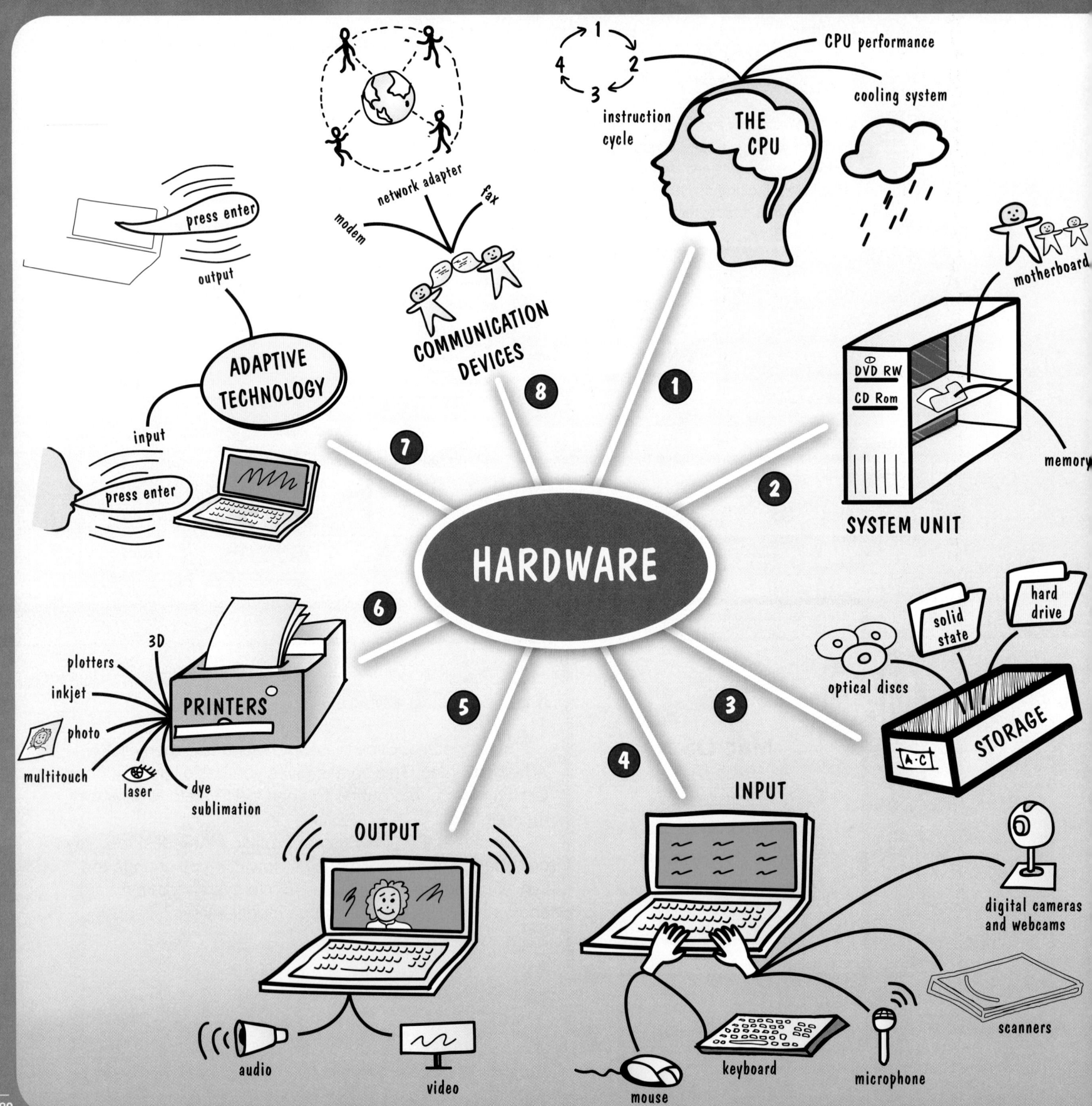

## Objectives Recap

1. Explain the function of the CPU.
2. Identify the parts of a system unit and motherboard.
3. Compare different types of storage devices.
4. List different input devices and their uses.
5. List different video and audio output devices and their uses.
6. Compare the features of different types of printers.
7. Explain and provide examples of the concept of adaptive technology.
8. Discuss the different communication devices that can be used.

## Key Terms

adaptive technology **172**
AGP (accelerated graphics port) **143**
arithmetic logic unit (ALU) **138**
biometric scanner **158**
BIOS (basic input output system) **145**
Bluetooth **145**
Blu-ray disc (BD) **149**
cache memory **147**
CD (compact disc) **149**
clock speed **139**
CMOS (complementary metal oxide semiconductor) **145**
CMYK **164**
communication device **176**
control unit **138**
CPU (central processing unit) **138**
CRT monitor **160**
data bus **143**
DLP (digital light-processing) projector **161**
DVD (digital video disc; digital versatile disc) **149**

drive controller **143**
dye-sublimation printer **165**
EIDE (enhanced integrated drive electronics) **143**
expansion card **143**
FireWire **145**
flash drive **149**
flash memory **149**
game controller **159**
gigahertz (GHz) **139**
hard drive **150**
hardware **137**
headphones **162**
hot-swappable **144**
IEEE 1394 **145**
inkjet printer **164**
input device **152**
instruction cycle **138**
joystick **159**
keyboard **152**
keypad **154**
laser printer **166**
LCD (liquid crystal display) **160**
LCD projector **161**
legacy technology **160**
memory **146**

memory card **150**
microphone **158**
modem **176**
monitor **160**
motherboard **142**
mouse **156**
multi-core processor **140**
multifunction device **166**
network adapter **176**
OLED (organic light-emitting diode) **161**
optical disc **148**
output device **160**
parallel processing **139**
PCI (peripheral component interconnect) **143**
PCI express (PCIe) **143**
peripheral device **137**
photo printer **164**
PictBridge **164**
pipelining **139**
pixel **160**
plasma monitor **161**
plotter **166**
port **144**
processor **138**

projector **161**
PS/2 port **144**
QR code reader **157**
RAM (random access memory) **146**
resolution **160**
RFID tag **158**
ROM (read-only memory) **145**
SATA (serial ATA) **143**
scanner **157**
serial and parallel ports **144**
solid-state drive (SSD) **149**
solid-state storage **149**
sound card **163**
speakers **162**
stylus **156**
system unit **142**
thermal printer **165**
touchpad **156**
touchscreen **156**
USB (Universal Serial Bus) **144**
USB hub **144**
video card **162**
webcam **157**

# Summary

1. **Explain the function of the CPU.**

   The CPU is the brain of the computer and consists of the control unit and arithmetic logic unit. It processes data through the instruction cycle: fetch, decode, execute, and store. Features such as parallel processing and multi-core processing increase the CPU's ability to process multiple instructions at the same time, increasing its speed.

2. **Identify the parts of a system unit and motherboard.**

   The system unit is the case that houses the power supply, motherboard, processor (CPU), heat sink and cooling fan, and memory of a computer. It also has drive bays to hold the storage devices and openings for peripheral devices to connect to expansion cards on the motherboard. The motherboard is the main circuit board of a computer. In addition to housing the CPU, it contains drive controllers and interfaces, expansion slots, data buses, ports and connectors, BIOS, and memory. A motherboard may also include integrated peripherals, such as video, sound, and network cards.

3. **Compare different types of storage devices.**

   Optical discs are removable and include CDs, DVDs, and Blu-ray discs. They range in capacity from 700 MB to 50 GB and are used to distribute music, programs, and movies as well as to archive data. Solid-state storage is a nonmechanical form of storage found in solid-state drives (SSDs), flash drives, memory cards, personal media players, and netbooks. Hard disks are a form of magnetic storage and can be mounted in the system unit or connected via USB or FireWire cable. They have the largest capacities of any current storage device and hold the operating systems, programs, and data on the computer.

4. **List different input devices and their uses.**

   Input devices include keyboards and keypads for entering text; pointing devices, such as the mouse, touchpad, stylus, and touch-sensitive screens that move the cursor on the screen; cameras and webcams for video input; optical scanners, RFID scanners, magnetic strip readers, and biometric scanners that read data and convert it into digital form; microphones that convert sound into digital signals; and video game controllers and joysticks to interact with games and other software programs.

5. **List different video and audio output devices and their uses.**

   The most common output devices are monitors (LCD and plasma) and projectors (LCD and DLP) attached to video cards that produce video output; printers that produce hard copies; and speakers and headphones attached to sound cards that produce audio output.

6. **Compare the features of different types of printers.**

   The most common personal printer is the inkjet, which works by spraying droplets of ink onto paper. Photo printers can be either inkjet or dye-sublimation printers and are specifically designed to produce high-quality photo prints. Dye-sublimation printers use heat to turn solid dye into a gas that's then transferred to special paper to primarily produce photos. Thermal printers use special heat-sensitive paper to produce receipts, postage, and bar code labels. Laser printers produce the sharpest text at a much lower cost per page than inkjet printers. A multifunction device combines a printer with a scanner and sometimes a fax machine. A plotter produces very large printouts, such as blueprints, posters, and maps.

7. **Explain and provide examples of the concept of adaptive technology.**

   Adaptive technology enables users with a variety of disabilities to access technology through special hardware and software. Input devices include head wands, mouth sticks, voice-recognition software, and on-screen keyboards. Output devices include Braille embossers (printers), screen readers, and enlarged screens.

8. **Discuss the different communication devices that can be used.**

   Communication devices serve as both input and output devices and include network adapters, modems, and fax devices. A network adapter connects a computer to a network. A modem connects a computer to a telephone line for dial-up Internet access. The cable and DSL modems are special modems that enable access to high-speed Internet. Fax devices, which can be stand-alone fax machines, part of a multifunction device, or built into a modem, scan and convert a document into a digital form that can be transmitted over telephone lines.

# Multiple Choice

Answer the multiple-choice questions below for more practice with key terms and concepts from this chapter.

1. The hardware components that serve the input, output, and storage functions of a computer are called
   a. control units.
   b. central processing units.
   c. peripheral devices.
   d. arithmetic logic units.

2. _____ plug directly into expansion slots on the motherboard and allow you to connect additional peripheral devices to a computer.
   a. Drive controller
   b. CPU
   c. CMOS
   d. Expansion cards

3. A single USB port can connect up to _____ devices.
   a. 4
   b. 26
   c. 127
   d. 256

4. Which type of memory is also referred to as primary storage?
   a. RAM
   b. Nonvolatile
   c. Cache
   d. CMOS

5. _____ are the main mass storage devices in a computer system.
   a. Flash drives
   b. Optical discs
   c. Hard drives
   d. ROM

6. Pointing devices, such as the mouse and _____, work by moving a cursor on the screen.
   a. scroll wheel
   b. touchpad
   c. ball
   d. LED

7. _____ scanners read human characteristics such as fingerprints and retinas.
   a. Optical
   b. RFID
   c. Magnetic
   d. Biometric

8. What type of monitor is considered legacy technology?
   a. CRT
   b. LCD
   c. Plasma
   d. DLP

9. What type of printer produces the highest quality photo prints?
   a. Inkjet
   b. Color laser
   c. Dye-sublimation
   d. Thermal

10. _____ are used to connect a computer to a telephone line for dial-up Internet access.
    a. Network adapters
    b. Modems
    c. Analog signals
    d. WiFi adapters

# Application Project

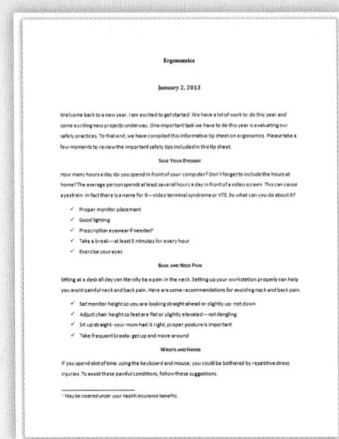

## Microsoft Office Application Project 1:
### Word Level 2

**PROJECT DESCRIPTION:** You have been asked to write an article on ergonomics using Microsoft Word. You will need modify formatting, find and replace text, and create and modify a footnote.

**INSTRUCTIONS:** For the purpose of grading the project you are required to perform the following tasks:

| Step | Instructions |
|------|--------------|
| **1** | Start Word. Download and open the Word file named *vt_ch04_word*. Save the file as **lastname_firstname_ch04_word**. |
| **2** | Change the left and right margins of the document to 1.0". Center the first two paragraphs (title and date). |
| **3** | Change the line spacing of the entire document to 1.5 lines and the paragraph spacing of the entire document to 6pt after. |
| **4** | Center the heading *Save Your Eyesight*. Using the Format Painter, apply the formatting from the heading *Save Your Eyesight* to the headings *Back and Neck Pain* and *Wrists and Hands*. |
| **5** | Use the Find and Replace dialog box to search for and replace all instances of the word *report* with **tip sheet**. There should be two replacements. |
| **6** | In the *Save Your Eyesight* section, format the list beginning *Proper monitor placement* and ending *Exercise your eyes* as a bulleted list using check mark bullets. |
| **7** | In the *Back and Neck Pain* section, format the list beginning *Set monitor height* and ending *Take frequent breaks* as a bulleted list using check mark bullets. |

| Step | Instructions |
|------|--------------|
| **8** | In the *Wrists and Hands* section, format the list beginning *Use an ergonomic keyboard and mouse* and ending *Rest elbows on chair arms* as a bulleted list using check mark bullets. |
| **9** | In the document header, add a page number using the Plain Number 2 style at the Top of Page. In the footer, add the FileName field using the default format. Ensure the header and footer are not displayed on the first page. |
| **10** | In the *Save Your Eyesight* section, in the bulleted list, insert a footnote immediately following the text *Prescription eyewear if needed*. Type: **May be covered under your health insurance benefits.** (include the period). |
| **11** | Use the Spelling and Grammar dialog box to correct the misspelling of the word *imporatn*. Ignore all other spelling and grammar suggestions. |
| **12** | Place the insertion point at the beginning of the last line of the document, before Sally. Insert the picture *ch04 _image1*. Change text wrapping to Square. Save and close the document. Exit Word. Submit the document as directed. |

Visit **pearsonhighered.com/Geoghan** for data files, simulations, VizClips, and additional study materials.

## Microsoft Office Application Project 2:
### PowerPoint Level 2

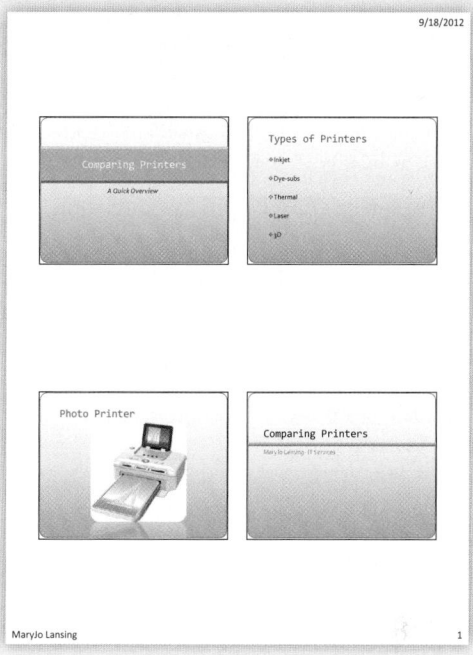

**PROJECT DESCRIPTION:** In this Microsoft PowerPoint project, you will create a presentation about printers. In creating this presentation you will apply design, font, and color themes. You will also change font colors, bullet symbols, and slide layout.

**INSTRUCTIONS:** For the purpose of grading of the project you are required to perform the following tasks:

| Step | Instructions | Step | Instructions |
|---|---|---|---|
| 1 | Start PowerPoint. Download and open the file named *ch04_ppt*. Save the file as **lastname_firstname_ch04_ppt**. | 9 | On Slide 1, copy the title text, Comparing Printers. On Slide 4, paste the copied text into the text placeholder using the Destination theme. |
| 2 | On Slide 1, type **A Quick Overview** in the subtitle placeholder. On Slide 2, type **Types of Printers** in the title placeholder. | 10 | On Slide 1, apply bold and italic formatting to the subtitle text, A Quick Overview. |
| 3 | Apply the Wisp theme to the presentation. | 11 | Change the layout of Slide 4 to Section Header. |
| 4 | Apply the blue Variant to the presentation. | 12 | On Slide 4, type **MaryJo Lansing—IT Services** in the subtitle placeholder. Change the font color of the title text, Comparing Printers, to Black, Text 1 (under Theme Colors). |
| 5 | On Slide 3, insert the downloaded *ch04_image2* in the content placeholder. | | |
| 6 | Apply the Reflected Rounded Rectangle picture style to the image. | 13 | Insert the page number and your name as the footer on the notes and handouts pages for all slides in the presentation. View the presentation in Slide Show view from beginning to end, and then return to Normal view. |
| 7 | On Slide 2, change the line spacing of the bullets to double. | | |
| 8 | On Slide 2, change the bullets to Star Bullets. Change the color of the bullets to Dark Blue, Accent 3, Darker 25% (under Theme Colors). | 14 | Save and close the presentation. Exit PowerPoint. Submit the presentation as directed. |

Visit **pearsonhighered.com/Geoghan** for data files, simulations, VizClips, and additional study materials.

Chapter 4 | 185

# True or False

Answer the following questions with T for true or F for false for more practice with key terms and concepts from this chapter.

1. The terms "CPU" and "system unit" mean the same thing.

2. Random access memory (RAM) loses the information stored in it when the power is turned off.

3. Blu-ray is a short-range, wireless technology used to connect peripheral devices to a computer.

4. Solid-state storage is mechanical.

5. CDs and DVDs store data magnetically.

6. QWERTY keyboards were designed to improve ergonomics.

7. LCD monitors are big, use a lot of energy, and are considered legacy technology.

8. Adaptive technology includes the hardware and software used by individuals with disabilities to interact with technology.

9. Network adapters may be onboard expansion cards or USB devices and may be wired or wireless.

10. Digital signals are superior to analog signals because they don't have to be converted for use by computers and other digital devices.

# Fill in the Blank

Fill in the blanks with key terms from this chapter.

1. A computer's clock speed is measured in _____.

2. The _____ performs arithmetic (addition and subtraction) and logic (AND, OR, and NOT) calculations, and the _____ manages the movement of data through the CPU.

3. A(n) _____ processor consists of two or more processors on a single chip.

4. The wires that transfer data across the motherboard are known as the _____.

5. The operating systems, programs, and data the computer is currently using are stored in _____.

6. _____ is the standard internal drive interface in use today.

7. The use of _____ increases the speed and accuracy of data entry and converts information into a digital format that can be saved, copied, and manipulated.

8. _____ monitors work by passing an electric current through gas sealed in thousands of cells inside the screen. The current excites the gas, which in turn excites the phosphors that coat the screen to pass light through an image.

9. _____ printers produce the sharpest text at a much lower cost per page than _____ printers.

10. _____ are used to connect a computer to computer network.

# Running Project ...

## ... The Finish Line

Use your answers to the previous sections of the Running Project to determine what you would need in a desktop system. Look at computer ads on some current retail websites and select a computer system that meets your needs. Pick a system in the $300–500 price range. Does it include everything you need? What's missing? What additional features does it have that you will find useful? Does it have extras that you could do without? Is it reasonably priced? What features would you get if you spent more money? What would you lose if you spent less? Justify why the system you chose is a good choice for you.

Write a report describing your selection and responding to the questions raised. Save your file as **lastname_firstname_ch04_ project**, and submit it to your instructor as directed.

# Do It Yourself 1

1. Windows 8 Display Color Calibration helps you set your monitor to display colors as accurately as possible. Press F1 to open Windows *Help and Support*, type **calibrate** in the search box, and press Enter. Click *Calibrate your display*. What is it? How does it work? What type of monitor is best suited for ClearType?

2. From the link in the Help screen, open Display Color Calibration. Note: You may need to supply an administrator password to continue.

3. Follow the directions on the next several screens to adjust your color. If you can't adjust the settings, read each screen for information only. What is gamma? What does brightness adjustment control? What is contrast? How does color balance work?

4. Prepare your response, save the file as **lastname_firstname_ch04_diy1**, and submit it as directed by your instructor.

# Do It Yourself 2

Windows and OS X provide several ways to reduce the energy consumption of your computer. In this activity, you'll examine the power settings on your computer.

1. Open the Control Panel, click *System and Security*, and click *Power Options.*

2. Click *Change plan settings* for each of the plans. Compare the settings to turn off the display and put the computer to sleep. Which power plan is your computer currently using? Is this the appropriate plan for your computer?

3. Use Windows Help and Support or the Internet to learn about sleep and hibernation. What is the difference between the two, and what purpose do they serve?
   If you have a Mac, from the Apple menu or dock, open *System Preferences, Energy Saver* to examine the settings. Use Apple Help to search for **safe sleep**. What is sleep mode?

4. Prepare your response, save the file as **lastname_firstname_ch04_diy2**, and submit it as directed by your instructor.

# File Management

1. Open File Explorer and click *Downloads*. Are there any files in this folder? If so, what types of files are they?

2. Search Windows Help and Support, or use the Internet to learn about the Downloads folder. What is the purpose of the Downloads folder?

3. Type up your answers, save the file as **lastname_firstname_ch04_fm**, and submit the assignment as directed by your instructor.

# Critical Thinking

Michael is a first-year student at a local community college. He's looking for a computer for doing schoolwork. He needs to run Microsoft Office and needs network access. Mike's also an avid computer gamer and wants a machine that can handle the latest computer games. He's looking for a machine that will get him through the next couple of years until he graduates and can afford to upgrade. Because you're taking this class, Mike has enlisted your help in choosing a computer that meets his needs. He has $600 to spend.

1. Evaluate three computer choices from current newspaper ads or websites and compare them with respect to Mike's requirements.

2. Use a word processor to create a table like the one provided, comparing the features of each computer, to organize your research.

3. In the same document, write up your recommendation for Mike in a two- to three-paragraph essay. Which computer should he buy and why? What other peripherals and software will he need to purchase? You should also recommend necessary peripherals, including a monitor and printer. Remember your budget is fixed, so you can't exceed $600.

4. Save your file as **lastname_firstname_ch04_ct**, and submit both your table and essay as directed by your instructor.

|  | Computer 1 | Computer 2 | Computer 3 |
|---|---|---|---|
| Website or store providing sales information (support issues) |  |  |  |
| Brand |  |  |  |
| Model |  |  |  |
| Price |  |  |  |
| Processor type |  |  |  |
| Processor speed |  |  |  |
| Memory type |  |  |  |
| Memory amount |  |  |  |
| Hard drive capacity |  |  |  |
| Additional equipment/ features |  |  |  |
| Additional purchases required to meet Mike's needs |  |  |  |

# Ethical Dilemma

The United States now issues RFID passports to its citizens. Many individuals and groups, such as the American Civil Liberties Union, have criticized this decision, claiming the passports pose security and privacy risk. In February 2009, Chris Paget, an "ethical hacker," used $250 worth of equipment to scan and copy the information on RFID passport cards (wallet-sized passport cards that can be used only to enter the United States from Canada, Mexico, the Caribbean, and Bermuda at land border crossings or sea ports-of-entry) and enhanced driver's licenses while he drove around San Francisco. Paget claims he did this to demonstrate the security weakness in the technology. You can watch the video of his experiment by searching for Chris Paget on YouTube.

1. What Paget did is illegal, but does the end justify the means?

2. Should the United States consider scrapping the RFID passport program? Why or why not?

3. There are several websites that suggest microwaving your passport to disable the RFID chip. Is this legal? Would you do it if you thought it would work? (By the way, it doesn't; but it will ruin your passport.) Are there other, legal ways to protect your information?

4. Type up your answers, save the file as **lastname_firstname_ch04_ethics**, and submit it as directed by your instructor.

# On the Web

The EPEAT website provides information to help you "evaluate, compare and select electronic products based on their environmental attributes." Visit the site **www.epeat.net**, and answer the following questions:

1. What types of devices are included in the system? How are they placed into the registry? What testing do they undergo?

2. What are the environmental performance criteria the devices must meet?

3. What manufacturers participate in the program? How is it funded? Is there any conflict of interest? Type up your answers, save the file as **lastname_firstname_ch04_web**, and submit it as directed by your instructor.

# Collaboration

**Instructors:** Divide the class into five groups, and assign each group one type of printer for this project. The topics include inkjet, dye-sublimation, laser, multifunction, and plotter.

**The Project:** Each team is to prepare a multimedia commercial for its printer type. The presentation should be designed to convince a consumer to buy the team's printer. Teams must use at least three references, only one of which may be this textbook. Use Google Docs or Microsoft Office to plan the presentation, and provide documentation that all team members have contributed to the project.

**Students:** Before beginning this project, discuss the roles each group member will play. Choose a team name, which you'll use in submitting your presentation. Be sure to divide the work among your members, and pick someone to present your project. You may find it helpful to elect a team leader who can direct your activities and ensure that all team contributions are collated through Google Docs or Microsoft Office as directed by your instructor.

**Outcome:** You're to prepare a multimedia presentation on your assigned topic in PowerPoint (or another tool, as directed by your instructor) and present it to your class. The presentation may be no longer than 3 minutes and should contain 5 to 7 slides. On the first slide, be sure to include the name of your presentation and a list of all team members. Turn in a final version of your presentation named as **teamname_ch04_presentation** and your file showing your collaboration named as **teamname_ch04_collab**. Submit your presentation to your instructor as directed.

# 5

# System Software

## OBJECTIVES

1. **Explain what an operating system does.**

2. **Compare the most common stand-alone operating systems.**

3. **Compare specialized operating systems.**

4. **Compare the most common network operating systems.**

5. **List and explain important disk utility software.**

## IN THIS CHAPTER

A computer is a programmable machine that converts raw data into useful information. Programming is what makes a computer different from a toaster. In this chapter, we look at the system software used to make computers run smoothly and securely.

# Who's the Boss?

## Explain what an operating system does.

We often hear about application software—software for the user. Software that makes the computer run is **system software**. The **operating system (OS)** is the most important type of system software because it provides the user with the interface to communicate with the hardware and other software on the computer and manages system resources. Without an operating system, a personal computer is useless.

## PROVIDES USER INTERFACE

The user interface is the part of the operating system that you see and interact with. Modern operating systems, such as Windows, Linux, and MAC OS X, have a **graphical user interface (GUI)**. Graphical because we interact with graphic objects such as icons and buttons to control the computer, a GUI allows a user to point to and click on objects to initiate commands. Older operating systems used a command-line interface, which required the user to type out all commands. If you look at the interface on most personal computers, you'll see that they have a lot in common. Figure 5.1 shows how the interface has changed from command line to GUI in Microsoft operating systems. This change made PCs more user-friendly, which helped them increase in popularity. A similar evolution occurred in the Apple systems. In fact, in 1988, Apple sued Microsoft for copyright infringement, but the case was later dismissed.

All user interfaces serve the same basic function: to allow the user to control the computer. If you want to play a game, for example, you navigate to the icon for the game and click (or double-click) on it to begin. The clicking tells the computer to open the file—in this case, to run the game. The procedure to open a Word document is very much the same. All these tasks require the OS user interface. GUIs use icons, menus, dialog boxes, and windows, and in many cases, there are multiple ways to perform the same task.

**FIGURE 5.1** The user interface of the Microsoft operating system has evolved.

WINDOWS 8

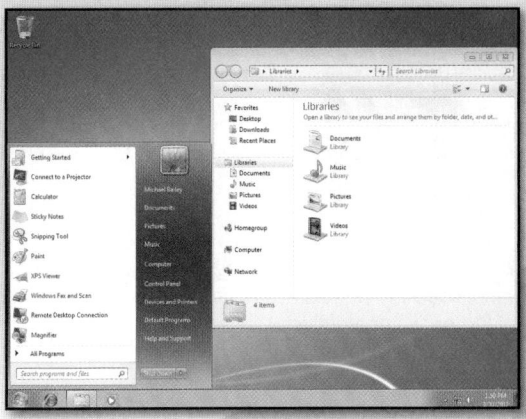

WINDOWS 7

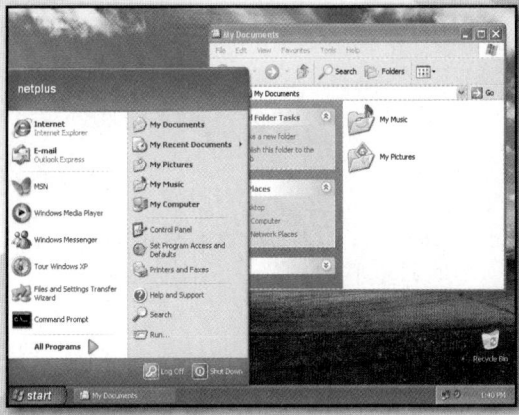

WINDOWS XP

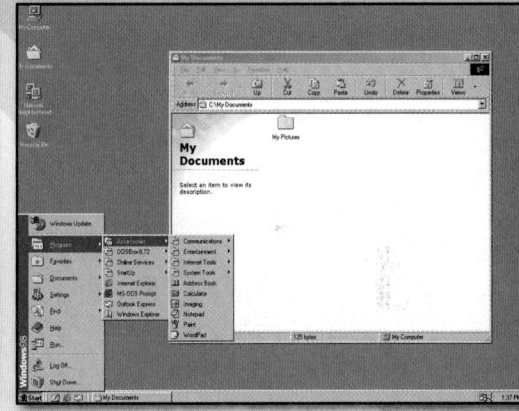

WINDOWS 98

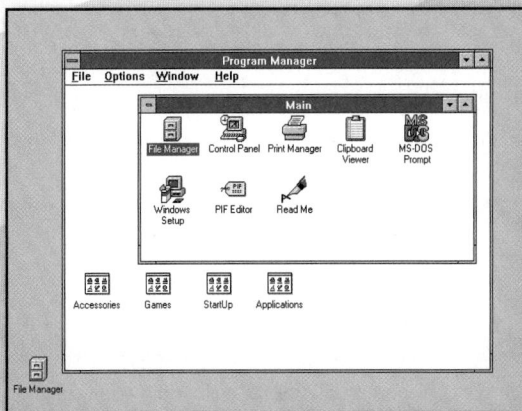

WINDOWS 3.1

MS-DOS

# MANAGES RESOURCES

The resources on your system include the processor and the memory. The operating system has the important job of managing how these resources are allocated to both hardware and software. The operating system makes sure that each process is allocated its own memory and manages the instructions that are sent to the processor (see Figure 5.2). Modern operating systems support **multitasking**, which is the ability to do more than one task at a time. A single processor can't actually do more than one thing at a time but switches between the tasks so quickly that it's transparent to the user. Each running application is assigned its own area of memory and is prevented from accessing the memory area of other programs. This prevents a program crash from affecting other processes running in other areas of memory.

# MANAGES AND CONTROLS HARDWARE

The operating system manages and controls the hardware. Early PCs were simple devices that had limited hardware: a keyboard, a monochrome monitor, a disk drive, and not much else. Today, we have a wide variety of peripheral devices, including printers, scanners, cameras, media players, video and sound cards, and storage devices. Windows 95 introduced a feature known as Plug and Play. **Plug and Play (PnP)** allows you to easily add new hardware to a computer system. When you plug in a new piece of hardware, the OS detects it and helps you set it up. An OS communicates with hardware by means of a **device driver**, which acts like a translator between the two. A device driver is software that enhances the capabilities of the operating system. It's what allows you to expand your computer with new hardware. If it were not for device drivers, there would be no way for you to install new hardware on your system. Figure 5.3 shows how Windows notifies you of the installation of new hardware. When you first connect the hardware, Windows detects it and informs you that it's installing the device driver software. If Windows cannot locate the device driver, it asks you for permission to search the Web or instructs you to insert the manufacturer's disc. The message *Device driver software installed successfully* indicates your new hardware is now ready to use.

**FIGURE 5.2** The operating system manages the instructions that are sent to the processor, much like a police officer manages the flow of traffic at a busy intersection.

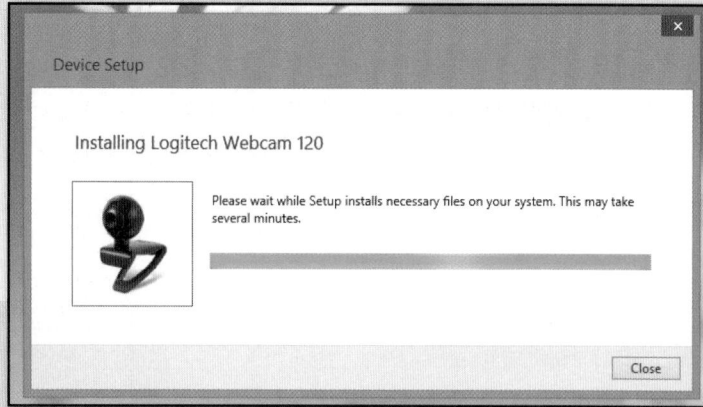

**FIGURE 5.3** Windows automatically installs the device driver for new hardware—in this case, a Logitech Webcam.

# INTERACTS WITH SOFTWARE

When you look at the system requirements to install software, you'll always see a list of supported operating systems. The OS on a computer interacts directly with the software you install, giving it access to resources it needs to run. This happens through the use of an **application programming interface (API)**, which allows the application to request services from the operating system, such as a request to print or save a file. An API lets a computer programmer write a program that will run on computers with different hardware configurations by sending such service requests to the OS to handle. Figure 5.4 shows Microsoft Word using the API to request save services from Windows.

An operating system manages interactions between the user, the software, and the hardware of a computer. These critical functions make the computer more user-friendly, flexible, and expandable. The OS is the most important piece of software on the computer because without it, the computer won't run at all.

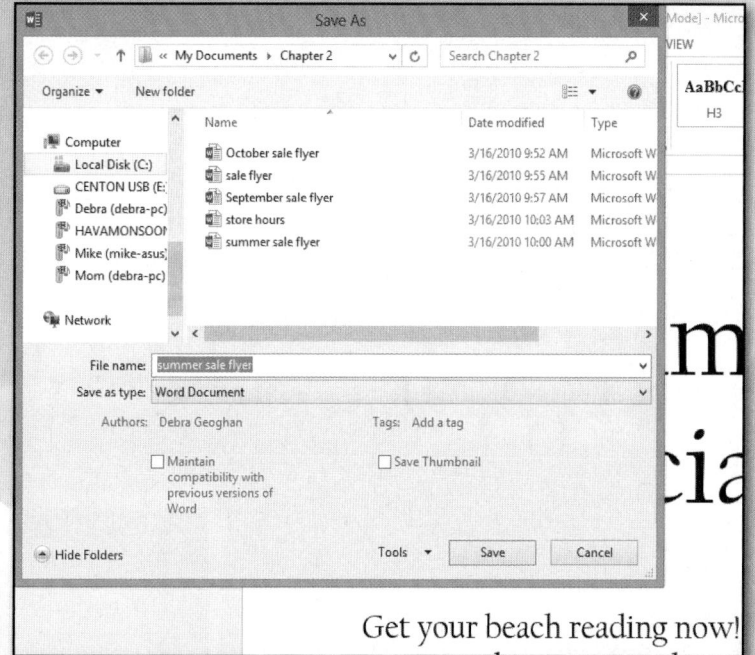

**FIGURE 5.4** Programs use the API to save files.

## Running Project

What operating system is on your computer? You can check a Windows computer by right-clicking on *Computer* in File Explorer and clicking *Properties*. To check a Mac, open the About This Mac window from the Apple menu. Is your OS the latest version? If you have not upgraded yet, why not? If you could change the OS, would you? Which OS would you use instead?

## 4 Things You Need to Know

- A GUI allows you to point and click to control your computer.
- The OS manages the system resources: processing and memory.
- PnP allows you to add new hardware easily.
- Application software communicates with the OS through an API.

## Key Terms

application programming interface (API)

device driver

graphical user interface (GUI)

multitasking

operating system (OS)

Plug and Play (PnP)

system software

# HOW TO

## Examine and Update Your Printer Driver

Having the right printer driver allows you to use the capabilities of your printer most effectively. While it might work fine to print using the generic operating system driver, the advanced features usually require you to install the driver and related utilities from the printer manufacturer. In this exercise you examine your printer drivers and learn how to update them if necessary. (Note: Security settings may prevent you from performing these steps in the lab.)

**1** Open your word processor, type your name and date in the document, and save it as **lastname_firstname_ch05_howto1**. Open File Explorer and click *Computer* in the Navigation pane. On the ribbon, click *Open Control Panel*. Under Hardware and Sound, click *View devices and printers*.

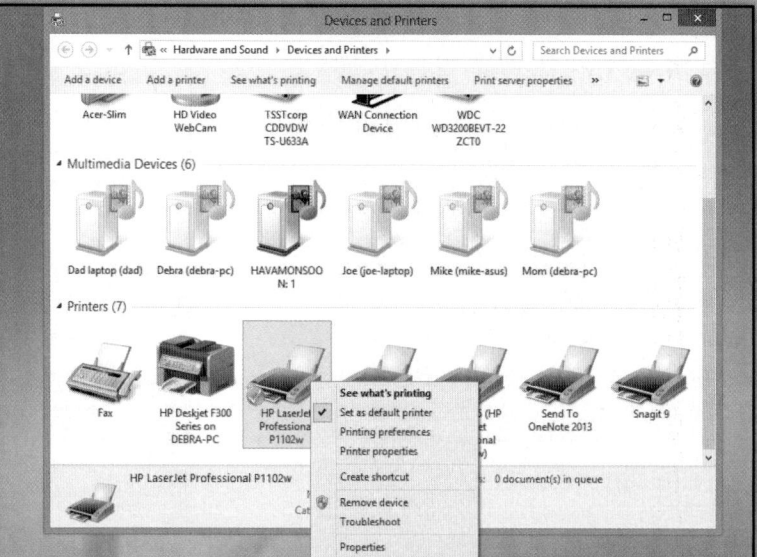

**2** How many printers are listed? Right-click on the default printer (identified by a green check) and choose *Printer properties*. What is the model of the printer you chose? Click the *Advanced* tab.

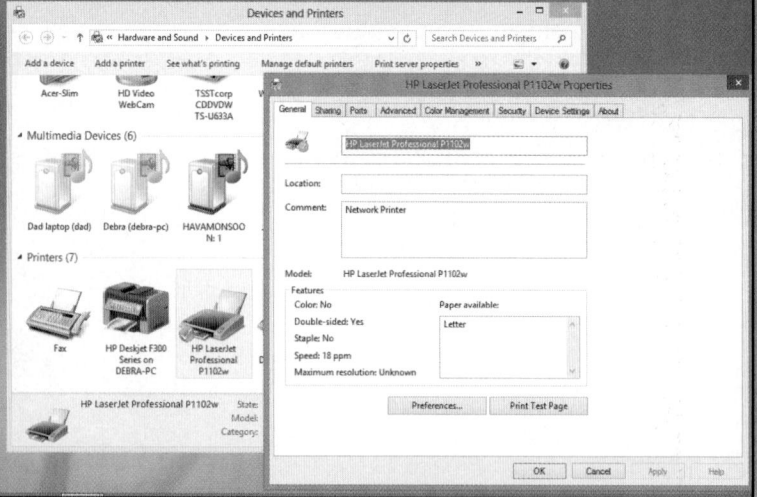

**3** What is the current driver? Click the *New Driver* button. On the Welcome window click *Next*. Click the link *Tell me why driver signing is important*. Read the information on the Help screen. What is a digitally signed driver and why is it important? Close the Help window. Take a screen shot of the Printer Driver Selection window and paste it into your document. Click *Cancel* twice to exit the wizard without changing any settings.

**4** Type up your answers, including the screen shot, save your file, and submit as directed by your instructor.

**If you are using a Mac:**

1. From the Apple menu, select *About This Mac*. Click *More Info* and then click *System Report*.
2. Under Hardware, click *Printers*. How many printers are listed? Select a printer in the right pane. What is the model of the printer you chose? Take a screen shot of this information. Locate the PostScript Printer Description files (PPDs) information. Does this match the printer description? (If it is listed as a Generic, you might be able to use more features of your printer by downloading the software from the printer manufacturer's website.)
3. Type up your answers, including the screen shot, save your file, and submit as directed by your instructor.

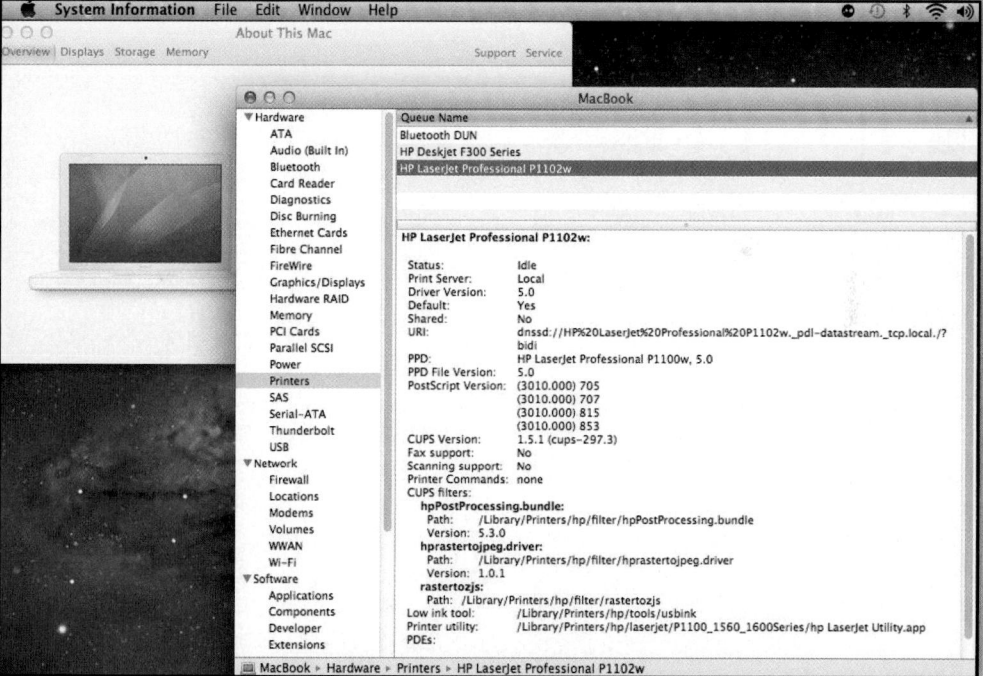

# Running the Show on Personal Computers

## 2 OBJECTIVE
## Compare the most common stand-alone operating systems.

There are many different stand-alone operating systems. In this article, we look at some of the most popular operating systems used on personal computers today.

## WINDOWS

The most common desktop operating system is **Microsoft Windows**. Figure 5.5 shows a timeline of the release of successive versions of the Windows desktop operating systems. The current version is Windows 8, although you'll still find many computers running previous versions of Windows, such as Windows 7 or even XP. It's estimated that over 90 percent of personal computers are running one of these versions of Windows. Windows XP was released in 2001 and was still the most widely used operating system in the world in 2010. However, sales of Windows XP ended in 2008. All Microsoft support for Windows XP will end in 2014. Windows Vista was released in 2006 (2007 to consumers) but was met with much resistance from both the public and business customers. The hardware requirements to install Vista are much more stringent than those for XP. In addition, software and device driver compatibility were problematic when Vista was first released, adding to the cost of upgrading. Windows 7 was greeted much more favorably, and both home and business users that were still using XP began to upgrade to it. Since its release in 2008 (2009 to consumers), Windows 7 has been steadily gaining, and the number of PCs running Windows XP and Vista has been declining. In 2012, Microsoft released Windows 8. The most obvious change is the introduction of the Metro interface. In this book, the Windows screen shots and exercises are based on Windows 7 and 8.

**FIGURE 5.5** Windows Release Timeline

| VERSION | YEAR |
|---|---|
| Windows 8 | 2012 |
| Windows 7 | 2009 |
| Windows Vista | 2007 |
| Windows XP | 2001 |
| Windows Me | 2000 |
| Windows 2000 | 2000 |
| Windows 98 | 1998 |
| Windows NT 4.0 | 1996 |
| Windows 95 | 1995 |
| Windows NT 3.5 | 1994 |
| Windows NT 3.1 | 1993 |
| Windows 3.1 | 1992 |
| Windows 3.0 | 1990 |
| Windows 2.0 | 1987 |
| Windows 1.0 | 1985 |

Each release of Windows added new features and security measures and was designed to be easier to use, more secure, and able to incorporate the new technologies.

- Windows 95 introduced Plug and Play (PnP), enhanced support for CD-ROMs, and the right mouse click.
- Windows 98 included Internet Explorer, better PnP support, and more multimedia features.
- Windows XP introduced a new interface, automatic updates, easier networking and Internet connectivity, and increased reliability.
- Windows Vista once again introduced a new interface, gadgets, enhanced networking, entertainment, and accessibility features.
- Windows 7 included a redesigned taskbar, new ways to manipulate windows, Remote Media Streaming, and Windows Touch multi-touch technology.
- Windows 8 has a totally new interface that uses a Start Screen with Live Tiles instead of a Start menu to access applications. Windows 8 also integrates your computer with the cloud through Skydrive and third party apps.

Moving from one version of Windows to the next usually requires a fairly small learning curve, and users adapt quickly to the changes.

# MAC

In 1984, Apple introduced its first Macintosh computer, which had a GUI interface. The OS at the time was called Mac System Software. New versions and updates that improved stability and hardware support were released between 1984 and 1991. Figure 5.6 shows a timeline of Mac releases.

- System 7 was released in 1991 with an updated GUI, multitasking support, built-in networking, better hardware and memory management, and new applications. Beginning with version 7.6, the name was changed to Mac OS.
- Mac OS 8 was released in 1997 and included a new interface, a better file system, searching, and Internet browsing.
- Mac OS 9 had improved wireless networking support, a better search tool, and the ability to be updated over the Internet. Mac OS 9 is referred to today as Mac Classic.

The **OS X** operating system was first released in 2001 as Mac OS X 10.0, also called Cheetah. This OS wasn't an updated version of the classic Mac OS but was an entirely new operating system based on UNIX. Early versions of OS X included a Mac OS 9 emulation to run older applications. Cheetah introduced iMovie and iTunes; Puma added iDVD. Each new version included more integrated applications for email, chat, Internet, and multimedia. The current version—OS X Mountain Lion (see Figure 5.7)—is faster, more reliable, and easier to use. The interface has been updated and includes the Time Machine backup utility, better file sharing and networking capabilities, and exceptional multimedia applications. It borrows popular features from the iPad such as a messaging app and iCloud. In this book, the OS X screen shots and exercises are based on Lion and Mountain Lion.

**FIGURE 5.6** Mac Release Timeline

| YEAR | VERSION |
| --- | --- |
| 2012 | OS X Mountain Lion |
| 2011 | OS X Lion |
| 2009 | Mac OS X 10.6 Snow Leopard |
| 2007 | Mac OS X 10.5 Leopard |
| 2004 | Mac OS X 10.4 Tiger |
| 2003 | Mac OS X 10.3 Panther |
| 2002 | Mac OS X 10.2 Jaguar |
| 2001 | Mac OS X 10.1 Puma |
| 2001 | Mac OS X 10.0 Cheetah |
| 1999 | Mac OS 9 Mac Classic |
| 1997 | Mac OS 8 |
| 1991 | System 7 |
| 1988 | System 6 |
| 1987 | System 4, System 5 |
| 1986 | System 3 |
| 1985 | System 2 |
| 1984 | System 1 |

The Mac OS is a secure, feature-rich operating system that only runs on Mac computers. If you don't have a Mac, then you can't use the Mac OS. Currently, Macs have about a 5 percent share of the personal computer market.

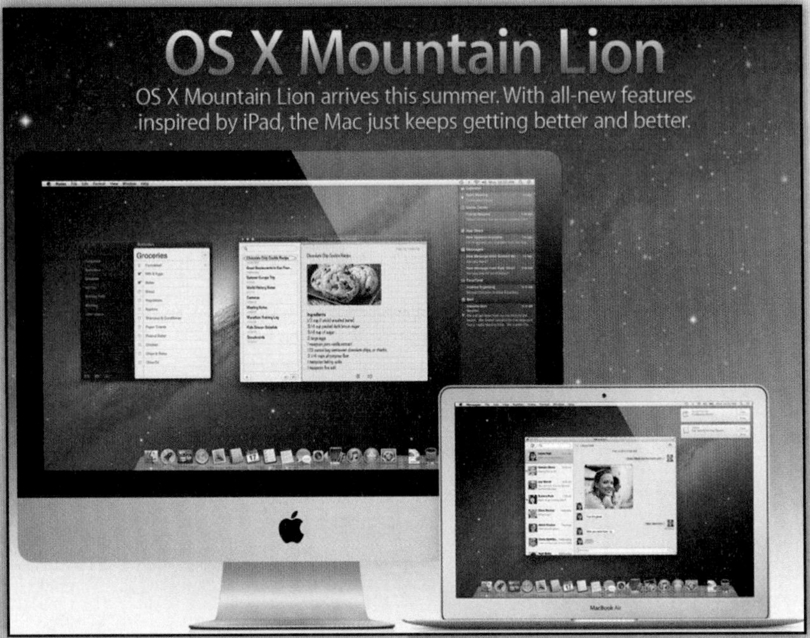

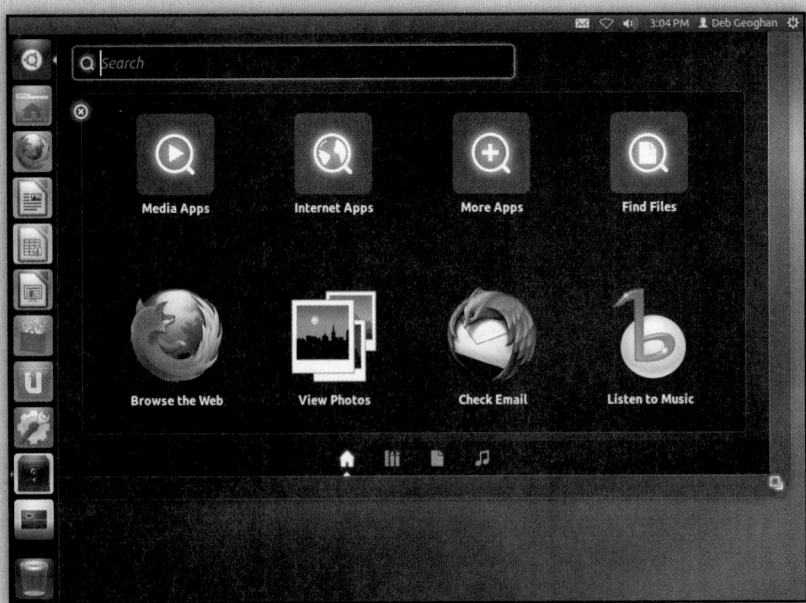

## OS X Mountain Lion

OS X Mountain Lion arrives this summer. With all-new features inspired by iPad, the Mac just keeps getting better and better.

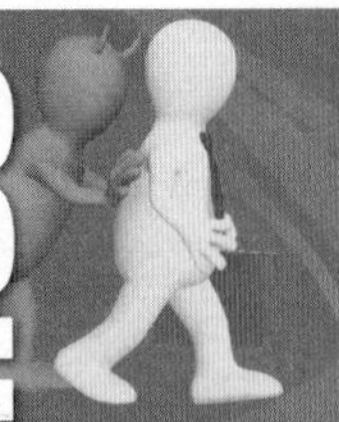

**FIGURE 5.7** OS X Mountain Lion

**FIGURE 5.8** The Ubuntu desktop features a GUI that's easy to navigate for most users.

## LINUX

Unlike Windows and Mac, Linux doesn't refer to a single operating system but rather many different versions or distributions that use the same kernel OS: Linux. **Linux** was first developed in 1991 by Linus Torvalds, then a graduate student at the University of Helsinki. It was designed to be similar to UNIX and is sometimes called UNIX-like. Unlike UNIX (and Windows and Mac OS), however, Linux is **open source**. The code is publicly available, and developers all over the world have created hundreds of Linux distributions (distros) with all kinds of features. Distros include the OS, various utilities, and software applications, such as Internet browsers, games, entertainment software, and an office suite. The most popular personal version of Linux is currently Ubuntu. Figure 5.8 shows the Ubuntu desktop with the Dash open. Most Linux distros come with a GUI that's similar to a Windows or OS X, and users can easily navigate through the system. Linux desktops make up a very small percentage of personal computers, but the number is growing all the time. Linux has found a niche in the netbook market. On machines with limited memory and processing power, Linux shines.

In businesses, Linux has a very small market share of desktop computers (less than 2 percent), but it has a larger share of the server market. Red Hat Enterprise Linux is the world's leading open source application platform.

In 2009, Google released a prerelease, or **beta version,** of its Chrome OS. "Chromium OS is an open source project that aims to provide a fast, simple, and more secure computing experience for people who spend most of their time on the web." In 2011, several manufacturers began shipping Chromebooks—notebooks that run the Chrome OS. These notebooks are designed to work best when connected to the Internet, and they rely on Web apps and cloud storage rather than traditional software. Figure 5.9 shows the desktop of the current version.

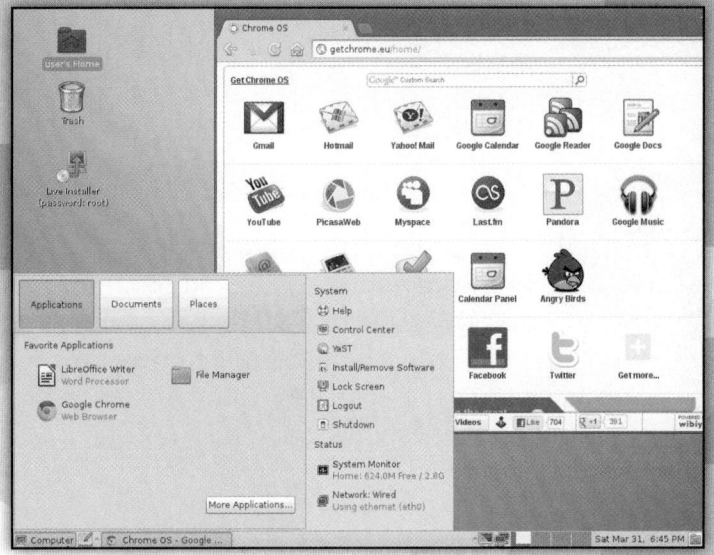

**FIGURE 5.9** Google Chrome OS

The operating system that you run largely depends on the hardware you have, but running the most recent version of your OS of choice ensures the best features and security.

**Try the System Software Simulation**

SIMULATION

## Running Project

Microsoft Windows is the primary desktop operating system installed on new personal computers, but not every consumer is happy with that choice. Some manufacturers sell Linux computers such as the Chromebooks mentioned in this article. Use the Internet to research the versions of Linux currently available preinstalled on new computers. Write a two- to three-paragraph essay summarizing your findings, which applications are included, the cost, and any other details you deem important.

## 3 Things You Need to Know

- Microsoft Windows is the primary OS installed on PCs.
- OS X is the proprietary Mac OS.
- Linux is an open source kernel OS that's distributed as part of many versions or distros.

## Key Terms

beta version

Linux

Microsoft Windows

open source

OS X

# HOW TO

## Keep Your Desktop OS Up To Date

One of the most important things you can do to protect your system is to keep your software up to date. Some programs will check automatically and prompt you when a new version or update is available. Windows includes Windows Update to do just that. It's important to set the utility up correctly and monitor it to be sure that your updates are being installed. Complete each step, and compare your screen to the figures that accompany each step.

**1** Open your word processor, type your name and date into the document, and save the file as **lastname_firstname_ch05_howto2**. Open Windows Update through the System and Security Control Panel. Take a screen shot of the Windows Update screen and paste it in your document. How many updates are available on your system?

**2** In the left pane, click *Change settings* to verify that you're getting the updates you need. In a business or school, this is likely handled centrally, and these settings might be disabled.

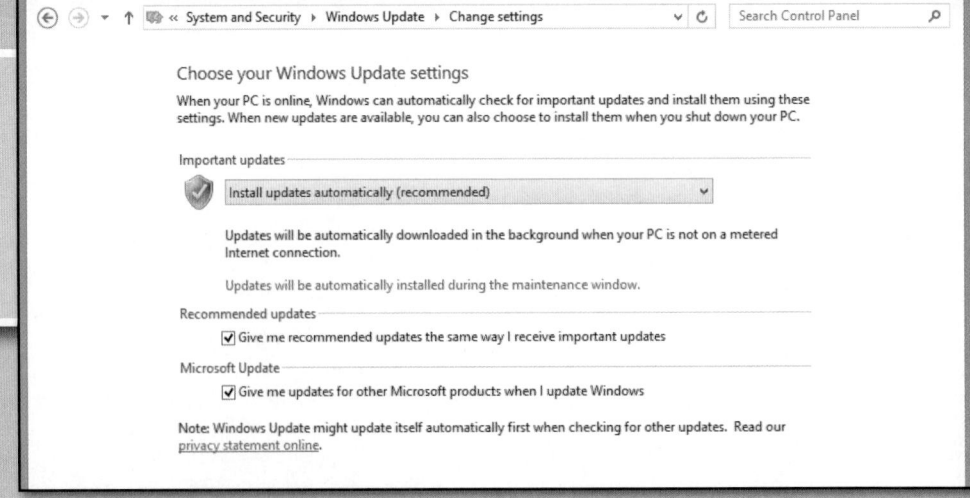

**3** Important updates can be installed automatically (the default) or you can change the settings by clicking the drop-down arrow on the right. I sometimes change this to *Check for updates but let me choose whether to download and install them* when I'm traveling and not connected to my broadband Internet connection at home. This prevents Windows from downloading files while I'm working on a slow dial-up or public WiFi connection. How is your computer configured to handle updates?

**4** Click the check boxes for the other options you want. If you enable *Recommended updates*, you'll get additional items, such as new device drivers. Microsoft Update will also get you updates for other Microsoft products, such as Office. When you're finished making your selections, take a screen shot of your choices, paste it into your document, and click *OK* to save your changes or *Cancel* to discard them.

**5** When you close the Change settings window, you're returned to the Windows Update screen. In this example, there are three updates ready to be installed. You can click the links for more information. The first figure shows two important updates ready to be installed. Important updates are checked by default. You can click on each for more information. If there are any updates available, take a screen shot of the Important updates, and paste it in your document below the previous screen shot.

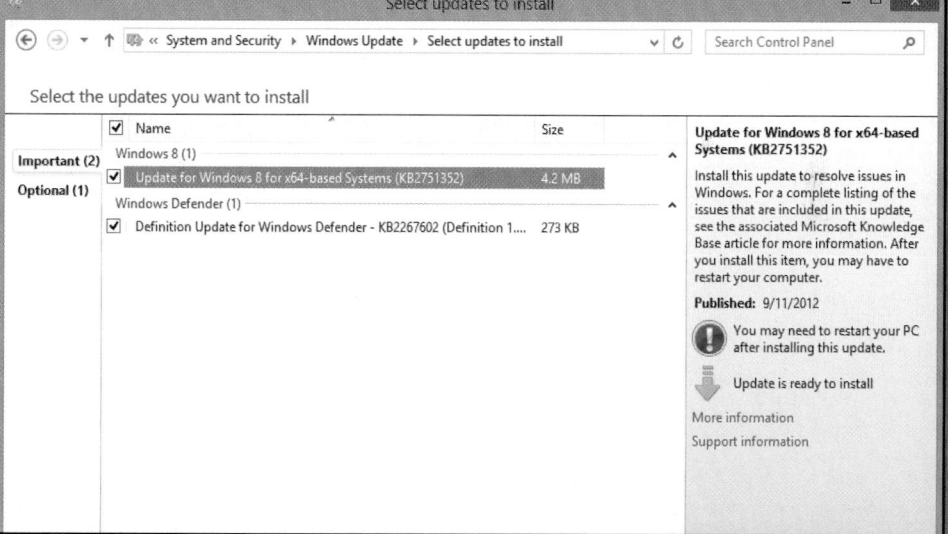

**6** The optional update in this example is an update for Microsoft Silverlight. If there are optional updates available on your system, click the *Optional* tab, take another screen shot, and paste it below the others in your document. Unlike the recommended updates, optional updates are not checked by default.

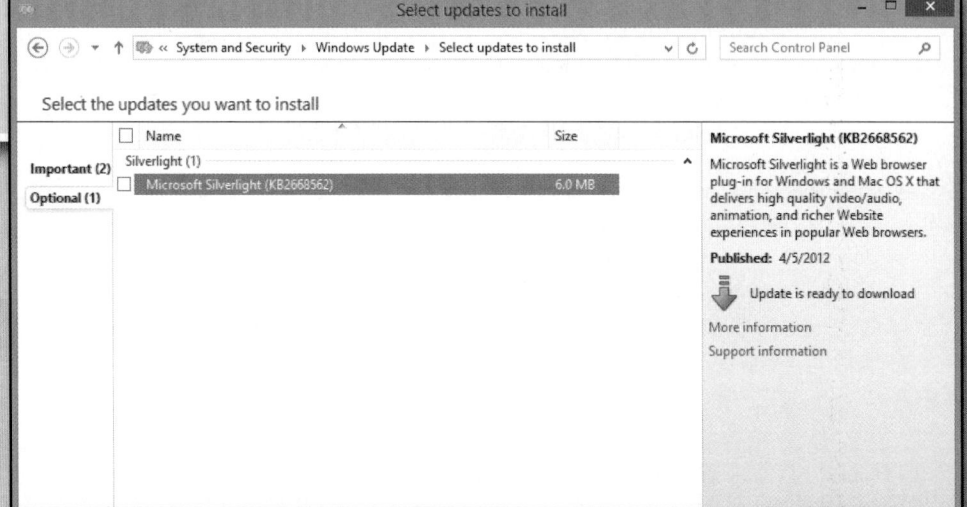

**7** If Windows is set to automatically install updates, you don't need to install them yourself, but you can choose to manually install them if there are updates available by clicking the *Install updates* button in the Windows Update window.

**8** Save your file and submit it as directed by your instructor.

### If you are using a Mac:

1. Open the Apple menu and choose *Software Update*.
2. Wait for OS X to check for updates. If there are updates available, click *Show Details* to display them. Take a screenshot of this window and paste it into your document.
3. Open System Preferences and click *Software Update*. Take a screenshot of this window and paste it into your document. How frequently does your computer check for updates?
4. Save your file as **lastname_firstname_ch05_howto2**, and submit it as directed by your instructor.

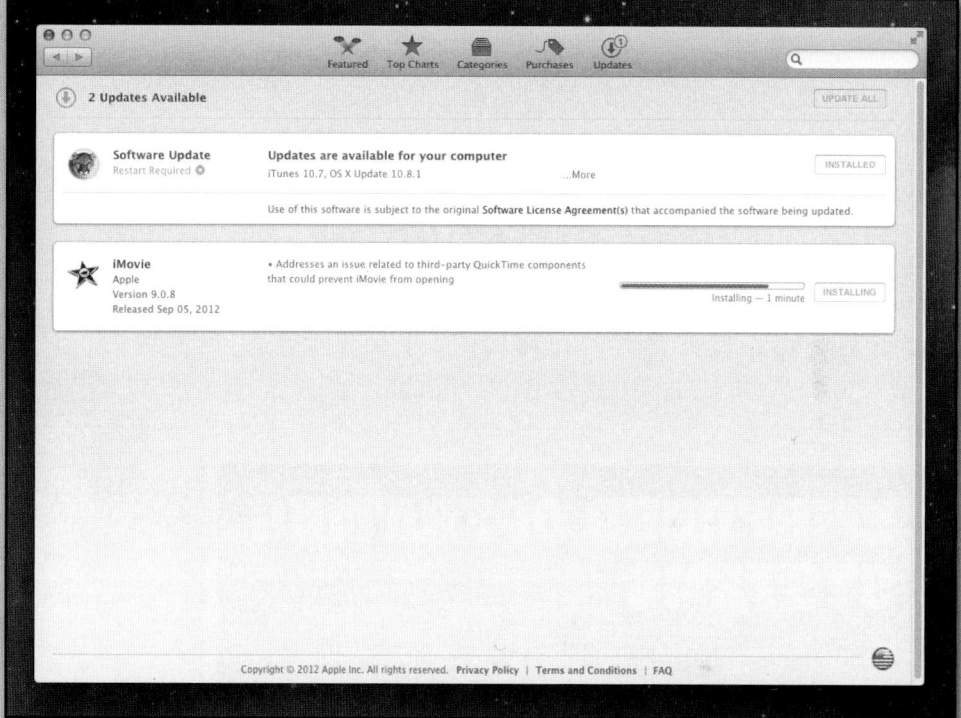

# Something Special For You

## 3 OBJECTIVE
## Compare specialized operating systems.

So far, we've discussed operating systems that run on personal computers. In this article, we look at embedded and mobile operating systems.

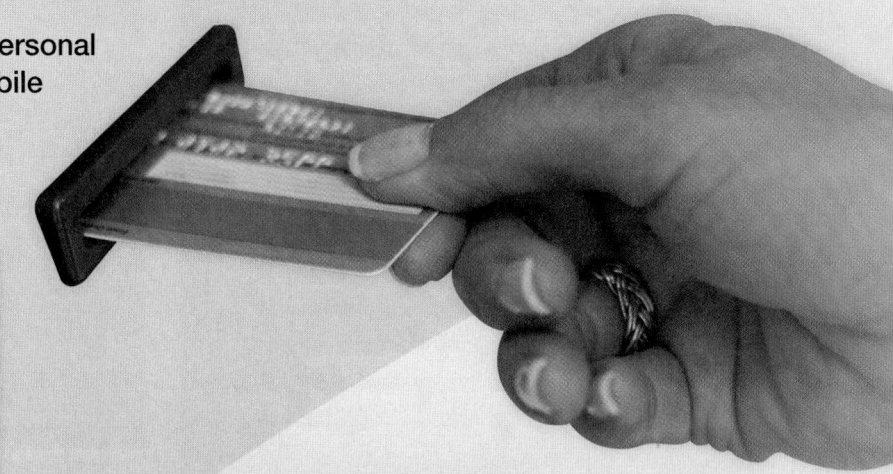

## EMBEDDED OPERATING SYSTEMS

Devices such as ATM machines, GPS devices, video game consoles, ultrasound machines, and even the communication and entertainment system in your car run **embedded operating systems**. Because they have specialized and limited functions, these operating systems can be very small and are able to run on simpler hardware.

The Windows Embedded OS has been around since 1996. It can be found on many devices from set-top cable boxes and GPS devices to complex industrial automation controllers and medical devices. The advantage to using an embedded version of Windows is that users recognize the familiar interface.

Mobile devices such as smartphones and tablets run embedded **mobile operating systems**. These are more full-featured than the versions on devices such as GPS and cable boxes. Windows Phone is based on Windows Embedded CE version and can be found on many smartphones. It first introduced us to the Metro interface.

The iPhone, iPad, and iPod Touch run **iOS**, a scaled-down version of Mac OS X that uses direct manipulation and multi-gesture touch such as swipe, tap, and pinch to control it. **Android** is an embedded version of Linux that runs on many phones and tablets. BlackBerry OS runs on smartphones from Research In Motion. These small operating systems have familiar interfaces and features, including touch-screen support, email, and Web browsers. As we have become more dependent on our mobile devices, these mobile OSs have become more full-featured and easier to use. The newer versions of our desktop operating systems have even begun to look more like their mobile cousins.

The most popular smartphone operating systems are illustrated in Figure 5.10. The market changes quite rapidly as new technologies are released.

**FIGURE 5.10** Smartphone Operating Systems

**OS VERSION**
RIM BlackBerry OS

**FEATURES**
Proprietary; the standard for business users.

**OS VERSION**
Apple iOS

**FEATURES**
Proprietary; found only on Apple devices such as iPhone, iPad, iPod Touch, and Apple TV.

**OS VERSION**
Microsoft Windows Phone

**FEATURES**
Based on Windows Embedded CE found on devices, such as this HTC Titan, from many companies.

**OS VERSION**
Google Android

**FEATURES**
Linux kernel found on devices from many companies including this Samsung Galaxy Nexus.

As technology becomes more mobile, smaller, faster, and less tethered to the desk, alternative operating systems become an important way for us to interface with our files and applications. Developers know this and strive to create the best interfaces—ones we can learn to use easily and come to depend on quickly.

## Running Project

What's the mobile OS on your favorite handheld device? What are some of the features that you like about it? Are there any features that are missing? What features do you (or would you) use the most often? Did you select your device because of the OS?

## 2 Things You Need to Know

- Embedded OSs are small and specialized for devices such as GPSs, ATMs, and cell phones.
- Mobile operating systems are embedded OSs on smartphones and tablets.

## Key Terms

Android

embedded operating system

iOS

mobile operating system

# The NOS Knows

OBJECTIVE

## 4 Compare the most common network operating systems.

In a business or school environment, a network server centralizes resources, storage, and, most importantly, security in what is known as a client-server network. These servers run a specialized operating system called a network operating system. In this article, we look at the most common network operating systems and their basic functions.

A **network operating system (NOS)** is a multiuser operating system that controls the software and hardware that runs on a network. It allows multiple computers (clients) to communicate with the server and each other to share resources, run applications, and send messages. A NOS centralizes resources and security and provides services such as file and print services, communication services, Internet and email services, and backup and database services to the client computers. Figure 5.11 details the most common network operating systems found today.

**FIGURE 5.11** Comparing Modern Network Operating Systems

| NETWORK (NOS) | CURRENT VERSION | COMMENTS |
| --- | --- | --- |
| Windows Server: First released as Windows NT in 1993 | Windows 2008 R2 and Windows Server 2012 | Scalable; found on many corporate networks; available in versions from Small Business edition to Enterprise and Datacenter editions |
| Linux: Linux kernel is part of many different distros | Some of the most popular server versions used in business are Red Hat Enterprise Linux and Novell SUSE. | It's impossible to know how many Linux servers are currently installed because there are so many versions that can be downloaded and installed for free and without registration. |
| UNIX: Developed in 1969; the oldest NOS | UNIX itself is not an OS but a set of standards that are used to create a UNIX OS. Apache Web server is the most widely used NOS found on Web servers. Apache can run on UNIX or Linux servers. | Found on servers from HP (HP-UX), IBM (AIX), and Sun (Solaris) |
| Novell | Novell Open Enterprise Server 11 | Novell was a leader in business servers throughout the 1980s and 1990s with its Netware products but moved to open source in the past decade. |

Your school network is most likely a client-server network. When you log in to the network, you're given access to certain resources, such as printers and file storage. Figure 5.12 shows the Windows 7 Welcome screen for a network login. The first part of the username NETPLUSLAB\ indicates the network domain. The second part, m.bailey, is the user. When the password is entered correctly, the user is granted access to network resources on the NETPLUSLAB network.

Centralized resources and security make a network operating system indispensable in today's business environment. When a client logs in to a network, the resources appear in the client's environment. In Figure 5.13, you can see network drives that appear in the Explorer window of a Windows 7 client.

At home, the network you set up is a peer-to-peer network that doesn't require a NOS. While your personal operating system has networking features, the files and services that are shared between your home computers aren't centralized. A NOS provides important security and resource management in a business environment. Without a NOS, businesses would have to rely on peer-to-peer networks, which are just not practical for more than a few computers.

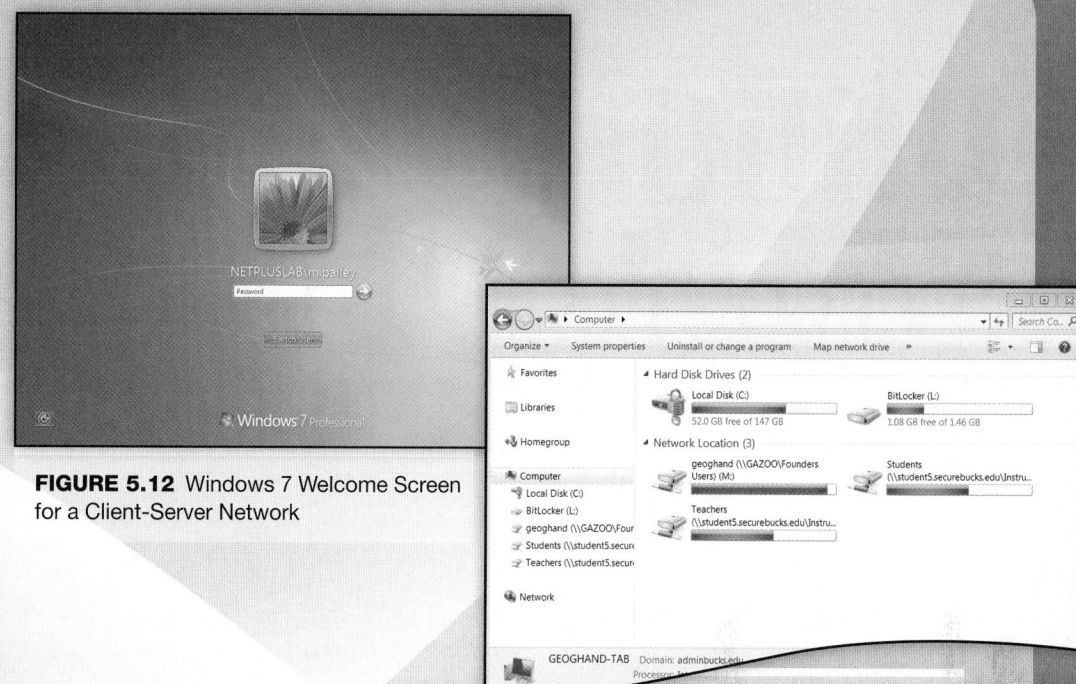

**FIGURE 5.12** Windows 7 Welcome Screen for a Client-Server Network

**FIGURE 5.13** This Windows 7 client has access to three network drives.

## Running Project

The one area of NOS usage that can be easily monitored is activity on Web servers. These are the servers that serve up web pages when you go to a URL, such as amazon.com. Netcraft does a monthly survey of Web servers. Go to the **netcraft.com** website and look at the current report. What are the three most popular Web servers for this month? How much has it changed in the past month? Are there any servers not mentioned in this chapter?

## 3 Things You Need to Know

- A NOS controls the software and hardware that runs on a client-server network.
- The most common NOSs are Windows Server, UNIX, and Linux.
- A NOS isn't needed on a peer-to-peer network.

## Key Term

network operating system (NOS)

# Utilities You Should Use

## 5 OBJECTIVE
## List and explain important disk utility software.

System software isn't just the operating system. **Utility software** helps you maintain your computer and is also considered system software. In this article, we look at some of the most important disk utilities that you should use. Security software such as antivirus software, firewalls, and antimalware software are also considered utility software and are discussed in the chapter on security and privacy.

## WHY USE UTILITIES?

Hard disks today are very large and can hold a lot of information. It's important to keep your disks healthy to keep your system running efficiently and to protect the files stored on them. When a disk is first **formatted** to hold files, a set of concentric circles called tracks are created. The disk is then divided up like a pie into sectors (see Figure 5.14). The files you save to your disk are stored in these sectors, called "clusters." This physical, low-level formatting occurs when the disk is manufactured. Think of this like a library full of empty bookshelves. The second part of formatting a disk is called high-level formatting. High-level formatting sets up the **file system** of the disk. You can think of it like a library catalog. When you save files to your disk, the file system keeps track of what you saved and where you saved it. The file system used on hard disks in Windows is the NTFS file system. External disks or those from older versions of Windows may be formatted with the FAT file system instead. The OS X file system is HFS+.

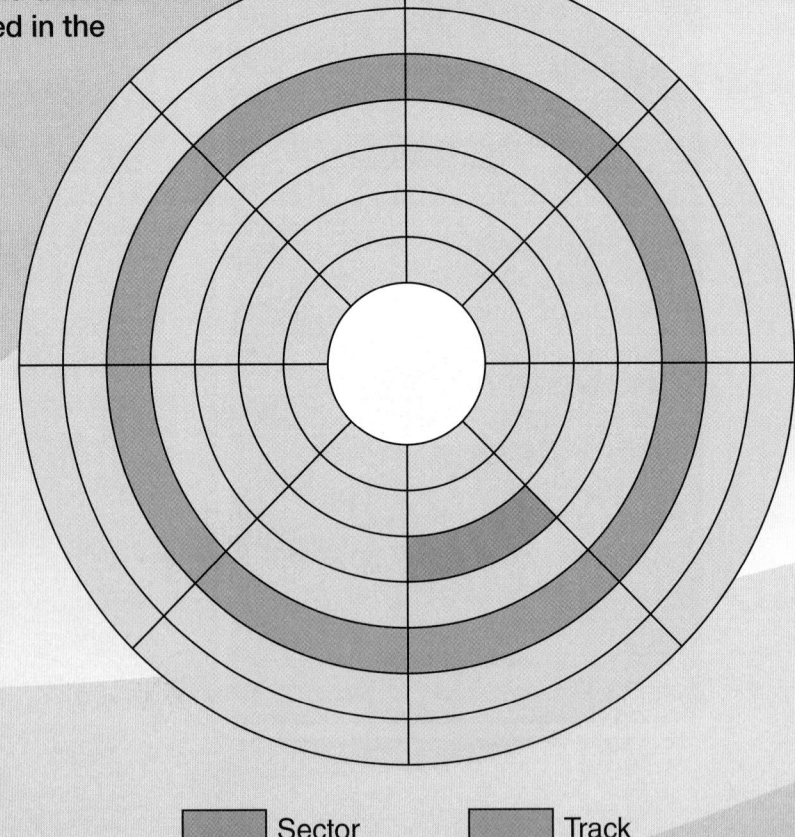

Sector          Track

**FIGURE 5.14** A Simplified View of Disk Formatting

# UTILITIES FOR DISK HEALTH

Windows includes several disk utilities to help you maintain your disks: Check Disk, Optimize Drives, and Disk Cleanup. To open these tools, first open the Computer window and then right-click on the disk you want to work with. Click *Properties* to open the Properties dialog box for the disk.

**DISK CHECKING** Disk-checking utilities monitor the health of the file system on a disk. To check a disk for errors in Windows, in the disk's Properties dialog box, click the *Tools* tab and then click *Check*. The Error Checking dialog box message indicates that I don't need to scan this drive (see Figure 5.15), but it allows me to run the scan anyway if I feel the need. If I choose to Scan drive, the scan runs right away and takes only a few minutes.

OS X comes with Disk Utility. You can access it from the Utilities folder in the Launcher. You can use this utility to get information about the disks on your computer and to verify and repair a disk you're having trouble with (see Figure 5.16).

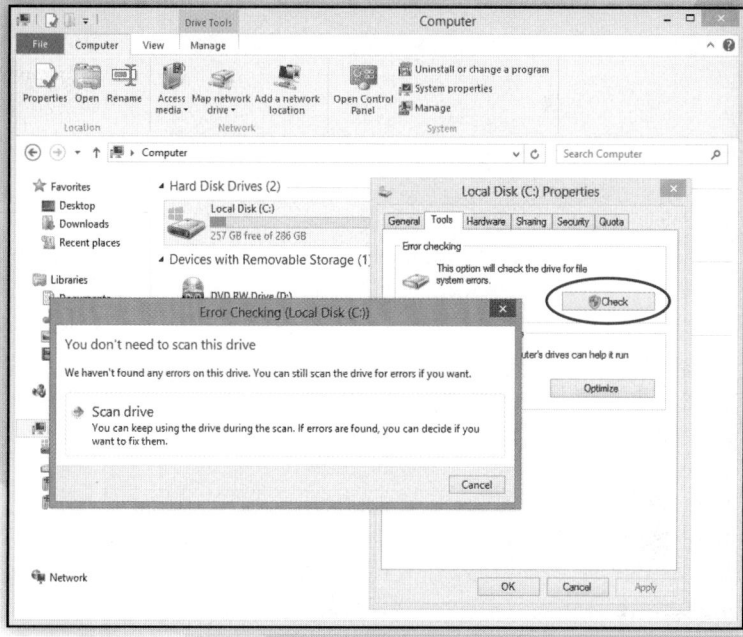

**FIGURE 5.15** The Windows Check Disk utility can check both the file system and the physical health of the disk.

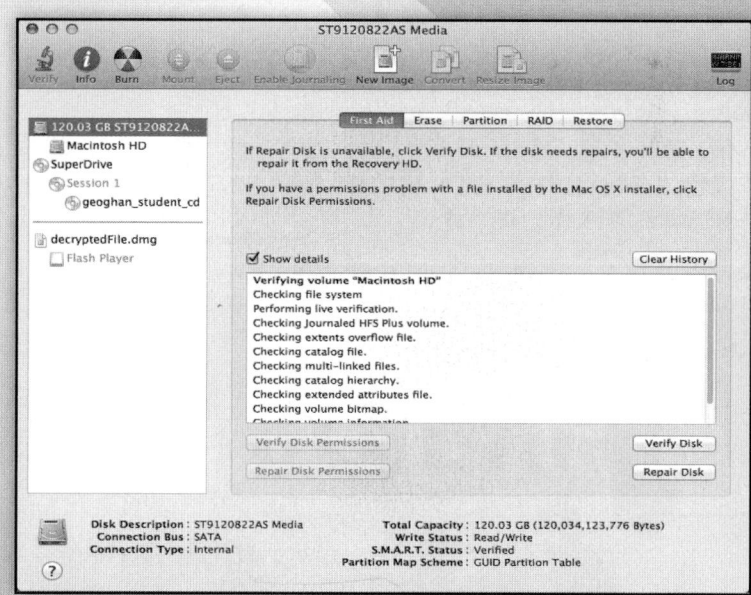

**FIGURE 5.16** The OS X Disk Utility

**OPTIMIZE DRIVES** Over time, the disk can become messy as files are created, edited, saved, and deleted. Staying with the library analogy, as books are checked out, lost, purchased, misplaced, and returned, the shelves can become disorganized and require someone to periodically go through and clean them up. In addition to being unorganized, files that are fragmented are broken into small pieces that are stored in nonadjacent or noncontiguous clusters on the disk. This is referred to as **file fragmentation**. A disk **defragmenter** is a utility that rearranges the fragmented files on your disk to improve efficiency. You should not run a defragmenter on a solid-state disk (SSD).

Windows 8 comes with a built-in utility to optimize and defragment drives that runs automatically on a weekly basis. You can also run it manually if you need to. Microsoft recommends that you defragment a drive that's more than 10 percent fragmented. Figure 5.17 shows the Optimize Drives utility. Like the Disk Check utility, the Optimize Drives utility can be accessed from the Tools tab of the disk's Properties dialog box.

Mac OS X's HFS+ file system has some safeguards against fragmentation, and Macs rarely need to be defragmented. OS X does not include a defragmenter utility, although there are third-party tools you can use.

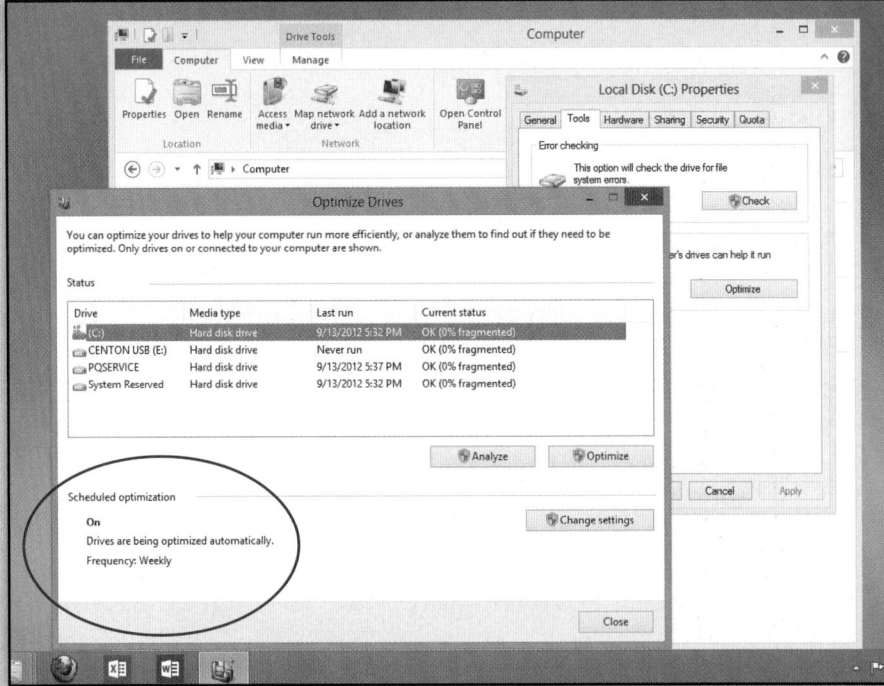

**FIGURE 5.17** The Windows Optimize Drives utility is scheduled to run automatically.

# Find Out MORE

Is defragmenting a disk really necessary? Some people say no. Use the Internet to research the controversy. Do you agree with the contention? Why or why not? What Web pages did you find supporting this argument? What credentials does the author have that makes you trust the information you found? Make sure you're using recent information.

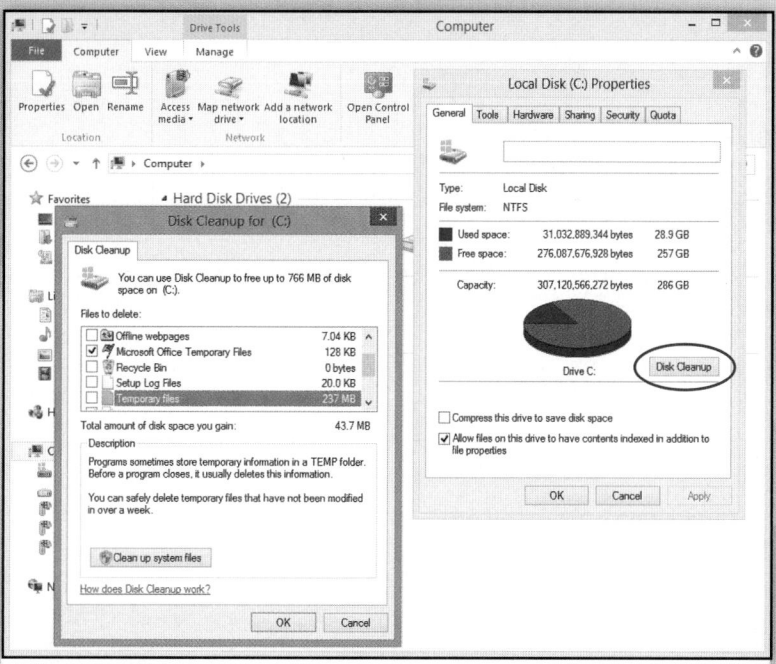

**FIGURE 5.18** The Windows Disk Cleanup utility identifies files that you might choose to delete to free up disk space.

**DISK CLEANUP** Back to the library. Over time, books become damaged, old, outdated, duplicated, and obsolete. A librarian will go through the stacks of books and remove those books. A disk cleanup utility looks for files that can be safely deleted to free up disk space so you have more space to store your files and to help keep your system running efficiently. The Windows Disk Cleanup utility is on the General tab of the disk's Properties dialog box. Click the *Disk Cleanup* button to begin. Figure 5.18 shows the result of running the Windows Disk Cleanup utility. During the first part of the process, the disk is analyzed and the results can be reviewed by the user. When you click on each file type listed, a description of these files displays. You should read each description carefully to help you decide which files you can delete safely. In this example, several types of files are checked

by default, and the total amount of disk space I would gain is a meager 43.7 MB. If I choose to delete the Temporary files, I can free up another 237 MB of space. To proceed with the cleanup, click *OK*.

Macs have daily, weekly, and monthly maintenance scripts that run automatically overnight, so you don't normally need to do any other disk cleanup of your own. That said, it still makes sense to delete unneeded files and empty the Trash to keep your disk clutter free.

The utilities discussed here are included with Windows and Mac; however, there are also third-party versions available. The important thing is to remember to use them. Like changing the oil in your car and checking the tire pressure, regular maintenance of your computer will keep it running more efficiently and make it last longer.

# GREEN COMPUTING

## POWER MANAGEMENT

Did you know that you could cut the energy used by your computer in half, saving between $25–75 a year in energy costs, by using its power management features? That would save more than lowering your home thermostat by 2 degrees or replacing 6 regular light bulbs with compact fluorescents (CFLs). Putting your computer into a low power mode can save on home cooling costs and even prolong the life of your notebook battery.

Energy Star power management features are standard in both Windows and Mac operating systems. Activating these settings is easy and saves both money and resources. The EPA recommends setting computers to sleep or hibernate after 30 to 60 minutes of inactivity. To save even more, set monitors to sleep after 5 to 20 minutes of inactivity. And don't use screensavers—they actually increase energy use!

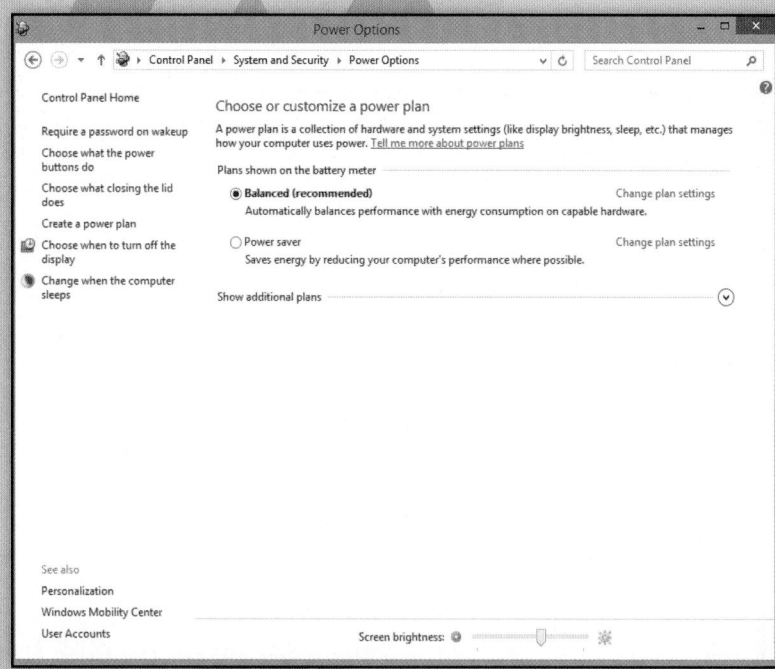

# CAREER SPOTLIGHT

An entry-level IT job that requires good OS skills is a computer support specialist working at a helpdesk. Helpdesk specialists are the folks you speak with when you call or email for tech support. Computer support specialists assist people with computer problems—both hardware and software related. As you can imagine, a good foundation in operating systems is a must. Helpdesk technicians typically have an associate's degree or certifications such as CompTIA A+. According to the U.S. Bureau of Labor Statistics, by 2016, the demand for helpdesk jobs will increase by 18 percent.

Calling:

## HELPDESK

## ▶ Running Project

Open the disk properties for your primary hard drive (C). What's the disk file system? What is its capacity, and how much disk space is used? If you are using a Windows computer, on the Tools tab, click *Optimize* to start the Optimize Drives utility. When was the disk last defragmented? What percentage of the disk is currently fragmented?

## 4 Things You Need to Know

- Utility software helps you maintain your computer.
- You format a disk to prepare it to hold data.
- Files that are broken up and stored in noncontiguous clusters are considered to be fragmented.
- NTFS is the file system used on Windows-formatted hard drives. HFS+ is the file system used on Macs.

## Key Terms

defragmenter

file fragmentation

file system

format

utility software

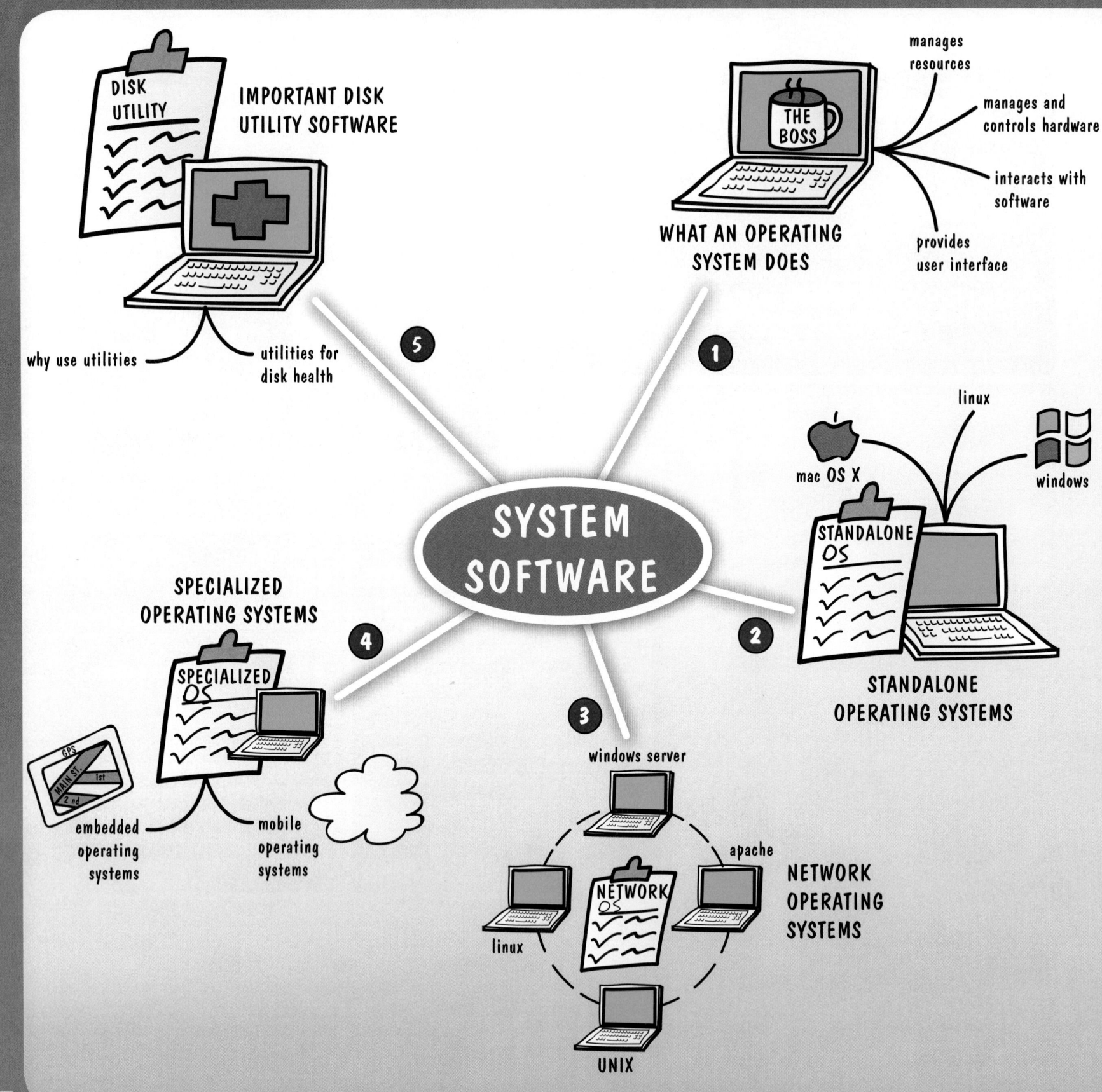

IMPORTANT DISK
UTILITY SOFTWARE

DISK
UTILITY

WHAT AN OPERATING
SYSTEM DOES

THE BOSS

manages
resources

manages and
controls hardware

interacts with
software

provides
user interface

why use utilities

utilities for
disk health

SYSTEM
SOFTWARE

① ②

③ ④ ⑤

linux

mac OS X

windows

STANDALONE
OS

STANDALONE
OPERATING SYSTEMS

SPECIALIZED
OPERATING SYSTEMS

SPECIALIZED
OS

GPS
MAIN ST.
1st
2nd

embedded
operating
systems

mobile
operating
systems

windows server

NETWORK
OS

linux

apache

UNIX

NETWORK
OPERATING
SYSTEMS

# Objectives Recap

1. Explain what an operating system does.
2. Compare the most common stand-alone operating systems.
3. Compare specialized operating systems.
4. Compare the most common network operating systems.
5. List and explain important disk utility software.

# Key Terms

# Summary

**1. Explain what an operating system does.**

The operating system (OS) is the most important type of system software because it provides the user with the interface to communicate with the hardware and other software on the computer. The operating system also manages the allocation of memory and processing resources to both hardware and software, manages and controls hardware using Plug and Play and device drivers, and provides services to applications through the use of an application programming interface (API).

**2. Compare the most common stand-alone operating systems.**

The three most common stand-alone operating systems are Microsoft Windows, Mac OS X, and Linux.

Windows has been around since 1985, and the current versions are Windows 7 and 8. Windows is installed on over 90 percent of personal computers.

The Mac OS has been around since the first Mac computer was released in 1984. The Mac OS only runs on Mac computers, which currently make up about 5 percent of the total personal computer market. The current versions are OS X Lion and OS X Mountain Lion.

Linux was first released in 1991 and is the OS kernel for hundreds of different distributions (distros) that come bundled with utilities and applications. The most popular Linux distro is Ubuntu.

**3. Compare specialized operating systems.**

Embedded operating systems run on devices such as ATM machines, GPS devices, video game consoles, ultrasound machines, and even the communication and entertainment system in your car. Because they have specialized and limited functions, these operating systems can be very small and run on simpler hardware.

A mobile operating system such as Windows Phone, iOS, or Android runs on devices such as smartphones and tablets and is more full-featured than other embedded OSs.

**4. Compare the most common network operating systems.**

A network operating system (NOS) is a multiuser operating system that controls the software and hardware that runs on a network. It allows multiple computers (clients) to communicate with the server and each other as well as to share resources, run applications, and send messages. A NOS centralizes resources and security and provides services such as file and print services, communication services, Internet and email services, and backup and database services.

Most servers run some version of Windows server, Linux, or UNIX. Apache Web server is the most widely used NOS found on Web servers.

**5. List and explain important disk utility software.**

Windows includes several disk utilities to help you maintain your disks: Check Disk, Optimize Drives, and Disk Cleanup. Disk-checking utilities monitor the health of the file system on a disk. OS X includes Disk Utility to verify and repair disk problems. A defragmenter is a utility that rearranges fragmented files on your disk to improve efficiency.

# Application Project

## Microsoft Office Application Project 1:
### PowerPoint Level 2

**PROJECT DESCRIPTION:** In this Microsoft PowerPoint project, you will create a presentation about upgrading your operating system. In creating this presentation you will apply design, font, and color themes. You will also change font colors, bullet symbols, and slide layout.

**INSTRUCTIONS:** For the purpose of grading of the project you are required to perform the following tasks:

| Step | Instructions |
|------|-------------|
| 1 | Start PowerPoint. Download and open the file named *vt_ch05_ppt*. Save the file as **lastname_firstname_ch05_ppt**. |
| 2 | On Slide 1, type **Questions to Ask** in the subtitle placeholder. On Slide 2, type **Will it Run?** in the title placeholder. |
| 3 | Apply the Facet theme, blue Variant, to the presentation. |
| 4 | On Slide 2, change the bullet style to Arrow Bullets, and change the line spacing of the bullets to double. |
| 5 | On Slide 3, change the title to **Check Hardware and Software**. |
| 6 | On Slide 3, insert the downloaded *vt_ch05_image1* in the content placeholder. Apply the Metal Rounded Rectangle picture style to the image. |
| 7 | Change the layout of Slide 4 to Two Content. |
| 8 | On Slide 4, in the left pane, type the following 4 item list. **Pros**, **Latest features**, **Modern interface**, **Security**. |

| Step | Instructions |
|------|-------------|
| 9 | On Slide 4, in the right pane, type the following 4 item list. **Cons**, **Hardware requirements**, **Software compatibility**, **Learning curve**. |
| 10 | On Slide 4, select the last three items in each list, and use the Increase List level button to indent them. |
| 11 | Insert a new Title and Content slide after Slide 4. |
| 12 | On Slide 5, in the title placeholder, type **For More Information**. Type **Contact IT Services** in the content placeholder and change the bullet to None. |
| 13 | Insert the page number and your name in the footer on the notes and handouts pages for all slides in the presentation. |
| 14 | Apply the Reveal slide transition to all slides, with a duration of 4.00. View the presentation in Slide Show view from beginning to end, and then return to Normal view. |
| 15 | Save and close the presentation. Exit PowerPoint. Submit the presentation as directed. |

Visit **pearsonhighered.com/Geoghan** for data files, simulations, VizClips, and additional study materials.

218 | APPLICATION PROJECT

## Microsoft Office Application Project 2:
## Excel Level 2

**PROJECT DESCRIPTION:** In this Microsoft Excel project, you will format cells and use functions and an absolute cell reference in a formula. You will also create and format a pie chart.

**INSTRUCTIONS:** For the purpose of grading the project you are required to perform the following tasks:

| Step | Instructions |
|------|--------------|
| **1** | Start Excel. Open the downloaded Excel file named *vt_ch05_excel*. Save the file as **lastname_firstname_ch05_excel**. |
| **2** | Select the range A1:C1 and set the text to wrap in the cells. Center and middle align the text in the selected range. |
| **3** | Set the width of columns A, B, and C to 20. Set the height of row 1 to 40. |
| **4** | Merge and center the text in cell A1 over columns A:C. Apply the cell style Heading 1. Merge and center the text in A2 over columns A:C. Apply the cell style Heading 2. |
| **5** | In cell A11, type **Total**. In cell B11, use the SUM function to calculate the 3rd Quarter 2011 sales. Select the range A11:C11 and apply the Total cell style. |
| **6** | In cell C4, create a formula using an absolute cell reference to calculate the Market Share of Android. |
| **7** | Copy the formula in cell C4 down to C5:C10. Apply the Percentage number format. |

| Step | Instructions |
|------|--------------|
| **8** | Select the range A4:B10 and insert a 3-D Pie chart. Move the chart so that its upper left corner aligns with the upper left corner of cell A13. |
| **9** | Change the layout of the chart to Layout 6. Change the chart title to **3rd Quarter Sales**. |
| **10** | Format the chart area with the default gradient fill. |
| **11** | Insert a header with the Sheet name in the center cell. Insert a footer with the file name in the left cell. Return to Normal View. |
| **12** | Change the orientation of Sheet 1 to Portrait. Center the worksheet horizontally and vertically on the page. |
| **13** | Rename Sheet 1 as 3Q11. |
| **14** | Ensure that the worksheets are correctly named and placed in the following order in the workbook: 3Q11, Source. Save the workbook. Close the workbook and then exit Excel. Submit the workbook as directed. |

Visit **pearsonhighered.com/Geoghan** for data files, simulations, VizClips, and additional study materials.

Chapter 5

219

# Multiple Choice

Answer the multiple-choice questions below for more practice with key terms and concepts from this chapter.

1. Which is a function of an operating system?
   a. Provide user interface
   b. Protect against malware
   c. Edit images
   d. Browse the Internet

2. What OS feature makes installing new hardware easy?
   a. Graphical user interface
   b. Application Programming Interface
   c. Plug and Play
   d. Multi-touch

3. _____ is the ability to do more than one task at a time.
   a. Graphical user interface
   b. Multitasking
   c. Plug and Play
   d. NOS

4. Which operating system is open source?
   a. Microsoft Windows
   b. Mac OS X
   c. Linux
   d. iOS

5. A limitation of Mac OS X is that it _____.
   a. does not have a GUI
   b. only runs on Mac computers
   c. can't be updated over the Internet
   d. can't be used in a home network

6. Which mobile operating system uses direct manipulation and multi-gesture touch such as swipe, tap, and pinch to control it?
   a. Windows Phone
   b. Android
   c. Linux Mobile
   d. iOS

7. On what type of device might you find an embedded OS?
   a. Desktop computer
   b. GPS
   c. Notebook computer
   d. Server

8. Which is the most popular NOS found on Web servers?
   a. Windows NT
   b. Novell Linux Enterprise
   c. Red Hat Enterprise
   d. Apache

9. What is the process of preparing a disk for storing files called?
   a. File system sectoring
   b. Defragmenting
   c. Disk cleanup
   d. Formatting

10. What utility should you use to reorganize the files on your disk to improve efficiency?
    a. Optimize Drives
    b. Disk Checker
    c. Disk Cleanup
    d. Disk Properties

# True or False

Answer the following questions with T for true or F for false for more practice with key terms and concepts from this chapter.

1. You can use a computer without an operating system installed.

2. Application software interacts with the operating system through the use of an API.

3. The OS communicates with hardware via device drivers.

4. Many people don't use Linux because it requires high-end hardware to run.

5. A network operating system is necessary to set up a peer-to-peer network.

6. Android is a mobile Linux operating system found on many smartphones and tablets.

7. A NOS centralizes resources and security and provides services such as file and print services to clients.

8. The file system used on hard disks in Windows is the HFS+ file system.

9. Using a screensaver reduces energy consumption on your computer.

10. The Windows Disk Cleanup utility identifies files that you might choose to delete to free up disk space.

# Fill in the Blank

Fill in the blanks with key terms from this chapter.

1. A(n) _____ allows a user to point and click on objects to initiate commands.

2. An OS communicates with hardware by means of a(n) _____.

3. Mountain Lion is the current version of _____.

4. Ubuntu is the most popular desktop version of _____.

5. Manufacturers sometimes release a prerelease or _____ of software before the final version is released.

6. To _____ is the process of preparing a disk to store files by dividing it into tracks and sectors and setting up the file system.

7. The OS on a smartphone is referred to as a(n) _____.

8. A(n) _____ runs on servers in a client-server network.

9. _____ occurs when unorganized files are broken into small pieces stored in nonadjacent or noncontiguous clusters on the disk.

10. The _____ of a disk keeps track of what files are saved and where they're stored on the disk.

# Running Project ...

## ... The Finish Line

Use your answers to the previous sections of the running project. Assume that you just got a new computer with no software on it. What operating system and version would you install? Select one utility that you consider indispensable to have. Which program did you pick and why?

Write a report describing your selections and responding to the questions raised. Save your file as **lastname_firstname_ch05_project**, and submit it to your instructor as directed.

# Do It Yourself 1

Utility software is important to protect and maintain your computer. In this activity, you'll examine your computer to determine what type of utility software is installed on it and if it's properly protected.

1. Open the Action Center by clicking on the white flag in the notification area of the Windows taskbar, or by opening the Control Panel and then choosing *System and Security*.

2. If necessary, click the arrow next to Security to open that section. What is your status for each category? Are there any important notices? What software is reported for virus protection and spyware?

3. If necessary, click the arrow next to Maintenance to open that section. What is your status for each category? Are there any important notices?

4. Write up your answers to the questions above. Include a screen shot of the Action Center. Save your file as **lastname_ firstname_ch05_diy1**, and submit your work as directed by your instructor.

**If you are using a Mac:**

Open the Utilities folder from the Launchpad. What utilities are in this folder? Explore the Activity Monitor, Network Utility, and System Information. Use Help to look up each of these utilities. What is the purpose of each of these? Write up your answers to the questions above. Save your file as **lastname_ firstname_ch05_diy1**, and submit your work as directed by your instructor.

# Do It Yourself 2

In this exercise, you'll perform a disk check on your flash drive.

1. Insert your flash drive into the computer. If necessary, wait until Windows finishes installing drivers. Close any windows that open automatically.

2. Open File Explorer. Right-click on your flash drive, and choose *Properties*. Open your word processor and type your answers to the following questions: What file system is on the disk? What's the capacity, and how much free space is on the disk? Take a screen shot of the Properties dialog box, and paste it into your document.

3. Click the *Tools* tab and click *Check*. Make sure that only the first box is checked, and click *Scan drive*.) When the scan is finished, click *Show Details*, and take a screen shot of the results. Paste it into your document.

4. Type up your answers to the questions. Save the file as **lastname_firstname_ch05_diy2**, and submit your work as directed by your instructor.

**If you are using a Mac:**

1. Insert the flash drive into the computer.

2. Open the Disk Utility from Launchpad, Utilities folder. Select the flash drive from the left pane of the Disk Utility. Open your word processor and type your answers to the following questions: What file system is on the disk? What's the capacity, and how much free space is on the disk? Take a screen shot and paste it into your document.

3. If necessary, click the *First Aid* tab and click *Verify Disk*, Make sure Show Details is checked. When the scan is finished, take a screen shot of the results and paste it into your document,

4. Type up your answers to the questions. Save the file as **lastname_firstname_ch05_diy2**, and submit your work as directed by your instructor.

# File Management

Utility software such as disk defragmenters and cleanup utilities help you keep your computer running efficiently. In this activity, you'll use the Windows Disk Cleanup utility to examine some of the files on your computer.

1. Open File Explorer and click *Computer*. What items are listed under *Hard Disk Drives*? Right-click on the *C*: drive, and click *Properties*. What is the capacity of the disk? How much free space is currently available?

2. Click the *Disk Cleanup* button. Allow the Disk Cleanup utility to analyze your system. When it's finished, take a screen shot of this dialog box. Note: This process may take several minutes to complete.

3. Click on each of the categories of files listed, and read the descriptions in the bottom of the dialog box. What types of files are included in Downloaded Program Files and Temporary Internet Files? What are Temporary Files, and is it safe to delete them? What other categories of files are listed? Which ones have check marks next to them? How much space could you free up if you cleaned up all the files found?

4. Type up your answers, including the screen shot from step 2. Save your file as **lastname_firstname_ch05_fm**, and submit it as directed by your instructor.

**If you are using a Mac:**

There is no disk cleaning utility in OS X. For this exercise, you will learn how to manually clean up your disk.

From the Help Center, search for **increase disk space**. What are the recommended methods for cleaning up your disk? Open the section Delete items you don't need. Where are these files located? Type up your answers, save your file as **lastname_firstname_ch05_fm**, and submit it as directed by your instructor.

# Critical Thinking

Your school is still running Windows 7 in the computer lab. It's considering upgrading to Windows 8. As a user of the computer lab, you've been asked to give some input into the decision process.

1. Use the Internet to research the improvements in Windows 8 over Windows 7. What are the improvements you feel are the most important? Do they require any special hardware or software to be installed?

2. Do you recommend the school upgrade the computer lab? Give two reasons supporting your recommendation.

3. Write up a one-page summary that includes the answers to the questions above. Save the file as **lastname_firstname_ch05_ct**, and submit your assignment as directed by your instructor.

## Ethical Dilemma

Miriam works at a small company and was just passed over for a promotion, which was given to a new employee, Bill, because he has a certification. Bill lets it slip that he easily passed the test because he paid $50 for a study guide that had all the test answers in it.

1. Miriam is confused. She has the experience in the company, but Bill got the job because he has the certification. What should she do? Should she report Bill to her employer? To the certification testing center? Borrow the questions and take the exam herself? What would you do?

2. Because this has been a common issue in the past, the certification tests have become stricter and more difficult to cheat on, but it still happens. Use the Internet to find out the penalty for cheating on one of the current IT industry exams.

3. Write up a one-page summary that includes the answers to the questions above. Save the file as **lastname_firstname_ch05_ethics**, and submit it as directed by your instructor.

## On the Web

In this activity, you'll compare the hardware requirements for different versions of Windows.

1. Use the Internet to research the hardware requirements for each of the following versions of Windows: Windows 3.1, Windows 95, Windows 98, Windows XP, Windows Vista, Windows 7, and Windows 8. When there are multiple versions of the OS, choose the original release and the Home (or Home Premium) version.

2. Create a table like the one below.

| Windows Version | Year Released | Minimum Processor | Minimum Memory | Minimum Free Disk Space | Optical Disc Type | Other Requirements |
|---|---|---|---|---|---|---|
| Windows 3.1 | | | | | | |
| Windows 95 | | | | | | |
| Windows 98 | | | | | | |
| Windows XP | | | | | | |
| Windows Vista | | | | | | |
| Windows 7 | | | | | | |
| Windows 8 | | | | | | |

3. What websites did you use to locate this information? Save the file as **lastname_firstname_ch05_web**, and submit your work as directed by your instructor.

# Collaboration

**Instructors:** Divide the class into groups of three to five members, and assign each group one topic for this project. The topics include Windows 8, OS X Mountain Lion, and Ubuntu Linux. For larger classes, assign multiple groups the same operating system.

**The Project:** Each team is to prepare a commercial that includes an explanation of its operating system and special features that aren't included in this book. Teams must use at least three references, only one of which may be this textbook. Use Google Docs or Microsoft Office to prepare the outline and script of your commercial, and provide documentation that all team members have contributed to the project.

**Students:** Before beginning this project, discuss the roles each group member will play. Choose a team name, which you'll use in submitting your commercial. Be sure to divide the work among your members, and pick someone to present your project. You may find it helpful to elect a team leader who can direct your activities and ensure that all team contributions are collated through Google Docs or Microsoft Office as directed by your instructor.

**Outcome:** You're to prepare a commercial on your assigned topic. The presentation may be no longer than 2 minutes. You may videotape it or perform it live for your class. On the first page of your written outline, be sure to include the name of your commercial and a list of all team members. Turn in a final version of your outline and script named as **teamname_ch05_collab**. Submit your project to your instructor as directed.

# 6

# Digital Devices and Multimedia

Visit **pearsonhighered.com/Geoghan** for data files, simulations, VizClips, and additional study materials.

## Running Project

In this chapter, you explore how to purchase and use different types of digital devices and share multimedia content you create. Look for instructions as you complete each article. For most, there is a series of questions for you to research. At the conclusion of the chapter you're asked to submit your responses to the questions raised.

1. **Explain the features of various types of digital cameras.**

2. **Compare different methods for transferring images from a digital camera.**

3. **List several ways to edit and print photos.**

4. **Recognize different audio file types.**

5. **Describe several ways to create videos.**

6. **Compare portable media players, tablets, and smartphones.**

# IN THIS CHAPTER

Digital devices, such as digital cameras, smartphones, and tablets, have become commonplace in our lives. **Multimedia**, which is the integration of text, graphics, video, animation, and sound, describes the type of content we view and create with these devices. In this chapter, we discuss digital devices and multimedia content and how we use these every day.

# Digital Camera Basics

## OBJECTIVE

## Explain the features of various types of digital cameras.

Over the past few years, digital cameras have become increasing popular as they've dropped in price and gotten easier to use. In fact, you don't even need to have a computer to use one. In this article we look at the different types of digital cameras on the market, the features that distinguish them, and how to use them to capture your memories.

VIZ CLIP

## KEY FEATURES

Choosing a digital camera can be bewildering with all of the choices available today. Three important features that can help you sort it all out are resolution, storage type, and zoom and lenses.

**FIGURE 6.1** Image Resolution for Photo Quality Prints

| RESOLUTION | PHOTO QUALITY PRINT SIZE |
|---|---|
| 1–2 megapixel | Up to $4 \times 6$ |
| 2–3 megapixel | Up to $5 \times 7$ |
| 4–5 megapixel | Up to $8 \times 10$ |
| 6–7 megapixel | Up to $11 \times 14$ |
| 8 megapixel | Up to $16 \times 20$ |
| 10 megapixel | Up to $20 \times 30$ |

**RESOLUTION** The quality of the images that a camera can take is determined by the resolution. **Resolution** is the measure of the number of pixels in an image and is expressed in megapixels. A 10-megapixel camera can take a picture containing 10 million pixels of information. The higher the resolution, the more detail in the image and the larger the prints you can make before the image quality suffers. Figure 6.1 lists the best resolution for various photo print sizes. Images that will only be viewed on a computer screen can be taken at a lower resolution (lower quality) than those intended for photo quality prints. This is important, because resolution also affects file size: the higher the resolution, the larger the file. A very high resolution image is not appropriate for use on a Web page because the larger file size takes longer to load onto the screen. This also affects storage. Many cameras allow you to select the image quality before you take a picture. Setting the camera to take lower resolution pictures will allow you to fit more pictures on your memory card.

**STORAGE** Digital cameras can store images internally or on removable memory cards. The internal memory on most cameras is relatively small compared to the capacity of removable media. The type of card you choose will depend on the camera. Flash memory cards come in capacities up to 100 GB in size, depending on the type of card. The cost of these cards has dropped dramatically, and many people now carry multiple cards with their cameras. The advantage to carrying these cards is that they can be easily read by most computers and in kiosks in many stores. In fact, consumers who don't have a computer can still use a digital camera and simply bring their memory cards to their local grocery store or drugstore to have the pictures printed or use a photo printer that can read memory cards. Once the images have been printed, saved to your computer, transferred to a CD, or uploaded to the Web, the memory card can be erased and reused.

**ZOOM AND LENSES** Most digital cameras have the ability to zoom in on an object before taking the picture. **Zoom** can be either optical or digital, and some cameras will combine both. Optical zoom uses a zoom lens to change the focal length of the camera, making objects appear closer (telephoto) or farther away (wide-angle). Typical low-end digital cameras have an optical zoom of 3–5x, while more advanced (and expensive) cameras may have 20–24x zoom. Some cameras have a macro setting, or close-focus, for taking pictures of objects that are very close. Digital SLRs (D-SLRs) allow you to change the lens. Zoom, telephoto, macro, and wide-angle lenses can cost hundreds or even thousands of dollars.

Digital zoom crops the image and enlarges a portion of it, resulting in a zoomed image of lower quality. Total zoom on a camera is determined by multiplying its optical by its digital zoom. So, a camera with a 3x optical zoom and a 10x digital zoom has a total zoom of 300x. Because digital zoom lowers the image quality, it's better to rely on optical zoom when taking picture. You can always use software to crop and enlarge the image later (see Figure 6.2).

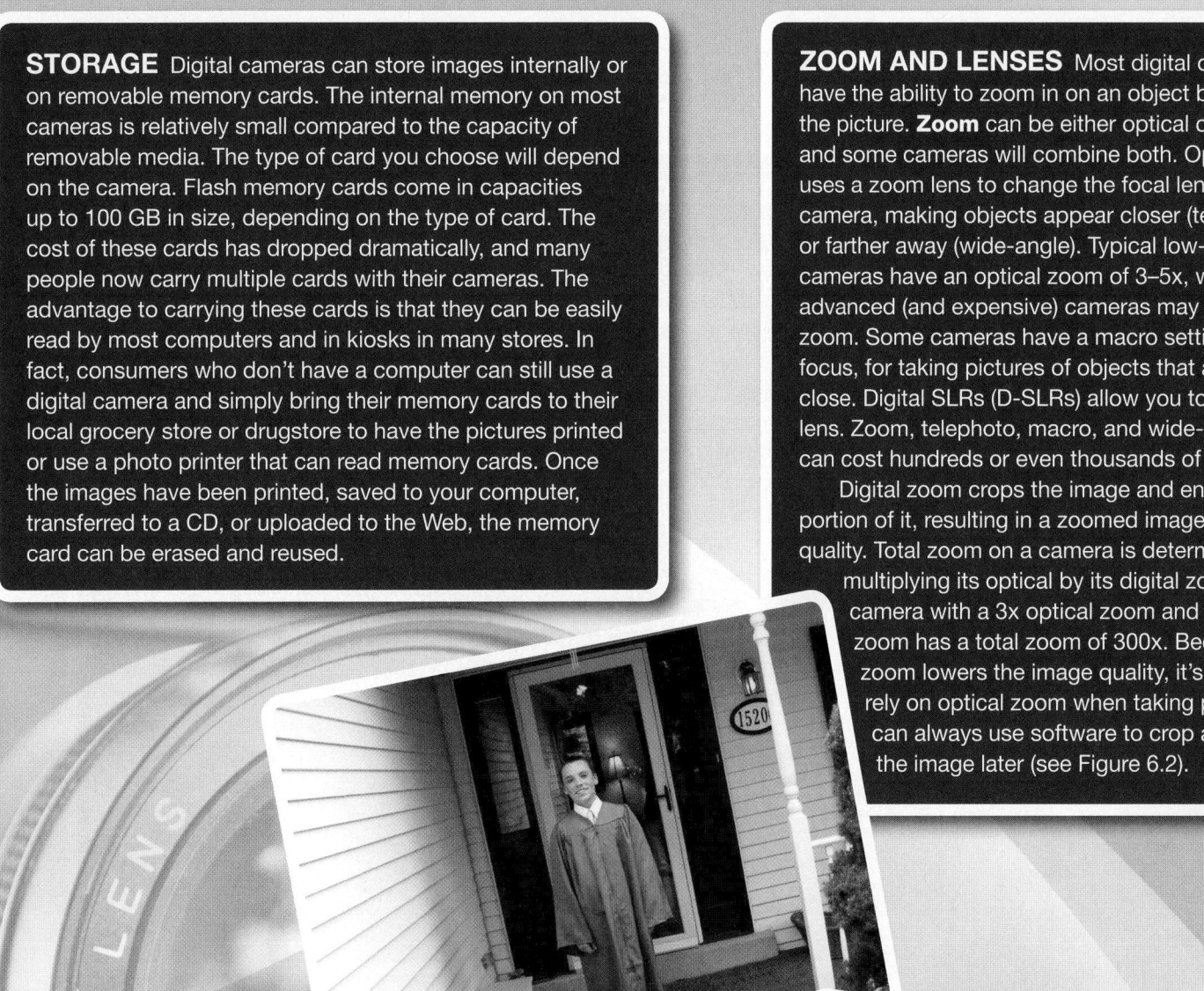

**FIGURE 6.2** These images illustrate how zoom can make the subject appear closer.

# TYPES OF DIGITAL CAMERAS

Not so long ago, digital cameras were expensive niche items. Today, they range from disposable cameras you can buy in a drug store for under $20 to high-performance digital SLR cameras costing thousands. Most fall somewhere in between the two. Choosing the camera that is right for you will depend on a number of factors, including the types of pictures you plan to take, ease of use, and cost.

**POINT-AND-SHOOT** The easiest cameras to use are point-and-shoot. They range from very simple and inexpensive cameras with limited features to high-end cameras with all the bells and whistles—and a price tag to match.

Basic **point-and-shoot cameras** are the simplest, least expensive, and have the fewest features. You can purchase one for as little as $20 or spend hundreds of dollars for more features. Basic cameras may not have a flash or viewfinder and may have limited or no optical zoom. Another drawback to these cameras is that they often suffer from noticeable **shutter lag**—the time between pressing the button and the camera snapping the picture. When your subject is smiling and waiting for the flash to go off, several seconds can seem like a long time, and shutter lag can cause you to miss that action shot. Some basic point-and-shoots have the ability to capture limited video and can be used as a webcam. Most point-and-shoot cameras don't have a viewfinder to help you frame your image. They rely instead on the LCD screen (see Figure 6.3). Most of the time this is fine, but some people feel that a true viewfinder does a better job of framing the shot.

Single-use disposable cameras are basic point-and-shoot cameras that can be purchased in drugstores and supermarkets. These are great to carry on trips, send to school with your kids, and put out on tables at weddings and other celebrations for the guests to take pictures. Keep one in your car for that once in a lifetime shot, or to document a fender-bender.

**FIGURE 6.3** Most point-and-shoot cameras use an LCD screen, rather than a viewfinder, to frame a shot.

**FIGURE 6.4** Comparison of Point-and-Shoot Digital Cameras

|  | BASIC POINT-AND-SHOOT | ADVANCED POINT-AND-SHOOT |
|---|---|---|
| **General** | Tiny, fits in a pocket or is part of a cell phone or tablet. | Produces better pictures, provides more control, zoom, and features, but still lets you point and shoot |
| **Resolution** | 1–8 megapixels | 10–18 megapixels and up |
| **Price** | $20–$200<br><br>Good for snapshots, especially outdoors and Web/email | $50–$600<br><br>Good for snapshots, portraits, and enlargements, Web/email |
| **Special features** | Low resolution video, may be used as a webcam | May capture short video clips and include macro (close-up) and other special effects, manually control settings, image stabilization, burst mode. Little or no shutter lag. |
| **Zoom** | Usually has little optical zoom, may not have a flash or viewfinder | Up to 24x optical and additional digital zoom (less expensive models may only have 4–5X optical zoom) and a built in flash. |

Basic point-and-shoot cameras take good pictures under normal conditions, but for better quality images and more features, you'll need a more advanced camera. Advanced point-and-shoot cameras are moderate in price, features, and quality. While still easy to use, they include better zoom, macro functions, viewfinders, and other special effects. Most also include the ability to capture video and may have other features such as image stabilization, which accounts for camera shake and results in sharper images, and burst mode, which allows you to take several pictures in a burst by holding down the shutter button. They may also include some of the features of professional D-SLR cameras, such as the ability to adjust speed and exposure settings. Although more expensive than basic cameras, advanced point-and-shoots are still relatively inexpensive.

Figure 6.4 compares features of different types of point-and-shoot cameras. Deciding which camera to purchase can be a difficult task with all of the options available today.

## COMPACT SYSTEM CAMERAS

Also known as superzooms, **compact system cameras (CSC)** are advanced point-and-shoot cameras that have interchangeable lenses (see Figure 6.5), some manual controls like a D-SLR, 10x to 26x optical zoom lenses, and the ability to capture HD video. They are smaller, less expensive, and easier to use than the D-SLRs, and they can produce better images than point-and-shoots. Other features include hot shoe and accessory ports to attach an external flash, microphone, or viewfinder. Priced from about $300 to $2,000, these cameras are more expensive than most point-and-shoot cameras but less expensive than most D-SLRs.

**FIGURE 6.5** A Compact System Camera with Interchangeable Lens

**DIGITAL SINGLE LENS REFLEX (D-SLR)** If you really want control and a more traditional type camera, then you'll want to look at a **digital single lens reflex (D-SLR) camera**. With D-SLRs, you can change the lens, which can cost hundreds or even thousands of dollars, to get the exact zoom you need. You can attach a hot-shoe flash, manually adjust focus and exposure, and look through the viewfinder to frame your shot, allowing you to create artistic images that auto focusing point-and-shoots can't. There is almost no shutter lag, so they are the best type of digital camera for shooting action stills. Older D-SLRs did not have the ability to shoot video, but processing power has increased and many newer D-SLRs can now shoot HD video. All this comes at a steep cost—from $700 to $5,000, plus hundreds or thousands of dollars for additional lenses (see Figure 6.6).

**FIGURE 6.6** A D-SLR Camera with Attached Lens and Hot-shoe Flash

## Running Project

Use the Internet to research digital cameras. What is the highest resolution available today in point-and-shoot cameras? CSCs? D-SLRs? Choose one point-and-shoot, one CRC, and one D-SLR camera with the same resolution. How do they compare in terms of price, features, and reviews? What other factors affect the price?

## 5 Things You Need to Know

- Resolution determines the quality of the print you can make and the size of the file.
- Optical zoom is better than digital zoom.
- Point-and-shoot cameras are the easiest to use.
- Compact system cameras blend the ease of point-and-shoot with some of the control and quality of a D-SLR.
- D-SLRs take the best pictures and cost the most.

## Key Terms

compact system camera (CSC)

digital single lens reflex
   (D-SLR) camera

point-and-shoot camera

resolution

shutter lag

zoom

# Bridging the Gap: Transferring Photos

## Compare different methods for transferring images from a digital camera.

Imagine you just came home from a vacation and have a camera full of pictures. What do you do next? If you have a computer, you'll want to transfer the pictures from the camera to your computer so you can view, edit, store, share, and print them. There are several ways to transfer your images to your computer.

## MEMORY CARDS

If your camera uses memory cards to store the images, you can take the card out of the camera and put it in a card reader attached to your computer. Many computers have a card reader built in, but you can purchase removable card readers for just a few dollars and plug into a USB port. When you put the memory card into the reader, Windows will detect it, and it will appear in the Computer window as a removable device. You can copy, move, and delete the pictures just like any other type of file. See Figure 6.7. Depending on your settings, Windows might automatically start the transfer process as described in the next section. If you are using a Mac, the memory card will appear as a disk on your desktop and you can simply open it and copy the images over to your computer, or iPhoto may open and give you the option to import the images.

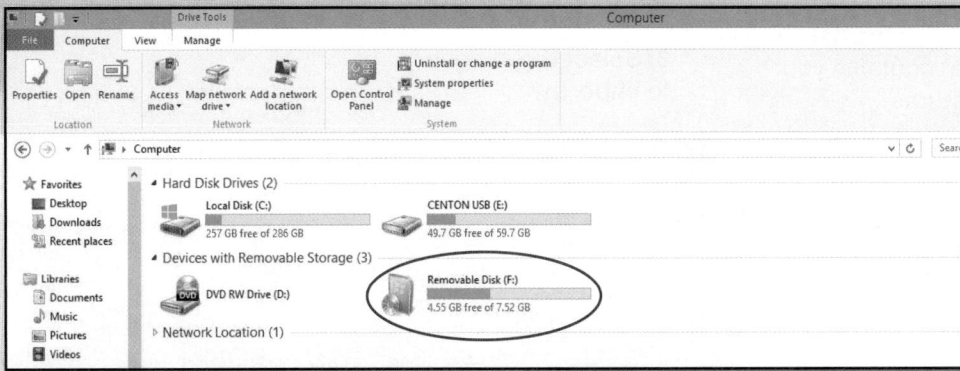

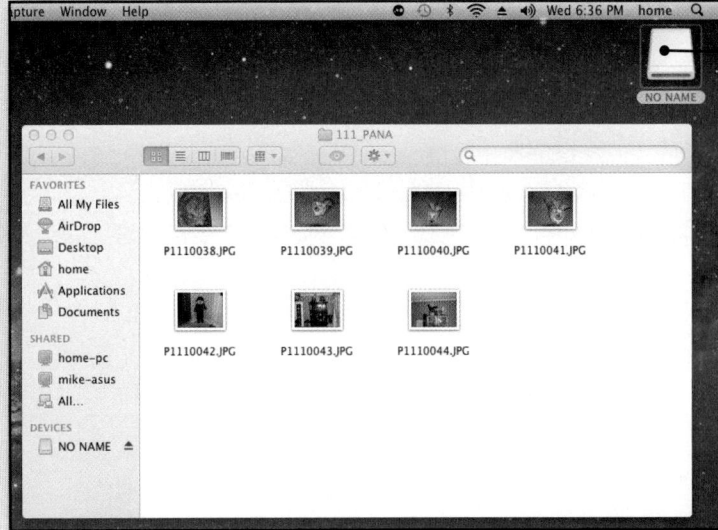

Mac OS X displays the memory card on the desktop. Double-click to open the disk in Finder.

**FIGURE 6.7** A memory card appears in the Computer window or on the Mac desktop.

**Try the Digital Devices and Multimedia Simulation**

# USB OR FIREWIRE CABLE

Digital cameras typically have a USB or FireWire connection that can be used to connect the camera directly to the computer, which requires you to install device driver software for the computer to be able to talk to the camera. The driver installation might happen through software that comes with your camera or through the operating system itself. Once the driver has been installed, the computer and camera can communicate and you can transfer the pictures. Windows automatically starts the process of transferring your pictures when you connect the camera to a computer (see Figure 6.8). You have the options of **tagging** the images with keywords and of erasing them from the memory card. If you are using Windows, the operating system will automatically create a new folder inside your Pictures folder and copy the pictures into it. The folder will be named based on the tags you provided and the date of the transfer so you can find your pictures easily later. If you are using a Mac, you can use iPhoto to download your photos. Once you connect your camera via USB to your Mac, iPhoto should open automatically or you can start it from the Dock or Applications stack.

**2. Click the device that contains your pictures.**

**3. Select the images to import.**

**FIGURE 6.8** Windows Picture Transfer Process

**1. If the import process doesn't start automatically, open the Photos app, right-click to open the menu, and then click *Import*.**

**4. Verify the correct folder, and then click Import.**

# WIRELESS TRANSFER

Wireless-enabled digital cameras can transfer photos using WiFi wireless technology, allowing you to connect to a computer network and save photos to your computer or even print photos without cables or card readers. For cameras that don't have built-in wireless, a company called Eye-Fi makes a WiFi-enabled SD (secure digital) card that is compatible with more than 1,000 camera models. The Eye-Fi card is set up once using a standard card reader and then inserted into your camera. The wireless transmission range is about 45 feet indoors. If you are in range of the stored network, your images will automatically "fly" to your computer.

# TRANSFERRING TO THE CLOUD

Cameras that are part of a mobile device, such as a tablet or cell phone, allow you to upload photos directly to the Internet, or cloud (see Figure 6.9). Android devices may upload to Photobucket, Facebook, or Google Picasa; Instagram and DropBox are two commonly used apps that work on multiple platforms. **iOS devices** (iPad, iPhone, iPod) use iCloud, which can sync your data among multiple devices—even a Mac or Windows PC. You can set up the process to be automatic or manually choose which images to upload. This type of transfer requires a working Internet connection on the device.

Email Photo

Message

Use as Wallpaper

Tweet

Print

Copy Photo

Save to Camera Roll

**FIGURE 6.9** From my iPad I can email, message, tweet a photo, or use iCloud to sync a photo to all of my devices.

We take photos for many reasons: to remember a special occasion, a vacation, friends and family, pets, and for more practical reasons such as documenting an accident or how to take apart (and put back to together) a car engine. Once the pictures have been transferred to your computer or the cloud, they can be saved, edited, printed, and shared, and moving the photos off the memory card of your camera frees up space to go out and take some more pictures.

## Running Project

Do any of the cameras you researched in the last section include wireless capabilities? If so, how fast can they transfer images? What are the limitations? If the cameras didn't include wireless, look up the current Eye-Fi card. Is your camera compatible with the card? How much will it cost to purchase the card? Find a similar model camera that includes wireless. How does the price compare to adding the Eye-Fi card instead?

## 4 Things You Need to Know

● Memory cards can be transported from camera to computer.

● USB and FireWire cables connect the camera directly to the computer.

● Wireless transfer uses a WiFi network to transfer photos to your computer.

● Mobile devices can transfer photos to the cloud.

## Key Terms

iOS device

tagging

# A Picture Is Worth a Thousand Words: Editing, Printing, and Sharing Photos

## OBJECTIVE 3
## List several ways to edit and print photos.

The beauty of digital photography is what you can do with the images after you transfer them from your camera. With film photography, unless you invest in expensive darkroom equipment, you are pretty limited to choosing the size and finish of your prints and maybe ordering double-prints to share with someone else. Cropping an image means taking a pair of scissors to it. Today, anyone can create amazing looking photos using a home computer and free or inexpensive software.

## EDITING PHOTOS

One of the biggest advantages of digital photography over film is the ability to edit the images. This can mean doing something as simple as cropping out unwanted parts of the image or removing red-eye or as advanced as using sophisticated software to create works of art, or anything in between.

## EDITING SOFTWARE
Photo editing software is available in simple, free programs, such as Picasa from Google, up to sophisticated (and expensive) professional programs, such as Adobe Photoshop. These programs are covered in more detail in the applications chapter. Older versions of Windows include the ability to perform basic editing on your pictures using the Windows Photo Gallery, but Windows 7 and 8 do not include this feature by default. Microsoft, instead, has a free download called Windows Essentials that includes Windows Photo Gallery, which will allow you to edit, organize, and share your digital photos. Macs include iPhoto (see Figure 6.10). Programs like Windows Photo Gallery, iPhoto, and Picasa also integrate online photo sharing.

FIGURE 6.10 iPhoto is free on Mac computers.

**ONLINE EDITING** Many online photo services, such as Shutterfly (see Figure 6.11) and Flickr, include basic editing tools you can use, including cropping, resizing, and red-eye removal. Editing options also often include special effects such as making the picture look black-and-white and adding special borders. You can also order photo prints and create personalized gifts such as calendars, books, and coffee mugs.

FIGURE 6.11 Online photo editing tools, such as Shutterfly, allow you to edit your images without installing software on your computer.

# PRINTING AND SHARING PHOTOS

The cost of creating prints of your photos varies depending on the paper, ink, and type of printer you use. At home, printing can cost 50 to 70 cents per print. Photo printers can be inkjet printers that use special ink cartridges or dye-sublimation printers, which produce lab-quality prints. Less expensive prints using regular ink and paper have a lower quality and shorter lifespan.

**PICTBRIDGE** **PictBridge** is an industry standard that allows a camera to connect directly to a printer, usually by a USB connection or special dock. Cameras that are compatible with this system don't require connecting to a computer. You can use a small, portable printer to print photos on the spot. You may also be able to do some limited editing either on the camera or printer before you print.

**KIOSKS** Photo kiosks in retail stores have built-in editing capabilities and are very easy to use. Gone are the days of having a whole roll of film developed only to find that most of the pictures are bad. The printing kiosks allow you to print only the pictures you want and to fine-tune your images without needing to use your own computer. You can connect your camera via USB or FireWire, or insert a memory card into the kiosk. These prints typically cost between 15 to 59 cents per print. Kiosks can even print photos you have stored in the cloud or on websites such as Facebook.

## ONLINE PRINTING AND SHARING

Websites such as Snapfish and Shutterfly are personal image-sharing sites. Their main goal is to get you to buy prints and other merchandise they offer. The advantage to using these sites is that you can share your photos with your friends and family, and they can order the items they want directly. The prints can be mailed or picked up at local retail partners. Companies such as Walgreens and Walmart allow you to upload your pictures at home and pick up the prints in the store. The standard prints from these sites cost about 15 cents.

Flickr is an online photo sharing community owned by Yahoo. Flickr has millions of users and millions of images in its vast repository. When you upload images to Flickr, you are able to tag them with keywords that you define. The tags link your images to other Flickr images with the same tag, and while you can choose to keep your pictures private, the majority of the images on Flickr are publically available. Another feature is geotagging (Figure 6.12), which allows you to add your photo to a location on a map.

**FIGURE 6.12** Geotagging Images on Flickr

Flickr also gives you the ability to control how other people can use your pictures legally by applying Creative Commons licensing (CC). You can search Flickr for images that have CC licensing applied. Another feature of Flickr is The Commons. There are currently dozens of institutions participating in The Commons, a project that is designed to make publicly held photography collections accessible to everyone. This is a great resource for you to use when you need an image for a school project. Images in The Commons have no known copyright.

# Find Out MORE

Creative Commons (**creativecommons.org**) is a project that has been developed as a way to increase sharing and collaboration by specifying how images and other materials can be used.

According to the Creative Commons website, Creative Commons "tools give everyone from individual creators to large companies and institutions a simple, standardized way to grant copyright permissions to their creative work. The Creative Commons licenses enable people to easily change their copyright terms from the default of 'all rights reserved' to 'some rights reserved.'"

You can visit the Creative Commons website to learn more about how it works.

One of the first institutions to embrace this idea was the Smithsonian Institution, which made hundreds of images available on Flickr under Creative Commons. Visit **flickr.com/photos/smithsonian** to see them. What copyright restrictions are in place on these images? How can they be used legally? How did you find this information? Are there any other public institutions that have made CC images available on Flickr? How did you find them?

---

For years, whenever we celebrated a special occasion with family and friends, I would take my film to be developed—always ordering a second set of prints so I could share them. The prints were expensive, and often there were several (OK, many) prints that were just awful, and I would throw them away. There was no way to decide ahead of time which prints I wanted—I had to pay for the whole roll. Not anymore. Now, if I take a lousy picture, I can review it right on my camera, and if need be, I can delete it and reshoot another. When I get home, I download the pictures to my computer, crop and enhance them, upload them to Facebook, and share away. That process is so much easier and faster, and much less expensive, because I print few pictures, but instead view and share them online.

## Running Project

Use the Internet to compare the cost and quality of photo prints from several home photo printers, online services, and local retailers in your area. Create a chart comparing them. Include the following information: cost per print, sizes available, finish available, expected lifespan of prints, water resistance, and any other details you think might be important. When might you choose to use each of these methods for prints?

## Key Term

PictBridge

## 4 Things You Need to Know

- Photo editing software can be used to enhance and fix your photos.

- Printing photos at home is easy but can be expensive.

- Kiosks in stores allow you to edit and print better quality photos less expensively than you could print them at home.

- Online printing and sharing sites enable you to edit and share your photos easily and are the least expensive way to print quality photos.

# HOW TO    Edit a Photo

In this exercise you will perform some basic editing on a photo. To complete this exercise, you will need to have Windows Photo Gallery installed on your Windows computer. If it is not, you can download it from **download.live.com** or you can use an online editing tool. If you have a Mac, you can use iPhoto.

**1** Locate the data files for this chapter. Right-click on the file *vt_ch06_kids* and point to Open with and then click *Photo Gallery*.

**2** Click *Edit, organize, or share* on the menu bar. Double-click the image to open the editing screen. Click *Make a copy* and save the copy as **lastname_firstname_ch06_howto1** in your work folder for this chapter. Close the original file and open the copy in Windows Live Photo Gallery. Click *Edit, organize, or share* on the menu bar. Double-click the image to open the editing screen.

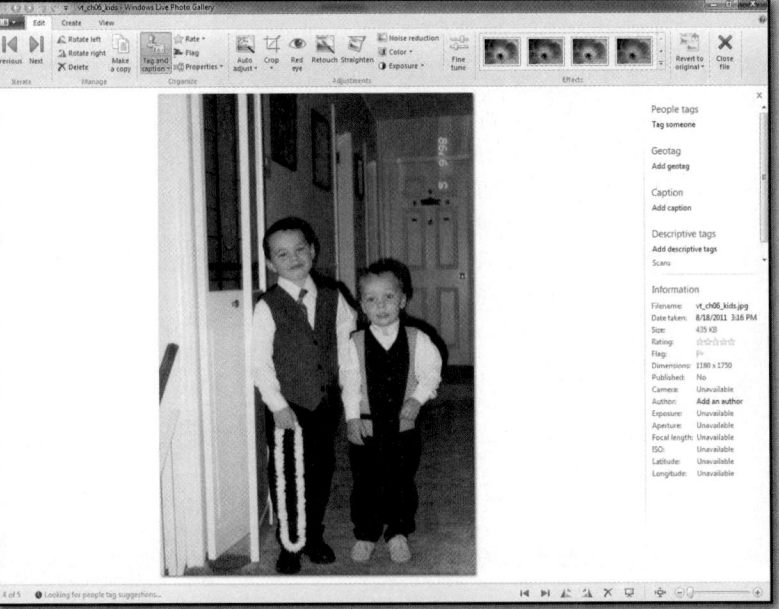

**3** In the Adjustments group, click *Auto adjust* and then click *Noise reduction*.

**4** Click the arrow below the Crop tool, point to Proportion, and select *4x6*. Drag the grid to crop the image so that the boys make up most of the image, and then press Enter (their feet will not fit). Click the *Red eye tool* and drag it around each eye to clean up the eyes.

**5** Use the Info pane on the right to add People and Geo tags. The boy on the left is Joey, and the boy on the right is Mikey. The Geotag is Maryland. Add an appropriate caption and two descriptive tags of your choice.

**6** Close the file (Windows will automatically save your changes). Submit your image as directed by your instructor.

**If you are using iPhoto on a Mac:**

1. Save a copy of *vt_ch06_kids* as **lastname_firstname_ch06_howto1** in your work folder and then import the image into iPhoto.
2. From the Photos menu, choose *Edit Photo*. Use the tools in Quick Fixes pane to Enhance, Fix Red-Eye, Straighten, and Crop as noted in steps 3 and 4 in the PC instructions.
3. Below the Edit pane, click the *Info* button. Change the description, name the faces, and assign a place using the information provided in step 5.

# Making Sense of Sound

## Recognize different audio file types.

Sound plays an important role in the multimedia experience. We listen to songs on our portable media players, use speech to control our computers and video games, and are alerted to new email with a ding. In this article we'll examine the differences in several audio files types and compare various media player programs and speech recognition programs.

## AUDIO FILE TYPES

There are many different audio file types. Music files are typically **MP3** (MPEG-1 Audio Layer 3) files. These files are a compressed format, allowing them to maintain excellent quality while being reasonably small. When you rip a CD, you transfer your music files to your computer. The files on an audio CD are very large, which is why there are typically only 10–12 songs per disc. An MP3 file is about 1/10th the size of a CD file. MP3 utilizes lossy compression, in which some of the detail is removed. There is a trade-off between file size and quality. MP3 files have the file extension .mp3.

The default file type used by Apple's iTunes software is **AAC (advanced audio coding)**, which are files compressed in a manner similar to MP3s. Because AAC files are somewhat higher quality than MP3 files, support for them is growing on other devices, such as the Sony Playstation3, Nintendo Wii, and newer cell phones and media players.

There are several other common file types that you may run into. Most commonly you will find windows media audio files (WMA), synthesized digital media files you might hear as a soundtrack to a video game (MIDI files), and real media files (RAM).

**Digital rights management (DRM)** is a technology that is applied to digital media files, such as music, e-books, and videos, to impose restrictions on the use of these files. This may mean that you cannot transfer the file from one device to another or make a backup copy, or that your access to the file will expire in a set amount of time. The companies that apply DRM to media files argue that it is necessary to protect the copyright holder. The Digital Millennium Copyright Act (DMCA) made it illegal to remove DRM from protected files. Opponents of DRM argue that it not only prevents copyright infringement but also restricts other lawful uses of the media.

Isaac purchased an e-book to use for his history course at school. He downloaded it to his desktop computer, intending to transfer it to his iPad to take it to class with him. To his surprise, the DRM protection on the file prevented him from reading it on any device other than the one he originally downloaded the file to. Because he can't bring his computer to class, Isaac sees no way to bring the e-book to school. His buddy Matt has a solution—a free program that he can use to strip the DRM from the file, making a new copy that Isaac can easily transfer to his iPad. Because Isaac is really in a bind, he takes Matt's advice, makes the copy of the book, and brings it to class with him. Isaac feels that this is OK, because he did pay for the file.

Was stripping the DRM rights from the book legal? Was it ethical? Was Isaac justified in what he did? Did he have any other alternatives?

# MEDIA SOFTWARE

Media software is used to organize and play multimedia files such as music, videos, and podcasts. You can transfer (rip) your music CDs to your computer; organize your songs into playlists for working out, driving, or dancing; and find new music that you might like using the online store feature. You can watch a movie trailer, a professor's lecture, or a music video. The content available to you grows daily. In this section we discuss three media programs: Apple iTunes, Windows Media Player, and Winamp Media Player.

Apple's iTunes is a program that you can use to organize your music if you have an iOS device, or even if you don't. If you do have an iOS device, then you will need to use iTunes to transfer music from your computer to your device. iTunes allows you to organize your music, videos, and other media files. You can use iTunes to shop for new music, find podcasts to subscribe to, rip your music CDs to your computer, and watch a movie trailer. **Podcasts** are prerecorded radio- and TV-like shows you can download and listen to or watch any time. There are thousands of podcasts you can subscribe to. Your instructors may even have podcasts of their class lectures. Figure 6.13 shows my iTunes U homepage, where students can find and subscribe to my classroom podcasts. With iCloud, items purchased using iTunes will automatically sync to all of your registered devices and computers.

Windows Media Player is included with Windows, and like iTunes, it can be used to organize and play all of your media files, find media on the Web to download and purchase, rip CDs, and transfer your media files to your media player (except if it's an iPod). Media Player has the ability to stream media files to computers and other devices on your home network. You can also burn CDs of your music.

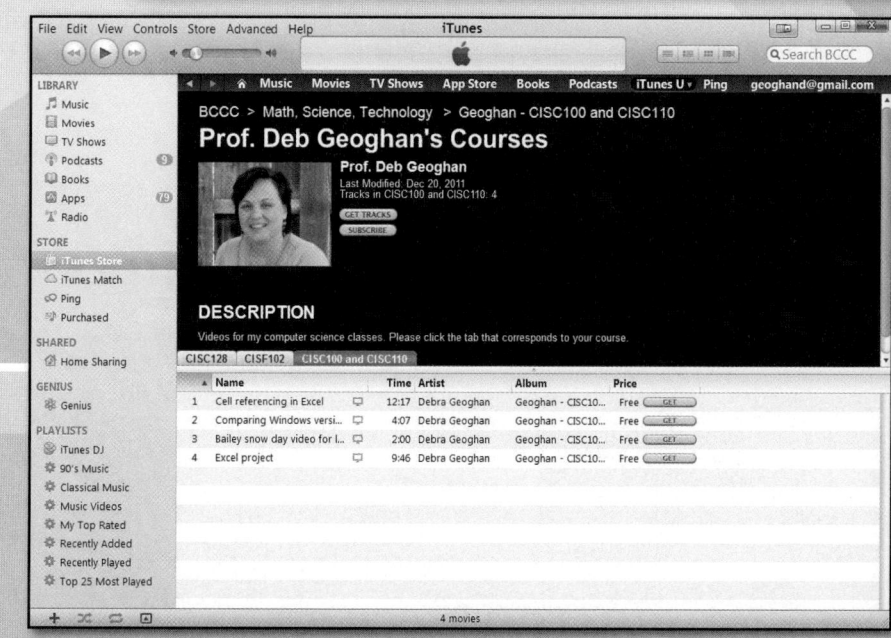

**FIGURE 6.13** My iTunesU Page

Connecting your music to the cloud allows you to listen to your favorite songs on any device with an Internet connection. There are many different music services out there—some that incorporate your own tracks and others that don't. Some radio stations stream live over the Internet. In fact, many radio stations broadcast exclusively over the Internet.

With a Pandora account, you can listen on an Xbox, Blu-ray player, computer, or mobile device. You create stations by selecting songs or artists that you like. Pandora has a massive collection of music that has been analyzed and classified by "musician-analysts." You can refine the results you get by giving each track a thumbs-up or down. Pandora also displays the lyrics so you can sing along to your favorite tunes.

Spotify uses both the music on your devices and millions of tracks stored in the cloud. It allows you to share playlists and recommend tracks to your friends. Spotify has a radio feature that will automatically create stations for you based on both your music collection and your most frequently played tracks (see Figure 6.14).

There are other services such as Grooveshark, Rhapsody, Slacker Radio, and Last.FM as well. Most services have free, ad-supported plans and premium subscriptions that eliminate ads and add more features. Connections to Facebook, Twitter, and other services make sharing and listening to music a social experience. Using one of these services allows you some control over the songs you listen to—unlike a normal radio broadcast.

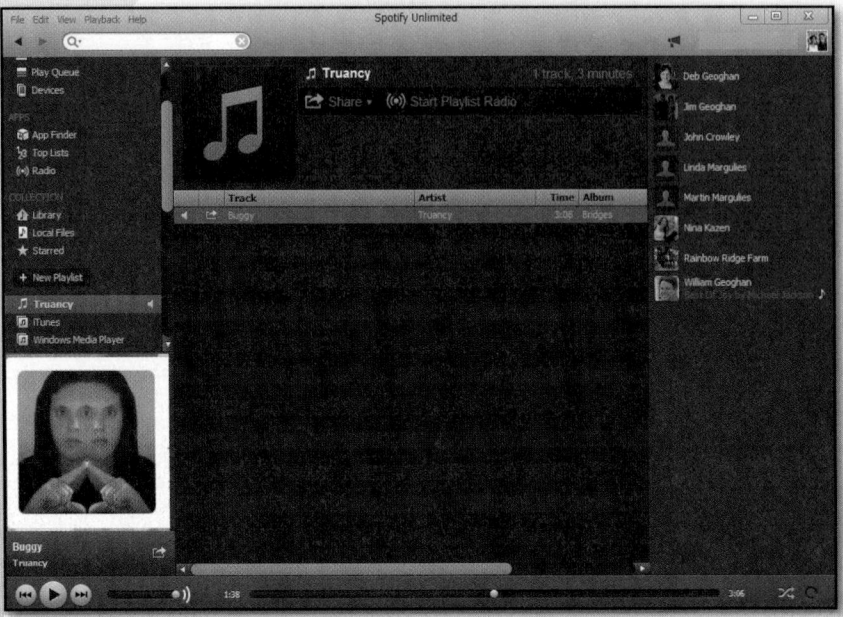

**FIGURE 6.14** Spotify is an alternative to using Apple iTunes or Windows Media Player and uses both your local tracks as well as those shared online by others.

# Find Out MORE

We have discussed some of the most popular streaming media and radio services, but there are many others. Use the Internet to find a list of Internet radio stations. How many did you find? Which of them have you used? Are any of your favorite local stations broadcasting over the Internet? Do you listen to them online?

# SPEECH RECOGNITION

**Speech recognition**, also known as voice recognition, has gone from a feature used in expensive software to a way to automatically provide customer service through a call center, dial a cell phone, or even dictate a term paper. Speech recognition allows disabled users to use a computer without a keyboard. Windows and OS X have built-in speech recognition, but there are also other software packages that provide similar services. The most recent releases of such software are becoming much more accurate and sophisticated. Speech recognition is often built into video games, allowing the player to control the action using voice commands. To use speech recognition software you generally need to train it to recognize your speech patterns. The more you use it, the better the software becomes at recognizing what you're saying. It takes time to use speech recognition efficiently to control your computer.

Apple iPhones include SIRI, an intelligent personal assistant app that allows you to speak using natural language to send messages, make phone calls, and ask questions. SIRI uses information from your contacts, music library, calendars, and reminders to make recommendations and perform other actions. It works with built-in apps and some third-party apps such as Facebook and Twitter. Unlike some other voice recognition software, SIRI works without tedious training or the use of special commands. Over time, SIRI learns your speech patterns and gets even better at understanding you.

Sound is an important component of multimedia content. Speech recognition allows us to interact with our systems with voice commands, making for easy access and increasing safety. The use of compression allows us to convert our music collection into digital files that are small enough to enable us to carry thousands of songs on a media player or cell phone, while still maintaining a high-quality sound. Media player software gives us control over how and what we listen to. How many songs do you have on your playlist?

## Running Project

Use Windows Help and Support or Mac Help Center to research Speech Recognition. What are three ways you can use Speech Recognition on your computer? What advantages can you see to using this feature? What disadvantages? Think about your interactions with technology every day and give an example of speech recognition that you use.

## 5 Things You Need to Know

- MP3 and AAC are the most common music file types.
- Digital rights management imposes restrictions on the use of DRM-protected media files.
- Media programs such as iTunes and Windows Media Player organize and play multimedia files.
- Streaming media services allow you to listen to music on any Internet connected device.
- Speech recognition allows you to interact with your systems using voice commands.

## Key Terms

AAC (advanced audio coding)

digital rights management (DRM)

MP3

podcast

speech recognition

# Lights, Camera, Action

## 5 OBJECTIVE
## Describe several ways to create videos.

It's estimated that one-third of all Internet traffic is video and that number is only expected to rise. Creating, viewing, and sharing video is not different from handling any other media, except that video files tend to be larger and require more storage and bandwidth.

## SCREEN CAPTURE

There are several ways to create videos. **Screen capture** software tools allow you to create a video of what happens on your computer screen. This is a handy way to create a how-to video or to capture a video of a problem that you are having. You don't need a camera to do it. Some programs, such as Jing and Screencast-O-Matic (both have free and paid versions), even allow you to share the video online. Machinima, the art of creating videos using screens captured from video games, is one creative use of screen capture software.

## WEBCAMS AND VIDEO CONFERENCING

**Webcams** are specialized video cameras that provide visual input for online communication. They can be used in live video chat sessions through an instant messaging (IM) tool, such as AIM or Skype, or through more sophisticated video conferencing software. Webcams allow you to have virtual meetings with people miles away, connect classrooms on different campuses, collaborate on projects with others in real time, or say goodnight to your family when you are far away. Such two-way interactions require both ends to have webcams and software setups that allow them to communicate with each other. Webcams are relatively inexpensive and come built-in to many notebooks today.

Broadcasting on the Web, or **webcasting**, can be used to monitor a child in daycare, stream a live performance or lecture, check out the waves on your favorite surfing beach, or watch a live feed from the International Space Station (see Figure 6.15). Webcasting is not interactive—it's a one-way process. The broadcast, known as a video stream, can be live or prerecorded. **Streaming** means that the media begins to play immediately as it is being received and does not require the whole file to be downloaded to your computer first.

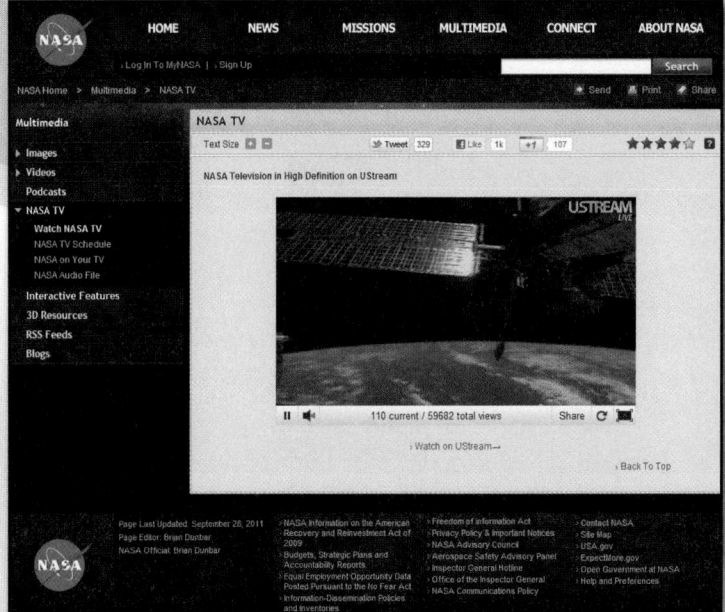

FIGURE 6.15 Live video from the International Space Station can be viewed at **www.nasa.gov/multimedia/nasatv/iss_ustream.html**

# SHARING VIDEO

As with photos, many people create videos intending to share them. This can mean using an online service or burning the video onto a DVD or Blu-ray disc. Regardless of how you decide to share your video, you may want to do some editing before you share it.

**VIDEO EDITING** Video-editing software, like photo-editing software, comes in a variety of forms. Video-editing software ranges from free online services, such as YouTube, to free programs, such as Microsoft Movie Maker and Apple iMovie, to very expensive professional-quality programs, such as Adobe Premiere and Sony Vegas. All video-editing software will capture, edit, and export video. Most programs have cool features you can add, such as captions, credits and titles, fades between scenes, music, and more. The software allows you to burn your creation to DVD or upload it to the Web. If you want more than the free programs offer, but don't want to spend the hundreds of dollars for professional software, programs in the $50 to $200 range usually have all the features an amateur would need.

DVD authoring is a feature of most video-editing software. Basic programs typically have design templates you can use to create attractive titles and menus and allow you to burn your creation to a DVD that can be played in any DVD player.

# VIDEO CAMERAS

You can also use webcams to record video, but if you want to record something that is not right in front of your computer, you will need a video camera. Today, most digital cameras and cell phones include a video mode. However, for the best quality, you will probably want a stand-alone video camera. A digital video camera will allow you to record video that can be easily uploaded to your computer, where is can be edited, stored, and shared. The features of video cameras (megapixels, storage, zoom) are similar to regular digital cameras, and the more money you spend, the more features you get.

An important thing to consider when buying a digital video camera is the media it records to. Some video cameras have a built-in hard drive or flash memory and do not use any removable media. While this is convenient, it also means that once the drive is full, you'll need a computer nearby to upload the video to before you can record any more. Another option is a camera that uses flash memory cards. Memory cards come in large capacities, are relatively inexpensive, and can be easily reused. In addition, it is easy to carry several with you. Cost, convenience, and the amount of storage you need will all affect your decision.

**YOUTUBE** YouTube (see Figure 6.16) is the most popular video-sharing site on the Internet. According to YouTube, 48 hours of video are uploaded every minute, resulting in nearly 8 years of content uploaded every day. The quality ranges from awful cell phone videos to professionally created music videos and movie trailers. You can upload your videos to YouTube and other video-sharing sites and share them with friends and family—or the world. Some of the photo sites will allow you to upload video, too.

In 1888, Thomas Edison filed a caveat with the U.S. Patent Office describing his plan to invent a motion picture camera that would "do for the eye what the phonograph does for the ear." In 1892 he opened a motion picture production studio to create motion pictures. One of the first motion pictures made there was called "Fred Ott's Sneeze," a recording of an Edison employee sneezing for the camera. You can watch the clip on YouTube today. Little could Edison have imagined the impact that video would have on society a century later.

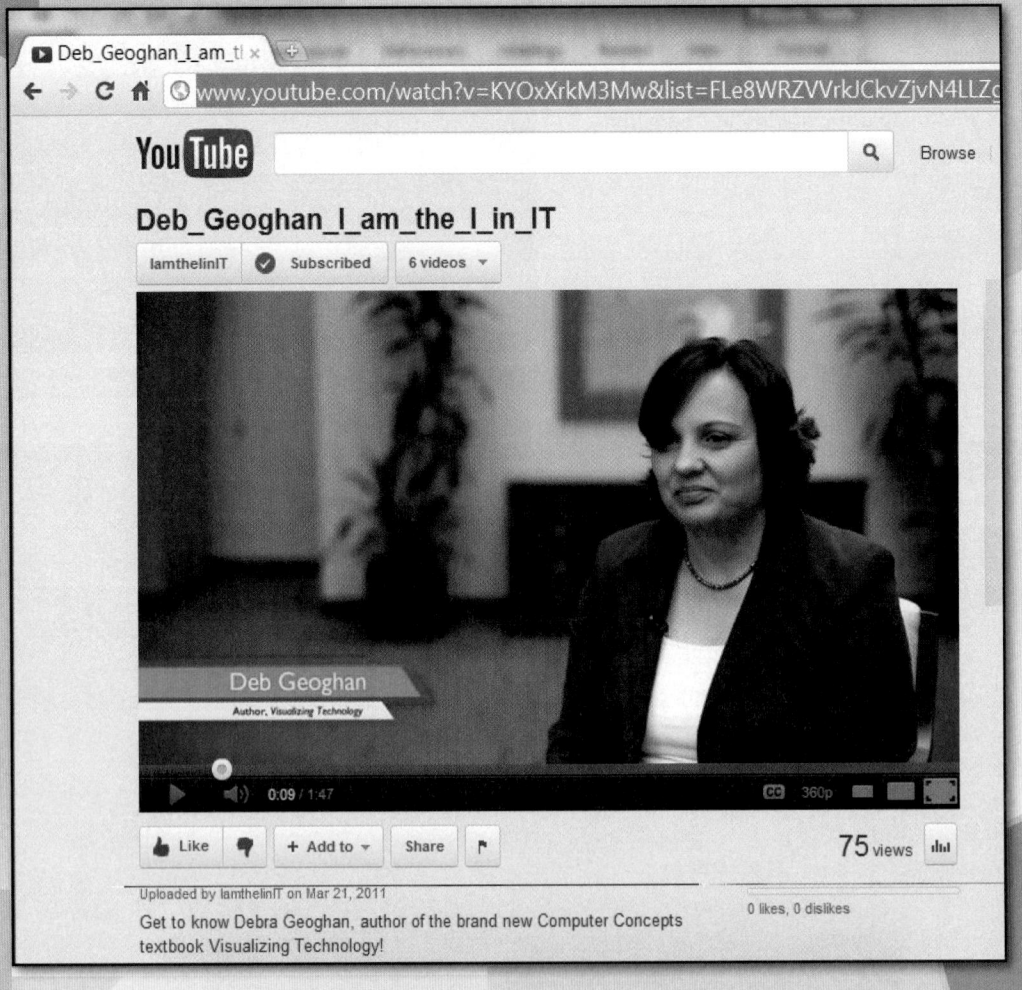

**FIGURE 6.16** YouTube Video of the Author

# Find Out MORE

YouTube not only includes home videos of kids singing and dogs riding skateboards, but it has also become a place where professional videos are hosted. Go to **youtube.com/news**. What are the top stories today? What news organizations have videos on YouTube? Are there any news organizations that you are not familiar with?

VIZ CLIP

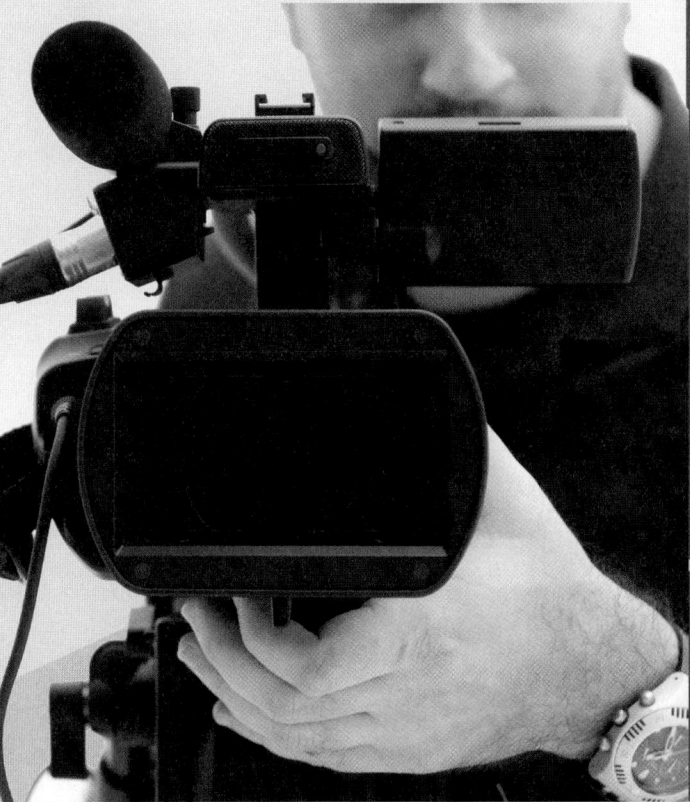

## Running Project

Use the Internet to research digital video cameras. Select a model in the same price range as the point-and-shoot camera you researched earlier. Compare the video capabilities of the two cameras. What features does a dedicated video camera have that the point-and-shoot does not? Is the video camera capable of taking still images? How do still images taken with a video camera compare to the image quality of a point-and-shoot camera? Do you think it is worth the money to purchase both types of camera? Explain your answer.

## 4 Things You Need to Know

- Screen capture software records what happens on your computer screen.
- Webcams allow you to video conference with others.
- Webcasting is broadcasting on the Web.
- YouTube is the most popular video-sharing site on the Web.

## Key Terms

screen capture

streaming

webcam

webcasting

# HOW TO

## Edit Videos Using the Youtube Editor

YouTube is the world's largest repository of online video. To complete this How To exercise you will need to set up a YouTube or Google account if you don't already have one.

**1** Log in to YouTube. Click *Upload*, click *Select files from your computer*, locate the data files for this book, and then navigate to the Chapter 6 folder. Locate the video file *vt_ch06_snowday*, and then click *Open* to upload the file.

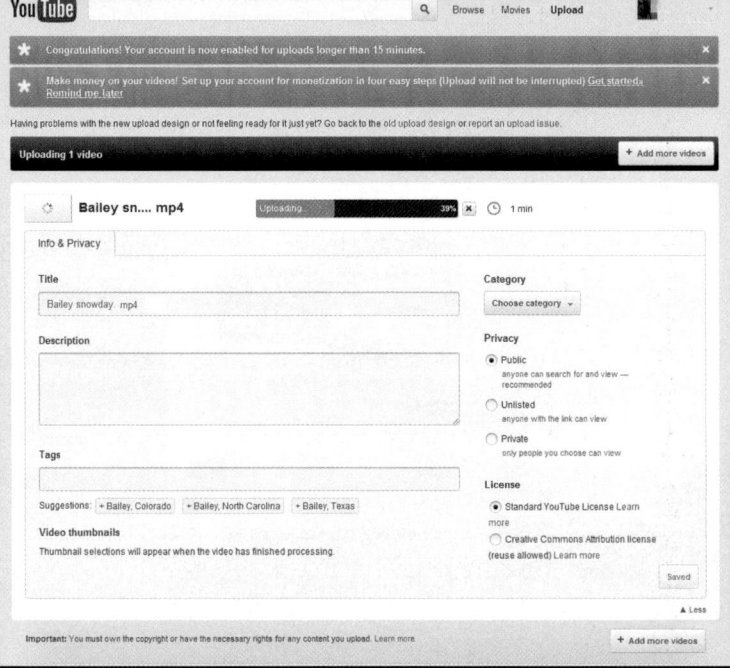

**2** On the Upload screen, fill in the description and tags.
- Title: Bailey the Corgi gets a snow day
- Description: Bailey gets some exercise on a snow day in January.
- Tags: Corgi, snow, dog
- Category: *Pets & Animals*
- Privacy: Set to *Unlisted*.
- License: *Standard YouTube License*.

**3** Scroll up to Video Tools and choose *Edit video*. On the Quick fixes tab, select *Stabilize* to reduce camera shake. Preview your change.

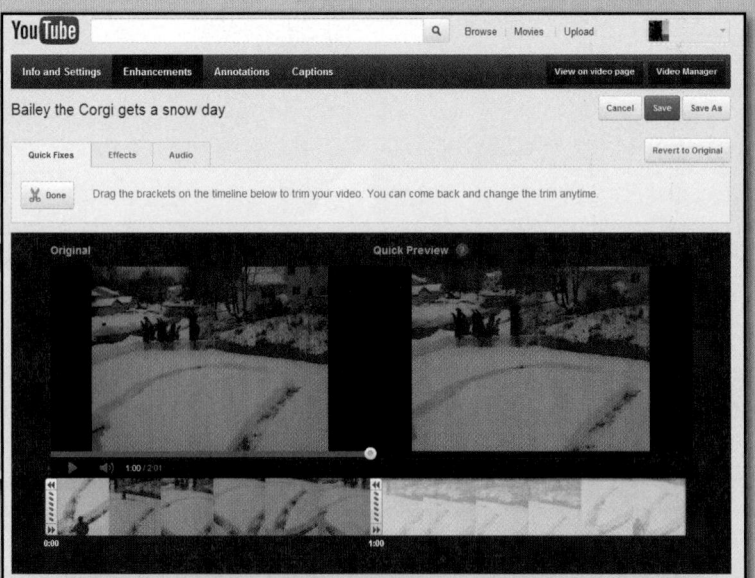

**4** Cut the video down to 1:00 minute using the Trim tool. Click the scissors image, and then drag the right-hand side of the window to 1:00. When you are finished, click *Done* to return to the editor.

**5** Adjust the color and lighting. Using the buttons on the editor, set the Contrast to +2, the Saturation to −2, and the Temperature to +1. Preview the changes. Examine the different effects available, but don't apply any of them.

**6** The audio is very bad in this video, so jazz it up with some music instead. Click the *Audio* tab. Check *Only show songs of a similar length to this video* and then press *Get recommended tracks*. Try out a few and select one that you think is appropriate for this video. Adjust the slider on the audio bar (only visible after you have selected a song) so that it says Equal and both the music and original audio can be heard.

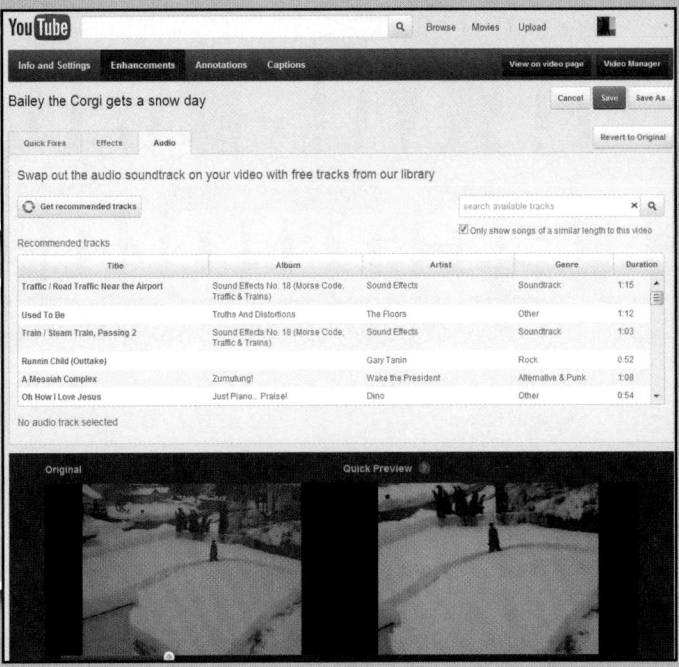

**7** Click *Save As*, and add your name to the video title. Click *Save changes*.

**8** Click the *Share* button. Copy the link in the box, paste it into a document, save the file as **lastname_firstname_ch06_howto2**, and submit the file as directed by your instructor.

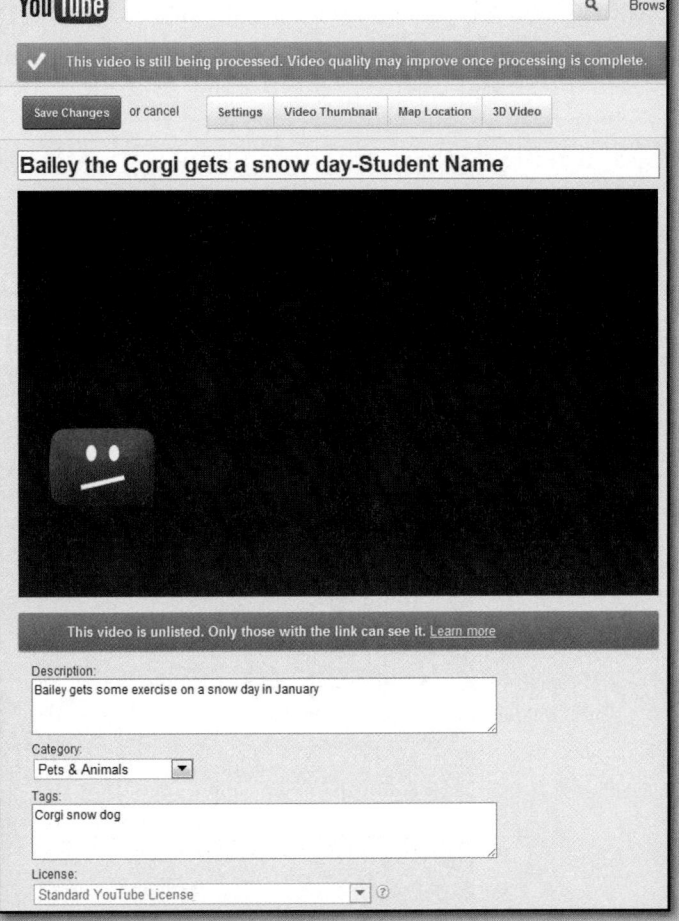

# On the Move with Technology

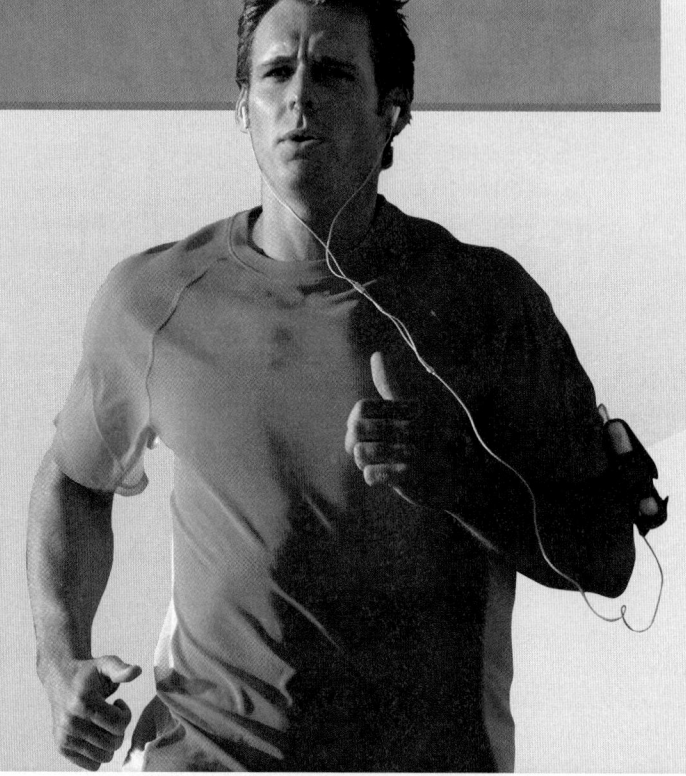

## Compare portable media players, tablets, and smartphones.

Digital mobile devices allow us to take technology with us everywhere we go. These mobile devices range from small, inexpensive MP3 players to multifunction devices costing hundreds of dollars. The rate at which technology advances is staggering. Apple's release of the iPod in 2001 changed the way we listen to music forever, and less than a decade later, the iPod is also changing how we watch videos, share photos, and much more.

## PORTABLE MEDIA PLAYERS

Today **MP3 players**, or **portable media players,** allow you to carry with you thousands of songs and podcasts (and perhaps photos, videos, and games), so you can access them wherever you are. You can plug portable media players into your computer, your home stereo, and even your car. Tablets and smartphones have built-in media players as well, and many people choose not to have a separate media player at all. But there are times when you might find it convenient to have a media player—for example, on a plane, in the gym, or by the pool. Playing music and videos on your phone can use a lot of battery, so using a separate device can keep you connected longer.

The simplest MP3 players, such as the iPod Shuffle and SanDisk Sansa Clip, have flash memory capacities from less than 2 GB to 4 GB, start at under $20, and have limited features. Midrange flash media players, with capacities ranging from 8 GB to 32 GB, can hold up to 2 days worth of music and may have more features, such as video and photo support. Because they use flash memory, they have no moving parts, which makes them ideal for high-impact activities such as jogging. Higher-end media players such as the iPod Touch and iPod classic can hold many days worth of music, video, and photos on flash memory up to 64 GB or hard drives up to 160 GB in size. These players also have other features such as built-in games and Internet access (see Figure 6.17).

# SMARTPHONES

**Smartphones** are multifunction devices that blend phone, PDA (personal digital assistant), and portable media player features and are popular in both the business and personal markets. Smartphones run a mobile operating system such as iOS, Android, BlackBerry, or Windows. Figure 6.18 shows the Samsung Galaxy S II. Smartphones like this one have the ability to download additional programs, called **mobile applications (mobile apps)**, to extend their capabilities, making them true convergence devices. The cellular networks offered by major carriers have improved dramatically and now offer data transfer speeds that rival home connections. This improved connection speed allows us to watch TV, video chat, and play online games from our phones.

**FIGURE 6.17** Portable media players are great for listening to music on the go.

**FIGURE 6.18** Mobile devices have the ability to download apps to extend their capabilities.

# TABLETS

Not to be confused with a tablet PC—which is a type of notebook computer—a **tablet** falls somewhere between a notebook and a smartphone. These handheld devices can be multifunctional devices or dedicated e-readers and cost from under $100 to nearly $1,000.

Tablets run a mobile operating system: the iPad runs iOS, and most other tablets, including the Motorola Xoom and Samsung Galaxy, run some version of Android or Windows. They have an LCD screen, a fairly long battery life, built-in WiFi, and possibly 3G or 4G cellular connectivity, making them great for travel. Tablets come with a variety of mobile apps preinstalled. Out of the box, you can surf the Web, send and receive email, watch videos, and much more. The coolest part is the vast collection of apps that you can download to your device—many for free or very little cost. At the time of this writing, the Apple App Store has more than 500,000 apps and the Google Play store has more than 200,000 (see Figure 6.19).

**FIGURE 6.19** Apple's App Store has more than 500,000 apps.

# GREEN COMPUTING

## E-WASTE

The efficient and ecofriendly use of computers and other electronics is called *green computing*. Green computing is good for the environment, but it also saves money, making it a win-win proposition.

The amount of **e-waste** (electronic waste) generated every year is staggering. Old computers, cell phones, TVs, VCRs, and other electronic devices make up e-waste, some of which is considered hazardous. CRT monitors can contain more than eight pounds of lead and cannot, by EPA regulations, be disposed of in landfills. eCyling, or recycling electronics, is one way to reduce the amount of e-waste and hazardous materials that end up in landfills, as well as reducing the cost to have it hauled away. The EPA provides information on its website about eCycling in your community (**epa. gov/epawaste/conserve/materials/ecycling**).

You can also dispose of e-waste in an altruistic manner by donating working electronics to worthwhile charities. Your donations of working electronics not only help reduce e-waste, but they also benefit the recipients as well.

# Find Out MORE

There are lots of places on the Web to find free books. Some notable resources include the Google Library Project, The Gutenberg Project, and the Online Computer Library Center. Choose one of these resources to research. When and why was it established? What types of books and other materials are included? Are there any partner institutions or projects? How can you access the materials? Where did you find this information?

# CAREER SPOTLIGHT

The use of technology has become commonplace in many careers. Nowhere is this more evident than in health care. Many medical schools and nursing programs now require their students to learn to use handheld devices, which gives them instant access to vast amounts of clinical information in one small mobile device. These devices can be loaded with drug and diagnostics manuals, calculators, and other medical reference materials—and they can also be used for patient tracking, ordering laboratory tests, and even billing. Handheld devices and other computing technology have changed the way health care providers practice medicine. Using digital technologies is a critical skill for practitioners to have.

**E-READERS E-readers** are a special class of tablets that are designed specifically to read books, magazines, and other publications. Dedicated e-readers are lightweight, inexpensive devices that can hold thousands of books. Through a wireless connection, users can browse an electronic bookstore and download a new book in seconds. Some libraries also lend e-books, and many textbooks come in e-book form that can be read on a computer or e-reader.

Some e-readers use e-ink technology to make screens that are easy to read and extend battery life for as long as two months. Others have an LCD screen like most tablets. E-ink creates a screen that is easy on the eyes and most like the experience of reading an actual book. The screen can easily be read, even in the brightest conditions—such as on the beach—but as with a paper book, you will need a booklight to read in bed at night because e-ink readers are not backlit. An LCD screen is backlit, and the brightness can be adjusted so you can read in bed at night—but the glossy screen is subject to glare and is harder to read in a brightly lit location.

The two main e-readers available are the Amazon Kindle and the Barnes and Noble Nook. Both come in several versions and cost anywhere from $79 to $300, depending on the features you choose. The Kindle Fire and the Nook tablet are full-fledged tablet computers. As prices have come down, the lines have blurred between the devices, but for someone who just wants a lightweight, inexpensive device to read and store a library collection, a dedicated e-reader is still a smart choice.

For most of us, mobile devices have become a part of everyday lives. Even the simplest cell phone is likely to have a built-in camera, the ability to send and receive text messages via Short Message Service (SMS) and multimedia text messages via Multimedia Messaging Service (MMS), and perhaps a game or two. Many people find that they are so plugged-in that they can never really relax. Sometimes it makes sense to just turn your mobile device off. Hey, leave a message. Beep.

## Running Project

Use the Internet to research the newest smartphones. Select two models you would like to purchase. Create a table comparing the features of each. Include the following information: cost, carrier, contract length, camera type, media player, video, games, Internet, email, mobile operating system, and any other information you think is important. How do the devices stack up? Write up a summary explaining which one you would buy and why.

## 4 Things You Need to Know

- Portable media players can carry music, videos, photos, and games.
- Flash-based media players have small capacities—up to 32 GB.
- Hard drive media players have larger capacities—up to 160 GB.
- Multifunction devices, such as tablets and smartphones, combine the features of different devices.

## Key Terms

e-reader

e-waste

mobile application (mobile app)

MP3 player

portable media player

smartphone

tablet

**DIGITAL MEDIA DEVICES**

features
- zoom lens 2x
- zoom lens 4x

types
- point-and-shoot
- compact system
- D-SLR

**DIGITAL CAMERAS** ①

smartphones

portable media devices

tablets

e-readers

**DIGITAL MOBILE DEVICES** ⑥

video camera

**VIDEO** ⑤

screen capture

webcam

**AUDIO** ④

file types
.mp3
.wav

media & software

speech

recognition

**TRANSFERRING PHOTOS TO YOUR COMPUTER** ②

memory cards

4 GB

USB & firewire

cloud

wireless

**EDITING, PRINTING AND SHARING PHOTOS** ③

editing

online

# Objectives Recap

1. Explain the features of various types of digital cameras.
2. Compare different methods for transferring images from a digital camera.
3. List several ways to edit and print photos.
4. Recognize different audio file types.
5. Describe several ways to create videos.
6. Compare portable media players, tablets, and smartphones.

# Key Terms

AAC (advanced audio coding) **244**
compact system camera (CSC) **232**
digital rights management (DRM) **244**
digital single lens reflex (D-SLR) camera **232**
e-reader **258**
e-waste **257**
iOS device **236**
mobile application (mobile app) **255**
MP3 **244**
MP3 player **254**

PictBridge **240**
podcast **245**
point-and-shoot camera **230**
portable media player **254**
resolution **228**
screen capture **248**
shutter lag **230**
smartphone **255**
speech recognition **247**
streaming **248**
tablet **256**
tagging **235**
webcam **248**
webcasting **248**
zoom **229**

# Summary

### 1. Explain the features of various types of digital cameras.

The main types of digital cameras are basic and advanced point-and-shoot, compact system camera, and D-SLR. Each type is progressively more expensive and complex. Resolution is the measure of pixels in an image, and higher resolution cameras can take higher quality pictures. Storage includes internal camera storage as well as flash memory cards. Zoom and lenses are important features that can make an object appear closer (telephoto) or farther away (wide-angle).

### 2. Compare different methods for transferring images from a digital camera.

Flash memory cards can be removed from a camera and plugged directly into a card reader in a computer or kiosk in a store. Most cameras can also be connected to a computer via USB or FireWire cable. The images can then be copied to a CD, the cloud, or a computer or made into prints.

### 3. List several ways to edit and print photos.

At home, you can print photos by first transferring the images to a computer or by directly connecting a PictBridge-enabled printer and camera. In-store kiosks can read most memory card types or access images on the Internet, and online services allow you to upload images to be printed that can be mailed home or picked up at a local retailer.

### 4. Recognize different audio file types.

The most common audio file types include MP3, which is the most common format for music files, and AAC, which is primarily used by Apple iTunes. Another common audio file is a MIDI file, which is often used for synthesized music in video games.

### 5. Describe several ways to create videos.

Screen capture software can be used to create a video of what is happening on your computer screen, but video cameras are needed to record action away from the screen. You can use a webcam to stream a live feed or to have a real-time video conference.

### 6. Compare portable media players, tablets, and smartphones.

Portable media players are small, handheld devices that play music, video, photos, and may also have games, Internet access, and other features. Tablet devices are multifunction devices that fall somewhere between notebook computers and smartphones and include built-in apps as well as the ability to download others. Smartphones are cell phones with PDA functions and portable media players built in. Smartphones can extend their capabilities with mobile apps and are true convergence devices.

Chapter 6 | 261

Visit **pearsonhighered.com/Geoghan** for data files, simulations, VizClips, and additional study materials.

# Application Project

**Make the Most Out of Your Mobile Camera**

July 21, 2012

With the summer season in full swing, our digital cameras are getting a full workout. The cameras built into our smartphones are always with us—allowing us to capture those special moments. But what to do with the images we capture? Fear not my friends. We are going to look at some amazingly easy ways to really make those photos something special to share.

**ANDROID DEVICES**

One of the coolest features of an Android phone is the ease of sharing media. The list of ways you can share depends upon the apps you have on your smartphone, but at minimum you can send an email or SMS message.

Some of the apps that you can use to share images are:

- Email
- Facebook
- Messaging
- Twitter[1]

Let's get started. Once you've taken the picture that you want to share, there are just a few easy steps you need to do.

1. Open the Gallery
2. Select the photo you want to share
3. If necessary, press Menu to display the Share option
4. Press Share to open the Share menu
5. Select the service you want to use to share the photo

[1] Facebook and Twitter require separate account setup.

## Microsoft Office Application Project 1: Word Level 2

**PROJECT DESCRIPTION:** In this Microsoft Word project, you have been asked to write an article on digital cameras. You will need to change alignment, line and paragraph spacing, margins, lists, and edit the header and footer. You will also find and replace text, create and modify a footnote, and use the Format Painter.

**INSTRUCTIONS:** For the purpose of grading the project you are required to perform the following tasks:

| Step | Instructions |
|------|--------------|
| **1** | Start Word. Download and open the Word file named *vt_ch06_word.* Save the file as **lastname_firstname_ch06_word**. |
| **2** | Change the left and right margins of the document to 1.25". |
| **3** | Change the line spacing of the entire document to 1.5 lines. Change the paragraph spacing (before and after) of the entire document to Auto. |
| **4** | Center the heading *Android Devices.* |
| **5** | Using the Format Painter, apply the formatting from the heading *Android Devices* to the headings *iOS Devices.* |
| **6** | Use the Find and Replace dialog box to search for and replace all instances of the word *cellphone* with smartphone. There should be two replacements. |

| Step | Instructions |
|------|--------------|
| **7** | In the Android Devices section, format the list beginning with *Email* and ending with *Twitter* as a bulleted list using solid round bullets. Increase the left indent of the bulleted list to 0.5". |
| **8** | In the Android Devices section, format the list beginning with *Open the Gallery* and ending with *Follow the service screens* as a numbered list using the 1., 2., 3. format. Increase the left indent of the numbered list to 0.5". |
| **9** | In the iOS Devices section, format the list beginning with *Email* and ending with *Tweet* as a bulleted list using solid round bullets. Increase the left indent of the bulleted list to 0.5". |

**Visit pearsonhighered.com/Geoghan** for data files, simulations, VizClips, and additional study materials.

| Step | Instructions |
|------|--------------|
| **10** | In the iOS Devices section, format the list beginning with *Open the Photo app* and ending with *Follow the service screens* as a numbered list using the 1., 2., 3. format. Increase the left indent of the numbered list to 0.5". |
| **11** | In the document header, add a page number using the Plain Number 2 style at the Top of Page. In the footer, add the FileName field using the default format. Ensure the header and footer are not displayed on the first page. |
| **12** | In the Android Devices section, in the bulleted list, insert a footnote immediately following the text *Twitter* reading **Facebook and Twitter require separate account setup.** (Include the period). |

| Step | Instructions |
|------|--------------|
| **13** | Use the Spelling and Grammar dialog box to correct the misspelling of the word *lsit* to *list*. Ignore all other spelling and grammar suggestions. |
| **14** | Place the insertion point after last line of the Android Devices section (*That's it!*). Press Enter and insert the picture *vt_ch06 image1.* |
| **15** | Place the insertion point at the beginning of the last paragraph (*As you can see*). Press Enter, move the insertion point up to the new blank line and insert the picture *vt_ch06_image2.* |
| **16** | Save and close the document. Exit Word. Submit the document as directed. |

Visit **pearsonhighered.com/Geoghan** for data files, simulations, VizClips, and additional study materials.

Chapter 6 | 263

# Microsoft Office Application Project 2:
## Excel Level 2

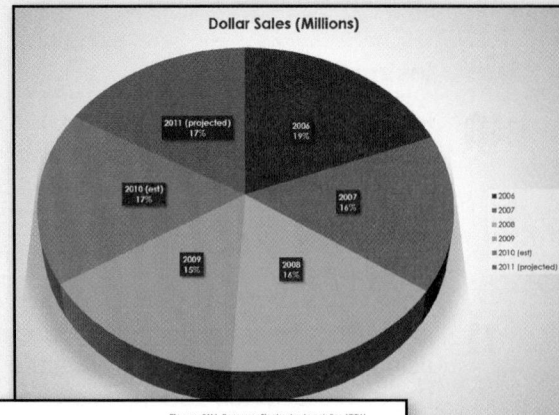

**PROJECT DESCRIPTION:** In this Microsoft Excel project, you will format cells and use functions. You will also create and format charts, and add WordArt to a worksheet.

**INSTRUCTIONS:** For the purpose of grading the project you are required to perform the following tasks:

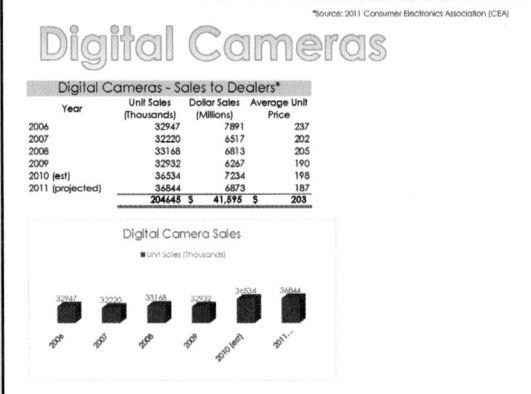

| Step | Instructions |
|------|--------------|
| 1 | Start Excel. Open the downloaded Excel file named *vt_ch06_excel*. Save the workbook as **lastname_firstname_ch06_excel**. |
| 2 | Apply the Ion theme to the workbook. |
| 3 | Merge and center the text in cell A7 over columns A:D. Increase the font to 16 pt. |
| 4 | Select the range A8:D8 and set the text to wrap in the cells. Center and middle align the text in the selected range. |
| 5 | Use the SUM function to calculate the Unit Sales from 2006–2011. Copy the function to sum the Dollar Sales. Use the AVG function in cell D15 to find the average unit price. |

| Step | Instructions |
|------|--------------|
| 6 | Select the range C15:D15. Apply the Accounting Number Format to the selected range. Decrease the decimals displayed to 0. Change the cell style of the range B15:D15 to Total. |
| 7 | Select the range A8:B14 and insert a 3-D Column chart. Move the chart so that its upper left corner aligns with the upper left corner of cell A17. |
| 8 | Change the layout of the column chart to Layout 2. Change the chart title to **Digital Camera Sales**. |

264 | APPLICATION PROJECT

Visit **pearsonhighered.com/Geoghan** for data files, simulations, VizClips, and additional study materials.

| Step | Instructions |
|------|-------------|
| **9** | Select the ranges A9:A14 and C9:C14 and insert a Pie in 3-D chart. Move the chart to a new sheet named **Dollar Sales Chart**. |
| **10** | Change the layout of the pie chart to Layout 1. Change the title to **Dollar Sales (Millions)**. Format the chart with the chart Style 3. |
| **11** | On the 2006–2011 sheet, insert the text **Digital Cameras** as WordArt using the Gradient Fill - Green, Accent 4, Outline - Accent 4. Move the WordArt so that its upper left corner aligns with the upper left corner of cell A1. |

| Step | Instructions |
|------|-------------|
| **12** | Change the scaling of the 2006–2011 worksheet so the width will fit to one page. Center the Expenses worksheet vertically on the page. And a footer with the file name in the center. |
| **13** | Ensure that the worksheets are correctly named and placed in the following order in the workbook: Dollar Sales Chart; 2006–2011. Save and close the workbook and then exit Excel. Submit the workbook as directed. |

Visit **pearsonhighered.com/Geoghan** for data files, simulations, VizClips, and additional study materials.

Chapter 6 | 265

# Multiple Choice

Answer the multiple-choice questions below for more practice with key terms and concepts from this chapter.

1. What feature allows you to connect a camera directly to a printer?
   a. Resolution
   b. Flash memory
   c. Optical zoom
   d. PictBridge

2. Which is a drawback of point-and shoot cameras?
   a. They don't use flash memory.
   b. You must take them to the store to process photos.
   c. They are expensive.
   d. You can't change the lens.

3. Which type of camera has the least shutter lag?
   a. Point-and-shoot
   b. Webcam
   c. D-SLR
   d. Digital video

4. What is necessary for your camera to connect to your computer using a USB or FireWire cable?
   a. Device driver
   b. PictBridge
   c. Card reader
   d. Tags

5. Which audio file type is most commonly used for music files?
   a. MIDI
   b. WAV
   c. RAM
   d. MP3

6. Which media player is designed to transfer media to an iOS device?
   a. Windows Media Player
   b. Real Player
   c. iTunes
   d. Spotify

7. What process allows media to begin to play immediately as it is being received?
   a. Streaming
   b. Webcasting
   c. Downloading
   d. Machinima

8. Which is not an iOS device?
   a. iPod
   b. Android
   c. iPhone
   d. iPad

9. Why might you carry a tablet instead of a notebook?
   a. Longer battery life
   b. To listen to music
   c. To take pictures
   d. All of the above

10. Why is a smartphone considered a convergence device?
    a. It includes support for multiple users.
    b. It includes support for multiple computers.
    c. It can connect users to other smartphones.
    d. It has features of a PDA and a portable media player.

# True or False

Answer the true-false questions below for more practice with key terms and concepts from this chapter.

1. You can change the lens on a compact system camera.

2. Resolution has the most impact on the size of photo print you can make.

3. D-SLRs are subject to shutter lag.

4. Once full, memory cards cannot be reused.

5. Editing digital images requires expensive software.

6. Once you post an image on an online photo sharing site, anyone can view it.

7. Webcasts can be live or prerecorded.

8. Speech recognition software is built into most modern operating systems.

9. Portable media players that use flash memory for storage have lower capacities than those that have hard drives.

10. An e-reader is a tablet designed for reading books.

# Fill in the Blank

Fill in the blanks using the words from the key terms.

1. _____ is the measure of the number of pixels in an image and is expressed in megapixels.

2. The time between pressing the button and the camera snapping the picture is called _____.

3. Optical _____ uses a lens to change the focal length of the camera.

4. Labeling images with keywords, or _____ them, makes it easier to find your pictures later.

5. An industry standard that allows a camera to connect directly to a printer is _____.

6. To use _____ software you might need to train it to recognize your speech patterns.

7. _____ is a technology that is applied to digital media files, such as music, e-books, and videos, to impose restrictions on the use of these files.

8. _____ software tools allow you to create a video of what happens on your computer screen.

9. Broadcasting on the Web, or _____, can be used to stream a live performance or lecture.

10. _____ allow you to carry with you thousands of songs and podcasts (and perhaps photos, videos, and games), so you can listen to them wherever you are.

# Running Project . . .

## . . . The Finish Line

In this chapter you researched a number of digital devices. Think about the career you are planning to pursue. What is one such device that would be important in your career? Using your answers to the previous sections of the Running Project, write a report describing your selections and responding to the questions raised. Save your file as **lastname_firstname_ch06_project** and submit it to your instructor as directed.

# Do It Yourself 1

Purchasing a tablet can be a difficult task, as there are so many different models to choose from. In this exercise, you will research several tablets and determine if a tablet is right for you.

1. Use the Internet to research three tablets. Create a chart like the one below.

|  | Tablet 1 | Tablet 2 | Tablet 3 | Comments |
|---|---|---|---|---|
| Tablet Model |  |  |  |  |
| Price |  |  |  |  |
| Mobile operating system |  |  |  |  |
| Wireless connectivity |  |  |  |  |
| Memory capacity |  |  |  |  |
| Expandability |  |  |  |  |
| Included apps |  |  |  |  |
| Additional app availability |  |  |  |  |
| Special features |  |  |  |  |
| Website where you found your information |  |  |  |  |

2. Write up a one-page summary of your findings. Which tablet is the best choice for you and why? If you had more money, would your choice change? Save your file as **lastname_firstname_ch06_diy1**. Submit your work as directed by your instructor.

# Do It Yourself 2

In this activity, you will search YouTube for podcasts. YouTube lists podcasts under Shows.

1. Open your browser and go to **youtube.com**.

2. Click *Browse* and then click *Shows*. What categories are listed on the Shows page? Where would you find shows to help you with this course?

3. Click the *Science and Tech* link, and then filter by Web Shows. Browse through some of the featured shows. Select one that interests you and watch it. What show did you pick and why? Is there a subscribe section on the show page? If so, what options are listed for subscribing to the show? Take a screen shot to capture the page.

4. Type your answers and include the screen shot from step 3. Save the file as **lastname_firstname_ch06_diy2**. Submit your work as directed by your instructor.

# File Management

Files stored on your computer have properties attached to them that make searching for and organizing files easier. In this exercise, you will examine the properties of several files, modify the tags, and use the Search feature to locate files.

1. Locate the data files for this chapter.

2. Select, but do not open, the file *vt_ch06_tags.jpg*.

3. Click *Add a tag* in the Details pane and type **logo**. Then click *Save*. Take a screen shot of this window and paste it into your document.

4. Click *Libraries* in the folder pane on the left. In the Search Libraries box, type **logo**. As you typed each letter, what happened? What filter options are available?

5. Did the Search locate the correct file? Did it locate any other files? If the Search did not yield the results you wanted, what other options are available? Take a screen shot of the Search results window and paste it into your document. Save your file as **lastname_firstname_ch06_fm** and submit as directed by your instructor.

# Critical Thinking

You are excited about the idea of using the cloud to stream your music, but before you begin, you need to do some homework to decide what the best option is for you.

1. Use the Internet to research the three music streaming services. What are the basic features of each? Do they require any special hardware or software to be installed? What is the difference between their free, ad-supported service and premium paid subscription? Is it worth the price?

2. Examine your own computer. Does it have all of the hardware you will need? If not, what will you need to purchase? What about your mobile devices?

3. Write up a one-page summary that includes the answers to the questions above. Save the file as **lastname_firstname_ch06_ct** and submit your assignment as directed by your instructor.

# Ethical Dilemma

Alaina received some music CDs of her favorite band for her birthday. She likes to listen to her music on her smartphone, so she ripped the music to her computer and transferred the songs to her phone. Because she no longer needs the CDs to listen to her music, her roommate Jessica suggested that she sell them on eBay. This would free up some space in their cramped dorm room and generate some much needed cash.

1. Alaina thinks this is a great idea, but is it? Is it ethical to sell the CDs and still keep the music? Is it legal?

2. Because Alaina and Jessica share a computer, is it OK for both of them to transfer the music files to their smartphones?

3. Write up a one-page summary that includes the answers to the questions above. Save the file as **lastname_firstname_ch06_ethics** and submit it as directed by your instructor.

# On the Web

Webcams have become common tools for scientists to use to monitor animals, weather conditions, and even volcanoes.

1. Search the Web for a webcam that is streaming a live feed of a place you would like to visit. Choose a webcam that is sponsored by a reputable organization. Visit the site and take a screen shot of the webcam feed. Are there any other webcam feeds on the same site?

2. What is the address of the webcam you chose? What location is being observed? What organization sponsors the webcam? How did you locate it?

3. Type your answers and include the screen shot from step 1. Save the file as **lastname_firstname_ch06_web** and submit your file as directed by your instructor.

# Collaboration

In this project you will create your own video podcast. You'll need a video camera and video editing software such as Windows Movie Maker (a free download from Microsoft) or Apple iMovie to complete this project.

**Instructors:** Divide the class into small groups of two to four students. The topic for each group is a smartphone or tablet that is used by a member of the group.

**The Project:** Each team is to prepare a video podcast that includes an explanation of their device, favorite features, and a demonstration of how to send and receive email using the device. Teams must use at least three references, only one of which may be the textbook. Write a script for a two- to five-minute presentation. Choose a format that best suits your group. For example, it can be a news magazine, talk show, game show, or any other format you'd like to use. Use Google Docs or Microsoft Office to prepare the script and provide documentation that all team members have contributed to the project.

**Students:** Before beginning this project, discuss the roles each group member will play. Decide on a team name, which you will use in submitting your presentation. Be sure to divide the work among your members and select someone to present your project. You may find it helpful to elect a team leader who can direct your activities and ensure that all team contributions are collated through Google Docs or Microsoft Office as directed by your instructor. Decide how you are going to record and edit your show and download and install any necessary software.

**Outcome:** You are to prepare a video podcast on your assigned topic. Submit a copy of the script. On the first page, be sure to include the name of your podcast and a listing of all team members. Save the file as **teamname_ch06_collab**. The podcast will be two to five minutes in length and uploaded to YouTube. It requires participation from everyone in the group. Save the final project as **teamname_ch06_podcast** and submit it as directed by your instructor.

# The Internet

Visit **pearsonhighered.com/Geoghan** for data files, simulations, VizClips, and additional study materials.

**OBJECTIVES**

1. **Recognize the importance of the Internet.**

2. **Compare types of Internet connections.**

3. **Compare popular Web browsers.**

4. **Demonstrate how to navigate the Web.**

5. **Discuss how to evaluate the credibility of information found on the Web.**

# IN THIS CHAPTER

If you're a typical college-aged student, then the Internet has always been around. It has become such a part of our everyday lives that you may already know a lot about it. But there's so much to know that most folks only scratch the surface. The goal of this chapter is to introduce you to the wide variety of tools and information that's literally at your fingertips. When you've finished this chapter, you'll have a broad understanding of the Internet as a whole as well as a good idea of the parts of the Internet that you find particularly useful. You'll have researched, evaluated, and discovered why the Web is so important in today's society and why you need to be fluent in the tools and language of the Internet to be an educated consumer, a better student, and a valuable employee.

# Internet Timeline

## Recognize the importance of the Internet.

Did Al Gore invent the Internet? Well, no, not really. Al Gore didn't *invent* the Internet, but early on, he recognized its potential and, as a congressman and vice president, promoted its development through legislation. In 2005, he received a Webby Lifetime Achievement Award for his contributions (Webbyawards.com). He was one of the first politicians to see the potential of the Internet, but it actually started much earlier.

## HOW IT ALL GOT STARTED

In 1957, the Soviet Union launched the first space satellite: Sputnik. The United States and the Soviet Union were, at the time, engaged in a political conflict—called the Cold War—and this launch led to fears that the United States was falling behind in the technology race. In 1958, President Eisenhower created the Advanced Research Projects Agency (ARPA) to jump-start U.S. technology for the military. One of ARPA's early projects was to create a Galactic Network that would connect smaller networks around the world.

The Internet started as a U.S. Department of Defense ARPA project in the 1960s to design a communications system that had multiple pathways through which information could travel so that losing one part of the system (for example, in a nuclear strike) wouldn't cripple the whole thing. It took about 10 years to develop the technology. The original system was called **ARPANET** and only had four nodes on it (see Figure 7.1). The four nodes were at UCLA, the Stanford Research Institute (SRI), the University of Utah in Salt Lake City, and UCSB (UC Santa Barbara).

In 1979, the National Science Foundation (NSF) created CSNET to connect the computer science departments at universities using the ARPANET technology. In the mid-1980s, NSF created NSFNET, giving other academic disciplines access to supercomputing centers and connecting smaller networks together. By the late 1980s, NSFNET was the primary **Internet backbone**—the high-speed connection points between networks. In 1995, NSF decommissioned the NSF backbone, the Internet backbone was privatized, and the first five large Network Access Points (NAPs) that made up the new backbone were established in Chicago, New Jersey, San Francisco, San Jose, and Washington, D.C. Today, the backbone of the Internet is composed of **Internet Exchange Points** around the world.

# WORLD WIDE WEB

Most people use the terms "Internet" and "World Wide Web" interchangeably, but they are, in fact, two different things. The **Internet**, or just **net**, is the physical entity—a network of computer networks. The World Wide Web, or just Web, is just one way that information moves on the Internet. Email, instant messaging, P2P (peer-2-peer) file sharing, and VoIP (voice over IP) are other ways that you might use the Internet.

In 1991, Tim Berners-Lee and CERN (European Organization for Nuclear Research) released the hypertext system we know as the **World Wide Web**. **Hypertext** is text that contains links to other text and allows you to navigate through pieces of information by using the links, known as **hyperlinks**, that connect them. The milestone of having a million Internet nodes (networks or ISPs) was reached in 1992, and commercial sites, such as Pizza Hut, began to appear. The first White House website was launched in 1994. In 1993, a group of graduate students led by Marc Andreessen released the Mosaic point-and-click graphical browser for the Web, which later became Netscape. These events led to a user-friendly Internet. A couple years later, Windows 95 was released, and existing online service companies such as AOL and CompuServe began offering Internet access.

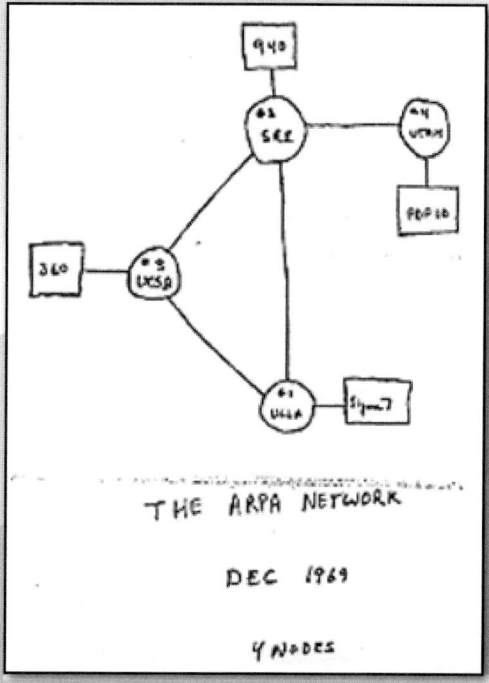

THE ARPA NETWORK

DEC 1969

4 NODES

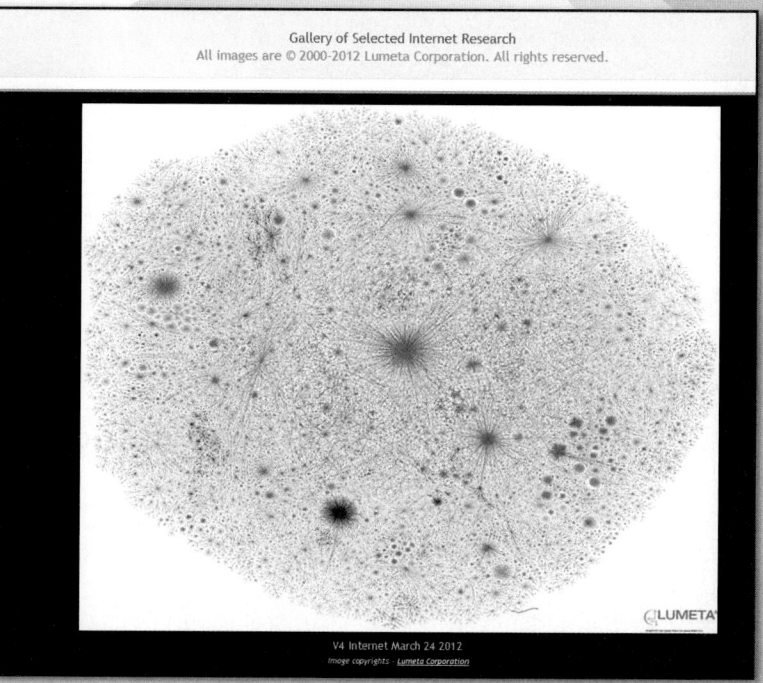

V4 Internet March 24 2012
*Image copyrights - Lumeta Corporation*

**FIGURE 7.1** This original drawing of ARPANET shows the first four nodes at UCLA, UCSB, SRI, and the University of Utah. Today's Internet has many millions of nodes, as illustrated on the Internet map captured on March 24, 2012.

As personal computers dropped in price and became more powerful, the Internet grew at an incredible rate, with an estimated 2.27 billion users at the beginning of 2012. Figure 7.2 shows the Internet penetration rate around the world at the end of 2011. Over the last several years, the widespread use of mobile devices such as tablets and smartphones has given Internet access to even more people.

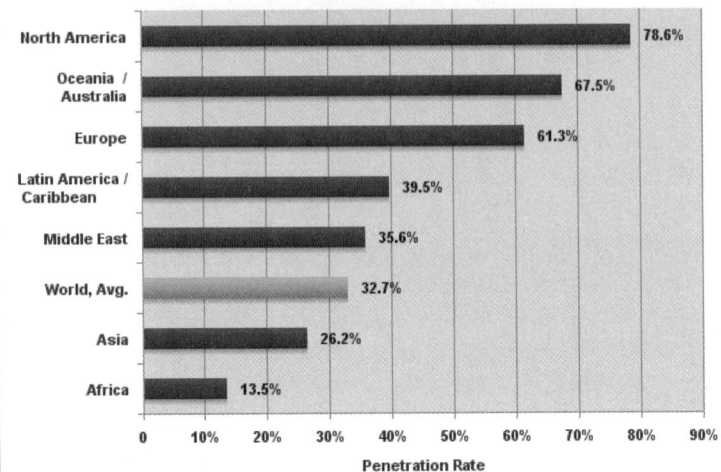

**World Internet Penetration Rates
by Geographic Regions - 2011**

| Region | Penetration Rate |
| --- | --- |
| North America | 78.6% |
| Oceania / Australia | 67.5% |
| Europe | 61.3% |
| Latin America / Caribbean | 39.5% |
| Middle East | 35.6% |
| World, Avg. | 32.7% |
| Asia | 26.2% |
| Africa | 13.5% |

Source: Internet World Stats - www.internetworldststs.com/stats.htm
Penetration Rates are based on a world population of 6,930,055,154 and 2,267,233,742 estimated Internet users on December 31, 2011.
Copyright © 2012, Miniwatts Marketing Group

**FIGURE 7.2** The Growth of the Internet (taken from internetworldstats.com/stats.htm)

# INTERNET2 (I2)

The original uses of the Internet—research and education—have been overtaken by commercial and social uses. Even as bandwidth and the Internet infrastructure increase, educational and research institutions have been unable to access the speed and resources they need. Thus, the Internet2 project was born. **Internet2 (I2)** is a second Internet designed for education, research, and collaboration, very much like how it all began—only faster. In 1995, when NSFNET was decommissioned, there was a small remnant retained just for research called the Very High Speed Backbone Network Service (vBNS), which later evolved into the Internet2 project. While the Internet is composed of a mix of older telephone cables and newer fiber-optics, the I2 backbone is all fiber. The data travels much faster and is less prone to corruption.

# Find Out MORE

Wondering what your favorite website used to look like? The Internet Archive WaybackMachine can show you. Go to **archive.org**, and enter the address of the website you want to see. The archives only go back to 1996, so you can't see the original Pizza Hut or White House site, but you can see the 1996 versions. Type in the address of your school's website, and click *Take Me Back*. Click on several available dates to see how it has changed over time. Try a few other sites that you visit regularly.

Membership in I2 is limited to colleges, universities, other educational institutions, museums and art galleries, libraries, hospitals, and other organizations that work with them. It's a pretty small group, and that's one of the reasons it's so fast. Collaboration, streaming video, and Web conferencing are just some of the applications that benefit from the faster speed. Figure 7.3 shows the muse K20 Connectivity Map. You can use this map to find out which institutions are using I2.

From its earliest inception, the Internet was designed to be a place for collaboration and information sharing. Today, it's an integral part of education, business, and communication. Even if you don't spend a lot of time surfing the Web, it's hard to deny the impact it has on your life.

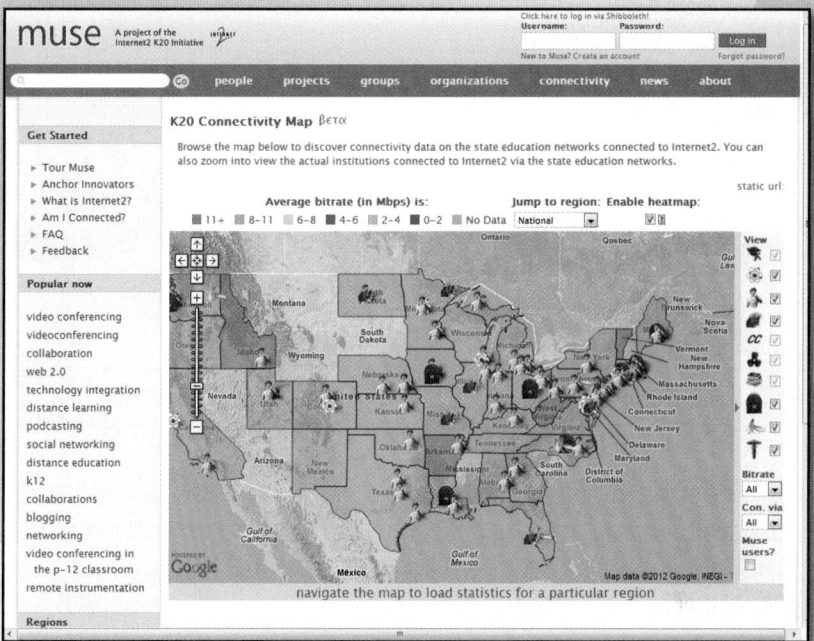

**FIGURE 7.3** Schools around the country are connected to I2.

## Running Project

Does your school participate in the I2 project? Ask your librarian or instructor. If yes, what features does your school use? If not, why not?

## 3 Things You Need to Know

- ARPANET was the original Internet.
- Hypertext is used to navigate the World Wide Web by using hyperlinks.
- Internet2 is a second Internet designed for education, research, and collaboration.

## Key Terms

| | |
|---|---|
| ARPANET | Internet backbone |
| hyperlink | Internet Exchange Points |
| hypertext | Internet2 (I2) |
| Internet (net) | World Wide Web |

# Get Connected

## Compare types of Internet connections.

There are many different ways to get on the Internet. If you have a personal computer, you have several options. **Internet service providers (ISPs)**—companies that offer Internet access—offer many different plans from which to choose. The options available to you depend on where you live and how much you have to spend.

## SO, HOW DO YOU GET CONNECTED?

A good place to find local ISPs is by searching the Web. If you don't have access at home, most schools and libraries offer free access (see Figure 7.4). Search for a list of ISPs that offer service in your area; there are many websites that compare services and prices for you. Before you begin your search, read the rest of this article to learn about the questions you should ask when comparing packages.

Ask yourself what you need based on how you use the net. Do you just check email and look up recipes? If so, a slower connection might work for you. But if you work from home, play games, share photos, or watch videos, then you'll need a faster connection. So, what are your options? Speed is essentially the data transfer rate and is measured in kilobits or megabits per second (Kbps or Mbps). For this measurement, the higher the number, the better.

**FIGURE 7.4** Most schools and libraries provide free Internet access.

**DIAL-UP** The least expensive type of connection is usually **dial-up**. With a dial-up connection, you use your regular phone lines to connect to the network. Plans range from about $10 to $30 per month. There are even some companies that will give you free access for up to 10 hours a month. This might be a good backup plan to have in case your normal connection should become unavailable. I have this set up on my notebook for when I travel, in case there's no another access where I am. For some people, a dial-up connection may be the only option available. Dial-up can be very slow, maxing out at 56 Kbps (kilobits per second), especially if you're trying to download a file or watch a video. Another drawback is that the connection ties up your phone line while you're online. Aging phone lines were not designed to carry data, so they do a poor job of it.

**BROADBAND** If you're looking for more speed, then you have several options: cable, DSL, FiOS, and wireless technologies. The FCC defines **broadband** as anything over 200 Kbps, which is at least four times faster than dial-up and often significantly more than that. Availability, speed, and costs vary depending on where you live. You'll have to do some research to get the best price and service.

**Cable Internet access** is generally offered by your cable TV provider and uses the same wires to carry both signals. Some cable companies also offer digital phone service. This requires older cable systems to be upgraded, so it's not universally available. Cable speeds range from 1 Mbps (megabit per second) to 100 Mbps but are typically 8 to 25 Mbps. One drawback to using cable Internet access is that you share the cable with your neighbors. This could potentially negatively impact your Internet speed if many neighbors are online at the same time.

**DSL (digital subscriber line)** uses telephone lines to carry digital signals. Unlike your normal phone line that's designed to carry analog signals (sound), DSL lines are designed to carry digital signals and thus are much faster than ordinary telephone lines. DSL averages speeds of 384 Kbps to 15 Mbps, which is slower than cable; however, it's generally less expensive. One of the biggest problems with DSL is its distance limitations. You must be within 3 miles of the DSL service provider's facilities. The farther away you are, the slower your connection will be. Aging phone lines can also significantly slow down DSL.

**Fiber-to-the-home (FTTH)** is the fastest of the broadband alternatives, with top speeds of 300 Mbps—but at a premium. Fiber can cost two to three times as much as DSL or cable for the highest speeds. It can carry Internet, TV, and phone calls to your home over fiber-optic cable and is available in limited areas—those where the fiber-optic cable has been installed. In the United States, the primary FTTH service is Verizon FiOS (Fiber Optic Service). Unlike cable and DSL lines, which many people already have, FTTH requires a contractor to lay a fiber-optic conduit directly to the home, which can be costly and involve digging up your lawn.

**WIRELESS** What if you live in a rural or remote area without cable, DSL, or fiber access? Are you stuck with dial-up? What about if you're on the road? There are several wireless alternatives available, too.

Mobile Internet access allows you to connect to the Internet using the cellular network standards 3G (third generation) and 4G (fourth generation). 4G is faster and includes **WiMAX Mobile Internet** and **LTE (Long Term Evolution)** technologies. The signals are transmitted by a series of cellular towers; thus, coverage isn't universal. Coverage maps are available on the providers' websites, allowing you to verify coverage exists where you need it before making the commitment. Although we tend to think about 3G/4G in terms of mobile devices, they can be used on personal computers with a special adapter. In some cases, the smartphone can serve as a wireless access point to share the connection with other devices via wireless or USB tethering. I often use my smartphone to provide Internet access to my iPad when I am traveling. Special modems make 4G available at home, too. Top speeds are considered broadband and can potentially equal those associated with wired broadband service.

**Satellite Internet access** is a more global and more expensive option. Satellite service speeds are comparable to DSL. You need a clear view of the southern sky, where the communications satellites are positioned, and weather conditions can affect your service. You would probably only consider satellite if there were no other option available where you live. In the next few years, several new satellites are scheduled to be launched, which will increase the availability and speed of satellite Internet.

**Municipal WiFi** is offered in some cities and towns. CBS Mobile Zone is available in central Manhattan. Wireless Philadelphia currently covers most of the city for free. WiFi **hotspots** are wireless access points that are available in many public locations, such as airports, schools, hotels, and restaurants, both free or for a fee. You can find hotspots by using a website such as jiwire.com (see Figure 7.5). **WiFi** is the same type of wireless networking you may have set up in your home.

**FIGURE 7.5** Jiwire's WiFi Finder can help you locate public hotspots.

# Find Out MORE

The National Broadband Plan—Connecting America—is an ambitious plan to assure that all Americans have fast, affordable Internet access. Go to **broadband.gov** to find out why the U.S. government considers this so important. What is the status of this project?

## CONNECTING WITHOUT A COMPUTER?

Today, most cell phones offer at least a limited ability to connect to the Internet. Smartphones, tablets, video game consoles, and even your media player may be able to connect via cellular or WiFi. Some e-readers include free 3G Internet access to shop for and download books and to access other resources. These devices generally have small screens and limited keyboards, which can make using them more difficult. However, they're becoming more powerful and easier to use. Many people rely on such devices as their primary Internet access device. While only about 25 percent of the world's population have personal computers, over 60 percent have cell phones.

Satellite phones connect to satellites instead of cellular towers, making them useful in places where cell service is lacking, such as remote locations. They need a clear view of the sky and don't work well indoors. Satellite phones and satellite phone services are very expensive.

According to the FCC, in 2012, 78 percent of adults in the United States are Internet users, and 65 percent of adults have home broadband access. For those who don't have broadband at home, cost and inaccessibility are often cited as the reasons. Of course, there are always some people that just aren't interested—they don't find any reason to have Internet access at home. But for the rest of us, not having a good Internet connection just isn't an option.

## Running Project

Use the Internet to research the current state of satellite Internet access. Have the newest satellites been deployed? What services and speeds are available and what is the cost? Is this a viable option where you live?

## 3 Things You Need to Know

- Dial-up is the slowest type of Internet access.
- Broadband Internet access includes cable, DSL, FTTH, and 3G/4G.
- The type of Internet access you choose largely depends on where you live.

## Key Terms

| | |
|---|---|
| broadband | Internet service provider (ISP) |
| cable Internet access | LTE (Long Term Evolution) |
| dial-up | municipal WiFi |
| DSL (digital subscriber line) | satellite Internet access |
| fiber-to-the-home (FTTH) | WiFi |
| hotspot | WiMAX Mobile Internet |

# Surf's Up VIZ CLIP

## 3 Compare popular Web browsers.

Some people use the Internet strictly for email, others for day-trading, and others for work. Some folks have specific websites that they visit regularly, while others like to surf and explore. However you use the Web, you need the right tools to access it and enjoy the content. In this article, we discuss the software you need.

### BROWSERS

Most information on the Web is in the form of basic **Web pages**, which are written in **HTML (hypertext markup language)**. HTML is the authoring language that defines the structure of a Web page. **Web browsers**, such as Microsoft Internet Explorer, Mozilla Firefox, and Apple Safari, are programs that interpret the HTML to display Web pages as you browse the Internet. Although these are the most widely used browsers for personal computers, there are actually many alternatives, including Chrome and Opera. The first Web browser, Mosaic, was released in 1993. Mosaic eventually became Netscape Navigator, which dominated the market until Microsoft got in the game. Some websites, tools, and technologies are optimized or better supported by a specific browser, so you may find it helpful to have more than one browser installed on your system.

**INTERNET EXPLORER** First released in 1995, Internet Explorer (IE) has become the leading Web browser. IE is included with Windows, so there's no special download needed. Figure 7.6 shows the NASA website displayed in IE10.

Navigation buttons     Address bar     Tabbed browsing     Favorites     Tools

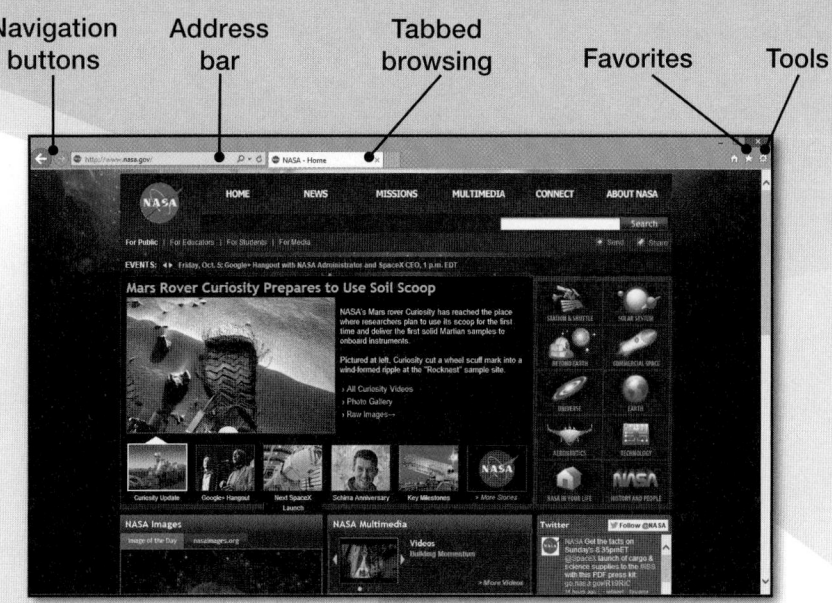

**FIGURE 7.6** Internet Explorer

Some important features of Internet Explorer are the following:

- **Navigation buttons:** Provide a means to navigate back and forward through browsed Web pages
- **Address bar:** Contains the Web address of the current Web page. You can also search the Web from the address bar without having to go to a search provider's website first.
- **Favorites:** Allows you to save Web addresses, giving you easy access to your favorite websites. Favorites are sometimes called bookmarks.
- **Tabbed browsing:** Allows you to have multiple Web pages open in tabs.
- **Settings:** Contains easy access to most settings and features of IE.

These features are fairly common across most browsers.

**FIREFOX** The first version of Mozilla Firefox was released in 2004. At the time, Internet Explorer had become the dominant Web browser and Netscape was at the end of its life. By 2007, Firefox had approximately 16 percent of the market share. By the beginning of 2012, Firefox has increased its market share to about 20 percent. Figure 7.7 shows the FBI website in Firefox 15.0. Firefox is available for Windows, OS X, and Linux.

If you compare the Firefox image with the IE image, you'll see that they're very similar. Many people use IE simply because it comes with Windows. Firefox is free and easy to install; however, it requires you to go out and download it.

Menu     Address bar     Tabbed browsing     Search bar     Bookmarks

**FIGURE 7.7** Mozilla Firefox

**CHROME** The newest browser is Google Chrome. Released in 2008, Google Chrome had about an 18 percent market share as of March 2012. Comparing it to the previous images, you'll see that it has a streamlined interface but is still similar to both IE and Firefox. Chrome's main focus is on speed, and it loads Web pages faster than other browsers. Figure 7.8 shows the Smithsonian website in Chrome 22.0. Chrome is available for Windows, OS X, and Linux.

**SAFARI** Safari is the most popular Web browser for Macs but has an overall market share of about 5 percent. It comes bundled with Mac OS X and is also available for Windows. One of the slickest features of Safari is the Top Sites preview of your most visited websites (see Figure 7.9).

**MOBILE BROWSERS** Small screen devices, such as tablets, e-readers, and smartphones, use **mobile browsers**, which are sometimes called **microbrowsers**. IE, Firefox, Safari, and Opera all come in mobile versions. Other microbrowsers are proprietary—such as the Kindle, Android, and BlackBerry browsers. Most websites today can be accessed with a mobile browser, and many websites offer alternative pages that are optimized to be viewed with a mobile browser. Figure 7.10 shows the Library of Congress website displayed in the iPad version of Safari.

Navigation    Tabbed browsing    Omnibox — both Address and Search bar    Tools menu

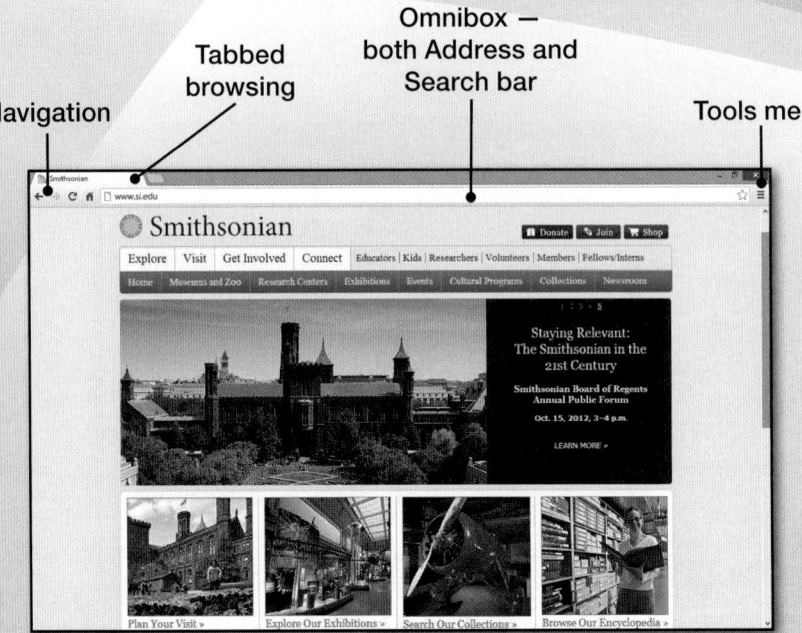

**FIGURE 7.8** Google Chrome

The Star indicates the page has changed since it was last viewed.

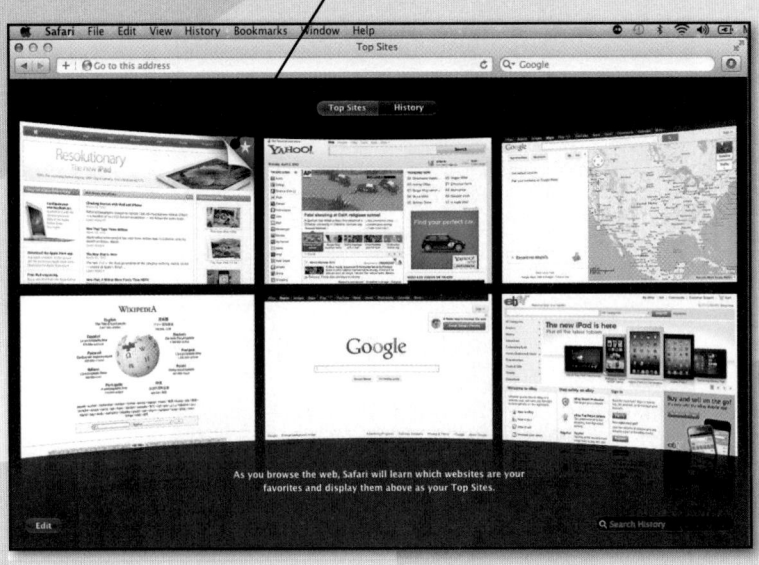

**FIGURE 7.9** Apple Safari Browser

# CONFIGURING YOUR WEB BROWSER

The first time you open any browser, it will have default settings, such as the home page and search provider, but you can (and should) customize it for your own use.

## SETTING THE HOME PAGE

The term **home page** has several meanings. It can mean the first page of a website, but in this case, it means the Web page that appears when you first open your browser. The default home page for IE is msn.com unless your computer manufacturer or ISP has altered it, in which case it is probably the company home page. You can set any page you want as your home page. In fact, because most browsers support tabbed browsing, you can actually set multiple home pages. Think about the things that you do as soon as you open your browser. Do you check Facebook? Web mail? Weather? Stock prices? Traffic? These are the things that will help you choose your home page(s). I have three home page tabs: MyITLab (where I save my links for this book), my work email, and Facebook (see Figure 7.11).

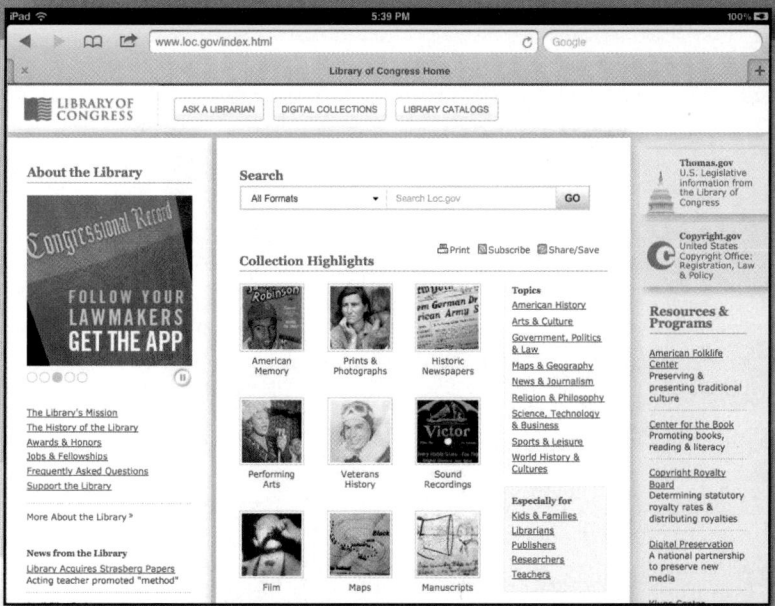

**FIGURE 7.10** Microbrowsers such as Safari for the iPad are optimized for small screens.

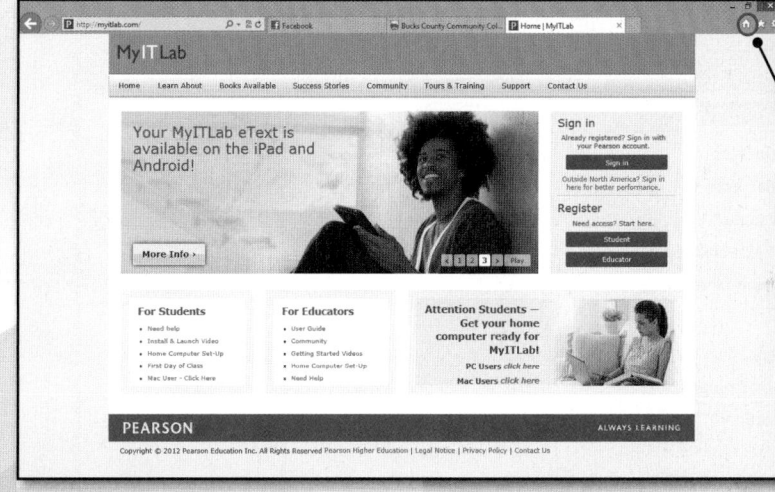

Click the house icon to go to your home page. Right-click the house to add or change your home pages.

**FIGURE 7.11** My Home Pages in IE

**SETTING THE SEARCH PROVIDERS** When you type a search term in the address bar or search box of your browser, what search provider is used? By default, the search provider will probably either be Microsoft Bing or Google—the provider your computer manufacturer or ISP chose. But as with your home page(s), you can modify this to your own favorites. In IE, click the arrow next to the magnifying glass in the address bar, and you'll see what search providers are already set up. You can choose any one of them during a search by clicking the name from the list, but if your favorite is missing, click *Add*. This will take you to a web page with numerous search providers that you can choose from (see Figure 7.12). Safari does not allow you to add search providers.

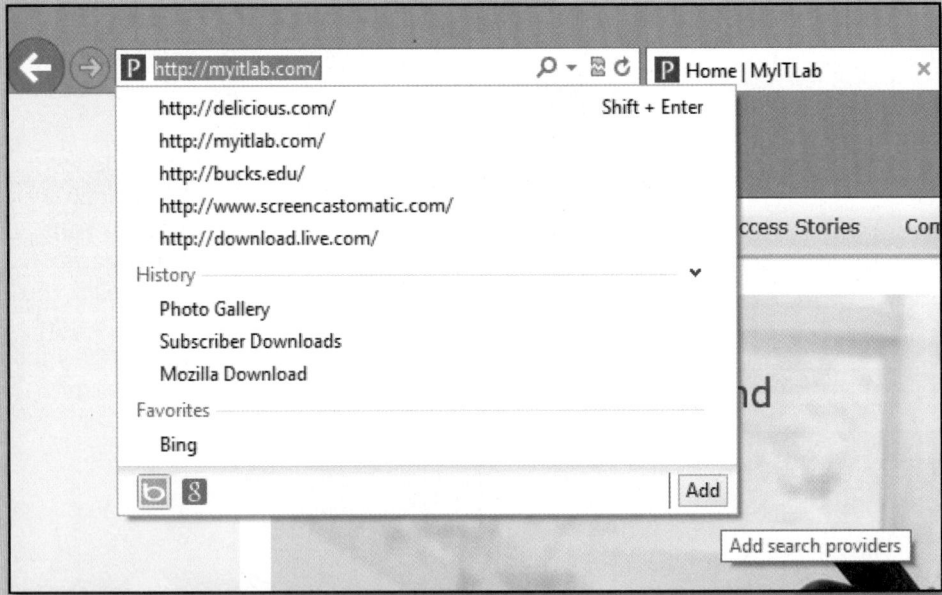

**FIGURE 7.12** You can easily modify the search providers in most browsers.

# ADD-ONS, PLUG-INS, AND TOOLBARS

You can extend the functionality of your Web browser by installing add-ons, plug-ins, extensions, and toolbars. The term "extension" tends to be used to refer to all of them. The distinction between the terms "add-on" and "plug-in" varies by browser. A **plug-in** is a third-party program, such as Adobe Reader. An **add-on** is created for a specific browser to add features to it. Firefox is the king of add-ons—there are hundreds of them available. My favorites allow me to capture video from the Web and block ads. IE has a smaller number of add-ons, but some of my favorites give me quick access to maps and shopping. Adding a toolbar to your browser gives you quick access to the features of the application that installed it—but be wary of toolbars that come bundled with software you install. Make certain you really want or need the toolbar before you agree to add it. Toolbars can be a source of malware and slow down your browsing as well.

Plug-in software, such as Adobe Flash Player, Microsoft Silverlight, and Sun Java, helps your browser to display the multimedia-rich, interactive, dynamic content that's increasingly common on the Internet. You don't need a plug-in to view a static Web page of text, such as a Wikipedia page; but dynamic content, videos, games, and even the flashy ads you see all rely on plug-ins. If you try to view a video on YouTube or play games on Facebook, you need Adobe Flash Player. If your school uses a learning management system such as Blackboard, you'll need to install Sun Java on your computer. Installing plug-ins is quick and free.

To see which add-ons and plug-ins are installed on your computer in IE, open the Tools menu, and click *Manage Add-ons*. In Firefox, choose *Add-ons* from the Firefox menu. Figure 7.13 shows the Add-ons Manager in the Firefox browser. From this window, you can discover new add-ons and disable those that you don't want.

For many people, choosing a browser is largely a matter of using whatever is available or preinstalled on their device. You do, however, have options if you're not happy with that choice. Also, remember that you can and should customize your browser to fit your needs. Make it work for you, and you'll enjoy the experience even more.

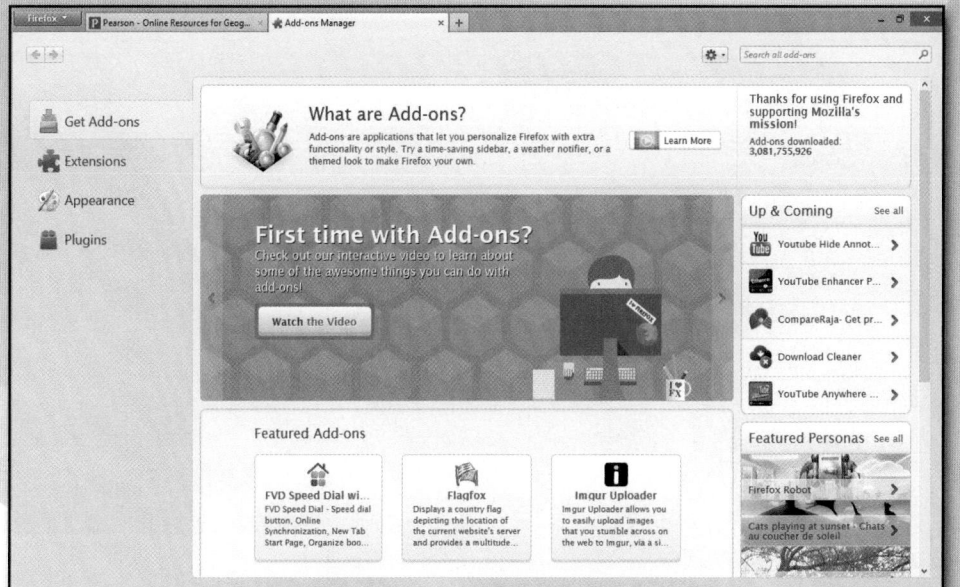

**FIGURE 7.13** Managing Firefox Add-ons

## Running Project

Research the version and market shares of the top five Web browsers. How has this changed since this article was written? Are there any in the current list of five that were not mentioned in this book?

## 4 Things You Need to Know

- The most popular Web browsers are Internet Explorer, Firefox, Chrome, and Safari.
- Mobile browsers are optimized for the small screens of mobile devices.
- You can customize the home page and other settings in most browsers.
- Add-ons and plug-ins extend the functionality of Web browsers.

## Key Terms

add-on

home page

HTML (hypertext markup language)

mobile browser
(microbrowser)

plug-in

Web browser

Web page

# HOW TO

## Manage Browser Home page, Favorites, and Search

In this exercise, you will look at and customize your browser settings using IE10. Directions for Safari users follow. *Note: You may be unable to perform some of these steps in a lab.*

**1** Open your word processor and type your name and date in the document. Save the file as **lastname_firstname_ch07_howto1**. Open Internet Explorer. Open the Tools menu and click *Internet Options*.

**2** On the General tab of the Internet Option dialog box, what page(s) are listed as Home page? Who decided which pages belong here? If you could change them, what changes would you make and why? Take a screen shot of this tab and paste it into your document.

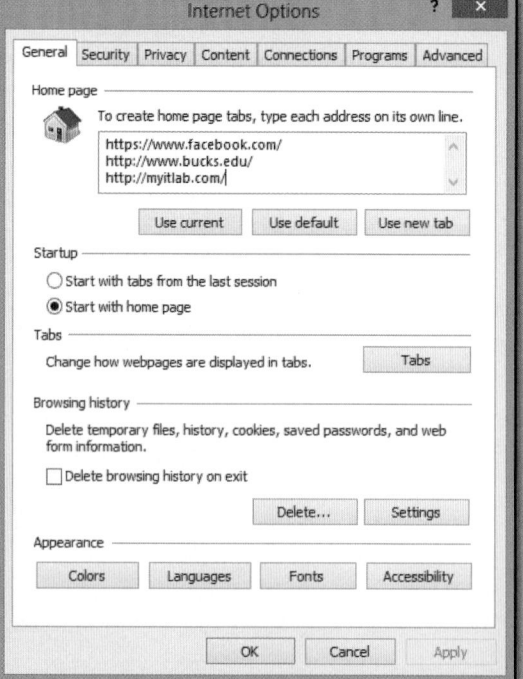

**3** Click the *Programs* tab and then click *Manage Add-ons*. Look through the Toolbars and Extensions that are installed. How many companies are listed? Are any disabled? At the bottom of the window, click *Learn more about toolbars and extensions*. What is their purpose? Close the Help window, take a screen shot of the Toolbars and Extension tab, and paste it into your document.

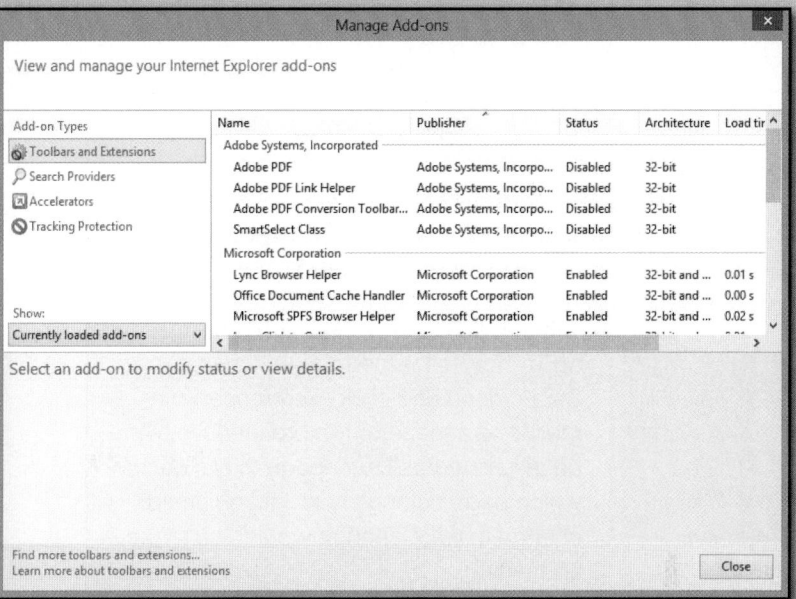

**4** In the Manage Add-ons window, under Add-on Types, click *Search Providers*. Which search providers are installed? At the bottom of the window, click *Find more search providers . . .* This will take you to the Internet Explorer Gallery. Select a search provider that is not already installed on your computer. Click the link to find out more about it. Which search provider did you choose and why? Click *Add to Internet Explorer*. Click *Add* in the dialog box and close the Gallery browser window and close the Manage Add-ons window. Reopen the Manage Add-ons window and click *Search Providers*. The search you added should now appear in the list. Take a screen shot of this window and paste it into your document. Save your file and submit as directed by your instructor.

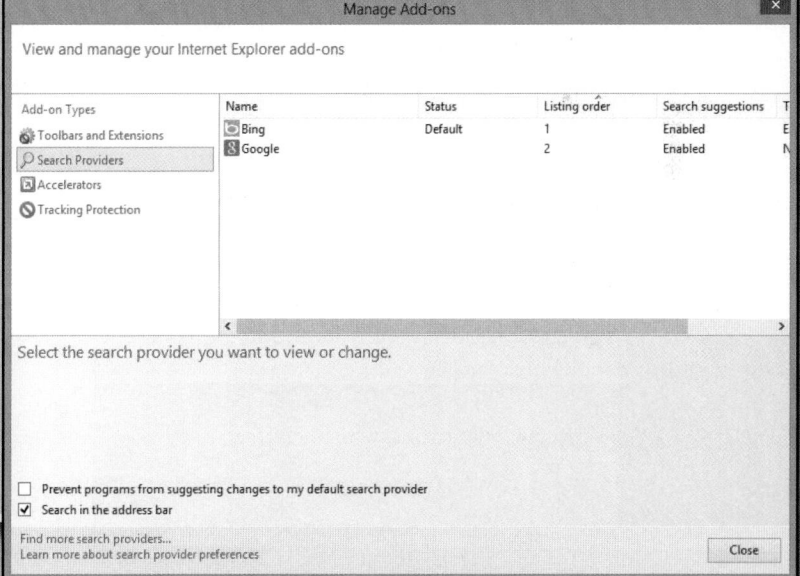

### If you are using a Mac:

**1** Open your word processor and type your name and date in the document. Save the file as **lastname_firstname_ch07_howto1**. Open Safari. Open the Safari menu and click *Preferences*. On the General pane of the preferences, what page is listed as Homepage? Who decided which page belongs here? If you could change it, what change would you make and why?

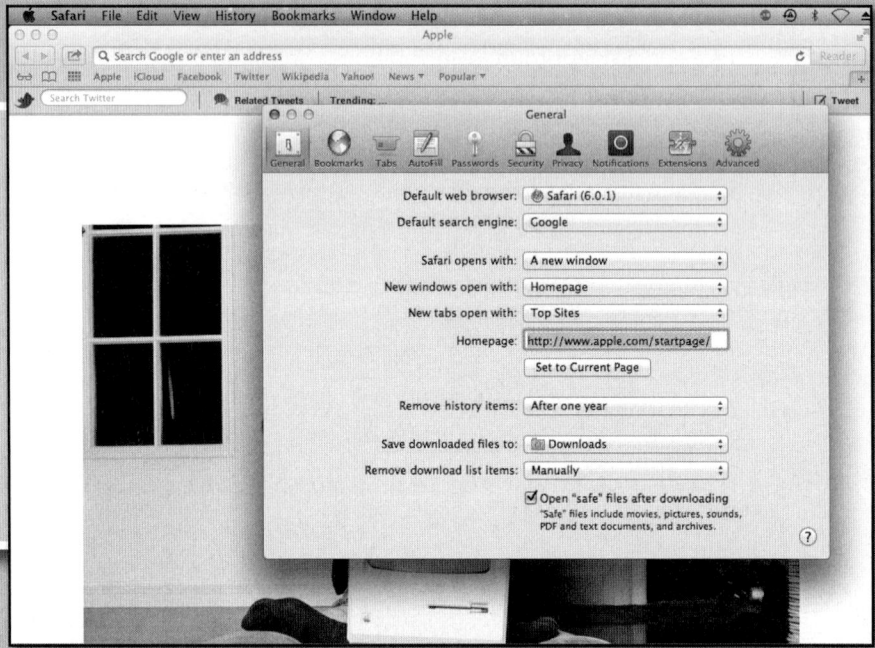

**2** Click the *Default search engine* option. Which search engines are installed? Which is set as your default? Take a screen shot of this pane and paste it into your document.

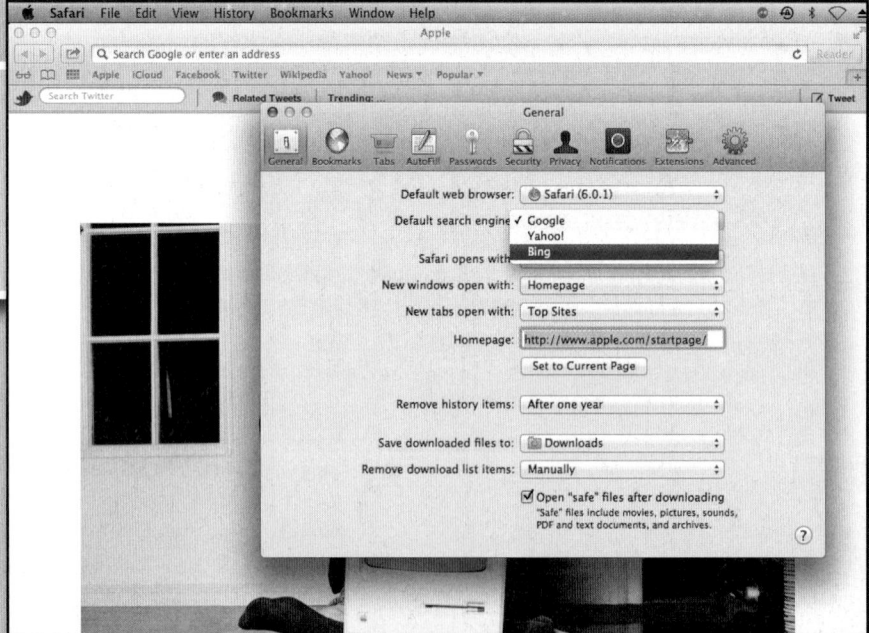

**3** Click the *Extensions* pane. Look through the Extensions that are installed. How many are listed? Are any disabled? What is their purpose? Take a screen shot of the Extension pane and paste it into your document.

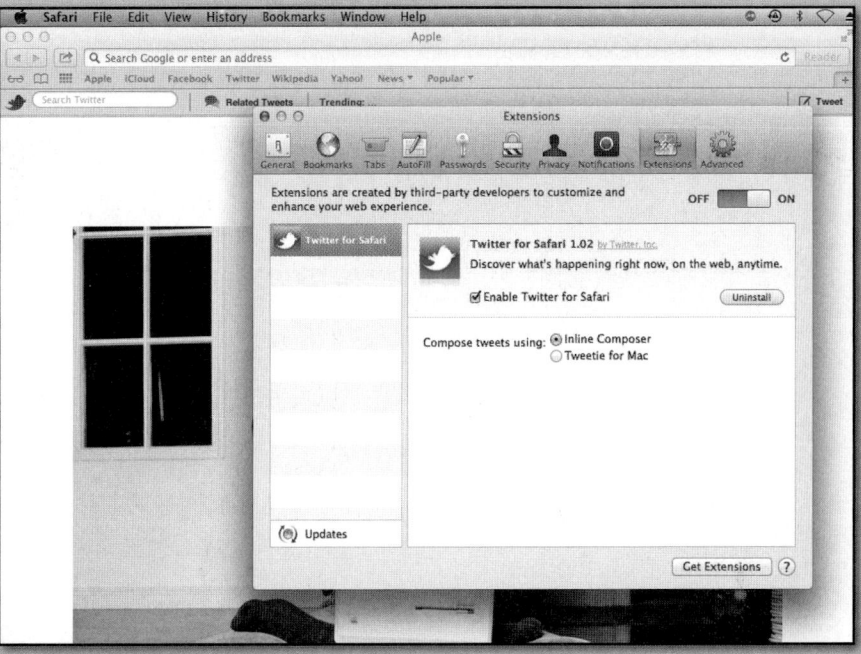

**4** Click *Get Extensions*. This will take you to the Safari Extension Gallery. Look through the list of Most Popular. Are any installed on your system? Select one that you would like to install. What is its purpose and why did you select it? Take a screen shot and paste it into your document. Save your file and submit as directed by your instructor.

# Navigating the Net

## 4 OBJECTIVE
## Demonstrate how to navigate the Web.

Congratulations—you're connected. Now what? There's so much information out there, it can be overwhelming. How do you know where to start? How do you find what you're looking for?

## WEB ADDRESSES

Let's start with the basics of how navigation works. There are two ways to move around the Web. First, you can type in the **URL (uniform resource locator)** or address of the website you want to visit (such as http://www.google.com) or you can follow links embedded in Web pages (remember Tim Berners-Lee) from one place to the next. Most people do both. A **website** consists of one or more Web pages that all are located in the same place. The **home page** of a website is the main or starting page. It's the page you see when you type in the Web address for a site.

Let's look at the parts of a URL.

http://www.google.com

*http* is the protocol that tells your computer what type of page you're looking at. This is almost always http (a Web page) but can be https (a secure Web page), ftp (file transfer protocol), or others. It is so likely to be http that you can actually leave this part of the address out when you type it.

http://www.google**.com**

**.com** is known as the **top-level domain (TLD)** and represents the type of website you're visiting. Common TLDs are .com (commercial), .edu (educational), and .gov (government). Today, there are so many websites that more TLDs are needed. Websites outside the United States often have a country code TLD, such as .ca (Canada) or .af (Afghanistan).

http://www.*google*.com

The *domain name* precedes the TLD and is sometimes called the second-level domain. In our example, google is the domain name. The **domain name** represents a company or product name and makes it easy for us to remember the address.

http://*www*.google.com

The *www* represents the computer on the google domain and is called the third-level domain. It is common to name the computer www, so this part of the URL is also often omitted.

So, typing http://www.google.com or merely google.com will result in the same thing. And from there, the fun begins. In this book, the http://www part of a URL is generally omitted.

When you visit other pages on a website, the URL will have an additional part after the TLD. For example, to view the page about the band Tom Petty and the Heartbreakers on Facebook, you can type **facebook.com/TomPetty**.

ICANN (Internet Corporation for Assigned Names and Numbers) coordinates the Internet naming system. Computers speak in numbers, so computers on the Internet are assigned **IP (Internet protocol) addresses**. Like phone numbers, these IP addresses must be unique.

IP addresses are composed of numbers, which can be hard for a person to remember, so the DNS system was developed. **DNS (Domain Name System)** allows us to use a friendly name such as google.com instead of an IP address such as 74.125.224.72 to contact a website. DNS works like a telephone directory. When you enter a URL in your browser, your computer requests the IP address of the computer. Your DNS server, which is probably provided by your ISP, locates the IP address information and sends it back to your computer, which then uses it to address your request (see Figure 7.14).

**FIGURE 7.14** The Domain Name System is a directory system for the Internet.

# SMART SEARCHING

When did Google become a verb? The verb google—to use the Google search engine to obtain information on the World Wide Web—was added to the Merriam-Webster Dictionary in 2001. With billions of Web pages on the Internet, how do you begin to find what you're looking for, and when you do find it, how can you trust it? Searching for information on the Internet is a crucial skill in today's world. While it may seem that everything you want to know is on Google, the fact is that Google only covers part of the Internet. Also, when you type in a search like the words "dog care" in a search page such as Google, you'll likely get *millions* of results or hits. So, the first part of the puzzle is knowing how to ask the right question.

# Find Out MORE

Check out the current list of TLDs at the **iana.org** website. What are some of the gTLDs in the list that are less common? What is the difference between a ccTLD and a gTLD?

**VIZ CLIP**

Let's use Google in our example. Typing in the word "eagles" on the Google website got me 216 million hits the day I wrote this (see Figure 7.15). Because the Web is constantly changing, if you perform the same search today, your numbers will probably be different. Also, if your browser or device is using location services, your results might be location specific. Because I live in Philadelphia, the Philadelphia Eagles football team is near the top of my results. If you live in Denver, the results will probably be different.

So, where do I start? A good approach is to look at the first few hits and see if what you want is there. If not, it's time to think about a better way to ask the question. To narrow down the results, I can add some more keywords to the search. The first few hits using the word "eagles" got me the football team and the rock band. I need to be more specific in my query if I'm really interested in the kind of eagles that fly! I can do this by adding more terms to my search, such as "birds," "raptors," or "bald." To get narrower search results, I can use the advanced search tool to filter the results. I can add or exclude terms as well as specify a language and date, among other things. The advanced search options are fairly common for different search sites, too.

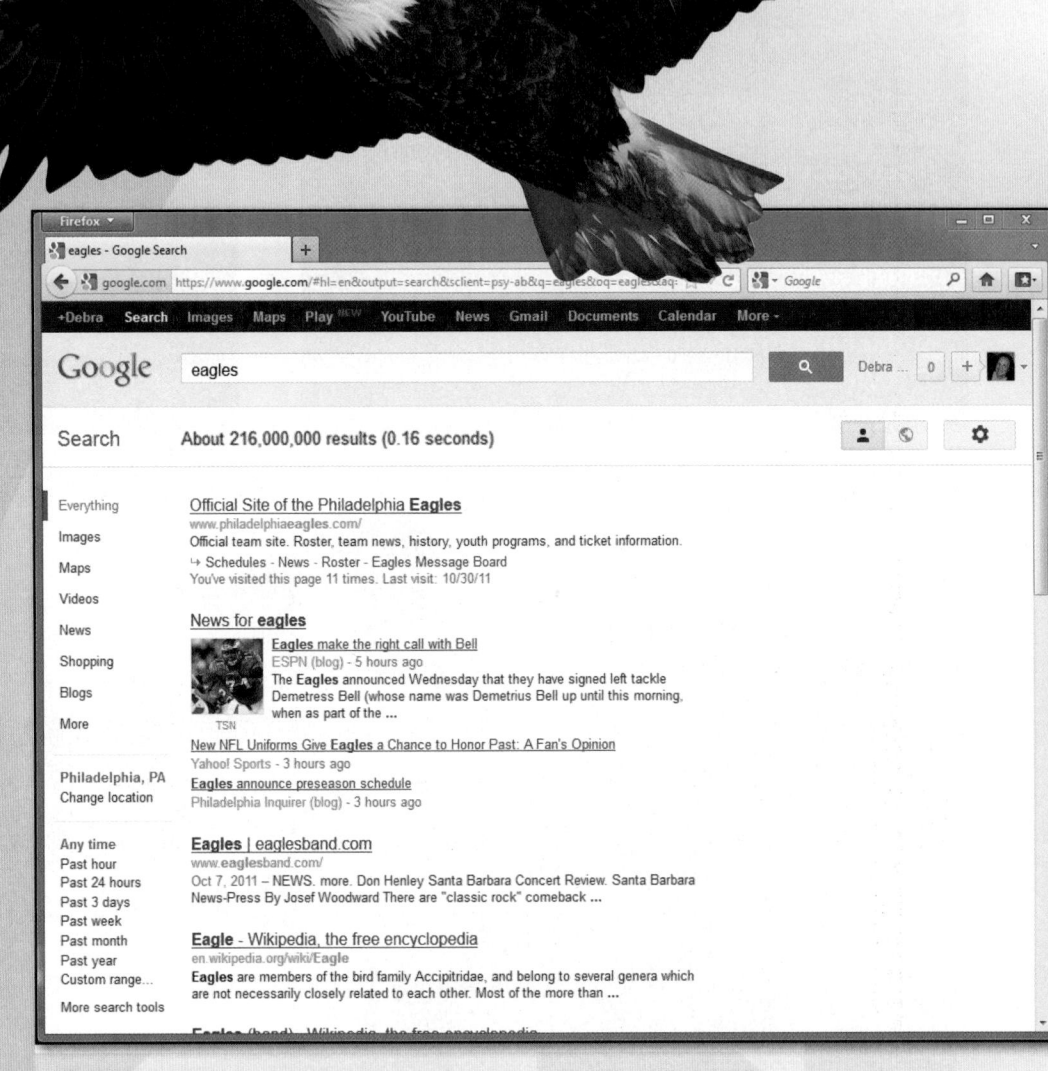

**FIGURE 7.15** Here are my Google results for the search term "eagles."

You can also use Boolean operators or Advanced Search to refine your search. Figure 7.16 shows the "eagles" search using various Boolean operators.

What's the difference between search tools? **Search engines** are huge databases. They send out software (called spiders or bots) to crawl the Web and gather information, which is then indexed. Because the Web is dynamic and constantly changing, this method helps the search engine stay up-to-date. Some search engines also accept submissions, and others use both methods to gather information. There are even metasearch engines that search other search engines. There may also be differences in the way the information is classified and categorized.

There are so many places to search for information that it can be hard to figure out where to start. Contrary to popular belief, Google doesn't index the entire Web, so it's wise to become familiar with at least a couple of other search tools you can use.

| TERMS | SEARCH FILTER/ BOOLEAN OPERATOR | RESULTS |
|---|---|---|
| eagles | None | 216,000,000 |
| eagles AND birds | AND | 32,600,000 |
| eagles OR birds | OR | 818,000,000 |

**FIGURE 7.16** Using Search Filters in Google

## Running Project

Think Google, Bing, and Yahoo! are the only search engines around? Try googling to see how many you get. How many of them have you used in the past? Select two that look interesting, and search for the name of your favorite sports team on each. Did you get the same results? How were they different? Read the About section of the search tool to determine how content is added. You can usually find this link at the bottom of a Web page. What are some of the unique features of each?

## 5 Things You Need to Know

- A Web address is also known as a URL.
- TLDs are .com, .edu, .gov, and so on.
- DNS allows us to use URLs instead of IP addresses to access websites.
- Every node on the Internet has a unique IP address.
- Search engines are databases that index the Web.

## Key Terms

domain name

DNS (Domain Name System)

home page

IP (Internet protocol) address

search engine

top-level domain (TLD)

URL (uniform resource locator)

website

# HOW TO

## Use Google Docs

Google provides free online applications you can use to create and share many types of documents. The first step is to sign in to your Google account. If you do not wish to use your Google account, create a new account for this exercise. You may delete it when you have finished the exercise, or keep it as an extra account. Creating a Google account is easy. Just go to Google.com, click *Sign in*, and click *Create an account now*. Answer a few questions, and you're all set.

Using Google Docs is an easy way to quickly create and share documents with others. There is no software to purchase or install; it all runs right from your browser. Google docs is an example of a SaaS application. It doesn't matter if you have a PC and your friend has a Mac. Because collaboration is so easy, you can work on the file together even if you are not in the same location.

**1** From the menu at the top of the screen, choose *Drive*.

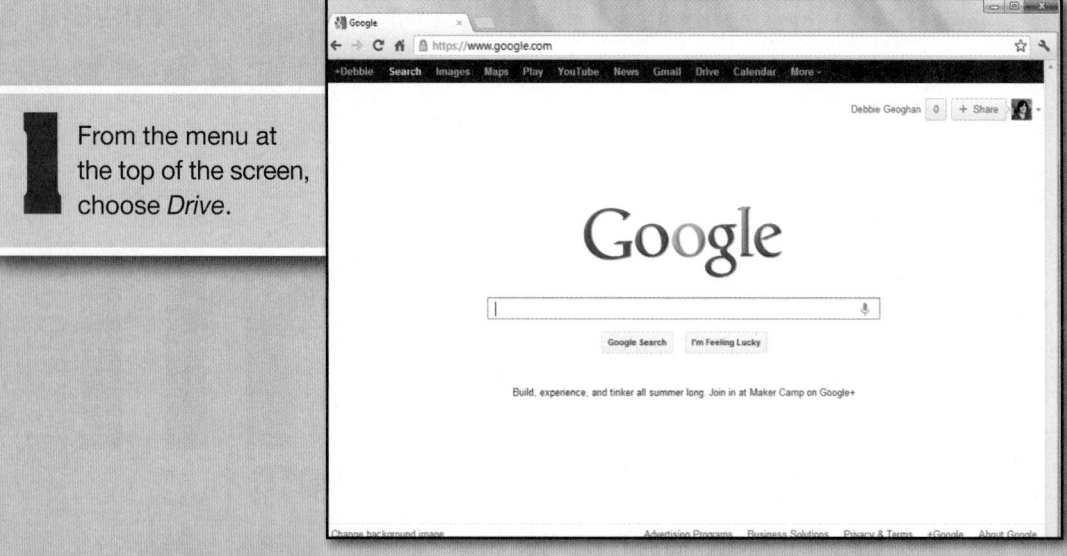

**2** On the Google Drive page, you can see the files you have created and shared, and files others have shared with you. To create a new file, click the *Create* button and choose the type of file you wish to create. You can create a document (word processor), presentation, spreadsheet, form, or drawing. For this exercise, choose *Document*.

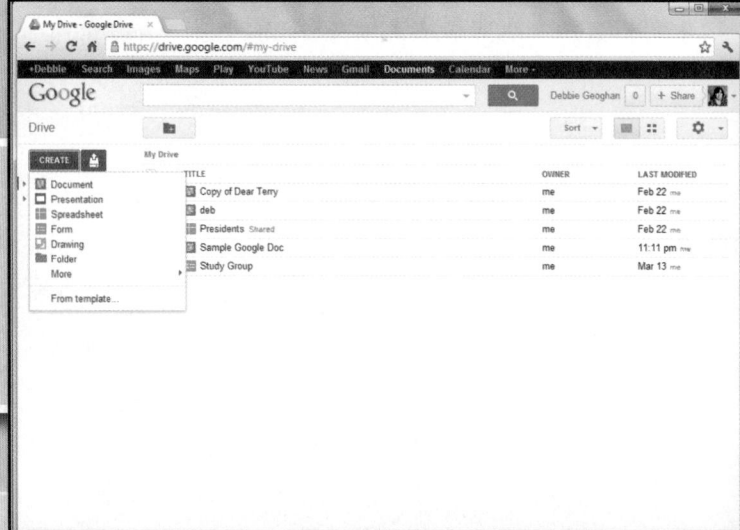

**3** The word processing (Document) tool includes standard formatting options and is easy to use. Enter the following text in the document:

**A simple Google document can be shared and used as an easy collaboration tool—no installation required!**

**The toolbar includes standard formatting options including font styles and alignment.**

**You can add elements such as links, images, and lists.**

**There is a built-in spell checker.**

**You can share your file with others using the blue Share button.**

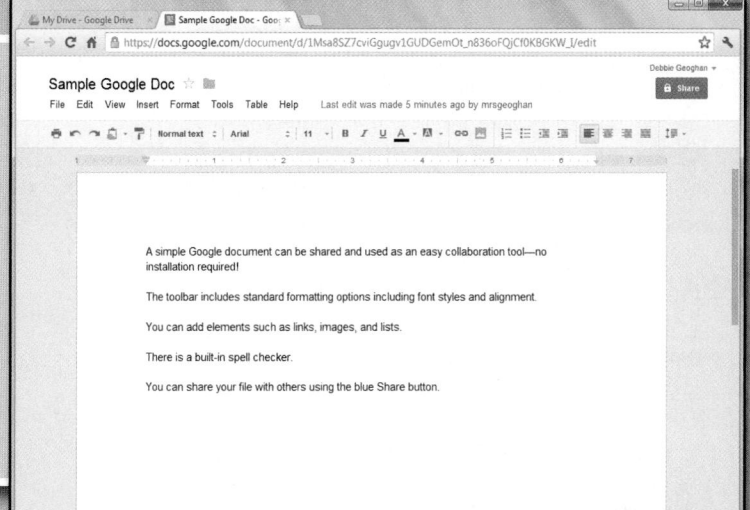

**4** Click *File* and then click *Rename . . .* Change the file name to **Lastname_Firstname_ch07_howto2**. Because Google automatically saves your file, as Untitled document, you need to rename the file.

**5** If possible, work with a classmate on this part of the activity. The Share button allows you to share your file with others for collaboration. Click the *Share* button and enter an email address to share the file with a classmate. Click *Share and Save*, and then click *Done*. Close the file to return to the Google Drive. Take a screen shot of your Google drive that shows the shared file.

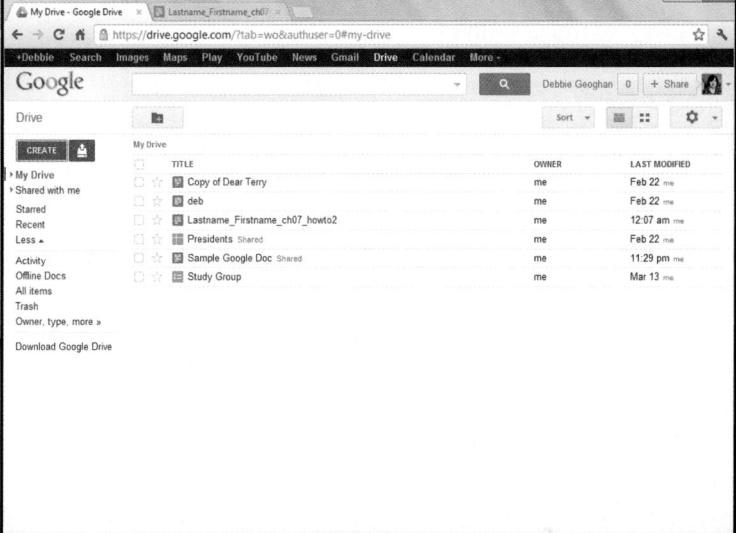

**6** To work on a shared file, open it from the Google Drive file list. If you are working with a classmate, you should both open the same shared file. If you are working alone, open the file you created for this exercise. Paste the screen shot from step 5 at the end of the document.

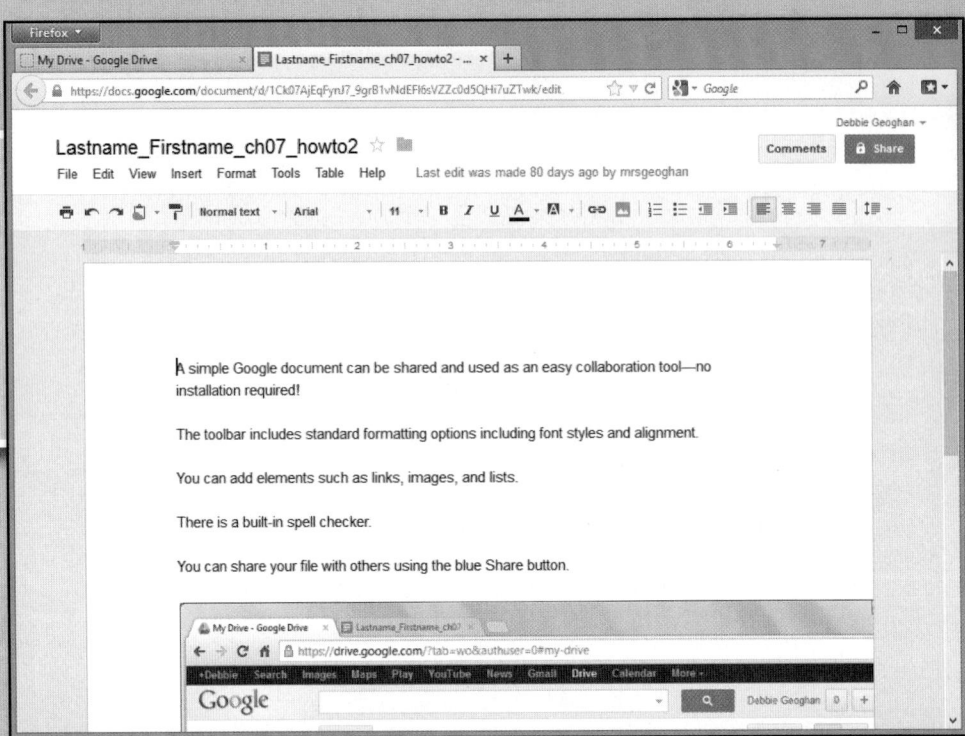

**7** From the File menu, choose *See revision history* to see each revision of the document.

**8** You can collaborate in real time. A list of people working on the document displays in the upper right corner, and you will see their edits in real time. Open the list to view and chat with collaborators in the current session.

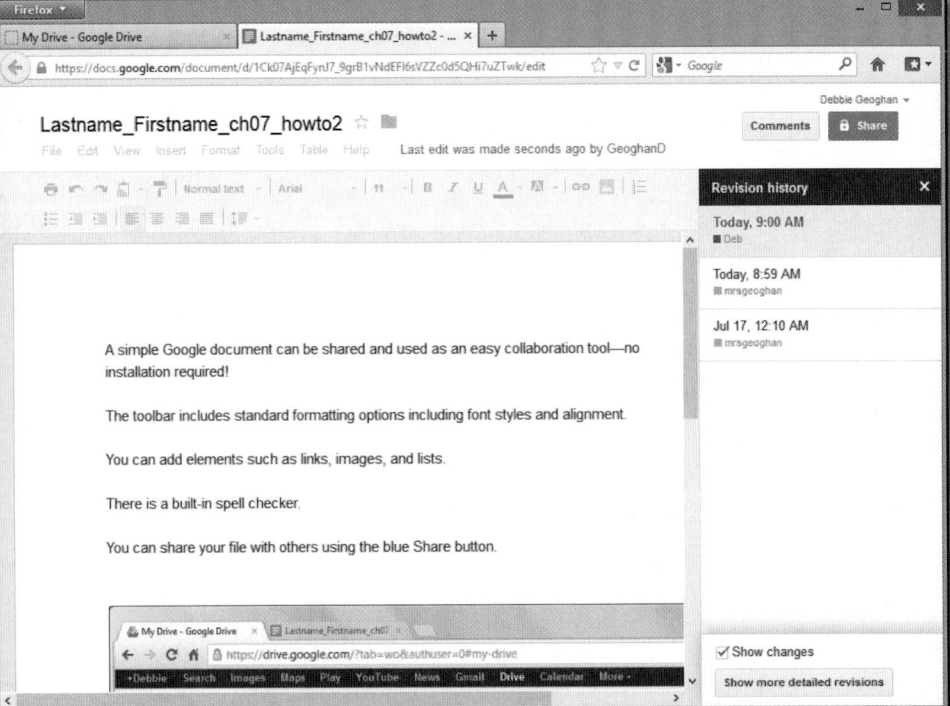

**9** You can download the file into many popular formats, including Microsoft Office formats, by clicking *Download as* on the File menu. Submit as directed by your instructor.

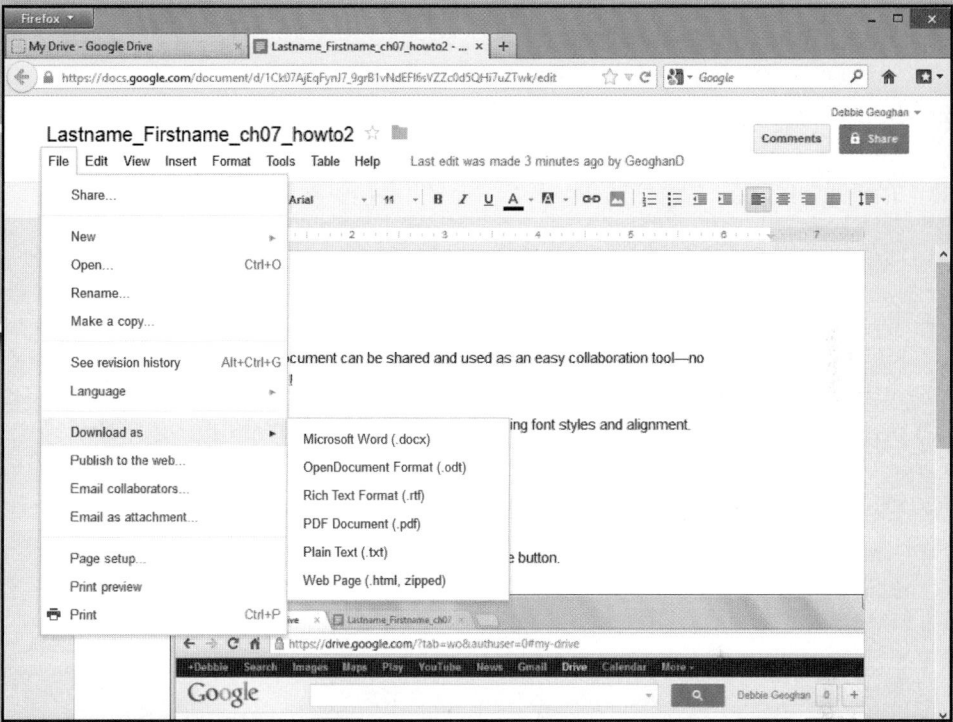

# Would I Lie to You?

## 5 OBJECTIVE
## Discuss how to evaluate the credibility of information found on the Web.

So, now that you have your three million hits, how do you know what to believe? The Internet is full of **user-generated content**—content that has been written by everyday users. While there's a lot of wonderful content out there, the truth is that anyone can say anything. You need to be able to evaluate the information you find. There are many clues to look for when deciding whether a website is one that you can trust. Here are just a few.

## WHO WROTE IT?

Do you believe everything you hear? Or everything you read? Do you evaluate the credentials of the people that you take advice from? How did Bernie Madoff scam so many people? He was convincing. He was believable, and nobody questioned his results until it was too late—even though what he promised was too good to be true. Be a skeptic when evaluating information you find on the Internet.

Look at the URL. Ask yourself: Is it a restricted TLD like .edu or .gov or a general one like .com? Take a look at **fda.gov** and **fda.com** and compare them (see Figure 7.17). The .com version isn't the Food and Drug Administration website. On the fda.com website, at the top of the page in small type you will see, "Food and Drug Assistance; Resources for Industry and Consumers." Because we're in the habit of typing .com, not .gov, sometimes we end up at a site we didn't intend to. Some organizations go so far as to own both domains so you can't make that mistake—for example, you can reach the U.S. Post Office website by typing usps.com or usps.gov. A restricted TLD such as .edu or .gov gives some authority to a site, but even that's not a guarantee that the author is credible.

**FIGURE 7.17** The FDA website, which is part of the restricted TLD .gov, is quite different from the fda.com website.

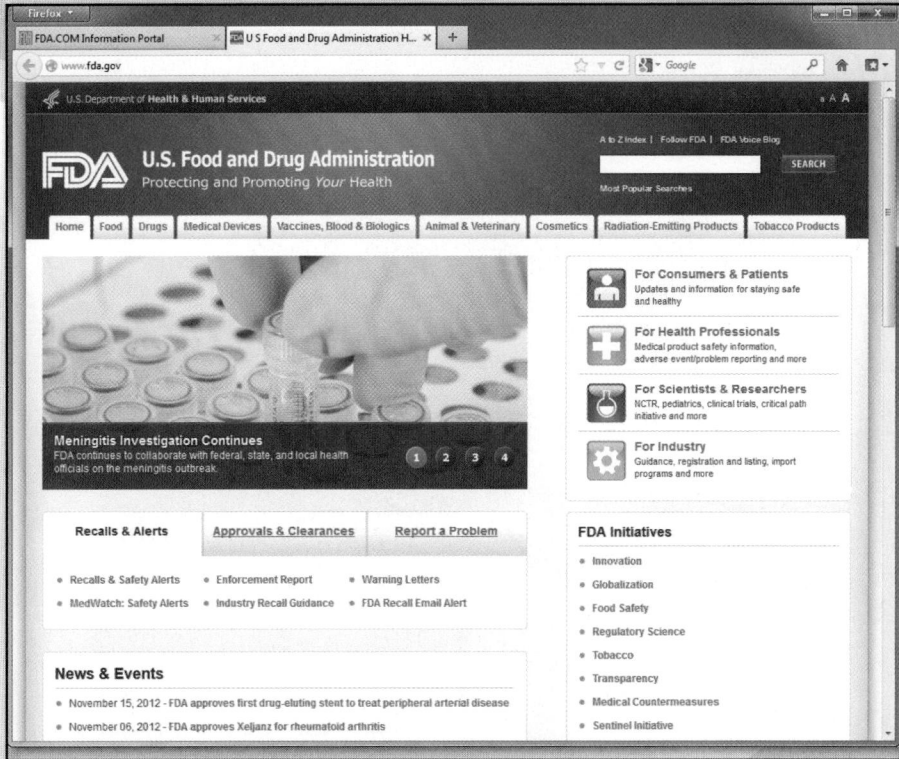

For more information, read the home page and About Us page, and look for the credentials of the author or organization. Ask yourself if there are any conflicts of interest or obvious biases. Is there contact information? How up-to-date is the website? You can usually find this information at the bottom of the home page. If you can't find any of this information, it should raise a red flag.

Stick to well-known sources for important information. If you're looking up health advice, WebMD and the American Cancer Society websites are trustworthy authorities. On the other hand, **skipyourselfhealthy.info** may not be. Then again, it might, but you'll need to do a bit of research before you can be sure.

A good search tool to use when doing scholarly research is Google Scholar (**scholar.google.com**) to search for articles, theses, books, abstracts, and court opinions. Or, check with your school library as well to see which databases and resources you have access to as a student.

**Try the Internet Simulation**

# WHAT ABOUT THE DESIGN?

Look at the design of the site, including its sophistication, grammar, and spelling. What impression do you get from the site? But don't be fooled—a well-designed and executed site can still have bad information, and a poorly designed site might have really good information. The Onion website (**theonion.com**), America's Finest News Source, is very well designed, but it is certainly not a valid news source.

Finally, take a look at other sites. Does this information match what you can find on other sites that cover the same topics? Does it make sense? This is really key. If it's too good to be true, it probably is.

Critically evaluating the information you find on a website is a skill that takes time to master. It may not be a big deal if you believe a website that says you should eat tofu to make your hair grow (although it probably won't work), but if you follow advice to invest all your money and it turns out to be a scam, then it will be a huge deal.

# CAREER SPOTLIGHT

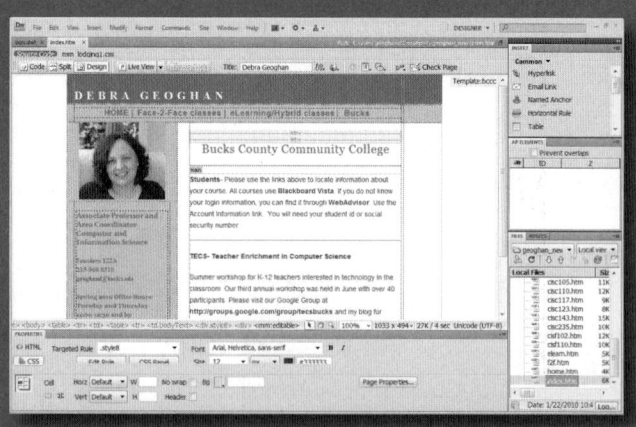

The person who decides how a website will look is called the Web designer. If the website is simple, the Web designer may also be the person who creates the website. If you have ever created your own Web page, then you were the designer.

Today, it's pretty easy to create a basic website. There are software programs, templates, and websites that can help you make something quickly and easily. A professional Web designer, however, goes beyond the basics and creates designs from scratch that are customized and branded for a business. A Web designer needs to have a good understanding of the capabilities of the Web to design an interesting, dynamic, and professional site. Some Web designers are self-taught; others have degrees in graphic arts, computer science, e-business, or marketing.

# GREEN COMPUTING

## TELECOMMUTING TO SAVE

As I write this, I'm sitting in my family room in my pajamas. I'm one of the millions of Americans who telecommute at least part-time. I do go in to school a few days a week to teach classes, but I also teach many online classes, especially in the summer, which allows me to work from home. While there are lots of arguments for and against telecommuting, there's no denying the positive impact it can have on the environment. It saves me a few days' worth of gas, which at today's prices really adds up. So, it's better for the environment to keep my car off the road, and it's better for my wallet, too.

Not every job lends itself to telecommuting, but according to one site created to provide resources to telecommuters, businesses, and individuals, if just 50 percent of the people who could work from home did so just half of the time, in the United States, we would:

- Save more than $650 billion a year
- Reduce greenhouse gases by the equivalent of taking 9 million cars off the road
- Reduce oil imports by 37 percent

Businesses that encourage telecommuting can also save on real estate expenses. Fewer employees onsite means smaller office space requirements and lower utility bills. Sun Microsystems has a large telecommuting program that saves more than 5,000 kilowatt hours per year for each person who works from home just two days a week.

## Running Project

Compare these two websites:

- **mypyramid.gov**
- **foodpyramid.com**

Use the guidelines discussed in this article to evaluate and compare the two. Pay special attention to the About Us section on each site.

## 4 Things You Need to Know

- User-generated content means anybody can create content on the Web.
- Use the home page, contact information, and About pages of a website to look for credentials of the author or organization.
- Restricted TLDs include .gov and .edu., and they add some credibility to the content.
- Good website design doesn't guarantee credible website content.

## Key Term

user-generated content

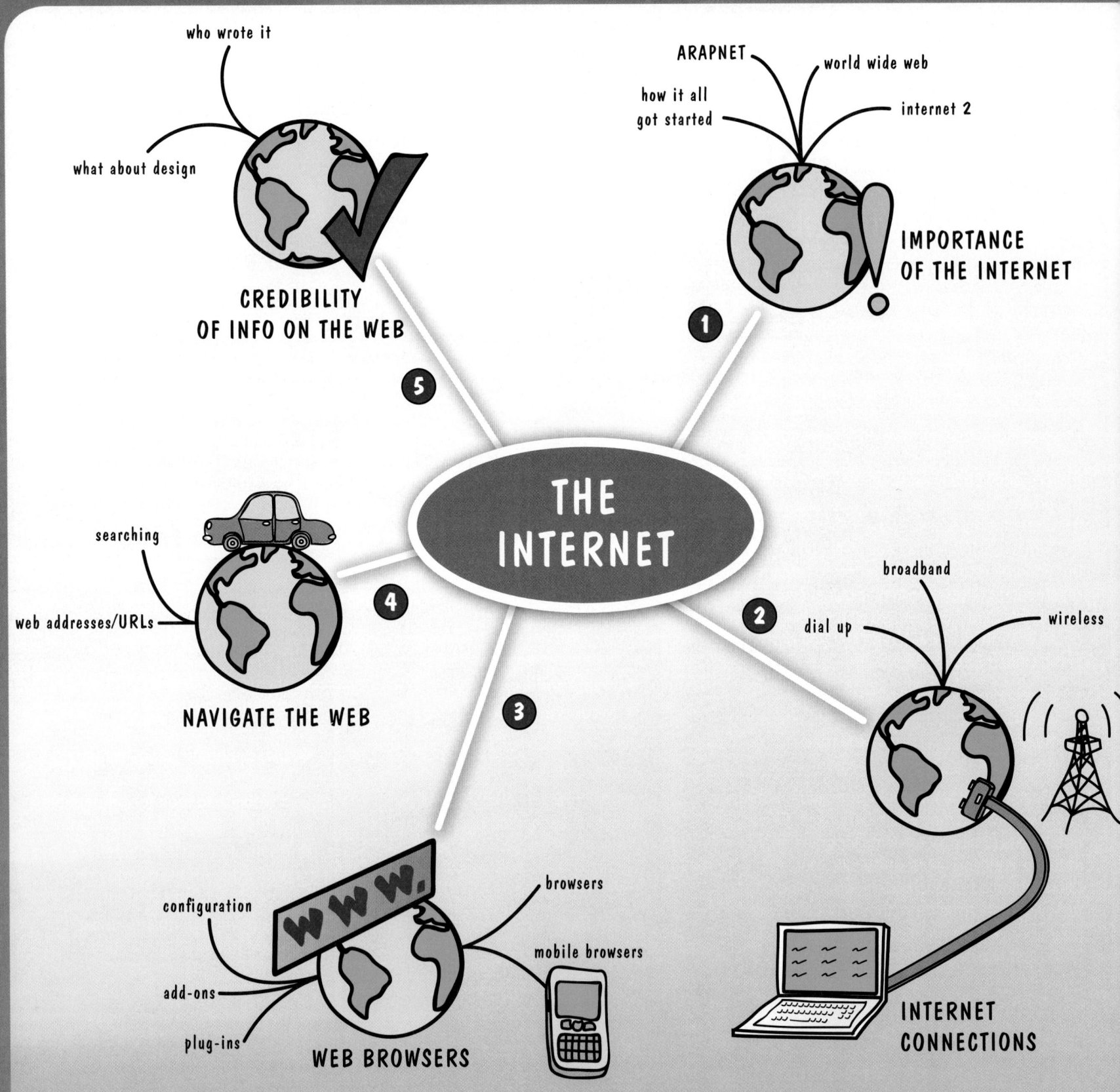

who wrote it

what about design

CREDIBILITY
OF INFO ON THE WEB

ARAPNET

world wide web

how it all
got started

internet 2

IMPORTANCE
OF THE INTERNET

①

THE
INTERNET

⑤

searching

web addresses/URLs

④

NAVIGATE THE WEB

②

broadband

dial up

wireless

③

configuration

browsers

mobile browsers

add-ons

plug-ins

WEB BROWSERS

INTERNET
CONNECTIONS

# Objectives Recap

1. Recognize the importance of the Internet.
2. Compare types of Internet connections.
3. Compare popular Web browsers.
4. Demonstrate how to navigate the Web.
5. Discuss how to evaluate the credibility of information found on the Web.

# Key Terms

add-on **284**
ARPANET **272**
broadband **277**
cable Internet access **277**
dial-up **277**
domain name **290**
DNS (Domain Name System) **291**
DSL (digital subscriber line) **277**
fiber-to-the-home (FTTH) **277**
home page **283, 290**
hotspot **278**
HTML (hypertext markup language) **280**
hyperlink **273**
hypertext **273**
Internet (net) **273**
Internet backbone **272**
Internet Exchange Points **272**
Internet2 (I2) **274**

Internet service provider (ISP) **276**
IP (Internet protocol) address **291**
LTE (Long Term Evolution) **278**
mobile browser (microbrowser) **282**
municipal WiFi **278**
plug-in **284**
satellite Internet access **278**
search engine **293**
top-level domain (TLD) **290**
URL (uniform resource locator) **290**
user-generated content **298**
Web browser **280**
Web page **280**
website **290**
WiFi **278**
WiMAX Mobile Internet **278**
World Wide Web **273**

# Summary

**1. Recognize the importance of the Internet.**

Since its invention in 1969, the Internet has grown to almost 2 billion users. It's now an integral part of research, education, commerce, and communication for people around the world. The Internet2 project is a second Internet that's limited to educational and research institutions.

**2. Compare types of Internet connections.**

Dial-up Internet uses regular telephone lines to access the Internet and is very slow. Broadband connections provide speeds at least four times faster than dial-up and include cable, DSL, and fiber. Cable is provided by the same company that provides you with cable TV and uses the same lines for both services. DSL (digital subscriber line) uses digital telephone lines to provide Internet access. DSL is slower than cable and is affected by the distance from the telephone company switch. Fiber-to-the-home (FTTH) delivers Internet access over fiber-optic cable. FTTH is the fastest and most expensive option. Wireless Internet access includes municipal WiFi, satellite, and 3G/4G cellular service.

**3. Compare popular Web browsers.**

The most popular Web browsers are Internet Explorer, Firefox, Chrome, and Safari. Mobile browsers are optimized for small screen devices, such as smartphones and tablets. Many people simply use the browser that's preinstalled on their device.

**4. Demonstrate how to navigate the Web.**

A Web address or URL (uniform resource locator) can be broken down into four parts: protocol, TLD (top-level domain), domain name, and the computer on the domain. URLs can be typed in or embedded into a Web page as a hyperlink that you can click on. When you type a URL in your browser, your computer sends a DNS (Domain Name System) request to find the IP (Internet protocol) address of the website. You can search for information using search engines—huge databases that index Web pages.

**5. Discuss how to evaluate the credibility of information found on the Web.**

Be skeptical. Look at the URL for restricted TLDs such as .gov and .edu. Read the About Us page and other website information to view the author's credentials. Look for professional design and writing style. Finally, verify information using other sources.

# Application Project

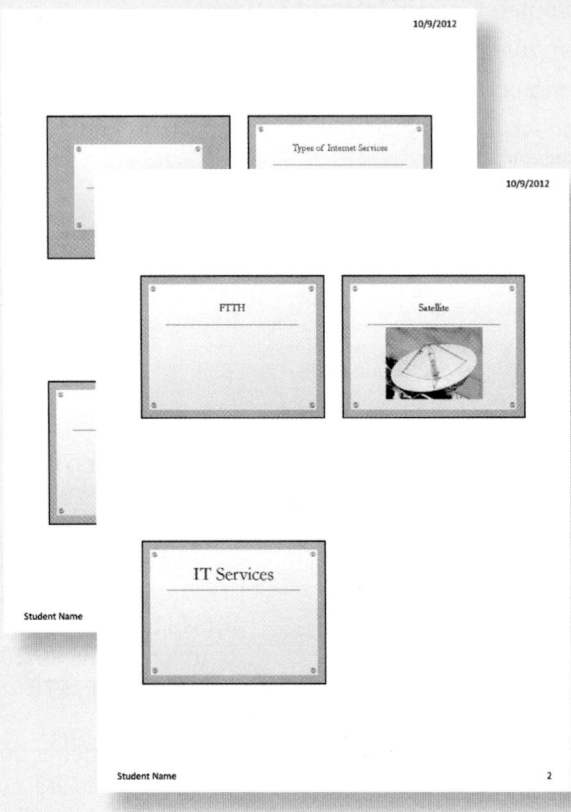

## Microsoft Office Application Project 1:
## PowerPoint Level 2

**PROJECT DESCRIPTION:** In this Microsoft PowerPoint project, you will create a presentation about Internet Services. In creating this presentation you will apply design, font, and color themes. You will also change font colors, bullet symbols, and slide layout.

**INSTRUCTIONS:** For the purpose of grading of the project you are required to perform the following tasks:

| Step | Instructions |
|------|--------------|
| **1** | Start PowerPoint. Download and open the file named *vt_ch07_ppt*. Save the file as **lastname_firstname_ch07_ppt**. |
| **2** | Apply the Organic theme to the presentation. |
| **3** | Apply the Vertical Striped Variant to the presentation. |
| **4** | On Slide 1, type your name in the subtitle placeholder, and apply bold and italic formatting to the subtitle text. |

| Step | Instructions |
|------|--------------|
| **5** | On Slide 2, type **Types of Internet Services** in the title placeholder. In the content placeholder, enter the following four bullet points: (note this theme does not use bullet symbols)<br>**Cable**<br>**DSL**<br>**FTTH**<br>**Satellite** |
| **6** | On Slide 2, change the bullet style to Star bullets and set the line spacing to 2.0. |
| **7** | Type **Cable** in the title placeholder on Slide 3. Type **DSL** in the title placeholder on Slide 4. |

Visit **pearsonhighered.com/Geoghan** for data files, simulations, VizClips, and additional study materials.

| Step | Instructions |
|------|--------------|
| 8 | Insert three new slides after Slide 4. Type **FTTH** in the title placeholder on Slide 5 and type **Satellite** in the title placeholder on Slide 6. |
| 9 | On Slide 6, insert the downloaded *vt_ch07_image1* in the content placeholder. Apply the Drop Shadow Rectangle picture style to the image. |
| 10 | Apply the Window transition to all slides with a duration of 2.00. |
| 11 | Change the layout of Slide 7 to Title Only. |
| 12 | On Slide 7, type **IT Services** in the title placeholder. Center the title and change the font size to 72. |
| 13 | Insert the page number and your name in the footer on the notes and handouts pages for all slides in the presentation. View the presentation in Slide Show view from beginning to end, and then return to Normal view. |
| 14 | Save and close the presentation. Exit PowerPoint. Submit the presentation as directed. |

Visit **pearsonhighered.com/Geoghan** for data files, simulations, VizClips, and additional study materials.

Chapter 7 | 305

# Microsoft Office Application Project 2:
## Word Level 2

**PROJECT DESCRIPTION:** In this MIcrosoft Word project, you have been asked to write an article on cellular Internet service. You will need to change alignment, line and paragraph spacing, margins, lists, and edit the header and footer. You will also find and replace text, create and modify a footnote, and use the Format Painter.

**INSTRUCTIONS:** For the purpose of grading the project you are required to perform the following tasks:

### Cellular Internet

**1G**, or first-generation cellular telephone technology was analog. It was introduced in the 1980s and was replaced by the digital **2G** or second-generation in the early 90s. **2G** not only carried voice signals, but also data such as text messages and email.

**3G**, or third-generation, access was launched in 2001 and was the first cellular technology that offered reasonably fast data transfer speeds[1]. Smartphones became increasingly popular and more websites began to support mobile access.

The first **4G** networks began appearing in 2009 and offer even faster data rates.

- **1G**- introduced 1979- Speed 28- 56 kbps
- **2G**- introduced 1991- Speed 56-384 kbps
- **3G**- introduced 2001- Speed At least 200 kbps
- **4G**- introduced 2009- Speed 1 Gbps for stationary and 100 Mbps for mobile operation

[1] Some earlier technologies were referred to as 2.5G and 2.75 G.

lastname_firstname_ch07_word

| Step | Instructions |
|------|--------------|
| **1** | Start Word. Download and open the Word file named *vt_ch07_word*. Save the file as lastname_firstname_ch07_word. |
| **2** | Change the left and right margins of the document to 1.25". |
| **3** | Change the line spacing of the entire document to 2.0 lines. Change the paragraph spacing (before and after) of the entire document to 6.0 point. |
| **4** | Apply the Title style and center the heading *Cellular Internet*. |
| **5** | Apply bold and underline formatting to the text 1G. Using the Format Painter, apply the formatting from the text *1G* to the text *2G, 3G, and 4G*. |
| **6** | Use the Find and Replace dialog box to search for and replace all instances of the word *wireless* with **cellular**. There should be two replacements. |
| **7** | Select the last four lines and format as a bulleted list using solid square bullets. |
| **8** | In the 3G paragraph, insert a footnote immediately following the period following the text *data transfer speeds* reading **Some earlier technologies were referred to as 2.5G and 2.75G.** (include the period). |
| **9** | Move the insertion point to the end of the document, press enter twice, and insert the picture *vt_ch07_image2*. |

| Step | Instructions | Step | Instructions |
|------|--------------|------|--------------|
| **10** | Resize the image to a height of 2.5". Center the image and apply the Double Frame, Black Picture Style. | **12** | Use the Spelling and Grammar dialog box to correct the misspelling of the word *genaration* to *generation*. Ignore any other spelling and grammar suggestions. |
| **11** | In the document footer, add the FileName field using the default format. | **13** | Save and close the document. Exit Word. Submit the document as directed. |

Visit **pearsonhighered.com/Geoghan** for data files, simulations, VizClips, and additional study materials.

Chapter 7

307

# Multiple Choice

Answer the multiple-choice questions below for more practice with key terms and concepts from this chapter.

1. The original Internet was called:
   a. ARPANET
   b. CSNET
   c. NSFNET
   d. Internet2

2. The broadband Internet service that runs over fiber optic cable is:
   a. Cable
   b. LTE
   c. FTTH
   d. WiMAX

3. A(n) _____ is a company that offers Internet access.
   a. ARPANET
   b. ISP
   c. Internet Exchange Point
   d. search engine

4. The default Web browser on a Mac is:
   a. Internet Explorer
   b. Firefox
   c. Chrome
   d. Safari

5. You can view multiple Web pages in most browsers using:
   a. Add-ons
   b. Extensions
   c. Plug-ins
   d. Tabs

6. A(n) _____ is a third-party program that extends the functionality of a Web browser.
   a. add-on
   b. microbrowser
   c. search provider
   d. tab

7. Examples of _____ include .com, .gov, and .edu.
   a. websites
   b. domains
   c. TLDs (top-level domains)
   d. protocols

8. The _____ allows you to type a URL in your browser instead of an IP address.
   a. DNS (Domain Name System)
   b. Hypertext
   c. ICANN
   d. TLD (top-level domain)

9. One way to evaluate a website's credibility is to look for a _____ TLD.
   a. .com
   b. restricted
   c. cc
   d. .net

10. Check the _____ on a website for the credentials of the author or organization.
    a. site map
    b. Contact page
    c. About Us page
    d. All the above

# True or False

Answer the following questions with T for true or F for false for more practice with key terms and concepts from this chapter.

1. The Internet was developed in 1991 by Tim-Berners Lee.

2. There are five Internet Exchange Points around the world.

3. The Internet2 project evolved from the original NSFNET.

4. Outside of your home, you share your DSL with your neighbors.

5. Because it uses satellites, WiMAX is available in remote locations.

6. Most Web pages can't be viewed in a mobile browser.

7. Adobe Flash Player is a popular Web browser.

8. It's generally not necessary to type http:// when entering a URL in your browser.

9. Every node on the Internet must have a unique IP address.

10. Much of the Internet consists of user-generated content that should be critically evaluated.

# Fill in the Blank

Fill in the blanks with key terms from this chapter.

1. The _____ is the high-speed connection point between networks.

2. The _____ is the part of the Internet that uses hypertext to connect pieces of information.

3. _____ is broadband over digital telephone lines.

4. Internet access that exceeds 200 Kbps is considered _____.

5. The two formats of 4G Internet access are _____ and _____.

6. Basic Web pages are written in _____.

7. Internet Explorer, Firefox, and Safari are examples of _____.

8. The _____ is the Web page that appears when you open your browser.

9. Another term for the address of a website is _____.

10. The _____ .gov is restricted to government websites.

# Running Project . . .

## . . . The Finish Line

Use your answers to the previous sections of the project. Why is the Internet important to you, and why is it important to be knowledgeable about it? Write a report describing how you use the Internet in your daily life and respond to the questions raised. Save your file as **lastname_firstname_ch07_ project**, and submit it to your instructor as directed.

# Do It Yourself 1

The actual Internet access speed that you get is rarely as high as your ISP advertises. In this activity, you'll use an online speed test to measure your speed.

1. Open your favorite browser. For this activity, close anything else that uses Internet access, such as your email or instant messaging programs. Close all but a single tab in your browser.

2. Navigate to **broadband.gov**, and run the Consumer Broadband Test on your connection. Because results can fluctuate, run your test at least twice. Try to use a different testing engine if you're given the option. Take a screen shot of the results screen for each of your tests.

3. Read the Privacy Statement and the About the Consumer Broadband Test screens. What is the purpose of the test and how are the results collected and used?

4. Write up a summary of your results. How do the results compare to your expected speeds? Paste your screen shots into a word processing document. Save the file as **lastname_firstname_ch07_diy1**, and submit it as directed by your instructor.

# Do It Yourself 2

There are many different search engines you can use to find information on the Web. In this activity, you'll perform a search using Bing and refine your search using advanced options.

1. Open your browser, and go to **bing.com**. In the search box, type **rose**, and press Enter.

2. Open a new word processing document, take a screen shot of this page, and paste it into the document. How many results did you get? Is this a practical number of results? What type of information is presented in the first page of results?

3. Click Advanced next to the results. Add the word **red** to the search. How does this affect the results? Type **King** and select None of these terms to exclude it from the search. How are the results affected? Take a screen shot of the results, and paste it into the document.

4. Type up your answers, save the file as **lastname_firstname_ ch07_diy2**, and submit it as directed by your instructor.

# File Management

Saving information from the Web can be tricky. In this exercise you will save a Web page in various formats and compare them.

1. Open Internet Explorer and go to your school's home page. From the Tools menu, choose *File* and then *Save as*. What is the default Save as type? Save the page as **Home1** using the default file format.

2. Repeat the procedure and save the page using each of the other Save as file types, changing the name each time to reflect the change.

3. Close your browser and open the folder that contains the saved files. Open each file by double-clicking it. What application opens each format? Compare how the page appears. Which format do you think is the best way to save this file and why?

4. Type up your answers, save the file as **lastname_firstname_ ch07_fm**, and submit as directed by your instructor.

# Critical Thinking

You just moved to a new apartment and need to get Internet access. In this exercise you will consider the options available where you live.

1. Use the Internet to determine which broadband services are available where you live. Some places to start include **dslreports.com** and **thelist.com**. Create a spreadsheet or chart comparing prices and features.

2. What questions should you ask to help you choose?

3. Write up a summary of the services available and the questions you would ask each company. Save the file as **lastname_firstname_ch07_ct**, and submit it as directed by your instructor.

# Ethical Dilemma

In the early days of the Web, it was common practice to buy up domain names to resell them. Speculators would buy domain names that they anticipated would be worth a lot of money to them. This practice is known as cybersquatting.

1. Intentionally buying a domain name that's the same as a trademark another company owns (for example, Avon or Hertz, which were both victims) for the purpose of selling it to the trademark owner at profit is a trademark infringement, but what about something that's not trademarked but still recognizable—like a catchphrase or a person's name? Is it legal to grab up these domain? Is it ethical? What about changing the TLD (nasa.com, for example)?

2. Suppose you purchase a domain name for your own use, and it turns out that a company wants to buy it from you? Is it legal to sell it to them? At a profit?

3. Type up your answers, save the file as **lastname_firstname_ch07_ethics,** and submit it as directed by your instructor.

# On the Web

Many websites will allow you to personalize the content that you see. Choose one of the following websites: espn.com, yahoo.com, msn.com, or use your ISP's home page. Join and customize the site.

1. If necessary, create an account on your chosen website and log in. (This might be a good time to use a secondary email account created just for such purposes.) What personalization and customizations are available to you?

2. Create your personal page on the site. What items did you choose to modify, add, or delete?

3. Type up your answers, take a screen shot of your customized page, and paste it in your document. Save the file as **lastname_firstname_ch07_web,** and submit it as directed by your instructor.

# Collaboration

**Instructors:** Divide the class into five groups, and assign each group one browser for this project. The topics include Internet Explorer, Firefox, Chrome, Safari, and Opera.

**The Project:** Each team is to prepare a multimedia commercial for its browser. The presentation should be designed to convince a consumer to use the browser. Teams must use at least three references, only one of which may be this textbook. Use Google Docs or Microsoft Office to plan the presentation and provide documentation that all team members have contributed to the project.

**Students:** Before beginning this project, discuss the roles each group member will play. Choose a team name, which you'll use in submitting your presentation. Be sure to divide the work among your members, and pick someone to present your project. You may find it helpful to elect a team leader who can direct your activities and ensure that all team contributions are collated through Google Docs or Microsoft Office as directed by your instructor.

**Outcome:** You're to prepare a multimedia presentation on your assigned topic in PowerPoint (or another tool if approved by your instructor) and present it to your class. The presentation may be no longer than 3 minutes and should contain 5 to 7 slides. On the first slide, be sure to include the name of your presentation and a list of all team members. Turn in a final version of your presentation named as **teamname_ch07_presentation** and your file showing your collaboration named as **teamname_ch07_collab**. Submit your presentation to your instructor as directed.

# Communicating and Sharing: The Social Web

Visit **pearsonhighered.com/Geoghan** for data files, simulations, VizClips, and additional study materials.

**OBJECTIVES**

1. **Compare different forms of synchronous online communication.**

2. **Demonstrate how to use email effectively.**

3. **Discuss the roles of social media in today's society.**

4. **Locate user-generated content in the form of a blog or podcast.**

5. **Discuss how wikis and other social media sites rely on the wisdom of the crowd.**

6. **Explain the influence of social media on e-commerce.**

## IN THIS CHAPTER

The first thing I do every morning is check my email and the notifications on my smartphone. Then, when I come downstairs, I open my browser. I have two home page tabs. The first is my My Yahoo! page, which includes my email, and the RSS feeds from my favorite blogs, news, and sports websites. The second tab is Facebook. I can find out everything I need to start my day in just a few minutes. Online communication has become an integral part of my life—and probably yours, too. In this chapter, we look at the world of online communication and the impact it has on society.

# Talk to Me

## Compare different forms of synchronous online communication.

Want to talk to someone right now? That's what chat and instant messaging allow you to do. The term **synchronous online communication** means communication that happens in real-time, with two (or more) people online at the same time. Face-to-face conversations or telephone calls are examples of synchronous communication. Online synchronous communication tools let us communicate in real-time on the Web.

### CHAT AND IM

Online **chat** allows you to talk to multiple people at the same time in a chat room. **Instant messaging (IM)** allows you to talk to one person at a time, although most IM software will also support group chats. The line between chat and IM has blurred over the years. For example, Facebook chat is really a form of IM by the definition used here.

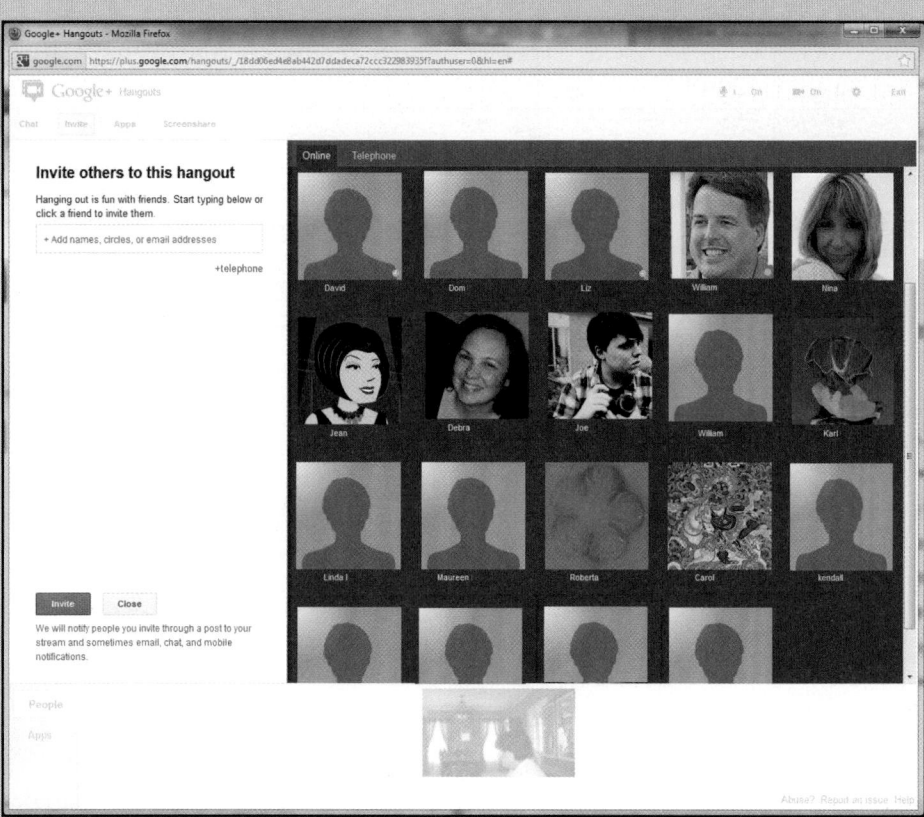

**FIGURE 8.1** Starting a Google+ Hangout

**CHAT** You can find chat rooms that are geared toward common interests, such as travel or cooking, or more general chats for people who just want to talk. There are chats that are moderated, where a moderator screens all content, or unmoderated, where anything goes. There are many chat rooms that are adult in nature, and unfortunately, sexual predators often find their victims in such chat rooms. That said, it's important to put safety first when using chat rooms (or any form of online communication, for that matter).

Traditional chat rooms are text-based, persistent, and users come and go, often not knowing each other. Client-based chats require you to install client software to access them. Some instant messaging programs, such as AIM and Windows Messenger, allow you to create group chats. Social media sites such as Facebook and Google+ also allow you to chat with others. In Figure 8.1, I'm in the process of creating a Google+ hangout. You can start a hangout by inviting people in your circles. Chat is a great way to talk with people in real time. It is perfect for a class discussion or getting a group of family members together to plan a reunion. And if you're on the go, there are mobile versions of all of these tools. So, you can start a chat while you're in front of your computer, and then continue the conversation from your smartphone or tablet when you're not.

**INSTANT MESSAGING** Instant-messaging (IM) sessions happen between buddies and disappear when they end, although some IM software will allow you to save the text of your conversation. There are Web-based IM tools, but many popular IM services, such as Microsoft Messenger, iMessage (OS X and iOS), AIM (see Figure 8.2), or Google Talk, use client software that must be installed on your computer or mobile device. Figure 8.3 shows the iChat client on a Mac. iChat—and other programs like it—allows you to access all your separate accounts in one place.

Today, businesses are finding IM and chat to be useful tools for holding meetings and providing customer support. This is often the case with websites that offer services, such as Internet access (Figure 8.4). In this example, the term "chat" really means IM.

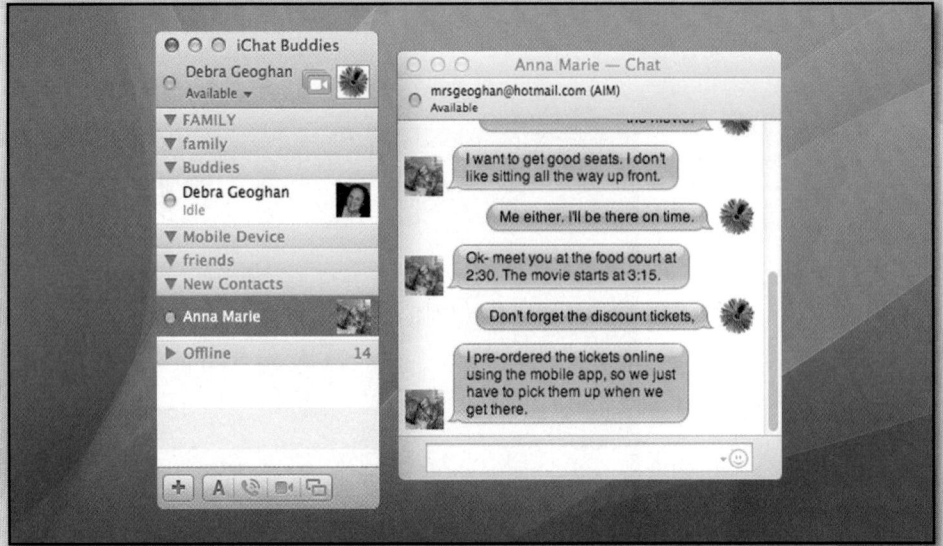

**FIGURE 8.3** The iChat client can connect with other IM systems, such as AIM.

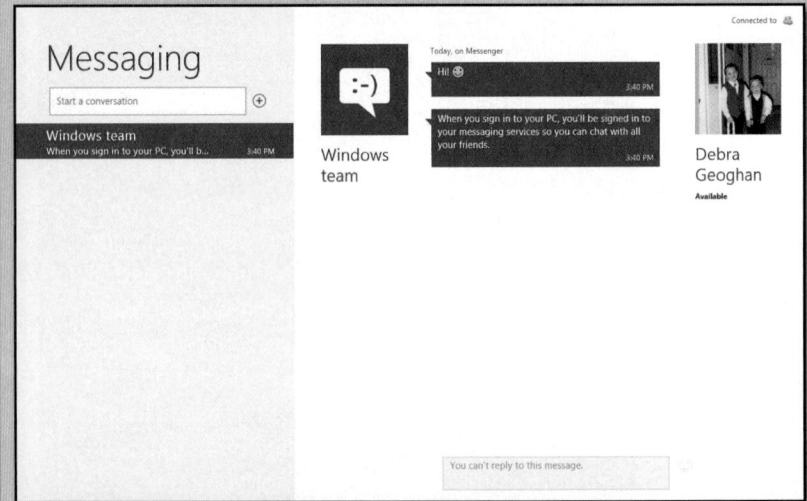

**FIGURE 8.2** Windows Messaging allows you to chat with friends.

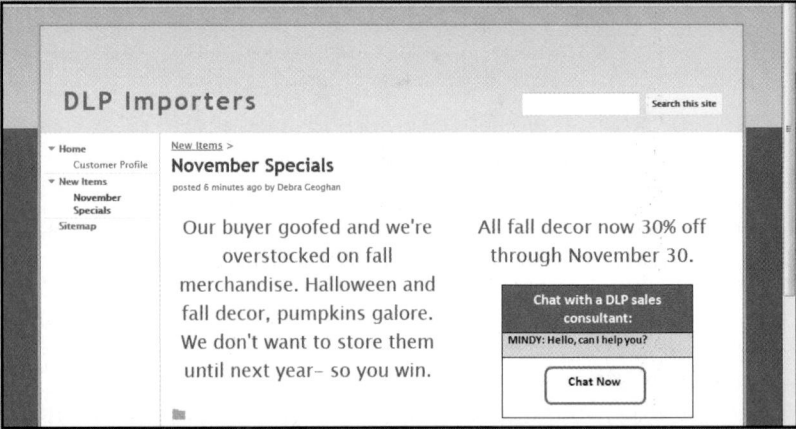

**FIGURE 8.4** Websites like this one allow you to chat via IM with a representative.

# VOIP

You can even make phone calls over the Internet. **VoIP (voice over IP)** allows phone calls to be transmitted over the Internet instead of via traditional phone lines or cellular towers. If you have broadband Internet access, your Internet Service Provider (ISP) may also offer VoIP phone service. Apple FaceTime is built into OS X and iOS and allows you to make video calls to other FaceTime users. A service such as Skype allows you to place calls to other Skype users for free or to regular phones for a small fee. Using Skype to talk to friends and family that are in other countries can save a lot of money over traditional telephone calls. My cousin, who lives in Australia, talks regularly with his sisters here in the United States, and his children are able to keep in touch with their faraway grandparents.

Using VoIP allows you to make calls from your computer or mobile device anywhere you have Internet access, even if you don't have phone service. You can even video chat if your device has a camera (see Figure 8.5).

Using the tools discussed in this article, you can communicate with people online in real time. These tools have made it easier (and cheaper) than ever to get instant help or advice and keep in touch with friends and family both near and far.

**FIGURE 8.5** VoIP helps people keep in touch when far away.

## Running Project

Use the Internet to research chat/IM safety rules for kids. Create a list of five rules you consider the most important when it comes to keeping kids safe.

## 3 Things You Need to Know

- Chat rooms can have many people in them at one time.
- IM occurs between two people at a time.
- VoIP uses the Internet to make phone calls.

## Key Terms

chat

instant messaging (IM)

synchronous online communication

VoIP (voice over IP)

# Leave a Message

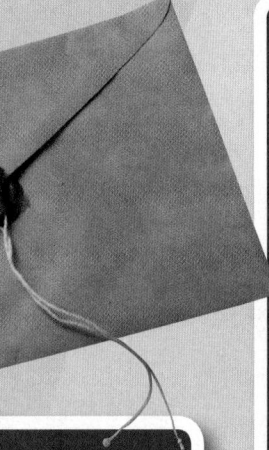

## Demonstrate how to use email effectively.

Asynchronous forms of communication don't require the participants to be online at the same time. Like leaving a voicemail or sending a letter, **asynchronous online communication** technology lets you send a message that the receiver can access later.

## HOW DO YOU READ AND SEND EMAIL?

At its roots, the Internet was designed for communicating and sharing. One of the first applications of it was email, which quickly became the most widely used Internet application. Using email to communicate has become an essential business skill.

**Email** is a system of sending electronic messages using store-and-forward technology. That means an email server holds your messages until you request them. Thus, someone can send you an email message even if you're not online at the time. There are two ways to access email: using an email client on your computer (or tablet, smartphone, or some other device) or reading it online through a webmail interface. When you use an email client, such as Outlook or Thunderbird, the email server sends a copy of the message to you. This makes it available to read even after you disconnect from the Internet. If you configure your client to leave a copy of the message on the email server, then you will still be able to access the messages from a webmail interface as well. The advantage to using a webmail interface is that your email is available to you from anywhere whenever you're online: home, school, vacation, or work.

Today, it makes sense to have multiple email accounts. This allows you to keep your private, work, school, etc., accounts separate. Think about the impression you'd make if you sent a job inquiry from cutiepie_cupcake@hotmail.com. I have one account just for shopping websites, another for friends and family, and yet another at work. One very important thing to remember about email is that it's not secure. As it travels from your computer over the Internet, it can be read by hackers along the way. Copies of the message exist on servers and routers it crosses on its journey, and those copies can be retrieved long after you've deleted the message from your Inbox. Your email provider might scan your messages to deliver you targeted advertising, and your employer or school network administrator might also read your email. A good analogy is to think of email as a postcard, not a letter in a sealed envelope.

Your ISP can provide you with at least one (and maybe up to 10) email accounts. Your employer or school may provide you with another. There are also many places where you can sign up for a free email account, such as Yahoo!, Google, and Hotmail. The advantage to using an email account not tied to your ISP is that, should you change your ISP, you will not lose your email account in the process. Figure 8.6 shows how easy it is to create a free email account on Windows Live. The hardest part of the process is getting the letters of the captcha right. A **captcha (Completely Automated Public Turing Test to Tell Computers and Humans Apart)** is a series of letters and numbers that are distorted in some way. This makes them difficult for automated software to read but relatively easy for humans to read.

Accessing your new Hotmail account is easy. Just log in to the live.com website and click on the Mail link. New email messages are in your Inbox. You can read a message by double-clicking on it (see Figure 8.7).

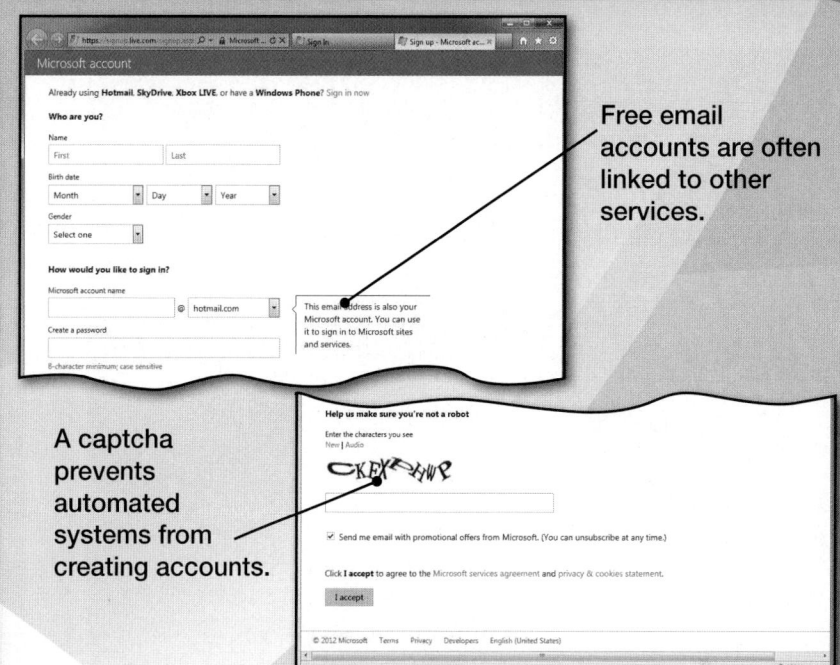

Free email accounts are often linked to other services.

A captcha prevents automated systems from creating accounts.

**FIGURE 8.6** Creating a Free Hotmail Email Account

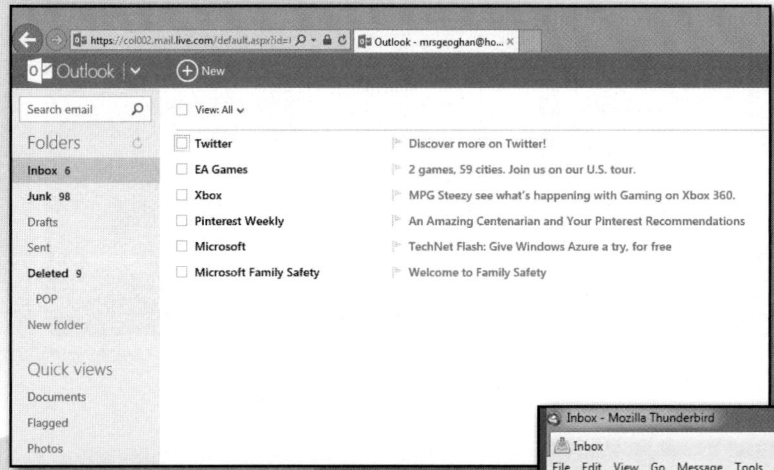

**FIGURE 8.7** Accessing a Webmail Account

You can also use an email program such as Mozilla Thunderbird or Microsoft Outlook to read your email on your computer, or a mobile app to read it on your smartphone or tablet. In a business environment, a program such as Outlook is a critical tool, but many home users don't feel the need for a local email program. Figure 8.8 shows Thunderbird configured for the same Hotmail account.

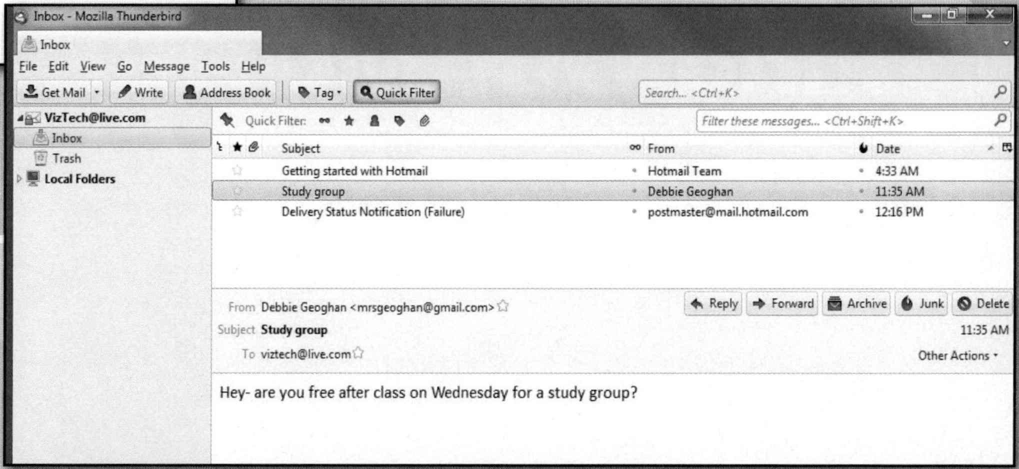

**FIGURE 8.8** The Mozilla Thunderbird Email Client

An email message has some distinct parts that you should be familiar with. Figure 8.9 has some of the important parts of a new email message labeled. This message has not yet been sent.

The most important part of the message is the address. If you don't address it correctly, the message will not reach its recipient. There are three address fields that you can use: To, Cc, and Bcc. To: is the field you normally use when sending an email to someone. Cc:, which stands for carbon copy, is the field you use to send to someone who's not the main addressee a copy—so he or she knows about a conversation, for example. It's like an FYI and generally means that a reply isn't expected. Functionally, there's no real difference in the way the message is sent or received. Bcc:, however, has an important difference. Did you ever have an email message forwarded to you that includes the addresses of dozens of other people? The sender should have used the Bcc field, not the To: or Cc: fields, to send that message. The B stands for blind. When you send an email out to several people, using the Bcc field keeps the addresses private.

Use the Subject line of an email message to give the recipient some idea of the content of the email. The body of the message should contain the rest of the information. The message in Figure 8.9 includes some formatted text and an image. Not all email programs will let you format text or include images, and not everybody will be able to view those elements. You need to use an email program that's configured to read HTML email messages for those elements to be visible. An email program that's configured to view only text email messages will only see the text in this message.

A signature line is a block of text that's automatically put at the end of the messages that you compose. It can be a simple message that just includes your name, but in business, it will usually contain more contact information and perhaps a privacy statement of some type. You need to create the signature and activate it for it to appear on your email messages.

When you receive an email message, you have the ability to reply to the message or forward it (see Figure 8.10). When you choose Reply, your response is sent back to the original sender. If you choose Reply all (or Reply to All, depending on the email program), then the response is sent to all the addressees of the original message and the original sender. Think carefully before you use this option. Do you really want everyone to receive your reply? The subject line for a Reply will include Re: before the original subject. If you want to send the message to someone else, then you would use the Forward option, which allows you to select new addresses and put Fw: before the subject.

# Find Out MORE

Is using Bcc: really protecting anyone? Use the Internet to find out if there are ways to decode the Bcc to see the email addresses it hides.

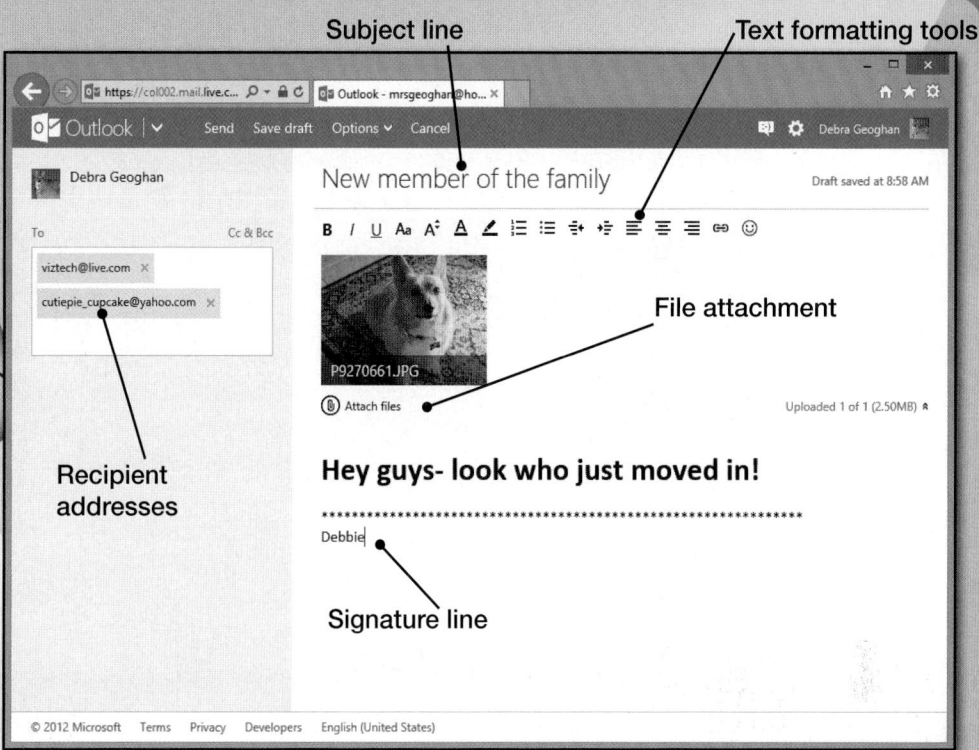

Subject line

Text formatting tools

File attachment

Recipient addresses

Hey guys- look who just moved in!

Signature line

**FIGURE 8.9** Composing an Email Message

Choose reply, reply all, or forward to respond to an email message.

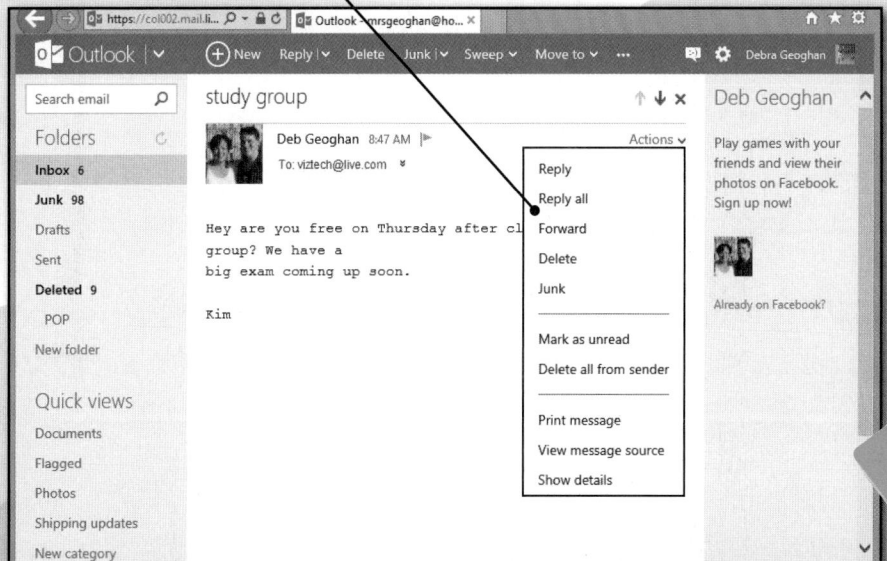

**FIGURE 8.10** Replying to an Email

Try the Communicating and Sharing on the Web Simulation

SIMULATION

SEND

# FORUMS AND DISCUSSION BOARDS

**Forums**, also known as discussion boards or message boards, were one of the first forms of social media. They're conversations much like chat but are not in real time. There are forums for people with common interests, such as sports, pets, travel, or video games. Many technology and product websites include forums, which may be used as a support system. Some websites refer to a forum as a community.

Participants post comments and questions, usually about a particular topic or problem, and other participants respond. Each conversation is called a thread, and the responses are posts. Forums are a great place to get help with problems, ask for advice, or just communicate with folks with similar interests. Threads can be searched and read long after the initial conversation has ended. Most forums are moderated and require you to create an account before you're allowed to post. Figure 8.11 shows the home page of the Ubuntu forums.

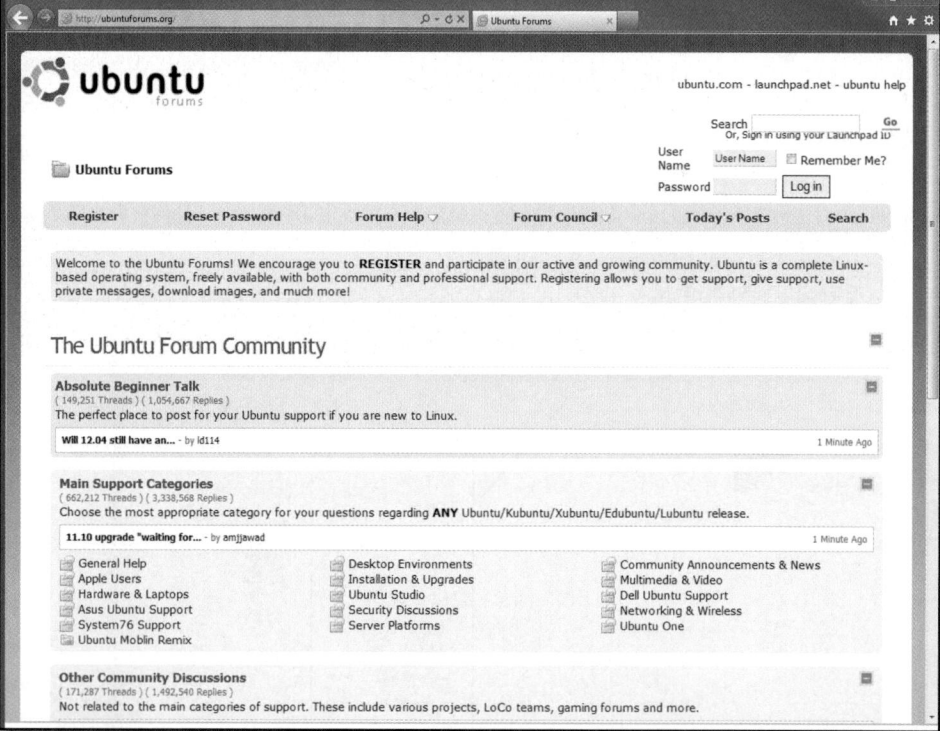

**FIGURE 8.11** Users can get help and information about Ubuntu through The Ubuntu Forum Community.

The advantage to using email or a forum over chat or IM is that the conversations have a longer life span. You can save emails indefinitely as long as you have the storage space, and forums can persist for years after a thread is started. These tools have become critical ways to communicate in all types of businesses.

## Running Project

Visit **tripadvisor.com/forum**. Select a destination that you have visited in the past. Read some of the threads. Select a thread that you would like to reply to. Do you agree with the replies posted? Would you find them helpful if you were deciding whether to visit this location?

## 5 Things You Need to Know

- Email is a store-and-forward technology that doesn't require you to be online when someone sends it to you.
- Webmail allows you to access your email from anywhere.
- You shouldn't expect that your email is private.
- A captcha assures that a person and not a machine is creating an account.
- Forums are online discussion boards.

## Key Terms

asynchronous online communication

captcha (Completely Automated Public Turing Test to Tell Computers and Humans Apart)

email

forum

# There's a Place for Everyone ...

## Discuss the roles of social media in today's society.

VIZ CLIP

So many ways to connect with people! Forums and email are old technologies, having been around almost as long as the Internet itself, but recently, newer technologies have emerged. These new tools are sometimes called **Web 2.0** and are changing the way we communicate and collaborate on the Web. These new tools rely on the wisdom of the crowd. What's important, interesting, or relevant is no longer decided by a few people sitting around a table but by the crowd of participants. Collectively, these tools—which enable users to create user-generated content, connect, network, and share—are called **social media**.

## SOCIAL NETWORK SITES

**Social networks**, such as Facebook, MySpace, and LinkedIn, are online communities that combine many of the features of the other online tools we have discussed. Social networks allow you to chat in real time and to post messages for all to see or to send a personal message similar to an email. There are hundreds of social networking sites. Some focus on business, others are language- or location-specific, and still others are available where anything goes. Social networking allows you to keep in touch with old friends and make new ones.

**FACEBOOK AND MYSPACE** The first social network sites began in the late 1990s, and today, there are hundreds of them. Facebook and MySpace are two of the most popular. MySpace was launched in 2003, and Facebook was launched in 2004 for Harvard students and in 2006 for the rest of us. Today, these two sites have hundreds of millions of users worldwide. Users create a profile that includes some personal information, pictures, and interests, and then they connect with other users or friends. You can also join groups within the networks that interest you. For some people, using a social network is all about the number of "Friends" that they have, but for others, it is a way to stay in touch with people.

I have accounts on many different social websites and use different accounts for my personal and professional communication. I have different friends on each and post different information on each. For example, on my professional profile, I might post a link to an interesting tech article and join a group related to technology or education. Because my personal profile is private, only my friends can see what I post there. I play games, post pictures, and chat with friends on my private profile. I belong to several groups that match my interests, such as the neighborhood I grew up in and martial arts (see Figure 8.12). My privacy settings are high, and I choose carefully the friend requests I send and accept.

If you have friends who tag you in their photos, even if your profile is private, you may be sharing more than you meant to. Be sure to use the security and privacy settings to keep your private life private, and consider creating a second public profile on a professional social network such as LinkedIn. Many employers will expect you to be technically literate and use social networking tools, so not having one could be a negative. I have had people tell me that they received friend requests from people who interviewed them for jobs and internships and from bosses at work. These are the people who should be in your professional social network.

## BUSINESS SOCIAL NETWORKS

Facebook and MySpace are great for making connections with friends and family, but for a more business-centered social network, consider a site such as LinkedIn. LinkedIn is designed for business connections. Figure 8.13 shows my LinkedIn profile. There are no games or silly applications, no place to post photos (except a profile image), and no chat. You have connections instead of friends. LinkedIn—or other business social networks that relate to your field of interest—should be part of your personal brand.

**FIGURE 8.12** My personal profile has posts and information that I share with friends and family.

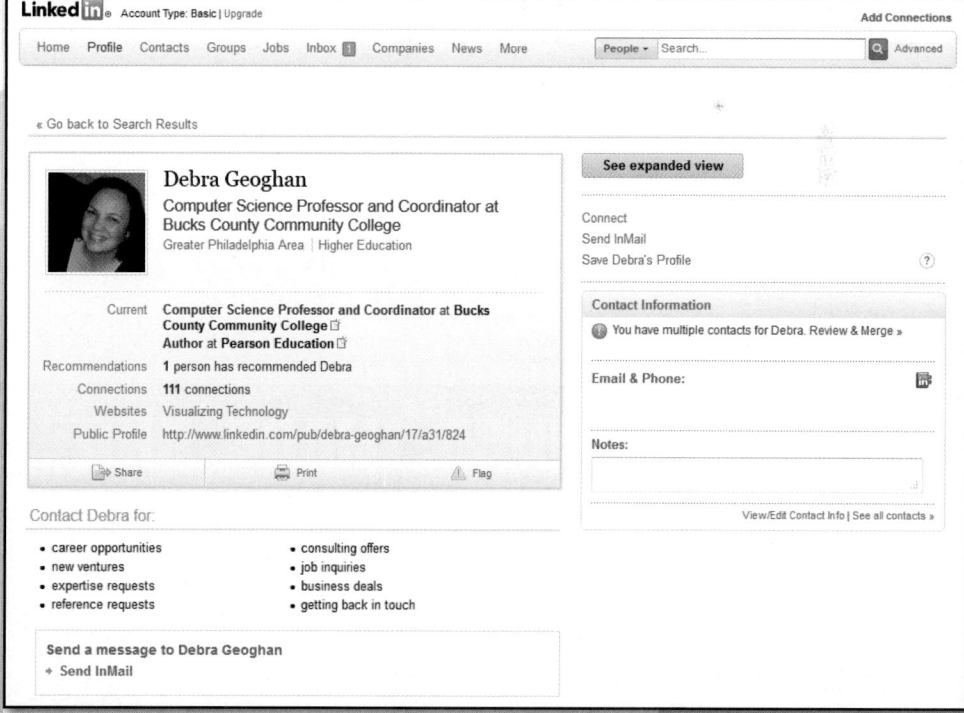

**FIGURE 8.13** LinkedIn is a business-oriented social network.

**VIRTUAL WORLDS** Virtual communities, such as Second Life and Webkinz, and **massively multiplayer online role-playing games (MMORPG)** games, such as Guild Wars 2 (see Figure 8.14), allow you to interact with people in real time using an **avatar**, or virtual body. Some schools even offer virtual classes in Second Life. Second Life and multiplayer games have pretty high system requirements and require fairly new and powerful systems.

**FIGURE 8.14** Avatars interact in a virtual world.

*Speech bubble:* Yes! And a trillion bytes is a terabyte, and a quadrillion bytes is a petabyte! Sorry, I get excited...

# SOCIAL VIDEO, IMAGE, AND MUSIC SITES

Social sharing sites, such as YouTube, Flickr, and Last.fm, allow anyone to create and share media. These sites are outside of social networks such as Facebook, although you can also share their content within them. One of the key features of these sites is the ability to tag items. This tagging, or **folksonomy**, makes the sharing even more social, as users begin to tag not just their own creations but also those of others.

FOLKSONOMY

**VIDEO** Let's face it: Everyone knows about YouTube. It's the largest online video hosting site in the world. It's also social in the sense that you can subscribe to other users' channels, send messages, and recommend videos. A **viral video** is one that becomes extremely popular because of recommendations and social sharing. Figure 8.15 shows a viral video from YouTube. There are other video sharing sites, including CollegeHumor, Vimeo, TeacherTube, and even Facebook and Flickr. Sites such as Hulu don't host user-created content but are still social in that they keep track of the popularity of videos and have users review and discuss the videos.

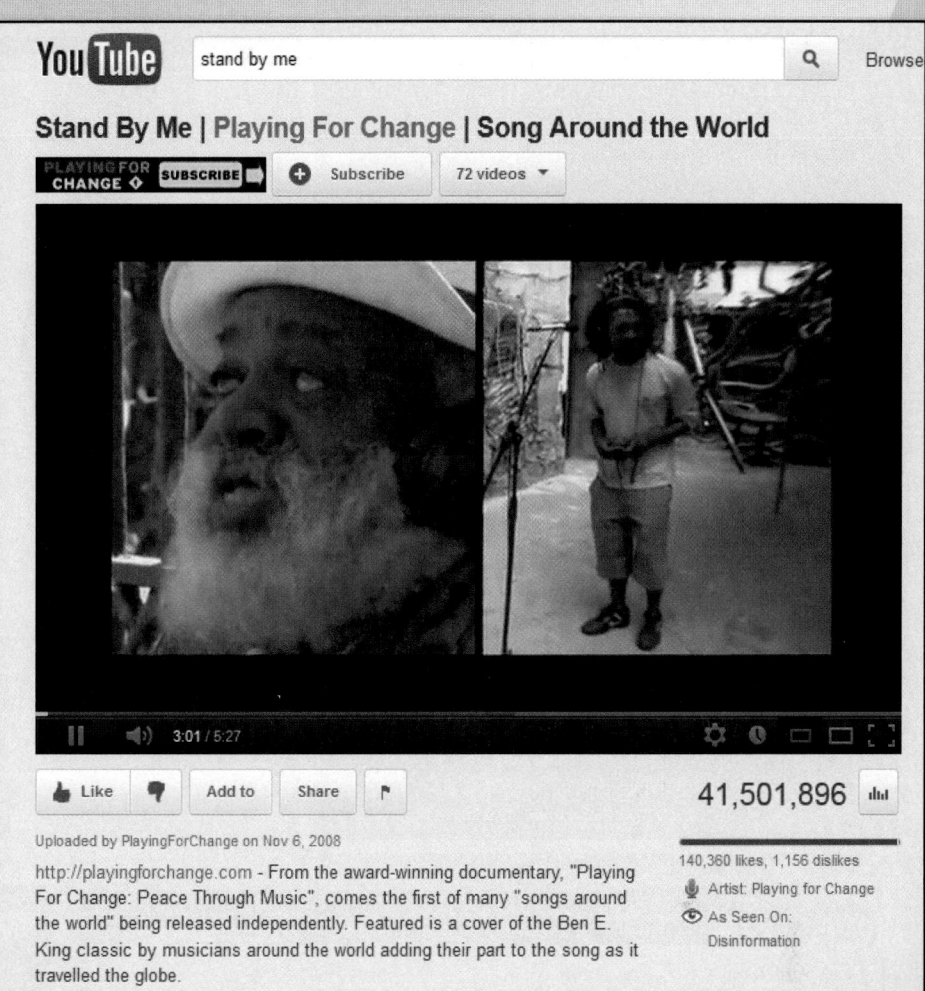

**FIGURE 8.15** YouTube is the largest video sharing network in the world.

# Find Out MORE

Some companies have a virtual presence on Second Life. Go to **secondlife.com** and click on *What Is Second Life?* and then click *Education & Enterprise* to find out which companies are using it and why.

**IMAGES** Flickr is the largest image sharing site. With a free account, you can post up to 200 images. You can mark your pictures as private or make them public. You can adjust the copyright to allow others to use your images legally. Images can be tagged, allowing you to search for something that interests you. Other popular photo sharing sites include Picasa and Photobucket. Instagram and other mobile apps allow you take and edit photos on your mobile device and upload them to the Web automatically. To share your photos, create an account (Flickr will let you use your Yahoo account, and Picasa uses your Google account), log in, and begin uploading your images. You can tag them with appropriate categories to make them easier to find using a search. In Figure 8.16, the image is tagged with Mike, Halloween, alien, and abduction. You can also comment on and share images that you like and add location information to them.

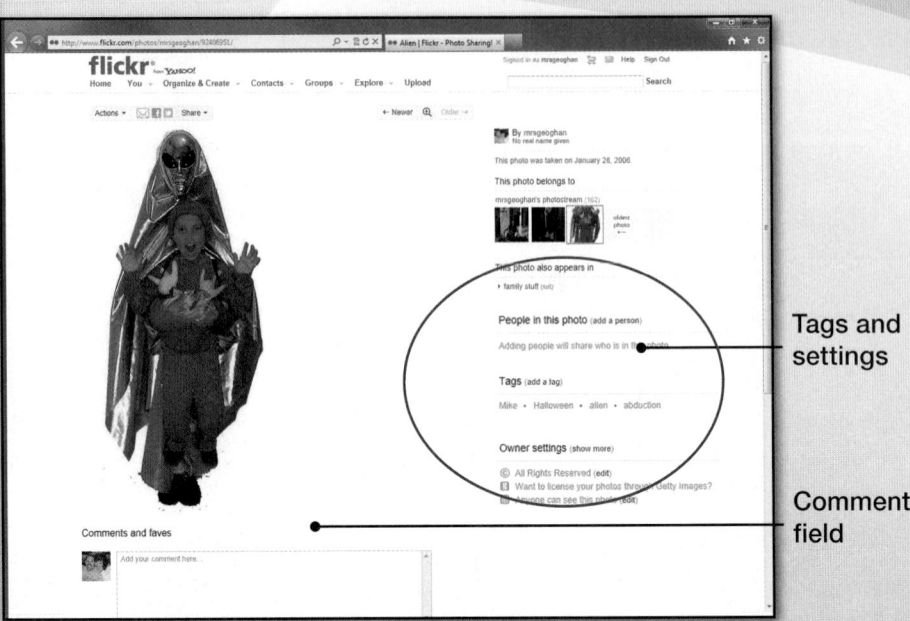

Tags and settings

Comment field

**FIGURE 8.16** A Flickr Image Showing Its Tags, Settings, and Comment Field

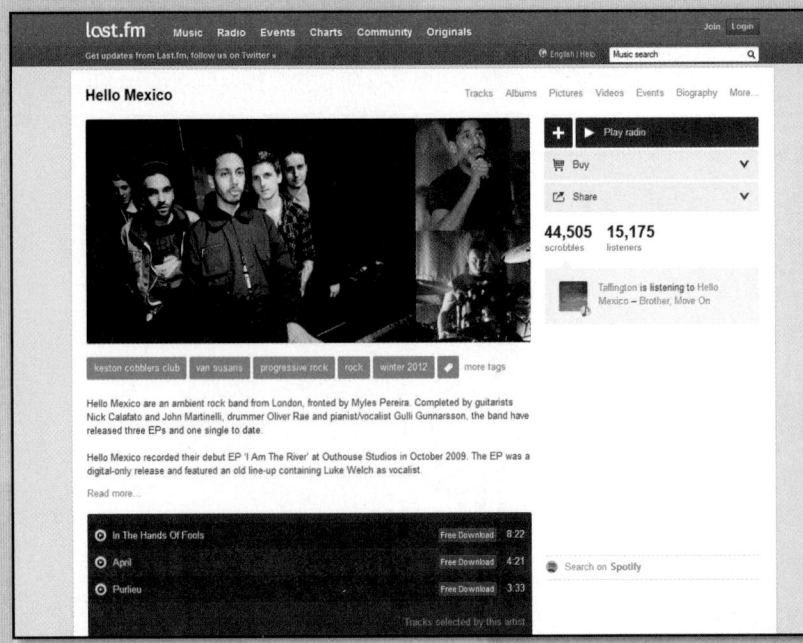

**FIGURE 8.17** Last.fm is a social music site.

**MUSIC** What is more social than music? There are lots of places on the Web to find music, but if you want a social experience, create an account on a site such as Last.fm or Pandora. These sites recommend music to you based on what you listen to. With Last.fm, you can browse users with similar music tastes and discover what they're listening to. You can mark tracks as "loved," which will help you get recommendations. The more you listen to and love tracks, the more recommendations you will get. You can add tag and shouts (comments) to music you like. Figure 8.17 shows the artist page for Hello Mexico, with links to concerts, albums, videos, and similar artists. I can tag and share this page easily using the tag and share buttons. This page was recommended to me because I have similar music in my personal collection.

If you like to make and share your own music, a website such as SoundCloud (**soundcloud.com**) will let you do just that. Using a browser or mobile app, you can upload sound files that you have created and share them with the community. Users can follow their favorites and comment and share new finds. Artists can communicate directly with their fans, and musicians can collaborate with each other, even if they are many miles apart.

It's really important to think about your digital footprint. Your **digital footprint** is all the information that someone could find out about you by searching the Web, including social network sites. Remember that once something has been posted on the Web, it's almost impossible to completely get rid of it. Suppose you were a prospective employer. Would you hire someone who has compromising pictures on Facebook? You need to develop your own brand and make sure that anything that's publically viewable fits into that brand.

## ▶ Running Project

Imagine that you're a prospective employer. Search the Web and major social networks to see what they would find. Log out of your social networking sites to see how an outsider would view you. How is your brand? Would you hire yourself? Was it easy to find things that you would rather keep private?

## 4 Things You Need to Know

- Social networks are online communities where people connect with each other.
- Video, image, and music sharing sites allow users to post their creations on the Web for others to see and use.
- Tagging, or folksonomy, creates a way to search for content on social websites.
- You should be very careful about your digital footprint.

## Key Terms

avatar

digital footprint

folksonomy

massively multiplayer online role-playing games (MMORPG)

social media

social network

viral video

Web 2.0

# HOW TO Create a LinkedIn Profile

In this exercise, you will create an account on LinkedIn. Because this is a business network, you should use a professional email address, not a cute nickname. If you don't have an appropriate email address to use, this would be a good time to create one using a free service as described in this chapter. (Note: You can't use a fake email address, as you will be required to confirm the email address before you can successfully complete your sign-up.)

**1** Open your word processor and type your name and date in the document. Save the file as **lastname_firstname_ch08_howto1**. Open your browser and go to **linkedin.com**. On the Get started— it's free page, type your name, email address, and select a password.

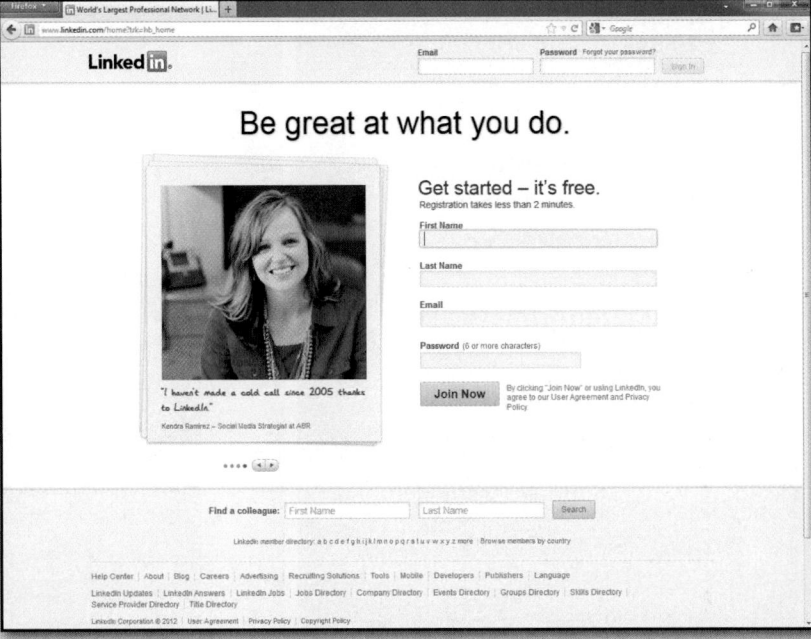

**2** Create your professional profile by completing the information on the next screen. Select *Student* and complete your school and dates attended information, and then click *Create my profile*.

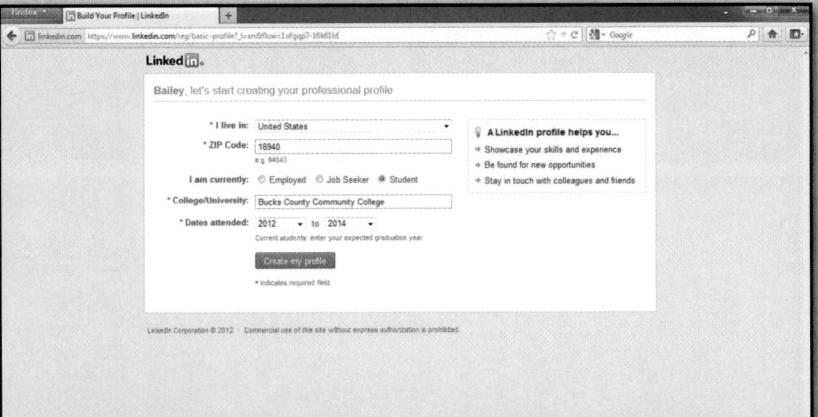

**3** For the sign-up Step 2, click *Skip this step* (you can always complete this later should you choose to). Click to receive a confirmation email. Open your email and follow the steps to confirm your email account. Once you have confirmed your email address, sign in to LinkedIn.

**4** For Step 4, you can choose to share your profile on Facebook or Twitter or click *Skip this step*. In Step 5, choose a Basic free account.

**5** Improve your profile by adding experience, education, and skills. Because you are a student, you can fill in information about your school work and future plans. Add a few items under Skills that you have gained from taking this course.

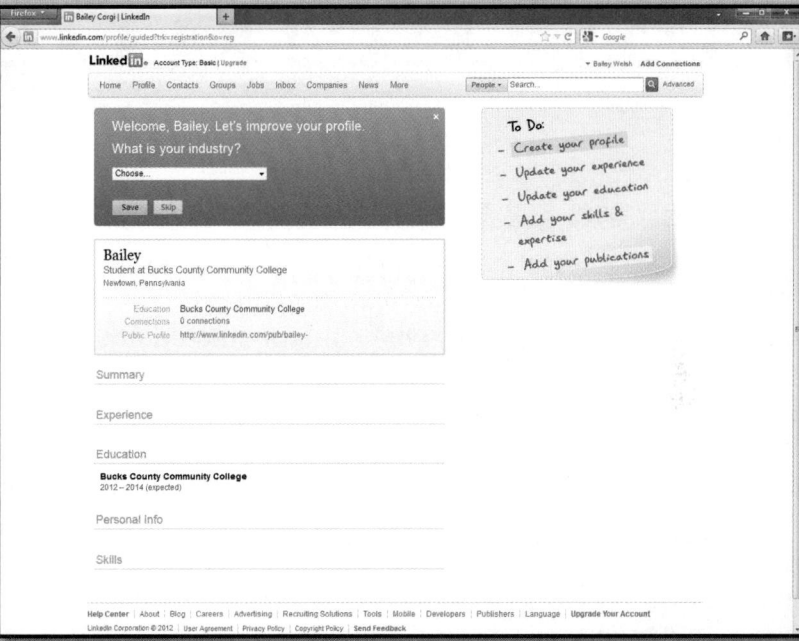

**6** When you get to the Looking good now! screen, click *Finished*. You can edit your profile any time by using the Profile option in the menu above.

**7** Take a screen shot of your finished profile and paste it into your document. Include your LinkedIn profile name. Save your file and submit as directed by your instructor.

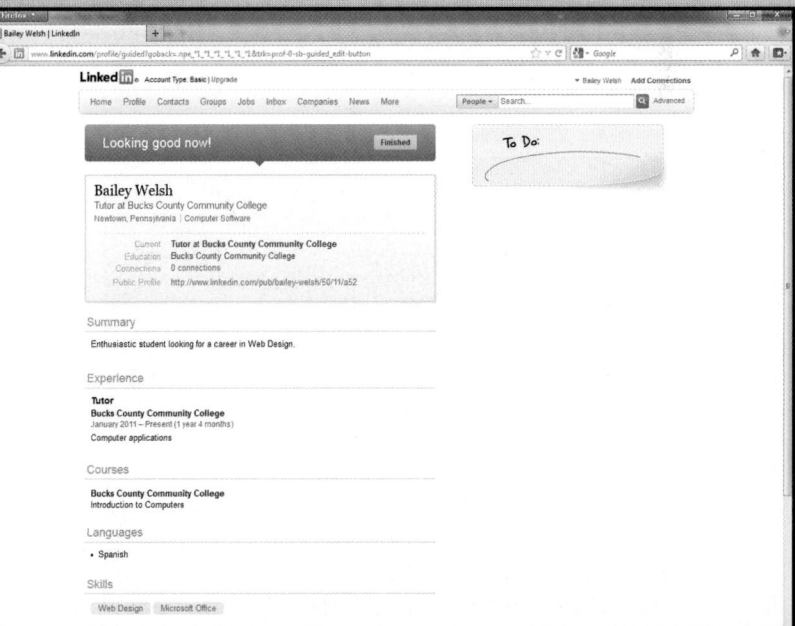

# Get Your Word Out

## 4 OBJECTIVE
## Locate user-generated content in the form of a blog or podcast.

**User-generated content** is the content created not by professional writers and photographers but by the rest of us. It includes the videos and photos we take and post online, but it also includes what we write and say. In the 2011 Arab Spring uprisings, social media played an important role in organizing and informing people across North Africa and the Middle East—particularly in Tunisia and Egypt. The number of tweets about political change increased dramatically, both in those regions and around the world. In the same year, the Occupy Wall Street movement used social media to organize and inform protestors around the country.

## BLOGS

A **blog** (**weblog**) is like an online journal. It's a Web page that's created with simple blog tools that anyone can set up, and people can pretty much talk about whatever they like. Vlogs, or video blogs, are just that—video journals instead of text. The idea is the same either way. The difference between just creating a Web page and writing a blog is that blogs can be interactive. Your readers can post comments about your blog posts.

There are a lot of prolific bloggers, and many even earn a living that way. There are lots of good blogs written by experts in many different fields, such as technology, education, and medicine. Technorati.com is a good place to start to search the **blogosphere** (see Figure 8.18), which consists of all the blogs on the Web and the connections among them. Many bloggers link to other related blogs. Two of the most popular blog sites are WordPress and Blogger. Both of these sites allow you to create an account and blog for free.

**Microblogging** sites such as Twitter and Tumblr are a more social form of blogging where posts are typically limited to a relatively small number of characters and users post updates frequently. Posts can be public or restricted to a group of users; sent from computers, mobile apps, and text messages; and they can be received the same ways.

VIZ CLIP

**FIGURE 8.18** Technorati.com keeps track of the blogosphere.

With Tumblr, you can post anything from photos to text, links, videos, and music. You can even link your Tumblr account to your Twitter account, so your posts appear on both sites. In Figure 8.19, you can see my Twitter page, with recent tweets from some of the folks I follow.

Twitter posts are called tweets and answer the question: What are you doing? Instead of friends, Twitter users have followers. You can link your Twitter account to your Facebook account, so your tweets will also appear in your Facebook feed. Unlike most social networks, you don't have to ask for permission to follow someone on Twitter or Tumblr (although they can block you).

**FIGURE 8.19** Twitter tweets are limited to 140 characters each.

# PODCASTS

A **podcast** is a digital media file of a prerecorded radio- and TV-like show that's distributed over the Web to be downloaded and listened to (or watched) on a computer or portable media player. Podcasts allow both time shifting (listening on your own schedule) and location shifting (taking it with you).

You can find podcasts using a **podcast client** or media player program, such as iTunes or Winamp, and download single episodes or subscribe to a podcast that's part of a series. There are hundreds of thousands of podcasts available. Two good sites to find podcasts are podcast.com and podcastalley.com. The White House (Figure 8.20) and the New York Times both produce regular podcasts that you can listen to using a podcast client or directly from their websites.

**FIGURE 8.20** The website for the President of the United States has podcasts that you can listen to right in your browser.

# RSS

So, how do you keep up with all your favorite websites? **RSS (Really Simple Syndication)** is a format used for distributing Web feeds that change frequently—for example, blogs, podcasts, and news. RSS saves you time by sending you the updates on the sites you subscribe to. Subscribing to the RSS feeds of your favorite blogs, podcasts, and other websites will bring the information right to you. You need a feed reader, such as Internet Explorer, Outlook, or Google Reader. To add a subscription, you usually just click the RSS icon at the top of the page.

## ▶ Running Project

Search for a podcast at **podcast.com** about a topic that interests you. Find out as much as you can about the podcast and its creators. Listen to an episode and write up a short summary of the contents. Did you enjoy it? Would you subscribe to it? Recommend it to a friend? Do you feel this is a good way to get this information? Explain your answers.

## 4 Things You Need to Know

- Anybody can create a blog to talk about almost anything.
- A microblog site restricts posts to a limited number of characters.
- Podcasts are radio- and TV-like shows that you can download and listen to or watch anytime.
- You can subscribe to the RSS feed of blogs, podcasts, and other sites to be notified of new content.

## Key Terms

blog (weblog)

blogosphere

microblogging

podcast

podcast client

RSS (Really Simple Syndication)

user-generated content

# HOW TO

## Create a blog with Blogger

A blog is like an online journal. It's a Web page that is created with simple blog tools that anyone can set up and pretty much talk about whatever they like. The difference between just creating a Web page and writing a blog is that blogs can be interactive. Your readers can post comments about your blog posts.

Setting up a blog is pretty easy. You don't need to know how to create a Web page. The blogging tools do all of the work for you. One website for creating free blogs is Blogger.com. To use Blogger, you need to have a Google account.

**1** Open your word processor, type your name and date in the document, and save the file as **lastname_firstname_ch08_howto2**. Go to **Blogger.com**. Use your Google account to log in to Blogger. (If you do not have a Google account, you can create one as part of the Blogger sign-up.) Sign in, then click *New Blog*.

**2** On the Create a new blog screen, create a blog title, address, and template. Try to select something that is easy to remember (and spell). You want it to be easy for people to find your blog. Choose a template that visually complements the style and content of your blog. Don't worry—you can change or customize it later. Take a screen shot of this window and paste it into your document. Click *Create Blog!*

**3** You now have a blog. Click *Start posting* or the orange edit button to begin.

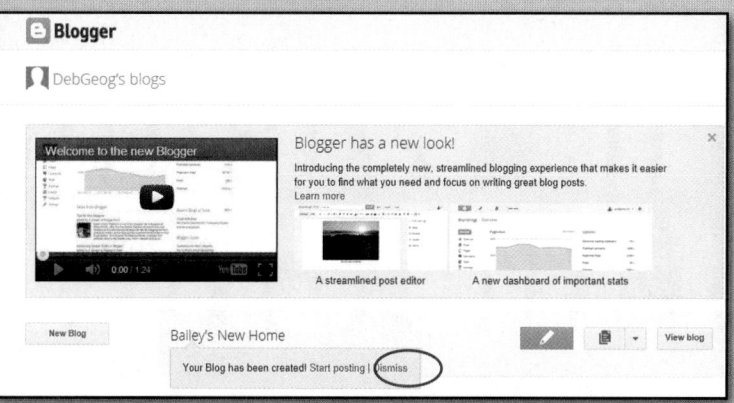

**4** The Post screen is where you compose and format your blog postings. Use the formatting toolbar to format your text. Include a title using the Heading Style, center align, and insert an image or video clip in your post. Under Post settings, allow comments (the default). Add at least one label (tag) to help your readers find posts that are related. When you are satisfied with your post, click *Publish*.

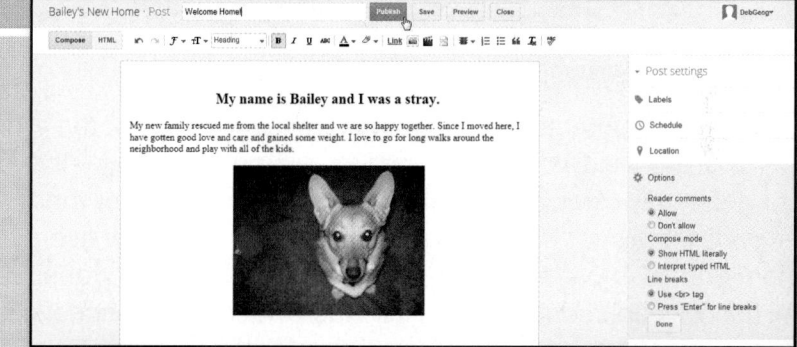

**5** Click *View blog* to view your finished product. Explain the steps you took to create your blog and include the URL of your blog and a screenshot of the finished blog. Save the file and submit as directed by your instructor.

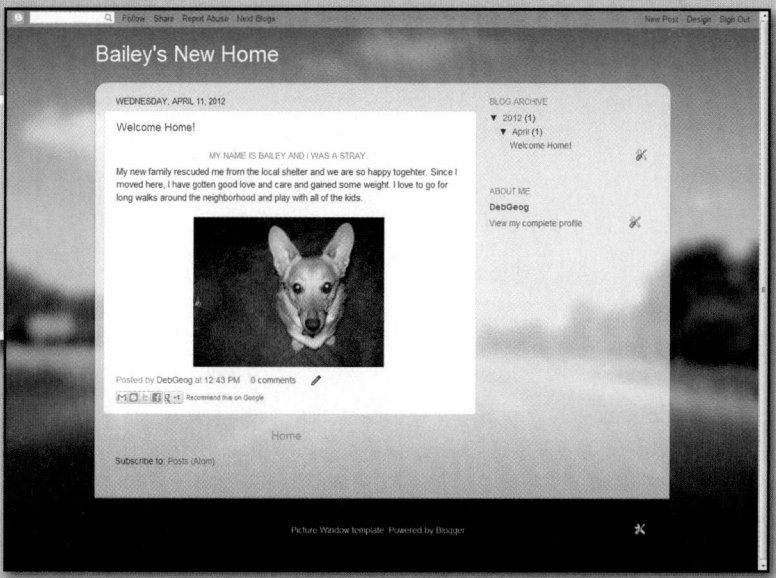

# The Wisdom of the Crowd

## Discuss how wikis and other social media sites rely on the wisdom of the crowd.

One of the most interesting aspects of the social uses of the Web is the idea of the wisdom of the crowd, or **crowd-sourcing**—the idea of trusting the collective opinion of a crowd of people rather than that of an expert. Sites such as Digg, reddit, and Slashdot allow users to share content and Web pages they find interesting. **Wikis** are websites that allow users to edit content, even if it was written by someone else. Review sites such as Yelp and TripAdvisor give us a voice and a place to get advice and recommendations from other folks who are just like us.

## WIKIS

Wikis differ from blogs and podcasts in that they're designed for collaboration, not just in posting responses to another post but in actually editing the content. The most well-known wiki is Wikipedia (see Figure 8.21), which is a massive free encyclopedia that is written by . . . anyone. What? How can you trust something that anyone can edit? Well, that's part of the design. The thought is that if many people are involved in a wiki, then the person that knows the right information will (eventually) be the one to write or edit it. In less than 10 years, Wikipedia grew to more than 3 million articles in English alone. Wikipedia is a great place to start but is generally frowned on for use as a source in academic research.

**FIGURE 8.21** The Wikipedia Main Page

Wikipedia is the most well-known wiki, but it's not the only one. Wikis abound and are often used as a way for a community to develop instructions. For example, wikiHow (see Figure 8.22) is a website that contains how-to wikis on thousands of topics. You can read, write, or edit an existing wikiHow article or request that someone else write one if you can't find what you're looking for.

FIGURE 8.22 wikiHow has thousands of articles.

FIGURE 8.23 Searching for a place to eat in Times Square is easy, using the Yelp app on my iPad.

# SOCIAL REVIEW SITES

**Social review sites** such as TripAdvisor and epinions let users review hotels, movies, games, books, and other products and services. Yelp allows users to review local businesses and places with physical addresses such as parks. I don't go anywhere without checking out some reviews first. I prefer reviews from regular people, not just expert food critics. Figure 8.23 shows a Yelp map of Times Square restaurants. The reviews here help me decide where to eat. I used the Yelp mobile app on my iPad, so I was able to get the information when I was right in the area.

# SOCIAL BOOKMARKING AND NEWS SITES

**Social bookmarking sites** allow you to save and share your bookmarks or favorites online. Delicious allows you to not only save and share your bookmarks online but to also search the bookmarks of others. It's a great way to quickly find out what other people find interesting and important right now. Figure 8.24 shows the Delicious page with links that I post for my students and readers of this book at **delicious.com/visualizingtechnology**. The links are organized into topics, or tags, to make it easier for you to find links. You can click the *Follow* button if you have a Delicious account, but you don't need an account to view the page.

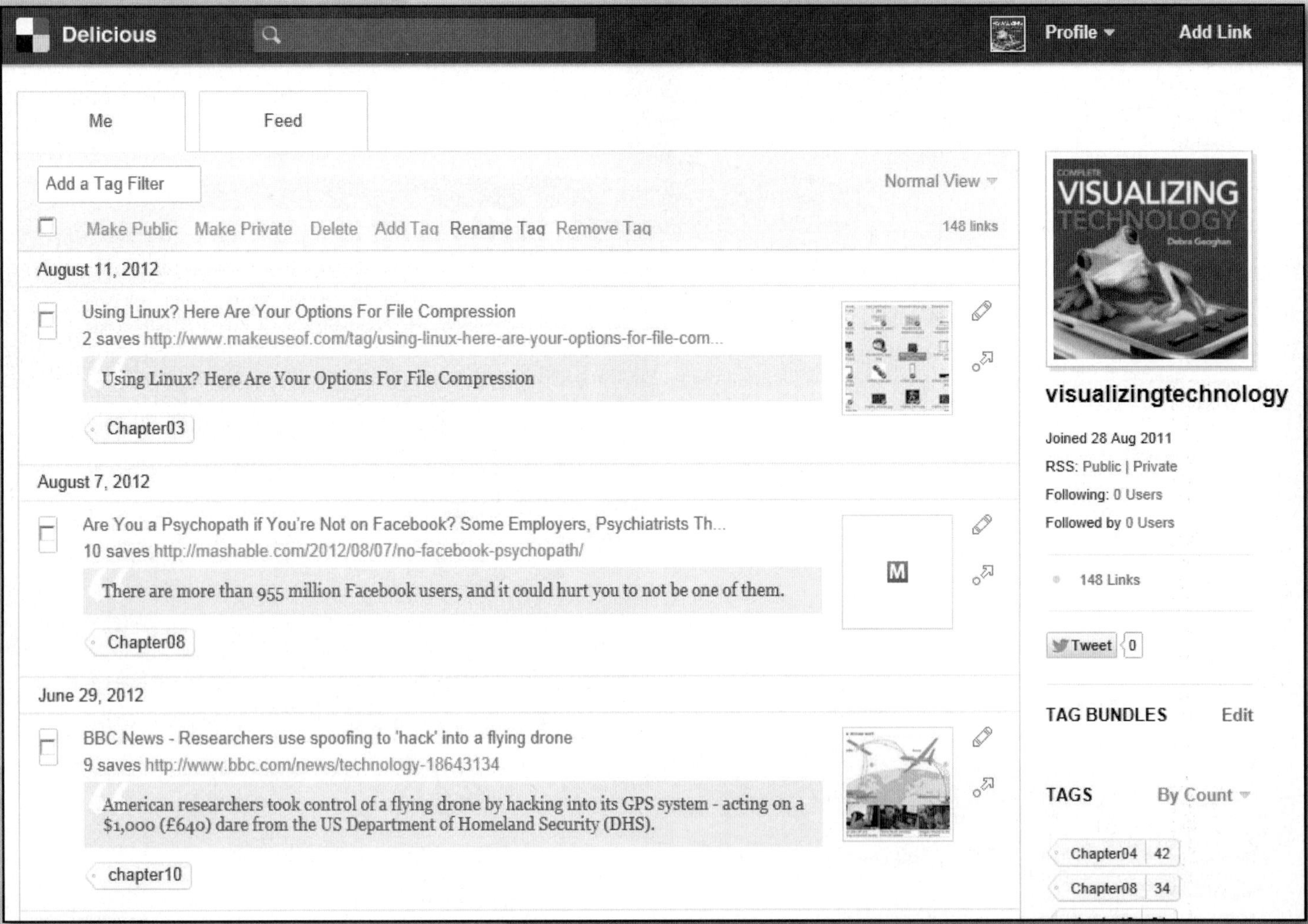

| ■ Delicious | 🔍 | | | | | 🖼 | Profile ▼ | Add Link |

| Me | Feed |

| Add a Tag Filter | | | | | | | Normal View ▼ |

☐  Make Public   Make Private   Delete   Add Tag   **Rename Tag**   Remove Tag                148 links

**August 11, 2012**

☐  Using Linux? Here Are Your Options For File Compression
2 saves http://www.makeuseof.com/tag/using-linux-here-are-your-options-for-file-com...

    Using Linux? Here Are Your Options For File Compression

‹ Chapter03

**August 7, 2012**

☐  Are You a Psychopath if You're Not on Facebook? Some Employers, Psychiatrists Th...
10 saves http://mashable.com/2012/08/07/no-facebook-psychopath/

    There are more than 955 million Facebook users, and it could hurt you to not be one of them.

‹ Chapter08

**June 29, 2012**

☐  BBC News - Researchers use spoofing to 'hack' into a flying drone
9 saves http://www.bbc.com/news/technology-18643134

    American researchers took control of a flying drone by hacking into its GPS system - acting on a $1,000 (£640) dare from the US Department of Homeland Security (DHS).

‹ chapter10

### VISUALIZING TECHNOLOGY

**visualizingtechnology**

Joined 28 Aug 2011
RSS: Public | Private
Following: 0 Users
Followed by 0 Users

  ●   148 Links

🐦 Tweet  ‹ 0

**TAG BUNDLES**               Edit

**TAGS**          By Count ▼

‹ Chapter04  42
‹ Chapter08  34

**FIGURE 8.24** The Delicious Page for This Book

StumbleUpon discovers websites based on your interests. When you sign up, you indicate topics that interest you. Then, as you visit websites, you can click the *StumbleUpon* button to be taken to a similar site. You can click *I like this* to improve the selection of pages you stumble onto. Pinterest is a newer website that is growing in popularity, notably among women. With Pinterest you create virtual cork boards and pin Web pages to them. You can share your boards with others and follow other people to see what they have pinned.

**Social news sites** are different than traditional media news sites in that at least some of the content is submitted by users. It's interactive in a way that traditional media isn't. It's like having millions of friends sharing their finds with you. Content that's submitted more frequently or gets the most votes is promoted to the front page.

Two of the most popular social news sites are reddit and Digg. Digg doesn't publish content but allows the community members to submit content they discover on the Web and puts it in one place for everyone to see and to discuss. Slashdot, which focuses primarily on technology topics, does produce its content but also accepts submissions from its readers. Whatever your interests, there's probably a social news site for you.

Relying on the wisdom of the crowd is much like asking your friends, family, and coworkers for advice. Did you enjoy the movie? Where should I go for the best ice cream? How do you change the oil in your car? Everybody's an expert in something. The Web just makes it easier for us to find and share that expertise with each other. But a word of caution: Like anything else you read on the Web, be critical in your evaluation of the credibility and reliability of its author.

## ETHICS

Some people create multiple accounts on social bookmarking and news sites so they can promote their own content. For example, a blogger might create several accounts on Digg and use each one to Digg a blog post, thereby artificially raising its popularity on Digg and driving more traffic to it. This violates the Digg terms of use. But what if the blogger had all his friends and family members create accounts and Digg his post? Is it ethical? Does it violate the terms of use? Is it fair to other bloggers?

## Running Project

Go to the Wikipedia article "Reliability of Wikipedia" at **wikipedia.org/wiki/Reliability_of_Wikipedia**. How does Wikipedia assure that the content is correct? What procedures are in place to remove or correct mistakes? How does Wikipedia compare to other online sources of information?

## 3 Things You Need to Know

● Social media relies on the wisdom of the crowd rather than that of an expert.

● A wiki can be edited by anybody.

● Social bookmarking and news helps users find content that others recommend.

## Key Terms

crowd-sourcing

social bookmarking site

social news site

social review site

wiki

# E-Commerce

## 6 OBJECTIVE
## Explain the influence of social media on e-commerce.

As we've seen, social media sites are used by businesses to provide support and interaction to customers. **Social media marketing (SMM)** is the practice of using social media sites to sell products and services.

## TYPES OF E-COMMERCE

**E-commerce** is business on the Web and is often broken into three categories: B2B, B2C, and C2C, where B stands for business and C stands for consumer. B2B, or business to business, services are ones that a business provides for another, for example, PayPal, Google Checkout, website hosting, and website design. B2B services allow smaller companies to have a Web presence or store without needing to have the in-house expertise or expense. A small business is able to have a professional-looking website and sophisticated shopping cart system because of B2B services it purchases from other companies (see Figure 8.25).

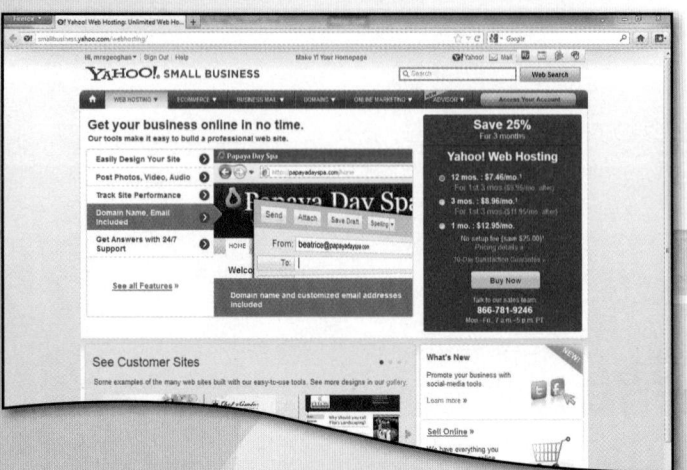

**FIGURE 8.25** Yahoo! Small Business provides B2B services for small companies that want a Web presence.

B2C, or business to consumer, is the most familiar form of e-commerce. Amazon.com, Overstock.com, and most brick-and-mortar retailers sell their goods and services online to you and me. This form of e-commerce has grown exponentially since Pizza Hut offered pizza ordering on its website in 1994. B2C companies leverage social media to help customers find out about their products, (see Figure 8.26).

**FIGURE 8.26** A small business can use the web to reach customers.

The third form of e-commerce is C2C, or consumer to consumer, electronic commerce. Websites such as eBay and craigslist have created a global yard sale, where you can find, sell, or trade virtually anything. eBay has a seller rating system that helps ensure honest transactions and a community (see Figure 8.27) that includes discussion boards, groups, and chats. An unscrupulous seller will quickly get a bad reputation, and a top-rated seller will see more sales as a result.

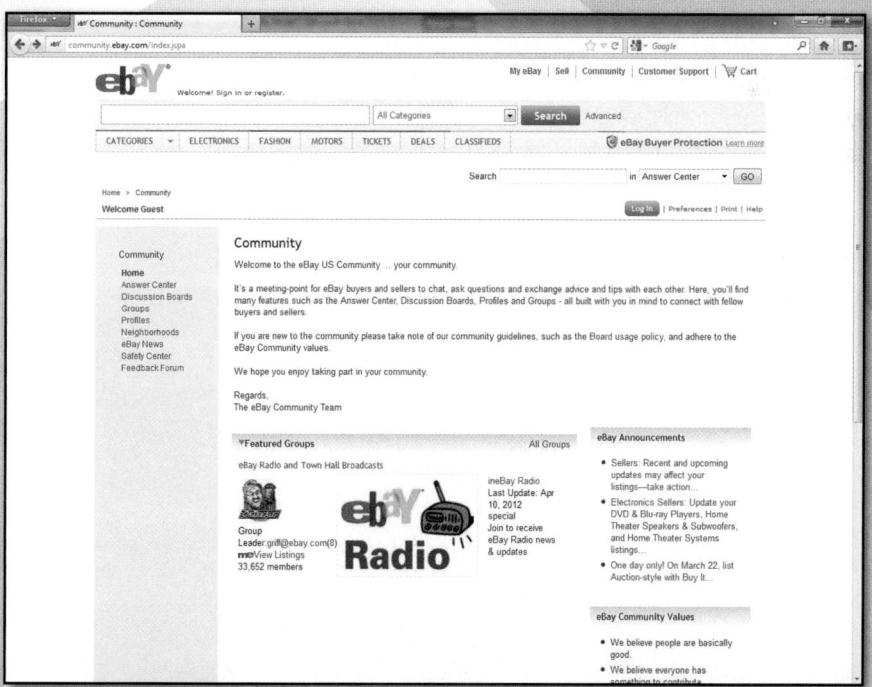

**FIGURE 8.27** The eBay community adds social media to the world's largest C2C site.

## HOW SAFE IS MY CREDIT CARD?

E-commerce on the Web requires you to hand over some sensitive information. So, is it OK to shop online? Yes, but just as you wouldn't leave your doors unlocked, you need to be sure that you're shopping wisely. Shop at well-known sites or use third-party payment sites such as Google Checkout and PayPal to protect credit card information. Make sure you're on a secure website when completing transactions. Look at your browser's address bar. If the URL begins with https, then the site is using SSL security. You'll also notice a padlock that indicates a secure site. Clicking on the padlock will open a security report about the website.

The Internet has changed how most companies do business, and the social Web has added a new dimension. Businesses that successfully leverage the power of social media are able to create customers who, in turn, create new customers.

## CAREER SPOTLIGHT

Although most blogs are personal in nature and earn the writer no compensation, some lucky folks are professional bloggers. These bloggers may be paid by a company to blog about a product or provide news or reviews, and their blogs are usually part of a bigger website. Some professional bloggers use their blogs to drive customers to their other products. Successful bloggers monetize the content on their sites in several ways, including placing ads and links to other sites. A professional blog may earn money by using Google AdSense to place ads and links on it. It takes a lot of time and work to write a good blog and even more to make money while doing it.

# GREEN COMPUTING

## RAISING SOCIAL AWARENESS

How much paper mail do you receive every week? And how much of it do you actually read? The cost of a direct-mail campaign is huge, and many people simply toss what they see as junk mail in the trash anyway, so the costs are also large in terms of the environment. SMM isn't just for businesses—it can also be used to raise awareness of important issues.

Not long ago, women all over Facebook posted one-word status updates. White, red, gray, black. What was going on? Women were sharing a message with each other that said: "Some fun is going on. . . . Just write the color of your bra in your status. Just the color; nothing else. It will be neat to see if this will spread the wings of breast cancer awareness. It will be fun to see how long it takes before people wonder why all the girls have a color in their status. . . . Haha." The message quickly spread, and thousands of women (and even some men) responded. The idea was to raise social awareness about breast cancer. Did it work? Well, it certainly didn't do any harm, and the story was also picked up by the news media. So, a simple act of social networking resulted in raising social awareness. The beauty of the idea was that it got women thinking about something we usually prefer not to at no cost to the environment. Facebook has an application called Causes that can be used to raise both awareness and funds for social causes without printing a single piece of paper.

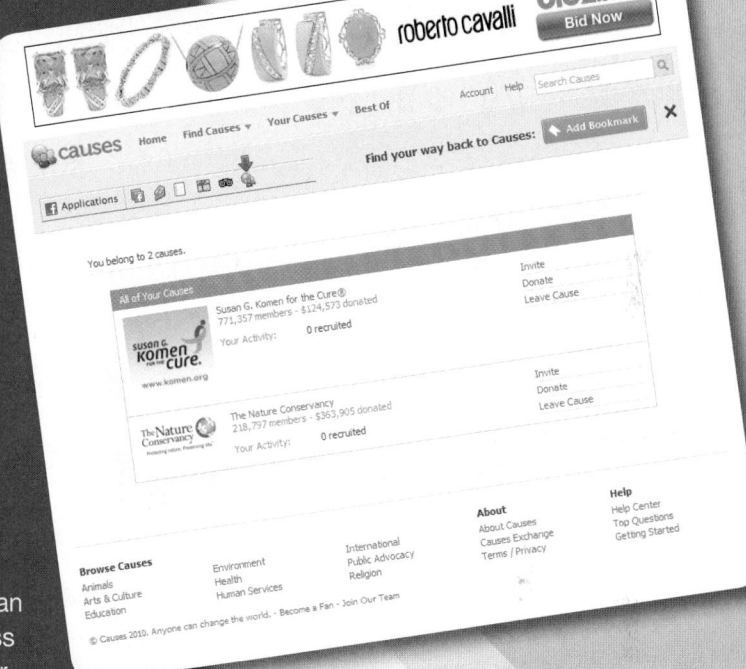

## Running Project

Visit Amazon.com. What are two ways that Amazon uses social media marketing? Can you find any other ways? How is this experience different from shopping in a store?

## 2 Things You Need to Know

- E-commerce is business on the Web.
- Social Media Marketing (SMM) uses social media sites to sell products and services.

## Key Terms

e-commerce

social media marketing (SMM)

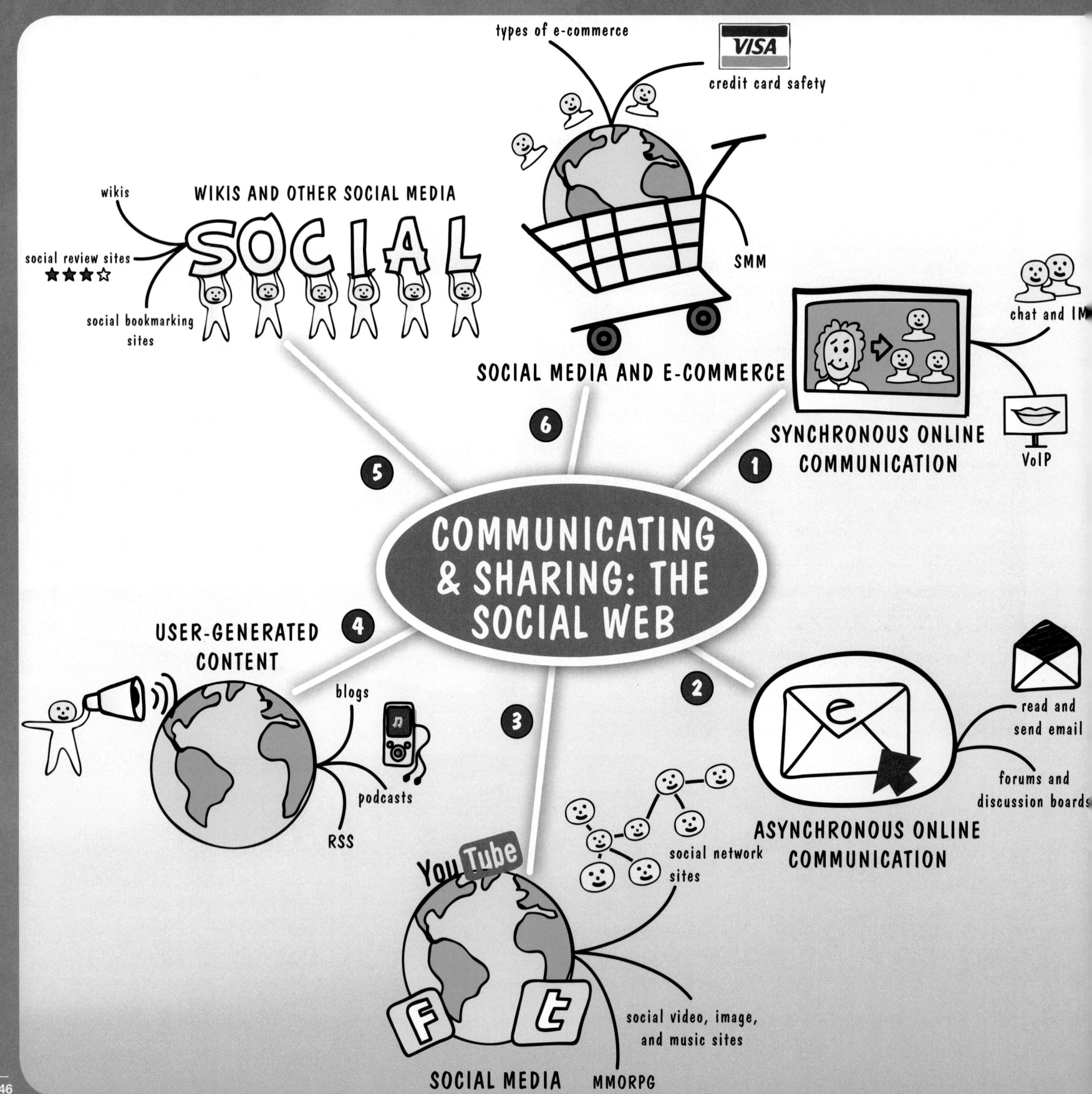

**types of e-commerce**

**credit card safety**
VISA

**WIKIS AND OTHER SOCIAL MEDIA**

wikis

social review sites
★★★☆

SOCIAL

social bookmarking sites

SMM

chat and IM

**SOCIAL MEDIA AND E-COMMERCE**

**SYNCHRONOUS ONLINE COMMUNICATION**

VoIP

5

6

1

## COMMUNICATING & SHARING: THE SOCIAL WEB

**USER-GENERATED CONTENT**

4

blogs

podcasts

RSS

2

3

read and send email

forums and discussion boards

**ASYNCHRONOUS ONLINE COMMUNICATION**

You Tube

social network sites

f  t

social video, image, and music sites

**SOCIAL MEDIA**    MMORPG

# Objectives Recap

1. Compare different forms of synchronous online communication.
2. Demonstrate how to use email effectively.
3. Discuss the roles of social media in today's society.
4. Locate user-generated content in the form of a blog or podcast.
5. Discuss how wikis and other social media sites rely on the wisdom of the crowd.
6. Explain the influence of social media on e-commerce.

# Key Terms

asynchronous online communication **318**
avatar **326**
blog (weblog) **332**
blogosphere **332**
captcha (Completely Automated Public Turing Test to Tell Computers and Humans Apart) **318**
chat **314**
crowd-sourcing **338**
digital footprint **329**
e-commerce **342**
email **318**
folksonomy **326**
forum **322**
instant messaging (IM) **314**
massively multiplayer online role-playing games (MMORPG) **326**

microblogging **333**
podcast **334**
podcast client **334**
RSS (Really Simple Syndication) **335**
social bookmarking site **340**
social media **324**
social media marketing (SMM) **342**
social network **324**
social news site **341**
social review site **339**
synchronous online communication **314**
user-generated content **332**
viral video **327**
VoIP (voice over IP) **317**
Web 2.0 **324**
wiki **338**

# Summary

1. **Compare different forms of synchronous online communication.**

   Synchronous communication happens in real time. Chat usually involves more than two people having a conversation in a chat room and is usually text-based. Instant messaging is similar to chat, but the conversation is between only two people. The terms "IM" and "chat" are often used interchangeably. VoIP service uses the Internet to place phone calls.

2. **Demonstrate how to use email effectively.**

   Email is an asynchronous, store-and-forward technology. You can access email using webmail or a desktop email program. You shouldn't expect that your email is private.

3. **Discuss the roles of social media in today's society.**

   Social networking and sharing allow us to keep in touch, create content, share ideas, and benefit from the expertise of others.

4. **Locate user-generated content in the form of a blog or podcast.**

   Blogs can be created on websites such as Blogger and WordPress and can be found using Technorati or similar sites. Podcasts can be found using a podcast program or by searching websites such as podcast.com. Content on many websites includes blogs and podcasts.

5. **Discuss how wikis and other social media sites rely on the wisdom of the crowd.**

   Wikis are unique because anyone can edit the content. Many types of social websites, including wikis, rely on the wisdom of the crowd rather than experts. Social review sites let users review hotels, movies, games, books, and other products and services; social bookmarking sites allow you to save and share your bookmarks or favorites online; and social news sites are different from traditional media news sites in that at least some of the content is submitted by users.

6. **Explain the influence of social media on e-commerce.**

   Businesses have begun to leverage social media through social media marketing strategies such as contests, fan pages, and review sites.

# Multiple Choice

Answer the multiple-choice questions below for more practice with key terms and concepts from this chapter.

1. What form of online communication happens in real time between two people?
   a. Email
   b. VoIP
   c. Instant messaging
   d. Flickr

2. What are synchronous online conversations between multiple people at the same time?
   a. Instant messaging
   b. Chats
   c. Forums
   d. Virtual worlds

3. Email is a _____ form of online communication.
   a. synchronous
   b. real-time
   c. private
   d. store-and-forward

4. Which field prevents multiple recipients from seeing each other's email addresses?
   a. To:
   b. Cc:
   c. Bcc:
   d. Fw:

5. A(n) _____ is an online game in which players interact with people in real time in a virtual world using an avatar.
   a. MMORPG
   b. chat room
   c. IM
   d. virtual world

6. Facebook and LinkedIn are examples of:
   a. Social networks
   b. Forums
   c. Social news sites
   d. Social media marketing

7. Your _____ is all the information that someone could find out about you by searching the Web, including social network sites.
   a. screen name
   b. profile
   c. digital footprint
   d. avatar

8. What service is used to distribute Web feeds to subscribers?
   a. RSS
   b. Folksonomy
   c. Podcasts
   d. Captcha

9. In which type of social media are posts limited to a small number of characters and users post updates frequently?
   a. Microblog
   b. Forum
   c. Podcast
   d. Wiki

10. _____ is the practice of using social media sites to sell products and services.
    a. Microblog
    b. B2B
    c. SMM
    d. Twitter

# True or False

Answer the following questions with T for true or F for false for more practice with key terms and concepts from this chapter.

1. VoIP is a service that allows phone calls to be transmitted over the Internet instead of traditional phone lines.

2. Email is private and can't be read by others.

3. Email is a form of synchronous communication.

4. A viral video spreads computer viruses.

5. The social tagging of Web media is known as folksonomy.

6. Social media is a collection of tools that enable users to create user-generated content, connect, network, and share.

7. You can listen to some podcasts directly from their websites without a podcast client.

8. Like a blog, a wiki usually has only one author.

9. Crowd-sourcing means trusting the collective opinion of a crowd of people rather than that of an expert.

10. Social media marketing is designed to get more subscribers on social networks.

# Fill in the Blank

Fill in the blanks with key terms from this chapter.

1. _____ online communication happens in real time.

2. A _____, or discussion board, is an asynchronous form of communication.

3. A(n) _____ is a series of letters and numbers that are distorted in some way.

4. New technologies used to communicate and collaborate on the Web are called _____.

5. Your _____ is all the information that someone could find out about you by searching the Web, including social network sites.

6. The _____ consists of all the blogs on the Web and the connections between them.

7. _____ is a format used for distributing Web feeds that change frequently—for example, blogs, podcasts, and news—to subscribers.

8. A(n) _____ is a digital media file of a prerecorded radio- or TV-like show that is distributed over the Web.

9. _____ sites allow you to save and share your favorites online.

10. _____ is doing business on the Web.

# Application Project

## Microsoft Application Project 1:
### PowerPoint Level 3

**PROJECT DESCRIPTION:** In this Microsoft PowerPoint project, you will create a presentation about desktop browsers. In creating this presentation you will apply design and color themes. You will also insert and format a chart and apply animations to objects on your slides, and transitions between slides.

**INSTRUCTIONS:** For the purpose of grading the project you are required to perform the following tasks:

| Step | Instructions |
|---|---|
| **1** | Start PowerPoint. Download and open the file named *vt_ch08*. Save the file as **lastname_firstname_ch08_ppt**. |
| **2** | On Slide 1, type **March 2012** in the subtitle placeholder. |
| **3** | Apply the Retrospect theme, green Variant, to the presentation. |
| **4** | On Slide 2, change the bullets to Hollow Square bullets and set the line spacing to 1.5. |

| Step | Instructions |
|---|---|
| **5** | Apply the Fly In animation with the From Left effect option and set a duration of 00.75 to the bullet list on Slide 2. |
| **6** | On Slide 3 in the title placeholder type **Share Trend May 2011–March 2012** and in the content placeholder, add a line chart. |
| **7** | Resize the data area by dragging to include column G. Use the following data to create the chart. |
| **8** | Change the chart to style 13. Change the chart layout of the chart to Layout 5. |

| Month | Internet Explorer | Firefox | Chrome | Safari | Opera | Other |
|---|---|---|---|---|---|---|
| May, 2011 | 57.15% | 22.87% | 13.19% | 4.37% | 2.10% | 0.31% |
| Sept, 2011 | 54.39% | 22.48% | 16.20% | 5.02% | 1.67% | 0.23% |
| Dec, 2011 | 51.87% | 21.83% | 19.11% | 4.97% | 1.66% | 0.55% |
| March, 2012 | 53.83% | 20.55% | 18.57% | 5.07% | 1.62% | 0.36% |

Visit **pearsonhighered.com/Geoghan** for data files, simulations, VizClips, and additional study materials.

| Step | Instructions |
|---|---|
| **9** | Insert a new slide after Slide 3. On Slide 4, in the title placeholder, type Source. In the content placeholder, type http://netmarketshare.com and press Enter. |
| **10** | Apply the Split transition to all slides in the presentation. |

| Step | Instructions |
|---|---|
| **11** | Insert the page number and your name in the footer on the notes and handouts pages for all slides in the presentation. View the presentation in Slide Show view from beginning to end, and then return to Normal view. |
| **12** | Save and close the presentation. Exit PowerPoint. Submit the presentation as directed. |

**Visit pearsonhighered.com/Geoghan** for data files, simulations, VizClips, and additional study materials.

Chapter 8 | 351

# MS Office Application Projects
## Excel Level 3

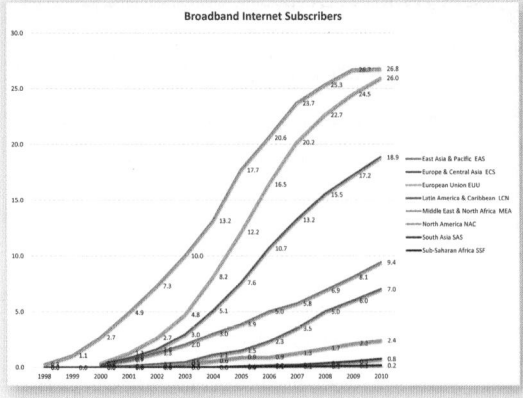

**PROJECT DESCRIPTION:** In this project, using data from The World Bank, you will format a Microsoft Excel spreadsheet and create and format a chart showing broadband growth from 1998 to 2010.

**INSTRUCTIONS:** For the purpose of grading the project you are required to perform the following tasks:

| Step | Instructions |
|---|---|
| **1** | Start Excel. Open the downloaded Excel file named *vt_ch08_excel*. Save the file as **lastname_firstname_ch08_excel**. |
| **2** | On the Regions sheet, Select the range C2:O10. Apply the Number Format to the selected range. Decrease the decimals displayed to 1. |
| **3** | Select A1:O1 and apply the Heading 4 Cell Style. |
| **4** | Adjust the width of columns A and B to fit the contents. |
| **5** | Select A10:O10 and apply a Bottom Double Border to the range. |
| **6** | In cell A11 type Highest. In cell A12 type Lowest. |

| Step | Instructions |
|---|---|
| **7** | In cell C11, use a function to calculate the highest number of broadband subscriptions of the range C2:C9. Copy the formula from C11:O11. |
| **8** | In cell C12 use a function to calculate the lowest number of broadband subscriptions of the range C2:C9. Copy the formula from C12:O12. |
| **9** | Select the range A1:O9 and insert a 2-D line chart. Move the chart to a new sheet named Line Chart. Format the chart as Style 4, Layout 9. |
| **10** | Change the Chart Title to Broadband Internet Subscribers and the vertical axis title to (per 100 people). |

| Step | Instructions | Step | Instructions |
|------|-------------|------|-------------|
| 11 | On the Regions sheet, apply the Gradient Blue Data Bar conditional formatting to the range E2:E10 and apply the Gradient Orange Data Bar conditional formatting to the range O2:O10. | 13 | Insert a header with the Sheet name in the center cell. Insert a footer with the file name in the left cell. Return to Normal view. |
| 12 | Change the orientation of the Regions worksheet to Landscape. Adjust the Scale option to change the Width to 1 page. | 14 | Ensure that the worksheets are correctly named and placed in the following order in the workbook: Line Chart, Regions, Source, All data. Save the workbook. Close the workbook and then exit Excel. Submit the workbook as directed. |

Visit **pearsonhighered.com/Geoghan** for data files, simulations, VizClips, and additional study materials.

Chapter 8 | 353

# Running Project ...

## ... The Finish Line

Use your answers from the previous sections of the chapter project to discuss the impact of social network on society. How has it changed the way we keep in touch with others? Do business? How has it personally changed the way you connect with others?

Write a report responding to the questions raised. Save your file as **lastname_firstname_ch08_project**, and submit it to your instructor as directed.

# Do It Yourself 1

Instant messaging and chatting have become popular tools for businesses to provide services to customers. Some schools also offer virtual advisors and librarians that you can chat with live online.

1. If your school or local library offers this service, use it to ask them about the success of this service. Take a screen shot of your conversation. If you don't have a local library that uses chat/IM, then use the Internet to find another library that does.

2. Type up your answers, and save the file as **lastname_firstname_ch08_diy1**. Submit your work as directed by your instructor.

# Do It Yourself 2

Some websites require you to provide an email address to register. While it's OK to use your normal email on sites that you trust and want communication from, it's a good idea to have a separate email address just to use for those sites that you don't want to hear from again.

1. Go to **yahoo.com**, and click *New here?* Sign Up. (If you're already logged in to Yahoo!, sign out first.)

2. Fill in the form. If you're nervous about using your personal information, you may use an alias and change your birthday. Click *Create My Account*.

3. Take a screen shot of the Congratulations page. Save the image as **lastname_firstname_ch08_diy2**, and submit it as directed by your instructor.

# File Management

Social sharing sites allow you to put your videos and images online. To help organize this content, these sites use social tagging. For this activity, you'll create tags for a group of images provided with this book.

1. Locate the data files for this chapter.

2. Navigate to the folder where you're keeping your student files for this chapter. Look at the 21 images in the file management folder. Create a table like the one below using a word processor or spreadsheet. For each image, list at least two tags that you would use to tag the file. Try to use the same tags for multiple files.

| Image | Tag1 | Tag2 |
|-------|------|------|
|       |      |      |
|       |      |      |

3. Go to the Flickr website, and search for the three tags that you used the most often in your table. Do you find images that are similar to the ones you tagged? Do you think you did a good job of tagging them? Take a screenshot of one of the images you found and paste it into your document or spreadsheet.

4. Save your file as **lastname_firstname_ch08_fm**, and submit it as directed by your instructor.

# Critical Thinking

Social networks such as Facebook and Google+ are often criticized in the media for their privacy settings. In this exercise you will examine the privacy policy of Facebook to determine the appropriate settings to use for your own profile. You do not need to have a Facebook account to do this exercise.

1. Go to **facebook.com** and click *Privacy* at the bottom of the page. Click the link for *Sharing and finding you on Facebook*. Read through the various topics on this page. How does Facebook protect your privacy? What are the default privacy settings and do you think they do a good job protecting you?

2. If you have a Facebook account, have you set your privacy settings to keep your personal information protected? When was the last time you checked and updated them? Have the terms of service changed since you first joined this network?

3. Type up your answers, save the file as **lastname_firstname_ch08_ct,** and submit it as directed by your instructor.

# Ethical Dilemma

Your digital footprint says a lot about you, but not everything is true or accurate. When you're a college (or high school) student, it's hard to think about the impact your digital life will have on future employment. Some potential employers will search the Web looking for information on job applicants.

1. Is it ethical for a potential employer to use the Internet this way? Is it legal? What if an angry ex-boyfriend or ex-girlfriend posted some things pretending to be you? How might this affect your chances for employment? Do you think it's OK to post things that make you look good, even if they're not true?

2. Type up your answers, save the file as **lastname_firstname_ch08_ethics**, and submit your work as directed by your instructor.

# On the Web

Social news sites are a great way to find out what other people think is important. Visit **Slashdot.org or Digg.com**, and look on the Recent page.

1. What are some of the recent stories? How do these compare to the headlines today in traditional mass media? Select two that you think are interesting or important, and write a short summary of each. Why did you select these stories?

2. Type up your answers, save the file as **lastname_firstname_ch08_web**, and submit your work as directed by your instructor.

# Collaboration

With a group of three to five students, research the history of social networks. Create a timeline showing five to seven important milestones of this development. Use a free online timeline generator, a drawing program, a word processor, or a presentation tool to create your timeline. Present your findings to the class.

**Instructors:** Divide the class into groups of three to five students.

**The Project:** Each team is to research the history of social networks. Create a timeline showing five to seven important milestones of this development. Teams must use at least three references, only one of which may be this textbook. Use Google Docs or Microsoft Office to plan the presentation, and provide documentation that all team members have contributed to the project.

**Students:** Before beginning this project, discuss the roles each group member will play. Choose a team name, which you'll use in submitting your presentation. Be sure to divide the work among your members, and pick someone to present your project. You may find it helpful to elect a team leader who can direct your activities and ensure that all team contributions are collated through Google Docs or Microsoft Office as directed by your instructor.

**Outcome:** Use a free online timeline generator, a drawing program, a word processor, or a presentation tool to create your timeline, and present it to your class. The presentation may be no longer than 3 minutes and should contain 5 to 7 milestones. Turn in a final version of your presentation named as **teamname_ch08_timeline** and your file showing your collaboration named as **teamname_ch08_collab**. Be sure to include the name of your presentation and a listing of all team members. Submit your presentation to your instructor as directed.

# 9

# Networks and Communication

Visit **pearsonhighered.com/Geoghan** for data files, simulations, VizClips, and additional study materials.

## Running Project

In this chapter, you'll learn about computer networks and communication. Look for instructions as you complete each article. For most, there is a series of questions for you to research. At the conclusion of this chapter you're asked to submit your responses to the questions raised.

**OBJECTIVES**

1. **Discuss the importance of computer networks.**

2. **Compare different types of LANs and WANs.**

3. **List and describe the hardware used in both wired and wireless networks.**

4. **List and describe the software and protocols used in both wired and wireless networks.**

5. **Explain how to protect a network.**

# IN THIS CHAPTER

The Internet is the largest computer network in the world, but it is actually a network of networks. On a much smaller scale, most of the computers that you use at school and in the workplace are part of a network, and it is likely that you also have a network at home. But only a few years ago, that was not the case. In this chapter, you'll learn about different kinds of computer networks.

357

# From Sneakernet to Hotspots

## OBJECTIVE

### Discuss the importance of computer networks.

A **computer network** is two or more computers that share resources. **Network resources** can be software, hardware, or files. Computer networks save us both time and money and make it easier for us to work, increasing productivity. Before computers were connected in networks, moving files between them involved physically putting the files on a disk and carrying the disk to the new machine. This is wistfully referred to as "sneakernet."

## PEER-TO-PEER NETWORKS

Figure 9.1 shows a small peer-to-peer network that you might have set up at home.

A **peer-to-peer network (P2P)** is one in which each computer is considered equal. Each device can share its resources with every other device, and there's no centralized authority. In this example, the computers might share music (files) and a printer (hardware). They don't necessarily have to connect to the Internet at all. This is the simplest type of network you can set up. Computers in a P2P network belong to a **workgroup**.

**FIGURE 9.1** A Simple Peer-to-Peer Network between Two Computers

Most P2P networks are found in homes or small businesses. They are easy to set up and configure and offer basic file and print sharing. A peer-to-peer network doesn't require a network operating system (NOS). While your personal operating system has networking features, the files and services that are shared between your home computers aren't centralized. Windows provides the Network and Sharing Center to help you configure your sharing options (see Figure 9.2). For example, if you have a printer in your house that's connected to your desktop computer, that printer can easily be shared with your notebook computer through your home network. The biggest problem with this type of network is that the computer that's sharing a resource must be turned on and accessible by the other computers in the network. If your desktop computer is turned off or in sleep mode, then the notebook will be unable to print.

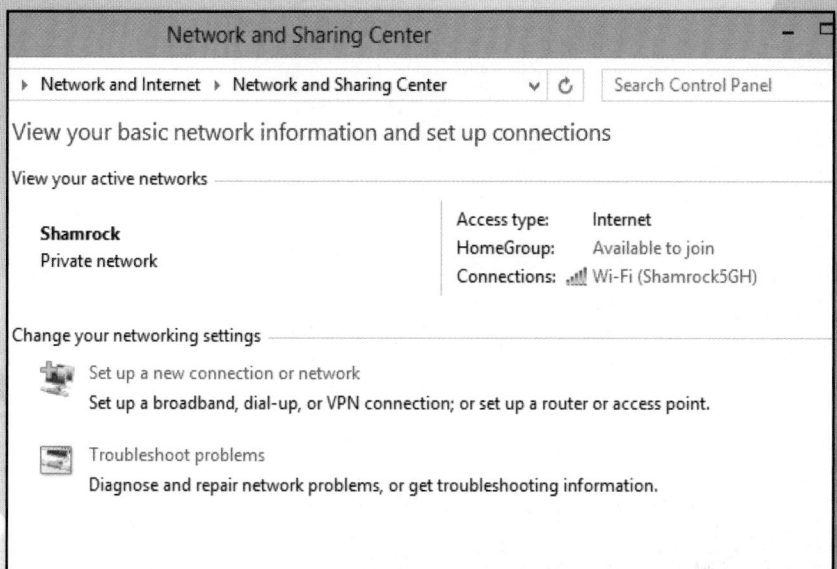

**FIGURE 9.2** The Windows Network and Sharing Center window allows you to view and configure your network.

Recent versions of Windows make setting up a home network an easy task. In fact, there's very little you have to do. When you add a new computer to your home and turn it on, Windows will automatically detect the other devices that are already on your network. Figure 9.3 shows the network from a Windows computer. Notice that is has detected both wired and wireless computers and even some devices that aren't personal computers at all, including a router, printer, and video game console. To see this view of your home network, click *Network* in the File Manager window.

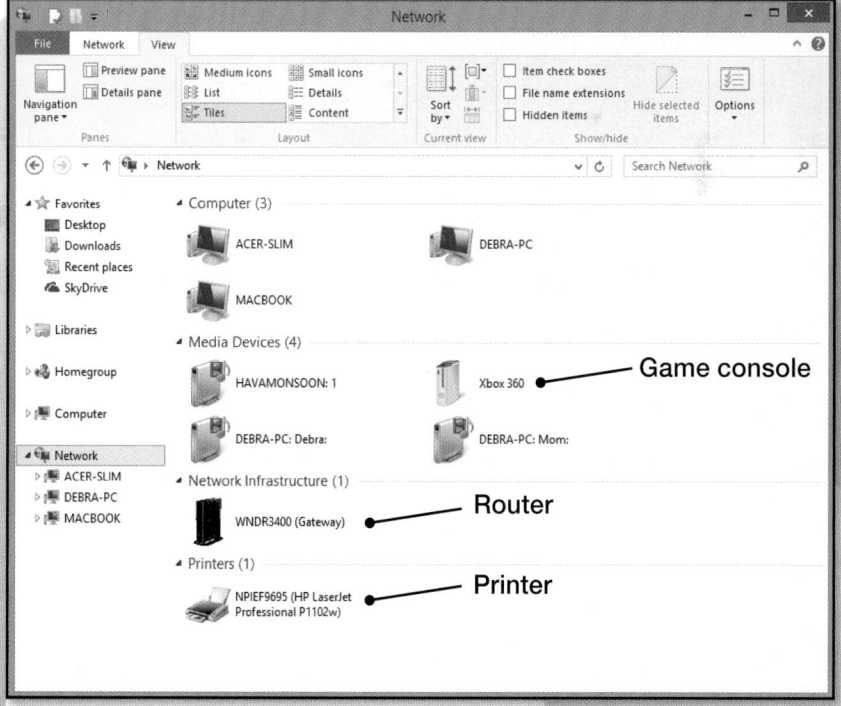

**FIGURE 9.3** This screen shows the computers and other devices detected on this network.

Windows comes with a networking feature called homegroup. A **homegroup** is a simple way to network a group of Windows computers that are all on the same home network. Members of a homegroup automatically share their picture, music, and video libraries and printers with each other without any additional configuration on your part. You can create a homegroup if your computer is running most versions of Windows 7 or 8. Once you create a homegroup, Windows will create a password that you can then use to join all your other Windows 7/8 computers to the homegroup. In Figure 9.4, you can see my homegroup setup in the Explorer window. In the navigation pane, MACBOOK is visible under Network but does not appear under Homegroup. This is because Macs and other computers not running Windows 7 or 8 can't join a homegroup. To share resources with other computers, I must use a workgroup. Although the Mac, running OS X, is visible in my Windows network, I must configure it to share files with Windows computers.

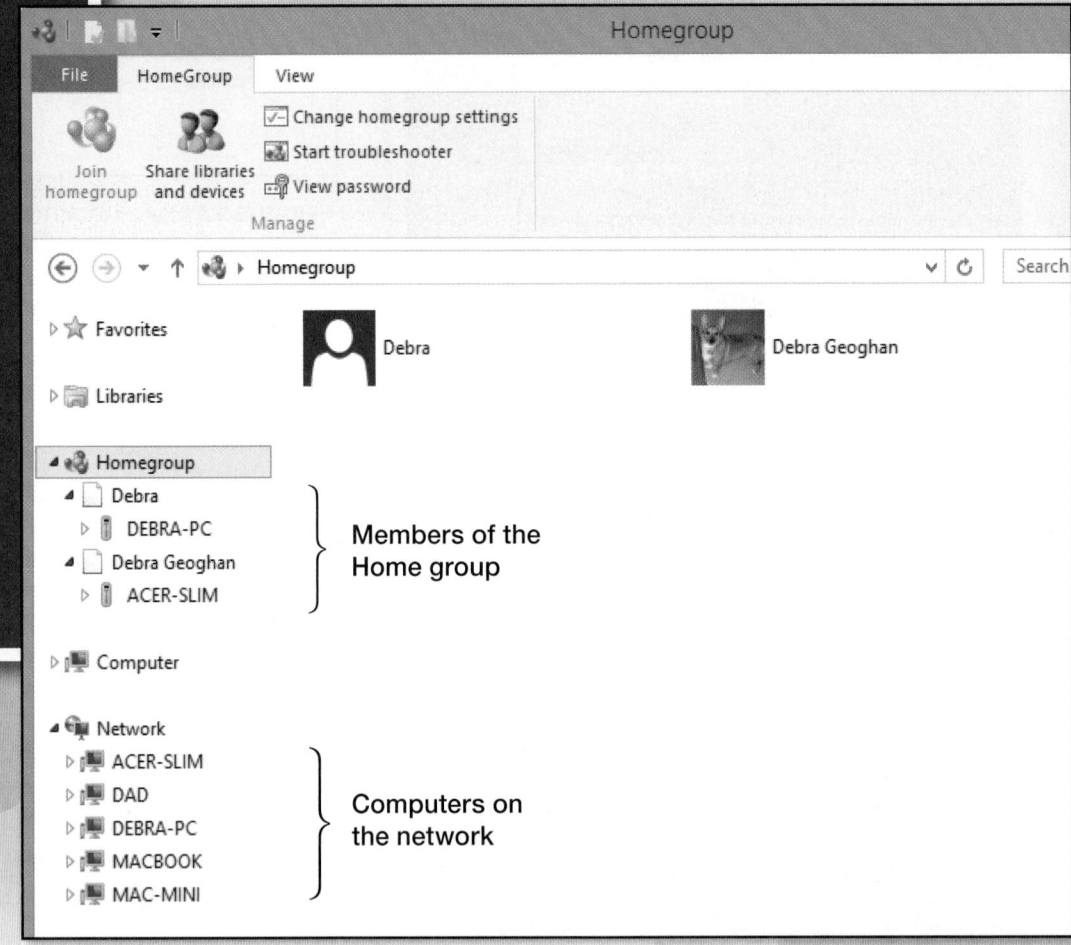

**FIGURE 9.4** My Homegroup and Other Network Computers

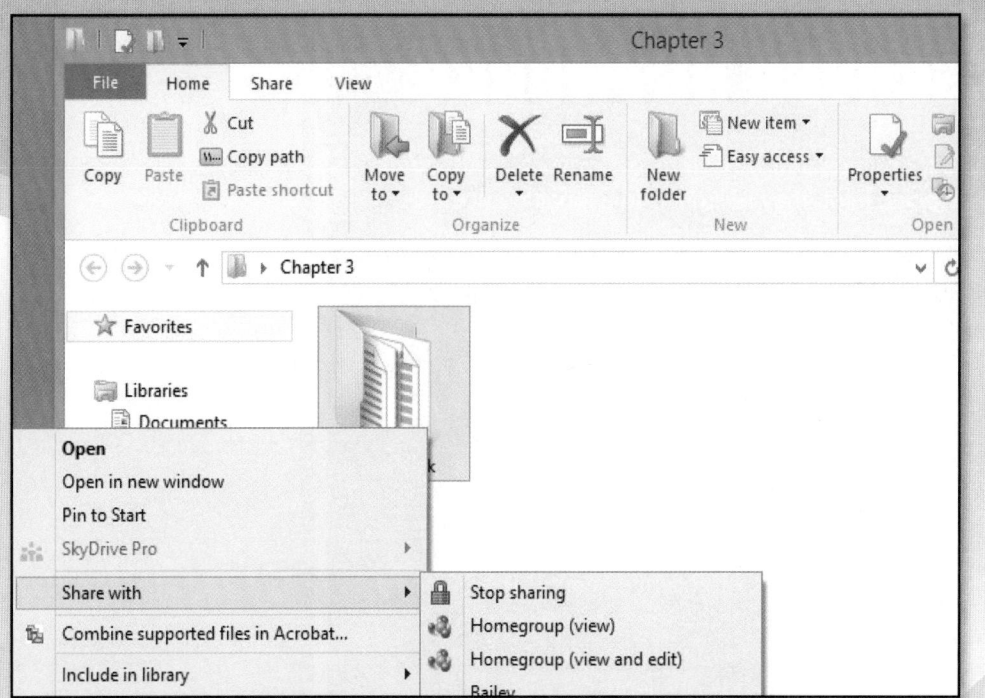

Setting up shared resources using a homegroup is easier than using a regular workgroup. You can choose to share Pictures, Music, Videos, Documents, and Printers. By default, Documents are not shared, but you can easily change this setting. If you have computers running other versions of Windows or Linux or Mac computers, then you will need to use a workgroup to share resources among them. Setting up the shares in a workgroup is not difficult but takes a bit more work than setting up a homegroup. Computers in a workgroup need to have the same workgroup and account information configured. By default, Windows computers belong to the workgroup called "workgroup." Mac and Linux computers will need to be configured to access the resources (see Figure 9.5).

**FIGURE 9.5** A Mac computer needs a username and password to access files on a Windows network.

To share a resource with computers in your workgroup, right-click the item to be shared and choose Share with (see Figure 9.6). Click *Specific people* to open the File Sharing dialog box. In the File Sharing dialog box, choose the users you want to give access to from the drop-down list box and click *Add*. You can grant read or read/write access to this folder. You can also remove users from this list.

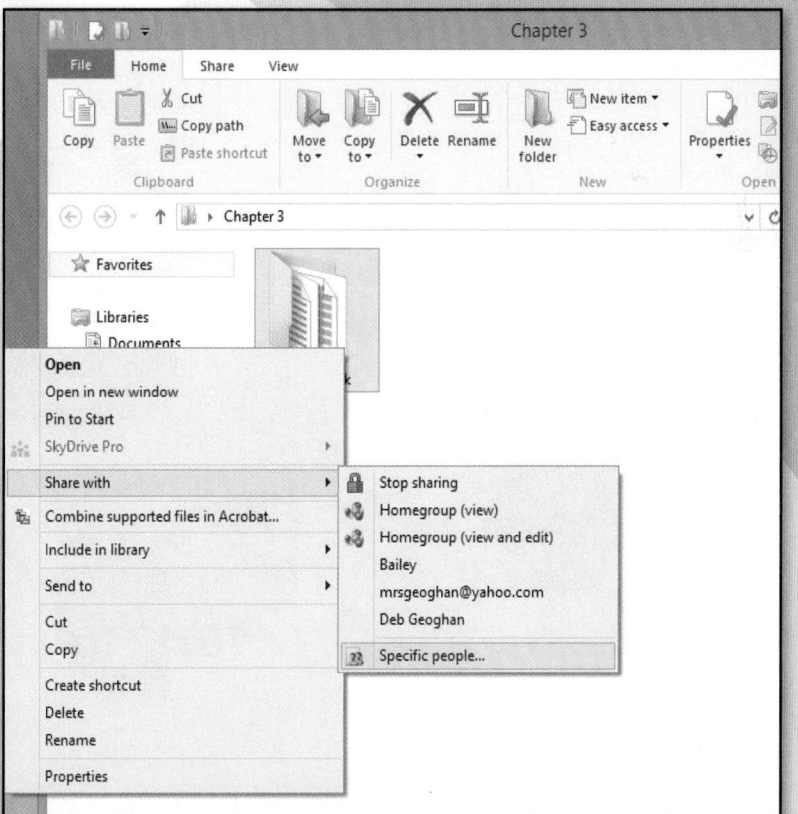

**FIGURE 9.6** Right click and select *Share* with to grant access to your files.

# CLIENT-SERVER NETWORKS

P2P networks are fine for homes and very small businesses, but they have two major drawbacks. First, they're limited to a small number of devices, and second, they provide no centralization of resources and security. In most business settings, a client-server network is a better choice.

A **client-server network** is one that has at least one server at its center (see Figure 9.7). The server provides a way to centralize the network management, resources, and security. In a client-server network, users log in to the network instead of their local computers and are granted access to resources based on that login.

A **server** is a multiuser computer system that runs a network operating system (NOS) and provides services—such as Internet access, email, or file and print services—to client systems. The personal computers and other devices that connect to the server are called **clients**. Servers range from very small to massive enterprise-level systems that serve hundreds of thousands of clients.

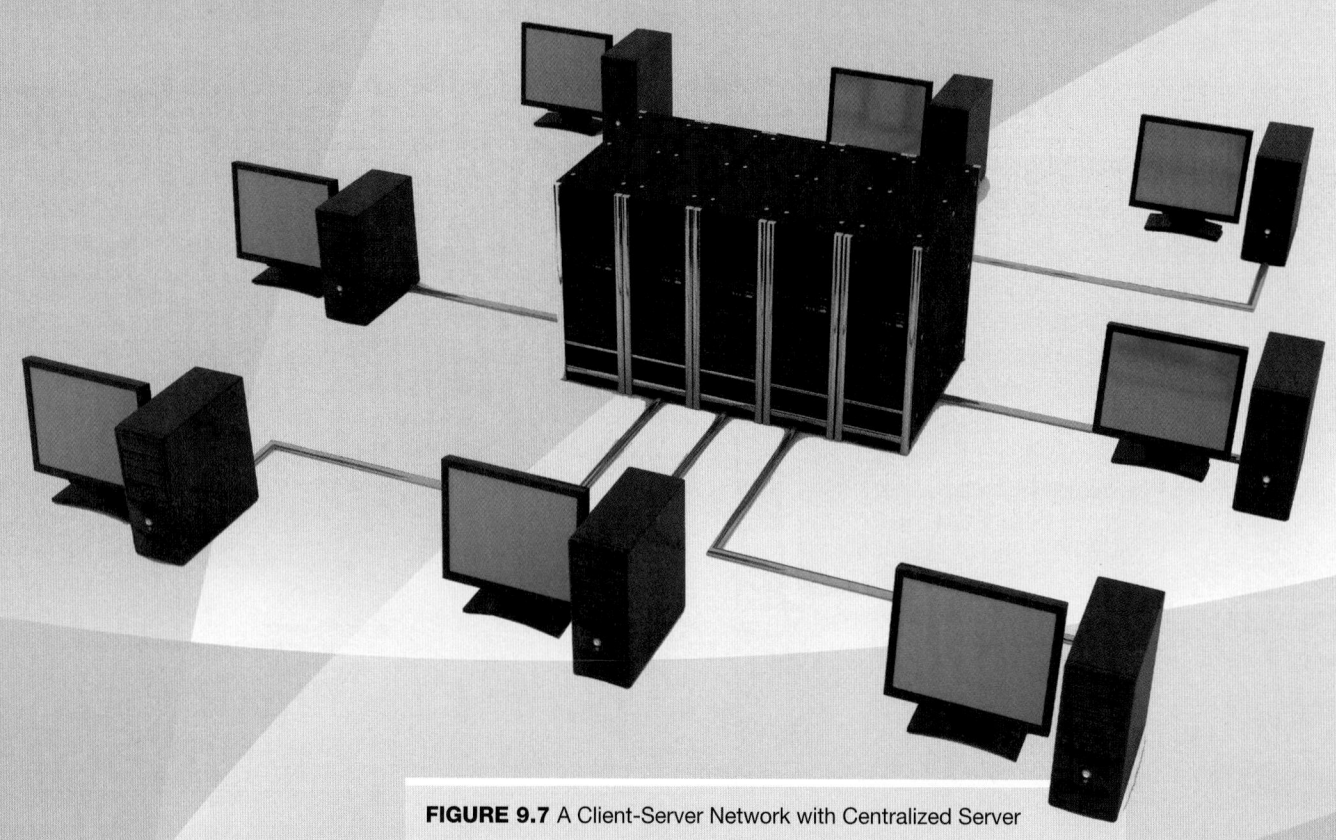

**FIGURE 9.7** A Client-Server Network with Centralized Server

# Find Out MORE

Windows Home Server is a NOS specifically designed to be used on a home network. Visit **windows.microsoft.com/en-US/windows/products/windows-home-server** to find out more about it. What features does it include? What are the hardware requirements? How much does it cost? Is it worth it?

## Try the Networks Simulation

SIMULATION

## Running Project

Select a computer network that you use (school, home, work). Is this a P2P or client-server network? How do you connect to it? What resources do you access/share on this network?

## 3 Things You Need to Know

- A computer network is two or more computers that share resources, such as software, hardware, or files.
- A peer-to-peer network (P2P) is one in which each computer belongs to the same workgroup and is considered an equal.
- A client-server network is one that has at least one server at its center that provides centralized management, resources, and security.

## Key Terms

client

client-server network

computer network

homegroup

network resource

peer-to-peer network (P2P)

server

workgroup

# HOW TO

## Share Files and Printers Using a Windows Homegroup

The Windows homegroup is an easy way to share files and printers on your home network. In this How To, you'll examine your current homegroup settings and share resources on your network. You must be using a Windows 7 or Windows 8 computer on a home network to complete this exercise. Before you begin, create a blank document named **lastname_firstname_ch09_howto1** to record your answers.

## PART A—CREATE A HOMEGROUP

**1a** First, check to see if your computer belongs to a homegroup. Open Explorer from the taskbar, and click *Homegroup* in the navigation pane. If there is no existing homegroup, Windows will give you the opportunity to create one. (Computers running Windows 7 Home Basic edition can join but can't create a homegroup.) If you see this message, click *Create a homegroup*. Take a screen shot of this window, and paste it into your document. If you do not see the option to *Create a homegroup*, skip to Part B.

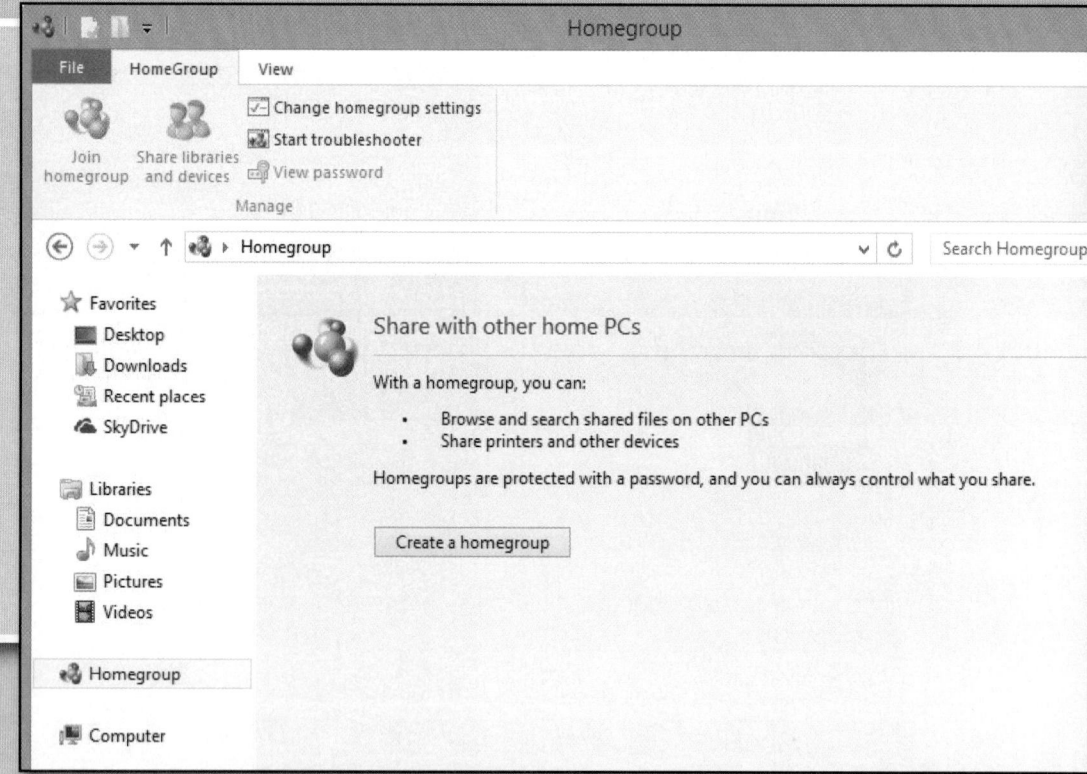

**2a** Choose what you want to share and then click *Next*. Which resources were shared by default? Which resources did you choose to share? A homegroup password is automatically generated. Use this password on your other Windows 7 or 8 computers to join the homegroup.

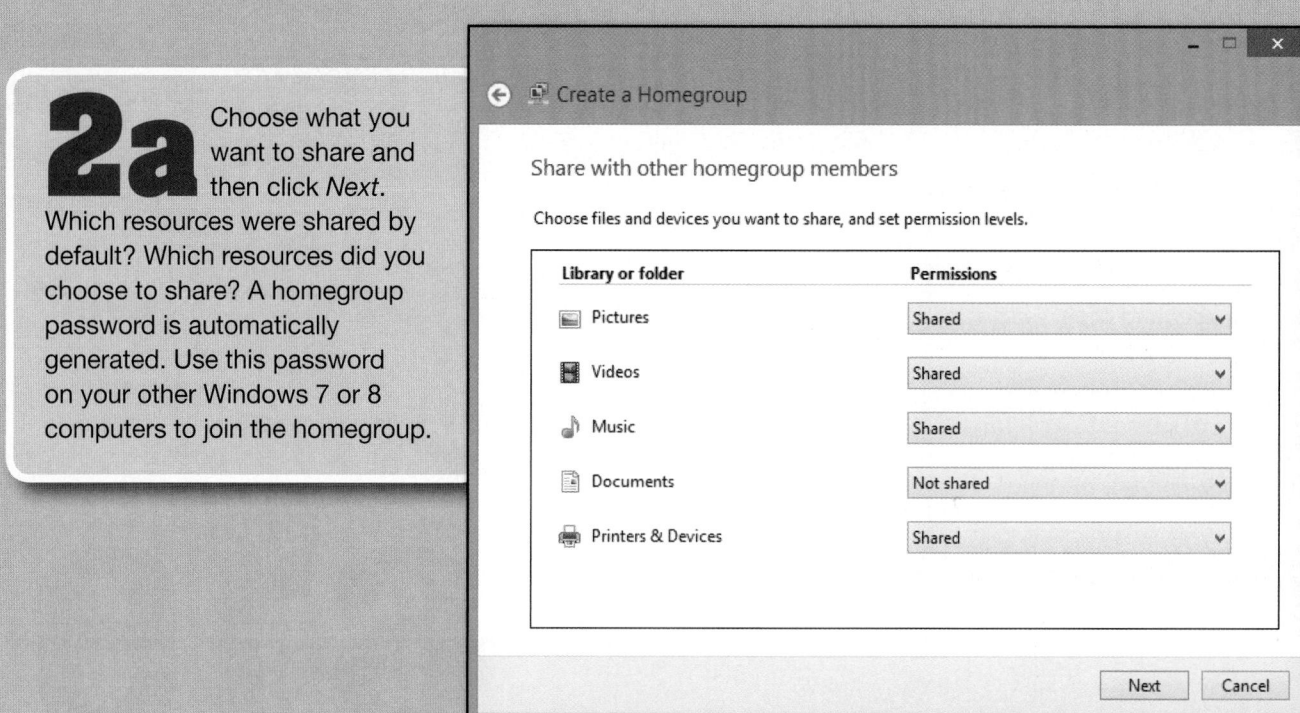

# PART B—JOIN A HOMEGROUP

**1b** Open Explorer from the taskbar, and click *Homegroup* in the navigation pane. If you don't belong to a homegroup but Windows detects one, you'll see the message Share with other home computers. Click *Join now*. (If you already belong to a homegroup, skip to Part C.)

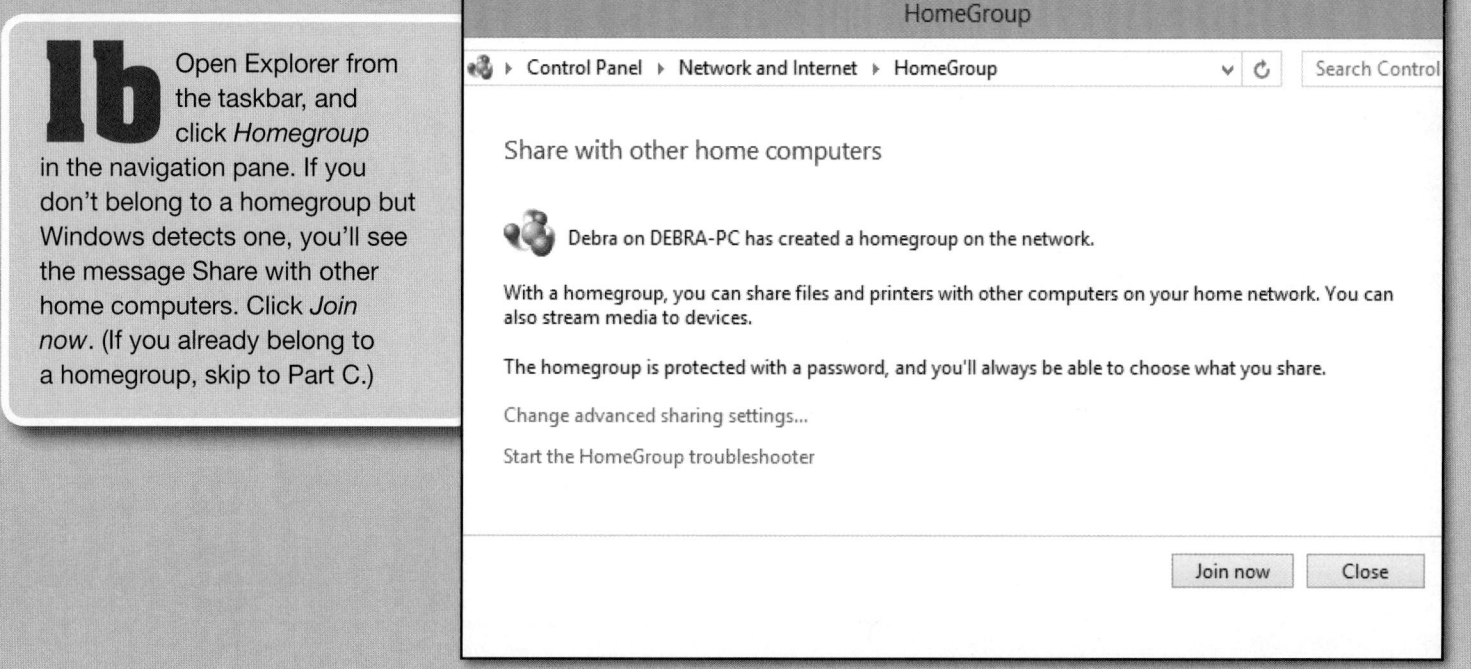

## 2b

Choose what you want to share, and click *Next*. You'll need the homegroup password to continue. Enter the homegroup password, and click *Next*. (If you don't have the homegroup password, you can find it on any computer that belongs to the homegroup by opening the Network and Sharing Center and clicking *Choose homegroup and sharing options* and then clicking *View or print the homegroup password*.)

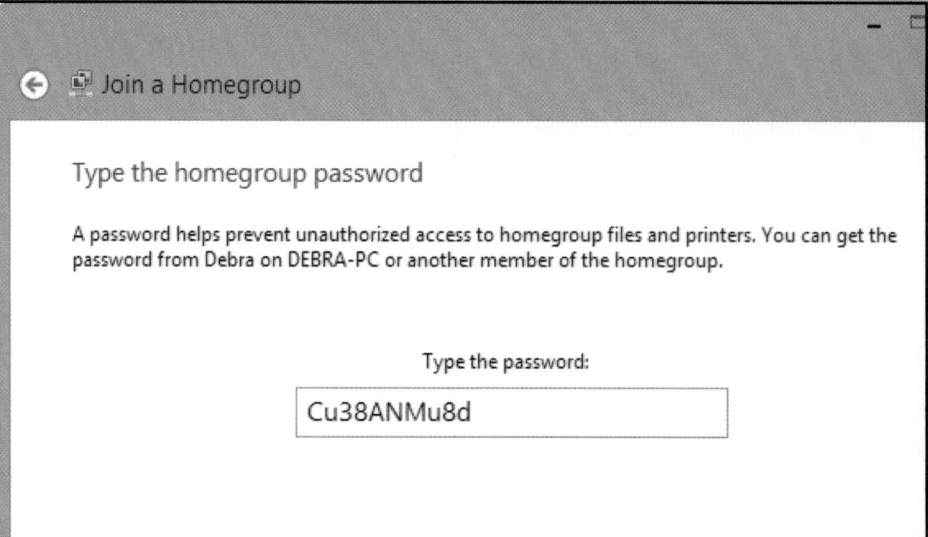

# PART C—EXAMINE HOMEGROUP SETTINGS

## 1c

On a computer that belongs to a homegroup, open File Explorer, click *Desktop*, and then open the Control Panel. Click *Choose homegroup and sharing options*.

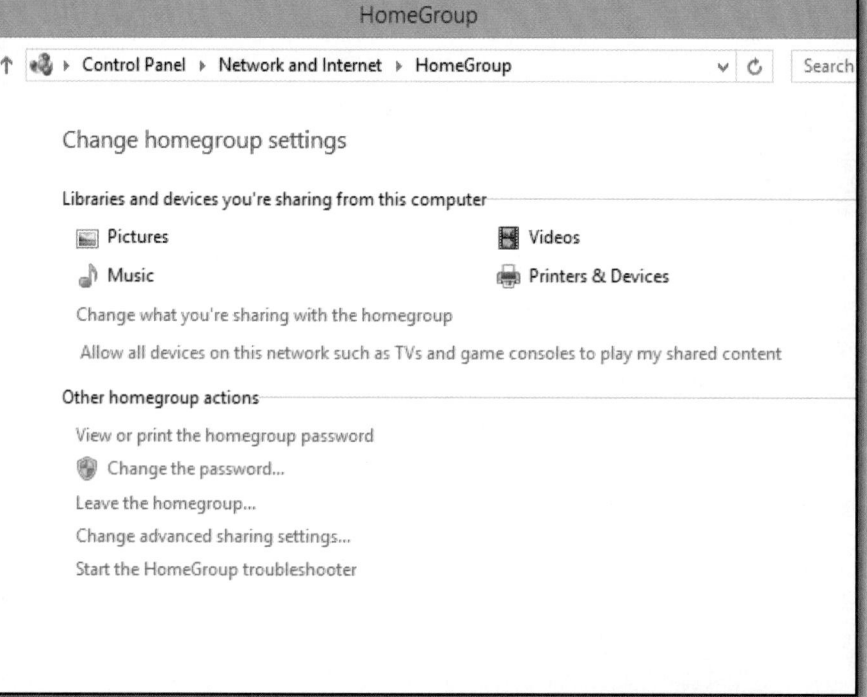

**2c** Under Libraries and devices you're sharing from this computer, click *Change what you're sharing with the homegroup*. Check the resources that you want to share, take a screen shot of this window, and paste it into your document. Click *Next* and then click *Finish*.

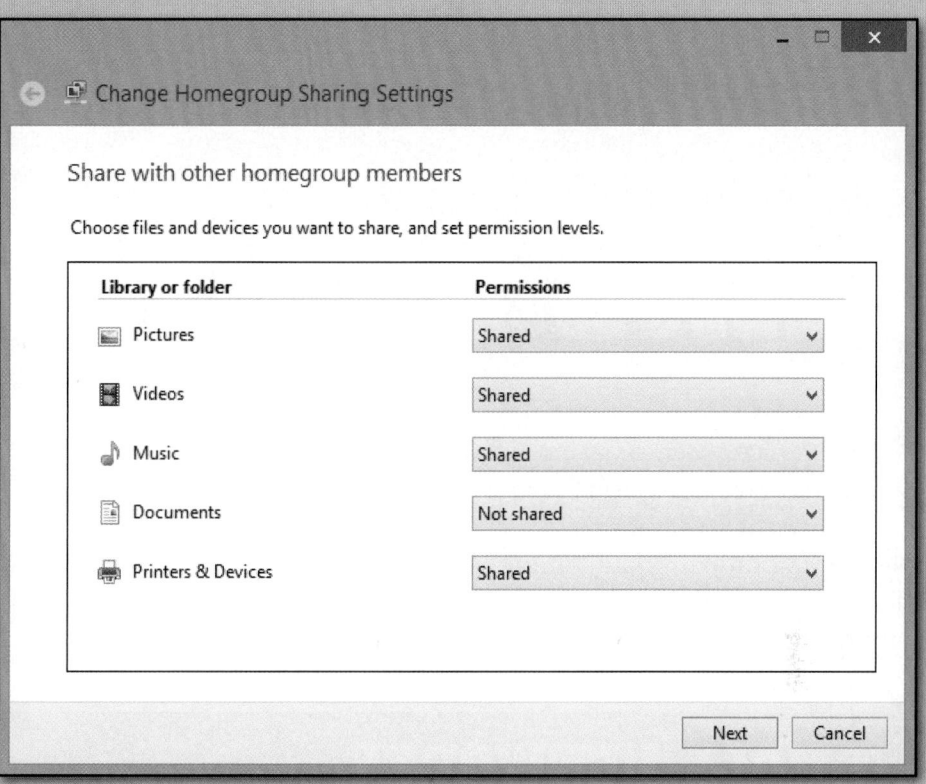

**3c** In the Homegroup Control Panel, click *Allow all devices on this network such as TVs and game consoles to play my shared content*. Are there any such devices on your network? Take a screen shot of this window and paste it into your document.

**4c** Type up your answers, including the screen shots, save your file as **lastname_firstname_ch09_howto1** and submit as directed.

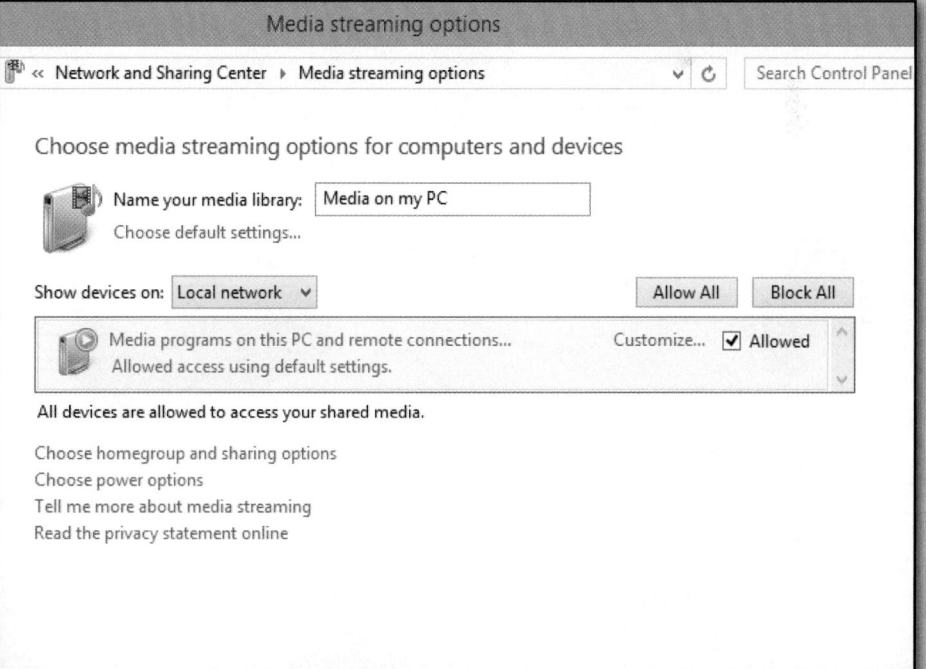

# LANs and WANs

## 2 OBJECTIVE
## Compare different types of LANs and WANs.

Networks come in many different shapes and sizes. In this article, we discuss some of the most common types of networks you'll find in both homes and businesses.

### SMALL NETWORKS

A **local area network (LAN)** is a network that has all connected devices or nodes located in the same physical location. On a small scale, a home network is a LAN. In a business, a LAN might consist of a single room, a floor, a building, or an entire campus. A home LAN is likely to be a peer-to-peer network, whereas a business LAN is more likely to be a client-server network and consist of computers, printers, and servers as well as the network hardware that connects them (see Figure 9.8). Devices on a LAN are connected using switches.

Servers

**FIGURE 9.8** A Client-Server LAN Configuration.

A small network that consists of devices connected by Bluetooth, such as a smartphone and a computer, is referred to as a **personal area network (PAN)**. Bluetooth has a very limited range of only about 10 to 100 meters (30 to 300 feet). The most common Bluetooth radio used for personal electronics is a low-power Class 2 radio, with a range of 30 feet and a data transfer rate of up to 3 Mbps. Bluetooth is designed to be easy to use, allowing devices to talk to each other securely over short distances. Each device in a PAN can connect to up to seven other devices at a time. Some common devices that might use Bluetooth include mice, keyboards, interactive whiteboards, headsets, cell phones, cameras, media players, video game consoles, and printers (see Figure 9.9). A **wireless LAN (WLAN)** is one that uses WiFi to transmit data. WiFi has a much larger range, higher speeds, better security, and supports more devices than Bluetooth, but it is also more expensive and complicated to set up.

**FIGURE 9.9** A Personal Area Network Using Bluetooth Devices: Mouse, Keyboard, and Headset

**LAN TOPOLOGIES** A home LAN uses the same Ethernet standards and equipment used in larger business networks. **Ethernet** defines the way data is transmitted over a local area network. Although there are other network standards, Ethernet is by far the most widely implemented. Standards are important because they assure that equipment that is made by different companies will be able to work together. Ethernet networks transmit signals over twisted-pair cable, fiber-optic cable, and WiFi at data transmissions speeds of 10 Mbps to as much as 10 Gbps. The maximum speed depends on the type of media and capability of the network hardware on the LAN. Most home networks use 100 Mbps Ethernet.

The physical layout of a LAN is called its **topology**. The devices, or nodes, on the LAN can be connected in many different configurations. The most common configurations are bus, ring, or star (see Figure 9.10). In a bus topology, the nodes are all connected via a single cable. The data travels back and forth along the cable, which is terminated at both ends. In a ring topology, the devices are also connected to a single cable, but the ends of the cable are connected in a circle and the data travels around the circle in one direction. Both buses and rings are simple networks that were popular in the past; however, you are not likely to find a pure bus or ring network today. Modern LANs use a physical star topology (or a hybrid star-ring or star-bus topology). In a star topology, every node on the network is attached to a central device such as a switch, router, or wireless access point. This connection device allows nodes to be easily added, removed, or moved, without disrupting the network.

**FIGURE 9.10** Bus, Ring, and Star Topologies

# LARGE NETWORKS

A **wide area network (WAN)** is a network that spans multiple locations and connects multiple LANs over dedicated lines using routers. A college that has multiple campuses would need to use WAN connections between them (see Figure 9.11). WAN technologies are slower and more expensive than LAN technologies. At home, the WAN you connect to is the Internet, and the port on your router that connects to the modem is labeled WAN (or Internet) port, distinguishing it from the LAN ports your other devices connect to.

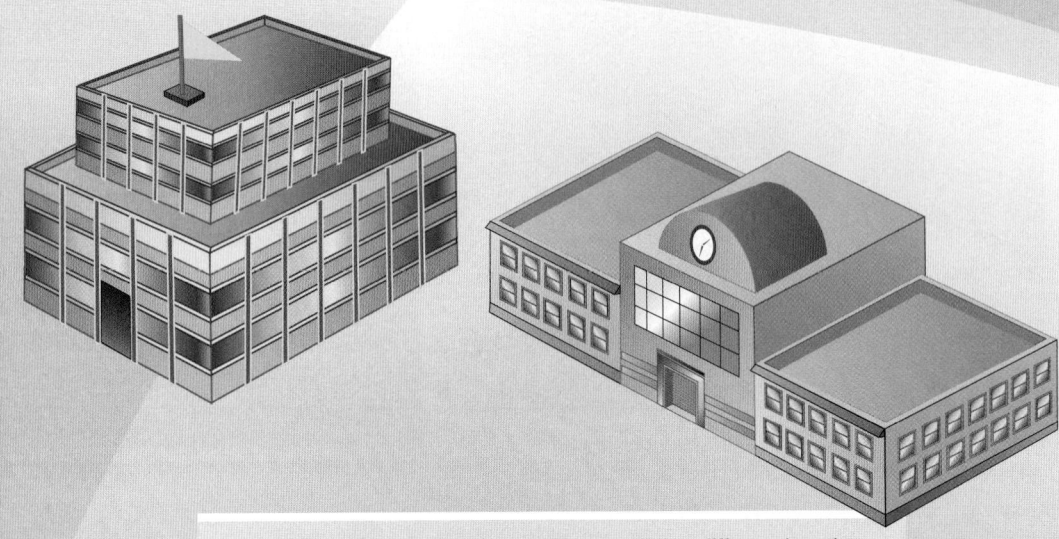

**FIGURE 9.11** A WAN connects LANs located at different locations.

Internet

VPN tunnel

**FIGURE 9.12** A VPN creates a virtual private network through the public Internet.

What if you need to connect to your work network from home or while on the road? Because you're located in a different location, you must use a WAN connection to access your work network, but it wouldn't be practical for a business to provide its employees dedicated WAN lines from every offsite location. Instead, companies use a special type of connection called a **virtual private network (VPN)** (see Figure 9.12). A VPN creates a private network through the public network (Internet), allowing remote users to access a LAN securely without needing dedicated lines. This is much less expensive and more practical for businesses, and in some cases, a VPN even replaces the need for dedicated lines completely. VPNs use encryption to ensure the data is secure as it travels through the public network.

Somewhere in between a LAN and a WAN is an enterprise network. In a business that is too large and has too many computers to manage a single LAN practically, there may be multiple LANs located in the same location. These LANs are connected to each other using routers—technically making them WANs. This hybrid is sometimes called a **campus area network (CAN)**. A network that covers a single geographic area—such as Wireless Philadelphia, which provides WiFi access over much of the city—is called a **metropolitan area network (MAN)**.

Companies that have massive amounts of information to move and store may have a **storage area network (SAN)** between the data storage devices and the servers on a network, making the data accessible to all servers in the SAN. Normal users are not part of the SAN but are able to access the information through the LAN servers.

**Cellular networks** use cell towers to transmit voice and data over large distances. The newest 4G networks have speeds that have made these networks a practical way for people on the move to connect to network resources, including the Internet and corporate VPNs from almost anywhere in the world.

Computer networks range from two personal computers sharing a printer to large enterprise networks to the Internet. The larger and more complex networks require more hardware, configuration, and expertise to manage, but they all have the same basic purpose: to share resources.

## Running Project

Make a list of networks that you use. Include home, cellular, work, and school networks. Label each as a LAN, WAN, or one of the other network types described in this article. List the devices you use to connect to each. What resources do you access?

## 5 Things You Need to Know

- A local area network (LAN) is a network that has all its nodes located in the same physical location.
- Wireless network types include Bluetooth personal area networks (PAN), WiFi wireless LANs (WLAN), and cellular networks.
- Ethernet is the standard that defines the way data is transmitted over a LAN. Topology describes the physical layout.
- A wide area network (WAN) is a network that spans multiple locations and connects multiple LANs.
- A VPN creates a private network through the public network (Internet).

## Key Terms

campus area network (CAN)

cellular network

Ethernet

local area network (LAN)

metropolitan area network (MAN)

personal area network (PAN)

storage area network (SAN)

topology

virtual private network (VPN)

wide area network (WAN)

wireless LAN (WLAN)

# Hardware

## List and describe the hardware used in both wired and wireless networks.

Every network has two major components: hardware to create the physical connections between devices and software to configure the resources and security. In this article, we look at the hardware needed to create different types of networks.

## NETWORK ADAPTERS

The hardware needed to set up a peer-to-peer network is much less complicated than what is needed in a client-server network. The simplest P2P network can consist of two devices sharing files using a wireless connection. For example, you can beam data from a smartphone or PDA directly to your computer or go head-to-head against a buddy by connecting your Nintendo DS games. Larger home networks with many types of devices require extra hardware to connect them.

Each device that connects to a network must have some type of network adapter. A **network adapter** is a communication device used to establish a connection with a network (see Figure 9.13). Most personal computers today come with a built-in Ethernet adapter. This type of connection, called an RJ-45, looks like a slightly larger phone jack. The cable used for this type of connection is called twisted-pair, Ethernet cable, or sometimes Cat-5e (or Cat-6). Depending on the size of the network you're connecting to, the other end of the cable might plug into a wall jack, a switch, a router, or a modem.

There are several advantages to using a wired network connection, including speed, location, and security. Network speed is measured in bits per second. Wired Ethernet connections can reach speeds of 1,000 megabits per second (also known as Gigabit Ethernet). Most home Ethernet connections use FastEthernet connections, which equal 100 Mbps. No wireless technology can currently reach the 1 Gbps speed, but some can equal or exceed the 100 Mbps speed. Another advantage is that a wired connection is less subject to interference and can travel long distances without slowing. A wireless connection that is 150 Mbps at close range might drop to less than half that speed at a distance of 300 feet. Buildings and other structures can slow or even prevent a wireless connection from working. Finally, a wired connection is more secure than a wireless connection, especially if the wireless connection is not configured with strong security settings.

There are several types of wireless network adapters. The WiFi networks found in homes and public hotspots use the IEEE 802.11 standards. The 802.11 standards ensure that devices developed by different vendors will work with each other. Notebook computers today come with a built-in

**FIGURE 9.13** A Built-in Ethernet Adapter Connected to an Ethernet Cable (left) and a USB Wireless Adapter (right)

wireless adapter. A USB wireless adapter can easily be connected to a desktop or notebook computer that does not have one built in. Wireless printers can be connected to a network directly, eliminating the need to be shared from an individual computer. Figure 9.14 compares the speeds of the most common types of WiFi connections.

The Wi-Fi Alliance certifies wireless devices to ensure interoperability. A WiFi network is also called a WLAN or Wireless Local Area Network. When two wireless devices connect to each other directly, they create an **ad hoc network**. In an **infrastructure wireless network**, devices connect through a wireless access point. A 3G or 4G adapter can be built into a smartphone or notebook computer and can be connected by USB to any computer, allowing you to use the cellular network for network access.

To view the network adapters that are installed on your computer, click the network icon on the taskbar, and click *Open Network and Sharing Center*. In the left pane, click *Change adapter settings*. This opens the Network Connections window, which lists all the network adapters on the machine and the status of each (see Figure 9.15). From here, you can manage your connections. This figure displays a 3G adapter, a Bluetooth adapter, a modem, a wired Ethernet adapter (Local Area Connection), and a wireless adapter. Most computers don't have all these.

| 802.11 STANDARD | MAXIMUM SPEED | DATE INTRODUCED |
|---|---|---|
| 802.11b | 11 Mbps | 1999 |
| 802.11g | 54 Mbps | 2003 |
| 802.11n | 300 Mbps–600 Mbps | 2009 |
| 802.11ac | 1.8–3.6 Gbps | 2012 |

**FIGURE 9.14** A Comparison of WiFi Standards

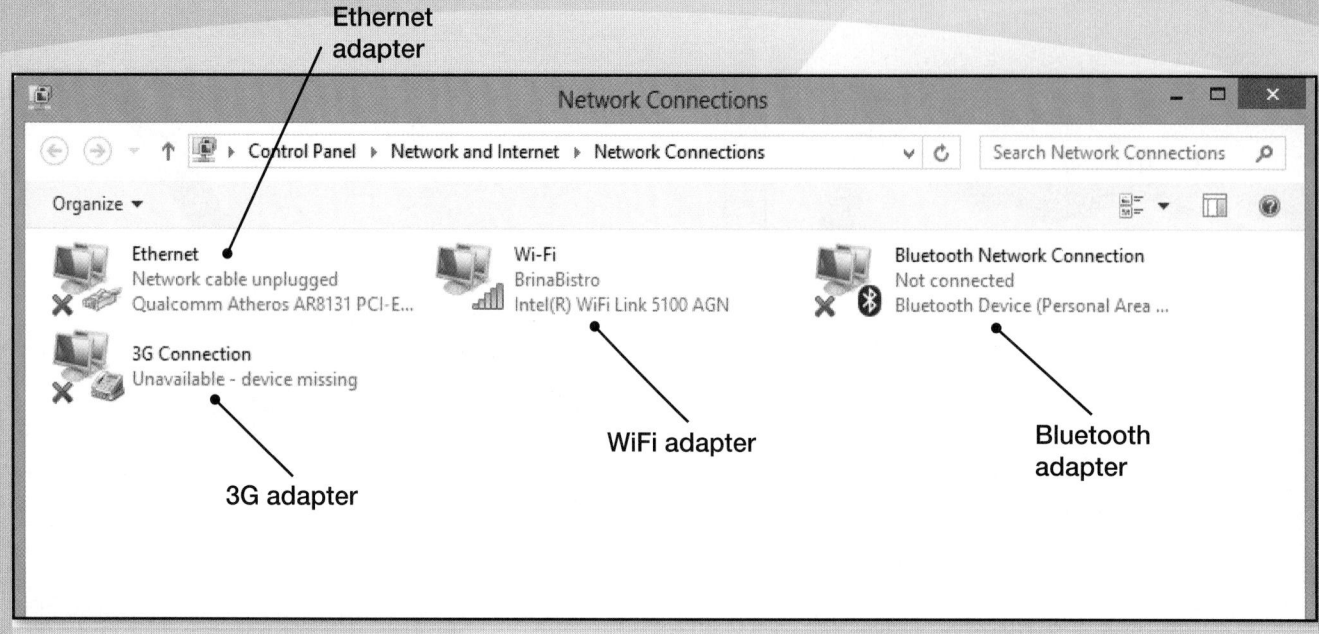

Ethernet adapter

3G adapter

WiFi adapter

Bluetooth adapter

**FIGURE 9.15** The Network Connections window shows several types of network adapters installed on this computer.

# NETWORK HARDWARE

To create networks with more resources and devices, you'll need some additional hardware. The first device on a network is usually the device that connects to the Internet. If you use a dial-up connection, this is an analog **modem**. Cable and DSL have special digital modems, and FTTH has an **optical network terminal (ONT)**. You can connect your computer directly to a modem or ONT, but you can share the connection with other devices more easily if you use a router instead.

A business network consists of routers, switches, wireless access points, and firewalls. Your home router serves all these functions. A **router** is a device that connects two or more networks together—for example, your home network and the Internet. A router uses address information to correctly route the data packets it receives. In a home network, the router is a convergence device that serves several functions: It shares the Internet connection, provides IP addresses to the other devices on the network, and, if configured correctly, provides security for your network.

Routers make up the backbone of the Internet and are responsible for sending the data packets along the correct route to their destination. If you think of the Internet as a map of highways, you'll realize that there are many different ways to get from one place to another. When you plan a trip, you take not only the distances into consideration but also traffic congestion and construction. You might make a detour if you run into a problem along your way. The shortest route is not always the fastest route. Routers serve the same function, routing data packets around traffic, collisions, and other impediments.

Home routers also include a built-in switch with several ports to connect multiple devices and can also serve as a wireless access point. A **switch** is a device that connects multiple devices on a LAN. Within the network, a switch uses address information to send data packets only to the port that the appropriate device is connected to. In the network shown in Figure 9.16, you can see a router with a built-in wired switch and wireless access point.

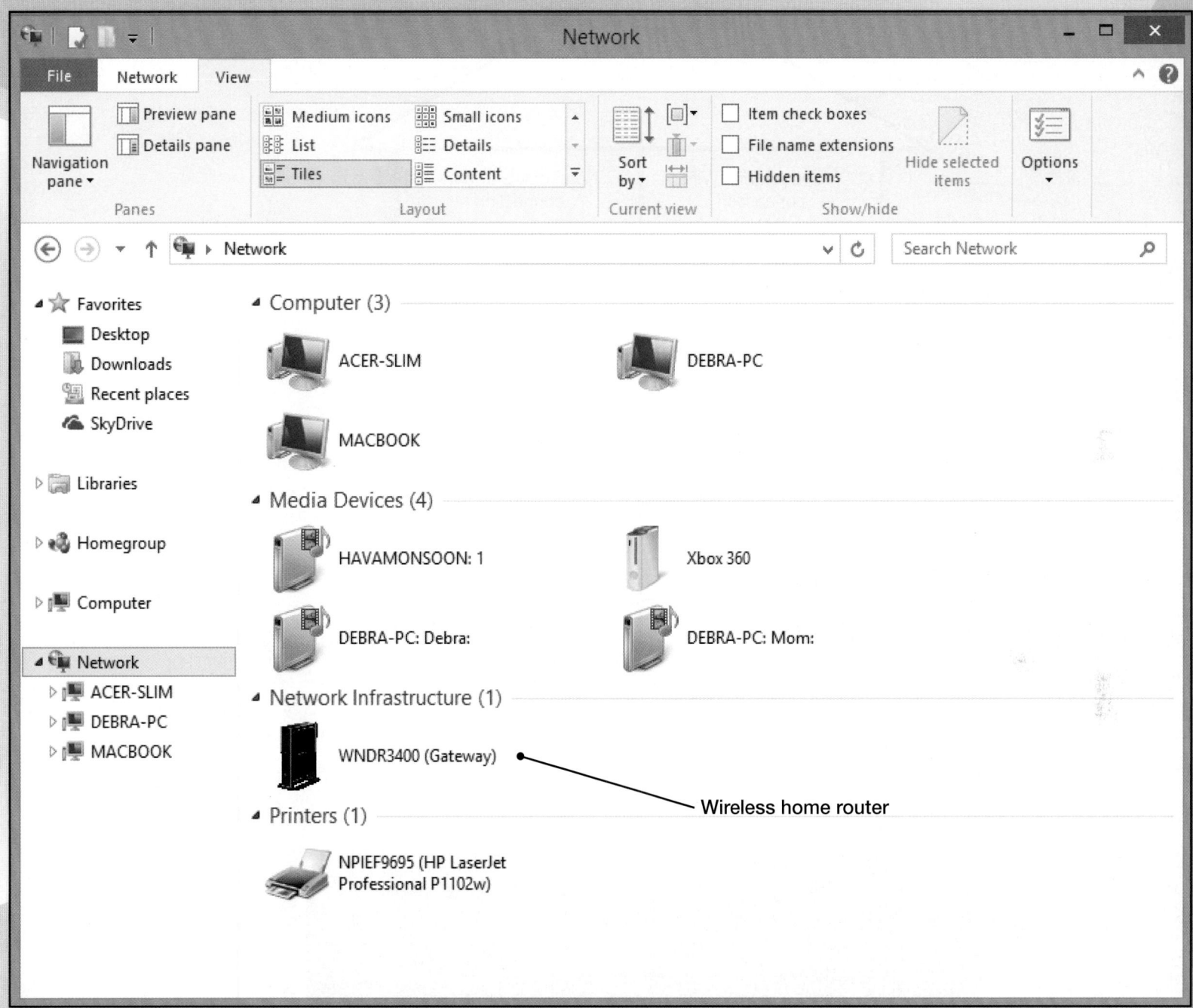

**FIGURE 9.16** In this network, a home network device serves as a router, wireless access point, and wired switch.

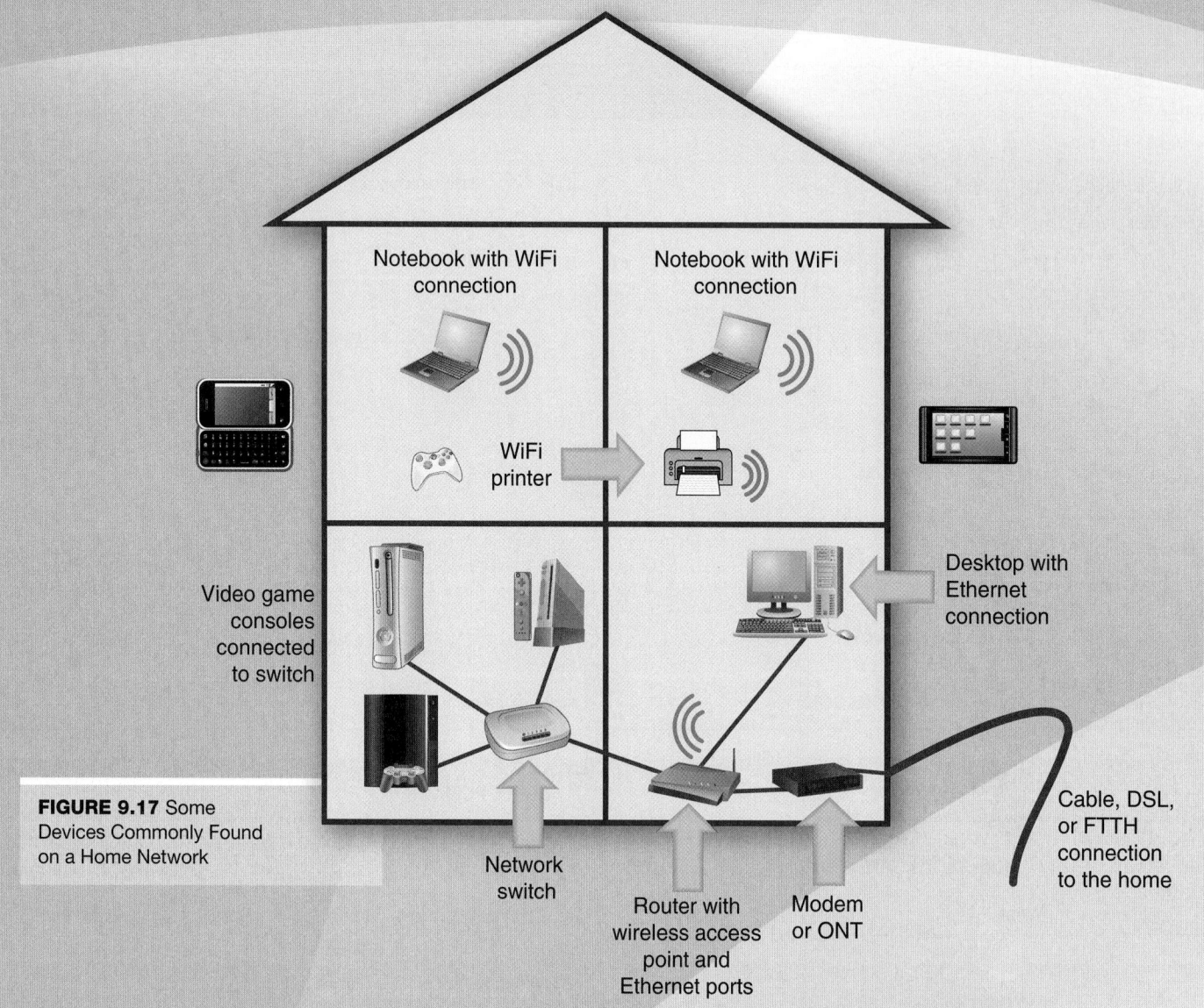

Notebook with WiFi
connection

Notebook with WiFi
connection

WiFi
printer

Desktop with
Ethernet
connection

Video game
consoles
connected
to switch

Network
switch

Router with
wireless access
point and
Ethernet ports

Modem
or ONT

Cable, DSL,
or FTTH
connection
to the home

**FIGURE 9.17** Some
Devices Commonly Found
on a Home Network

The switch has four ports so I can connect multiple devices (in my case: a Blu-ray player, Xbox 360, and PlayStation 3) to it using a single connection. These devices could also be connected wirelessly to my network if I didn't have a wired connection available.

To set up a WiFi network, you'll need a wireless access point. A **wireless access point (WAP)** is a device that allows wireless devices to join a network much like a switch. It can be built into a router or it can be a separate device. In a large wireless network, there may be many WAPs installed. In a home, one or two is usually enough to provide coverage, but in a larger building, many WAPs may be needed. Figure 9.17 shows a home network that includes both wired and wireless devices.

A **firewall** blocks unauthorized access to a network. There are both software firewalls, such as the one included with Windows, and hardware firewalls. A hardware firewall may be part of a router or a stand-alone device. Firewalls can check both outgoing and incoming data packets. A firewall can be configured with filters to allow/deny various kinds of traffic. Firewall filters can be based on IP address, protocol type, domain names, and other criteria. For example, a firewall might block access to certain websites or deny Internet access to certain computers during certain hours. Incoming packets that try to access restricted data will be denied access to the network.

The larger and more complex a network, the more hardware is necessary to assure the flow of data. These devices work together to transmit and filter data packets around the network and eventually to their destination. Without the network hardware, computers could not connect to each other.

## Running Project

Open the Network Connections window as described in this article. What adapters are installed on your computer? What type of networks do they connect to? Which of them are connected now? Include a screen shot of the window.

## 4 Things You Need to Know

- Each device that connects to a network must have a network adapter.
- The first device on a network connects to the Internet, typically a modem or optical network terminal (ONT).
- A router connects two or more networks together; a switch connects multiple devices on a network.
- A firewall blocks unauthorized access to a network.

## Key Terms

ad hoc network

firewall

infrastructure wireless network

modem

network adapter

optical network terminal (ONT)

router

switch

wireless access point (WAP)

# Software and Protocols

## OBJECTIVE

## List and describe the software and protocols used in both wired and wireless networks.

Network hardware allows devices to physically connect to each other, but it's the software and protocols that allow them to communicate with and understand each other. In this article, we look at network operating systems, communication software, and protocols that make a network work.

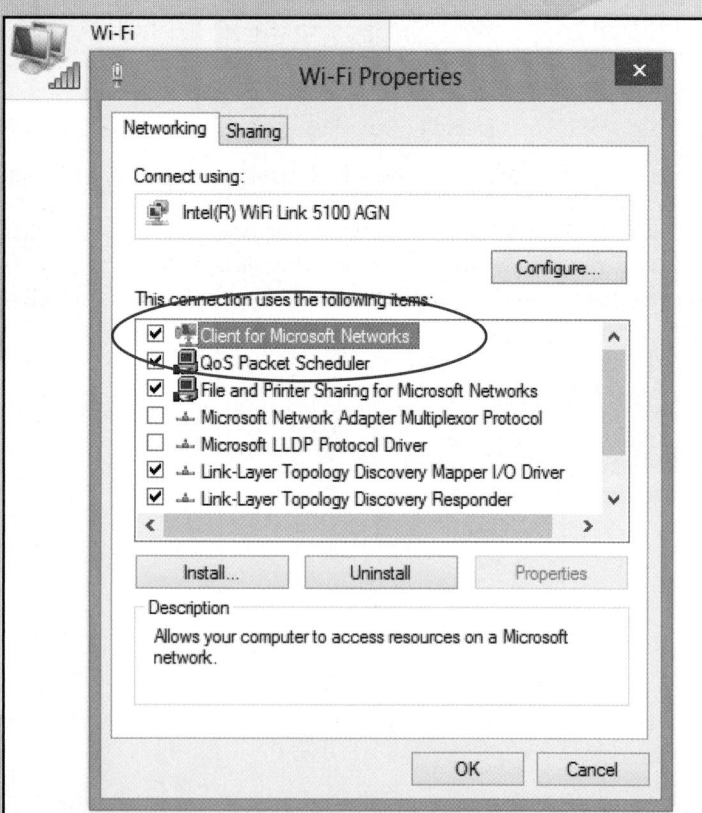

FIGURE 9.18 The properties for the Local Area Connection show the Client is installed.

## PEER-TO-PEER NETWORK SOFTWARE

No special software is required to create a simple peer-to-peer network. Modern desktop operating systems have networking capabilities built into them. When Windows is installed on a computer, it includes a feature called Client for Microsoft Networks, which allows it to remotely access files and printers on a Microsoft network. To verify that the Client for Microsoft Networks is installed on your computer, you can view the network adapters that are installed on the computer. Open the Network and Sharing Center from the taskbar, click *Change adapter settings* in the left pane, right-click the active adapter, and choose *Properties* to open the properties dialog box for the connection (see Figure 9.18).

Using the workgroup feature of Windows allows you to share and remotely access files on a Windows network. To connect to computers running Mac OS X to a Windows network, you may need to change some configuration settings on the Mac. In particular, you'll need to be sure the Mac has account information and Windows file sharing (SMB) configured. OS X includes Windows File Sharing, and its network discovery tool should locate your Windows computers automatically. It's also possible to include a Linux computer on a Windows network, but each version has a somewhat different method to do so. Figure 9.19 shows an Ubuntu Linux computer connecting to a Windows network. If your network consists of computers running the same OS, then network configuration should be easy. These computers are able to detect and share resources with each other with little or no configuration on your part.

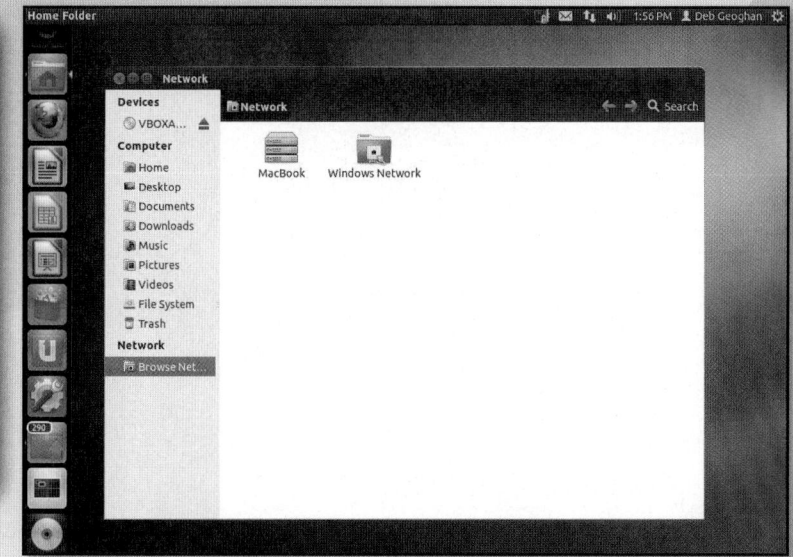

**FIGURE 9.19** An Ubuntu Linux computer can detect a Windows network.

# CLIENT-SERVER NETWORK SOFTWARE

As the name implies, both client software and server software are needed on a client-server network. The client software makes requests, and the server software fulfills them.

In a network where the servers run the Microsoft Server OS, Windows clients don't need any special client software for basic file and print services. Instead, they use the same Client for Microsoft Networks used in peer-to-peer networks to connect to the servers. A **domain** is a network composed of a group of clients and servers under the control of one central security database on a special server called the domain controller. You only need to log in to the domain once to have access to all the servers in the domain. So, in a network with multiple servers, you don't need to log in to each one individually. The security database includes your user information—who you are, what your password is, and what your access and restrictions are.

Clients log in to a server and request access to resources. For many types of servers, a special client is needed. When you use your Web browser to access your email, it serves as an email client. The browser can also act as an FTP client (when you download a file), a database client (when you access your bank transactions), and an HTTP client when you access a Web page. Other client software you may use includes VPN software, desktop email programs, instant messaging/chat programs, and even video and photo software that includes an upload feature.

Server software is also known as a network operating system. A **network operating system (NOS)** is a multiuser operating system that controls the software and hardware that runs on a network. It allows multiple computers (clients) to communicate with the server and each other, to share resources, run applications, and send messages. A NOS centralizes resources and security and provides services such as file and print services, communication services, Internet and email services, and backup and database services to the client computers.

Servers are classified by the type of services they provide. Some common services are file and print services, email, database, Web, chat, audio/video, and applications. Whenever you log in to a website such as Facebook or Gmail (see Figure 9.20), you're connecting to a server.

The most common network operating systems are Microsoft Windows Server, Linux servers (Red Hat, SUSE), UNIX servers (HP-UX, IBM AIX, Sun Solaris), and Novell servers (Netware, SUSE).

# NETWORK PROTOCOLS

Network hardware is what allows devices to connect to each other, but network protocols allow them to communicate. **Protocols** define the rules for communication between devices. These rules determine how data is formatted, transmitted, received, and acknowledged. Without protocols, devices could be physically connected and still unable to communicate.

Think about a meeting between two people. When you walk into the meeting, you greet the other person, perhaps shake hands, and exchange names. There are mutually agreed-on protocols as to how you begin the conversation (see Figure 9.21). Network protocols also define how a "conversation" between devices begins. This ensures that both are ready to communicate and agree on how to proceed. During the meeting, you also follow rules: what to say, how to say it, what language to speak, what's appropriate, and what's not. Protocols also define how devices converse in much the same way. Finally, at the end of your meeting, you likely stand up, shake hands, say good-bye, and depart. Protocols also define the method to end an electronic conversation.

Although there are hundreds of different protocols, the most important ones belong to the **TCP/IP protocol stack**. This is a suite of protocols that define everything from how to transfer files (FTP) and Web pages (HTTP) to sending (SMTP) and receiving (POP) email. **TCP** stands for transmission control protocol, and it's responsible for assuring that data packets are transmitted reliably. **IP** stands for Internet protocol, and it's responsible for addressing and routing packets to their destination. Both pieces are needed for data to move between devices. Figure 9.22 lists some of the important protocols in the TCP/IP stack and their functions.

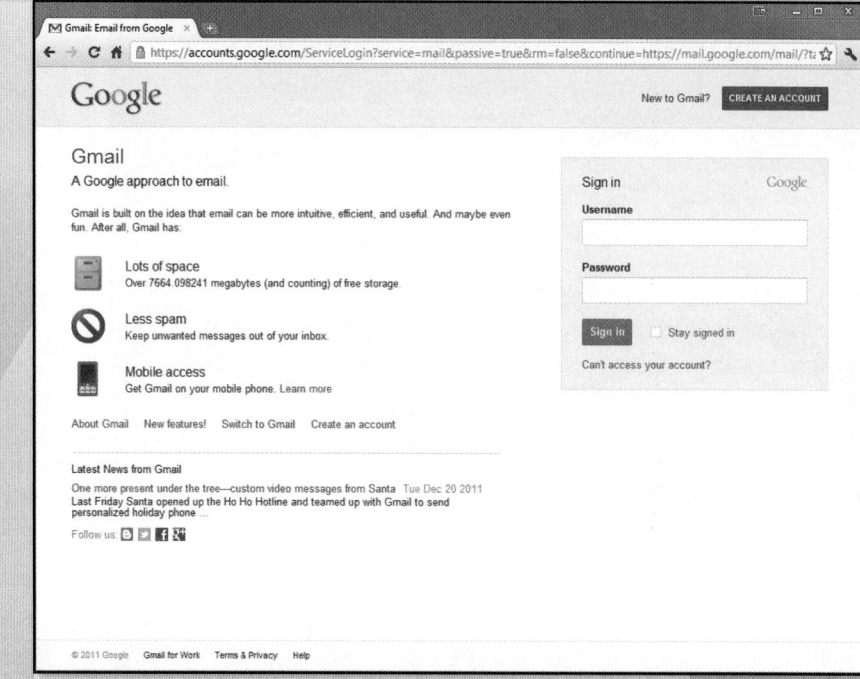

**FIGURE 9.20** You can use a Web browser as an email client.

**FIGURE 9.21** Protocols define how two devices (or people) communicate.

| PROTOCOL | FUNCTION |
|---|---|
| TCP (transmission control protocol) | Assuring that data packets are transmitted reliably |
| IP (Internet protocol) | Addressing and routing packets to their destination |
| HTTP (hypertext transfer protocol) | Requesting/delivering Web pages |
| FTP (file transfer protocol) | Transferring files between computers |
| POP (post office protocol) | Receiving email |
| SMTP (simple mail transfer protocol) | Sending email |
| DHCP (dynamic host configuration protocol) | Requesting/receiving an IP address from a DHCP server |
| DNS (domain name system) | Resolving a domain name such as www.ebay.com to an IP address |

**FIGURE 9.22** Some Important Network Protocols in the TCP/IP Stack

TCP/IP is the protocol stack that runs on the Internet, and because of this, it's also the protocol stack that runs on most LANs. TCP/IP is the default protocol stack installed on Windows, Mac, and Linux computers, and it's what allows them to communicate with each other easily. Figure 9.23 shows the adapter properties for the Local Area Connection. You can see that both TCP/IPv6 and TCP/IPv4 are installed. Currently, TCP/IP version 4 is used on the Internet and most LANs. Although many devices don't currently support TCP/IP version 6, that version is slowly being implemented and will eventually replace version 4 altogether. By default, Windows computers are set to Obtain an IP address automatically using the DHCP protocol. The computer sends out a DHCP request that's answered by a DHCP server (likely a router at home). Every computer on the network must have a unique IP address. This automatic configuration makes it easy to create a home network.

# Find Out MORE

Before the need for Internet access necessitated the use of TCP/IP, Mac computers used different protocols to talk to each other. Use the Internet to find out how they did this.

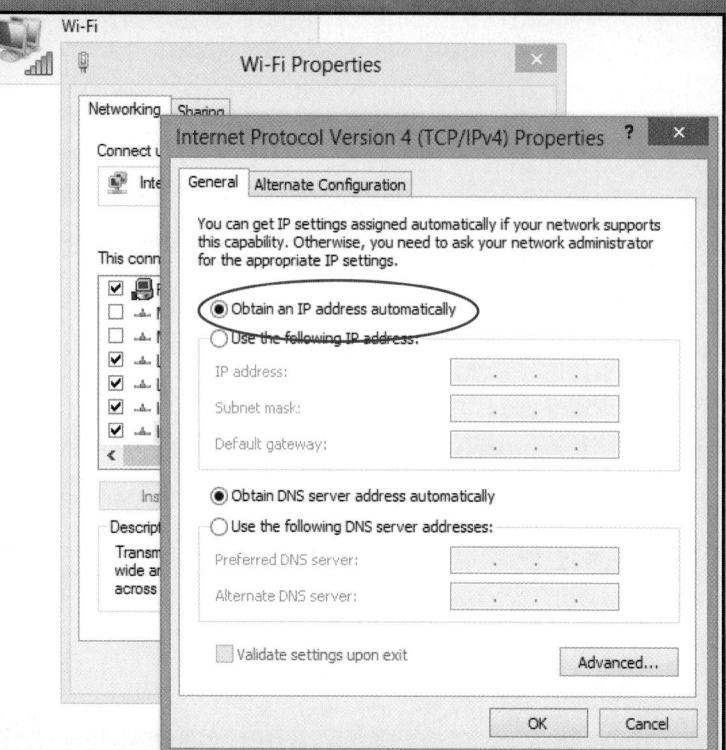

**FIGURE 9.23** Windows computers are set to use DHCP to obtain an IP address.

# GREEN COMPUTING

## SERVER VIRTUALIZATION

Technically, the term *server* refers to the server *software* on a computer, not to the hardware it runs on. So, a network server computer might actually run mail server, Web server, and file and print server software. The advantage to this is that a single physical computer can be several different servers at once. Server computers are high-end, with fast processors and lots of storage. Sometimes, the computer's capabilities aren't fully utilized, and its processors are idle much of the time. Virtualization takes advantage of this unused resource. A good example might be running both a Microsoft Exchange email server and an Apache Web server on the same computer. Each virtual server runs in its own space, sharing the hardware but not necessarily interacting with each other in any way. To the client, they appear to be separate servers.

Server virtualization is a big component of cloud computing. A company that offers IaaS (Infrastructure as a Service) can set up virtual servers for many small companies on a large enterprise server. This saves money and reduces the amount of hardware (and thus e-waste) needed for each business. Keeping servers in one location can also save in cooling and electric costs. IaaS is not just good for small companies. Joyent, one of the largest IaaS providers, hosts the social network LinkedIn and the online retailer Gilt Groupe.

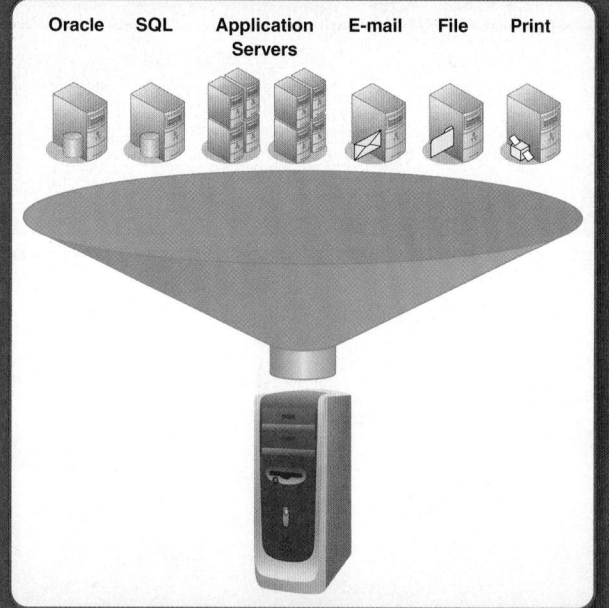

As with any computer system, the hardware of a network is useless without the software to make it work. In a network, that software also includes protocols to define the rules of communication. Together, the hardware, software, and protocols allow devices to share resources securely, efficiently, and (hopefully) easily.

## Running Project

Make a list of the networks you use. Include home, cellular, work, and school networks. List the software clients that you use to connect to each. What resources do you access? Do you use different clients to access different resources?

## 5 Things You Need to Know

- Peer-to-peer computers are able to detect and share resources with each other with little or no configuration.
- A domain is a network composed of a group of clients and servers under the control of the domain controller.
- Clients log in to a server and request access to resources.
- Server software allows clients to communicate with the server to share resources, run applications, and send messages.
- Protocols define the rules for communication between devices. TCP/IP is the protocol stack that runs on the Internet and on most LANs.

## Key Terms

domain

IP (Internet protocol)

network operating system (NOS)

protocol

TCP (transmission control protocol)

TCP/IP protocol stack

# HOW TO

## Examine Network and Sharing Settings

In this How To, you'll examine your current network settings and share resources on your network. (Note that in a school network, security settings may prevent you from being able to perform parts of this exercise.) Before you begin, create a blank document to record your answers. Save this file as **lastname_firstname_ch09_howto2.**

**1** Open the Network and Sharing Center from the taskbar or from the Control Panel, and click *Change adapter settings* in the Navigation pane. How many Network Connections do you have on this computer? Which ones are connected? Take a screenshot and paste it into your document.

**2** Locate the connection that you are currently using and double-click it to open the Connection Status window. Is this connection wired or wireless? What speed is the connection? Click the *Details* button. What is the IP address of this connection? What other information can you locate here? Take a screenshot and paste it into your document. Close the open dialog boxes and the Control Panel window.

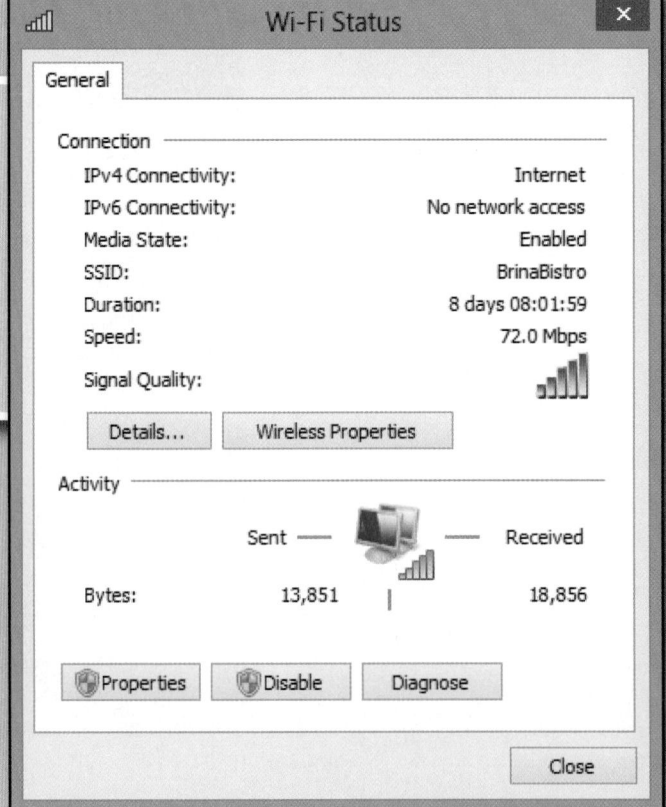

**3** Open File Explorer and click *Network* in the Navigation pane. List the other devices in your network. What resources do you access/share from/with these devices? Take a screenshot and paste it into your document.

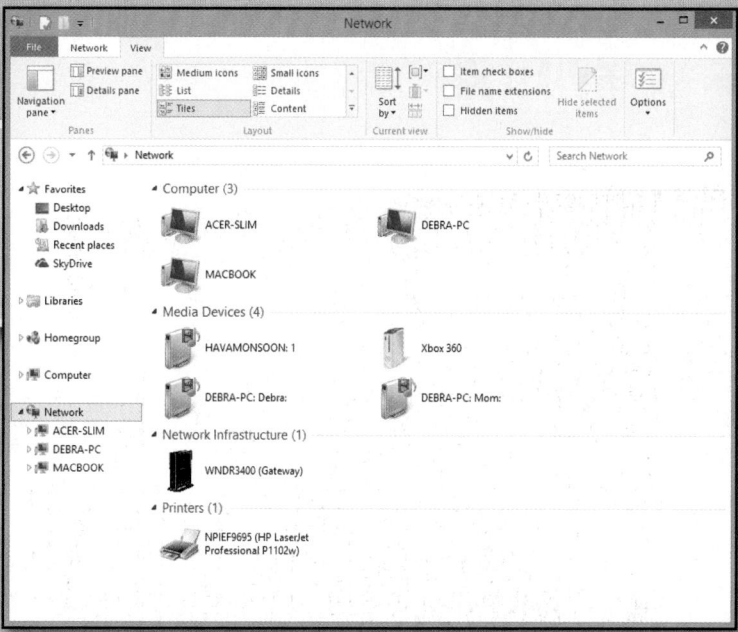

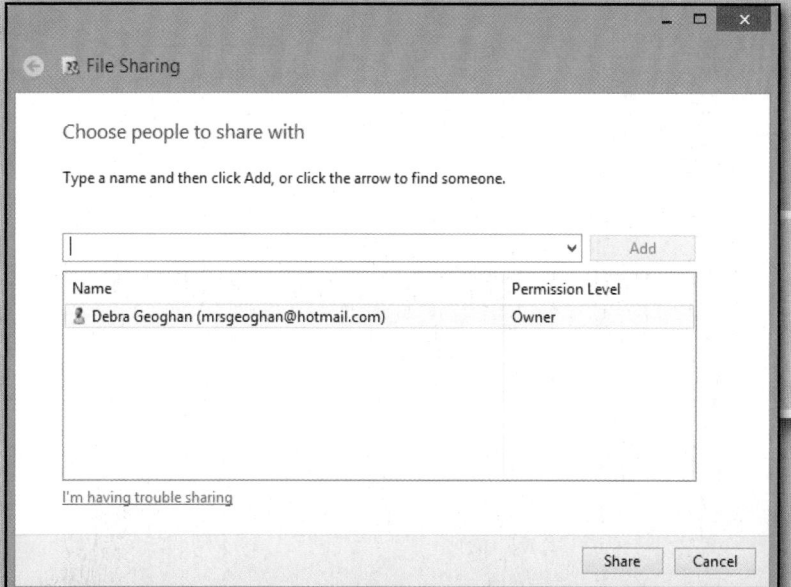

**4** In the Navigation pane, click *Homegroup*. Does your computer belong to a homegroup? If you see any other homegroup computers in the Explorer window, double-click to open one. What resources are shared with you?

**5** Right-click on the desktop and create a new folder called **myshare**. Right-click the new folder and point to Share with. By default, who is this folder shared with? Click *Specific people…* to open the File Sharing control panel. Click the down arrow next to Add. Who can you share this folder with? Choose *Everyone* and click *Add*. By default, what permissions are granted to Everyone? Take a screenshot and paste into your document. Click *Cancel* and then delete the folder.

**6** Save your file, including screen shots, as **lastname_firstname_ch09_howto2** and submit as directed.

**If you are using a Mac:**

1 Click the Apple menu, click *System Preferences*, and then click *Network*. How many network connections do you have on this computer? Which ones are connected? Take a screen shot and paste it into your document.

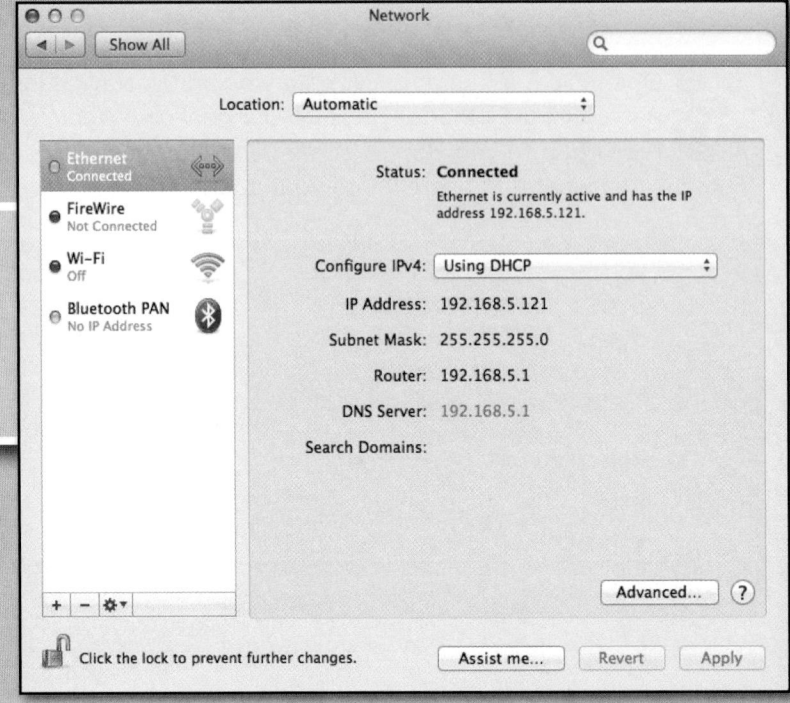

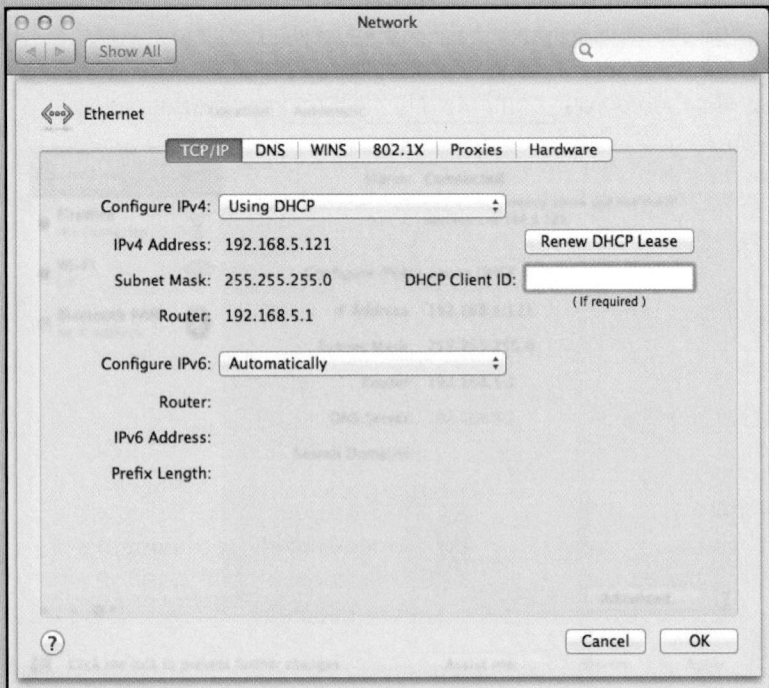

2 Click the connection that you are currently using. Is this connection wired or wireless? Click *Advanced*. What is the IP address of this connection? What other information can you locate here? Take a screen shot and paste it into your document.

**3** Open Finder from the Dock. In the Navigation pane, under SHARED, click *All*. List the other devices in your network. What resources do you access/share/ from/with these devices? Take a screen shot and paste it into your document.

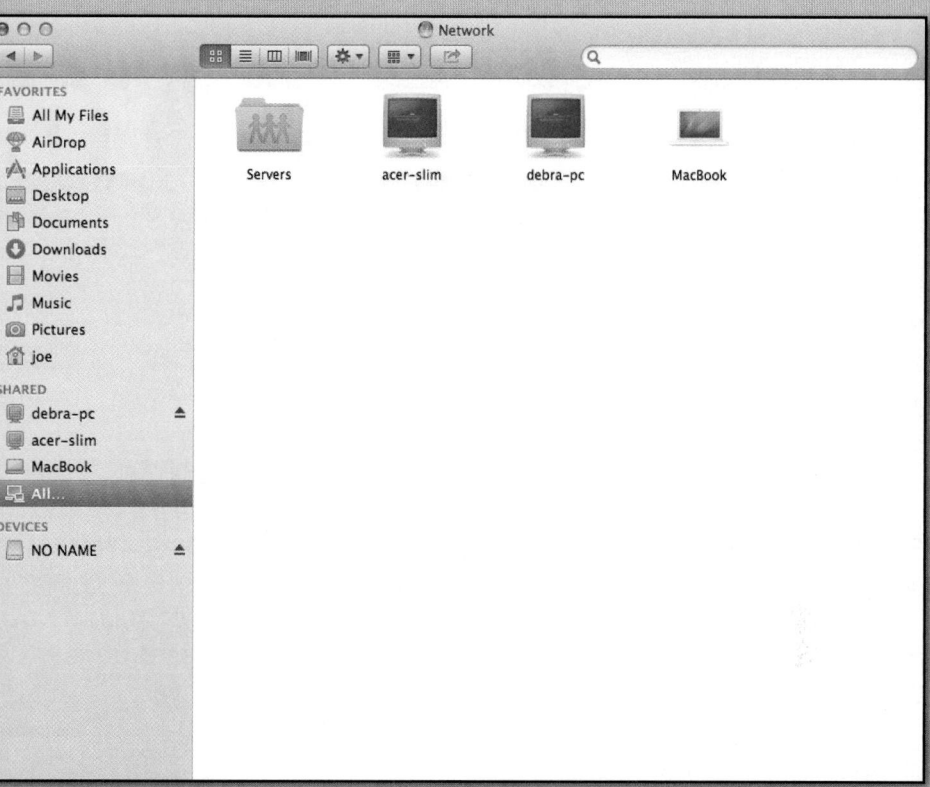

**4** In Finder, click *Desktop*. Click *File, New Folder*, and name the new folder **myshare**. Return to the System Preferences window and click *Sharing*. What resources are you sharing? Click *File Sharing*. What folders are shared?

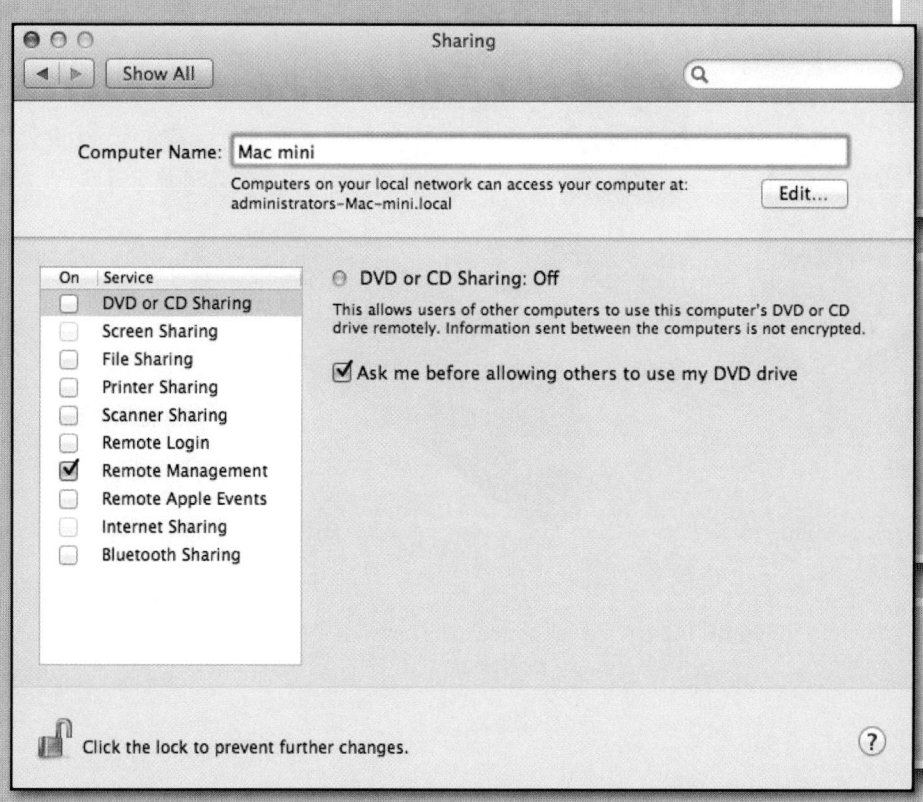

**5** Click *Options* and select *Share files and folders using SMB (Windows)* to make your shares accessible to Windows computers on your network. Click the + sign to share your new folder. Take a screen shot and paste it into your document. If you have a Windows computer on the same network, see if you can access your Mac files from it.

**6** Save your file, including screen shots, as **lastname_firstname_ch09_howto2** and submit as directed.

# Protecting Your Network

## 5 OBJECTIVE
## Explain how to protect a network.

A few years ago, network security was only a concern to network administrators in large businesses; today, with networks everywhere, it has become a larger problem. Just as you use layers of security at home—fences, door locks, alarm systems, and even guard dogs—the same approach should be used with network security.

## LAYER 1: THE FENCE

In a network, the fence is the hardware at the access point to your network (see Figure 9.24). In a home network, the hardware firewall is probably part of your router. In a business, the firewall is a stand-alone device. The firewall examines the data packets as they enter or leave your network and will deny access to traffic based on rules the network administrator defines. It also shields your computers from direct access to the Internet, hiding them from hackers looking for an easy target.

**FIGURE 9.24** A firewall protects the network.

# LAYER 2: DOOR LOCKS

In a network, door locks are represented by the network configuration, determining what's shared and who's granted access to it. Your usernames should have strong passwords that are hard to crack, and each user should be granted access only to what the user needs. Using no passwords, or passwords that are easy to guess—such as birthdays or pets' names—is equivalent to leaving your doors unlocked.

Windows and OS X allow you to create Standard users or Administrators, and also include Parental Controls. For normal use, it is wise to use a standard user account, which has less access to change system and security settings. An administrator account should be used only when necessary and be protected by a strong password (see Figure 9.25).

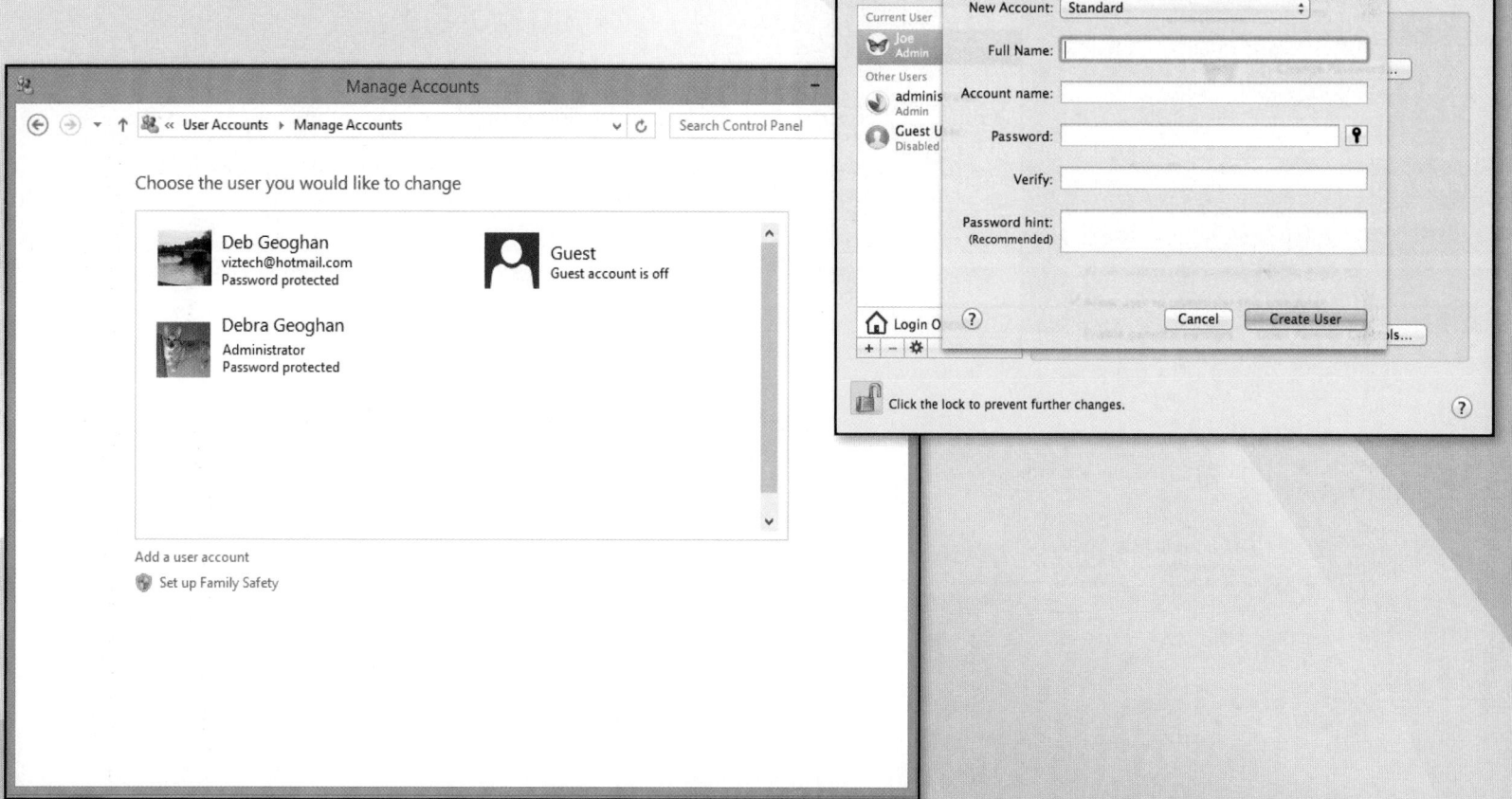

**FIGURE 9.25** Create a standard user for normal day-to-day computing.

# LAYER 3: ALARM SYSTEMS

The alarm system on a computer network includes software-based firewalls and antivirus and antimalware software on the individual computers on the network (see Figure 9.26). Your individual computers should be protected by software firewalls such as those included with Windows or OS X. If an intruder somehow breaches your network, software will detect unauthorized actions and prevent them.

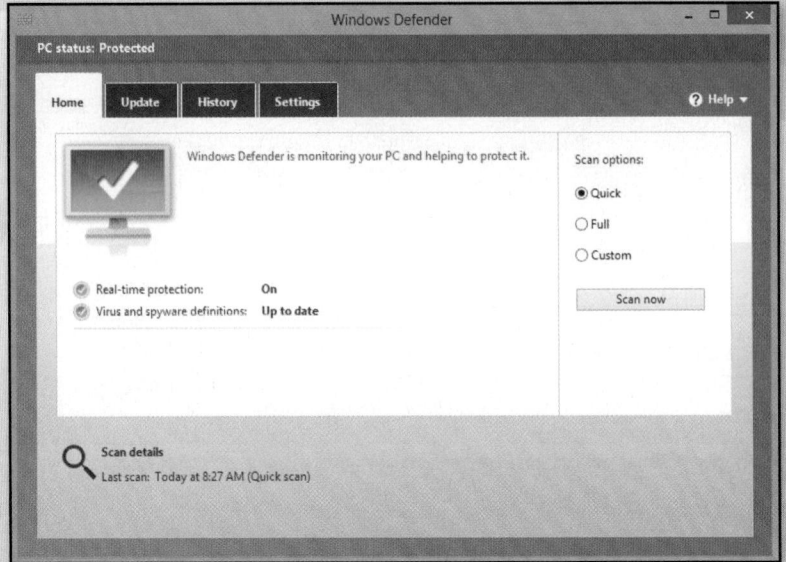

**FIGURE 9.26** Each computer on the network should have its own up-to-date security software installed.

# LAYER 4: GUARD DOGS

The network administrator (on a home network, that's you) needs to be diligent in keeping the systems on the network up to date and secure. Windows and OS X can be configured to automatically check for and install updates (see Figure 9.27), but other software applications can also be potential vulnerabilities and should be kept up to date as well. Unpatched systems are easy targets for hackers and can allow them access into your network.

Although you can never be completely secure, it *is* possible to make your home so difficult to break into to that the thief moves on to an easier target. That's also the goal with network security.

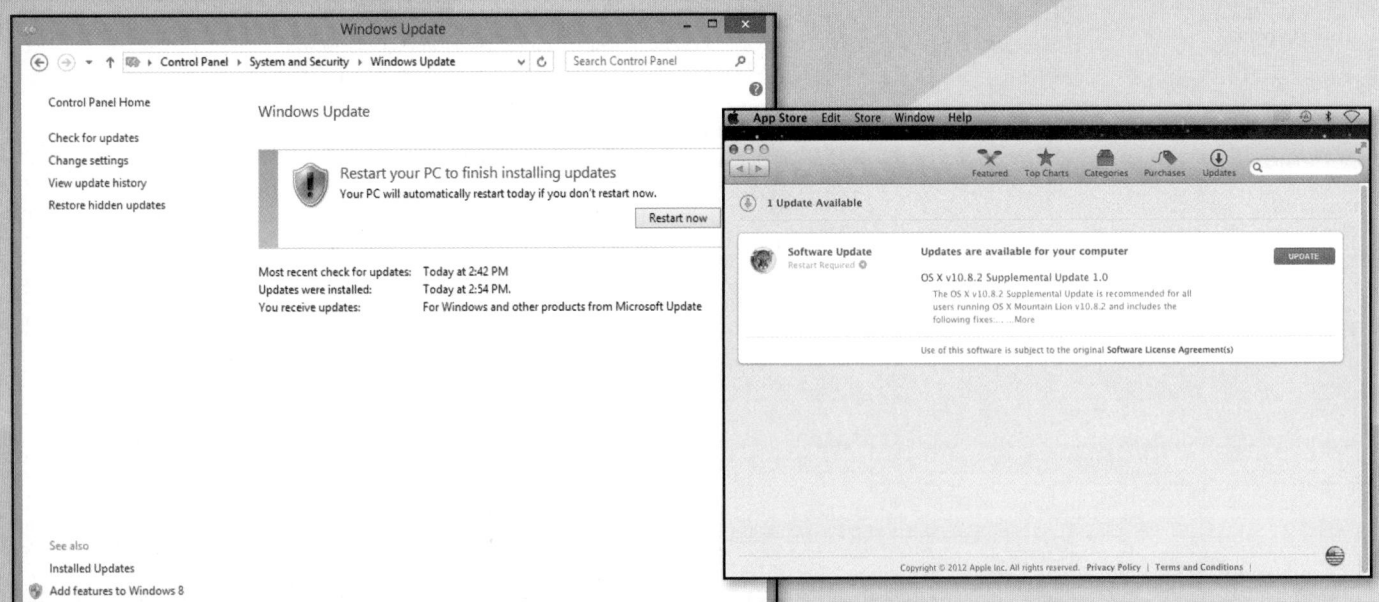

**FIGURE 9.27** Installing updates is a critical part of securing your systems.

ETHICS

The term **piggybacking** means using an open wireless network to access the Internet without permission. Many times, people intentionally use open wireless access. If an access point is left unsecured, they figure, "Why not?" In some places, it's illegal to use a network without authorization, but many statutes—if they exist at all—are vague. It's difficult to detect someone that's piggybacking. Still, it's unethical to use someone's connection without his or her knowledge.

To make things more confusing, some free hotspots—such as in cafes and hotels—might be accessible beyond the premises. So, a person sitting in a car parked on the street might be able to access the coffee shop hotspot intended for patrons of the shop.

The practice of wardriving is closely related. **Wardriving** means driving around and locating open wireless access points. There are communities on the Internet where wardrivers post maps of the open networks they find, along with free software that makes it easy to locate wireless networks. Wardrivers don't actually access the wireless networks, so the practice isn't illegal—but is it ethical? You decide.

# CAREER SPOTLIGHT

You'll find computer networks in every type of business, and knowing how to access network resources is a critical skill for most employees. A network administrator is the person responsible for managing the hardware and software on a network. The job may also include troubleshooting and security. Although not required, a two- or four-year college degree is helpful in this field, as are certifications. According to Salary.com, the average salary for a person in this field with 2–5 years of experience is about $64,000. As with any technical field, you should expect to continue your training to keep up with the changes in technology. An entry-level person may be called a network technician rather than an administrator.

The importance of networks and connectivity for most businesses requires employees that are experts at making networks secure and reliable. The *Occupational Outlook Handbook* predicts that network-related jobs will grow faster than the average for all occupations over the next decade, so considering a career in this field might be a good choice for you.

## 4 Things You Need to Know

- A firewall examines the data packets as they enter or leave your network.
- Network users should have strong passwords that are hard to crack and be granted access only to what they need.
- Individual computers on the network must be protected with firewalls and antivirus and antimalware software.
- Systems on the network must be kept up to date and secure.

## Key Terms

piggybacking

wardriving

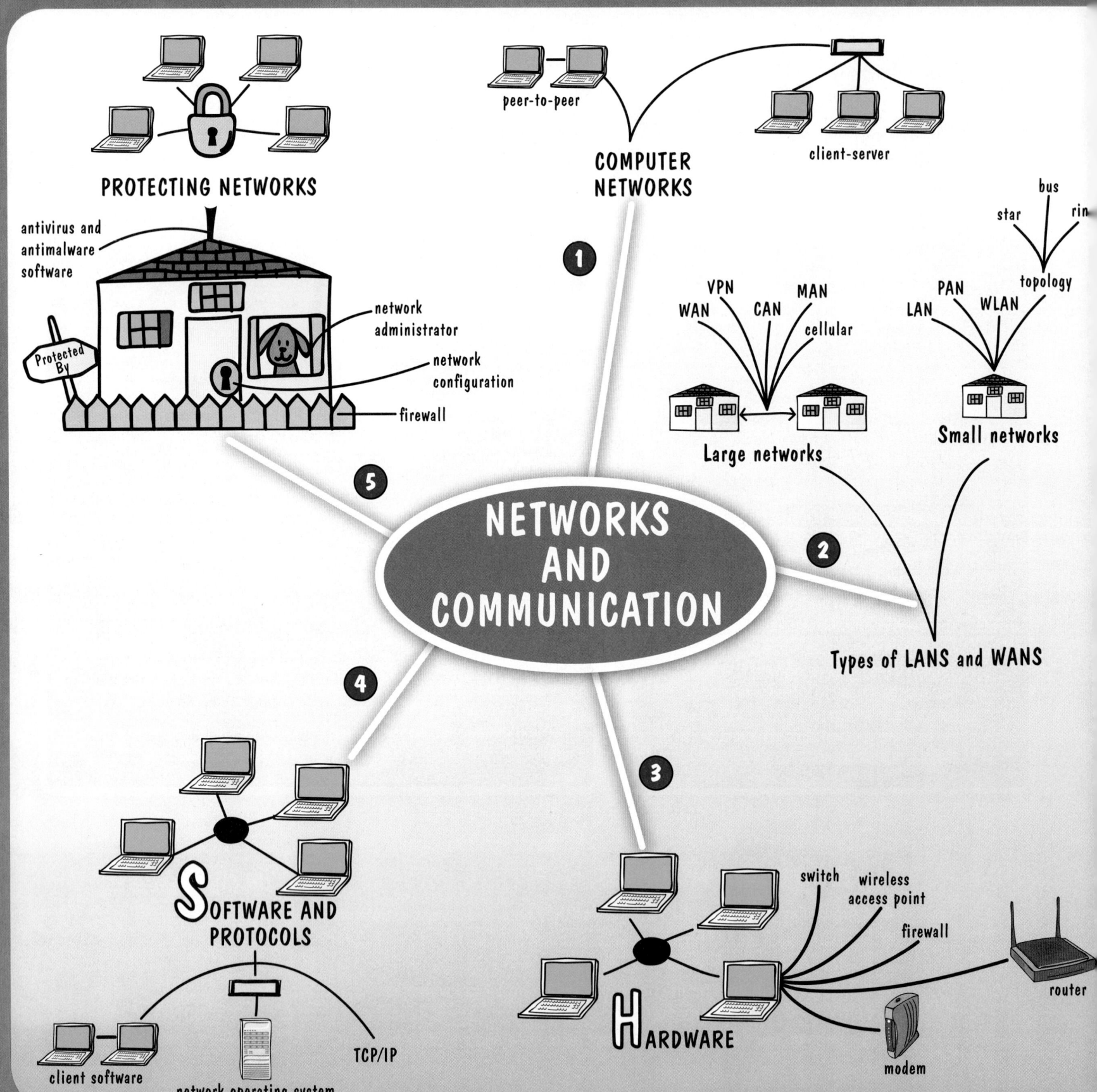

PROTECTING NETWORKS

antivirus and antimalware software

Protected By

network administrator

network configuration

firewall

COMPUTER NETWORKS

peer-to-peer

client-server

bus

star

ring

topology

VPN

WAN

CAN

MAN

cellular

PAN

LAN

WLAN

Large networks

Small networks

NETWORKS AND COMMUNICATION

1

2

3

4

5

Types of LANS and WANS

SOFTWARE AND PROTOCOLS

client software

network operating system

TCP/IP

HARDWARE

switch

wireless access point

firewall

router

modem

# Objectives Recap

1. Discuss the importance of computer networks.
2. Compare different types of LANs and WANs.
3. List and describe the hardware used in both wired and wireless networks.
4. List and describe the software and protocols used in both wired and wireless networks.
5. Explain how to protect a network.

# Key Terms

ad hoc network **373**
campus area network (CAN) **371**
cellular network **371**
client **362**
client-server network **362**
computer network **358**
domain **379**
Ethernet **369**
firewall **377**
homegroup **360**
infrastructure wireless network **373**
IP (Internet protocol) **380**
local area network (LAN) **368**
metropolitan area network (MAN) **371**
modem **374**
network adapter **372**
network operating system (NOS) **379**
network resource **358**
optical network terminal (ONT) **374**

peer-to-peer network (P2P) **358**
personal area network (PAN) **369**
piggybacking **391**
protocol **380**
router **374**
server **362**
storage area network (SAN) **371**
switch **374**
TCP (transmission control protocol) **380**
TCP/IP protocol stack **380**
topology **369**
virtual private network (VPN) **370**
wardriving **391**
wide area network (WAN) **370**
wireless access point (WAP) **376**
wireless LAN (WLAN) **369**
workgroup **358**

# Summary

**1. Discuss the importance of computer networks.**

A computer network is two or more computers that share resources: software, hardware, or files. Computer networks save us both time and money and make it easier for us to work, increasing productivity. A peer-to-peer network (P2P) is one in which each computer is a member of a workgroup and is considered equal. A client-server network is one that has at least one server at its center that provides a way to centralize the network management, resources, and security.

**2. Compare different types of LANs and WANs.**

A local area network (LAN) is a network that has all nodes located in the same physical location. Devices on a LAN are connected using switches. A wireless LAN (WLAN) uses WiFi to transmit data, and a personal area network (PAN) uses Bluetooth. Ethernet defines the way data is transmitted over a local area network and topology is the physical layout. A wide area network (WAN) is a network that spans multiple locations and connects multiple LANs over dedicated lines using routers. A VPN creates a private network through the public network (Internet), allowing remote users to access a LAN securely without dedicated lines. A campus area network (CAN) connects multiple LANs located in the same location. A network that covers a single geographic area is called a metropolitan area network (MAN). A storage area network (SAN) connects data storage devices and servers on a network. Cellular networks use 3G and 4G cell towers to transmit voice and data over large distances.

**3. List and describe the hardware used in both wired and wireless networks.**

Each device that connects to a network must have a network adapter. The first device on a network is usually the device that connects to the Internet: a modem or optical network terminal (ONT). A business network consists of routers, switches, wireless access points, and firewalls. Your home router serves all these functions. A router is a device that connects two or more networks together. It uses address information to correctly route the data packets it receives. A switch is a device that connects multiple devices on a LAN. A wireless access point (WAP) is a device that allows wireless devices to join a network, much like a switch. A firewall is a device that blocks unauthorized access to a network.

**4. List and describe the software and protocols used in both wired and wireless networks.**

Clients log in to a server and request access to resources. A Web browser can act as an FTP, a database client, and an HTTP client. Other client software you may use includes VPN software, desktop email programs, instant messaging/chat programs, and video and photo software that include an upload feature. Server software—also known as a network operating system (NOS)—is a multiuser operating system that controls the software and hardware that runs on a network. Protocols define the rules for communication among devices and determine how data is formatted, transmitted, received, and acknowledged. The most important protocols belong to the TCP/IP protocol stack and define everything from how to transfer files (FTP) and Web pages (HTTP) to

sending (SMTP) and receiving (POP) email. TCP stands for transmission control protocol, and it's responsible for assuring that data packets are transmitted reliably. IP stands for Internet protocol, and it's responsible for addressing and routing packets to their destination.

**5. Explain how to protect a network.**

Use a layered approach to security. Protect the access point to your network with a firewall. Ensure correct network configuration—that is, what is shared and who is granted access to it. Secure individual computers with software-based firewalls as well as antivirus and antimalware software, and be diligent in keeping the systems on the network up to date and secure.

# Multiple Choice

Answer the multiple-choice questions below for more practice with key terms and concepts from this chapter.

1. Computers in a peer-to-peer network belong to a _____.
   a. workgroup
   b. domain
   c. personal area network
   d. client-server group

2. Which resources are not shared by default in a homegroup?
   a. Pictures and videos
   b. Music
   c. Documents
   d. Printers

3. Which type of network consists of data storage devices and servers?
   a. PAN
   b. MAN
   c. VPN
   d. SAN

4. Which type of network spans multiple locations and connects multiple networks?
   a. MAN
   b. WAN
   c. LAN
   d. VPN

5. Which topology connects devices in a single line?
   a. Bus
   b. Ring
   c. Star
   d. Hybrid

6. When two Bluetooth devices connect to each other directly, they form a(n) _____.
   a. ad hoc network
   b. infrastructure wireless network
   c. WAN
   d. personal area network (PAN)

7. The device needed to connect two or more networks together is called a(n) _____.
   a. modem
   b. router
   c. optical network terminal
   d. access point

8. A(n)_____ connects multiple devices on a LAN.
   a. modem
   b. switch
   c. firewall
   d. ONT

**9.** Which protocol is responsible for assuring that data packets are transmitted reliably on a network?

a. TCP

b. IP

c. POP

d. SMTP

**10.** Which device examines data packets as they enter and leave a network and denies unauthorized packets access?

a. Modem

b. Switch

c. Router

d. Firewall

# True or False

Answer the following questions with T for true or F for false for more practice with key terms and concepts from this chapter.

1. In a client-server network, each computer is considered equal.

2. It's possible to share files between computers running Windows, Mac OS X, and Linux.

3. Most LANs are configured in a ring topology.

4. A campus area network (CAN) consists of multiple LANs in the same location connected to each other using routers.

5. When two wireless devices connect to each other directly, they form an ad hoc network.

6. Computers can have multiple network adapters installed at one time.

7. A switch is a device that connects two or more networks together.

8. You must install special software to create a peer-to-peer network.

9. TCP/IP is the default protocol installed on Linux computers.

10. Using an open wireless network to access the Internet without permission is called wardriving.

# Fill in the Blank

Fill in the blanks with key terms from this chapter.

1. _____ include software, hardware, and files.

2. A(n) _____ creates a private network through a public network.

3. A(n) _____ has at least one server at its center.

4. In a(n) _____, devices connect through a wireless access point.

5. A(n) _____ is a network that has all devices located in the same physical location.

6. _____ is the physical layout of a local area network.

7. Every device on a network must have a(n) _____ to establish a connection with a network.

8. An analog _____ is the first device on a network that connects to the Internet via telephone lines.

9. A group of clients and servers under the control of one central security database is called a(n) _____.

10. _____ define the rules for communication between devices.

# Application Project

my**it**lab
grader

## Microsoft Office Application Project 1:
### Word Level 3

**PROJECT DESCRIPTION:** In this Microsoft Word project, you will format a document with columns, outline and shade text, create and apply styles, work with Clip Art and SmartArt graphics, and insert and format a table.

**INSTRUCTIONS:** For the purpose of grading the project you are required to perform the following tasks:

### Creating a Secure Password

We are all responsible for system security!

**Password Policy**

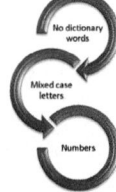

IT Services provides you with security and tech support for all school systems. In order to ensure the security of college resources, all users are required to create a secure password that must be changed at the start of each semester.

No dictionary words

Mixed case letters

Numbers

**Creating Your Password**

Here are some guidelines for creating (and remembering) a secure password. You must use a combination of letters and numbers. You must use at least one uppercase and one lowercase letter. Your password must be between 8-12 characters. Try using a combination of words that you can easily remember, but that someone else cannot easily guess. So don't use your kid's name (or your pet's, spouse's...) Everybody knows who your favorite sports team is (because you wear the team shirt to class every day). Instead, go for less obvious choices. One idea: pick a famous song lyric and use the first letter of each word. So, for example, Mary Had a Little Lamb becomes MHaLL. Mix up the case and add a few numbers and you have MhAlL34S.

| Tech | Extension |
|---|---|
| Sue | X 5421 |
| Charlie | X 5422 |

For help with your password or other security questions, contact IT Services. (702) 555-1234.

| Step | Instructions |
|---|---|
| **1** | Start Word. Download and open the file named *vt_ch09_word*. Save the file as **lastname_firstname_ch09_word**. |
| **2** | Select the subtitle *Password Policy* and all of the remaining text in the document. Modify the selected text so that it displays in two columns. |
| **3** | Insert a column break immediately to the left of the subtitle *Creating Your Password*. |
| **4** | Position the insertion point at the end of the paragraph beginning *Here are some guidelines…* Insert a 2x3 table. Apply the Grid Table 6 colorful—Accent 3 table style. Enter the following in the table:<br>**Tech Extension**<br>**Sue x5421**<br>**Charlie x5422** |

| Step | Instructions |
|---|---|
| **5** | Apply the Title style to the title of the document, *Creating a Secure Password*. Apply the Fill—Red, Accent 2, Outline—Accent 2 text effect to the title of the document. Center the title and change the font size to 36. |
| **6** | Left align the subtitle *Password Policy* and change the font size to 20. Change the font color of the selected text to Orange, Accent 6, Darker 25%. Format the text as bold. |
| **7** | Create a new style based on the formatting of the subtitle *This Year's Show*. Name the style **Password**. Apply the Password style to the subtitle *Creating Your Password*. |

**Visit pearsonhighered.com/Geoghan** for data files, simulations, VizClips, and additional study materials.

| Step | Instructions |
|------|--------------|
| **8** | Position the insertion point immediately to the left of the paragraph beginning *IT Services*. Search for clip art images using the phrase *computer* and then insert the image of the emoticon on the laptop computer into the document. For your reference, the image is included with the project starting materials with the file name *vt_ch09_image*. |
| **9** | With the image selected, change the text wrapping to tight. Resize the image height to 1.5", lock aspect ratio. |
| **10** | Add a box border to the paragraph beginning *For help with your password* and then change the shading to Olive Green, Accent 3, Lighter 60%. |
| **11** | Position the insertion point at the end of the paragraph beginning *IT Services provides*. Insert a SmartArt graphic using the Circle Arrow Process style from the Cycle category. |

| Step | Instructions |
|------|--------------|
| **12** | Use the Position button to move the SmartArt graphic in the bottom left of the page with square text wrapping, and then increase the height of the graphic to 4.3". |
| **13** | Apply the 3-D Inset to the SmartArt graphic. Change color to Colored Fill, Accent 4. |
| **14** | Display the text pane for the SmartArt graphic and insert the following text as the three bullet items (in this order): **No dictionary words**, **Mixed case letters**, **Numbers**. Close the text pane. |
| **15** | Save and close document and then exit Word. Submit the document as directed. |

Visit **pearsonhighered.com/Geoghan** for data files, simulations, VizClips, and additional study materials.

Chapter 9 |

397

# Microsoft Office Application Project 2:
## Excel Level 3

**PROJECT DESCRIPTION:** In this Microsoft Excel project, using data from the World Bank, you will format and summarize a large spreadsheet showing mobile cellular subscription growth from 2000 to 2010.

**INSTRUCTIONS:** For the purpose of grading the project you are required to perform the following tasks:

| Step | Instructions |
|---|---|
| 1 | Start Excel. Open the downloaded Excel file named *vt_ch09_excel*. Save the file as **lastname_firstname_ch09_excel**. |
| 2 | On the N. America sheet, Select the range C2:M5. Apply the Number Format to the selected range. Decrease the decimals displayed to 1. |
| 3 | In cell C6, use the AVG function to average the values in the range C2:C5. Copy the formula from C6:M6. |
| 4 | In cell C7, use a function to calculate the highest number of cellular subscriptions of the range C2:C5. Copy the formula from C7:M7. |

| Step | Instructions |
|---|---|
| 5 | In cell C8 use a function to calculate the lowest number of cellular subscriptions of the range C2:C5. Copy the formula from C8:M8. |
| 6 | In cell N2, insert a Line Sparkline. Use the data range C2:M2. Format Sparkline Style Accent 2 (no dark or light). Copy the sparklines down the column N2:N7. |
| 7 | Copy the Average row C6:M6 from the N. America sheet. Use the Paste link function to paste it into row 3 of the Summary sheet. Repeat for the remaining regions on the Summary sheet. |
| 8 | Format the values on the Summary sheet B2:L8 with the Number Format. Decrease the decimals displayed to 1. |

| Step | Instructions |
|------|--------------|
| 9 | Select the range A3:L8 and insert a 2-D line chart. Move the chart so the top left corner is in the top left corner of cell B10. Format the chart Style 10. |
| 10 | Format the data in the range A1:L8 in the Summary worksheet as a table with headers using Table Style Dark 10. Sort the 2010 column from the smallest to the largest value. |
| 11 | On the C. America sheet, apply the Gradient Green Data Bar conditional formatting (under Gradient Fill) to the range C2:M22. |
| 12 | On the Europe sheet, click cell A2 and then freeze the panes of the worksheet so that when you scroll down, the headings in row 1 remain visible. |

| Step | Instructions |
|------|--------------|
| 13 | Change the sheet options on the Europe worksheet so that row 1 repeats at the top of multiple printed pages. |
| 14 | Select the Summary, N. America, C. America, and S. America worksheets. Prepare the four worksheets for printing by changing the orientation to Landscape. Adjust the Scale option to change the Width to 1 page. |
| 15 | Ensure that the worksheets are correctly named and placed in the following order in the workbook: Summary, N. America, C. America, S. America, Europe, Asia, Middle East, N. Africa. Source. Save the workbook. Close the workbook and then exit Excel. Submit the workbook as directed. |

Visit **pearsonhighered.com/Geoghan** for data files, simulations, VizClips, and additional study materials.

Chapter 9 | 399

# Running Project...

## ... The Finish Line

Assume that you just moved into a new house with several roommates. Use your answers to the previous sections of the project to help you decide the best type of network setup to use so you can all share an Internet connection and printer as well as stream media files. Describe the hardware and software requirements for your setup. What other devices might you also connect to the network?

Write a report describing your selections and responding to the questions raised. Save your file as **lastname_firstname_ch09_project**, and submit it to your instructor as directed.

# Do It Yourself 1

1. Network security includes keeping your system up to date and installing antivirus and antimalware software. In this exercise, you will examine these settings on a Windows computer. (Note that in a school network, security settings may prevent you from being able to perform parts of this exercise.) Open the Action Center from the taskbar or Control Panel window. If necessary, click the arrow next to Security. What are the categories listed in this section? Are there are categories that are Off on your computer? If so, which one(s)? Is there a firewall on this computer and if so, which one? What about antivirus and antispyware software?

2. In the left pane, click *Windows Update*. Are there any updates that need to be installed? When was the last time updates were installed? How do you receive updates?

3. Type up your answers, save the file as **lastname_firstname_ch09_diy1**, and submit the assignment as directed by your instructor.

# Do It Yourself 2

Most of us use multiple networks at home, work, and school. In this exercise, you'll examine a network you use and the devices that are part of it.

1. Make a diagram of a network you use. If you don't have a home network, you may draw a friend's network or one you work on at school or work instead. You can use a program such as MS Paint, Google SketchUp, or even PowerPoint to create the diagram. Be sure to label the devices (including printers, cell phones, game consoles, and so on).

2. If your network connects to the Internet, label the LAN and WAN parts. What resources do you access/share on this network? What other resources would you like to be able to access through it?

3. Save the file as **lastname_firstname_ch09_diy2**, and submit it as directed by your instructor.

# File Management

1. Open File Explorer. Are there any items listed under Network in the Navigation pane? If so, what are they? (On a Mac, use finder and list items under SHARED.)

2. Search Help and Support or Google for Map network drive. Click on *Create a shortcut to (map) a network drive*. What's the purpose of mapping a drive? Read through the article (but don't perform the steps described). To what other places can you create shortcuts?

3. Type up your answers, save the file as **lastname_firstname_ch09_fm**, and submit the assignment as directed by your instructor.

# Critical Thinking

You work for a small accounting office. Your boss wants to ensure that everyone in the office knows the basics of keeping the office network secure.

1. Use the Internet and the information you learned in this chapter to create a list of five rules that employees should follow to ensure the security of the office computers. Use a word processor or drawing software to create a poster that can be displayed in the office to remind the employees of these rules.

2. Save the file as **lastname_firstname_ch09_ct**, and submit your work as directed by your instructor.

# Ethical Dilemma

A help desk technician received a call from an upset customer, Samantha. Samantha had been accessing the Internet at home with her tablet for months but was suddenly unable to connect. The technician asked her some questions to help her troubleshoot the problem. Did she try turning off her router and turning it back on? No—she didn't have a router. What about a wireless access point? Nope—she didn't have one of those either. Did she call her ISP for help? You guessed it—she didn't have one of those either! After some more questions, the technician finally realized that Samantha had been piggybacking off her neighbor's wireless network.

1. Samantha was very upset to have lost her Internet connection, and a few days later when her neighbor returned from vacation, it was restored. Her neighbor is unaware that Samantha is using the connection. Is it acceptable for Samantha to continue to use her neighbor's network now that she understands what she's doing?

2. Look up the laws where you live. Is it legal? Is it ethical? Would you do it?

3. Type up your answers, save the file as **lastname_firstname_ch09_ethics**, and submit it as directed by your instructor.

# On the Web

IPv6 is designed to replace IPv4.

1. Go to the Internet Society website (**internetsociety.org/**) and search for IPv6. What are some advantages of switching to IPv6? What was World IPv6 Day, and what were the results?

2. How does the number of IPv6 addresses compare to the number of IPv4 addresses?

3. Type up your answers, save the file as **lastname_firstname_ch09_web**, and submit it as directed by your instructor.

# Collaboration

**Instructors:** Divide the class into small groups, and provide each group with a large piece of paper or poster board or access to computers.

**The Project:** Each team is to prepare a Venn diagram that compares the features of peer-to-peer and client-server networks. Teams must use at least three references, only one of which may be this textbook.

**Students:** Before beginning this project, discuss the roles each group member will play. Choose a team name, which you'll use in submitting your presentation. Be sure to divide the work among your members, and pick someone to present your project. You may find it helpful to elect a team leader who can direct your activities and ensure that all team members contribute to the project.

**Outcome:** You're to prepare a Venn diagram using a large piece of paper or a computer drawing program. The diagram must have at least four items in each of the three areas of the diagram. Present your findings to the class. Be sure to include a listing of all team members. Turn in your diagram named as **teamname_ch09_collab**. Submit your presentation to your instructor as directed.

# Security and Privacy

Visit **pearsonhighered.com/Geoghan** for data files, simulations, VizClips, and additional study materials.

## Running Project

In this project, you'll explore security and privacy. Look for instructions as you complete each article. For most, there's a series of questions for you to research. At the conclusion of the chapter, you're asked to submit your responses to the questions raised.

## OBJECTIVES

1. **Discuss various types of cybercrime.**

2. **Differentiate between different types of malware.**

3. **Explain how to secure a computer.**

4. **Discuss safe computing practices.**

5. **Discuss laws related to computer security and privacy.**

## IN THIS CHAPTER

Do you leave your doors unlocked? Do you let strangers into your home? Do you hand out business cards with your Social Security number on them? Of course not. We all take steps to protect our security and privacy in the real world, and it's just as important to do so in the electronic world. In this chapter, we look at some of the threats we all face and how you can protect yourself in this digital age.

403

# Cybercrime: They Are Out to Get You

## I OBJECTIVE
## Discuss various types of cybercrime.

The term **cybercrime** means criminal activity on the Internet. Most of these types of crime existed in some form long before computers came along, but technology has made them easier to commit and more widespread. In this article, we discuss some of the most common forms of cybercrime that you should be on the lookout for.

## PERSONAL CYBERCRIME

Personal cybercrime is perpetrated against individuals, as opposed to businesses and other organizations. These are the crimes that affect you directly and that you need to be alert to.

**HARASSMENT** Cyberbullying and cyberstalking fall into the category of harassment. When the exchange involves two minors, it is called **cyberbullying**, but between adults, it becomes **cyberstalking**. The harassers use email, text messages, IMs, and social networks to embarrass, threaten, or torment someone—often because of his or her gender, race, religion, nationality, or sexual orientation. Unlike traditional schoolyard bullying, cyberbullying follows a child beyond the schoolyard and beyond the school day.

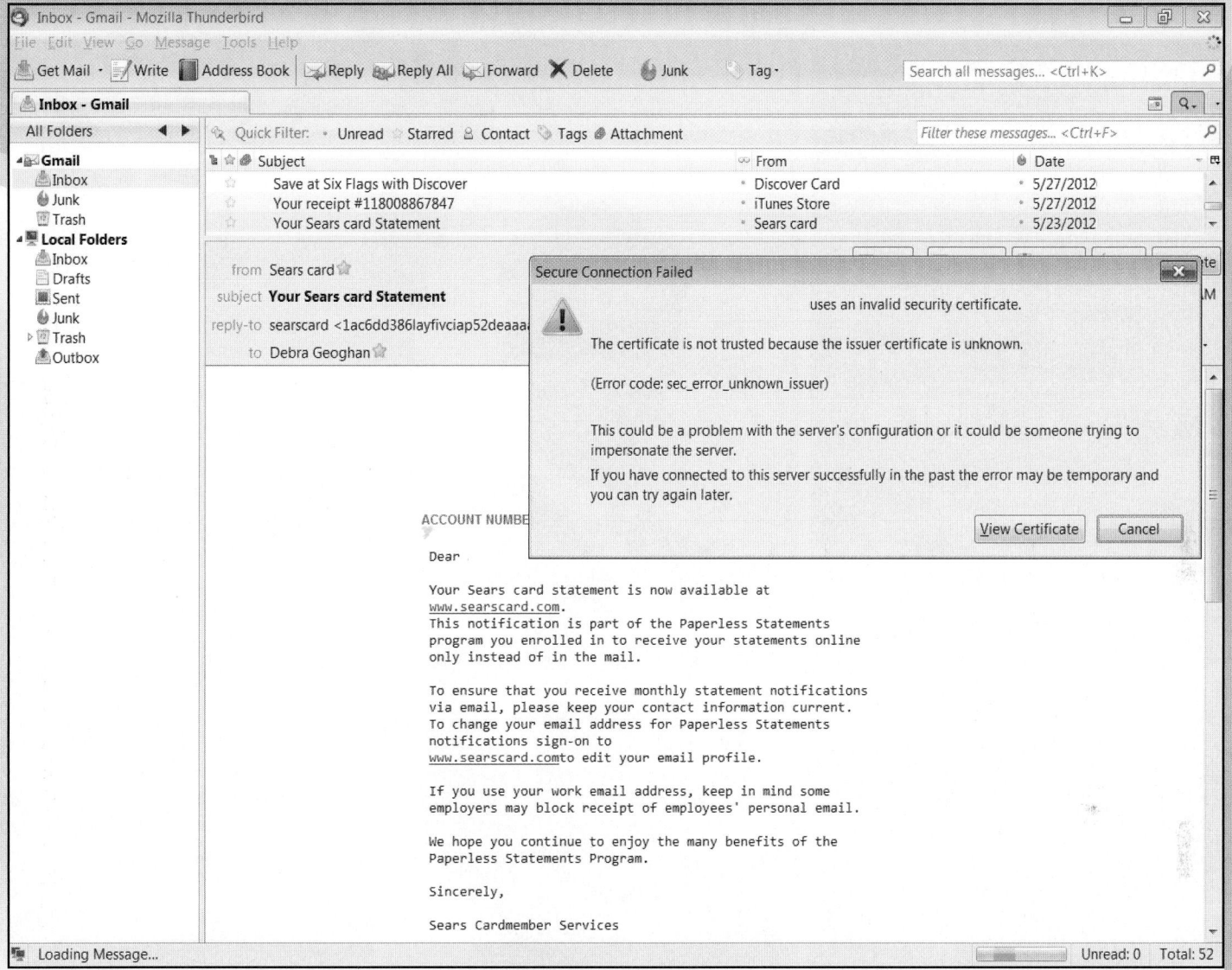

**FIGURE 10.1** This phishing message appears to be from a legitimate company, but the email program warns me that it might be a problem.

**PHISHING AND PHARMING** **Phishing** uses email messages and IMs that appear to be from those you do business with, such as your bank, credit card company, social network, auction site, online payment processor, or IT administrator. They're designed to trick you into revealing information, such as usernames and passwords for your accounts. **Pharming** redirects you to a phony website even if you type the right address into your browser. They do this by hijacking the domain name of a company that has either not renewed its registration or has security-compromised Web servers or by poisoning the DNS server references to a site, much like having the wrong phone number listed in the phone book. Both phishing and pharming work because they seem to be messages for legitimate websites. Figure 10.1 shows a phishing email message that appears to be from my credit card company.

## SOCIAL NETWORK ATTACKS

Social networks are vulnerable to many types of attacks. Because we are "friends" with other users, we trust what they post and send us, and it is easy to be fooled into clicking on something malicious. You'll notice that many of these types of attacks are not specifically social network attacks, but because many of us spend so much of our online time in social network sites where we lower our guards, the attacks tend to be more successful. Some common attacks include the following:

- Adware and other malware
- Suspicious emails and notifications— Appear to be from the site administrator asking for your password or threatening to suspend your account
- Phishing and "Please send money" scams—Fool you into downloading malware or sending money
- Clickjacking—Clicking on a link allows this malware to post unwanted links on your page
- Malicious script scams—Copy and paste some text into your address bar and you might just be executing a malicious script that creates pages and events or sends spam out to your friends

You can read more on the Facebook Security site at **facebook.com/help/ security** (it's not necessary to have an account or be logged in).

**Try the Security and Privacy Simulation**

SIMULATION

**FRAUD** In this type of cybercrime, the victim voluntarily and knowingly gives money or property to a person. Some of the more well-known **computer fraud** schemes on the Internet involve emails claiming you have won a lottery or inherited money. Figure 10.2 shows a message that claims to be from a friend of mine, and it even came from her email address. The language is the first giveaway that this is phony because my friend also happens to be an elementary school teacher and would never use such poor grammar. While most people are smart enough to ignore messages as obvious as this one, the messages are often more personal and believable, and many people fall victim to the scams. This scam can also occur on social networks when a cybercriminal hacks into a user's account and sends messages to friends asking for help.

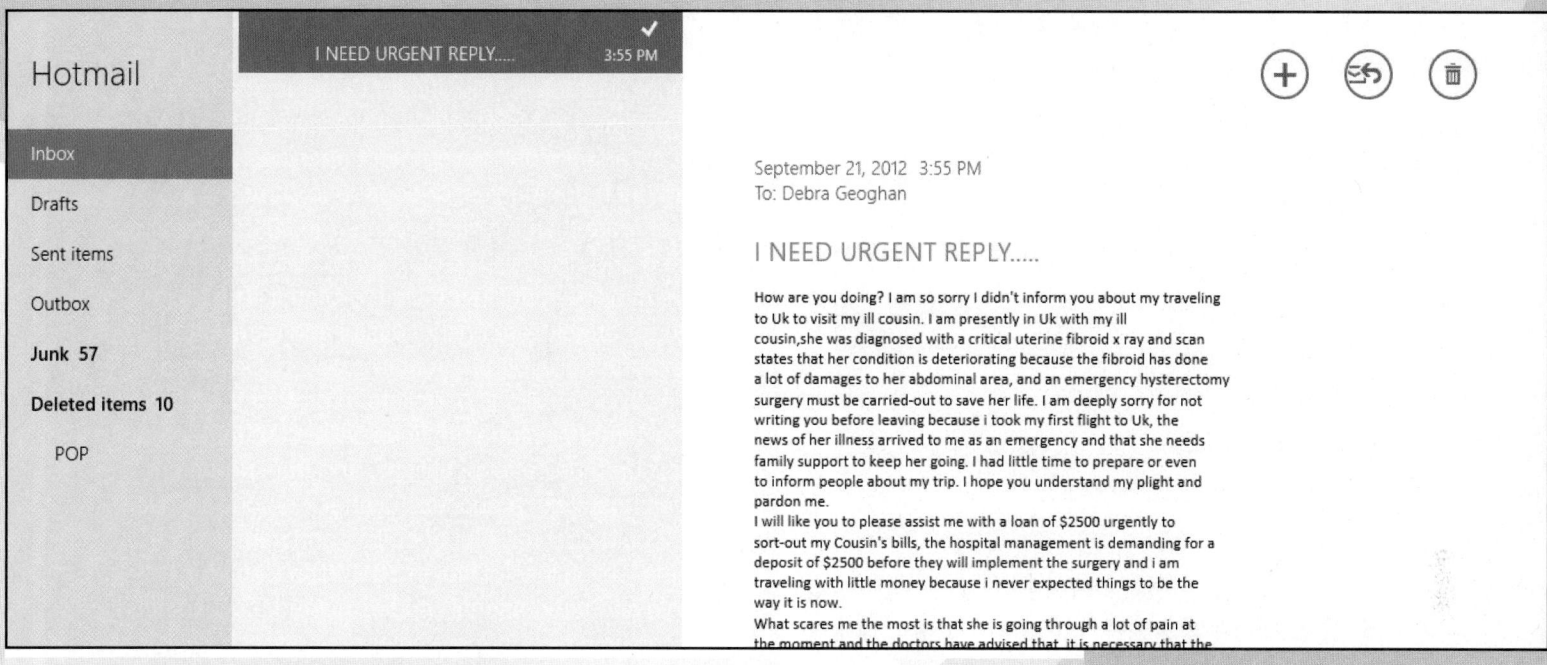

Hotmail

I NEED URGENT REPLY.....    3:55 PM

Inbox

Drafts

Sent items

Outbox

Junk 57

Deleted items 10

POP

September 21, 2012  3:55 PM
To: Debra Geoghan

I NEED URGENT REPLY.....

How are you doing? I am so sorry I didn't inform you about my traveling
to Uk to visit my ill cousin. I am presently in Uk with my ill
cousin,she was diagnosed with a critical uterine fibroid x ray and scan
states that her condition is deteriorating because the fibroid has done
a lot of damages to her abdominal area, and an emergency hysterectomy
surgery must be carried-out to save her life. I am deeply sorry for not
writing you before leaving because i took my first flight to Uk, the
news of her illness arrived to me as an emergency and that she needs
family support to keep her going. I had little time to prepare or even
to inform people about my trip. I hope you understand my plight and
pardon me.
I will like you to please assist me with a loan of $2500 urgently to
sort-out my Cousin's bills, the hospital management is demanding for a
deposit of $2500 before they will implement the surgery and i am
traveling with little money because i never expected things to be the
way it is now.
What scares me the most is that she is going through a lot of pain at
the moment and the doctors have advised that it is necessary that the

**FIGURE 10.2** An example of computer fraud is an email scam that appears to be a plea for help from a friend.

**IDENTITY THEFT** The form of cybercrime many people most fear is identity theft. **Identity theft** happens when someone uses your name, Social Security number, or bank or credit card number for financial gain. The identity thief may purchase items, open new accounts, or commit a crime using your identity. Using password-stealing software, keyloggers, and phishing and pharming scams, criminals can easily obtain enough personal information to wreak havoc on an individual. Victims of identity theft often spend years and thousands of dollars to clear up the mess. Companies that claim to protect you from identity theft have sprung up, but all they really do are things you can and should do yourself.

1. Monitor your bank and credit card statements, carefully checking each charge every month. Also watch for charges on your phone bills.

2. Monitor your credit report. By law, you're entitled to one free credit report per year from each of the three major credit reporting companies. Instead of requesting them all at once, space them out every four months to keep an eye out for suspicious activity throughout the year. Make sure to use the correct website: **annualcreditreport.com**.

3. If you suspect you might be the victim of identity theft, immediately place a fraud alert on your credit reports.

4. Protect your personal information. Be smart about the information you share and with whom you share it.

If you decide to pay for identity theft protection, you should compare products and services carefully and be sure that you're getting the right service for you.

# CYBERCRIME AGAINST ORGANIZATIONS

**Hacking** is the act of gaining unauthorized access to a computer system or network. Some people categorize hackers as white-hat, gray-hat, and black-hat depending on their motivation and the results of their hacking. A white-hat hacker's motivation is to find security holes in a system for the purpose of preventing future hacking. These are security experts who are paid to hack systems, and they're sometimes called "sneakers." Black-hat hackers hack into systems for a malicious purpose, such as theft or vandalism. Black-hat hackers are sometimes referred to as "crackers." Gray-hat hackers fall somewhere in between. They hack into systems illegally but not for malicious intent. A gray-hat hacker might break into a system to prove he can or to expose a system's vulnerability. **Hacktivism**, such as that committed by Anonymous (Figure 10.3), is hacking to make a political statement. Although it's possible to hack into an individual's computer, the biggest prizes are large companies and government agencies.

An unlawful attack against computers or networks that's done to intimidate a government or its people for a political or social agenda is known as **cyberterrorism**. Although many terrorist groups use technology such as the Internet and email to do business, cyberterrorism is more than just using computers as a tool. Cyberterrorists actually attack the information systems to cause harm. According to a report by the Center for Strategic and International Studies, "Significant Cyber Incidents Since 2006," updated in March 2012, there were nearly 100 significant attacks on "government agencies, defense and high tech companies, or economic crimes with losses of more than a million dollars." In 2012, Congress proposed and discussed a number of bills designed to improve cybersecurity in the United States. The majority of cyberterror attacks are unsuccessful and unreported, and most experts believe the threat is growing. Government agencies spend millions of dollars to protect themselves. Potential targets include the financial sector; infrastructure, such as communications, utilities, and transportation; and even hospitals. A successful attack on one of these targets could cost millions of dollars and cause major problems—even loss of life. In 2012, The Center for Strategic and International Studies hosted a cybersecurity simulation, in which former senior government officials participated. Such simulations help governments and security experts plan a response should such an attack occur and highlight places where more work is needed. You can view the video of the results at **csis.org/multimedia/video-united-states-prepared-cyber-attack**.

According to General Keith Alexander, the head of the U.S. Cyber Command, the Pentagon systems are attacked 250,000 times an hour, or 6 million times a day. The attacks come from ordinary hackers, criminal enterprises, and foreign intelligence agents.

# Find Out MORE

Research the hacktivist group Anonymous. Who are they? What do they stand for? What are some of their most recent exploits? How effective have they been?

**FIGURE 10.3** The group Anonymous uses hacktivism to make a political statement.

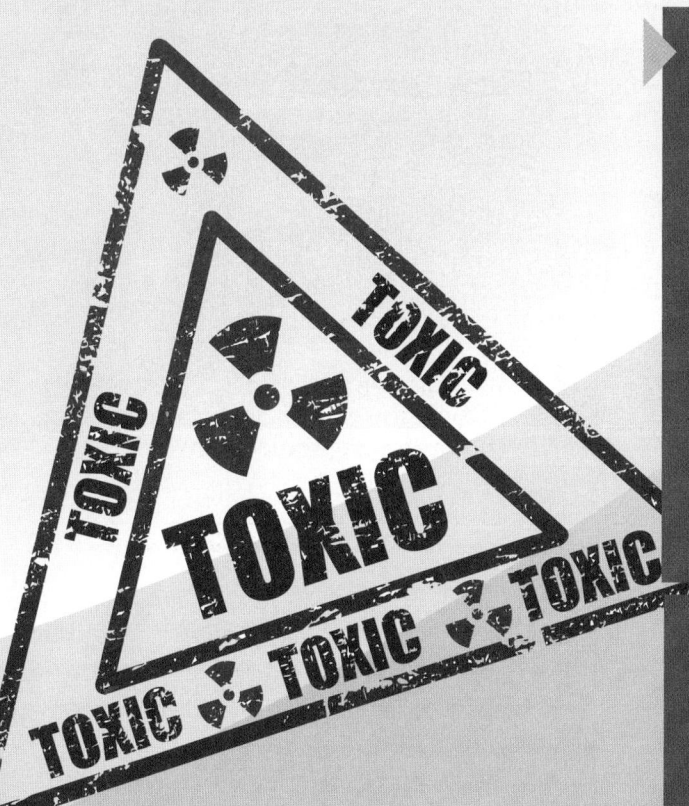

## Running Project

What steps should you take to prevent identity theft? How have you implemented these in your activities? Are there other things you should be doing? Has identity theft happened to you or someone you know? If so, describe what happened.

## 4 Things You Need to Know

- Cybercrime means criminal activity on the Internet.
- Harassment, phishing, pharming, fraud, and identity theft are forms of cybercrime against individuals.
- Hackers gain unauthorized access to computer systems or networks.
- Cyberterrorism attacks have political or social agendas.

## Key Terms

| | |
|---|---|
| computer fraud | hacking |
| cyberbullying | hacktivism |
| cybercrime | identity theft |
| cyberstalking | pharming |
| cyberterrorism | phishing |

# Malware: Pick Your Poison

VIZ CLIP

## 2 OBJECTIVE
## Differentiate between different types of malware.

The term **malware** (malicious software) includes many different types of programs that are designed to be harmful or malicious. Protecting your computer from these nasties can be a difficult task. In this article, we discuss various types of malware you should be on the lookout for.

## SPAM AND COOKIES

Sending mass, unsolicited emails is called **spam**. It's so popular because it's easy and inexpensive to do—no paper to print, no envelopes to stuff, and no postage. The same things that make email a good thing for all of us make it good for spammers. There are other forms of spam too: IM spam (spim), fax spam, and text message spam, to name a few. While spam may seem to be just a nuisance, in fact, it costs businesses millions of dollars each year (including ISPs). It's estimated that over 80 percent of all email messages are abusive in some way. That includes not just ads but also phishing messages and malware, such as viruses, Trojans, and spyware. Figure 10.4 shows a sample of the spam messages I received in just the past few days.

Many websites put a small text file called a **cookie** on your computer when you visit them. Cookies help the website identify you when you return. Your personal information, such as credit card numbers, isn't stored in the cookie. Figure 10.5 shows an e-commerce site. The site recognizes me because there's a cookie on my computer.

Whenever you visit a site and click the Remember me or Keep me logged in button, the website puts a cookie on your computer. But cookies are also used without your choosing them. While cookies are useful, they could be used to collect information that you don't want to share. Modern browsers include protection against potentially harmful cookies.

| | | |
|---|---|---|
| ☐ | Paxil Lawsuit Information | Paxil linked to serious side effects, find out your rights to compensation for s |
| ☐ | SUV Sales | Don't miss these prices on sport utility vehicles. - Please click "Not Spam" abov |
| ☐ | Champion Windows | Champion Windows - $750 Off...free in-home estimate - Please click "Not Spar |
| ☐ | Tax Defense | Tax Relief Notification - Please click "Not Spam" above if delivered to spam folder |
| ☐ | Car Search Assistance | Find the Right Car for You. Search for every make, every model, every detai |
| ☐ | Clever Claw | Revolutionary reaching tool retrieves small items that fall |
| ☐ | MeshPatchLegalRecall | Settlements for Mesh Implant injuries - Mesh Implants If you are experiencing di |
| ☐ | Free Foreclosures-can do. | Browse through foreclosed homes in your area - Please click "Not Spam" abov |
| ☐ | Business Blog | Proven work at home opportunity - Please click "Not Spam" above if delivered to |

**FIGURE 10.4** Spam in My Gmail Account

# ADWARE AND SPYWARE

One of the most annoying forms of malware you can get on your computer is called Adware. **Adware**, as its name implies, shows you ads—usually in the form of pop-ups or banner ads on websites or in software. Adware is not all bad. Some free software that's distributed as adware gives you the option to purchase a full version without ads. The ads generate income for the software developer and allow the user to try a program for free. Many mobile apps are ad supported—meaning the app is free to use and the developer earns money by displaying ads on your screen. The revenue from the ads allows the software publisher to distribute the software for free. For the minor nuisance of a few ads, users can listen to free music legally (see Figure 10.6).

Adware can use CPU cycles and Internet bandwidth and, as a result, can reduce your computer's performance. Some adware is more insidious because it monitors your Internet connection and slows down your browsing dramatically. For this reason, adware is sometimes lumped together with spyware.

**Spyware** is a form of malware that secretly gathers personal information about you. The information is sent back to a third party that may use it for anything from targeted advertisements to identity theft. Spyware is usually installed inadvertently by a user who clicks on a pop-up or installs a freeware program that includes tracking features. The information about the tracking feature might be buried in the license agreement that most people simply accept without reading or understanding. Sometimes, you can choose not to install these extra features by simply unchecking them in the installer. One common spyware infection is Cool Web Search, which is a browser hijacker—it changes your homepage and redirects you to other websites. Spyware can be very difficult to remove and can even cause your security programs to stop running.

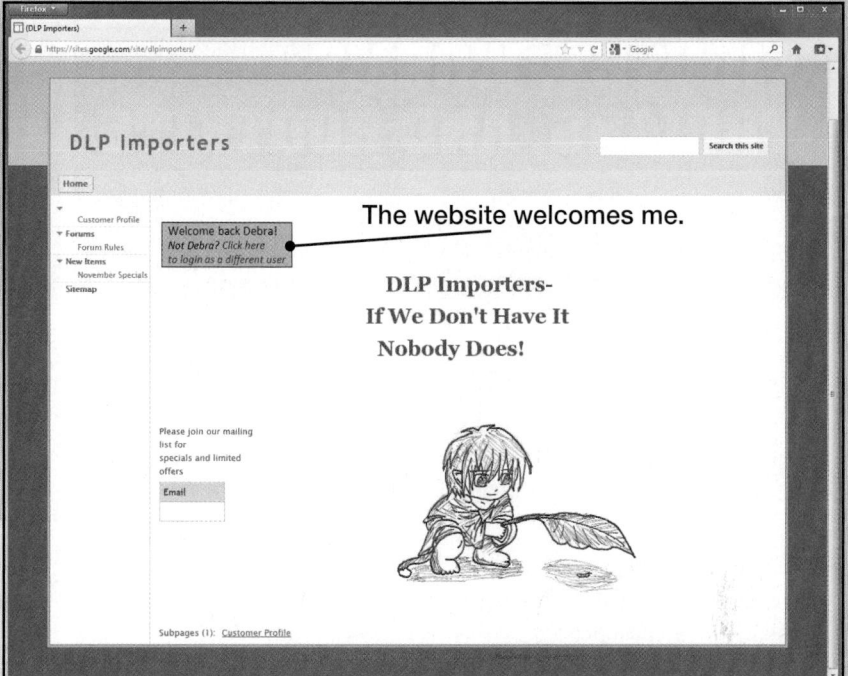

**FIGURE 10.5** A cookie on my computer allows this website to recognize me and personalize the site.

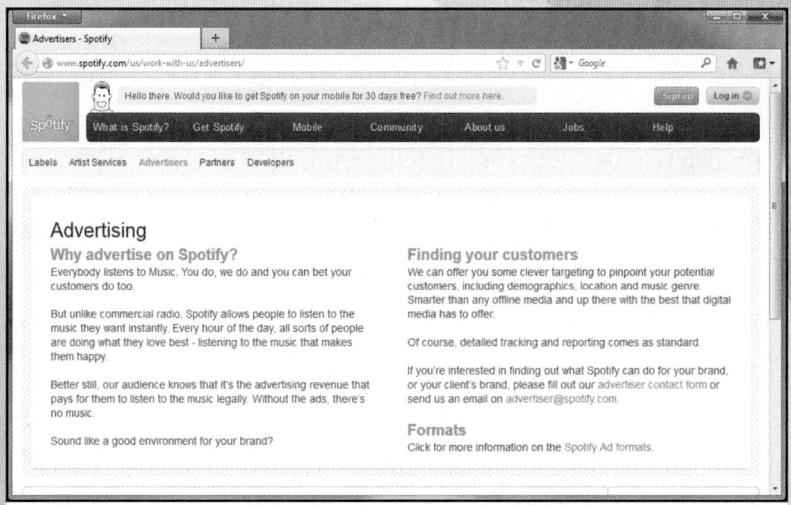

**FIGURE 10.6** Spotify makes money on ads and provides free music.

# VIRUSES, WORMS, TROJANS, AND ROOTKITS

A computer **virus** is a program that replicates itself and infects computers. A virus needs a host file to travel on, such as a game. The attack, also known as the **payload**, may corrupt or delete files, or it may even erase an entire disk. A virus may use the email program on the infected computer to send out copies of itself and infect other machines. Virus hoaxes are common in email messages. Although they don't contain a virus, they often trick users into behavior that can be harmful, such as searching for and deleting files that the computer actually needs. Another danger of hoaxes is that, like the boy who cried wolf, we can get desensitized and ignore the true virus alerts when they do occur. You can check to see if a message is a hoax at Snopes.com, hoax-slayer.com, or lookstoogoodtobetrue.com (see Figure 10.7).

A **logic bomb** behaves like a virus in that it performs a malicious act, such as deleting files. However, unlike a virus, it doesn't spread to other machines. A logic bomb attacks when certain conditions are met, such as when an employee's name is being removed from a database. Logic bombs are often used by disgruntled IT employees. When the trigger is a specific date and time, a logic bomb may be called a **time bomb**. A virus may have logic bomb characteristics in that it can lay dormant on a system until certain conditions are met. There have been viruses and Trojans triggered on April Fool's Day and Friday the 13th.

A **worm**, like a virus, is self-replicating, but it doesn't need a host to travel. Worms travel over networks, including the Internet. Once a system on a network is infected, the worm scans the network for other vulnerable machines to infect and spreads over the network connections without any human intervention. Conficker is a computer worm, first released in 2008, that has had many different variations. It initially took advantage of a flaw in several versions of Windows. Conficker prevented infected computers from connecting to software update websites and disabled antivirus software. In 2010, when it appeared that the virus was waning, it instead changed its behavior, making it even more difficult to prevent. It's estimated that millions of computers are infected with Conficker.

On April 1, 2009, millions of email spam messages were sent out by computers infected with the Conficker worm. These computers were part of a massive **botnet**—a network of computer zombies or bots controlled by a master (see Figure 10.8). The message was an advertisement for a fake antispyware program that, when installed, infected many more machines. Fake security notifications are one of the most common ways to infect computers. The ability to control millions of machines has the potential to cause real harm. A botnet could be used to send out spam and viruses or to launch a **denial-of-service attack,** which is perpetrated by sending out so much traffic that it cripples a server or network. Denial-of-service attacks have taken down Twitter, Yahoo, CNN, eBay, and Amazon, just to name a few.

A **Trojan horse**, or simply Trojan, is a program that appears to be a legitimate program but is actually something malicious instead. A Trojan might install adware, a toolbar, a keylogger, or open a back door to allow remote access to the system. A famous example of a Trojan is the Sinowal Trojan horse, which was used by criminals to steal more than 500,000 banking passwords and credit card numbers over 3 years.

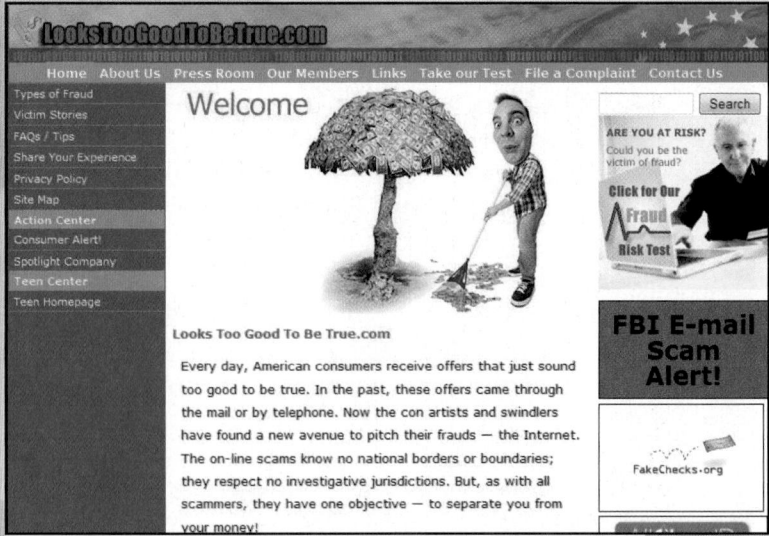

**FIGURE 10.7 lookstoogoodtobetrue.com** is a reliable place to check for hoaxes.

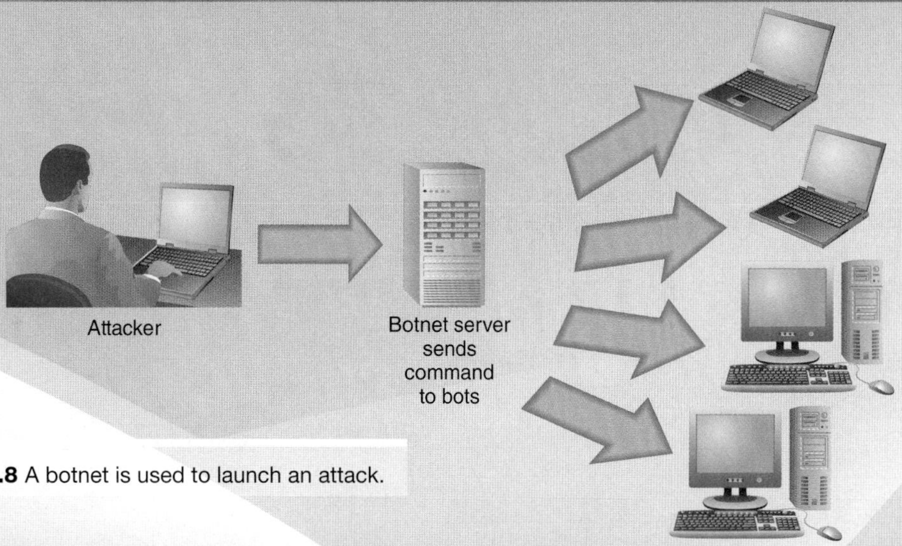

**FIGURE 10.8** A botnet is used to launch an attack.

Attacker

Botnet server
sends
command
to bots

Infected bot
computers
launch attack

A computer program that captures information a user enters on a keyboard is called a **keylogger**. A keylogger may be installed as a Trojan and reside unnoticed on an infected machine. When a user enters usernames and passwords or credit card numbers, the keylogger gathers that information. Some people install keyloggers on their own computers to monitor the activity of other users. There are also hardware keyloggers that plug in between the keyboard and computer. These USB devices are small and unnoticeable, and they can't be detected by security software.

A **rootkit** is a set of programs that allows someone to gain control over a computer system while hiding the fact that the computer has been compromised. A rootkit can be almost impossible to detect and also allows the machine to become further infected by masking the behavior of other malware.

More than one million computer viruses/Trojans/worms have been identified, and the number has grown exponentially in the past few years. Understanding the threats your computer faces is the first step in preventing these programs from infecting your machine.

## Running Project

Visit the U.S. Computer Emergency Readiness Team website at **us-cert. gov/cas/tips/**. Select the Guidelines for Publishing Information Online link and read about it. Write a 2- to 3-paragraph summary of the tip. Which of these suggestions do you follow? Are there any that you disagree with?

## 5 Things You Need to Know

- Malware is the term for harmful and malicious software.
- Spam is a common way to distribute other malware.
- Spyware secretly gathers personal information about you.
- Viruses, worms, Trojans, and rootkits are the most dangerous types of malware.
- Malware may damage your system or make it part of a botnet that attacks other systems.

## Key Terms

| | |
|---|---|
| adware | rootkit |
| botnet | spam |
| cookie | spyware |
| denial-of-service attack | time bomb |
| keylogger | Trojan horse |
| logic bomb | virus |
| malware | worm |
| payload | |

# Shields Up!

## 3 OBJECTIVE
## Explain how to secure a computer.

Protecting your computer from intrusion or infection can be a daunting task. In this article, we discuss important steps to keep your system secure.

## SOFTWARE

Because there are so many kinds of malware that can infect your computer, it takes a multilevel approach to safeguard your system from these and other threats. Most of the time, a machine becomes infected because of software exploits, lack of security software, or unpatched programs.

A **firewall** is designed to block unauthorized access to your network, but a software firewall—such as the one that comes with Windows—also blocks access to an individual machine. It's a good idea to use both forms to protect your systems. The Windows firewall monitors both outgoing and incoming network requests and protects you from local network threats as well as those from the Internet. It's turned on by default and can be used with a hardware-based firewall, such as one you might have in a home router. You shouldn't run another software-based firewall at the same time because they can conflict with each other, causing connectivity issues. The settings block connections to programs that aren't on the allowed list of programs. The first time a new program tries to access the network, you're asked whether to allow or deny access. In this way, the firewall program learns which programs should be allowed access and denies access to any unauthorized programs (such as a backdoor Trojan). OS X has a built-in firewall as well, but it is turned off by default. Use Security and Privacy Preferences to turn it on. Figure 10.9 shows the Windows and OS X firewall settings.

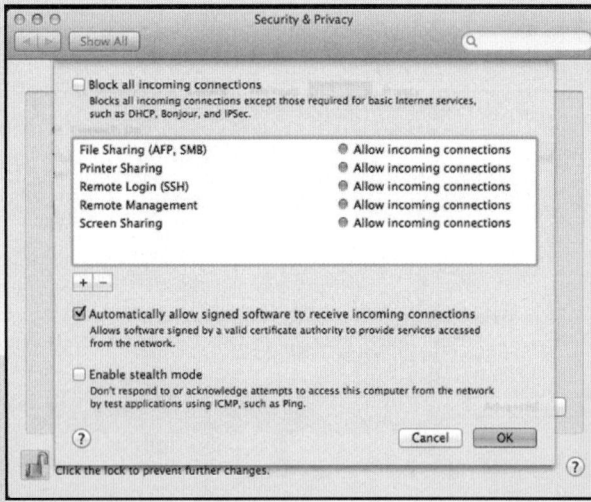

**FIGURE 10.9** The Windows Firewall Control Panel and OS X Firewall Advanced Settings

Today, many **antivirus programs** protect against viruses, Trojans, worms, and even some spyware. Most new Windows computers come with a trial version of antivirus software installed. Unfortunately, when these free trials run out, many people fail to pay for a subscription or replace them with something else, leaving outdated virus definition files on the machine. Antivirus software scans files on your computer, called "signature checking," to search for known viruses. It uses virus definition files to keep track of the newest threats. Outdated definition files leave a machine vulnerable to attack. Good antivirus software also uses heuristic methods, such as monitoring your machine for suspicious activity, to catch new viruses that are not in the definition files. Good antivirus programs can cost from nothing to $100 or more depending on the features included in the package you buy. Some very good free programs include AVG Free, Avast, and Microsoft Security Essentials. Windows 8 has built-in antivirus protection. Also, many ISPs provide free antivirus and other security software to their customers; be sure to check and see what you may be eligible for. It's important to only have one antivirus program running on your machine because multiple programs will interfere with each other and slow down your computer's performance.

**Antispyware software** is necessary to prevent adware and spyware software from installing itself on your computer. These infections aren't always caught by ordinary antivirus programs. Windows comes with Windows Defender, an antispyware program that includes both real-time protection and scanning. Real-time protection monitors your system for suspicious behavior (such as a program trying to change your home page or other Windows settings). You can run scans to detect and remove any spyware that's already installed on a computer. Other popular, effective, and free antispyware programs for personal use include Ad-Aware, Spybot Search & Destroy, and Malwarebytes Anti-Malware. You can download these and other programs from CNET's **download.com** website (see Figure 10.10).

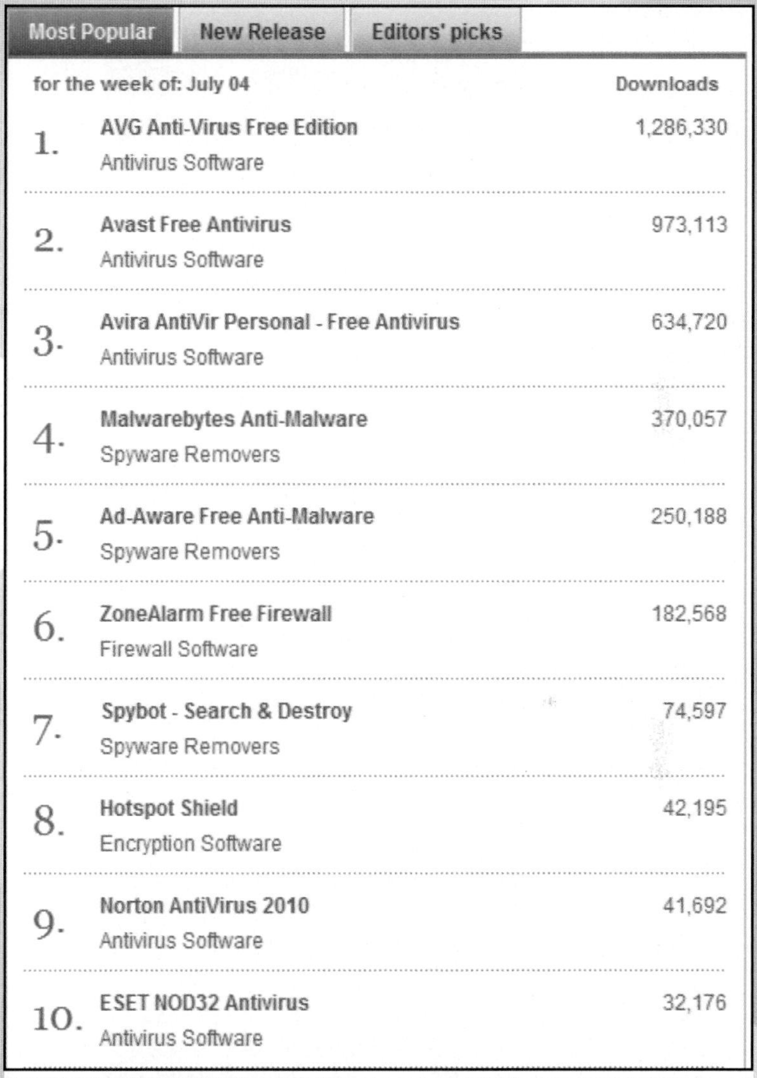

| Most Popular | New Release | Editors' picks |
| --- | --- | --- |

| for the week of: July 04 | Downloads |
| --- | --- |
| 1. AVG Anti-Virus Free Edition<br>Antivirus Software | 1,286,330 |
| 2. Avast Free Antivirus<br>Antivirus Software | 973,113 |
| 3. Avira AntiVir Personal - Free Antivirus<br>Antivirus Software | 634,720 |
| 4. Malwarebytes Anti-Malware<br>Spyware Removers | 370,057 |
| 5. Ad-Aware Free Anti-Malware<br>Spyware Removers | 250,188 |
| 6. ZoneAlarm Free Firewall<br>Firewall Software | 182,568 |
| 7. Spybot - Search & Destroy<br>Spyware Removers | 74,597 |
| 8. Hotspot Shield<br>Encryption Software | 42,195 |
| 9. Norton AntiVirus 2010<br>Antivirus Software | 41,692 |
| 10. ESET NOD32 Antivirus<br>Antivirus Software | 32,176 |

**FIGURE 10.10** The CNET download.com website features many categories of security software that you can download.

**Security suites** are packages of security software that include a combination of features. The advantage to using a suite is that you get "complete" protection, but they can be expensive and use a lot of system resources. The main complaint many people have is that they decrease the system performance. This may not be a big deal if you have a fast machine with lots of RAM, but if you have an older, slower machine, the effects could be quite noticeable. In the past, I've uninstalled programs that negatively affected my system's performance in favor of programs with less impact.

Macs come preconfigured to provide protection against malicious software and security threats, and there are far fewer threats to Macs to begin with, so many Mac users don't feel the need to install additional security software on their computers. Although less common than attacks on Windows computers, Macs can still be targeted. Between September 2011 and March 2012, more than 550,000 Macs were infected with a Trojan that exploited a flaw in Java and downloaded itself when the Mac user visited a website containing the malware. The Trojan stole usernames, passwords, and other data. Using the Security and Privacy preferences, you can lock your Mac down even more by requiring passwords, enabling the firewall, and turning off location services. Businesses that have both Mac and Windows computers should consider adding another layer of security to prevent the Macs from becoming hosts that spread viruses to Windows systems. Also, some people run both Mac and Windows on the same computer, which requires extra security measures.

# HARDWARE

At home, you should use a router between your computers and the Internet. The router provides several important security functions. A **router** is a device that connects two or more networks together—in this case, your home network and the Internet.

First, the router acts like a firewall. It can prevent unauthorized access to your network. The default setup of most home routers has this feature enabled, and you can customize it by using the router utility. For example, you might set restrictions on the type of traffic that can access your network, restrict the time of day that a computer can access the Internet, or define which sites can or cannot be accessed (think parental controls). You might need to customize your router to allow certain applications through—especially if you like to play online games.

Another important security feature of a router is called **network address translation (NAT)**. The router faces the public network (Internet) and has a public IP address that it uses to communicate with the network, but inside your house, the router supplies each device with a private IP address that's only valid on your private network. To the outside world, only the router is visible, so it shields the rest of your devices. The devices inside your network can communicate with each other directly, but any outside communication must go through the router.

A wireless router has all the features described but also provides a wireless access point to your network. This can be a potential security risk if it's not properly secured. Use the router setup utility to change the **SSID (service set identifier)**, or wireless network name, and enable and configure wireless encryption (see Figure 10.11). **Wireless encryption** adds security to a wireless network by encrypting transmitted data. You should use the strongest form of wireless encryption that's supported by the devices and operating systems on your network.

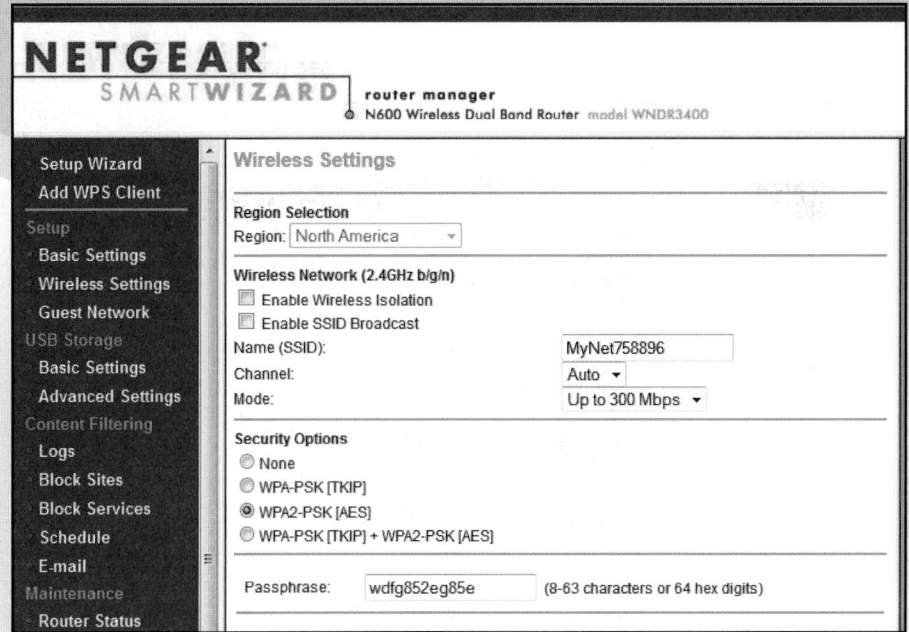

**FIGURE 10.11** Use the router utility to secure wireless access.

When setting up a wireless network, you should put security at the top of your list. Older routers came with no encryption configured and a default user name and password that anyone could find on the Internet. Newer routers come preconfigured with security in place.

WiFi Protected Setup (WPS) is a way to set up a secure wireless home network. Routers with WPS use a push button, Personal Identification Number (PIN), or USB key to automatically configure your devices to connect to your network. Using this method, you don't need to manually type (or remember) the network name (SSID) and wireless security passphrases (see Figure 10.12).

You should strive to use the highest level of security on your network, even though configuring all of your devices can be tricky. The harder it is to find and guess the settings on your network, the less likely it will be that someone will access it without your permission. Some things that you can do to secure your network:

- Change the SSID and disable SSID broadcast so that your network is not visible to others.
- Change the default administrator name and password.
- Use WPA2 encryption and a difficult passphrase.
- Set up Mac address filtering so that only devices in the list are allowed.

**FIGURE 10.12** Enter the security key or press the button on the router to use WiFi Protected Setup to join this network.

# OPERATING SYSTEM

The most important piece of security software on your computer is the operating system itself. It's absolutely critical that you keep it patched and up to date (see Figure 10.13). Many times, malware threats are only capable of infecting machines that are unpatched. For example, the Conficker worm can't infect a properly patched Windows computer, yet it infected millions of machines because they were unpatched. By default, Windows and OS X computers are configured to automatically install updates, but you have the option to change that setting. In most cases, you shouldn't change this setting on a home computer. In a school or business environment, this may be changed by the system administrator, who uses another method to update the machines.

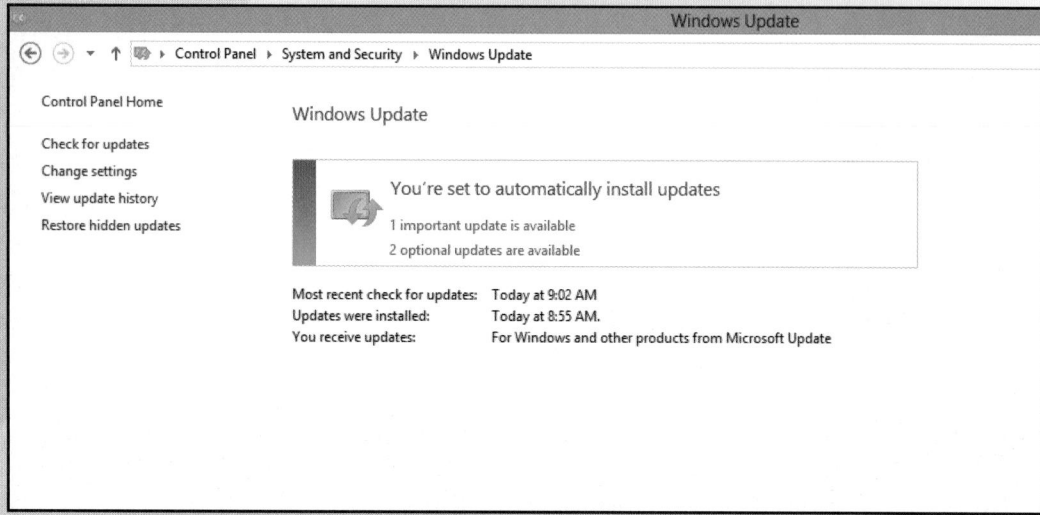

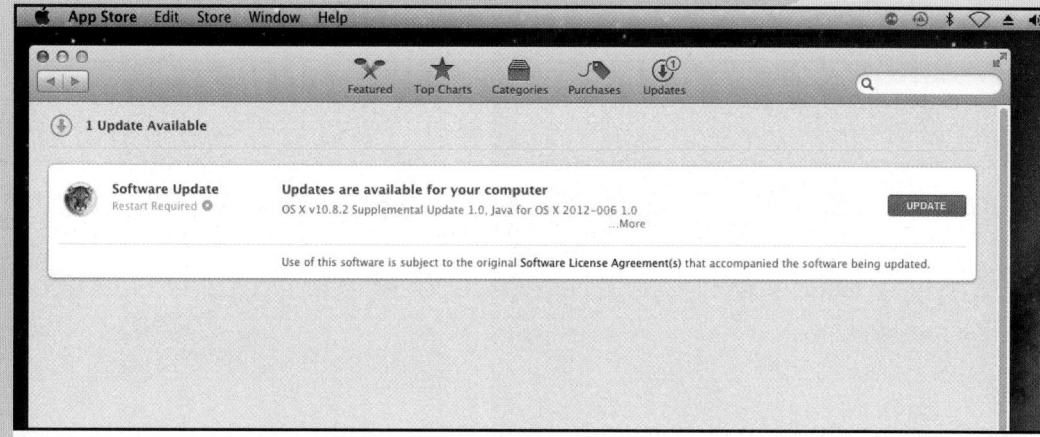

**FIGURE 10.13** Both Windows and OS X need to be kept up to date.

A security warning red flags a potential firewall problem.

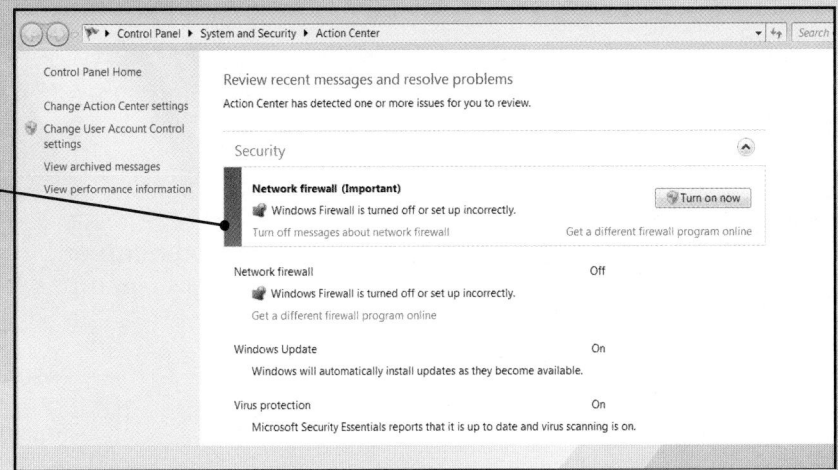

**FIGURE 10.14** The Action Center notifies you and helps resolve potential security problems.

The Windows Action Center is the place to look to verify that your computer is adequately protected. You can access it through the Control Panel or by clicking the white flag in the notification area of the taskbar in Windows 7. Figure 10.14 shows that my computer isn't protected because the firewall is turned off. There's a button I can use to easily correct the problem. Use the Apple menu to check your Mac for software updates.

Adequately protecting your computer systems requires you to be diligent and proactive, installing and maintaining security software and monitoring it for important messages. Even with the best protection, it's possible to get an infection on your machine, but without protection, it's almost a certainty that you will.

## Running Project

Use the Internet to find out what might happen if you use the Windows firewall and another firewall at the same time.

## 5 Things You Need to Know

- A software firewall blocks access to an individual machine.
- Antivirus programs protect against viruses, Trojans, worms, and even some spyware.
- Antispyware software is necessary to prevent adware and spyware infections.
- Network address translation shields your computers from the public network (Internet).
- Use the strongest form of wireless encryption that's supported by your network.

## Key Terms

antispyware software

antivirus program

firewall

network address translation (NAT)

router

security suite

SSID (service set identifier)

wireless encryption

# HOW TO

## Configure Secure Internet Explorer Browser Settings

Microsoft Internet Explorer comes with security features and settings to help protect your computer as you browse the Web. In this How To activity, we examine and configure these settings.

**1** Open a new, blank Word document and save it as **lastname_firstname_ch10_howto1**. Use this file to answer the questions in this exercise. Open Internet Explorer. If the Set Up Windows Internet Explorer dialog box opens, click *Ask me later* and then close the Welcome tab that opens. Open the Tools menu, and click *Internet Options*.

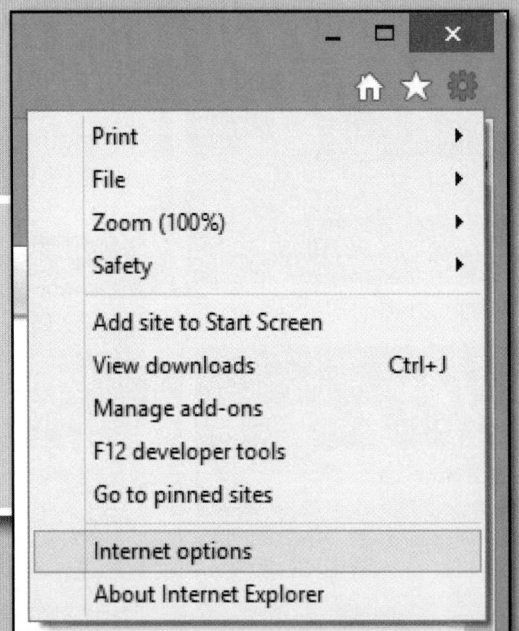

**2** On the General tab, verify that the correct home page is set. Some browser hijackers may change this. Under Browsing history, what type of information is stored? Click the *Delete* button. What are the options available? Which options are checked by default? Click *About deleting browsing history*, and read the Help page. If this is your own computer, you may choose to delete some of these objects. Which would you choose? Don't delete anything in a school lab unless directed by your instructor. Close the Help screen and cancel the Delete Browsing History dialog box.

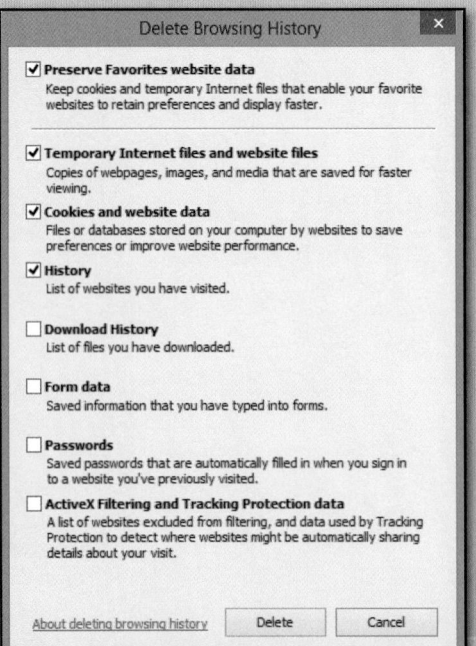

**3** In the Internet Options dialog box, click the *Security* tab. In the Select a zone to view or change security settings box, click *Internet*, and read the description below it. Click *Local intranet*, and read the description. How is the security level for this zone different from the Internet zone? Click the *Sites* button and then click the *Advanced* button. Are there any websites in this zone? If not, are there any that you believe should be there? Click *Close* and then *Cancel*.

Click *Trusted sites*, and read the description. How is the security level for this zone different from the Internet zone? Click the *Sites* button. Are there any websites in this zone? If it's not already listed, add the site pearsoned.com to the Trusted sites. In the Add this website to the zone box, type **pearsoned.com**, uncheck the box that says Require server verification (https:) for all sites in this zone, and then click *Add*. Take a screen shot of this window and paste it into your document. Click *Close*. You may be required to add your school website or learning management system (such as BlackBoard or Canvas) as a trusted site in order to use it effectively.

**4** Click the *Privacy* tab. What is the Settings level set to? Slide the slider up and down, and read each description. How do you think increasing the level would affect your browsing experience? Click *Sites*. Are there any sites listed? Click *OK*.

Is the Pop-up Blocker on? Click *Settings*. Click *Learn more about Pop-up Blocker*. What's a pop-up? Even with the Pop-up Blocker turned on, you might see some pop-ups—why? Close the Help window and the Pop-up Blocker Settings dialog box.

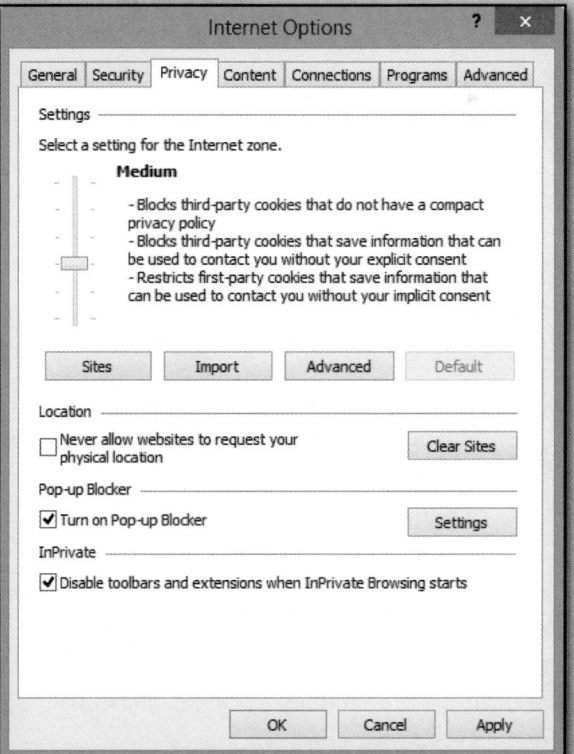

**5** Click the *Advanced* tab. Scroll down to the Security section in the Settings dialog box. If not checked, check the boxes for Do not save encrypted pages to disk and Empty Temporary Internet Files folder when browser is closed. Both of these options will increase your security. Take a screen shot of this window and paste it into your document. Click *OK*. Type up your answers and submit your file as directed by your instructor.

**MAC** If you are using a Mac, you can configure Safari in a similar manner.

**1** Open Safari and click the Safari menu. What options are available in this menu?

**2** Click *Private Browsing* and read the description in the window that opens. How does Private Browsing protect you? Click *Cancel* and reopen the Safari menu. Click *Reset Safari*. What items does this remove? Click *Cancel*.

**Do you want to turn on Private Browsing?**

Safari can keep your browsing history private. When you turn on private browsing, Safari doesn't remember the pages you visit, your search history, or your AutoFill information.

Cancel     OK

**3** Click the Safari menu and select *Preferences*. On the *General* tab, verify that the correct search engine and home page is set. How long do items remain in History?

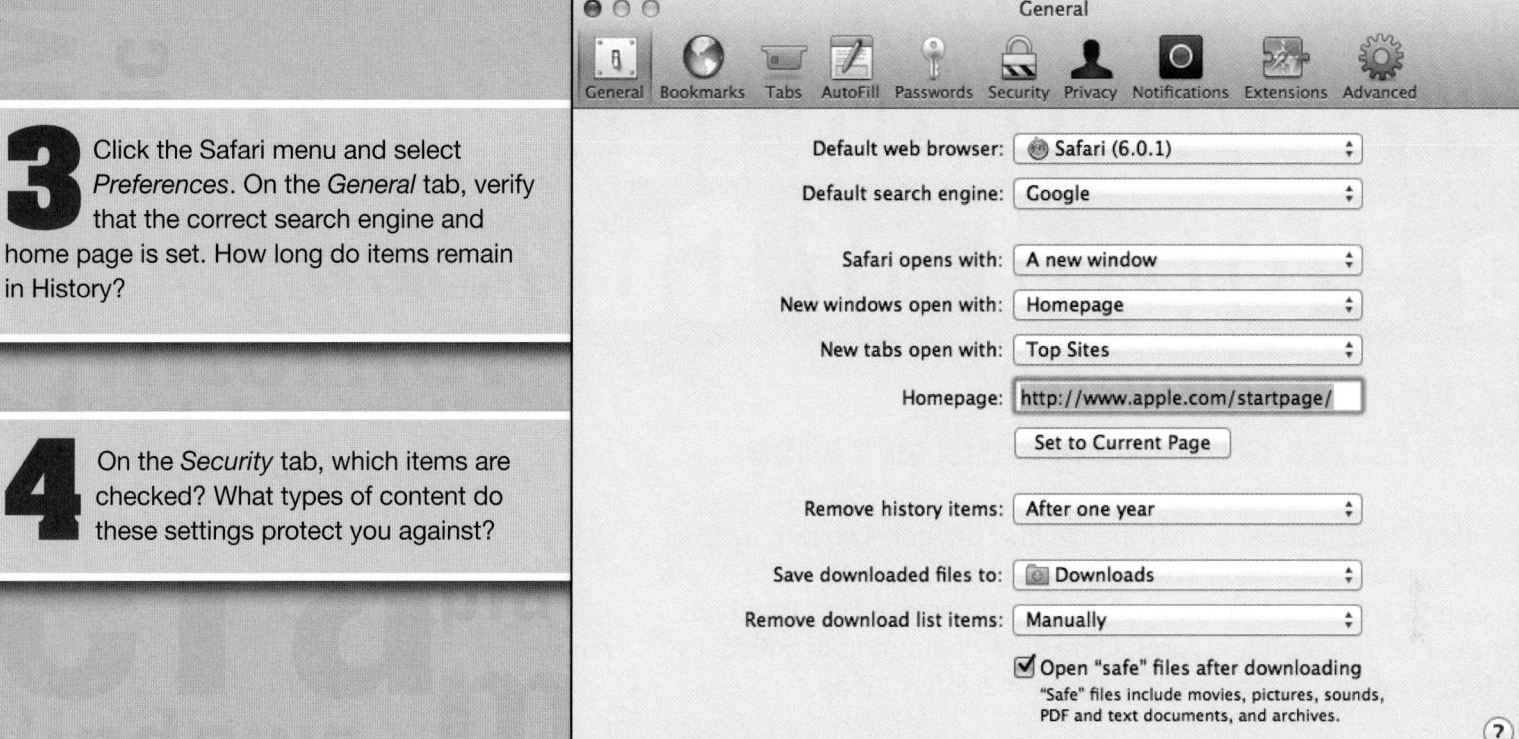

**4** On the *Security* tab, which items are checked? What types of content do these settings protect you against?

**5** On the *Privacy* tab, how many websites have stored data or cookies on your computer? Click *Details* and take a screen shot of this window and paste it into your document. What other settings are found on this tab? Click the help symbol on this screen and read about the Privacy preferences. How do websites use location services? Type up your answers, including the screen shot, save the file as **lastname_firstname_ch10_howto1,** and submit it as directed by your instructor.

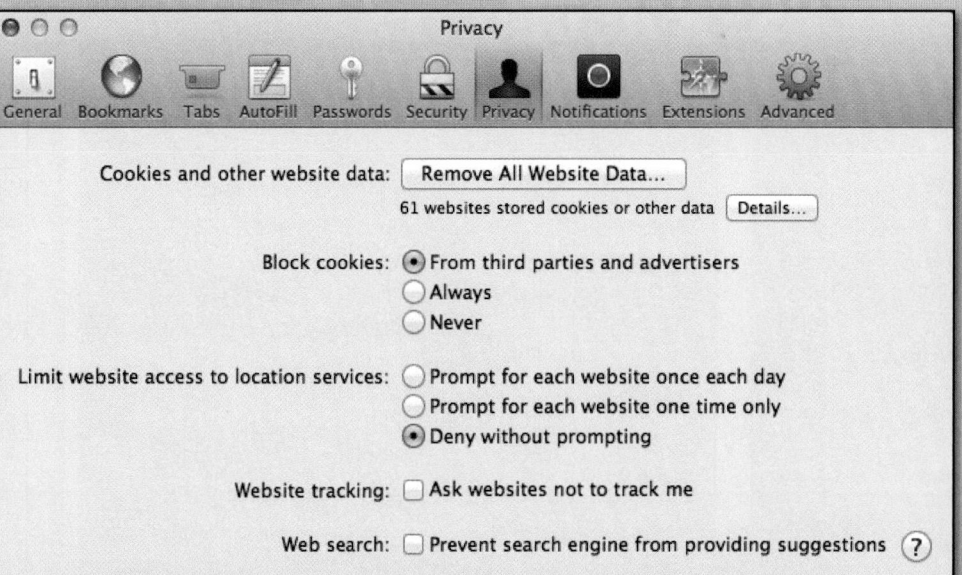

# An Ounce of Prevention Is Worth a Pound of Cure

**4 OBJECTIVE**
## Discuss safe computing practices.

The list of threats grows daily in size and danger. The only way to be truly safe is to unplug your computer and never connect it to a network (especially the Internet), but because this isn't practical for most computer users, practicing safe computing is critical to protecting your system and your personal information.

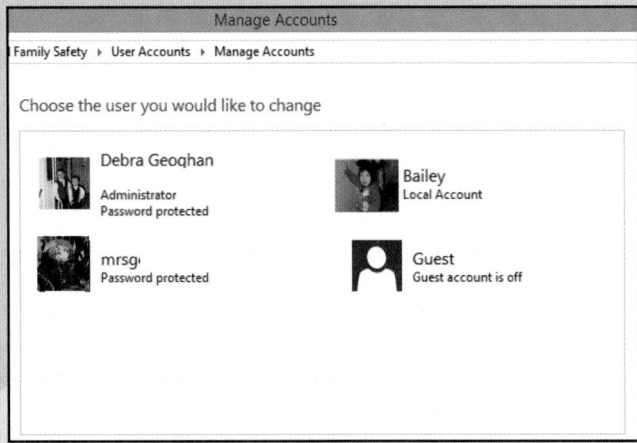

## USER ACCOUNTS

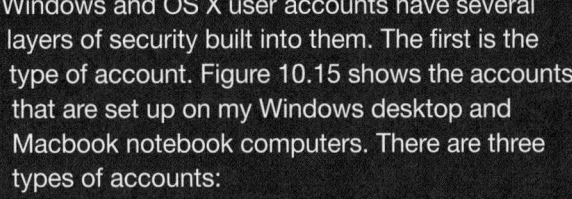

Windows and OS X user accounts have several layers of security built into them. The first is the type of account. Figure 10.15 shows the accounts that are set up on my Windows desktop and Macbook notebook computers. There are three types of accounts:

- Standard account—for everyday computing.
- Administrator account—for making changes, installing software, configuring settings, and completing other tasks—called Admin on a Mac.
- Guest account—for users who need temporary access to a system. This account is off by default.

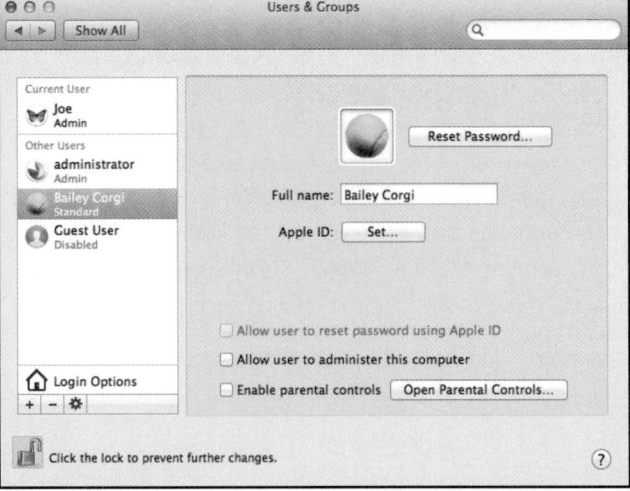

**FIGURE 10.15** User Accounts on a Windows and OS X Computer

When you create an account on a Windows 8 computer, you have the option to use your email address linked to your Microsoft account, or to create a local user. Either account type can be set up as an administrator or a standard user. Using your Microsoft account links you to your cloud resources such as Skydrive.

It's generally a good idea to create a Standard user account for your day-to-day tasks and use the Administrator account only when necessary. Tasks that require administrator-level permission, such as installing a new program, will prompt you for administrator credentials. Also, on a Windows computer, **User Account Control (UAC)** will notify you before changes are made to your computer (see Figure 10.16). While this may seem like a nuisance, it prevents malware from making changes to your system without your knowledge. You should *not* turn it off. It's important to always read the message in the UAC box before clicking Yes. Some malware infects computers by tricking users into clicking fake Windows notification boxes. Parental Controls allow you to put limits on your children's user accounts. Of course, if your child knows the administrator password, he or she can easily change these settings.

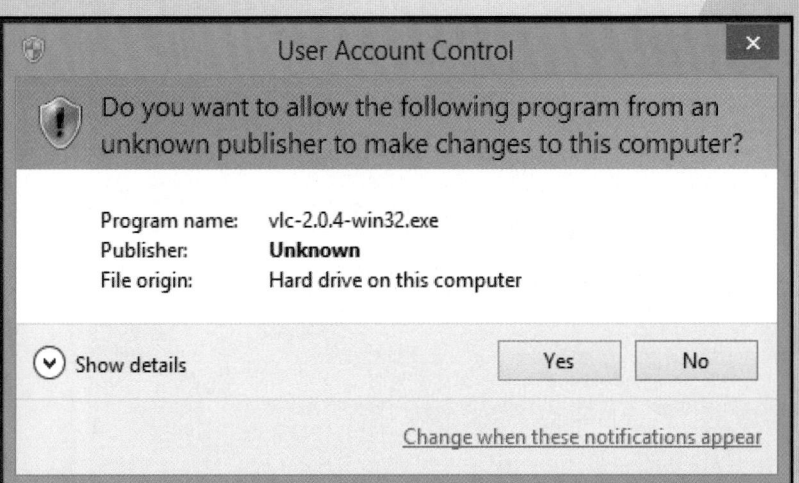

**FIGURE 10.16** User Account Control asks for permission to make changes on your computer.

# SECURING A USER ACCOUNT

What's the password on your computer user account? Do you even have one? Is it your pet's name, your birthday, your middle name, or something else that someone who knows you could easily guess? Is it written on a sticky note and affixed on your monitor or hidden under your keyboard? We all have multiple accounts that we need to log in to and so many usernames and passwords to remember that it's not a surprise that we try to make it easier for ourselves by making our passwords easy to recall. How well we protect our accounts goes a long way toward protecting the information they contain.

To make matters worse, different systems have different rules for acceptable passwords. The more places we have accounts, the more complicated it gets. As humans, we try to use the same password on multiple accounts, but this also makes them less secure. If a hacker manages to get the password to your email account, he or she may also have just gotten the password to your bank account. And it's pretty easy for someone to get your password. Don't think so? Ask Sarah Palin. In 2008, her personal Yahoo! email account was hacked by a college kid. He reset her password by correctly answering her security questions. The security questions on most sites are things that are easy to find out about a person: high school mascot, mother's maiden name, favorite color, birth date. In Palin's case, she's a public figure, so the information was pretty much common knowledge, but how much of this information could I find on your Facebook profile? Password-cracking software can crack even the strongest passwords that are 6–8 characters long in a matter of minutes.

Strong passwords are still the best way to secure your accounts. A deadbolt on your door could be thwarted by someone breaking the door in but will make less determined thieves look for easier targets. A strong password works in much the same way.

Here are some rules for good passwords:

- Use at least eight characters.
- Use a mixture of upper- and lowercase letters.
- Use at least one number.
- If allowed, use at least one special character.
- Don't use any words that can be found in a dictionary.
- Don't use anything personally identifiable.
- Don't write it down.
- Answer security questions with unexpected answers (but remember what you answered).
- Use different passwords for different accounts.
- Use more difficult passwords for accounts such as banks and credit cards.
- Always change default passwords.
- Change your passwords regularly.

Some people prefer to use a password manager to store passwords rather than trying to remember them all individually. Some of these programs can also generate passwords for you, which are more secure than the passwords people normally create because they're randomly generated. If you choose to use a password manager, do your homework to be sure the program you choose is very secure and your passwords are safe. There is always potential for someone to find your passwords using a password stealing program easily found online. OS X includes a feature, called Keychain, which stores various passwords and passphrases in one place and makes them accessible through a master password.

Many computers come with fingerprint scanners adding an additional layer of security to gain access to your computer, or allowing you to bypass entering a password. Biometric scanners that measure human characteristics, such as fingerprints, retina, or voice patterns, may someday replace the need to enter passwords. Requiring a magnetic card swipe is another way that businesses control access. You may have seen an example of this when you returned an item to a store. To allow a transaction that takes money out of a cash register, the clerk often will swipe an ID card to complete the transaction. Only users with the authority to reverse a transaction, such as a manager, will be able to do so.

When you create a new account (see Figure 10.17), you're asked for a lot of information to help identify you. Think about your answers carefully so they are hard for someone to guess but also so you're not giving away too much personal information. Select questions that are hard for other people to answer, and use good passwords following the rules of the site.

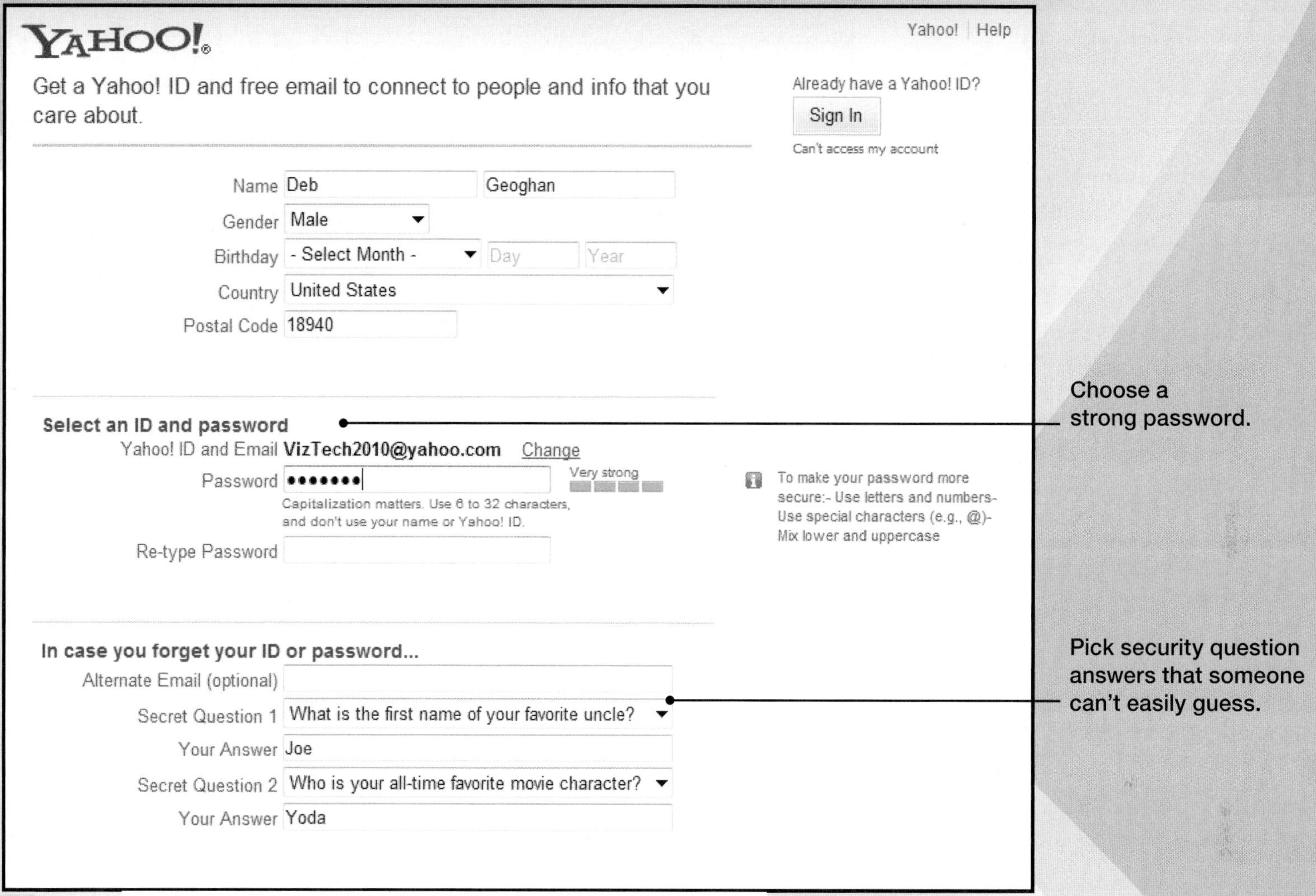

**YAHOO!**®

Yahoo! | Help

Get a Yahoo! ID and free email to connect to people and info that you care about.

Already have a Yahoo! ID?

Sign In

Can't access my account

Name  Deb          Geoghan

Gender  Male          ▼

Birthday  - Select Month -  ▼  Day    Year

Country  United States          ▼

Postal Code  18940

**Select an ID and password** ————————●

Yahoo! ID and Email  **VizTech2010@yahoo.com**   Change

Password  ●●●●●●|          Very strong ▬▬▬▬▯

Capitalization matters. Use 6 to 32 characters, and don't use your name or Yahoo! ID.

ⓘ  To make your password more secure:- Use letters and numbers- Use special characters (e.g., @)- Mix lower and uppercase

Re-type Password

**In case you forget your ID or password...**

Alternate Email (optional)

Secret Question 1  What is the first name of your favorite uncle?  ▼  ————●

Your Answer  Joe

Secret Question 2  Who is your all-time favorite movie character?  ▼

Your Answer  Yoda

Choose a strong password.

Pick security question answers that someone can't easily guess.

**FIGURE 10.17** Registering for a new account requires you to create a password and answer security questions.

When you create an account on a website that requires registration, such as a forum, don't use the same password that you use for other websites that need more security. It also makes sense to have an alternate email account to use just for website registrations. This will help keep the amount of spam down in your regular email account, and if it gets too bad, you can always delete the account without losing your personal contacts. While it's probably fine to have your passwords to such sites saved in your browser, don't have your browser save your passwords to websites such as bank and credit cards companies. Storing secure passwords in a browser leaves them open to potential hackers and other users of your computer.

# ENCRYPTION

Any time you send information across a network, there's the potential for someone to intercept it. **Encryption** converts unencrypted, plain text into code called **ciphertext**. To read encrypted information, you must have a key to decrypt it. This prevents the thief from being able to read the information. When you log in to a website, be sure that you're using a secure connection. Verify that the address bar of your browser shows *https*, which indicates that the site is encrypted (see Figure 10.18). This assures that your information is safe to send. If the connection uses regular old *http*, then your information is sent in plain text.

File and drive encryption secure the data in your files. Windows includes Encrypting File System (EFS), which enables you to encrypt individual files, and BitLocker, which encrypts the entire drive. You can use BitLocker To Go to encrypt removable drives. OS X has a similar feature called FileVault, which when turned on encrypts the contents of your hard disk.

Https in URL                                              Lock in the address bar

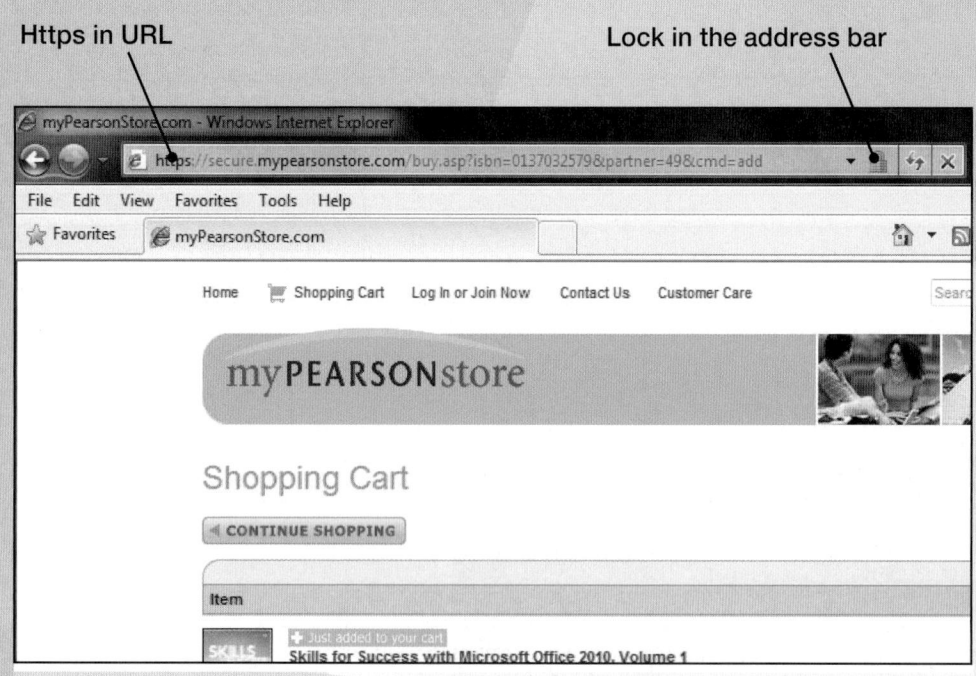

**FIGURE 10.18** This site uses encryption to safeguard the information you send.

# ACCEPTABLE USE POLICIES

Many businesses and schools have an **acceptable use policy (AUP)** that computer and network users must abide by. Although you might find them restrictive and annoying, from the business perspective, they force users to practice safe computing and thus prevent a lot of potential problems from affecting the systems. The restrictions you have depend on the type of business and the type of information you need access to. In a highly secure business, the AUP would likely prohibit all personal use of systems, including checking email, shopping online, using social networks, and playing online games. All these activities potentially could lead to malware being introduced into the system.

It's a good idea to have a personal AUP in place, too. It doesn't need to be a formal document, but all the users of your computers and home network should follow safe computing guidelines. It's a lot easier to prevent damage than it is to fix it.

- Be smart when reading email: Open attachments only if they're expected and you know exactly where they came from, and be sure your antivirus software scans them before you open them.
- Be wary of phishing and fraud scams, and delete any suspicious email right away.
- Make sure your normal user accounts are standard user accounts, and only use administrator accounts when necessary.
- Use good, strong passwords, and change them regularly.
- Be cautious of the information you enter on websites, and look for https encrypted pages.

## ETHICS

When criminals use encryption to hide their illegal activities, law enforcement officials often need to crack the codes. The U.S. government has tried to require encryption companies to provide them with a backdoor key that would allow them to unlock anything that uses the encryption. Thus far, they've been unsuccessful in making this happen and are forced to use brute-force methods to try to guess the criminal's passwords. Over the years, there have been allegations that the National Security Agency (NSA) has embedded a back door into various versions of encryption and random number generators used to create encryption algorithms.

In 2010, after a year of failed attempts, the U.S. government was unable to crack the password of a Brazilian banker who had been seized by Brazilian authorities. Should the government have the right to require a company to provide them with the key to unlock such types of evidence? What if it also enables them to decrypt any information that's encoded with the same key (such as yours)? What if the encryption hides suspected terrorism information? Or the hard drive of a suspected pedophile? Does the type of crime change your answer?

## ► Running Project

Visit **http://staysafeonline.org/teach-online-safety/higher-education/** and read the Internet Safety and Security Tips for College Students and the STOP. THINK. CONNECT. tips and advice sheet. Use this advice to craft an AUP for your college classmates.

## 4 Things You Need to Know

- Use a standard account for everyday computing.
- User Account Control (UAC) will notify you before changes are made to your computer.
- Strong passwords are still the best way to secure your accounts.
- Encryption converts plain text into code.

## Key Terms

acceptable use policy (AUP)

ciphertext

encryption

User Account Control (UAC)

# HOW TO

## Secure a Microsoft Word Document

Microsoft Office allows you to set different levels of protection on your documents.

- Encrypt with Password uses encryption to protect the document. Once the correct password is entered, the document can be viewed and edited.
- Restrict Editing allows you to control which parts of the document can be edited.
- Restrict Access allows you to grant people access to view, but not edit, copy, or print the document.

In this activity, you will secure your document with a password and restrict editing.

**1** Open a new, blank Word document and type your name and date in the file and save it as **lastname_firstname_ch10_howto2**. Type the information in the three bullet points provided at the beginning of this How To exercise. Click the *File* tab, then click *Info*. Under Permission, click *Protect Document* and Click *Encrypt with Password*.

**2** In the Encrypt Document dialog box, type the password **password1** and then Click *OK*. Re-enter the password and click *OK* again. Your document will now require the password to open it. (To remove the password from a file, repeat the process and delete the password in the Encrypt Document dialog box.)

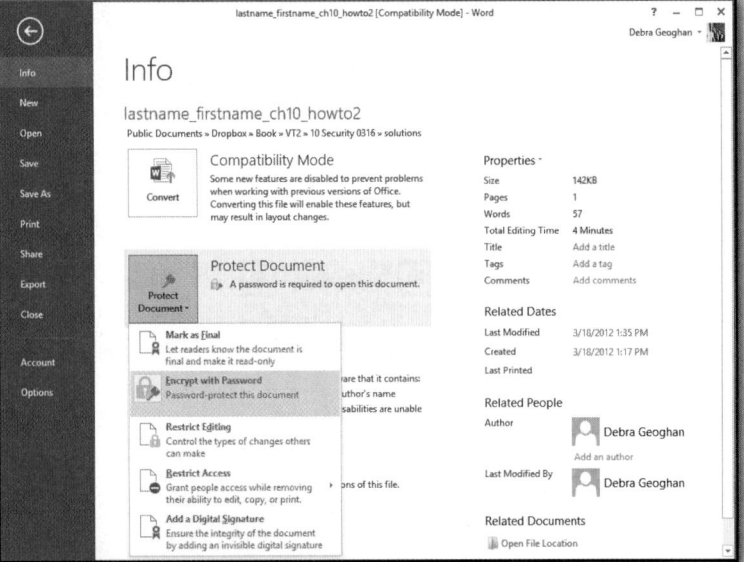

**3** Save and close your document, and then reopen it. When prompted for a password, enter **password1** to check that your password works. Take a screenshot of this prompt and then click *Open*. Paste your screenshot in your document below the bulleted list.

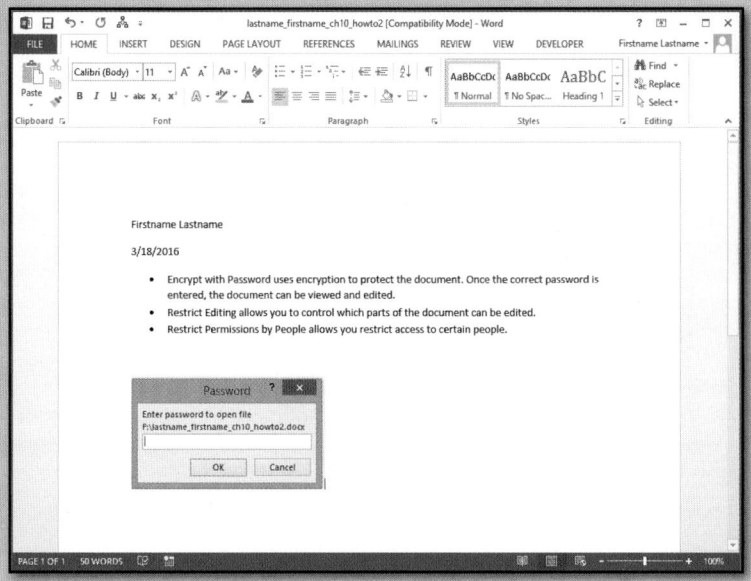

**4** Click the *File* tab. On the Info page, click *Protect Document*, and then click *Restrict Editing.* In the Restrict Editing pane, check the *Allow only this type of editing in the document* box, and if necessary select *No changes (Read only).*

**5** Check to make sure that your document is correct and complete, and then click the *Yes, Start Enforcing Protection* button. Verify that Password is selected and type **password2** in the dialog box.

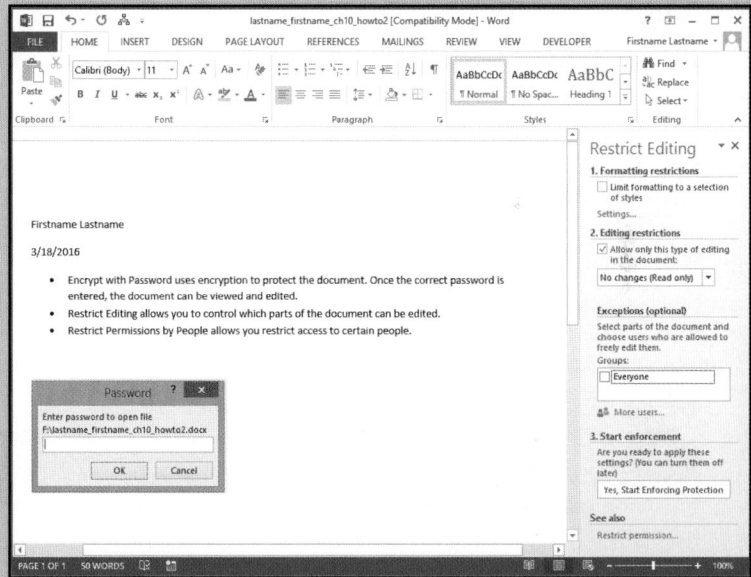

**6** Try to edit your document to verify that your protection was enforced. What happened? Click *Stop Protection* and enter **password2** in the dialog. Type **I can edit after I Stop Protection.** Save your file and submit as directed by your instructor.

**MAC**

## If you have a Mac:

**1** Open a new, blank Word document, and type your name and date in the file and save it as **lastname_firstname_ch10_howto2**. Type the information in the three bullet points provided previously. Click the Word menu, and select Preferences.

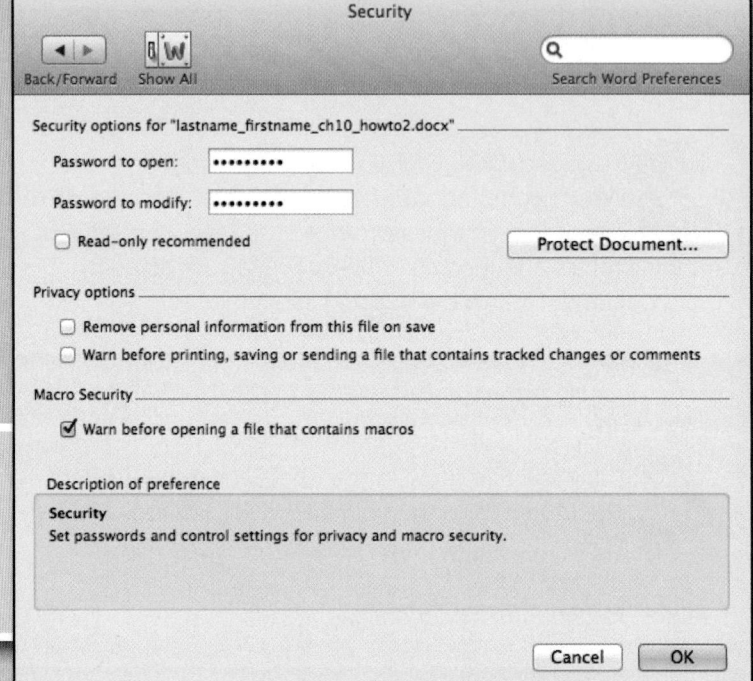

**2** Under Personal Settings, click *Security*. In the Password to open box, type **password1** and then click *OK*. Re-enter the password and click *OK* again. Your document will now require the password to open it.

**3** Save and close your document, and then reopen it. When prompted for a password, enter **password1** to check that your password works. Take a screenshot of this prompt and then click *Open*. Paste your screenshot in your document below the bulleted list.

Student Name
3/18/2013

- Encrypt with Password uses encryption to protect the document. Once the correct password is entered, the document can be viewed and edited.
- Restrict Editing allows you to control which parts other document can be edited.
- Restrict Permissions by People allows you to restrict access to certain people.

**4** Click the *Tools* menu, then click *Protect Document*. Under Protect document for, click *Read Only*. In the Password (optional) box, type **password2** and then click *OK*. Re-enter the password and click OK again. Your document will now require the password to edit it.

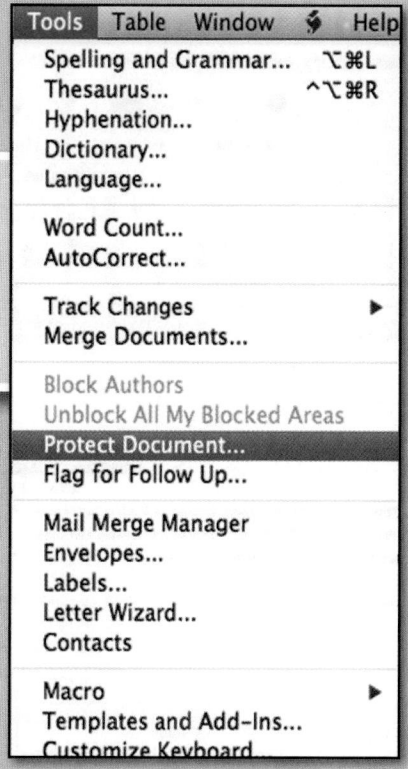

**5** Try to edit your document to verify that your document is protected. What happened? From the Tools menu, click *Unprotect Document* and enter **password2** in the dialog box. Type **I can edit after I click Unprotect Document.** Save your file and submit it as directed by your instructor.

Firstname Lastname
May 6, 2016

- Encrypt with Password uses encryption to protect the document. Once the correct password is entered, the document can be viewed and edited.
- Restrict Editing allows you to control which parts of the document can be edited.
- Restrict Access allows you to grant people access to view, but not edit, copy, or print the document.

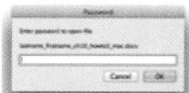

I can edit after I click Unprotect Document.

# The Law Is on Your Side

## 5 OBJECTIVE

### Discuss laws related to computer security and privacy.

Because computer crimes are so closely related to ordinary crime, many laws that already exist also apply to computer crimes. For example, theft and fraud are illegal whether a computer is used or not. However, cybercrime has also created new crimes that aren't covered by existing laws, and over the past two decades, the United States has enacted several important laws.

## THE ENFORCERS

Because the types of crimes are so varied, there's no single authority that's responsible for investigating cybercrime. The federal agencies that investigate cybercrime include the Federal Bureau of Investigation (FBI), the United States Secret Service, the United States Immigration and Customs Enforcement, the United States Postal Inspection Service, the Bureau of Alcohol, Tobacco, Firearms and Explosives (ATF), and the United States Department of Justice Computer Crime and Intellectual Property Section (CCIPS). Numerous local agencies and task forces also exist. To make it easier for victims to report cybercrimes, the **Internet Crime Complaint Center (IC3)** provides a website (**ic3.gov**) on which to file a report (see Figure 10.19). The IC3 will then process it and forward it to the appropriate agency.

**FIGURE 10.19** The IC3 is the place to report an online crime.

### INTERNET SAFETY ALERT

# FBI
## INTERNET CRIME COMPLAINT CENTER

### ARE YOU A SAFE INTERNET USER?
### YOU MAY BE AT RISK
### IF YOU ANSWER "YES" TO ANY
### OF THE FOLLOWING QUESTIONS:

➢ Do you visit websites by clicking on links within an email?

➢ Do you reply to emails from companies or persons you are not familiar with?

➢ Have you received packages to hold or ship to someone you met on the Internet?

➢ Have you been asked to cash checks and wire funds to an employer you met online?

➢ Would you cash checks or money orders received through an online transaction without first confirming their legitimacy?

➢ Would you provide your personal/banking information as a result of an email notification?

## DON'T BE AN INTERNET CRIME VICTIM!

**FOR MORE INFORMATION AND
TO TEST YOUR ONLINE PRACTICES VISIT:**

www.LooksTooGoodToBeTrue.com

**TO REPORT AN ONLINE CRIME VISIT:**

# www.IC3.gov

**BROUGHT TO YOU BY THE FOLLOWING:**

   MRC

# CURRENT LAWS

In 1986, recognizing the growth and potential of cybercrime, the U.S. Congress passed the Computer Fraud and Abuse Act, making it a crime to access classified information. Amendments between 1988 and 2002 added additional cybercrimes, including theft of property as a part of a fraud scheme; intentionally altering, damaging, or destroying data belonging to others; distribution of malicious code; denial-of-service attacks; and trafficking in passwords and other personal information. The USA Patriot antiterrorism legislation in 2001 and the Cyber Security Enhancement Act (part of the Homeland Security Act) in 2002 included many provisions for fighting cybercrime. In 2012, a simulated cyberattack on New York City's power supply was used to help gain senate support for the Cybersecurity Act of 2012. The bill, and others like it, created cybersecurity regulations for companies critical to U.S. national and economic security, such as banks and infrastructure (electricity, water, and communications).

One of the things that makes it difficult to catch cybercriminals is that many of them attack from outside of the United States. Countries around the world have been trying to create a united system to fight cybercrime. The Convention on Cybercrime is a treaty drafted by the Council of Europe, signed by more than 40 countries, including the United States, Canada, and Japan, but to date, there's little progress in stemming the tide of cybercrime.

# Find Out MORE

Visit **lookstoogoodtobetrue.com**, and click *Take our Test*. Take several of the tests to evaluate your risks. How well did you do? Are there steps that you should be taking to better protect yourself?

# CAREER SPOTLIGHT

IT security is a great field to consider if you have an interest in technology and like to solve problems. According to the *Occupational Outlook Handbook*, "[T]he responsibilities of computer security specialists have increased in recent years as cyber attacks have become more sophisticated." And employment prospects are good, with this and related occupations expected to grow much faster than the average. Upper-level positions require several years of experience, at least a bachelor's degree, and industry certifications, but there are also entry-level positions that have less demanding requirements.

In 2009, CNNMoney.com ranked Computer/Network Security Consultant as 8th in the top 50 Best Jobs in America, citing the challenge, excitement, job opportunities, and big paycheck. The article recommends a computer science degree and security certifications as minimum qualifications.

# GREEN COMPUTING

## BOTNETS

How do security and privacy relate to green computing? If you leave your computer turned on but idle, you expect it to go into sleep mode. If your computer becomes infected with malware and becomes part of a botnet, then it may be using energy even when you think it's in sleep mode. Imagine the amount of energy that's consumed by the thousands of compromised systems all over the world that are part of botnets. So, keep your machine clean and secure, assure that it's not part of a botnet, and when you'll be away from it for long periods of time, simply turn it off.

## ▶ Running Project

As of this writing, the Cybersecurity Act of 2012 was still being debated. What's the status of this act? Have there been any other cybercrime laws passed since then?

## 3 Things You Need to Know

- Existing laws (such as theft and fraud laws) apply to cybercrime.
- The Internet Crime Complaint Center (IC3) is the place to file a cybercrime report.
- Because many attacks originate from outside the United States, international cooperation is needed.

## Key Terms

Internet Crime Complaint Center (IC3)

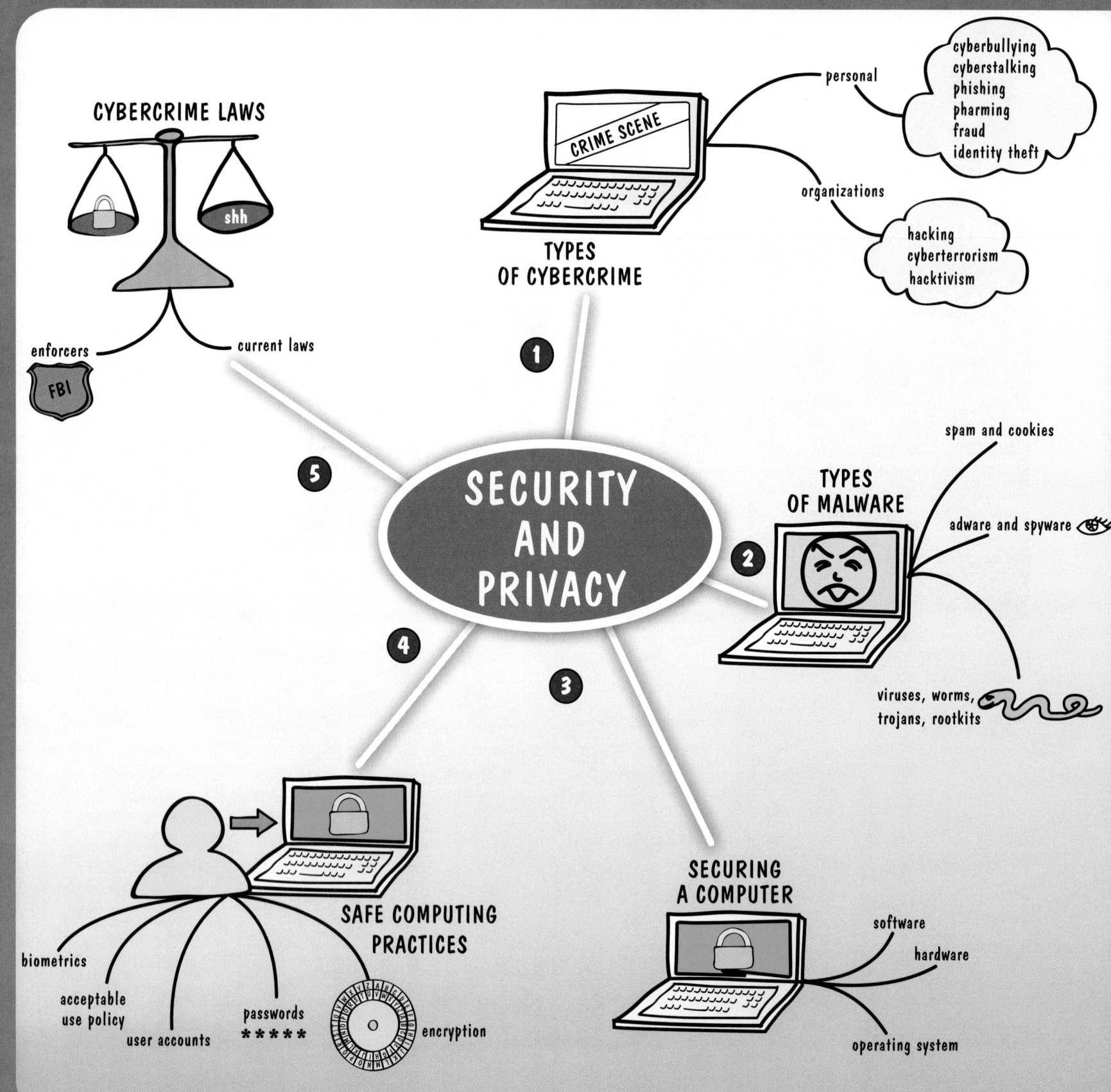

CYBERCRIME LAWS

shh

enforcers — current laws

FBI

TYPES OF CYBERCRIME

CRIME SCENE

personal — cyberbullying, cyberstalking, phishing, pharming, fraud, identity theft

organizations — hacking, cyberterrorism, hacktivism

SECURITY AND PRIVACY

1

2

3

4

5

TYPES OF MALWARE

spam and cookies

adware and spyware

viruses, worms, trojans, rootkits

SECURING A COMPUTER

software

hardware

operating system

SAFE COMPUTING PRACTICES

biometrics

acceptable use policy

user accounts

passwords *****

encryption

438

# Objectives Recap

1. Discuss various types of cybercrime.
2. Differentiate between different types of malware.
3. Explain how to secure a computer.
4. Discuss safe computing practices.
5. Discuss laws related to computer security and privacy.

# Key Terms

acceptable use policy (AUP) **428**
adware **411**
antispyware software **415**
antivirus program **414**
botnet **412**
ciphertext **428**
computer fraud **406**
cookie **410**
cyberbullying **404**
cybercrime **404**
cyberstalking **404**
cyberterrorism **408**
denial-of-service attack **412**
encryption **428**
firewall **414**
hacking **408**
hacktivism **408**
identity theft **407**
Internet Crime Complaint
    Center (IC3) **434**

keylogger **413**
logic bomb **412**
malware **410**
network address translation
    (NAT) **416**
payload **412**
pharming **405**
phishing **405**
rootkit **413**
router **416**
security suite **416**
spam **410**
spyware **411**
SSID (service set identifier) **416**
time bomb **412**
Trojan horse **412**
User Account Control (UAC) **425**
virus **412**
wireless encryption **416**
worm **412**

# Summary

1. **Discuss various types of cybercrime.**

   Cybercrime is any crime that happens via the Internet. Cybercrime against individuals includes cyberbullying, cyberstalking, phishing, pharming, fraud, social network attacks, or identity theft. Cybercrime against organizations includes hacking and cyberterrorism.

2. **Differentiate between different types of malware.**

   Malware is malicious software. It ranges from spam, cookies, and adware to spyware, viruses, worms, Trojans, and rootkits. Most malware carries a payload that causes harm to your system or causes your system to attack others.

3. **Explain how to secure a computer.**

   Software to secure a system includes firewall, antivirus, and antispyware programs. It's also critical to keep operating systems and other software up to date. Hardware protection includes a router with firewall functions, network address translation (NAT), and wireless encryption.

4. **Discuss safe computing practices.**

   Standard user accounts should be used for normal computing, and administrator accounts should be used only when needed. Passwords should be strong and changed frequently. Accounts that require more security should not share a password with less secure accounts. Encryption should be used to transmit data securely, and acceptable use policies should outline permitted activities.

5. **Discuss laws related to computer security and privacy.**

   The Internet Crime Complaint Center accepts victim reports and sends them to the proper authorities. Normal theft and fraud laws apply to cybercrime. Federal laws that cover cybercrime include the Computer Fraud and Abuse Act, the U.S. Patriot Act, and the Homeland Security Act. International agreements are also in place to fight cybercrime.

Chapter 10

439

Visit **pearsonhighered.com/Geoghan** for data files, simulations, VizClips, and additional study materials.

# Application Project

## Microsoft Office Application Project 1:
## Word 2010 Level 3

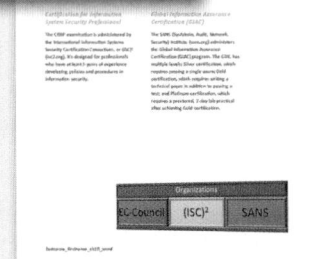

**PROJECT DESCRIPTION:** In this Microsoft Word project, you will format a Word document with columns, outline and shade text, apply styles, work with Clip Art and SmartArt graphics.

**INSTRUCTIONS:** For the purpose of grading the project you are required to perform the following tasks:

| Step | Instructions |
|------|--------------|
| **1** | Start Word. Download and open the file named *vt_ch10_word*. Save the file as **lastname_firstname_ch10_word**. |
| **2** | Change the orientation of the document to landscape. |
| **3** | Select all of the remaining text (except the title) in the document. Modify the selected text so that it displays in three columns. |
| **4** | Insert a column break immediately to the left of the subtitles: Computer Hacking Forensic Investigator, Certified Ethical Hacker; Certification for Information System Security Professional; and Global Information Assurance Certification (GIAC). |
| **5** | Apply the Title style to Security Certifications. Center it and change the font size to 36 point. |

| Step | Instructions |
|------|--------------|
| **6** | Apply the Subtitle style to the four subtitles: CompTIA and Cisco Certifications; Computer Hacking Forensic Investigator, Certified Ethical Hacker; Certification for Information System Security Professional; and Global Information Assurance Certification (GIAC). |
| **7** | Move the insertion point to the end of the third column on the first page and press Enter. Search for clip art images using the phrase **security badge** and then insert the image of a gold and black security badge into the document. Close the Clip Art task pane. For your reference, the image is included with the project starting materials with the file name *vt_ch10_image1*. |
| **8** | Apply the Drop Shadow Rectangle picture style to the graphic. Resize the image height to 2.5", and center align the image. |

| Step | Instructions | Step | Instructions |
|---|---|---|---|
| **9** | Move the insertion point to the end of the document and insert a column break. | **12** | Apply the Metallic Scene style to the SmartArt graphic. Change color to Colorful Accent Colors. |
| **10** | Position the insertion point at the top of the last column and insert a SmartArt graphic using the Table List style from the List category. | **13** | Display the text pane for the SmartArt graphic, type **Organizations** in the top bullet, and insert the following text as the three bottom bullets (in this order):<br>**EC-Council**<br>**(ISC)2**<br>**SANS**<br>Close the text pane. |
| **11** | Use the Position button to move the SmartArt graphic in the bottom center of the page with square text wrapping, and then increase the width of the graphic to 6". | **14** | Insert a footer with the filename, save and close document, and then exit Word. Submit the document as directed. |

Visit **pearsonhighered.com/Geoghan** for data files, simulations, VizClips, and additional study materials.

Chapter 10

441

# Microsoft Office Application Project 2:
## PowerPoint Level 3

**PROJECT DESCRIPTION:** In this Microsoft PowerPoint project, you will create a presentation about Windows user accounts. In creating this PowerPoint presentation you will apply design and color themes. You will also insert and format a table and apply animations to objects on your slides, and transitions between slides.

**INSTRUCTIONS:** For the purpose of grading the project you are required to perform the following tasks:

| Step | Instructions |
|------|--------------|
| 1 | Start PowerPoint. Download and open the file named *vt_ch10_ppt*. Save the file as **lastname_firstname_ch10_ppt**. |
| 2 | On Slide 1, type **Windows 8** in the subtitle placeholder. |
| 3 | Apply the Ion theme, purple Variant, to the presentation. |
| 4 | On Slide 2, convert the bulleted list in the content placeholder to Increasing Arrows Process SmartArt graphic. |
| 5 | Change the SmartArt style to Bird's Eye Scene Effect. |

| Step | Instructions |
|------|--------------|
| 6 | On Slide 3 in the content placeholder, add the following 3 bullets:<br>**Provide the most control over a computer.**<br>**Can change security settings, install software and hardware, and access all files on the computer.**<br>**Should only be used when necessary.** |
| 7 | On Slide 4, in the content placeholder, add the following 3 bullets:<br>**For everyday computing.**<br>**Protects your computer by preventing users from making changes that affect everyone who uses the computer.**<br>**Should create one for each user.** |

| Step | Instructions |
|------|--------------|
| **8** | On Slide 5, in the content placeholder, add the following 3 bullets:<br>**Intended primarily for people who need temporary use of a computer.**<br>**Can't install software or hardware, change settings, or create a password.**<br>**Turned off by default.** |
| **9** | Apply the Float In animation with the Float Down effect option and a duration of 01.50 to the bullet list on Slides 3, 4, and 5. |
| **10** | Insert a new slide after Slide 5. Add the title Purpose. In the content pane, add a 3x3 table. |

| Administrator | Standard | Guest |
|---------------|----------|-------|
| Security | Everyday computing | Temporary access |
| Installation and maintenance | Modify own settings | |

| Step | Instructions |
|------|--------------|
| **11** | Change the table style to Medium Style 2—Accent 6 and align it with the middle of the slide. |
| **12** | Apply the Push transition to all slides in the presentation. |
| **13** | Insert the page number and type your name in the footer on the notes and handouts pages for all slides in the presentation. View the presentation in Slide Show view from beginning to end, and then return to Normal view. |
| **14** | Save and close the presentation. Exit PowerPoint. Submit the presentation as directed. |

**Visit pearsonhighered.com/Geoghan** for data files, simulations, VizClips, and additional study materials.

Chapter 10 | 443

# Multiple Choice

Answer the multiple-choice questions below for more practice with key terms and concepts from this chapter.

1. _____ uses email messages that appear to be from trusted websites to trick you into revealing personal information.
   a. Phishing
   b. Pharming
   c. Spam
   d. Botnet

2. A scheme perpetrated over the Internet or by email that tricks a victim into voluntarily and knowingly giving money or property to a person is _____.
   a. phishing
   b. computer fraud
   c. cyberterrorism
   d. a botnet

3. A _____ is a small text file placed on your computer when you visit a website.
   a. cookie
   b. spim
   c. payload
   d. token

4. A _____ allows someone to gain control over a computer while hiding the fact that the computer has been compromised.
   a. virus
   b. spyware
   c. rootkit
   d. worm

5. A _____ is the form of malware that spreads over network connections without any human intervention.
   a. virus
   b. logic bomb
   c. rootkit
   d. worm

6. A _____ is a program that replicates itself and infects computers.
   a. rootkit
   b. denial-of-service attack
   c. time bomb
   d. virus

7. You should use a(n) _____ program to protect your computer from Trojan horses and worms.
   a. adware
   b. rootkit
   c. antivirus
   d. spam

8. You should use a(n) _____ user account for everyday computing.
   a. standard
   b. administrator
   c. guest
   d. public

9. Which password is the strongest?
   a. password
   b. mypassword
   c. myPwa0$r$d
   d. pwa05r5d

10. A _____ blocks unauthorized access to a network or an individual computer.
    a. SSID (service set identifier)
    b. firewall
    c. keylogger
    d. UAC

# True or False

Answer the following questions with T for true or F for false for more practice with key terms and concepts from this chapter.

1. Security experts paid to find security holes in a system are called white-hat hackers.

2. Sending mass, unsolicited email is called spam.

3. A worm is the form of malware that secretly gathers personal information about you.

4. If you have a hardware firewall, you shouldn't also use a software firewall.

5. A logic bomb is an attack that occurs when certain conditions are met.

6. If you keep your operating system up to date, it's not necessary to use security software.

7. Administrator credentials must be used to install software and configure settings on a Windows computer.

8. Wireless encryption adds security to a wireless network by encoding the transmitted data.

9. You should use the same password for all of your accounts.

10. The IC3 is the place for victims to report cybercrimes.

# Fill in the Blank

Fill in the blanks with key terms from this chapter.

1. An unlawful attack against computers or networks done to intimidate a government or its people is _____.

2. Using email and other technologies to embarrass, threaten, or torment an adult is called _____.

3. _____ happens when someone uses your name and other information for financial gain.

4. A(n) _____ is a network of computer zombies controlled by a master.

5. A(n) _____ is a program that replicates itself and infects computers.

6. A(n) _____ appears to be a legitimate program but is actually something malicious.

7. A router uses _____ to shield your devices from the outside world.

8. _____ is a form of malware that shows ads in the form of pop-ups and banners.

9. Businesses and schools require computer users to abide by (an) _____.

10. _____ is plain text that has been encrypted.

# Running Project ...

## ... The Finish Line

Use your answers from the previous sections of the chapter project to discuss the impact of cybercrime on society. How has it changed the way we keep in touch with others? How has it affected the way we conduct business? How has it changed the way you, personally, conduct yourself online?

Write a report responding to the questions raised. Save your file as **lastname_firstname_ch10_project**, and submit it to your instructor as directed.

# Do It Yourself 1

Security software is important to protect your computer from malicious attacks. In this activity, you'll examine your computer to determine what type of security software is installed on it and whether your computer is properly protected.

1. Open a new document and save it as **lastname_firstname_ch10_diy1.**

2. Open the Action Center by clicking on the white flag in the notification area of the Windows taskbar or from the System and Security control panel. If necessary, click the arrow next to Security to open that section. What's your status for each category? Are there any important notices? What software is reported for virus protection and spyware?

3. If necessary, click the arrow next to Maintenance to open that section. What's your status for each category? Are there any important notices? Take a screen shot of the Action Center and paste it into your document.
   If you are using a Mac, open Security and Privacy from System Preferences. Examine each tab and record your settings for each. Take a screen shot of the General tab and paste it into your document. Return to System Preferences and open Software Update. Examine each tab and record your settings for each. Take a screen shot of the Scheduled Check tab and paste it into your document.

4. Type up your answers. Save your file and submit your work as directed by your instructor.

# Do It Yourself 2

The amount of information that someone can find out about you is incredible. In this activity, you'll investigate yourself.

1. Google yourself. Try different variations of your name. Did you find any information about yourself? Do you have a common name that gave you lots of results or an uncommon one that netted you fewer? If you had no luck, try using your parents' names (property owners are likely to yield more results).

2. Now try a few more websites. Choose any two (if you have an account on any of these sites, make sure you're logged out): zabasearch.com, spokeo.com, wink.com, pipl.com, whitepages.anywho.com, addresses.com. Did you find any information about yourself (or your parents)? Was it correct? Is there a way to have the entry removed from the site?

3. Take screen shots of the results pages of your searches. Use an editing tool to obscure any information that you don't wish to submit. Type up your answers, paste the screen shots in the document, save the file as **lastname_firstname_ch10_diy2**, and submit it as directed by your instructor.

# File Management

One of the most common ways to spread malware is by email attachment. It's important to recognize the types of attachments that potentially contain malware.

1. Go to **office.microsoft.com/outlook-help**. Click *Attachments* and then click *Blocked attachments* in Outlook.

2. What are some of the file types that are blocked by Outlook? Why are they blocked? What should you do if you need to send someone a blocked file type?

3. Save your file as **lastname_firstname_ch10_fm**, and submit it as directed by your instructor.

# Critical Thinking

Think about the ways you and your family use your home computers and network.

1. Who are the users of computers in your family? For what purpose(s) does each family member use computers? What type of accounts do they each have? Are they password-protected?

2. Think about the ways each person uses the computer. What are the most likely threats that their usage leaves them vulnerable to? Why?

3. What security software is installed on your computer(s)? How effective has it been in protecting your system? Have you or your family members ever had a virus or other malware infection?

4. Create a family AUP with 6–8 rules that everyone should follow. Are there different rules for different users?

5. Type up your answers, save the file as **lastname_firstname_ch010_ct**, and submit it as directed by your instructor.

# Ethical Dilemma

There's a fine line between white-hat and gray-hat hackers and between gray-hats and black-hats. If a gray-hat hacker breaches a system and posts a warning to the site administrator about the vulnerabilities, the intent isn't malicious.

1. It's illegal to hack into a system without authorization, but is it ethical for a gray-hat to hack into a system if the intent is to help it become more secure? Some experts consider gray-hat hackers an essential part of securing the Internet because they often expose vulnerabilities before they're discovered by the security community. What do you consider the dividing line?

2. Type up your answers, save the file as **lastname_firstname_ch10_ethics**, and submit your work as directed by your instructor.

# On the Web

There are hundreds of known malware threats. Visit the website of two antivirus software vendors such as McAfee (mcafee.com), Norton (norton.com), TrendMicro (trendmicro.com), Panda (pandasecurity.com), or CA (ca.com).

1. What websites did you use? What's the current threat level? Of the top threats, how many can be classified as viruses? Worms? Trojans? How many of them were discovered today? In the past week? How many are at least 1 year old? Are the threats and threat level the same on both sites?

2. Type up your answers, save the file as **lastname_firstname_ch10_web**, and submit your work as directed by your instructor.

# Collaboration

With a group of 3 to 5 students, create a public service announcement on a current cyberthreat. You must receive approval for your topic from your instructor.

**Instructors:** Divide the class into groups of 3 to 5 students, and approve the topics they propose.

**The Project:** Each team is to prepare a Public Service Announcement that teaches your community about a current cyberthreat. You may use any multimedia tool that you're comfortable with. Here are just a few ideas:

- Create a video. You can write a script and cast your group members in it. Use Movie Maker (part of Windows Live Essentials) if you have a PC or iMovie (part of iLife) if you have a Mac.
- Use an online presentation tool, such as SlideRocket, Google Docs, or Zoho.
- Use a screen capture tool, such as Screencast-O-Matic or Jing.
- Create a PowerPoint presentation.

Don't be limited by the above suggestions; pay attention to both the content and the delivery method.

**Students:** Before beginning this project, discuss the roles each group member will play. Choose a team name, which you'll use in submitting your materials. Be sure to divide the work among your members. You may find it helpful to pick a team leader who can direct your activities and ensure that all team contributions are collated through Google Docs or Microsoft Office as directed by your instructor.

**Outcome:** Record the public service announcement using the script you've written. The announcement should be 1–2 minutes long. Save this video as **teamname_ch10_project**.

Turn in a final text version of your script named as **teamname_ch10_script** and your file showing your collaboration named as **teamname_ch10_collab**. Be sure to include the name of your presentation and a listing of all team members. Submit your presentation to your instructor as directed.

# 11

# Databases

**OBJECTIVES**

1. **Identify the parts of a database.**

2. **Compare the four types of databases.**

3. **Explain database management systems.**

4. **Discuss important information systems used in business.**

5. **List examples of databases used in law enforcement and science.**

# IN THIS CHAPTER

We live in the information age. The amount of information we all deal with every day can be overwhelming, and it's growing exponentially every year. A **database** is a collection of related information. It allows us to organize, sort, filter, and query the data in it and make useful information out of it. In this chapter, we discuss electronic databases, what they are, how they're created, and what they're used for.

# Database Basics

I have a coupon organizer that I use to sort my coupons. It's a small folder that has divider labels: Produce, Health and Beauty, Meat, Dairy, Frozen Food, Snacks and Sweets, Household, and Pets. When I clip my coupons, I place them in the appropriate sections so they're easy to find when I'm in the store. The system works pretty well—until I get an item like ice cream. Is it Frozen Food, Dairy, or Snacks and Sweets? The coupon organizer is a simple database that works reasonably well for the narrow type of information stored in it. An electronic version of the coupon organizer would give me more ways to manage my coupons. I wouldn't be limited to a single category for my ice cream; I could search for coupons from a particular manufacturer or sort them by expiration date, and I could create custom shopping lists based on the coupons I have. Let's begin by looking at the parts of a database.

## TABLES, FIELDS, AND RECORDS

A **table** is a database object in which data is stored. It's arranged in rows and columns. The simplest databases consist of a single table—such as a greeting card address list—but a database can also have multiple tables. The tables can be distinct, or they can be related by common information. The database in Figure 11.1 consists of two tables that contain the data as well as several other database objects that are used to manipulate, sort, query, and present the data. We'll explore this database throughout this article.

Two tables: Vehicles and Expenses

Other database objects include queries, forms, and reports.

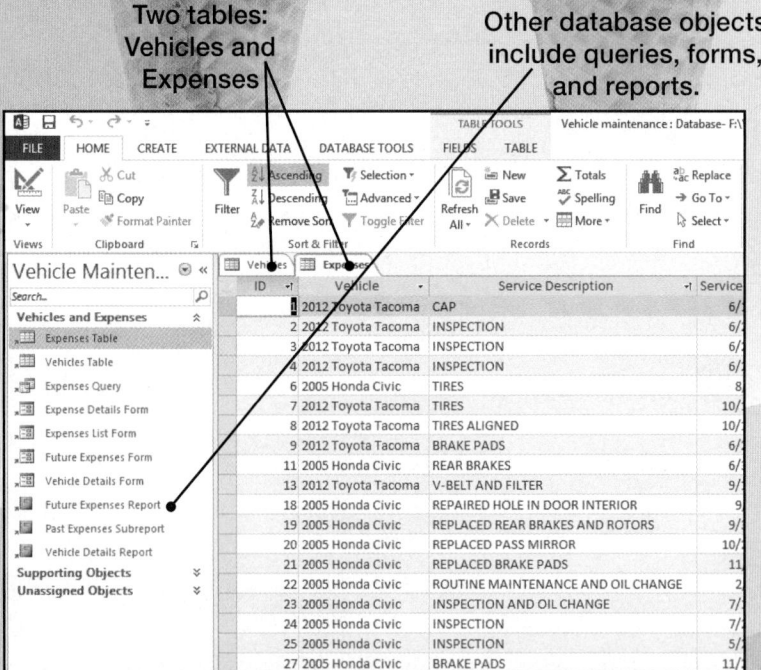

**FIGURE 11.1** An Access Database with Many Database Objects

The two tables in this database are Expenses and Vehicles. Each column in a table is known as a **field**. A field is a single piece of information in a record within a database. In the Vehicles table (see Figure 11.2), the fields include Make, Model, Year, Color, and so on. Each row— called a **record**—contains the information for a single entry in the database (person, place, thing, event, or idea). This table has five records in it—each representing a different vehicle. All five records have the same fields, but the data—or field values—vary. For example, in records 1 and 2, the Make fields contain the same field value (Ford), but the Model, Year, and other field values are different.

The first field in a record is called the **primary key**, or ID, and it uniquely identifies the record in the table. The primary key in this example is just an index number, but it might be a student ID, Social Security number, order number, or other unique identifier associated with the record.

While the table is an easy way to look at small amounts of information, it's not the best way to look at large amounts of data. Even in this small example, several fields are cut off and not displayed on the right.

| | ID | Make | Model | Year | Color | Notes | Pu |
|---|---|---|---|---|---|---|---|
| ⊞ | 1 | Toyota | Tacoma | 2012 | Black | Joe | |
| ⊞ | 3 | Honda | Civic | 2005 | Silver | Mike | |
| ⊞ | 4 | Mercury | Cougar | 1973 | Blue | Joe | |
| ⊞ | 5 | Ford | Taurus | 2009 | White | Joey | |
| ⊞ | 6 | Mazda | CX-7 | 2010 | Black | Deb | |
| ⊞ | 10 | | | 2012 | | | |
| * | (New) | | | | | | |

**FIGURE 11.2** Records in a table can have the same field values.

# FORMS, QUERIES, AND REPORTS

The tables contain all the data, but other database objects are used to manage the information. Forms, reports, and queries are some of the ways we can interact with the table data and use it in constructive ways.

**Forms** serve two purposes: They make data entry easier, and they make it easy to look at specific information on the screen. Figure 11.3 shows a form called Vehicle Details. It shows a single record in an easy-to-view layout. Compare the form in Figure 11.3 to the fifth record in the table in Figure 11.2. All the fields for this record are visible in the form, unlike in the table, where some fields are cut off.

**FIGURE 11.3** A form shows a record in an easy-to-read layout.

A form also makes it easier to enter a new record into a database. In Figure 11.4, a new record has been created, and data is being entered. Forms can be created so they match the layout of a paper form, making it easy to match the fields on the screen with those on the paper. Data entry errors can be reduced by including dropdown lists for fields such as the car model in this example.

In a large database, you often need to pull out information to answer a question. A **query** retrieves specific data from one or more tables. You use a query to ask a question. In this example (see Figure 11.5), the question asked is: "What are the expenses for the 2008 Ford F-150?" The results are presented in a new datasheet.

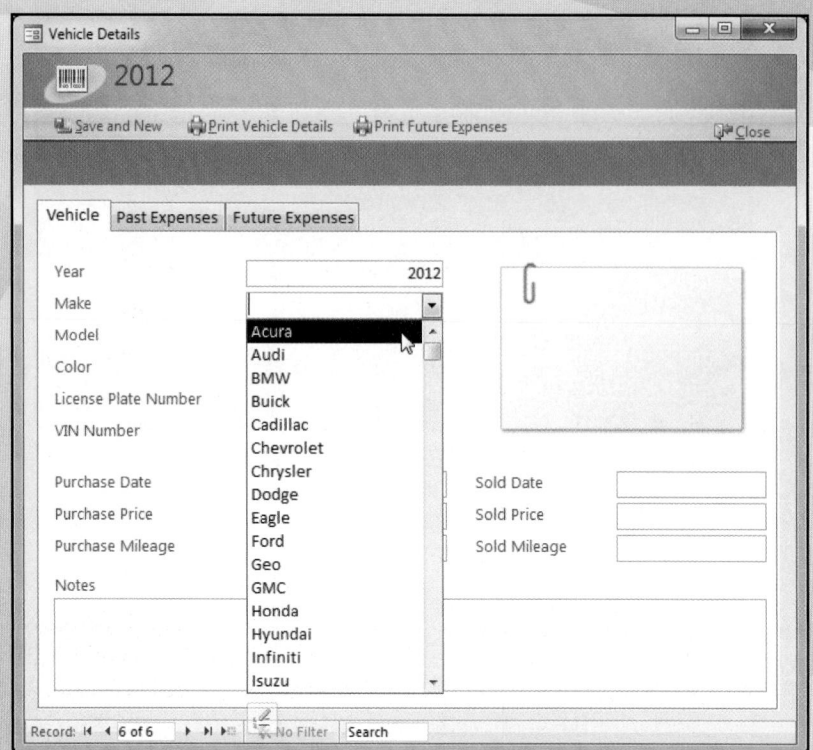

**FIGURE 11.4** A Form Used to Enter Data

| Vehicle | Service Description | Cost |
|---|---|---|
| 2012 Toyota Tacoma | CAP | $996.40 |
| 2012 Toyota Tacoma | INSPECTION | $84.69 |
| 2012 Toyota Tacoma | INSPECTION | $84.69 |
| 2012 Toyota Tacoma | INSPECTION | $84.69 |
| 2012 Toyota Tacoma | TIRES | $839.69 |
| 2012 Toyota Tacoma | TIRES ALIGNED | $0.00 |
| 2012 Toyota Tacoma | BRAKE PADS | $70.28 |
| 2012 Toyota Tacoma | V-BELT AND FILTER | $71.13 |
| 2012 Toyota Tacoma | OIL CHANGE | $60.00 |
| * | | $0.00 |

Expenses Query

**FIGURE 11.5** The Results of a Query

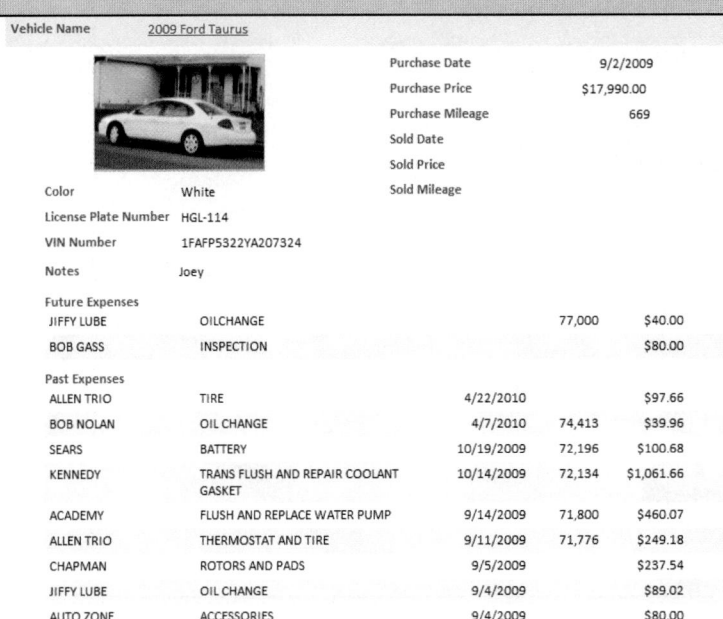

| Vehicle Name | 2009 Ford Taurus | | | |
|---|---|---|---|---|
| | | Purchase Date | 9/2/2009 | |
| | | Purchase Price | $17,990.00 | |
| | | Purchase Mileage | 669 | |
| | | Sold Date | | |
| | | Sold Price | | |
| Color | White | Sold Mileage | | |
| License Plate Number | HGL-114 | | | |
| VIN Number | 1FAFP5322YA207324 | | | |
| Notes | Joey | | | |
| **Future Expenses** | | | | |
| JIFFY LUBE | OILCHANGE | | 77,000 | $40.00 |
| BOB GASS | INSPECTION | | | $80.00 |
| **Past Expenses** | | | | |
| ALLEN TRIO | TIRE | 4/22/2010 | | $97.66 |
| BOB NOLAN | OIL CHANGE | 4/7/2010 | 74,413 | $39.96 |
| SEARS | BATTERY | 10/19/2009 | 72,196 | $100.68 |
| KENNEDY | TRANS FLUSH AND REPAIR COOLANT GASKET | 10/14/2009 | 72,134 | $1,061.66 |
| ACADEMY | FLUSH AND REPLACE WATER PUMP | 9/14/2009 | 71,800 | $460.07 |
| ALLEN TRIO | THERMOSTAT AND TIRE | 9/11/2009 | 71,776 | $249.18 |
| CHAPMAN | ROTORS AND PADS | 9/5/2009 | | $237.54 |
| JIFFY LUBE | OIL CHANGE | 9/4/2009 | | $89.02 |
| AUTO ZONE | ACCESSORIES | 9/4/2009 | | $80.00 |

**FIGURE 11.6** A Professional-looking Report

A **report** displays the data from a table or a query in an easy-to-read-and-print format. In Figure 11.6, the professional-looking Vehicle Details report shows data from both the Expenses and Vehicles tables.

A database is nothing more than a collection of information that's organized in a useful way. You interact with databases every day without even being aware of it. Online shopping, email contact lists, store catalogs, patient records in a doctor's office, online class registration, and Internet search engines are all examples of commonly used databases. Without databases, our lives would be very different.

## Running Project

Design a table for a simple database that you might use to organize your video or music collection. Include at least five fields. Use a word processor table for your design, and complete at least two records.

## 4 Things You Need to Know

- A database is a collection of related information.
- A table is a database object in which data is stored. It's arranged in rows (records) and columns (fields).
- The primary key uniquely identifies the record in a table.
- Forms, reports, and queries are some of the ways we can interact with the table data.

## Key Terms

| | |
|---|---|
| database | query |
| field | record |
| form | report |
| primary key | table |

# A Database for Every Purpose

**2** OBJECTIVE
## Compare the four types of databases.

Databases can be very simple or very complex. There are different database models that store and access data differently. The appropriate type of database to use depends on the type of data stored in it and the way in which the data will be used and accessed.

## FLAT FILE DATABASES

The simplest form of database is a flat file database. A **flat file database** consists of a single list of items. It can be a list or table in a document or a spreadsheet. Any time you make a to-do list, a wish list, or a shopping list, you've created a simple flat file database. Figure 11.7 shows a flat file database created in Excel. While it's possible to use Excel to create a simple database that might be suitable for a home user, for more complex data and relationships, it's necessary to use a database management system such as Access instead.

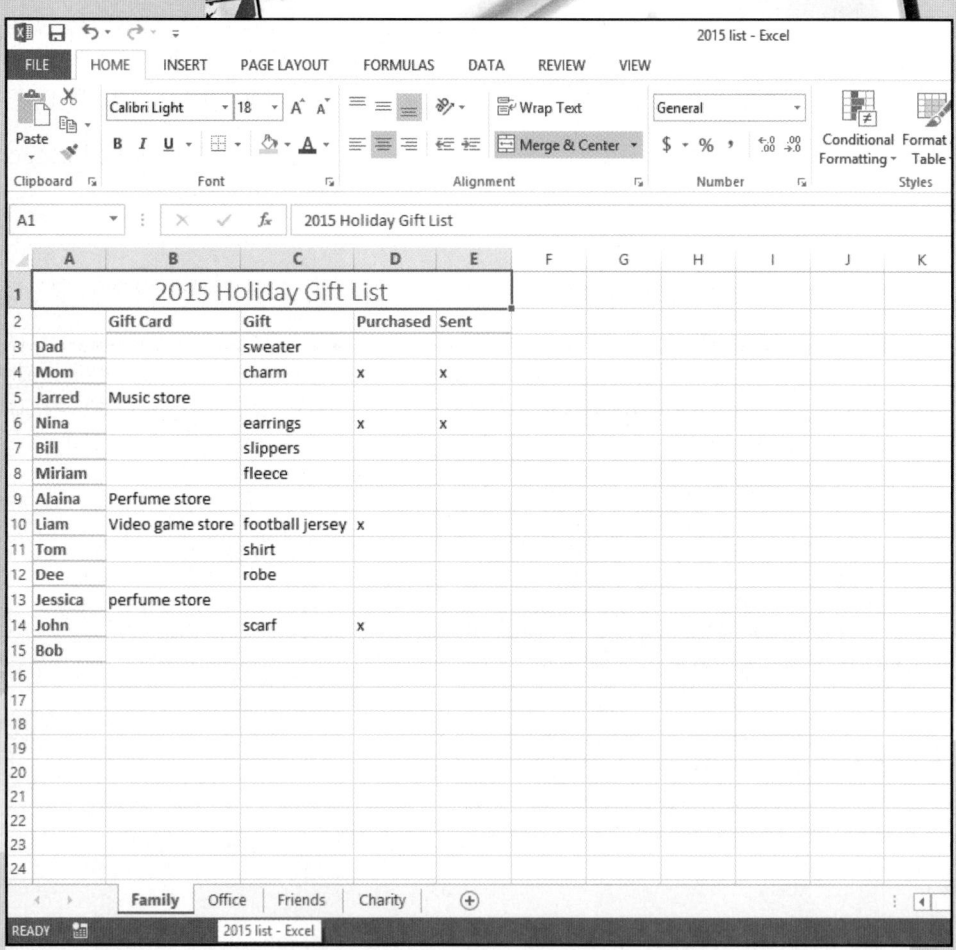

**FIGURE 11.7** An Excel spreadsheet can be used to create a simple flat file database.

# RELATIONAL DATABASES

The majority of databases today are relational databases. A **relational database** consists of multiple tables or relations, which are related by common information. A large database might contain thousands of tables. This type of database reduces the amount of data redundancy. Figure 11.8 illustrates a school database created in Access. It contains two tables that are related by the Student ID. The Students table (top) includes information such as name, address, and teacher. The Discipline table (bottom) includes disciplinary information such as infraction and action taken. Each student record may link to multiple discipline records, but each discipline record is linked to only one student record. This is known as a one-to-many relationship, and it's the most common type of relationship in a relational database.

**FIGURE 11.8** A one-to-many relationship exists between these two tables.

Student_ID ←
Student_major
Student_GPA

→ Student_ID
Student_Name
Student_medical_alerts
Student_prescriptions

**FIGURE 11.9** A one-to-one relationship links a single record in both tables.

A less common type of relationship is a one-to-one relationship. In a one-to-one relationship, a record in one table is linked to a single record in another table. Both tables use the same primary key to link them. For example, a school might keep student medical records in one table and student academic records in another and then use the student ID number as the primary key in both (see Figure 11.9). This is common when the data in a table requires restricted access. In this example, the medical records are confidential and restricted to the student health center.

In a many-to-many relationship, multiple records from a table can link to multiple records in another table. In a library catalog, each author may have written multiple books, and each book can have multiple authors, creating a many-to-many relationship between an author table and a book table. In a school, each teacher has multiple students, and each student can have multiple teachers (see Figure 11.10). The table between them is called a bridge table, and it breaks the many-to-many relationship up into two one-to-many relationships.

Bridge Table

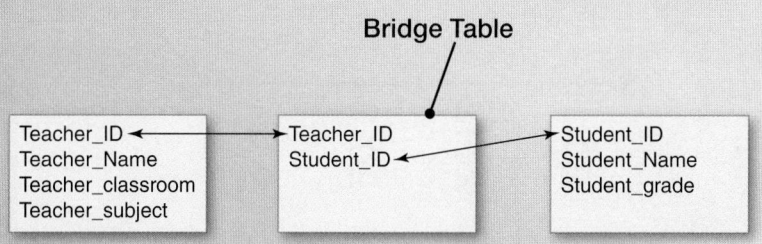

Teacher_ID ←
Teacher_Name
Teacher_classroom
Teacher_subject

→ Teacher_ID
Student_ID ←

→ Student_ID
Student_Name
Student_grade

**FIGURE 11.10** A many-to-many relationship between teachers and students uses a bridge table.

# OBJECT-ORIENTED DATABASES

In an **object-oriented database (OODB)**, data is stored as objects, which are used by modern programming languages such as C++ and Java. An object consists of both the data that describes the object and the processes that can be applied to it. The object-oriented database model is used to create databases that have more complicated types of data, such as images, audio, and video, and is common in industries with complex database needs, such as science, engineering, telecommunications, and finance. For very complex database needs, object-oriented databases are much faster than relational databases. Some relational database systems incorporate the ability to handle more complex data types by using objects.

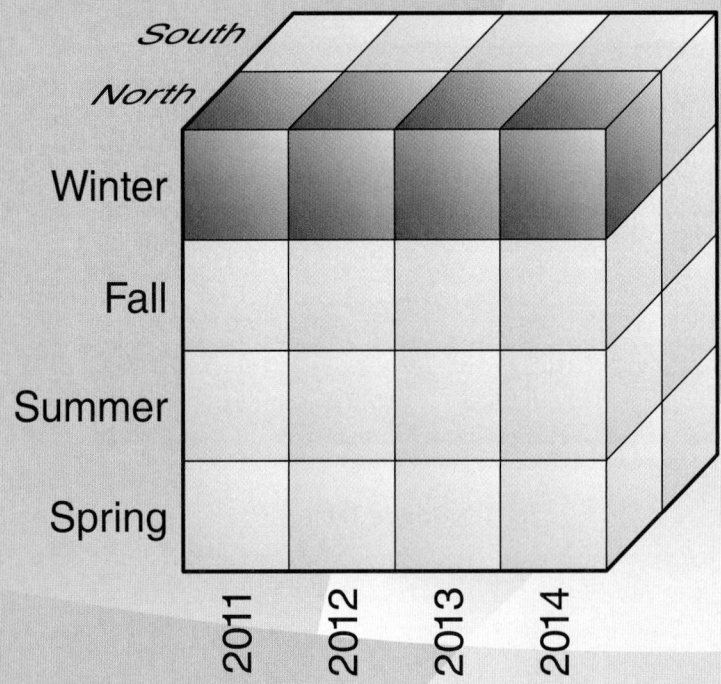

# MULTIDIMENSIONAL DATABASES

A **multidimensional database (MDB)** is optimized for storing and utilizing data. Such databases may be created using input from existing relational databases, but they structure the information into multidimensional data cubes (see Figure 11.11) instead of two-dimensional tables. The data can be accessed in a number of different ways depending on the user's needs. One important feature of MDBs is the ability to allow a user to ask questions in question form—rather than using a more complex query language. For example, "How many students visited the student health center on the north campus during the winter semester over the past four years?"

**FIGURE 11.11** Data in an MDB is structured as a multidimensional cube.

Multidimensional databases are ideal for use with data warehouses and **online analytical processing (OLAP)** applications, which enable a user to selectively extract and view data from different points of view. OLAP can be used for data mining or discovering relationships between data items. A **data warehouse** is a central repository for all the data that an enterprise uses: internal databases and external sources such as vendors and customers. The data is organized for use with queries, analysis, and reporting.

The best type of database to use depends on the type of data to be entered, the type of processing that's needed, and the expertise of the users and administrators. The relational database model is by far the most popular for most business applications. The object-oriented model has its niche in science and telecommunications (although it's also used in other industries), and the multidimensional model is used where query performance is critical. Many enterprises use a combination of these models to meet their needs.

## ▶ Running Project

Give an example of each of the four types of databases described in this article. Which of these have you used recently? Explain.

## 4 Things You Need to Know

- A flat file database consists of a single list of items.
- A relational database consists of multiple tables related by common information.
- In an object-oriented database (OODB), data is stored as objects.
- A multidimensional database (MDB) structures the information into multidimensional data cubes.

## Key Terms

data warehouse

flat file database

multidimensional database (MDB)

object-oriented database (OODB)

online analytical processing (OLAP)

relational database

# HOW TO

## Create a Form Using Google Docs

Google Docs includes an easy way to create a form, distribute it, and then collect the results. In this activity, you'll create a form you can use to plan a study group with your classmates. You will need a Google account to complete this exercise.

**1** Open your word processor and type your name and date in the document. Save the file as **lastname_firstname_ch11_howto1**.

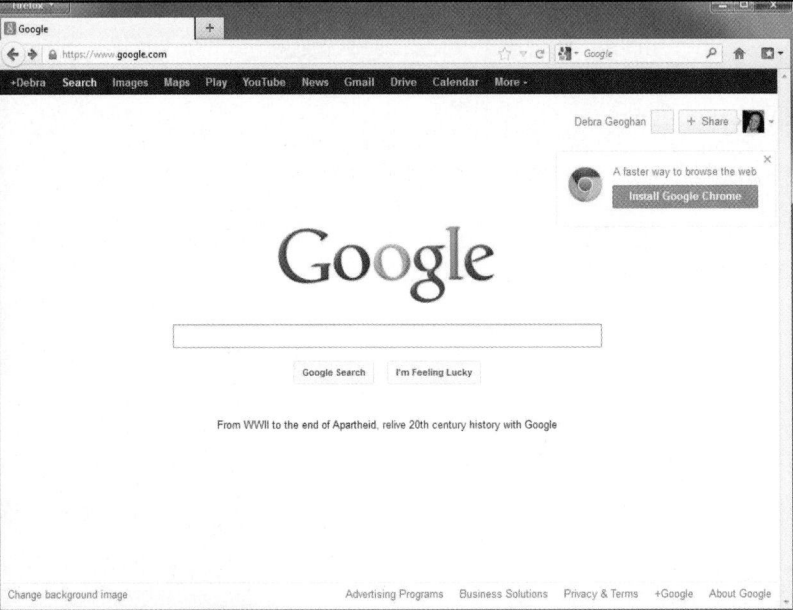

**2** Open your browser, and go to **google.com**. If necessary, sign in to your Google account. From the menu at the top of the screen, click *Drive*.

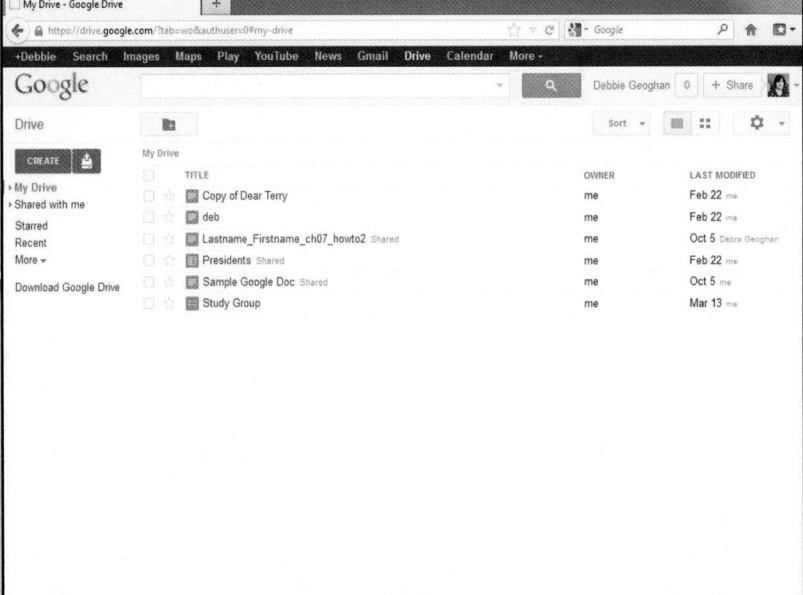

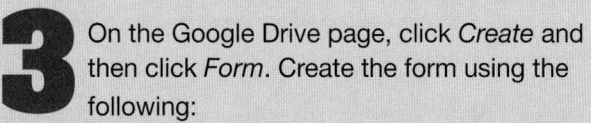

**3** On the Google Drive page, click *Create* and then click *Form*. Create the form using the following:

| Form Title | Study Group |
|---|---|
| Information | We are forming a study group for Mrs. Marshal's Intro to Computers class. Please fill out this form if you want to join the group. |
| Question Title (Sample Question 1) | Name and contact information |
| Help Text | Please provide the best way to reach you. |
| Question Type | Paragraph text |

**4** Select the *Make this a required question* check box, and click *Done*.

**5** If necessary, point to the Sample Question 2 and click the pencil to edit it.

| Question Title (Sample Question 2) | Availability |
|---|---|
| Help Text | Please select the times you're available to study. |
| Question Type | Check boxes |
| Option 1 | Before class |
| Option 2 | After class |

**6** Select the *Make this a required question* check box, and click *Done*.

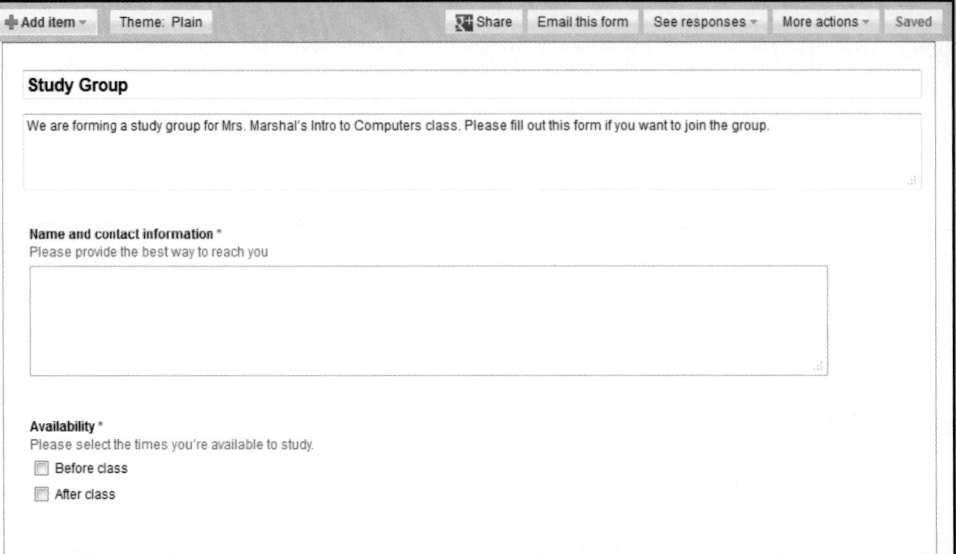

**7** Click *Theme* and select an appropriate theme and then click *Apply*.

**8** Click *Email this form* and email the form to yourself. Open your email; click the link to fill out the form online. Fill out the form, take a screen shot of your responses, and then submit the form. Paste your screen shot into your answers document. Email the form to at least three classmates and have them respond as well.

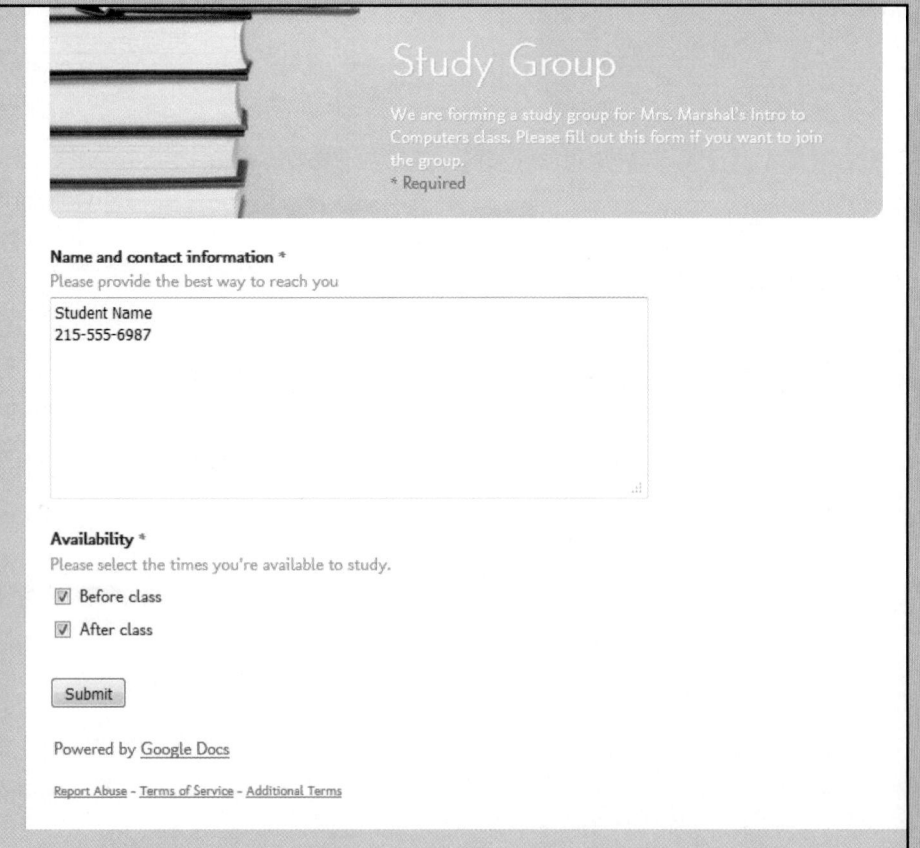

**9** Return to Google Drive, click on *Owned by me*, and then click the flat file database (spreadsheet) that contains the results. Take a screen shot of the results and paste it into your document.

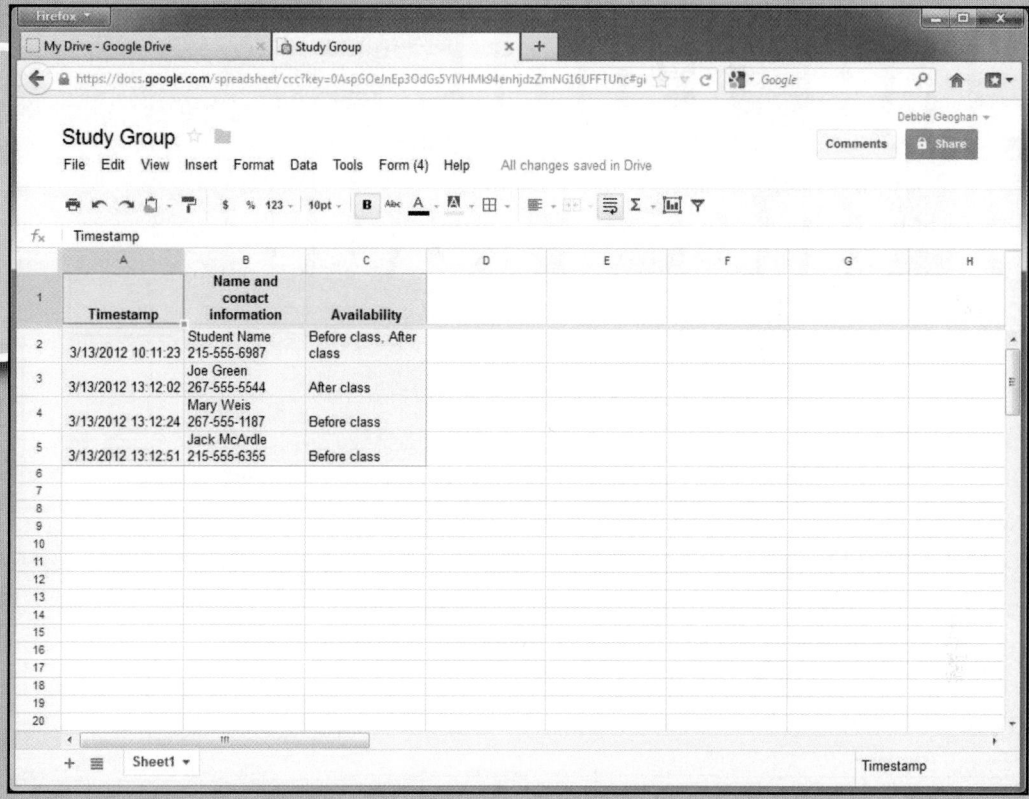

**10** Save your file and submit it as directed by your instructor.

# The Tools of the Trade

VIZ CLIP

## 3 OBJECTIVE
## Explain database management systems.

A **database management system (DBMS)** is the software used to create and manage the data in a database. The Vehicle maintenance database used throughout this chapter was created using Microsoft Access 2010. Access is an example of a DBMS.

### CREATING A DATABASE

A database management system such as Access, FileMaker Pro (see Figure 11.12), Oracle, or MySQL is needed to create a database. The DBMS is used to create tables, reports, forms, and queries. Planning is an essential first step to designing a database that can be used effectively.

The design of a database starts with the schema, or data dictionary. The **data dictionary** defines all the fields and the type of data each field contains. A field should be created for each independent piece of information. For example, first name and last name should be separate fields. This makes it easier to sort and filter the data. The type of data in a field also should be defined. While many fields are simply text, others might be numbers.

A major goal of good database design is to reduce data redundancy, or duplicate information, in multiple places. This process is known as **data normalization**. Normalization reduces the size of the database, makes it easier to keep records up to date, and increases query speed.

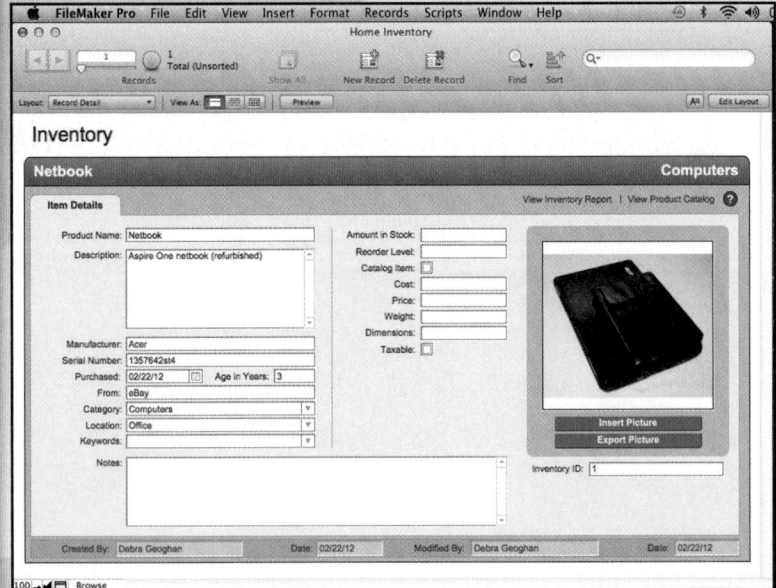

**FIGURE 11.12** FileMaker Pro is the most popular Mac DBMS.

# DATA VALIDATION

**Data validation** reduces data-entry errors using validation rules. The rules can include data type, data length, acceptable values, and required fields. Specifying the data type, such as text, number, or currency, prevents a user from entering the wrong type of information into a field. Creating a Lookup list goes even further by providing a drop-down list of items such as state, year, or vehicle model to choose from. In Figure 11.13, the data type is Date/Time and the data validation rule for the Service Date field will prevent an entry date before 1/1/1900. Figure 11.14 shows the errors displayed when either of these validations fails.

Once a table has been designed and the data dictionary created, it's time to enter the data. Data can often be imported from other places, such as a Word table, an Excel spreadsheet, or another database. This is useful if the data is already in an electronic format. For example, I can import a file that contains the student roster that I downloaded from my school website. Figure 11.15 illustrates the process of importing data into a new table in Access.

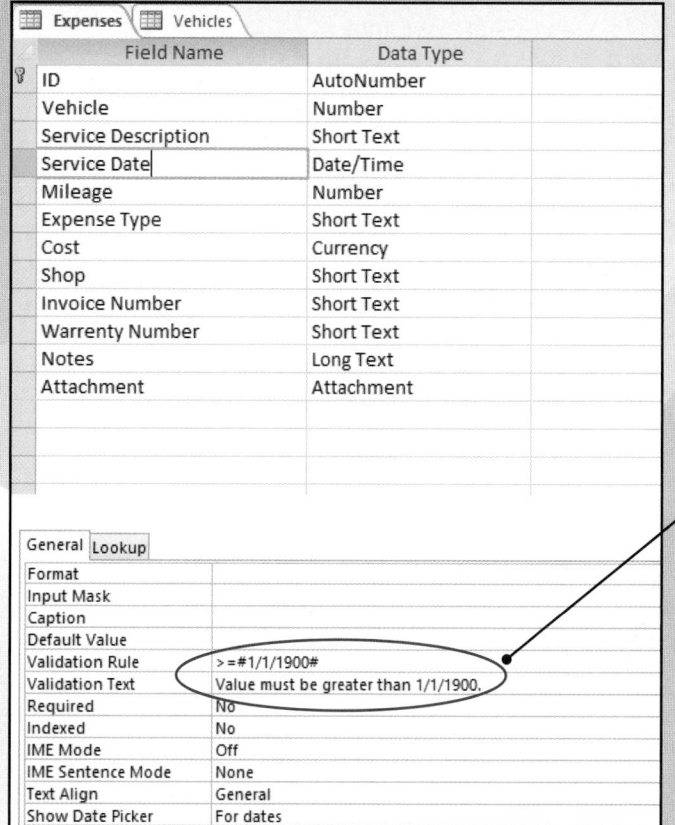

Validation Rule prevents a date prior to 1/1/1900 from being entered.

**FIGURE 11.13** Data Validation Rules in Access

| ID | Vehicle | Service Description | Service Date | Mileage | Cost | Shop | Invoice Num |
|----|---------|---------------------|--------------|---------|------|------|-------------|
| 1 | 2012 Toyota Tacoma | CAP | Tuesday | 250 | $996.40 | COTTMAN | |
| 2 | 2012 Toyota Tacoma | INSPECTION | | | | | |
| 3 | 2012 Toyota Tacoma | INSPECTION | | | | | |
| 4 | 2012 Toyota Tacoma | INSPECTION | | | | | |
| 6 | 2005 Honda Civic | TIRES | | | | | |
| 7 | 2012 Toyota Tacoma | TIRES | | | | | |
| 8 | 2012 Toyota Tacoma | TIRES ALIGNED | 10/18/2015 | 46,147 | $0.00 | SEARS | |
| 9 | 2012 Toyota Tacoma | BRAKE PADS | 6/22/2013 | 52,000 | $70.28 | KENNEDY FORD | |
| 11 | 2005 Honda Civic | REAR BRAKES | 6/30/2009 | | $85.00 | BOB GASS | |
| 13 | 2012 Toyota Tacoma | V-BELT AND FILTER | 9/19/2014 | | $71.13 | CHAPMAN FORD | |

The value you entered does not match the Date/Time data type in this column.
Enter new value.
Convert the data in this column to the Text data type.
Help with data types and formats.

| ID | Vehicle | Service Description | Service Date | Mileage | Cost | Shop | Invoice Nu |
|----|---------|---------------------|--------------|---------|------|------|-------------|
| 1 | 2012 Toyota Tacoma | CAP | 6/18/201 | 250 | $996.40 | COTTMAN | |
| 2 | 2012 Toyota Tacoma | INSPECTION | 6/24/2013 | 17,108 | $84.69 | BOB GASS | |
| 3 | 2012 Toyota Tacoma | INSPECTION | | 25,831 | $84.69 | BOB GASS | |
| 4 | 2012 Toyota Tacoma | INSPECTION | | | $84.69 | BOB GASS | |
| 6 | 2005 Honda Civic | TIRES | | 33,448 | $699.66 | SEARS | |
| 7 | 2012 Toyota Tacoma | TIRES | | 45,301 | $839.69 | SEARS | |
| 8 | 2012 Toyota Tacoma | TIRES ALIGNED | | 46,147 | $0.00 | SEARS | |
| 9 | 2012 Toyota Tacoma | BRAKE PADS | | 52,000 | $70.28 | KENNEDY FORD | |
| 11 | 2005 Honda Civic | REAR BRAKES | | | $85.00 | BOB GASS | |
| 13 | 2012 Toyota Tacoma | V-BELT AND FILTER | | | $71.13 | CHAPMAN FORD | |

Microsoft Access
Value must be greater than 1/1/1900.
OK    Help
Was this information helpful?

**FIGURE 11.14** Data validation rules prevent incorrect data from being entered.

**1. Data downloaded from the school server exists in a CSV (comma separated values) text file, viewed here in Excel.**

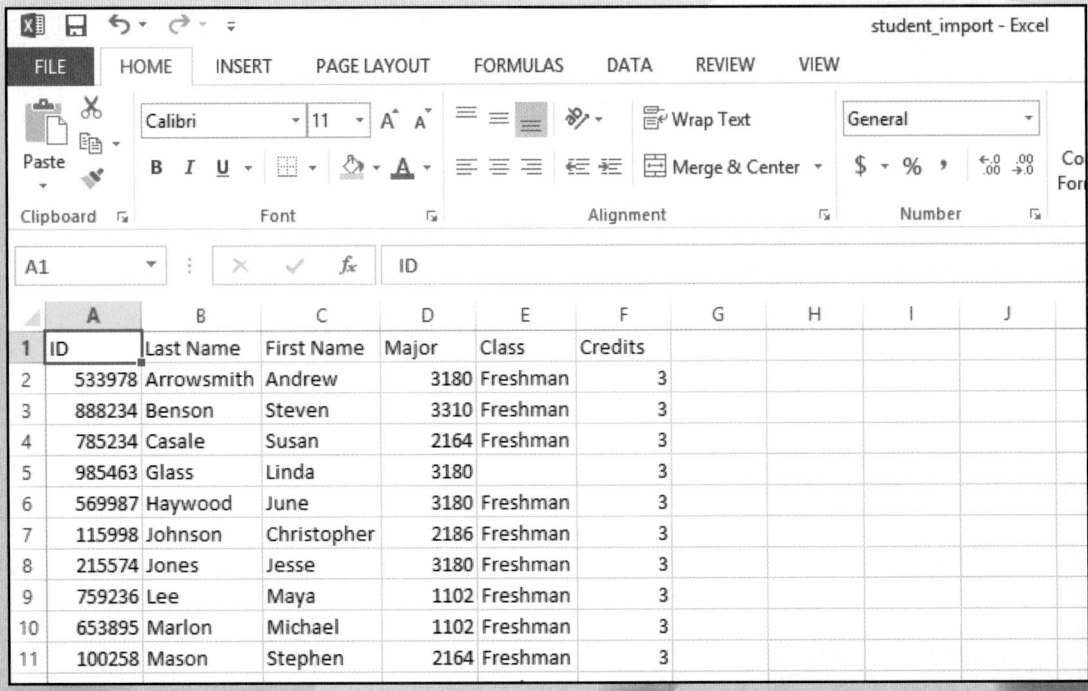

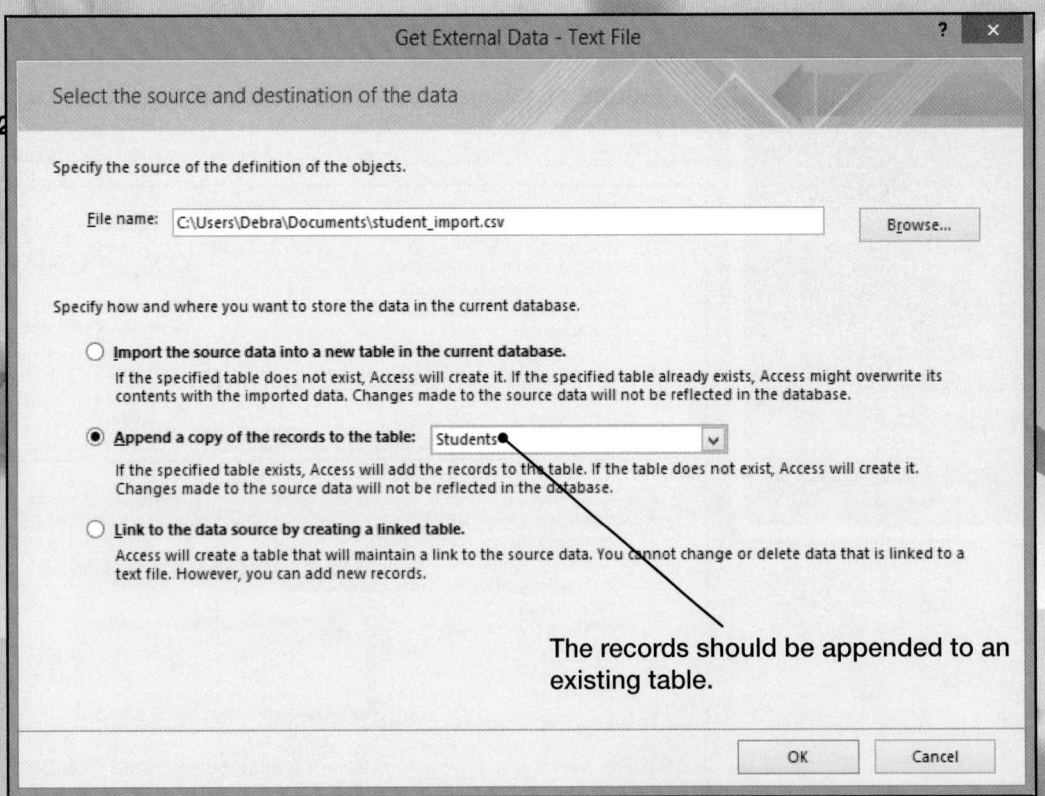

The records should be appended to an existing table.

**FIGURE 11.15** The Steps to Import a File into Access

OBJECTIVE 3

**3. Use the Import Text Wizard to correctly identify the fields and data.**

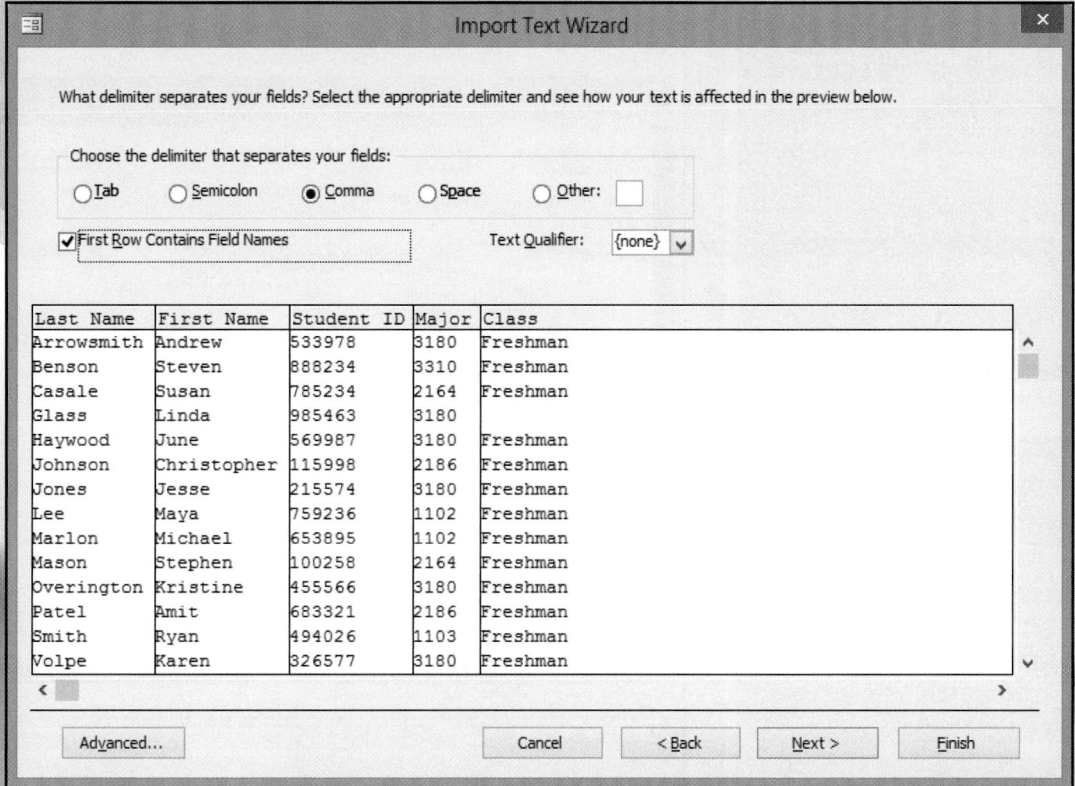

**4. The file was successfully imported into the Students table in the database.**

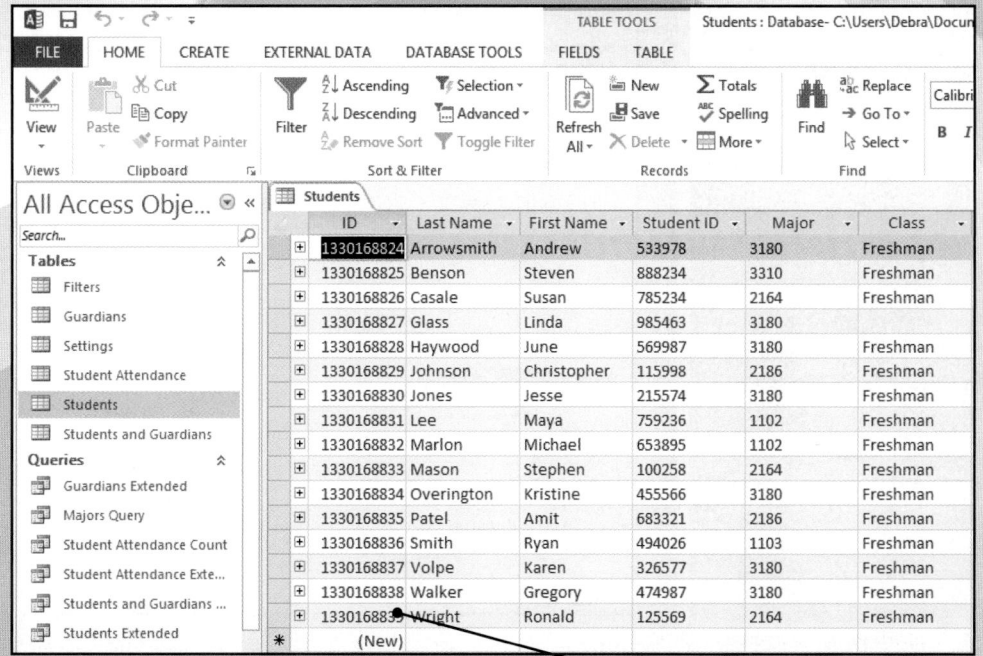

Access automatically sorts by the primary key.

Manually entering data can be a tedious and error-prone activity. In addition to using data validation rules, an input form can be used to make it easier to enter data. The validation rules apply to the data entered into the form, further reducing the potential for data-entry errors. Figure 11.16 shows a Student input form in both Access and FileMaker Pro. A form can contain dropdown lists and data pickers, and it can have some default information already filled (such as State).

# SQL

Once the data has been entered into the database, the DBMS helps to turn it into useful information. To ask a question, a query is designed using a query language. Most DBMSs today—including MySQL, SQL Server, Access, and Oracle—use **Structured Query Language (SQL)**. In Access, you can use the Query Wizard or Design view to help form the query, and Access will create the SQL for you (see Figure 11.17). In this example, the question asked is: "Which students are in the major 3180?"

SQL statements use relational keywords, such as SELECT, FROM, WHERE, and AND, to manipulate, query, and update data in relational databases. It isn't necessary for ordinary users to be able to write complex SQL statements, but it's helpful to be able to understand them. In a large organization, a database programmer would be responsible for writing most SQL statements to create customized queries and reports.

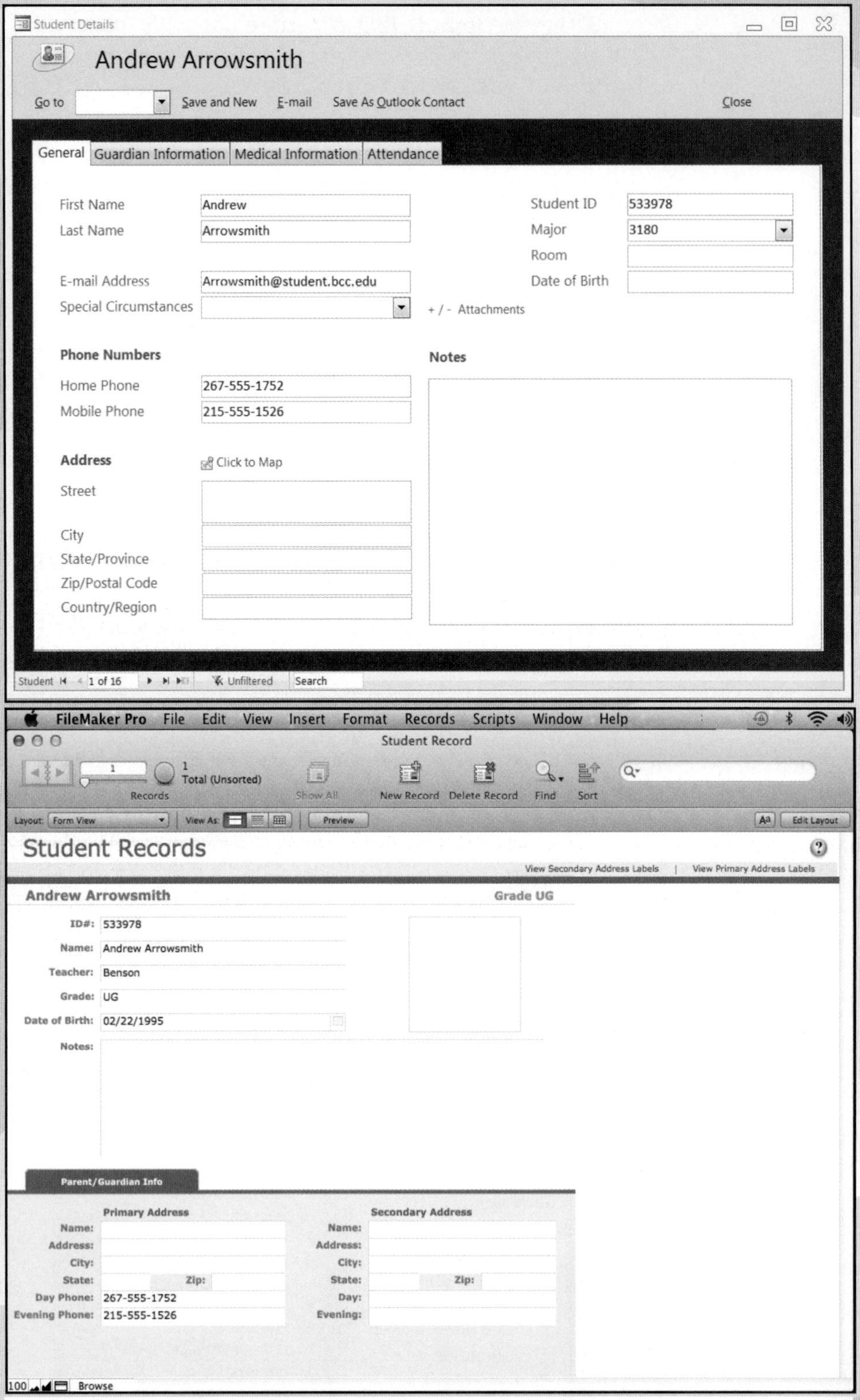

**FIGURE 11.16** An input form makes data entry easier and less error-prone.

**A. Majors Query in Design view**

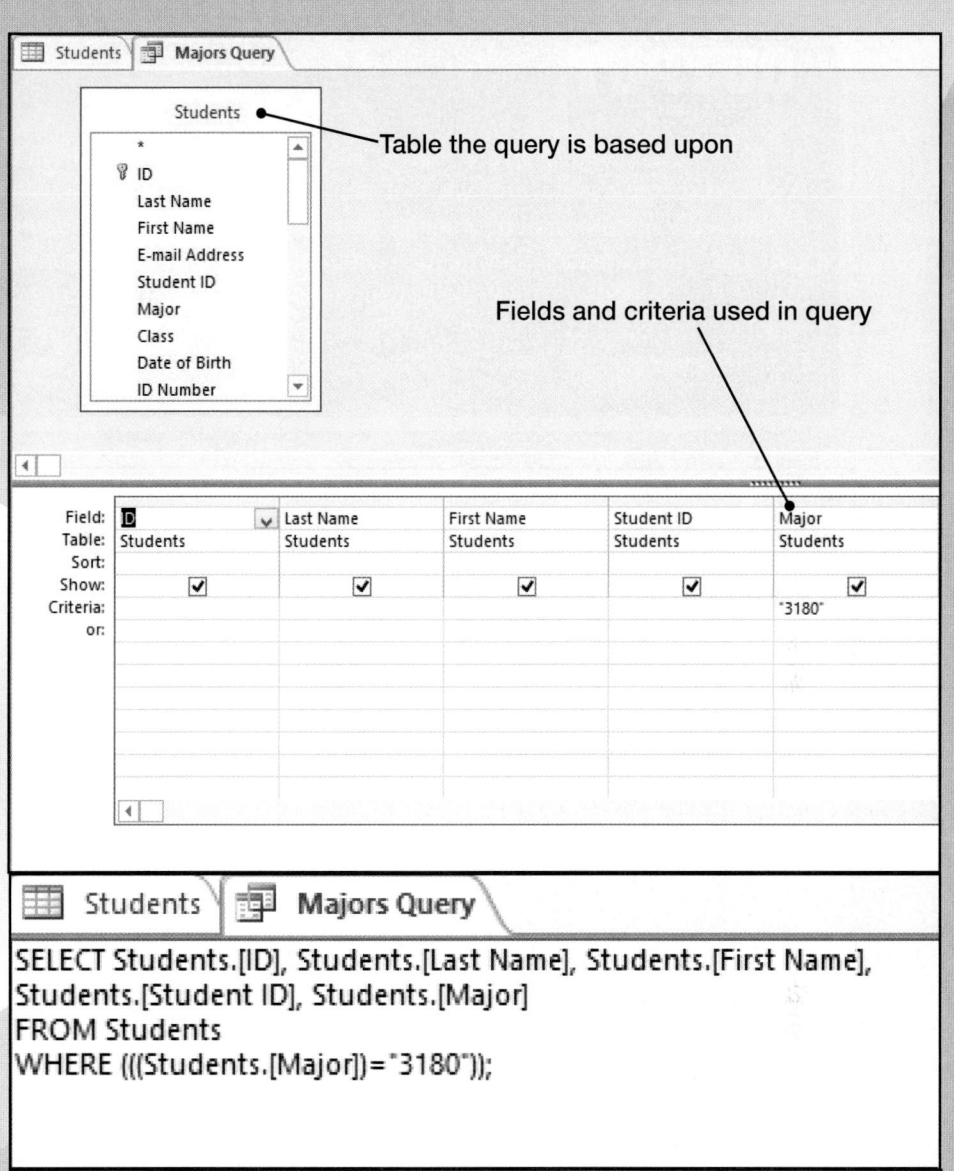

Table the query is based upon

Fields and criteria used in query

**B. Access Created SQL for Majors Query**

**C. Results of Majors Query**

**FIGURE 11.17** Using Design view (A) and SQL (B) to create a query (C) in Access

A DBMS is also used to create reports. Reports take information from tables or queries and present it in a way that's easy to read and print. They can be distributed to others without granting them access to the database, providing them with just the information they need in a format that is user friendly and doesn't require any database knowledge to use. Reports are often used to help in decision-making. The report in Figure 11.18 includes information from both the Vehicles and Expenses tables.

Future Expenses Report

# Future Expenses Report

Friday, November 9, 2012

| Vehicle Name | Make | Model | Year | License Plate Number |
|---|---|---|---|---|
| 2012 Toyota Tacoma | Toyota | Tacoma | 2012 | WR9030E |

| Service Description | Estimate |
|---|---|
| OIL CHANGE | $60.00 |
| Total Estimate: | $60.00 |

| Vehicle Name | Make | Model | Year | License Plate Number |
|---|---|---|---|---|
| 2009 Ford Taurus | Ford | Taurus | 2009 | HGL-114 |

| Service Description | Estimate |
|---|---|
| OILCHANGE | $40.00 |
| INSPECTION | $80.00 |
| Total Estimate: | $120.00 |

| Vehicle Name | Make | Model | Year | License Plate Number |
|---|---|---|---|---|
| 2010 Mazda CX-7 | Mazda | CX-7 | 2010 | DFS-5249 |

| Service Description | Estimate |
|---|---|
| OIL CHANGE AND TIRES ROTATE | $0.00 |
| Total Estimate: | $0.00 |

**FIGURE 11.18** A DBMS is used to create reports like this future expenses report.

# Find Out MORE

SQL can be difficult to learn, but it's a powerful tool. To learn more about SQL, visit **http://w3schools.com/sql**.
To test yourself on SQL, visit **http://w3schools.com/sql/sql_tryit.asp**, and use the online tool to write and test a few SQL statements and see the results.

## Running Project

Specialized database management systems are used by many libraries. Visit your school or local library and find out what DBMS is used for the circulation desk. Do the librarians have special database training? Is anyone trained as a database administrator?

## 5 Things You Need to Know

- A database management system (DBMS) is used to create and manage databases.
- The design of a database starts with the schema, or data dictionary.
- Good database design uses normalization to reduce data redundancy.
- Data validation reduces data-entry errors.
- SQL is used to manipulate, query, and update data in relational databases.

## Key Terms

data dictionary

data normalization

data validation

database management system (DBMS)

Structured Query Language (SQL)

# HOW TO

## Create a Home Inventory

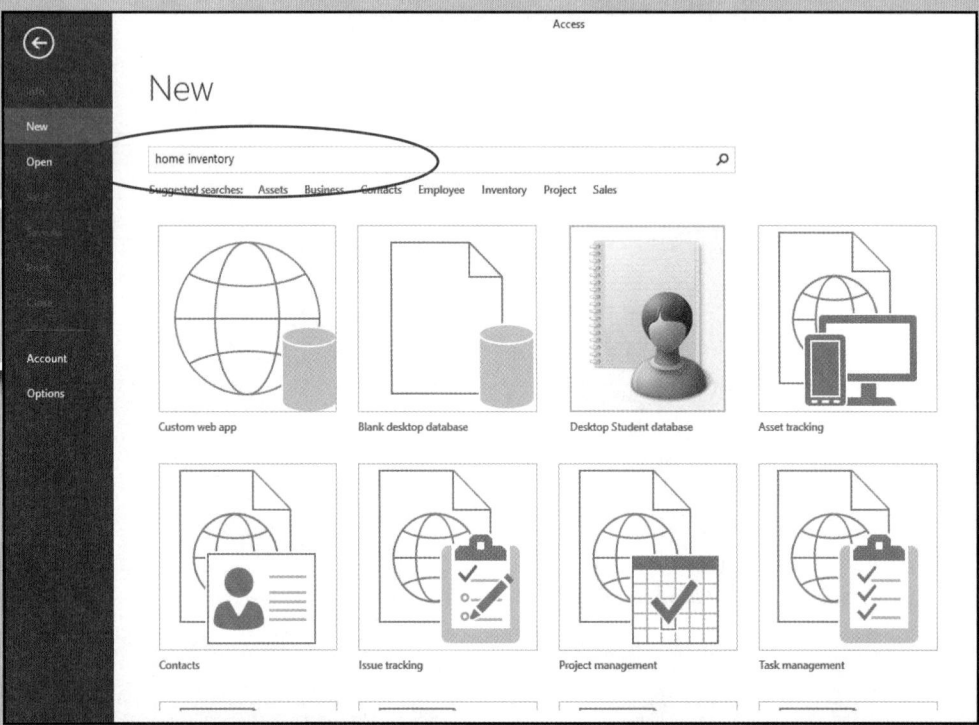

**1** Open Access, and type **home inventory** in the Search for online templates box.

**2** Click the *Desktop Home inventory* template. In the File Name box, click the small yellow folder icon, and browse to the location of your files for this chapter, name the file **lastname_firstname_ch11_howto2**, click *OK*, and then click *Create*. Read the information in the Help window that appears and then close it. (If this template is unavailable, you may use the file provided in your student data files for this text.

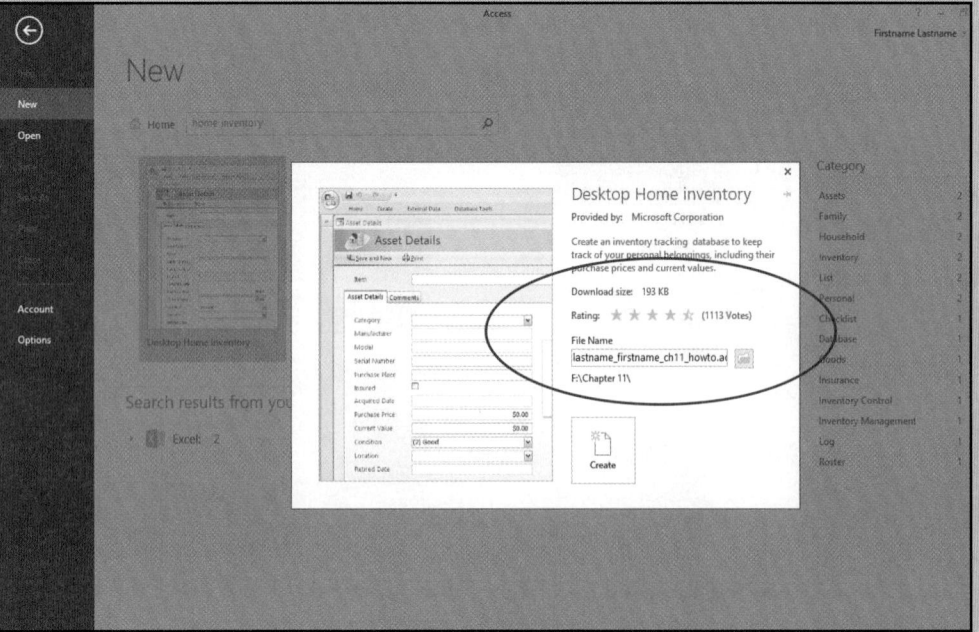

**3** If necessary, click *Enable Content* on the yellow Security Warning bar. Expand the Navigation Pane by clicking the *Shutter Bar*. Click the arrow next to Supporting Objects to expand the section. Close the Home Inventory List report.

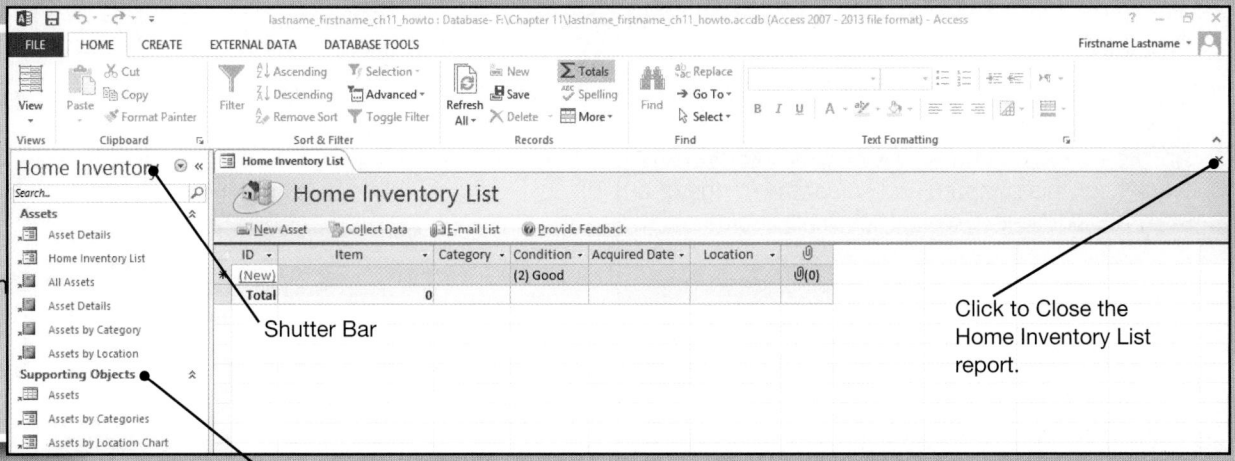

Shutter Bar

Click to expand the group.

Click to Close the Home Inventory List report.

**4** Double-click *Asset Details* (the first item in the Navigation Pane) to open the Asset Details form. Enter the information in the second column in the form.

| Item | **Microwave** |
|---|---|
| Category | **Appliances** |
| Manufacturer | **Buymore** |
| Model | **Counter Top (39012)** |
| Serial Number | **1X3498T2** |
| Purchase Place | **Mike's Discount Appliances** |
| Acquired Date | **today's date** |
| Purchase Price | **$39.00** |
| Current Value | **$39.00** |
| Condition | **(1) Great** |
| Location | **Kitchen** |
| Retired Date | **leave blank** |
| Description | **White 18" .6 cu. ft. countertop microwave** |

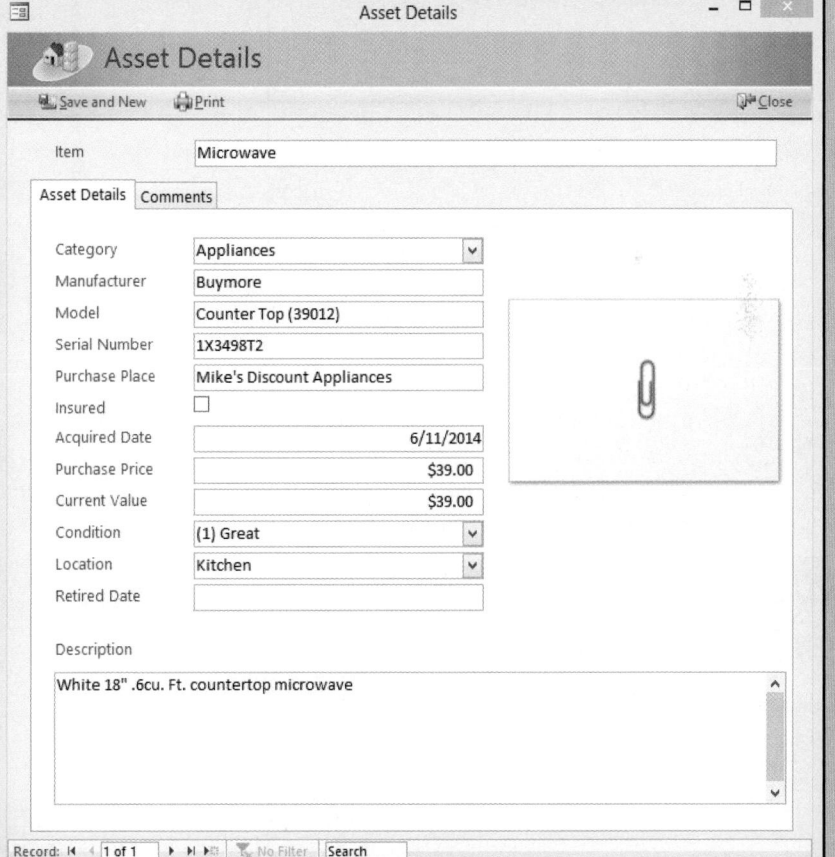

**5** Double-click the paperclip to attach an image. Click *Add*, browse to the data files for this chapter, and select the image of a microwave. Click *Open* and then click *OK*.

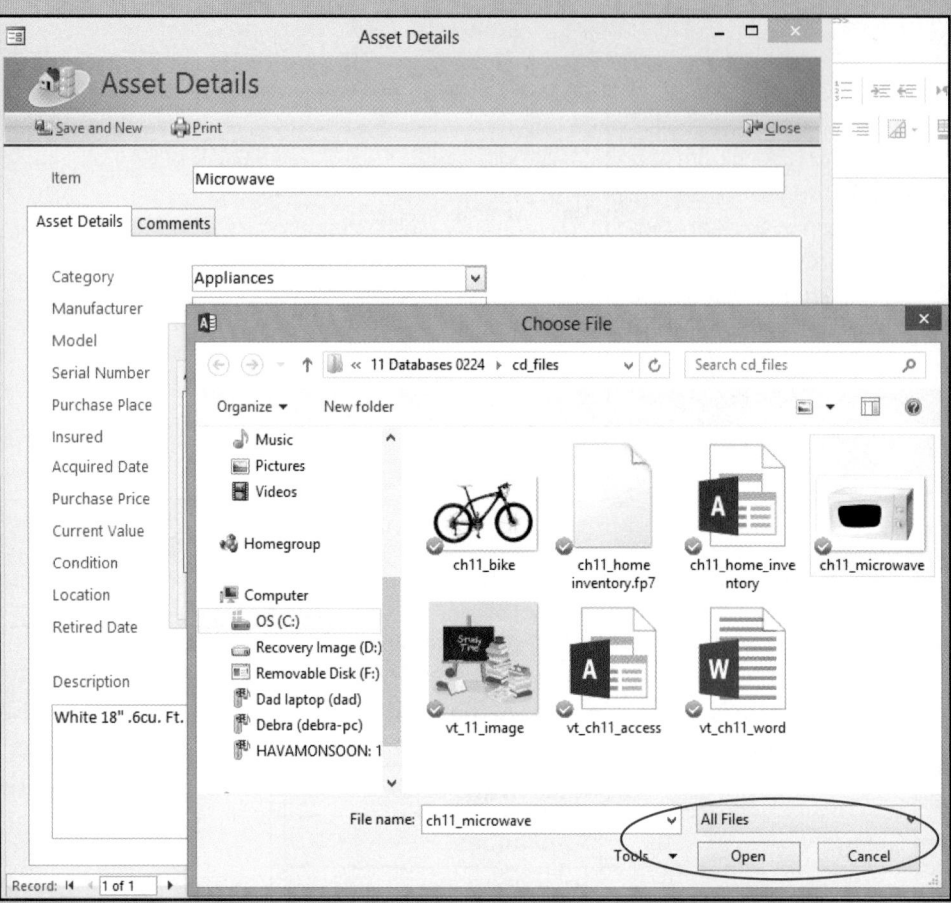

**6** To enter another item, click the *New (blank) Record* button.

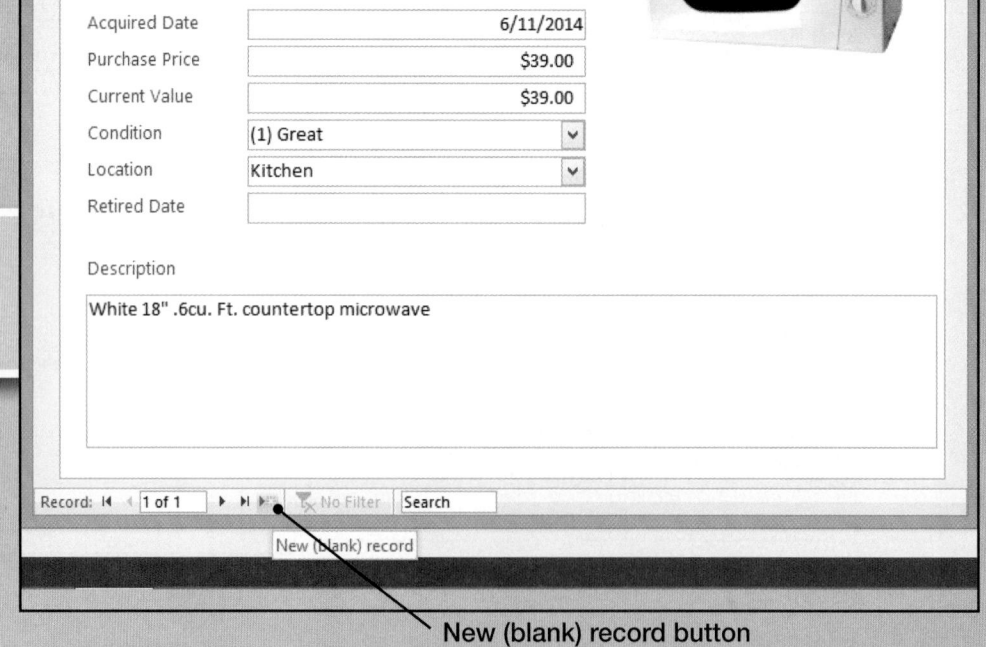

New (blank) record button

**7** Complete the new record as illustrated. The bike image can be found in your student data files. When finished, close the Asset Details form. The records will be automatically saved to the database.

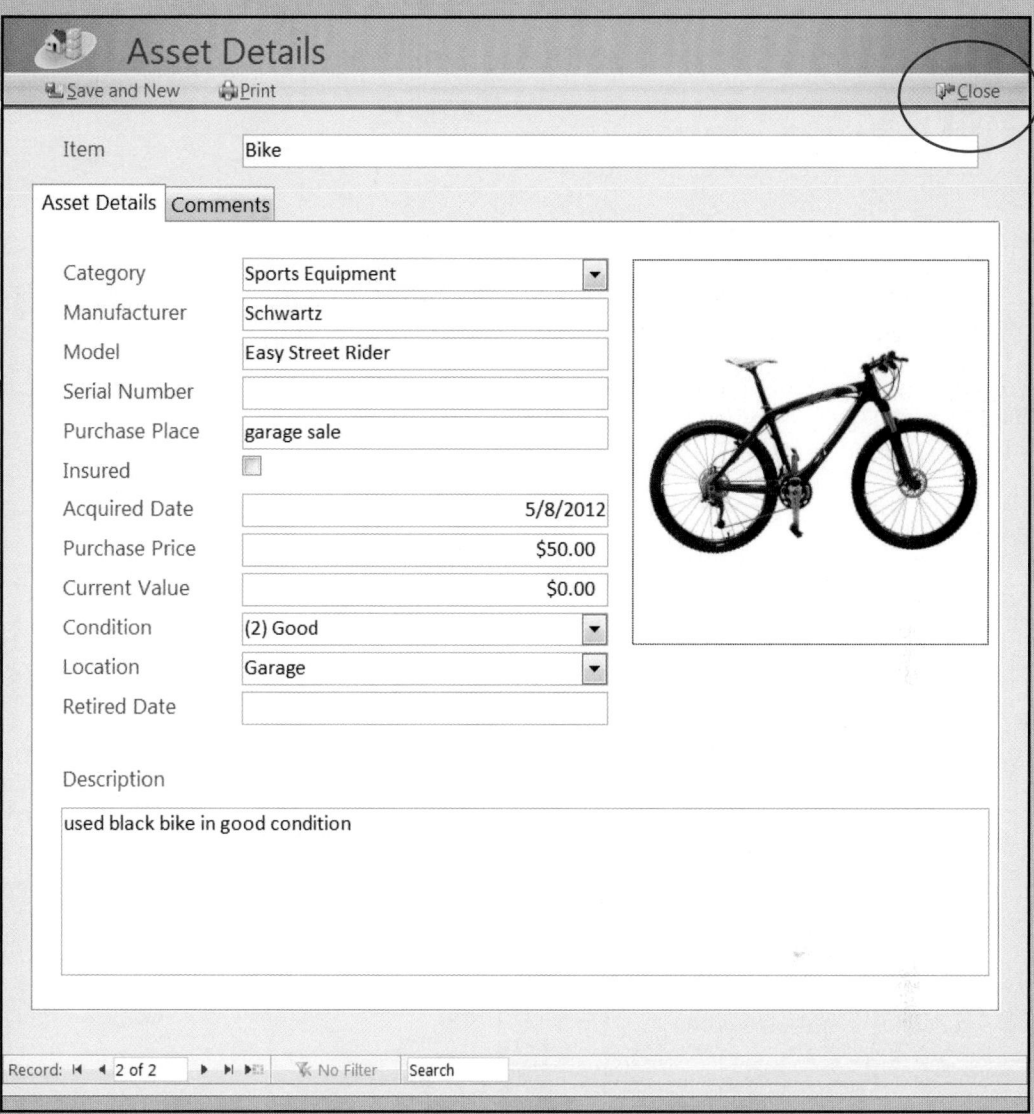

**8** Double-click the *Home Inventory List* to verify that your items have been added. Explore each of the database objects that were created. Close your database, and submit it as directed by your instructor. Unlike other applications, Access saves your database as you make changes, so you don't need to save the file before you close it.

### If you are using a Mac

FileMaker Pro is the most common Mac DBMS, but it can be expensive. The same publisher also has a personal product called Bento available for Macs as well as iPad and iPhone. They even provide a 30-day free trial so you can test it out to see if it is useful to you before you purchase it. If you have Bento on your Mac, you can complete this how-to exercise.

**1** Start Bento and click *File, New Library from Template*. Then do the following:
Select the Home Inventory Template.
Click the (–) sign to delete the sample record.
Click the (+) sign to add a new record.

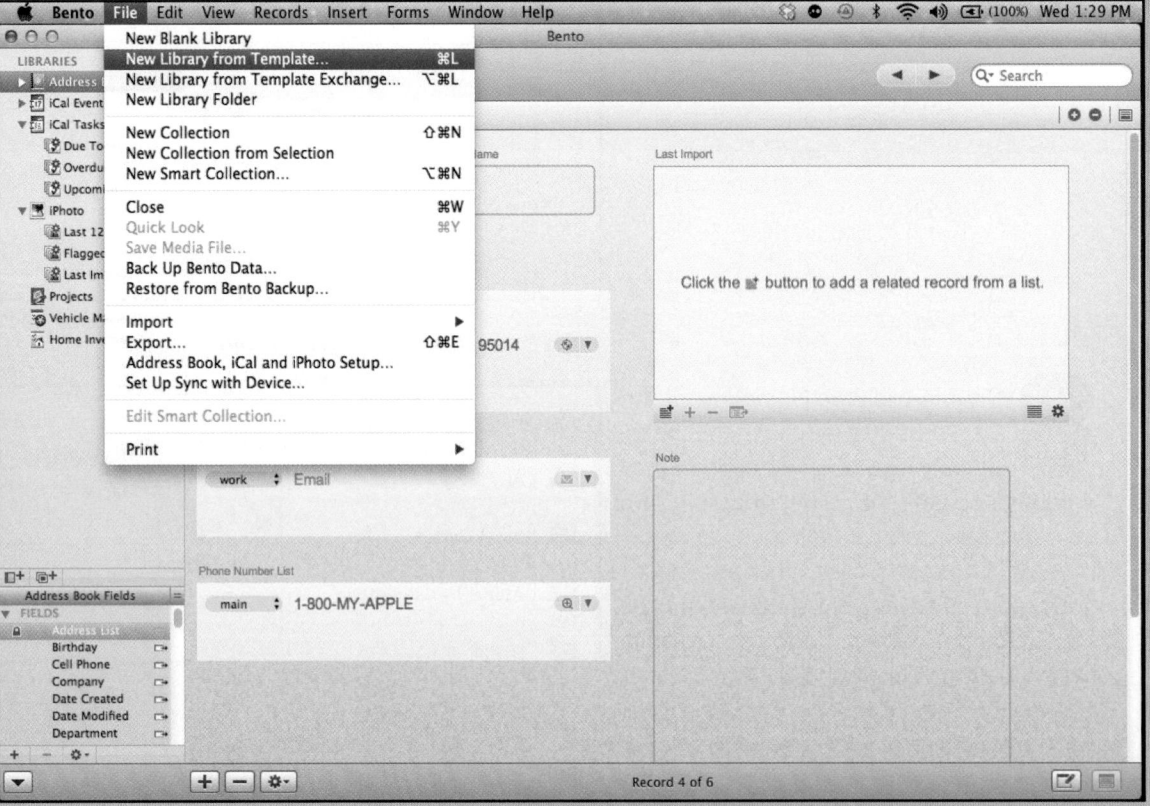

**2** Fill in the fields using the information in step 4. For the microwave, choose the *Other* category. For the bike, choose *Vehicle*. Use the notes area for model number.

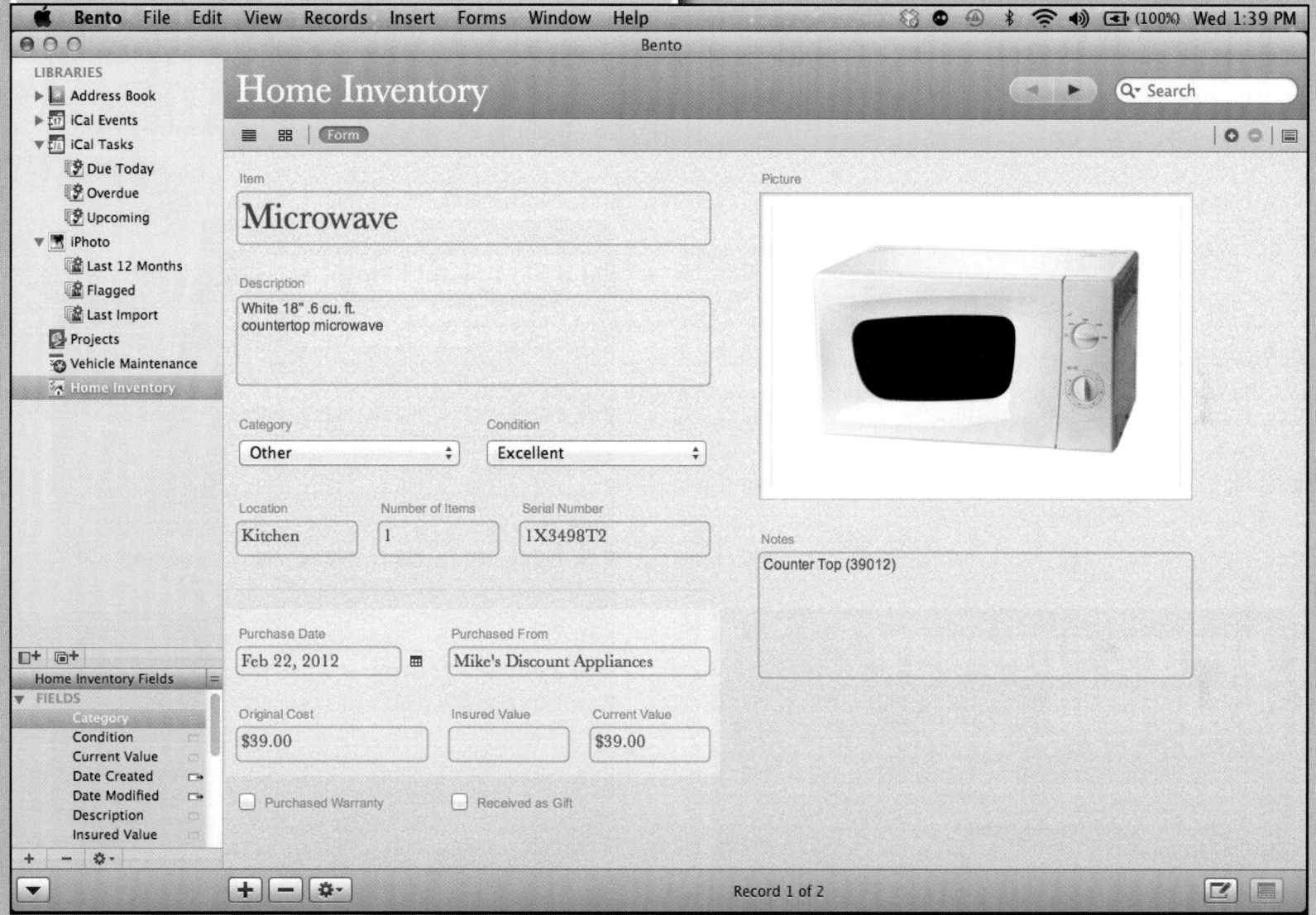

**3** Take screen shots of both records and paste them into a document. Save the file as **lastname_firstname_ch11_howto2** and submit as directed by your instructor.

# Data In . . . Information Out

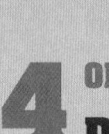

## 4 OBJECTIVE
## Discuss important information systems used in business.

An **information system** is the people, hardware, and software that support data-intensive applications, such as financial accounts, human resources, and other business transactions. Information systems include databases with special functions. In this article, we look at some of the most common information systems.

## OFFICE SUPPORT SYSTEMS

**Office support systems (OSS)**—sometimes called office automation systems—include software and hardware that improve the productivity of employees by automating common tasks such as the exchange of information; management of documents, spreadsheets and databases, collaboration, meeting, planning; and management of schedules. An OSS requires a network for electronic communication and storage. The most obvious software example is an office suite, such as Microsoft Office. Systems that allow employees to work remotely can also be considered office support systems.

## TRANSACTION PROCESSING

Businesses rely on **transaction-processing systems (TPS)** to respond to user requests. Usually, a transaction involves the exchange of goods, services, or money. A single transaction may consist of multiple, dependent operations. Transaction processing links multiple operations together and ensures that all operations in a transaction are completed without error.

Transaction-processing systems must pass tests for atomicity, consistency, isolation, and durability (the ACID test).

- Atomicity: Transactions are atomic—the transaction will either happen or not. If one account is debited, then another account has to be credited. The TPS assures that transactions are fully completed or aren't undertaken at all.

- Consistency: The TPS must always be consistent with its own operating rules (or integrity constraints). If errors occur in the transaction on either side, then the transaction will fail.

- Isolation: Each transaction must occur in isolation and must be independent.

- Durability: Transactions must be durable. Once transactions are completed, they can't be undone. This means that when that airline ticket has been booked, it's permanently recorded.

An example of transaction processing is paying your tuition bill from your bank account. The process of paying a bill from your account consists of two operations: debiting your account and crediting your school's account. The TPS links these two separate operations into the transaction. The success of the transaction depends on both of the operations being successful. If the debit from your account is successful but the credit doesn't go through to the college's account, then the transaction fails. Your money would be lost somewhere in the transaction, so the TPS would roll back your debit, essentially undoing the operation (see Figure 11.19).

# MANAGEMENT INFORMATION SYSTEMS

A **management information system (MIS)** includes software, hardware, data resources (such as databases), decision support systems, people, and project management applications. An MIS provides information on daily operations; takes data from the transaction-processing systems, other internal databases, and external sources; and puts it into reports and simulations used by managers to organize, evaluate, and efficiently run their departments.

An MIS has two important functions:

- Generate reports—such as financial statements, inventory reports, and performance reports—needed for routine or non-routine purposes, putting unmanageable volumes of data into a form that can be used by decision-makers.

- Create simulations of hypothetical scenarios that answer "what if" questions regarding alterations in business strategy.

MIS systems are typically used by mid-level managers. An MIS used by a marketing department might be used for product development, distribution, pricing, and sales forecasting. A human resources MIS might be used for hiring and recruiting decisions.

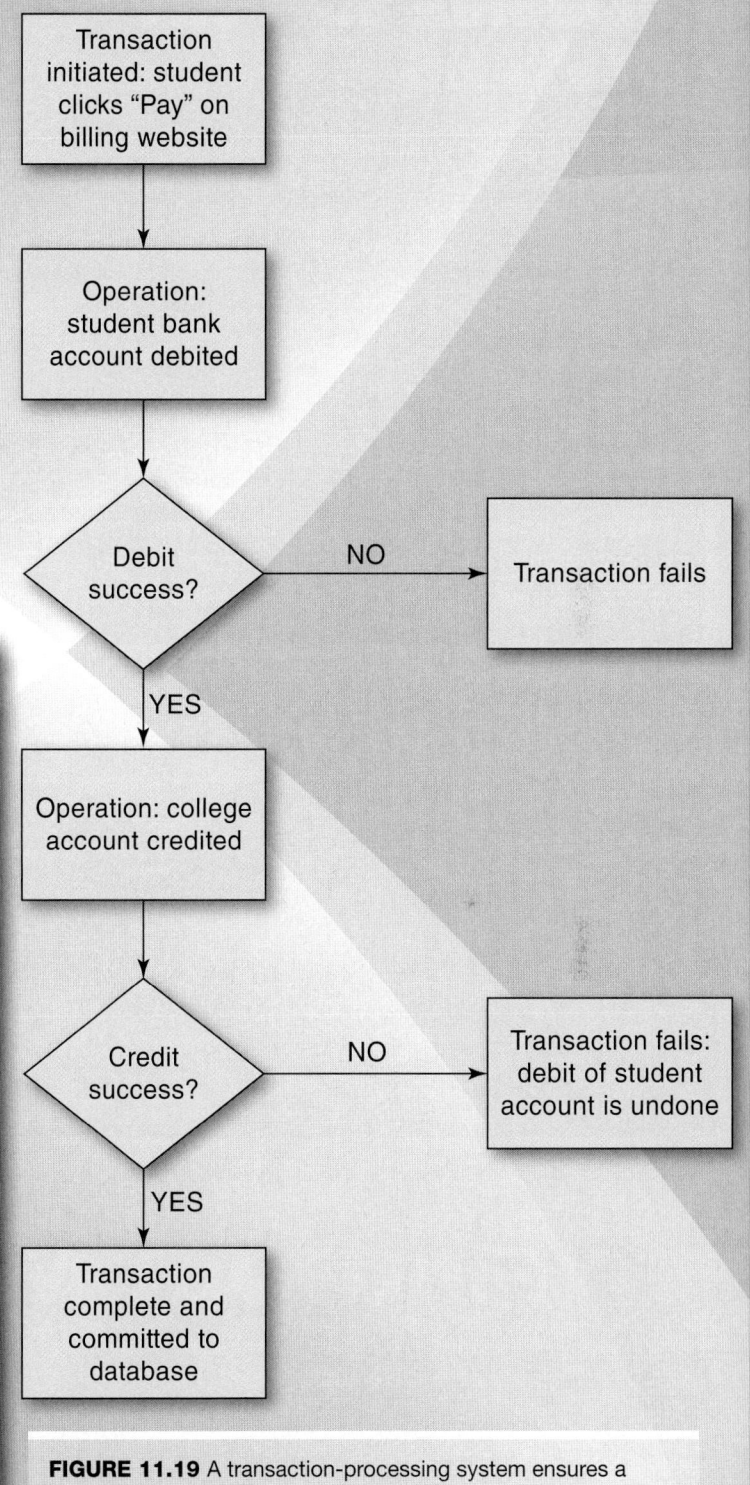

**FIGURE 11.19** A transaction-processing system ensures a transaction is completed.

# DECISION SUPPORT SYSTEMS

**Decision support systems (DSS)** are designed to help make decisions in situations where there is uncertainty about the possible outcomes of those decisions. For example, a local cookie bakery wants to begin selling its products nationally. Before making an investment in a website and online ordering system, the business manager needs to be sure that it's practical. The bakery business manager can use a DSS to gather information from internal sources (such as sales figures, account balances, and employees) to determine if the bakery has the ability to expand its business as well as external sources (such as industry data) to determine if there's a national market for cookies. The DSS organizes the data to help the manager analyze it and make the decision.

# EXPERT SYSTEMS AND ARTIFICIAL INTELLIGENCE

The branch of science concerned with making computers behave like humans is **artificial intelligence (AI)**. One important part of AI is the **expert system**: a computer programmed to make decisions in real-life situations (for example, diagnosing diseases based on symptoms).

An expert system simulates the judgment and behavior of a human expert and consists of two parts:

- **Knowledge base:** Contains expert knowledge and accumulated experience in a particular field
- **Inference engine:** A set of rules for applying the knowledge base to each particular situation

The most well-known example of an expert system is IBM's chess program Deep Blue. In 1997, Deep Blue won a six-game match against Garry Kasparov, the reigning world champion (see Figure 11.20). Deep Blue won because it was able to run through every calculation—derived from the rules of chess plus the expert's knowledge base—for every possible move.

Information systems used in business are as diverse as the types of businesses that use them, but there's no doubt that most modern businesses couldn't be successful without them.

**FIGURE 11.20** Deep Blue was an expert system designed to play chess.

# Find Out MORE

What's the Music Genome Project? Visit the Pandora Internet Radio website (pandora.com), and click on Music Genome Project. How is the data collected? How is it used? On the Pandora home page, enter the name of an artist that you enjoy, and click *Create*. Listen to a few of the songs that Pandora plays. Do you like them? Would you put them together?

## Running Project

Research the current state of AI. What breakthroughs have occurred in the past 5 years?

## 5 Things You Need to Know

- Information systems consist of people, hardware, and software.
- Transaction processing links multiple operations together and ensures that all operations in a transaction are completed without error.
- An MIS generates reports and simulations used by managers.
- A decision support system is designed to help make decisions in situations where there's uncertainty about the possible outcomes.
- An expert system is programmed to make decisions in real-life situations.

## Key Terms

artificial intelligence (AI)

decision support system (DSS)

expert system

information system

management information system (MIS)

office support system (OSS)

transaction-processing system (TPS)

# Real World Databases

## 5 OBJECTIVE
## List examples of databases used in law enforcement and science.

While a database to track your vehicle expenses or keep a home inventory is useful, many industries rely on databases for far more critical information. In this article, we discuss some of the exciting ways that databases are used in law enforcement and science.

## LAW ENFORCEMENT

You can hardly turn on the TV these days without hearing how DNA or fingerprints helped to solve a crime. It's on the news and in the plotline of every police drama. Today, law enforcement officers have technology on their side with two very powerful databases: CODIS and IAFIS, which are growing in size and helping in more cases every day.

**COMBINED DNA INDEX SYSTEM (CODIS)** The **CODIS (Combined DNA Index System)** (see Figure 11.21) searches across multiple local, state, and national DNA profile databases. It consists of three geographic levels: the National DNA Index System (NDIS) maintained by the FBI, the State DNA Index System (SDIS), and the Local DNA Index System (LDIS).

CODIS consists of five indices: Forensic, Arrestee, Detainee, Offender, and Missing Persons.

- The Forensic index contains DNA profiles obtained from crime scene evidence.

- The Arrestee, Detainee, and Offender indices contain DNA profiles of individuals arrested, detained, or convicted of various offenses (which vary by jurisdiction).

- The National Missing Persons DNA Database (NMPDD) consists of three parts: Unidentified Human Remains, Missing Persons, and Biological Relatives of Missing Persons.

CODIS searches across these indices for a potential match. Matches found between the Offender and Forensic indices can identify a suspect. Matches found in the Forensic index can link crime scenes—and thus cases—to each other. According to the FBI, as of May 2010, CODIS had nearly eight million offender profiles, more than 300,000 forensics profiles, and aided in approximately 120,000 investigations.

**FIGURE 11.21** The CODIS is used by law enforcement to link cases and identify suspects.

**Integrated Automated Fingerprint Identification System (IAFIS)** The **IAFIS (Integrated Automated Fingerprint Identification System)** is a national fingerprint and criminal history system maintained by the FBI and used by local, state, and federal law enforcement. IAFIS (see Figure 11.22) was launched in 1999 and is the largest biometric database in the world. It consists of a criminal database that includes the fingerprints of more than 66 million criminal subjects and a civil database of some 26 million subjects that have served in the armed forces or work in the federal government, law enforcement, finance, and other sensitive industries. The records include not only fingerprints but also mug shots, criminal histories, and physical characteristics.

IAFIS is an automated system. It takes only minutes to search the massive database for potential matches. In the past, the process was done by hand and could take months to complete. Today, fingerprints can be taken from a suspect at a crime scene or a suspected terrorist in a country across the globe using a handheld scanner and sent to IAFIS remotely, with the results returned in about 10 minutes.

**BLUE C.R.U.S.H** In 2005, Memphis police instituted Blue C.R.U.S.H. (Crime Reduction Utilizing Statistical History). The program uses a database of historical crime data to predict "hot spots" of crime allowing the department to effectively deploy its resources. The pilot was so successful it has become a department-wide system.

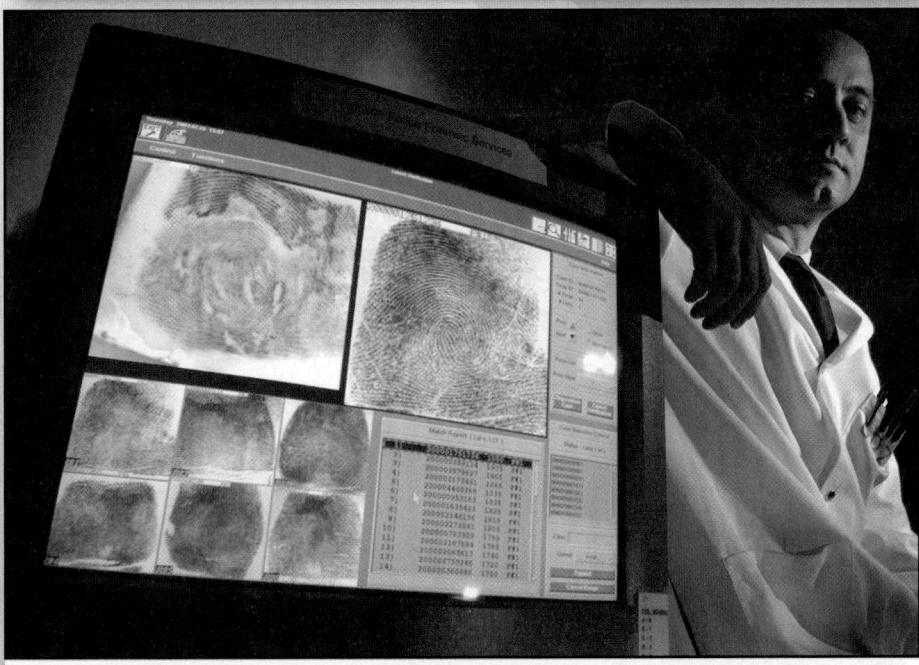

**FIGURE 11.22** A fingerprint technician uses IAFIS to search for a fingerprint match.

# SCIENCE

Modern advances in the sciences are closely linked to advances in technology. In some cases, the technology leads to scientific discoveries, and in others, the science drives technology development. Two areas where this is evident are bioinformatics and geography.

**HUMAN GENOME PROJECT** The **Human Genome Project (HGP)** (see Figure 11.23) ran from 1990 to 2003 and was coordinated by the U.S. Department of Energy and the National Institutes of Health (NIH).

The HGP goals were to:

- Identify all the approximately 20,000–25,000 genes in human DNA.
- Determine the sequences of the three billion chemical base pairs that compose human DNA.
- Store this information in databases.
- Improve tools for data analysis.
- Transfer related technologies to the private sector.
- Address the ethical, legal, and social issues (ELSI) that may arise from the project.

When the project began, the technology to store and analyze the data collected simply didn't exist, and the field of bioinformatics was born. **Bioinformatics** is the application of information technology to the field of biology. The project finished 2 years ahead of schedule, largely due to the advances in technology the project necessitated.

The data collected and analyzed from the project is being used in the development of new technologies and major advancements in biotechnology, agriculture, energy production, environmental science, and medical research.

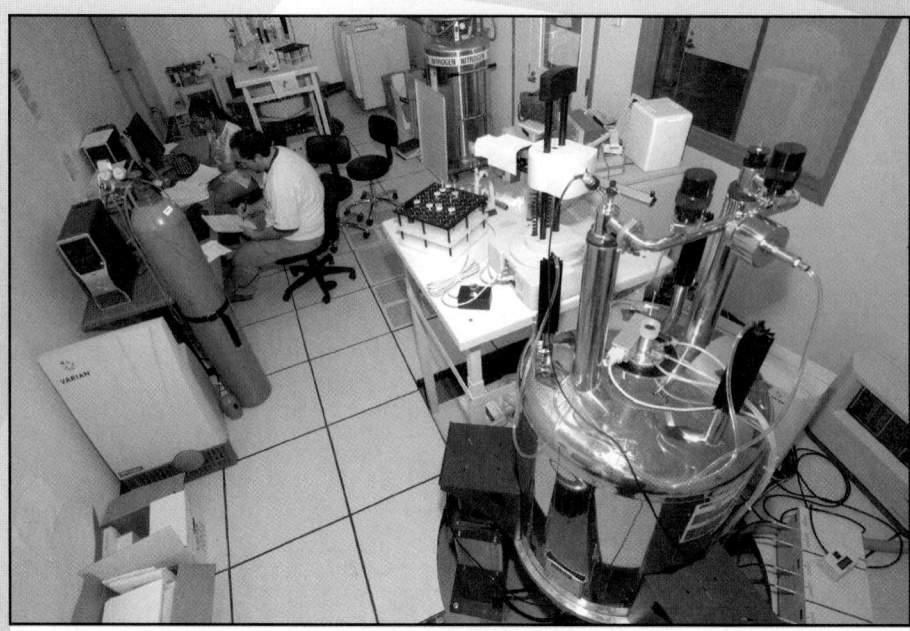

**FIGURE 11.23** The HGP combines biology and technology.

# ETHICS

Some states collect the DNA profiles of convicted violent offenders, others collect samples from all convicted offenders, and still others collect DNA from anyone arrested. DNA samples may be collected from suspects that are never arrested—often, simply to eliminate them. What happens to the DNA of someone who's not convicted can be a cause for concern. Unlike fingerprints, which merely establish identity, DNA can be used to establish paternity, susceptibility to disease, and other genetic predispositions. The information in DNA profiles could potentially be used to deny someone a job or insurance. What do you think should be done with samples of innocent persons?

# GREEN COMPUTING

## GREEN DATA CENTERS

All the computing power required to maintain large databases uses a lot of energy and has a large impact on the environment. And, the energy costs for a business with large data centers can be staggering. A **data center**—sometimes called a server farm—is a facility designed to house a company's servers and other equipment in a secure and controlled environment. One of the largest expenses in a data center is energy costs.

A green data center's mechanical, lighting, electrical, and computer systems are designed for maximum energy efficiency and minimum environmental impact. Green data centers can be certified by the U.S. Green Building Council (USGBC). Many companies look for data center locations with cheaper energy to lower power costs. In 2006, Google moved its data centers to rural Oregon with cheap, renewable, hydroelectric energy, and according to Google, their data centers use about half the energy of a typical data center. Locations near wind farms, hydroelectric plants, and geothermal plants are good places to build new data centers. Building green also involves other steps, such as low-emission building materials, sustainable landscaping, recycling, and the use of alternative energy technologies, such as heat pumps and evaporative cooling.

There are steps that can make existing data centers greener:

- Redesign cooling system. Channel heat away from servers, seal leaks, and use high-efficiency cooling units.
- Scale back equipment. Use smaller and more energy efficient systems.
- Consolidate and virtualize. Move equipment to one central location, and consolidate equipment to fewer, more efficient machines.
- Use Energy Star–rated appliances, computers, and servers.

**GEOGRAPHIC INFORMATION SYSTEMS (GIS)** A **GIS (geographic information system)** combines layers, or datasets, of geographically referenced information about Earth's surface. Each layer holds data about a particular kind of feature, such as rainfall, land use, land cover, census figures, or satellite imagery. The datasets may exist as graphic information such as maps or as database tables.

The U.S. Geological Survey has created the National Map (**nationalmap.gov**), which is available to the public on the Web. You can use the free online viewer (a simple GIS interface) to look at each of the layers (see Figure 11.24). You can also download the map data into a desktop GIS program. The National Map includes eight primary layers:

- Aerial photographs
- Elevation
- Geographic names
- Hydrography
- Boundaries
- Transportation
- Structures
- Land cover

GIS applies database operations—such as queries—on different types of data to see patterns, trends, and spatial relationships. The analysis of GIS information is used in decision-making. Municipalities use a GIS to design emergency routes, locate waste management facilities, and plan future development. Environmental management uses include natural resources management and environmental impact assessment.

Data is used to make decisions across many different disciplines, and databases have become an integral part of the process. From catching criminals to emergency management and medical breakthroughs, databases have made an impact on all our lives.

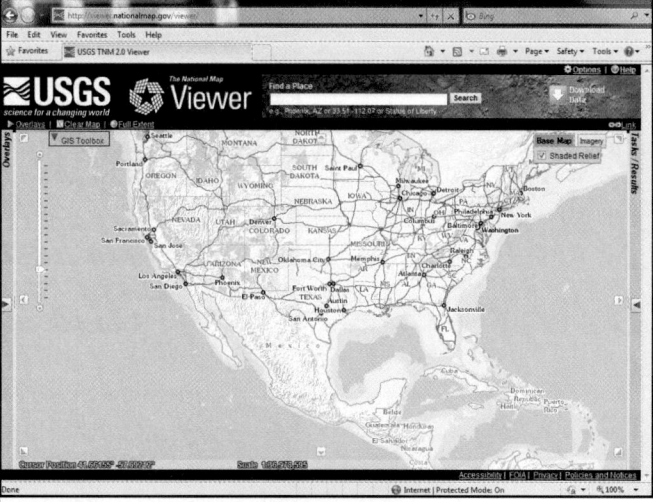

**FIGURE 11.24** The National Map Viewer

# CAREER SPOTLIGHT

As you have learned, databases are found in virtually every industry. As a result, there's a great need for people with expertise in designing, maintaining, and using them. According to the *Occupational Outlook Handbook*, jobs in this field are expected to grow much faster than the average for all occupations.

A **database administrator (DBA)** is the person who manages existing database systems. A DBA sets up databases, manages the installation and ongoing functions of the database system, upgrades database software, monitors performance, and performs maintenance, backup, and recovery of databases. A DBA may also create user accounts, manage database security, and provide login administration. A DBA generally requires at least a bachelor's degree. Industry certifications are also desirable.

## Running Project

Visit the FBI website (fbi.gov) to find out how CODIS has been used to solve cold cases. Type CODIS in the search box, and read through the results. Select one case, and write a short summary of the investigation.

## 4 Things You Need to Know

- CODIS searches across multiple DNA indexes for a potential match.
- IAFIS is the largest biometric database in the world.
- Bioinformatics is the application of information technology to the field of biology. The HGP mapped the approximately 20,000–25,000 human genes.
- GIS combines layers or datasets of geographically referenced information about Earth's surface.

## Key Terms

bioinformatics

CODIS (Combined DNA Index System)

data center

database administrator (DBA)

GIS (geographic information system)

Human Genome Project (HGP)

IAFIS (Integrated Automated Fingerprint Identification System)

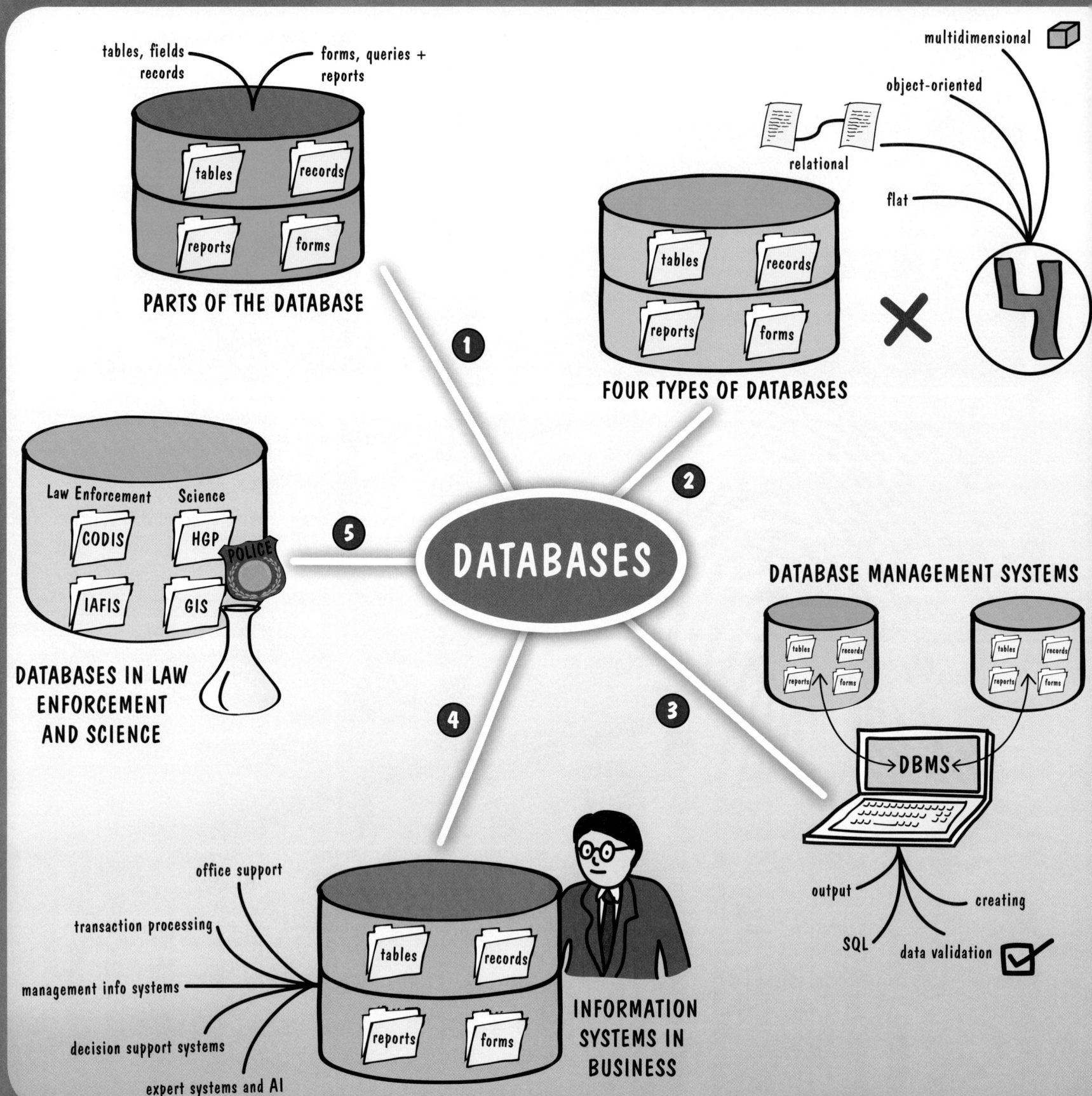

PARTS OF THE DATABASE

tables, fields records

forms, queries + reports

tables

records

reports

forms

FOUR TYPES OF DATABASES

multidimensional

object-oriented

relational

flat

tables

records

reports

forms

× 4

DATABASES

DATABASE MANAGEMENT SYSTEMS

tables
records
reports
forms

tables
records
reports
forms

DBMS

output

creating

SQL

data validation

DATABASES IN LAW ENFORCEMENT AND SCIENCE

Law Enforcement

Science

CODIS

HGP

IAFIS

GIS

POLICE

INFORMATION SYSTEMS IN BUSINESS

office support

transaction processing

management info systems

decision support systems

expert systems and AI

tables

records

reports

forms

1
2
3
4
5

486

# Objectives Recap

1. Identify the parts of a database.
2. Compare the four types of databases.
3. Explain database management systems.
4. Discuss important information systems used in business.
5. List examples of databases used in law enforcement and science.

# Key Terms

artificial intelligence (AI) **478**
bioinformatics **482**
CODIS (Combined DNA Index System) **480**
data center **483**
data dictionary **462**
data normalization **462**
data validation **463**
data warehouse **457**
database **449**
database administrator (DBA) **485**
database management system (DBMS) **462**
decision support system (DSS) **478**
expert system **478**
field **451**
flat file database **454**
form **451**
GIS (geographic information system) **484**
Human Genome Project (HGP) **482**
IAFIS (Integrated Automated Fingerprint Identification System) **481**

information system **476**
management information system (MIS) **477**
multidimensional database (MDB) **456**
object-oriented database (OODB) **456**
office support system (OSS) **476**
online analytical processing (OLAP) **457**
primary key **451**
query **452**
record **451**
relational database **455**
report **453**
Structured Query Language (SQL) **466**
table **450**
transaction-processing system (TPS) **476**

# Summary

1. **Identify the parts of a database.**

   A database consists of tables arranged in rows and columns. A row is a record that contains the information for a single entry. A column is a field, which is a single piece of information in a record. Forms, queries, and reports are database objects used to manage the information in tables.

2. **Compare the four types of databases.**

   The simplest type of a database is a flat file database consisting of a single list of items. A relational database consists of multiple tables or relations, which are related by common information. Relational databases are the most common type. In an object-oriented database (OODB), data is stored as objects, which consist of both the data that describes the object and the processes that can be applied to it. A multidimensional database (MDB) is optimized for storing and utilizing data. It may be created using input from existing relational databases, but it structures the information into multidimensional data cubes.

3. **Explain database management systems.**

   A database management system (DBMS) is the software used to create and manage the data in a database. The data dictionary defines all the fields and the type of data each field contains. Data normalization is used to reduce data redundancy, making it easier to keep records up to date, and increases query speed. Data validation reduces data-entry errors using validation rules. A DBMS helps users design queries using a query language, such as SQL, and create reports.

4. **Discuss important information systems used in business.**

   Office support systems (OSS) include software and hardware that improve the productivity of employees by automating common business tasks. Businesses rely on transaction-processing systems (TPS) to respond to user requests. Transaction processing links multiple operations together and ensures that all operations in a transaction are completed without error. A management information system (MIS) includes software, hardware, data resources (such as databases), decision support systems, people, and project management applications. Decision support systems (DSS) are designed to help make decisions in situations where there's uncertainty about the possible outcomes of those decisions. An expert system is a computer programmed to make decisions in real-life situations (for example, diagnosing diseases based on symptoms).

**5. List examples of databases used in law enforcement and science.**

The CODIS (Combined DNA Index System) consists of multiple local, state, and national DNA profile databases and has five indices: Forensic, Arrestee, Detainee, Offender, and Missing Persons. The Integrated Automated Fingerprint Identification System (IAFIS) is a national fingerprint and criminal history system maintained by the FBI and used by local, state, and federal law enforcement. It's the largest biometric database in the world. Blue C.R.U.S.H. uses a database of historical crime data to predict "hot spots" of crime. The Human Genome Project (HGP) determined the sequence of chemical base pairs that compose DNA and mapped the approximately 20,000–25,000 human genes. A GIS (geographic information system) combines layers or datasets of geographically referenced information about Earth's surface.

## Multiple Choice

Answer the multiple-choice questions below for more practice with key terms and concepts from this chapter.

1. A _____ is a database object in which data is stored.
   a. field          c. table
   b. record         d. primary key

2. A _____ retrieves specific data from one or more tables.
   a. field          c. report
   b. form           d. primary key

3. A database object that's used to pull out information to answer a question is a _____.
   a. table          c. report
   b. form           d. query

4. What type of database is optimized for storing and utilizing data?
   a. Flat file           b. Relational
   c. Object-oriented     d. Multidimensional

5. _____ reduces data redundancy.
   a. Schema
   b. Data normalization
   c. Data validation
   d. Data warehousing

6. A DBMS uses _____ to create a query.
   a. forms          c. dictionaries
   b. SQL            d. schemas

7. What is the set of rules in an expert system for applying a knowledge base to a particular situation?
   a. Inference engine
   b. Artificial intelligence
   c. Decision support system
   d. Information system

8. A(n) _____ is designed to help make decisions.
   a. OSS (office support system)
   b. TPS (transaction-processing system)
   c. MIS (management information system)
   d. DSS (decision support system)

9. _____ is the application of information technology to the field of biology.
   a. Bioinformatics
   b. TPS (transaction-processing system)
   c. MIS (management information system)
   d. DSS (decision support system)

10. A(n) _____ layers datasets that may include maps, imagery, and tables.
   a. CODIS
   b. IAFIS
   c. HGP
   d. GIS

# True or False

Answer the following questions with T for true or F for false for more practice with key terms and concepts from this chapter.

1. Each database consists of a single table of information.

2. A table is used to display data in an easy-to-read-and-print format.

3. In a relational database, all records are linked by a one-to-one relationship.

4. A field should be created for each independent piece of information.

5. A multidimensional database is optimized for storing and utilizing data.

6. An object-oriented database generates reports and simulations that answer "what if" questions.

7. SQL statements use relational keywords such as SELECT, FROM, WHERE.

8. Data validation reduces data-entry errors.

9. Data can often be imported from other sources.

10. IAFIS and CODIS contain information only from convicted offenders.

# Fill in the Blank

Fill in the blanks with key terms from this chapter.

1. A(n) _____ is a collection of related information.

2. A(n) _____ contains the information for a single entry in a database (person, place, thing, event, or idea).

3. The _____ uniquely identifies a record in a table.

4. A(n) _____ makes data entry easier.

5. A(n) _____ database is best for handling complex data such as images, audio, and video.

6. A(n) _____ is a central repository for all the data an enterprise uses.

7. The software used to create and manage data in a database is called a(n) _____.

8. The schema, or _____, defines all the fields and type of data they contain.

9. _____ improve the productivity of employees by automating common tasks.

10. The branch of science concerned with making computers behave like humans is _____.

# Application Project

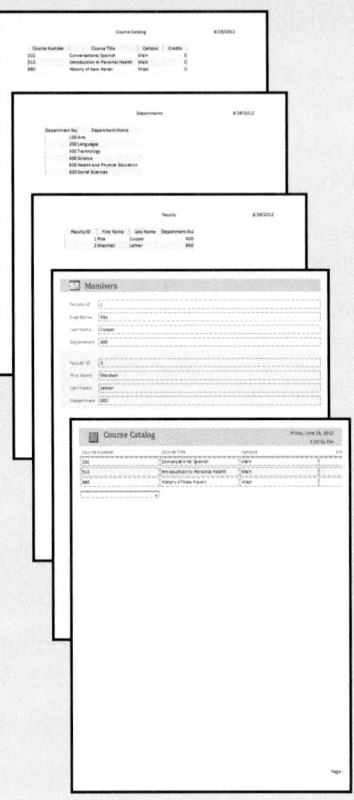

## Microsoft Application Project 1:
## Access Level 1

**PROJECT DESCRIPTION:** In this Microsoft Access project, you will add a second table to an Access database, add records through tables and a form, and change the field sizes in Design view of a table. You will also create a simple report.

**INSTRUCTIONS:** For the purpose of grading of the project you are required to perform the following tasks:

| Step | Instructions |
|------|--------------|
| 1 | Start Access. Open the downloaded file named *vt_ch11_access* and save the file as **lastname_firstname_ch11_access**. If necessary, click *Enable Content*. |
| 2 | In Design view of the Faculty table, change the First Name and Last Name field sizes to 35. Save and close the table. |
| 3 | Add the following two records to the Departments table:**500 Health and Physical Education 600 Social Sciences** |

| Step | Instructions |
|------|--------------|
| 4 | Resize the Department column to give it the best fit automatically. Save and close the Departments table. |
| 5 | Open the Faculty Data Entry Form. Add a new record, entering **Rita** as the First Name, **Cooper** as the Last Name, and **400** as the Department Number. Add a second record to the form, entering **Marshall** as the First Name, **Lehrer** as the Last Name, and **600** as the Department Number. Close the form. |

**Visit pearsonhighered.com/Geoghan** for data files, simulations, VizClips, and additional study materials.

| Step | Instructions |
|------|--------------|
| **6** | Create a new table in Datasheet view. Change the field name of the ID field to **Course Number**. Name the next fields **Course Title** and **Campus** (in that order), using the Text data type. Add **Credits**, using the number data type. |
| **7** | Change the Data Type of the Course Number field to Text, Save the table as **Course Catalog**, switch to Design view and ensure that the Course Number field is set as the Primary Key. Switch back to Datasheet view. |
| **8** | Add the following three records to the Course Catalog table: |

| Course Number | Course Title | Campus | Credits |
|---------------|--------------|--------|---------|
| 512 | Introduction to Personal Health | Main | 2 |
| 680 | History of New Haven | West | 3 |
| 202 | Conversational Spanish | Main | 3 |

| Step | Instructions |
|------|--------------|
| **9** | Resize all of the columns in the table to have the best fit. Save the table. |
| **10** | With the Course Catalog table open in Datasheet view, create a simple report that will open in Layout view. Sort the records from smallest to largest by the Course Number field. Save the report with the name **Course Catalog Report**. |
| **11** | Close all database objects. Close the database and then exit Access. Submit the database as directed. |

**Visit pearsonhighered.com/Geoghan** for data files, simulations, VizClips, and additional study materials.

Chapter 11 | 491

# Microsoft Office Application Project 2: Word Level 3

**Study Group Contact List**

| Name | Cell Phone | Email |
|---|---|---|
| [1]Sandy Blackwood | 267-555-2225 | blackwoods@phhe.edu |
| Marty Fratelli | 609-555-8663 | fratellim@phhe.edu |
| Jake Giambi | 215-555-9875 | giambij@phhe.edu |
| Mary Koch | 267-555-6345 | kochm@ phhe.edu |

[1] Group leader

**PROJECT DESCRIPTION:** In this Microsoft Word project, you will format create a flat file database using a Word table, apply a table style, sort a table, format text, and add a footnote.

**INSTRUCTIONS**: For the purpose of grading the project you are required to perform the following tasks:

| Step | Instructions |
|---|---|
| 1 | Start Word. Download and open the file named *vt_ch11_word*. Save the file as **lastname_firstname_ch11_word**. |
| 2 | Select the three contacts and convert the text to a 3X3 table. |
| 3 | Insert a row title above. Enter the text **Name**, **Cell Phone**, **Email** in the three top cells. Insert: Format using table style Grid Table 6 Colorful - Accent 5. |
| 4 | Be sure Header Row and Banded Rows are both checked. Uncheck First Column. |

| Step | Instructions |
|---|---|
| 5 | Sort the table by Email, ascending. |
| 6 | Format the first line Study Group Contact List using the Title style. Apply the text effect Fill - Aqua, Accent 2, Outline - Background 1, Hard Shadow - Accent 1, and center align. |
| 7 | Move the insertion point to the end of the last email address and press tab to create a new row. Enter the record: **Sandy Blackwood 267-555-2225 blackwoods@ phhe.edu** |

| Step | Instructions |
|------|-------------|
| 8 | Re-sort the table by email address ascending. |
| 9 | Search for clip art illustrations using the phrase **study time** and then insert the image of the Study time sign and supplies into the document. For your reference, the image is included with the project starting materials with the file name *vt_ch11_image.png*. |
| 10 | Resize the image height to 3", lock aspect ratio. Position the image Middle Center with Square Text Wrapping. |

| Step | Instructions |
|------|-------------|
| 11 | Apply the Reflected Bevel White picture style. |
| 12 | Position the insertion point before Sandy and insert a footnote: **Group leader**. |
| 13 | Save and close document and then exit Word. Submit the document as directed. |

# Running project...

## ... The Finish Line

Use your answers to the previous sections of the project. Why are databases important to you, and why is it important to be knowledgeable about them? Write a report describing how you use databases in your daily life, and respond to the questions raised. Save your file as **lastname_firstname_ch11_project**, and submit it to your instructor as directed.

# Do It Yourself 1

In addition to the physical collection in your library, many resources today are available in online databases. Visit your school library (in person or virtually) to find out what online databases are available to you as a student.

1. What databases are available to you? How many of these databases have you used in the past? Are any related to your chosen field? Select one that you haven't used before, and create a query using the online form. Search for an article related to your career choice. If possible, use the system to create a citation.

2. Write up a summary of your results. How difficult did you find it to create a query using the online form? Paste your citation into your document. Save the file as **lastname_firstname_ch11_diy1**, and submit it as directed by your instructor.

# Do It Yourself 2

Access has numerous templates that you can use to create your own database. In this exercise, you'll use a template to create a personal contact manager database.

1. Open Access. Type **personal contact manager** in the Search Office.com for templates box. Name the file **lastname_firstname_ch11_diy2**, navigate to the folder where you save you work for this chapter, and click *Download*.

2. Close the Help window, click *Enable Content*, and expand the Navigation Pane. Explore the database. List the objects that were created.

3. Close the Contact List. Use the Contact Details form to add three new contacts (you can make up the data). Take a screen shot of one of them. Open the Contact Address report and the Contact Phone List report.

4. Type up your answers, and include screen shots of the form and both reports. Save the file as **lastname_firstname_ch11_diy2_answers**, and submit both your database and answers as directed by your instructor.

# File Management

Now that you have learned about databases, you can see that the file system on your computer is actually a database.

1. Click the *Start* button and then click your username to open Windows Explorer. Open the Documents library. If necessary, change the view to Details using the Change your view menu. How does this view resemble a table? What fields are in this table?

2. Right-click next to the Name column heading. What other fields can be displayed in this window? List two that you think would be valuable to display.

3. Type up your answers, save the file as **lastname_firstname_ch11_fm,** and submit as directed by your instructor.

# Critical Thinking

You have a large collection of DVD and Blu-ray movies you often loan to friends and family. Create a simple flat file database to store the information.

1. Think about the information you'll need to organize. Design a simple flat file database you can use. Your table should have at least eight fields.

2. Use a spreadsheet or DBMS of your choice to create your table. Define the data type to be used for each field and any data validation rules you think are needed.

3. Save the file as **lastname_firstname_ch11_ct**, and submit it as directed by your instructor.

# Ethical Dilemma

It's standard business practice for a company to send you targeted advertisements based on information it has about you in a database. The information may be gleaned from your shopping habits, surveys you fill out, or information purchased from another company.

1. Retailers competing for your loyalty offer club cards and other incentives for you to shop in their stores. Most people don't realize that when they use those perks, the companies build a profile that includes information about where and when they shop—and what they buy. This is so the stores can send targeted ads and offers. In 2012, a story broke about a large company that was data mining its customer databases to try to determine if a woman was pregnant. This was a good time for the store to grab the customer with specials on baby items, maternity clothing, toys, and the like. Because the information is public, is it OK for a business to use the information to send unsolicited emails or advertisements or to contact the people in others ways? How would you feel if you (or someone you are close to) received coupons for diapers before you told anyone that you (or she) were pregnant?

2. Type up your answers, save the file as **lastname_firstname_ch11_ethics**, and submit it as directed by your instructor.

# On the Web

1. Visit the Zoho Creator website at **zoho.com/creator**. Sign in using one of the account options or create a new account for this activity. On the Creator page, under How do you want to create the application? click *Browse Gallery* and then click *Visit marketplace* to view all applications. Select the Education category. Browse through the applications available. How many are there? What are a few that you would find useful?

2. Select one and click *Watch Demo* to learn more about it. Write a 2–3 sentence summary of this database. Is it well designed? Useful? Easy to use? Would you recommend it?

3. Type up your answers, save the file as **lastname_firstname_ch11_web**, and submit it as directed by your instructor.

# Collaboration

**Instructors:** Divide the class into five groups, and assign each group one topic for this project. The topics are CODIS, IAFIS, Blue C.R.U.S.H., HGP, and GIS.

**The Project:** Each team is to prepare a poster for its database project. Teams must use at least three references, only one of which may be this textbook. Use Google Docs or Microsoft Office to prepare the final version of your presentation, and provide documentation that all team members have contributed to the project.

**Students:** Before beginning this project, discuss the roles each group member will play. Choose a team name, which you'll use in submitting your presentation. Be sure to divide the work among your members, and pick someone to present your project. You may find it helpful to elect a team leader who can direct your activities and ensure that all team contributions are collated through Google Docs or Microsoft Office as directed by your instructor.

**Outcome:** You're to prepare your poster using any tool that your instructor approves. In addition, turn in a final version of your file showing your collaboration named **teamname_ch11_collab**. Submit your presentation to your instructor as directed.

# 12

# Program Development

## Running Project

In this chapter, you learn about program development. Look for project instructions as you complete each article. For most, there's a series of questions for you to research. At the conclusion of the chapter, you're asked to submit your responses to the questions raised.

1. **Describe the system development life cycle.**

2. **Describe the program development cycle.**

3. **Compare various programming languages.**

4. **Explain the term *artificial intelligence*.**

## IN THIS CHAPTER

An **information system** is the people, hardware, and software that support data-intensive applications such as financial accounts, human resources, and other business transactions. In this chapter, we look at the process of developing an information system and the tools used to create it.

# Getting from Idea to Product

## OBJECTIVE
## Describe the system development life cycle.

There are many different models for developing an information system. In this article, we look at the traditional model and also discuss some of the alternative models.

## SYSTEM DEVELOPMENT LIFE CYCLE (SDLC)

The traditional model for system development is known as the System Development Life Cycle. As the name implies, it follows the system over time from inception to retirement or replacement. The **System Development Life Cycle,** or **SDLC**, consists of five phases (see Figure 12.1). It's sometimes called a waterfall approach, where each phase is completed in order before the next can begin. This method is rigid and doesn't allow for modification and revisions to occur to previous phases but it provides tight managerial control. The process begins when there's a request for a new system or a replacement for an old one in response to a business opportunity or problem.

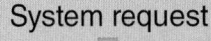

System request

Planning

Replace system

Analysis

Design

Implementation

Maintenance

**FIGURE 12.1** The Traditional SDLC Model

**PLANNING PHASE** The SDLC begins in the planning phase. In this phase, the project team is assembled, and feasibility studies are completed. Sometimes, this phase is referred to as the feasibility stage.

**Project Team** A **stakeholder** is someone who has an interest in and will be affected by the successful completion of the project, such as a manager, owner, user, security professional, telecommunications staff member, and software development specialist. A project team consists of stakeholders from multiple areas. The leader of the project team is the **project manager (PM)**. Throughout the project, the PM coordinates the project team and keeps the project on track. A large project may include a business project manager and a technical project manager. The team tries to answer the following questions: What are the purpose and goals of the project? How will we know if the project is successful? If the decision is made to proceed, then a project plan and budget estimates are produced.

**Investigation/Feasibility Studies** The project team works to define the objectives and scope of the project. Feasibility studies are used to determine if the project should proceed. They typically focus on economic feasibility (Can we afford it?), technical feasibility (Do we have the technical resources to build it?), operational feasibility (Will it work within our business model?), and political feasibility (Can we get buy-in for the project?). A **feasibility study** involves several steps, including the creation of the terms of reference or project charter, which states the objectives and scope of the project, the timeline for the project, risks, participants, deliverables, and budget.

**ANALYSIS PHASE** The goal of the analysis phase is to produce a list of requirements for the new system. This process involves evaluating the current system's weaknesses and strengths and defining the requirements of the new system.

**Analyzing the Current System** If there's an existing system in place, its strengths, weaknesses, and key features are evaluated by interviewing users and support staff. **Data flow diagrams (DFD)** are created to show the flow of data through the current system and to highlight its deficiencies. Figure 12.2 shows a DFD that illustrates the process of a student applying to a school. The Approval process circle could then be broken down into more detailed DFDs.

**Requirements Analysis** Once the old system has been analyzed, it's time to define the requirements for the new system. What will the system do? Tools such as data flow diagrams help define the flow of data in the system. Any deficiencies found in the current system will be addressed in the requirements of the new system. This process also looks at the existing business processes and how they might need to be changed. The system requirements generated guide the design of the new system and need to be as comprehensive as possible. The result is a logical model of the new system called a *system specification report*.

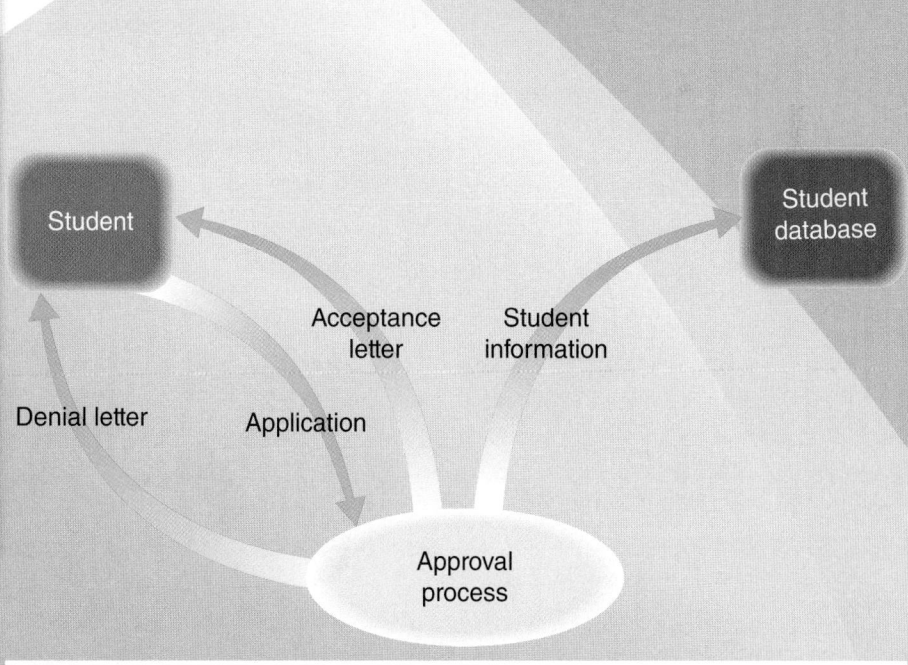

**FIGURE 12.2** A data flow diagram illustrates how data flows through a system. Analysis of each stop along the way helps in evaluating systems.

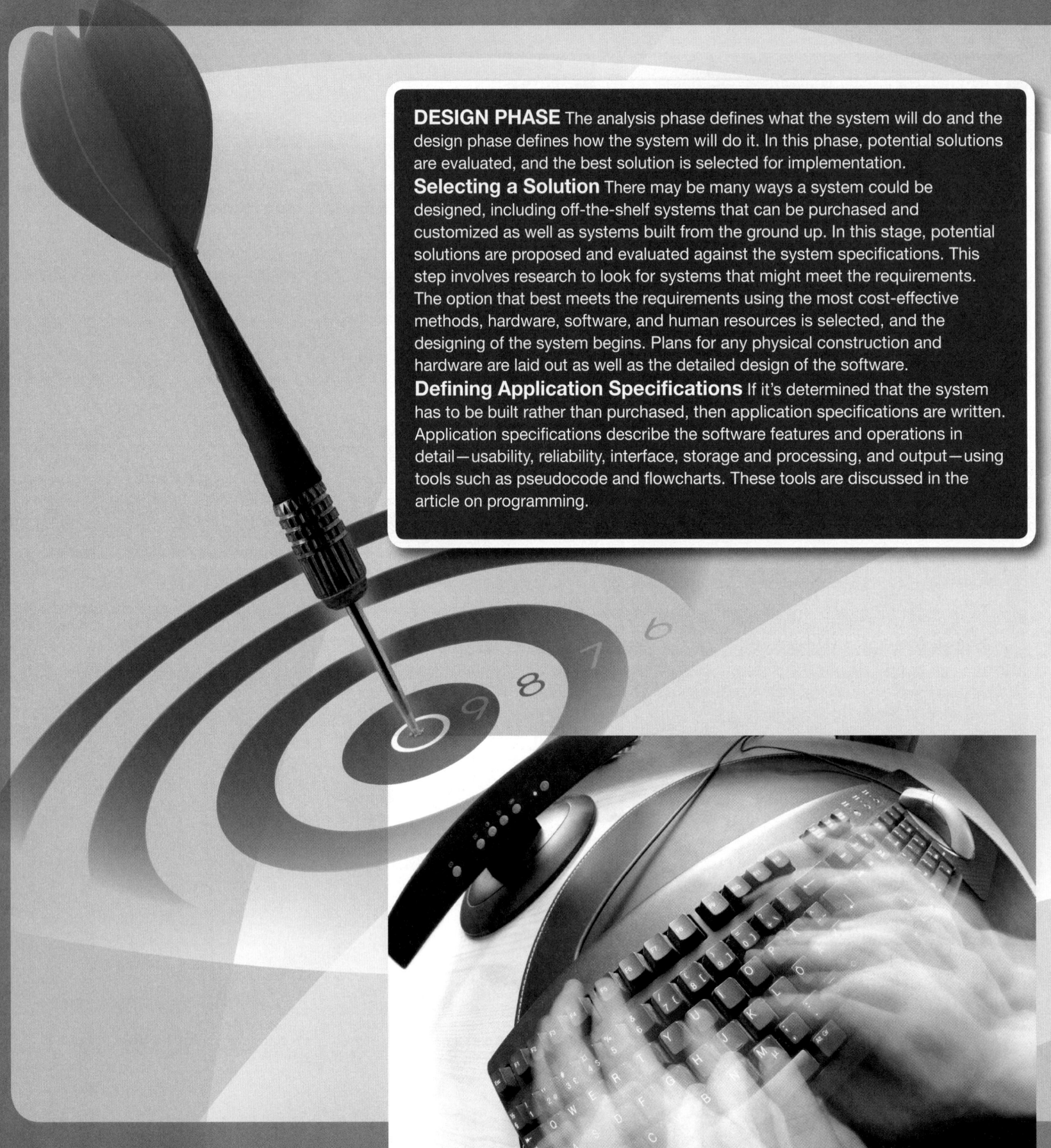

**DESIGN PHASE** The analysis phase defines what the system will do and the design phase defines how the system will do it. In this phase, potential solutions are evaluated, and the best solution is selected for implementation.

**Selecting a Solution** There may be many ways a system could be designed, including off-the-shelf systems that can be purchased and customized as well as systems built from the ground up. In this stage, potential solutions are proposed and evaluated against the system specifications. This step involves research to look for systems that might meet the requirements. The option that best meets the requirements using the most cost-effective methods, hardware, software, and human resources is selected, and the designing of the system begins. Plans for any physical construction and hardware are laid out as well as the detailed design of the software.

**Defining Application Specifications** If it's determined that the system has to be built rather than purchased, then application specifications are written. Application specifications describe the software features and operations in detail—usability, reliability, interface, storage and processing, and output—using tools such as pseudocode and flowcharts. These tools are discussed in the article on programming.

## IMPLEMENTATION PHASE

The implementation stage is when the actual coding takes place and the system is installed and tested. During this phase, users are trained to use it.

**Development and Testing** In this phase, the programmers use the designs and specifications to create the system. The documentation and help system is created, and the system is tested to ensure it meets the project requirements. Programs are usually written in small pieces or modules that undergo individual unit testing. Integration or link testing assures that the modules work together. Volume testing runs the system under normal usage conditions to assure it can handle the expected volume of data. Finally, acceptance testing assures that the system does what it's supposed to do. If you've ever been a software beta tester, then you've participated in acceptance testing. During this phase, adjustments to the system are common.

**Installation and Training** The system is installed, and user training takes place. During training, the users learn how to interact with the system (see Figure 12.3). This is a critical step to the success of the system. The implementation of the new system can occur in several different ways depending on the needs of the business; each method has its pros and cons:

- It may be phased in over time, bringing individual modules online one at a time or using a pilot group of users.
- It may be run in parallel with the old system to assure that the new system is working correctly before retiring the old one.
- It may be brought online all at once, shutting off the old system at the same time.

**MAINTENANCE PHASE** The last phase of the SDLC is the maintenance phase. The system should undergo periodic reviews to ensure it still meets the needs of the business. During this period, the system may change or be updated, security holes and bugs fixed, and new features added. Users may need to be retrained and documentation updated as a result of these changes. Day-to-day operational maintenance includes monitoring performance, installing updates and patches, and creating and restoring backups. Help desk technicians support users in the use of the system and also collect feedback from the users that can identify bugs that were missed by testing or used to improve the system. The maintenance phase is the longest phase of the SDLC and lasts until the system is retired or replaced.

**FIGURE 12.3** User training is a critical part of the SDLC.

# OTHER DEVELOPMENT MODELS

The SDLC is the oldest system development model, but because each phase proceeds in order, there's little opportunity to revise the project as it moves through the development process. Newer models include iterative steps—meaning earlier phases can be revisited as needed.

## JOINT APPLICATION DEVELOPMENT (JAD)

**Joint Application Development (JAD)** is a more collaborative process than the SDLC and involves the end user throughout the design and development of the project through a series of JAD sessions (see Figure 12.4). Using JAD results in shorter development times because of continued involvement of users throughout the development process. The user input throughout the process helps the developer better understand the user's needs and resolve any usability problems early in the process.

## RAPID APPLICATION DEVELOPMENT (RAD)

**Rapid Application Development (RAD)** is an iterative process that uses prototyping and user testing of the designs. Multiple prototypes that look and behave like the final product are created (using RAD tools) and tested. Once a prototype is approved, the real software is written. RAD uses object-oriented programming (OOP) with reusable software components to help speed up development.

**FIGURE 12.4** JAD sessions are collaborative meetings throughout the design and development phases.

Development projects may use some combination of these and other methods to meet the specific needs and goals of the project. Regardless of the model used, all projects follow a similar progression from initial planning through system maintenance.

WORK IN PROGRESS

## Running Project

Another development model is the synchronize-and-stabilize model. Use the Internet to find out about this model. Explain how it works and detail its advantages. What advantages does the synchronize-and-stabilize model have over the traditional SDLC model?

## 4 Things You Need to Know

- The System Development Life Cycle (SDLC) consists of five phases: planning, analysis, design, implementation, and maintenance.

- A project team includes stakeholders from all the areas that have a stake in the successful completion of the project. The project manager is the team leader.

- Joint Application Development (JAD) involves the end user throughout the design and development.

- Rapid Application Development (RAD) is an iterative process that uses prototyping and user testing.

## Key Terms

data flow diagram (DFD)

feasibility study

information system

Joint Application Development (JAD)

project manager (PM)

Rapid Application Development (RAD)

stakeholder

System Development Life Cycle (SDLC)

# Coding the System

## Describe the program development cycle.

A **computer program** is a sequence of instructions for a computer to follow. It's written in a language that the computer can understand and includes any data the computer needs to perform the instructions.

## PROGRAM DEVELOPMENT CYCLE

The **Program Development Cycle** is a set of five steps that a programmer follows to create a computer program (see Figure 12.5). It's considered a cycle because the steps can be iterative—causing the programmer to go back and repeat them throughout the process.

**DEFINING THE PROBLEM** As with any problem-solving exercise, the first step is to define the problem. To a large extent, the success or failure of the program depends on getting this step right. A programmer must determine what data will be provided (input) and what the program will do (processing and output).

Defining the problem

Designing the solution

Coding

Debugging

Testing and documentation

**FIGURE 12.5** The Program Development Cycle

1. Gather the grades for all assignments.

2. Total the points earned.

3. Calculate the average.

4. Determine your grade based on the average.

5. End.

**FIGURE 12.6** An algorithm to solve the grade problem shows the steps written in plain English.

**DESIGNING THE SOLUTION** An **algorithm** is a set of steps to solve a problem. It should be a clear and simple statement that breaks down the solution into small modules, each of which performs a single task. A well-written algorithm lays out the logic and processes the program will include, the sequence of steps to be performed, and any choices or alternatives that might occur. An algorithm written in plain English for determining your grade in a class might look something like Figure 12.6.

Once a good algorithm has been written, it can be mapped out using flowcharts and pseudocode. **Control structures** are used in flowcharts and pseudocode to show logic and the flow of data processing. Common control structures include sequence (lines of code are executed one after the other); selection (determine which lines of code to execute based on certain conditions being met); and loop (repeat certain lines of code a specific number of times). A **flowchart** is a graphic view of the algorithm. Flowcharts use arrows to show direction and other symbols to show actions and data. There are standard flowchart symbols used by most programmers.

Figure 12.7 is a flowchart that illustrates the algorithm used to calculate your grade and includes a selection control structure.

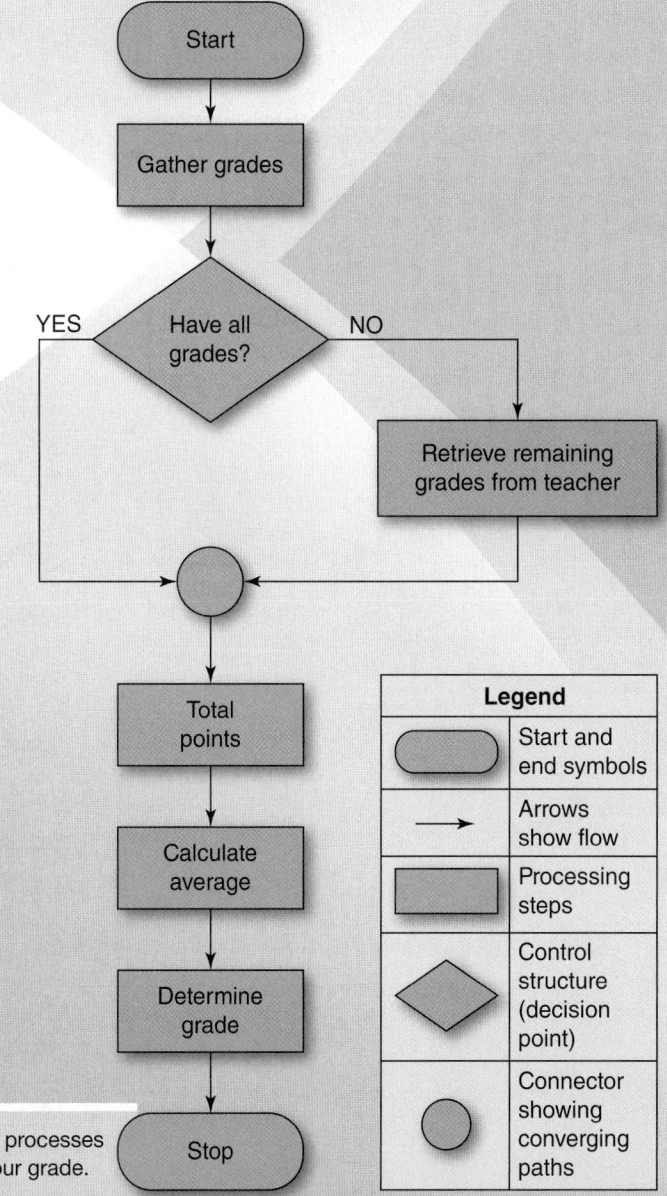

**FIGURE 12.7** A flowchart maps out the logic and processes of an algorithm—in this case, how to determine your grade.

**Pseudocode** expresses the steps of an algorithm using English-like statements that focus on logic, not syntax. Although it is closer to what a program will look like, pseudocode is not specific to any one programming language and is not executable. Figure 12.8 illustrates the pseudocode for the grade problem. There's much more detail, with each step in the process defined, and an IF-THEN and CASE control structure are used to make processing decisions.

The design process helps create the organization for the coding to come. A poor design will lead to frustration and poor coding, so it's essential to take the time to do this right.

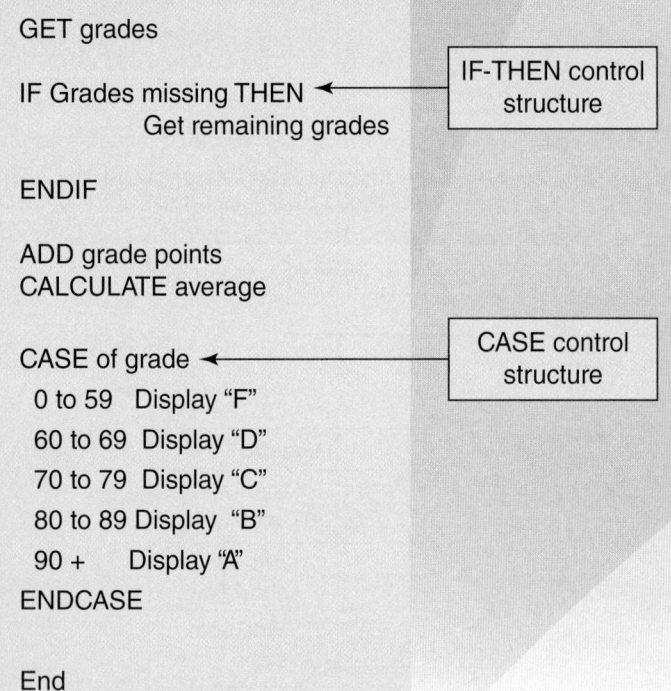

GET grades

IF Grades missing THEN            **IF-THEN control structure**
      Get remaining grades

ENDIF

ADD grade points
CALCULATE average

CASE of grade            **CASE control structure**
  0 to 59   Display "F"
  60 to 69  Display "D"
  70 to 79  Display "C"
  80 to 89 Display  "B"
  90 +     Display "A"
ENDCASE

End

**FIGURE 12.8** The Grade Problem in Pseudocode

**CODING Computer programming,** or **coding**, is the process of converting the algorithm into instructions the computer can understand. First, the appropriate programming language must be selected, taking into account such factors as the type of task, the platform it needs to run on, and the expertise of the programmer. Different languages are optimized for different tasks, so choosing the right language will result in a better solution. Programming is accomplished using one of two models: **Procedural programming** uses a step-by-step list of instructions, whereas **object-oriented programming (OOP)** defines objects and the actions or methods that can be performed on them. Objects can be reused in other programs, making OOP more efficient. Finally, the instructions are coded following the syntax of the chosen language. **Syntax rules** define the correct construction of commands in a programming language.

**DEBUGGING** It's rare that a program runs error-free the first time through. **Debugging** is the process of detecting and fixing errors, or bugs, in a computer program. There are three types of errors: syntax errors, logic errors, and runtime errors. Debugging occurs throughout the coding process and can be considered alpha testing.

**Syntax errors** are errors in the way the code is written. They may be typos, missing parameters, or the incorrect use of symbols, such as brackets. Such errors are generally easy to spot. Syntax errors can be found by reviewing the code line by line, but they'll also prevent a program from running and will generate a syntax error message.

A **logic error** is an error in programming logic that results in an unexpected outcome. The commands may be syntactically correct but logically incorrect. For example, a mathematical formula may add up a column of numbers, but the wrong numbers are used. So, the formula is not a syntax error (it's written correctly) but a logic error (it uses the wrong input, so it results in the wrong result). A common logic error is creating a loop that has no end. Logic errors are more difficult to detect than syntax errors because they don't prevent a program from running.

A **runtime error** occurs when the program is running and something entered causes it to crash. For example, a user may enter invalid data that causes the program to divide by zero. Memory issues are also a common cause of runtime errors. Good computer programming anticipates these possible errors and adds control structures to trap or prevent them.

**TESTING AND DOCUMENTATION** Once the program has been debugged, it needs to be tested under actual working conditions. This is **beta testing**, and undetected logic and runtime errors are often found at this point. Documentation is created throughout the programming cycle and is written both for the user and for programmers (those who work on the project and those who may maintain or update it in the future). Common documentation includes the following:

- For users of the system: user manuals (print or online)
- For programmers: comments within the code that explain what each section is designed to do as well as external documentation that outlines the project, problem, and design logic

Not every project will follow all these steps exactly, and there's often much overlap and iteration in the process, but in general, programming requires good organization to result in a complete and stable program.

# Find Out MORE

Mobile application development is a hot topic today. The three main platforms are iPhone, Windows Phone, and Android. Use the Internet to compare how the Google Play Store (Android), Windows Phone Marketplace, and the iPhone App Store differ. As a potential mobile app developer, which platform would you choose and why?

## Try the Program Development Simulation

SIMULATION

## Running Project

Use the Internet to find out more about the differences between procedural programming and object-oriented programming.

## 4 Things You Need to Know

- A computer program is a sequence of instructions for a computer to follow.
- The Program Development Cycle is a set of steps that a programmer follows to create a computer program.
- An algorithm is a set of steps to solve a problem; flowcharts and pseudocode show logic and processing flow.
- There are three types of errors: syntax, logic, and runtime. These errors are detected and resolved during the debugging process.

## Key Terms

algorithm

beta testing

computer program

computer programming (coding)

control structure

debugging

flowchart

logic error

object-oriented programming (OOP)

procedural programming

Program Development Cycle

pseudocode

runtime error

syntax error

syntax rules

# HOW TO

## Create a Flowchart

Creating a flowchart using a word processor can be a tedious process. In this exercise, you will use Creately—a free online tool.

**1** Point your Internet browser of choice to Creately. com. In the banner material, click *Try Creately now!*

**2** On the Welcome screen, click *New* on the menu bar.

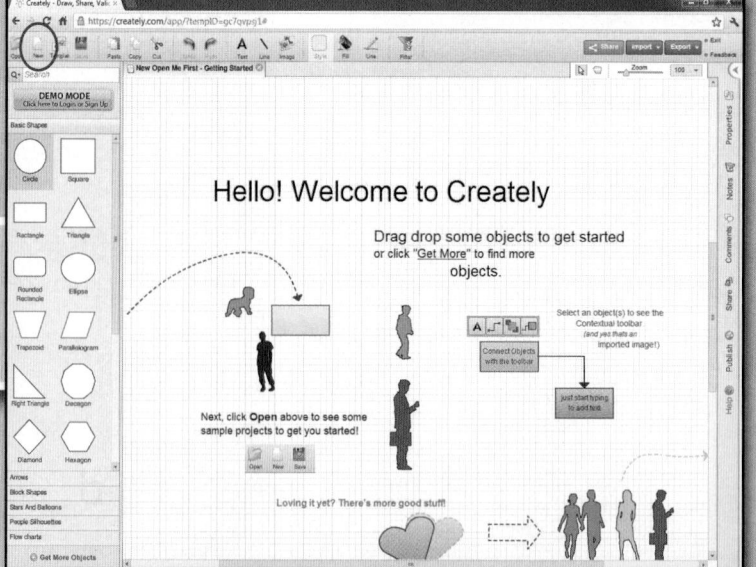

**3** In the What do you plan to draw box, type **flow-chart**, then click *Blank Diagram*. Name the flow-chart **Chapter 12 How To**, type your name in the description, and then click *Create Document*.

**4** In the left pane, select *Flow charts* to display the shapes used in a flowchart. Using Figure 12.7 as a guide, drag the correct shapes onto the canvas to create the flowchart that maps out the process to determine a grade (you may need to switch the pane to Basic shapes for the circle shape). As you add each shape, drag the corners to adjust the size and click on the *Connect* symbol above it to connect it to the symbol below it. Type the correct statement in each shape.

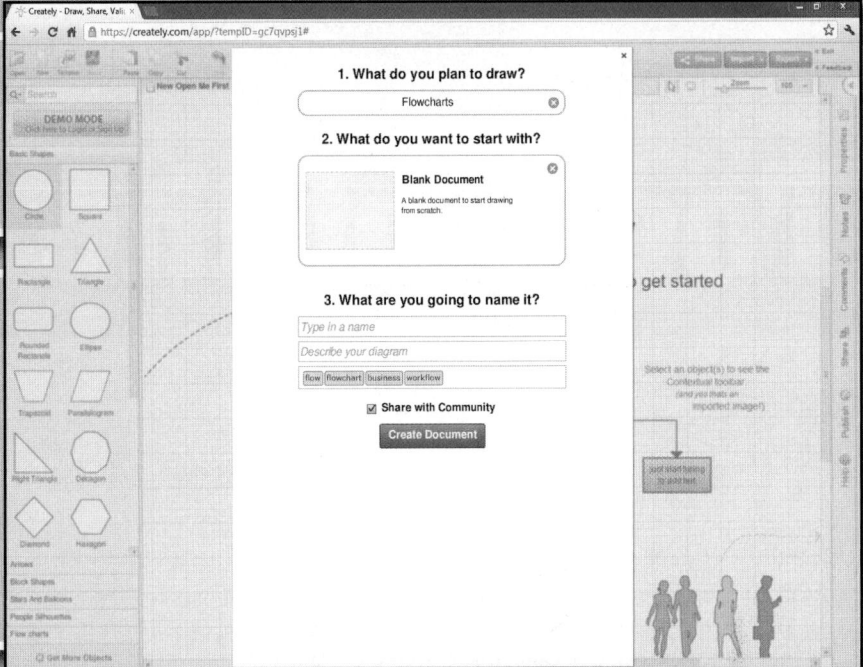

**5** On the toolbar above the canvas, click the *Text* button to add the YES and NO to the decision point.

**6** On the right hand side, click *Properties* to open the Properties pane. Take a screen shot of this window and paste it into a document. Under Direct Link To Diagram, click *Copy Link* and paste it into your document.

**7** Save the file as **lastname_firstname_ch12_howto1**, and submit it as directed by your instructor.

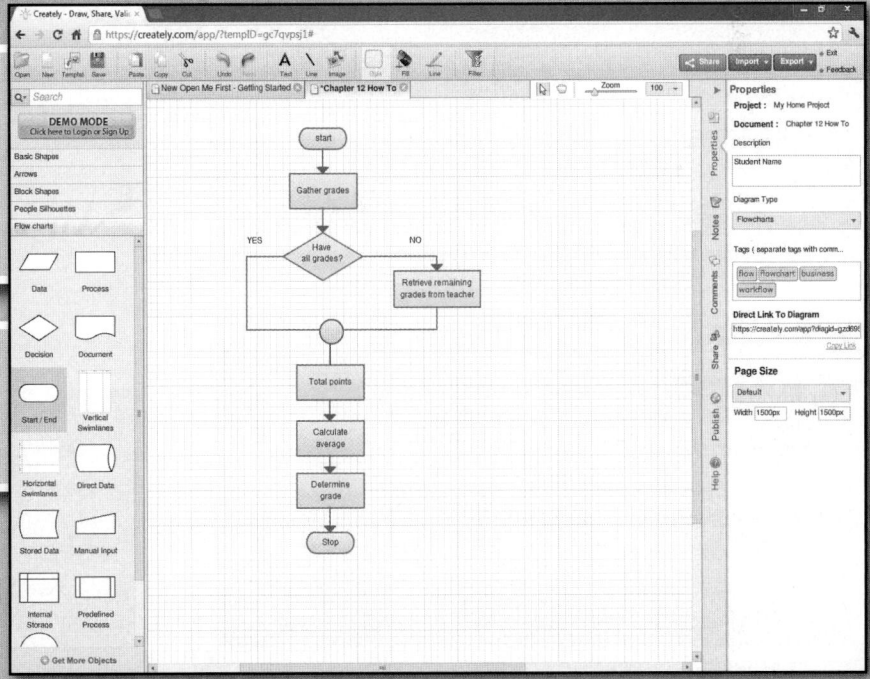

# Tools of the Trade

## Compare various programming languages.

The right tool gets any job done faster and better, whether it's building a deck or writing a computer program. There are many different programming languages to choose from, and selecting the right one will result in a better product. In this article, we discuss several different ways a programmer might choose to code a program.

## PROGRAMMING LANGUAGES

Programming languages can be divided into two levels: low level and high level. Within the levels, the languages can be further categorized into generations. Each generation is more sophisticated and moves from the 0s and 1s that a computer can easily understand (low level) to language that is more human-like (high level). Figure 12.9 lists some examples of each level.

| PROGRAMMING LANGUAGES | | |
|---|---|---|
| 1st Generation | Low Level | Machine language |
| 2nd Generation | Low Level | Assembly language |
| 3rd Generation | High Level | FORTRAN C++ Java |
| 4th Generation | High Level | SQL, Visual Basic |
| 5th Generation | High Level | Prolog, LISP |

**FIGURE 12.9** Computer Programming Languages

**LOW LEVEL** When the first computers were built, programs were wired directly into them. This was very inefficient and time-consuming. The first programming languages were written in the language a computer speaks—binary. A **first-generation language (1GL)** is a **machine language** written in binary that can execute quickly but takes a lot of effort to write and debug.

A **second-generation language (2GL)** is an **assembly language**. It's written with statements closer to what humans speak and has to be converted into a machine language by an assembler before the computer can execute it. An example of an assembly language command is: ADD 4,7. Assembly languages are difficult to use for large applications.

**HIGH LEVEL** The majority of computer programming today is done using high-level languages for everything from small scripts and applets that make a Web page dynamic, to **macros** used to automate tasks in applications such as Word and Excel, to the creation of complex artificial intelligence systems. These languages are probably what you're more familiar with. The distinction between third-, fourth-, and fifth-generation languages isn't clearly defined, and some languages can fall into more than one generation.

Most modern programming languages are **third-generation languages (3GL)**. These include both procedural and object-oriented languages, such as FORTRAN, C++, and Java. Programming in a 3GL requires a considerable amount of programming knowledge. While simple programs can be written with just a few statements, complex applications can have thousands of lines of code. Large projects often involve multiple programmers working together. A **compiler** is needed to convert the code into machine language the computer can read and execute.

A **fourth-generation language (4GL)** is designed to be closer to natural language than 3GLs; however, some programming knowledge is still needed to work effectively with 4GLs. Many 4GLs are used to access databases, such as SQL, PowerBuilder, and OLAP (online analytical processing) tools. Visual Basic is sometimes considered a 4GL. Visual Basic is an event-driven programming language, which means that it responds to events such as a user pushing a button or selecting an item from a list.

A **fifth-generation language (5GL)** is a system that allows the user to work with it without writing code. The 5GL creates the code. 5GLs are primarily used in artificial intelligence applications and in combination with Platform-as-a-Service (PaaS) application development.

Figure 12.10 shows the classic "Hello World!" program written in C++, Java, and Visual Basic. The program simply displays Hello World! on the screen and is often used as a first program when learning a programming language. Although the syntax is different, after compiling and running the programs, the results would be essentially the same.

### HELLO WORLD! PROGRAM IN C++

```
#include <iostream.h>

main()
{
   cout << "Hello World!";
   return 0;
}
```

### HELLO WORLD! PROGRAM IN JAVA

```
class HelloWorld {
   public static void main(String[] args)
   {
      System.out.println("Hello World!");
   }
}
```

### HELLO WORLD! PROGRAM IN VISUAL BASIC

```
Module Hello
   Sub Main()
   MsgBox("Hello, World!")
   End Sub
End Module
```

**FIGURE 12.10** The Hello World! program illustrates the syntax differences in C++, Java, and Visual Basic.

VIZ CLIP

# PROGRAMMING TOOLS

Tools that help a programmer create programs include software development kits and integrated development environments.

A **software development kit (SDK)** is provided (often for free download) to encourage programmers to develop software using a bundle of libraries and tools that are developed for a particular platform. For example, SDKs are available for creating iPhone and Android mobile apps and for developing Java applications and Facebook applications.

An **integrated development environment (IDE)** is a complete system for developing software, typically consisting of the following:

- A code editor
- One or more compilers
- One or more SDKs
- A debugger

Popular IDEs include Eclipse and NetBeans—which are free and open source—and Microsoft Visual Studio. Each of these IDEs has support for multiple languages (see Figure 12.11).

**Platform-as-a-Service (PaaS)** is an online programming environment used to develop, test, and deploy custom applications. Two of the most popular PaaS platforms are Force.com and WorkXpress. PaaS systems vary from those that require a lot of programming knowledge using 3GL and 4GL languages to those that have a point-and-click 5GL interface that requires little or no actual coding. The advantages to using a PaaS system are the same as for other cloud computing systems: the elimination of local administration, hardware, and software.

| IDE | LANGUAGES | WEBSITE |
|-----|-----------|---------|
| Eclipse | Java, Java EE, C/C++, PHP, JavaScript | eclipse.org |
| NetBeans | Java, JavaFX, PHP, JavaScript and Ajax, Ruby, Ruby on Rails, Groovy, Grails, C/C++ | netbeans.org |
| Visual Studio | Visual Basic, Visual C#, Visual C++, Visual F# | microsoft.com/visualstudio |

**FIGURE 12.11** Language Support of Popular IDEs

# WEB PROGRAMMING

As with any programming, developing Web applications requires selecting the right language for the task. But there are different concerns when the application is designed for the Web.

The simplest form of a Web page is a static HTML page. The client browser calls (requests) the page and the Web server sends it. The browser then reads the HTML and displays the page. However, modern Web pages are rarely static. Dynamic elements such as menus, rollovers, searches, videos, and animations make Web programming more complex.

## Find Out MORE

Adobe Flash is an important Web technology. Visit the Flash website **adobe.com/flashplatform** to read more about it. What are some of the types of applications that can be created using Flash?

**SERVER SIDE** A **server-side program** runs on a Web server. An example would be a Web search. When a user types in keywords in a search engine, the search is executed on the database on the server and the results are then formatted into a new HTML page and sent to the  client. The processing can't take place on the client side because the database isn't on the client computer. Server-side programming languages include Perl, ASP, PHP, JSP, and Cold Fusion. Because the processing takes place on the server side and the results are sent to the client as HTML, the client doesn't need to have special software (other than a browser) to see the results.

**CLIENT SIDE** A **client-side program** runs on the client computer. The coding is within a Web page, downloaded to the client computer, and compiled and executed by a browser or plug-in. The most popular client-side elements are JavaScript, ActiveX controls, and Java applets. Client-side programming (often called scripts) requires the user to have the proper browser and plug-ins installed. Because the processing takes place on the client system, it's not necessary to reload the Web page to see the changes.

Even if you never intend to write a computer program, understanding how they're developed will help you make decisions regarding the purchase and development of software—perhaps as a member of an SDLC project team.

## Running Project

There's some disagreement over the definition of a 5GL. Go to the WorkXpress website (**workxpress.com**), and click on Empower Me and then Build & Deploy Apps. What features of the platform would classify it as a 5GL? Do you agree that it's a 5GL?

## 5 Things You Need to Know

- A 1GL is a machine language; a 2GL is an assembly language.

- Most modern programming languages are 3GL and require a considerable amount of programming knowledge.

- A 4GL is designed to be closer to natural language and is often used to access databases. 5GLs are primarily used in artificial intelligence and in PaaS development.

- Tools that help a programmer create programs include software development kits (SDKs), integrated development environments (IDEs), and Platform-as-a-Service (PaaS).

- In Web programming, a server-side program runs on a Web server, and a client-side program runs on the client computer.

## Key Terms

assembly language

client-side program

compiler

fifth-generation language (5GL)

first-generation language (1GL)

fourth-generation language (4GL)

integrated development environment (IDE)

machine language

macro

Platform-as-a-Service (PaaS)

second-generation language (2GL)

server-side program

software development kit (SDK)

third-generation language (3GL)

# HOW TO

## Automate a Task Using a Macro in Word

A macro is an easy way to automate tasks in applications such as Word and Excel, which include Visual Basic for Applications (VBA) to create and edit macros. In this activity, you'll record and edit a macro in Word.

**1** Start Microsoft Word. Click the *File* tab and then click *Options*. Click *Customize Ribbon*. In the right pane, under Main Tabs, make sure there's a check mark next to Developer. Click *OK*.

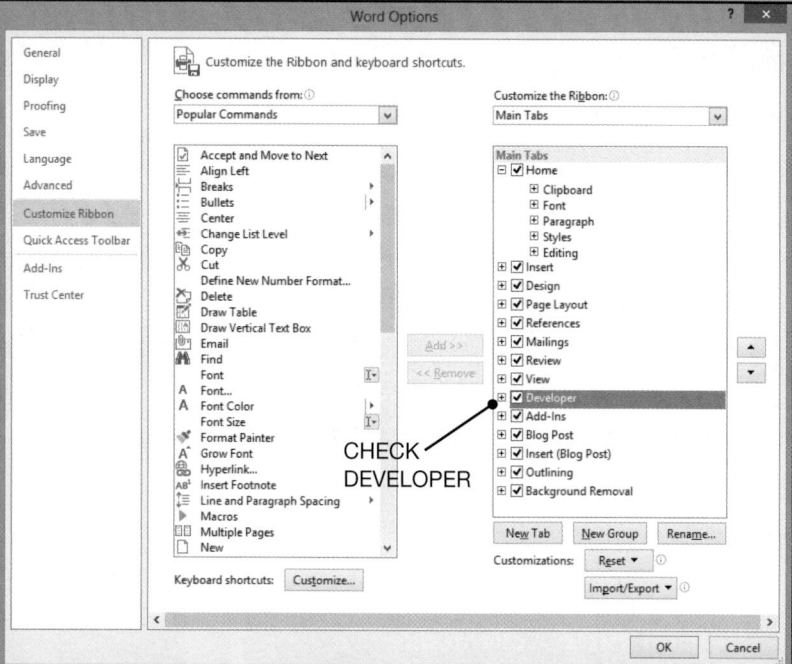

CHECK DEVELOPER

**2** Click the *Developer* tab and then click *Record Macro*. Create a new macro named **ContactInfo** and then click *Button* under Assign macro to.

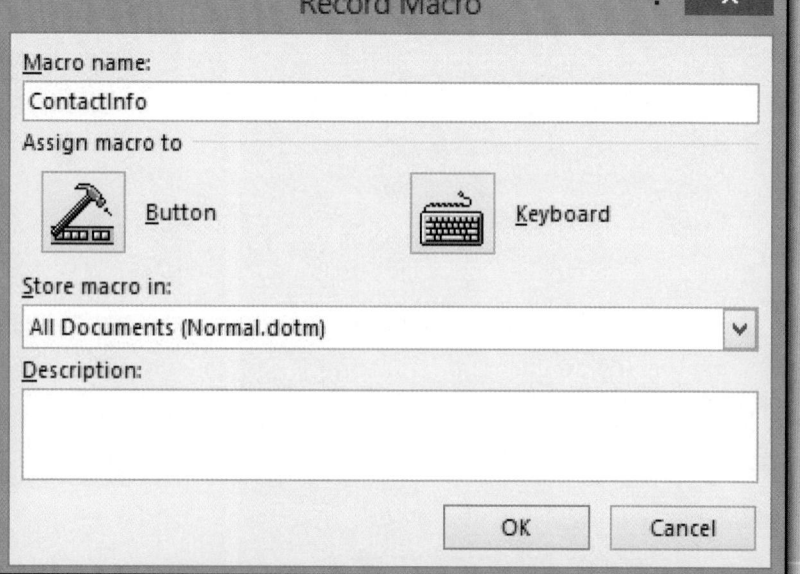

**3** Select your macro from the left column, click *Add>>* to place it in the right column, and then click *OK*. A new button will now appear on your Quick Access Toolbar above the File tab.

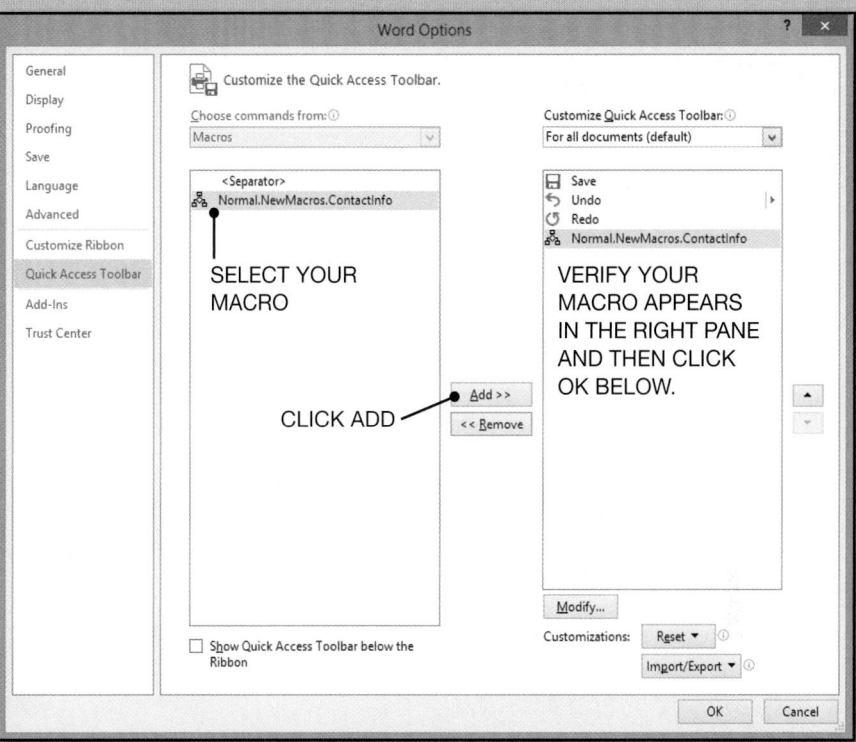

SELECT YOUR MACRO

CLICK ADD

VERIFY YOUR MACRO APPEARS IN THE RIGHT PANE AND THEN CLICK OK BELOW.

**4** Click the *Insert* tab and then click *Table*. Create a small, 1x1 table by clicking in the first box of the Insert Table menu.

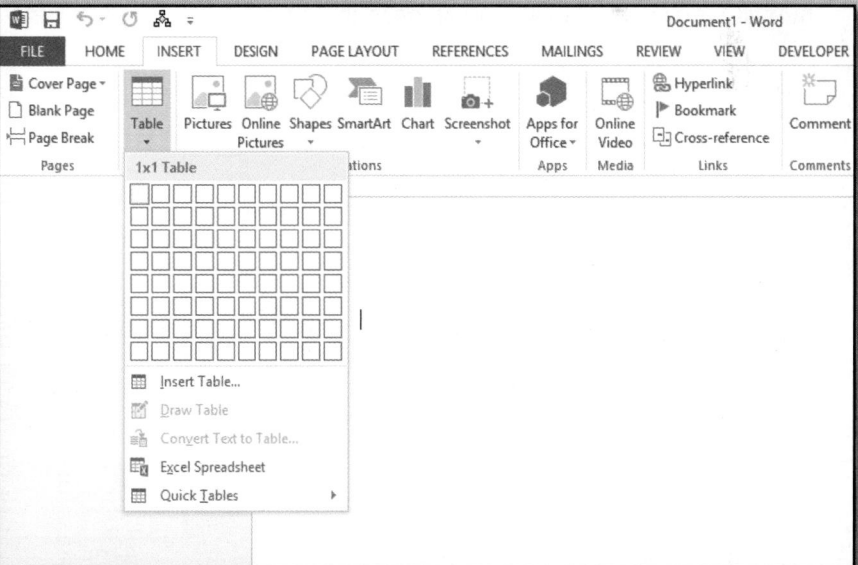

**5** Click the *Home* tab, and format the text in Times New Roman, size 12.

**6** Type your contact information in the table (name, email address, phone number). From the Table Styles section on the Design tab, click the *More* button and then select an appropriate table style.

**7** Click the *Table Tools Layout* tab and then in the Cell Size group, click *AutoFit*. Select *AutoFit Contents*.

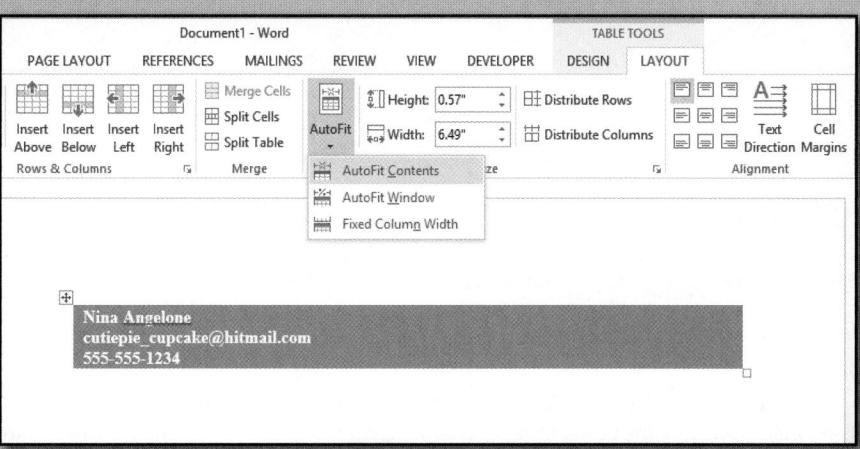

CLICK THIS BUTTON TO
RUN YOUR MACRO.

**8** Click the *Developer* tab, and click *Stop Recording*. Click the *File* tab, click *New*, and then click *Create* to open a new blank document. Save the file as **lastname_firstname_ch12_howto2**. Click the macro button you created on the Quick Access Toolbar to test your macro.

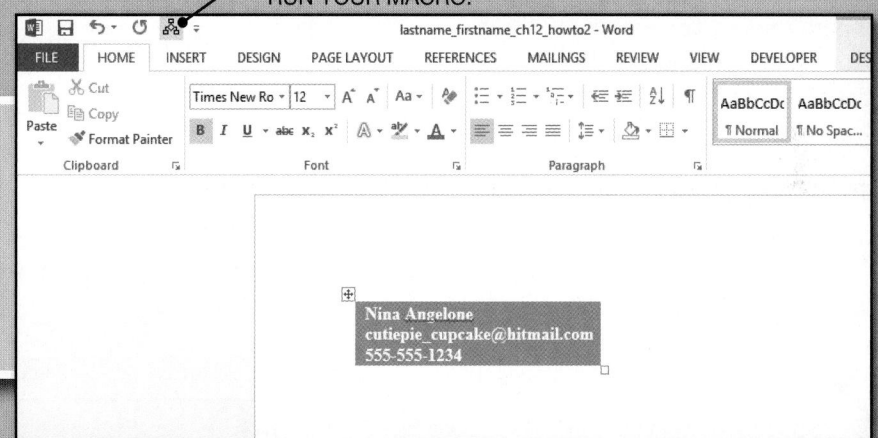

**9** Click the *Developer* tab, click *Macros*, select your macro from the list, and then click *Edit*.

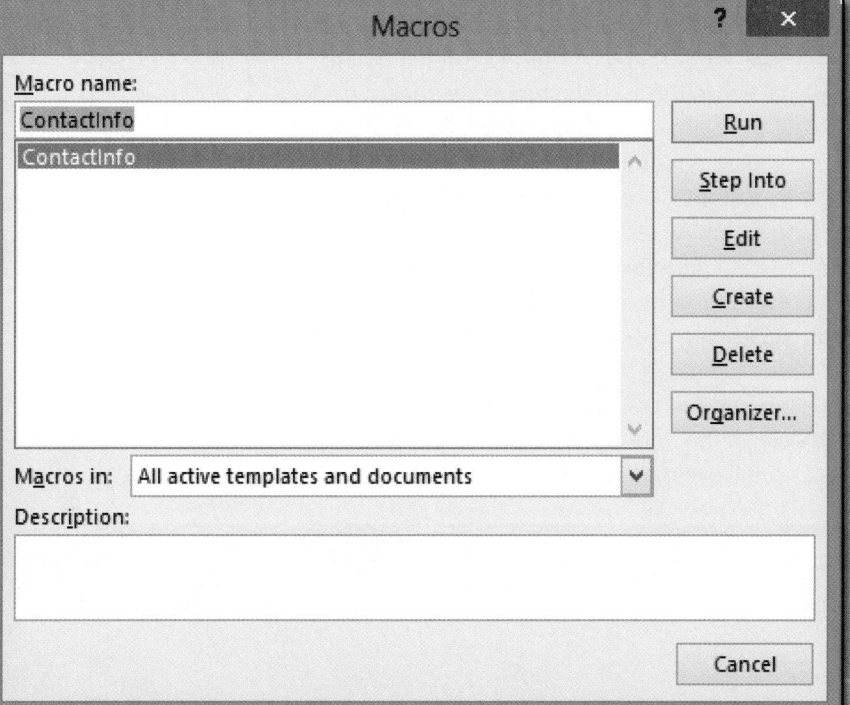

VIEW MICROSOFT
WORD BUTTON

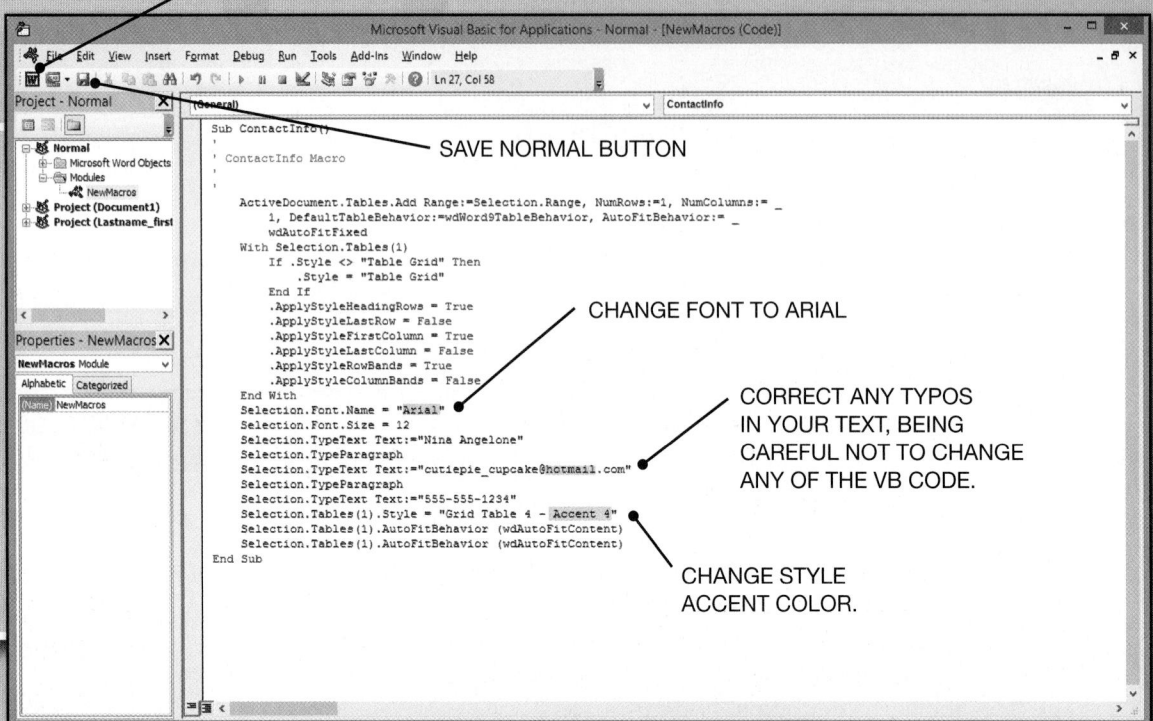

SAVE NORMAL BUTTON

CHANGE FONT TO ARIAL

CORRECT ANY TYPOS
IN YOUR TEXT, BEING
CAREFUL NOT TO CHANGE
ANY OF THE VB CODE.

CHANGE STYLE
ACCENT COLOR.

**10** Correct any typos in your text (I corrected hitmail in this example). Change the font from "Cambria" to "Arial." (Make sure to leave the quotation marks.) Change the Accent color of the table style. Take a screen shot of the macro code. Click the *Save Normal* button and then click the *View Microsoft Word* button to return to the document.

MACRO BUTTON AND
DEVELOPER TAB REMOVED

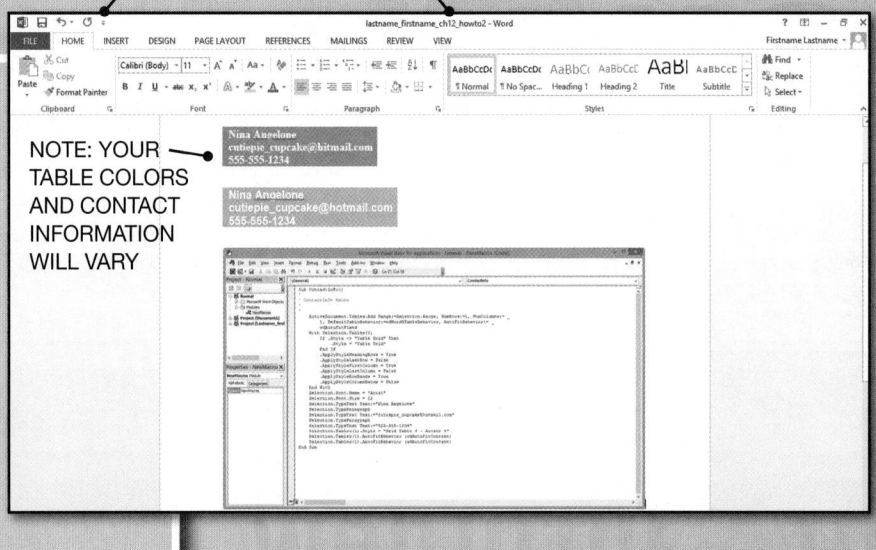

NOTE: YOUR
TABLE COLORS
AND CONTACT
INFORMATION
WILL VARY

**11** Move the insertion point below the table and press Enter. Click the *Macro* button you created to run the edited macro. Paste the screen shot of the macro code below the two tables. Save your file and then submit it as directed by your instructor.

To restore Word to its original configuration, on the Quick Access Toolbar, right-click on the *Macro* icon and then choose *Remove from Quick Access Toolbar* from the shortcut menu. Click the *Developer* tab, click *Macros*, and then delete the macro. To remove the Developer tab, click the *File* tab and then click *Options*. Click *Customize Ribbon*. In the right pane, under Main Tabs, uncheck Developer. Click *OK*.

**If you are using a Mac**

1. Click the Word menu and then click *Preferences*. Click *Ribbon* and make sure there's a check mark next to Developer. Click *OK*.
2. Click the *Developer* tab and then click *Record*. Create a new macro named **ContactInfo** and then click *Toolbars* under Assign macro to.
3. Select your macro from the right column, and drag it to the toolbar next to the Help? Symbol.
4–11. Follow directions above—except for steps 6 and 10. Instead, use these steps:
    6. Format the table using Borders and Shading. Apply a 1 pt, box border and use the shading color Green.
    10. Change the shading color to "blue."

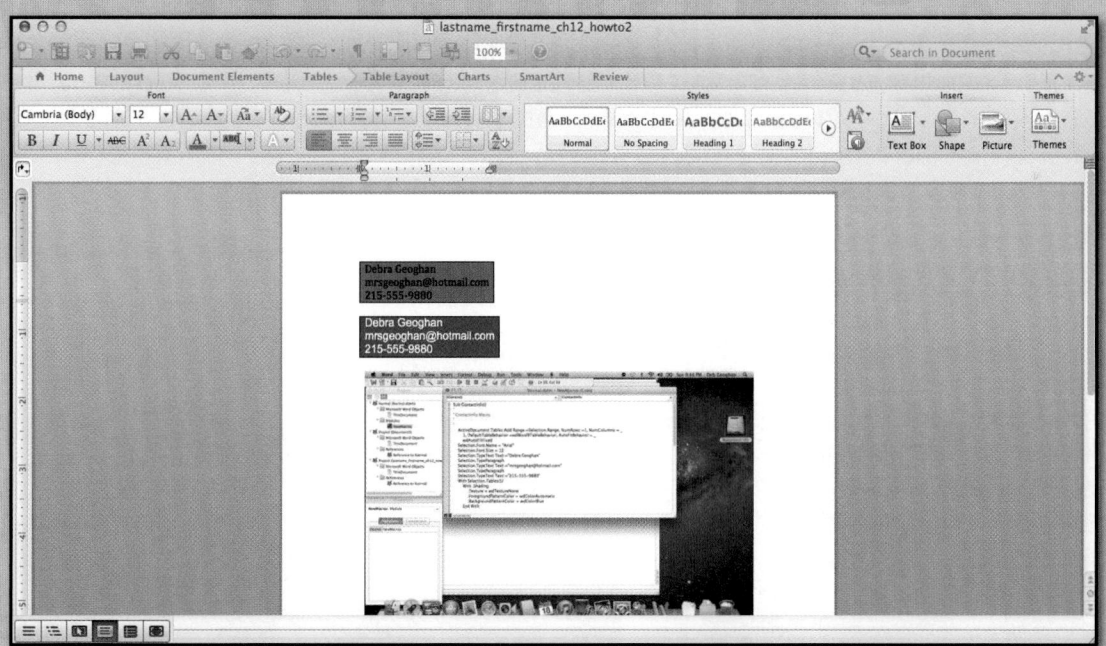

To restore Word to its original configuration, press CTRL + click on the toolbar and select *Reset Toolbar*. Then click *OK*. Click the *Developers* tab, click *Macros* and delete your macro from the list. Close the dialog box. Click the Word menu and then click *Preferences*. Click *Ribbon* and uncheck *Developer*. Click *OK*.

# Artificial Intelligence

## Explain the term *artificial intelligence*.

On the surface, it might seem that computers are smarter than people. After all, they can solve complex mathematical and scientific problems that humans couldn't solve without their help. But the truth is, computers are really good at computation, but they can't think like humans. So, for example, humans can easily read something that another human scribbled on a piece of paper. We can figure out what the person meant, even if the words are spelled wrong, the penmanship is sloppy, and the paper is torn or wrinkled. This process is something we don't really have to think about, but a computer has a much harder time recognizing what's on the paper. Facial recognition is even harder for a computer. When you see someone you know walking across the street, you can recognize him or her even if that person has a new haircut, has lost some weight, got new glasses, and so on. Any of those changes are enough to confound a computer's facial recognition system. Contrary to what's portrayed in popular TV and movies, there's not a good facial recognition system currently available. Computers are just not that good at performing tasks that require human judgment, and that's what the science of **artificial intelligence (AI)** is all about: making computers behave like humans.

## APPLICATIONS

Today, AI is being used in game playing, speech recognition, smart appliances such as air conditioners and refrigerators, medical and engineering research, weather forecasting (see Figure 12.12), robots and automation, detecting credit card fraud, and the list goes on. While we're a long way from a computer that has a mind of its own, AI systems are helping humans solve problems that range from entertaining to life-saving. The two most common programming languages used in AI development are the 5GL languages LISP and Prolog.

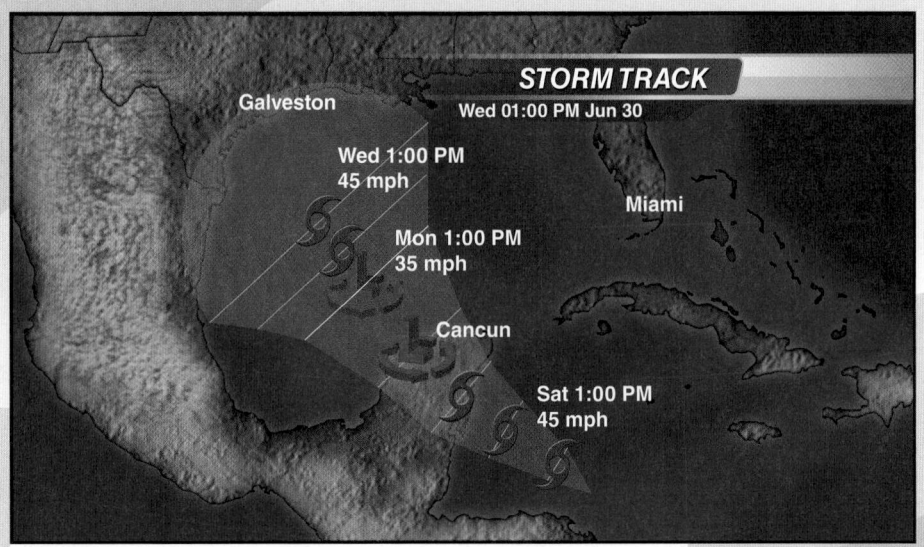

**FIGURE 12.12** One application of AI is weather forecasting.

# EXPERT SYSTEMS

An **expert system** is a computer programmed to make decisions in real-life situations. It's developed by a knowledge engineer who studies the way humans make decisions in an area and translates that process into a set of rules that are programmed into the system. There are expert systems used to help diagnose illness, decide whether to approve a mortgage application, schedule delivery routes most efficiently, and even play chess (see Figure 12.13). The more information the knowledge engineer has to program into the system, the more accurate the system will be. An expert system simulates human judgment to solve a problem using fuzzy logic.

   **Fuzzy logic** recognizes that not everything can be broken down to a true or false answer. Some things fall somewhere in between. For example, answer the question "Is it sunny out?" The answer isn't necessarily a clear yes or no. Maybe it's *partly sunny* or *partly cloudy*—terms you often see on the local weather forecast (see Figure 12.14). Fuzzy logic is similar to the way humans think.

**FIGURE 12.13** An expert system is used to program a computer to play chess.

**FIGURE 12.14** Fuzzy logic helps determine whether the day is sunny, partly cloudy, partly sunny, or cloudy.

## ETHICS

Whenever people start talking about making computers more human, there's controversy about just what that means. Ethical concerns about AI are common arguments against the research and have been the topic of many science fiction novels and movies. For many people, the images of HAL (*2001: A Space Odyssey*) or iRobot are all too real and are frightening enough to prevent us from even continuing to pursue AI at all. There's fear that AI computers would soon become smarter than humans and eventually become sentient beings. What rights would they have? How would they be assimilated into our society? Do we have the ability to create such beings? Not yet, certainly, but in the future, it is likely. The ethical questions need to be addressed before that happens. What do you think?

# NEURAL NETWORKS

A **neural network** is a system that simulates human thinking by emulating the biological connections—or neurons—of the human brain. A neural network consists of several layers (see Figure 12.15). The input layer consists of the data that's being put into the system and the output layer is the results. The magic happens in the middle, hidden layer(s). A neural network is first trained by feeding it large amounts of data—both the input and expected output—that it then uses to create the processes (or weights) of the middle layer. Neural networks are used for pattern recognition, speech recognition, automation and control systems, and data-mining applications.

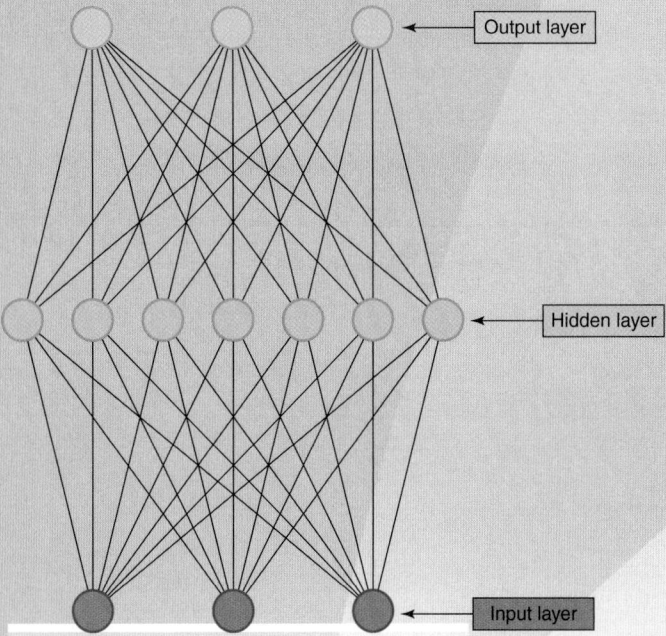

Output layer

Hidden layer

Input layer

**FIGURE 12.15** A neural network consists of at least three layers.

# CAREER SPOTLIGHT

According to the Occupational Outlook Handbook, computer software design and development is among the fields expected to grow the fastest over the next decade. The more experience and education you have, the better the job prospects and pay will be. Certifications also help to show your skills in specific platforms.

A computer software engineer is responsible for the design and development of computer software. Typically, the software engineer is responsible for the first parts of the SDLC—planning, analysis, and design. This field requires a minimum of a bachelor's degree, but a master's degree is preferred. A computer programmer writes the actual code based on the design work completed by the software engineer. A programmer should have at least an associate's degree, but a bachelor's degree is preferred. Often, the term *developer* is used instead of *programmer*. This implies that the person both designs and codes the system, and this is very often the case, especially on smaller projects or in smaller organizations.

# GREEN COMPUTING

## PROGRAMMING EFFICIENCY

When we think of green computing, we usually think hardware—turn off your monitor, lower cooling costs, and recycle—but efficient programming is an important part of green computing, too. Programmers can code efficiently so the program runs on the hardware with minimal impact, for example, using the processor efficiently and accessing data using the fewest interactions with the drives by using memory buffers. Think about how you perform a task as mundane as washing dishes. There are ways to do this inefficiently (washing each dish one at a time, leaving the water running continuously, drying each dish by hand) and methods you can use to make it more efficient (using a basin of water, washing a bunch of dishes, rinsing them all at once, and then allowing them to air-dry).

On a small scale, **green code**—which is written to be efficient so the program runs on the hardware with minimal impact—results in extending battery life for mobile devices, which have fewer resources to begin with. This is both a boon to the user and saves energy in the long run. On a large scale, it's estimated that green code can lower the energy requirements at data centers by 25–30%.

The field of artificial intelligence has been around since the 1950s. The idea of a computer that can think on its own and interact with us using natural language is still science fiction, but expert systems and neural networks are used in many applications, including voice and image recognition systems, robotics, data mining, and many scientific applications. Fuzzy logic systems are used in everything from camcorders to washing machines to smart weapons.

## Running Project

Visit the Association for the Advancement of Artificial Intelligence (AAAI) at **aaai.org**. Click on *AITopics*. Under Browse Topics, select *Games & Puzzles*. What are some of the ways AI is being used in games?

## 4 Things You Need to Know

- Artificial intelligence is the science of making computers behave like humans.
- An expert system is a computer programmed to make decisions in real-life situations.
- Fuzzy logic recognizes that not everything can be broken down to true or false answers.
- A neural network is a system that simulates human thinking by emulating the biological connections of the human brain.

## Key Terms

artificial intelligence (AI)

expert system

fuzzy logic

green code

neural network

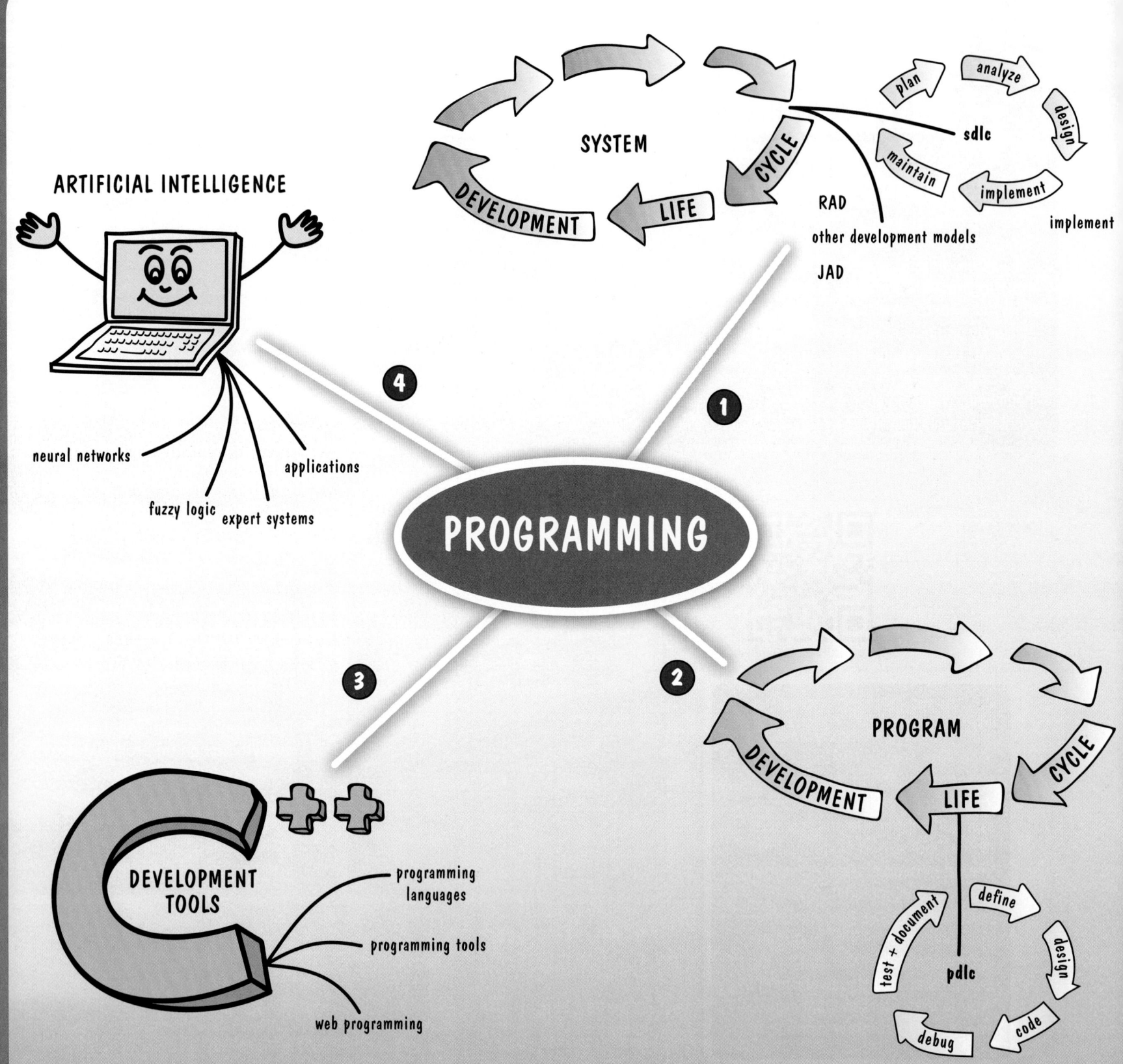

ARTIFICIAL INTELLIGENCE

neural networks
applications
fuzzy logic    expert systems

SYSTEM

DEVELOPMENT    LIFE    CYCLE

plan    analyze    design
sdlc
maintain    implement
implement
RAD
other development models
JAD

PROGRAMMING

④

①

③

②

DEVELOPMENT TOOLS

programming languages
programming tools
web programming

PROGRAM

DEVELOPMENT    LIFE    CYCLE

test + document    define
pdlc
debug    code    design

524

# Objectives Recap

1. Describe the system development life cycle.
2. Describe the program development cycle.
3. Compare various programming languages.
4. Explain the term *artificial intelligence*.

# Key Terms

algorithm **505**
artificial intelligence (AI) **520**
assembly language **510**
beta testing **507**
client-side program **513**
compiler **511**
computer program **504**
computer programming
(coding) **506**
control structure **505**
data flow diagram (DFD) **499**
debugging **506**
expert system **521**
feasibility study **499**
fifth-generation language (5GL)
**511**
first-generation language (1GL)
**510**
flowchart **505**
fourth-generation language
(4GL) **511**
fuzzy logic **521**
green code **523**
information system **497**
integrated development
environment (IDE) **512**
Joint Application Development
(JAD) **502**

logic error **506**
machine language **510**
macro **511**
neural network **522**
object-oriented programming
(OOP) **506**
Platform-as-a-Service (PaaS)
**512**
procedural programming **506**
Program Development Cycle
**504**
project manager (PM) **499**
pseudocode **506**
Rapid Application Development
(RAD) **502**
runtime error **506**
second-generation language
(2GL) **510**
server-side program **513**
software development kit (SDK)
**512**
stakeholder **499**
syntax error **506**
syntax rules **506**
System Development Life
Cycle (SDLC) **498**
third-generation language
(3GL) **511**

# Summary

### 1. Describe the system development life cycle.

The traditional SDLC consists of five phases: planning, analysis, design, implementation, and maintenance. The design phase includes the assembly of the project team and feasibility studies. During analysis, data flow diagrams help analyze the current system and highlight its deficiencies, and new system requirements are defined. The design phase defines what the new system will do and how it will do it. The implementation stage is when the coding takes place and the system is installed and tested. The final and longest phase is maintenance, when the system is in place, periodically reviewed, updated, and bugs fixed until the system is no longer adequate and the cycle begins again. JAD and RAD are other development systems in use.

### 2. Describe the program development cycle.

The program development cycle consists of five steps: defining the problem; designing the solution using tools such as algorithms, flowcharts, and pseudocode; coding the program using the appropriate language and programming tools; debugging the code for syntax, logic, and runtime errors; and testing and documentation of the program.

### 3. Compare various programming languages.

Computer programming languages can be classified into five generations. 1GL is machine language, the binary code a computer can understand. 2GL is assembly language that must be converted to machine language using an assembler. 3GL is a high-level language that can be procedural or object-oriented and requires a compiler to convert it to machine language. Most modern programming languages are 3GLs that require a lot of programming knowledge. A 4GL is closer to human language but still requires substantial programming knowledge and is often used to access databases. A 5GL uses tools that don't require programming on the user's part. 5GLs create the code and are used in AI applications.

### 4. Explain the term *artificial intelligence*.

Artificial intelligence is the branch of science concerned with making computers behave like humans. Modern applications include speech and pattern recognition, science and engineering applications, and financial predictions. Fuzzy logic is used by AI to help answer questions that don't have a clear yes or no answer. Neural networks simulate the way humans think by emulating the biological connections in our brains.

# Application Project

## Microsoft Office Application Project 1:
## PowerPoint Level 3

**PROJECT DESCRIPTION:** In this Microsoft PowerPoint project, you will create a presentation about the SDLC. In creating this PowerPoint presentation you will apply design and color themes. You will also insert and format a SmartArt graphic and apply animations to objects on your slides, and transitions between slides.

**INSTRUCTIONS:** For the purpose of grading of the project you are required to perform the following tasks:

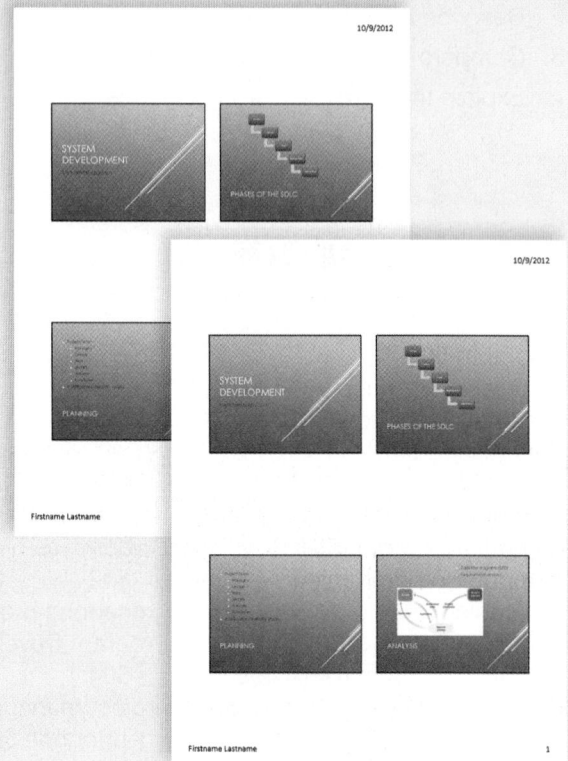

| Step | Instructions |
|---|---|
| **1** | Start PowerPoint. Download and open the file named *vt_ch12.* Save the file as **lastname_firstname_ch12**. |
| **2** | On Slide 1, type your name in the subtitle placeholder. |
| **3** | Apply the Slice theme, gold Variant, to the presentation. |
| **4** | On Slide 2, convert the bulleted list in the content placeholder to a Step Down Process SmartArt graphic. Delete the text placeholders to the right of the shapes. |

| Step | Instructions |
|---|---|
| **5** | Open the Text Pane and type the five phases of the SDLC: **Planning, Analysis, Design, Implementation, Maintenance**. You will need to add two bullets to the list for a total of 5 shapes in the SmartArt graphic. Close the Text Pane. Change the SmartArt style to Intense Effect. |
| **6** | On slide 3, under Project team, add the following 6 bullets: **Managers, Owners, Users, Security, Telecom, Developers**. Increase the List Level indent of these bullet points. |

**Visit pearsonhighered.com/Geoghan** for data files, simulations, VizClips, and additional study materials.

526 | APPLICATION PROJECT

| Step | Instructions |
|------|-------------|
| **7** | Apply the Fly In animation with the From Top-Right effect option and a duration of 01.00 to the bullet list on Slide 3. |
| **8** | On slide 4, change the layout to Two Content. Insert the downloaded file *vt_ch12_image1* in the right content pane. |
| **9** | Proportionally resize the image so that the height is 3". Move the image so that its top right corner is aligned with the 2.0-inch mark to the right of zero on the horizontal ruler and the 1.5-inch mark below zero on the vertical ruler. Apply the Drop Shadow Rectangle Picture Style to the image. |
| **10** | Insert a new slide after slide 7. On slide 8, type **Other Development Models** in the title placeholder. Insert a 2-column, 3-row table in the content placeholder. Type the following text into in the table (one line in each row): |

| LEFT COLUMN | RIGHT COLUMN |
|-------------|--------------|
| **JAD** | **JAD sessions involve end users throughout** |
| **RAD** | **Prototyping and user testing** |
| **Extreme Programming** | **Delivers the software as it is needed** |

| Step | Instructions |
|------|-------------|
| **11** | Resize the table so that the bottom edge aligns with the 0-inch mark on the vertical ruler. Distribute the rows in the table evenly. Center the text in the table both vertically and horizontally. |
| **12** | Apply the Reveal transition to all slides in the presentation. |
| **13** | Insert the page number and your name in the footer on the notes and handouts pages for all slides in the presentation. View the presentation in Slide Show view from beginning to end, and then return to Normal view. |
| **14** | Save and close the presentation. Exit PowerPoint. Submit the presentation as directed. |

Visit **pearsonhighered.com/Geoghan** for data files, simulations, VizClips, and additional study materials.

527

# Microsoft Office Application Project 2:
## Access Level 2

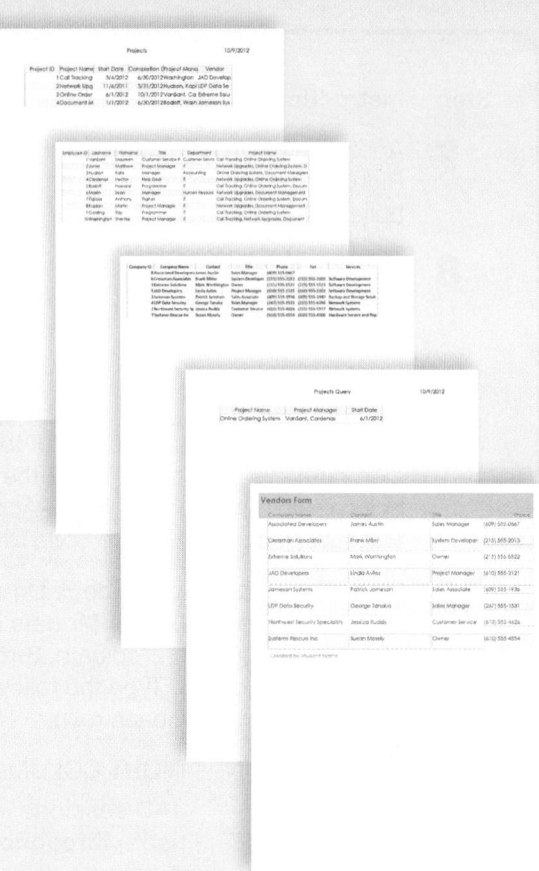

**PROJECT DESCRIPTION:** In this Microsoft Access project, you will manage a datasheet, build a form and query, and modify a query by defining query criteria.

**INSTRUCTIONS:** For the purpose of grading the project you are required to perform the following tasks:

| Step | Instructions |
|---|---|
| 1 | Start Access. Open the downloaded Access database named *vt_ch12_access*. Save the file as lastname_firstname_ch12_access. If necessary, click *Enable Content*. |
| 2 | With the Vendors table open in Datasheet view, sort the records in ascending order by Company Name. Use Filter by Selection to filter the records so that only those in the *Software Development* category are displayed. |
| 3 | With the Vendors table open in Datasheet view, change the font size of the whole table to 12. Resize all of the columns in the Vendors table to give them the best fit. Save and close the table. |

| Step | Instructions |
|---|---|
| 4 | Use the Form Wizard to create a form based on the Vendors table. Add the Company Name, Contact, Title, and Phone fields to the Selected Fields list (in that order). Click *Next*. Change to Tabular layout. Click *Next*. Name the form **Vendors Form** and then click *Finish*. |
| 5 | Change the theme to Austin. Select the title, *Vendors Form*. Change the font size to 16, apply bold formatting. |

| Step | Instructions |
|------|-------------|
| **6** | View the Vendors Form in Design view. Increase the height of the Form Footer section to 0.5 inches. Add a label control to the Form Footer section so it is left aligned with the other controls in the form. Type **Created by Your Name**. |
| **7** | In the Detail section of the form, drag the right border of the Title control to the 6.5-inch mark on the ruler and then drag the left border of the Phone control to the 6.5-in mark. Save the form. |
| **8** | View the Vendors Form in Form view. Add the following record to the form: |

| | | |
|--|--|--|
| *Company Name* | Associated Developers | |
| *Rep First Name* | James | |
| *Rep Last Name* | Austin | |
| *Job Title* | Sales Manager | |
| *Phone Number* | (609) 555-0667 | |

Save and close the form.

| Step | Instructions |
|------|-------------|
| **9** | Use the Simple Query Wizard to create a query based on the Projects table. Include the following fields (in this order): Project Name, Project Manager, and Start Date. Name the query **Projects Query**. |
| **10** | View the Projects Query in Design view. Modify the query criteria so that only records for Projects after **4/21/2012** are displayed. Run the query. Resize the columns to give the best fit. Save and close the query. |
| **11** | Close all database objects. Close the database and then exit Access. Submit the database as directed. |

Visit **pearsonhighered.com/Geoghan** for data files, simulations, VizClips, and additional study materials.

Chapter 12

529

# Multiple Choice

Answer the multiple-choice questions below for more practice with key terms and concepts from this chapter.

1. The traditional model for system development is the
   _____.
   a. SDLC
   b. JAD
   c. RAD
   d. DFD

2. Testing is an important part of the _____ phase of the SDLC.
   a. planning
   b. analysis
   c. design
   d. implementation

3. A(n) _____ is used to show the flow of data through a system and highlights its deficiencies.
   a. SDLC
   b. JAD
   c. RAD
   d. DFD

4. A _____ is a graphic view of an algorithm.
   a. DFD
   b. flowchart
   c. pseudocode
   d. control structure

5. _____ focuses on logic, not programming syntax.
   a. Algorithm
   b. Flowchart
   c. Pseudocode
   d. Control structure

6. _____ are errors in the way the code is written.
   a. Syntax errors
   b. Logic errors
   c. Runtime errors
   d. Code errors

7. A _____ is also known as a machine language.
   a. 1GL
   b. 2GL
   c. 3GL
   d. 4GL

8. A _____ is often used in artificial intelligence applications.
   a. 2GL
   b. 3GL
   c. 4GL
   d. 5GL

9. Which programming tool is an online programming environment used to develop, test, and deploy applications?
   a. Assembly language
   b. Software development kit (SDK)
   c. Integrated development environment (IDE)
   d. Platform-as-a-Service (PaaS)

10. A(n) _____ simulates human thinking by emulating the biological connections in the brain.
    a. fuzzy logic
    b. expert system
    c. neural network
    d. pattern recognition

# True or False

Answer the following questions with T for true or F for false for more practice with key terms and concepts from this chapter.

1. The SDLC development system uses prototyping.

2. The leader of a project team is the project manager.

3. No changes to the system can be made during the maintenance phase.

4. The JAD development system uses prototyping.

5. Flowcharts focus on logic, not programming syntax.

6. Object-oriented programming defines objects and the actions that can be performed on them.

7. 4GLs are often used to access a database.

8. An advantage to using a server-side program is that the client doesn't need to have special software to see the results.

9. AI is the science of making computers behave like humans.

10. An expert system is a computer programmed to make decisions in real-life situations.

# Fill in the Blank

Fill in the blanks with key terms or concepts from this chapter.

1. _____ take place during the planning phase of the SDLC and are used to determine if a project should proceed.

2. A(n) _____ is a set of steps to solve a problem.

3. A(n) _____ is a graphic view of an algorithm.

4. _____ define the correct construction of commands in a programming language.

5. _____ is the process of detecting and fixing errors in a computer program.

6. _____ is the testing of a program under actual working conditions.

7. A(n) _____ is a bundle of libraries and tools that are developed for a particular platform.

8. A(n)_____ is a small program created to automate a task in an application such as Word or Excel.

9. Coding within a Web page that is compiled and executed by the browser or a plug-in is a(n) _____.

10. Artificial intelligence applications use _____ to answer questions that don't have a clear yes or no answer.

# Running Project ...

## . . . The Finish Line

Use your answers to the previous sections of the project. Why is it important to understand the project development process? Save your file as **lastname_firstname_ch12_project**, and submit it to your instructor as directed.

# Do It Yourself 1

The **w3schools.com** website has free Web development tutorials and a Try it Yourself editor that lets you try code in your browser. In this exercise, you'll work with JavaScript.

1. Open a new document and then save it as **lastname_ firstname_ch12_diy1**. Go to the **w3schools.com** website, and click *JavaScript Examples* at the bottom of the page. Click *Write to the Document with JavaScript* to open the editor. The JavaScript code on the left results in the output on the right. Replace My First Web Page in the left with: **Hello World! I wrote my first JavaScript!** (do not delete the <h1> and </h1> tags. Press the *Edit and Click Me* button to see your results. Take a screen shot, and paste it into your document.

2. Return to the JavaScript examples page, and click *Alert* box. Edit the code in the left so the alert displays your name. Click the *Show Alert Box* button, take a screen shot, and paste it into your document. (You may need to allow pop-ups.) Compare the lines of code in the two examples. How are they different? Why is there more code in the alert box example?

3. Try out the If statement and the If ... else statement examples and then compare them. Include screen shots of each. Which is a better control structure for this example and why?

4. Type up your answers, including the four screen shots. Save your document, and submit it as directed by your instructor.

# Do It Yourself 2

In this exercise, you'll create a mind map to compare the features of three models of system development.

1. Using a word processor, online website, or paper and pencil, create a mind map that compares the features of three models of system development: SDLC, JAD, and RAD.

2. For each model, be sure to include the following information:
   - process
   - advantages
   - disadvantages

3. Save your file as **lastname_firstname_ch12_diy2**. Submit your work as directed by your instructor.

# File Management

Client-side programming can result in small files being downloaded to your computer. In this activity, you'll examine your computer for evidence of these files.

1. Open Internet Explorer, open the Tools menu, and choose *Internet Options*. On the General tab, in the Browsing history section, click *Settings*. In the Temporary Internet Files and History Settings dialog box, click *View objects*. Take a screen shot of this window.

2. What types of files are listed here? Are there any that you recognize? Look at the dates of the files. How old is the oldest file? The most recent?

3. Type up your answers and include the screen shot. Save your file as **lastname_firstname_ch12_fm**.

Visit **pearsonhighered.com/Geoghan** for data files, simulations, VizClips, and additional study materials.

# Critical Thinking

1. Your company needs software to track inventory of its widgets. Your boss has asked you to help decide between using an off-the-shelf program and paying a programmer to create something new. Write an algorithm to help make the decision to buy or create the software. What are the questions/decisions that need to be considered (cost, expertise, etc.)? List three, making sure each decision point is distinct.

2. Create a flowchart to show the steps in the algorithm. Use control structures to make decisions in your flowchart. You may sketch by hand and scan your chart or use another tool, such as Creately or Shapes in Word, to create it.

3. Write the pseudocode for the steps in your flowchart.

4. Save your file as **lastname_firstname_ch12_ct**, and submit it as directed by your instructor.

# Ethical Dilemma

When creating a program, it is important to include detailed and accurate documentation within the code. This is crucial for the programmer who later might need to edit or debug the code.

1. Some programmers deliberately make the code difficult to follow, using limited or cryptic documentation to protect their code. What are the implications of such practice? Is it legal? Is it ethical? Is it justified?

2. Type up your answers, save the file as **lastname_firstname_ch12_ethics**, and submit it as directed by your instructor.

# On the Web

Alice is a free scripting and prototyping environment program for 3D object behavior. It was created at Carnegie Mellon University as a tool for teaching programming.

1. Visit the **alice.org** website, and read the All about Alice section. Watch the promotional video to learn about Alice. Do you think this is a good approach to engaging students in programming? Did it pique your interest?

2. Type up your answers. Save the file as **lastname_firstname_ch12_web**, and submit it as directed by your instructor.

# Collaboration

**Instructors:** Divide the class into four groups. Each group is to create a presentation that explains the roles of the project team members: project manager, business manager, users, and programmers.

**The Project:** Each team is to prepare a presentation that explains the roles of the team members. Teams must use at least three references, only one of which may be this textbook. Use Google Docs or Microsoft Office to plan the presentation, and provide documentation that all team members have contributed to the project.

**Students:** Before beginning this project, discuss the roles each group member will play. Choose a team name, which you'll use in submitting your presentation. Be sure to divide the work among your members, and pick someone to present your project. You may find it helpful to elect a team leader who can direct your activities and ensure that all team contributions are collated through Google Docs or Microsoft Office as directed by your instructor.

**Outcome:** You're to prepare a presentation as a team and present it to your class. The presentation may be no longer than 3 minutes. Turn in a final version of your presentation named **teamname_ch12_project_team** and your file showing your collaboration named **teamname_ch12_project_collab**. Submit your presentation to your instructor as directed.

# Microsoft® Office Applications Projects in *Visualizing Technology, Second Edition*

| CHAPTER | APP 1 | TOPIC | APP 2 | TOPIC |
|---|---|---|---|---|
| 1. What Is a Computer? | Word level 1 | Letter to boss | PPT level 1 | Comparing types of computers |
| 2. Application Software | PPT level 1 | PowerPoint design | Excel level 1 | Comparing Office suite costs |
| 3. File Management | Excel level 1 | Municipal waste | Word level 1 | Importance of file management |
| 4. Hardware | Word level 2 | Ergonomics | PPT level 2 | Printers |
| 5. System Software | PPT level 2 | Should you upgrade your OS? | Excel level 2 | Mobile OS sales |
| 6. Multimedia and Digital Devices | Excel level 2 | Camera sales | Word level 2 | Cellphone cameras |
| 7. The Internet and World Wide Web | Word level 2 | Cellular Internet service | PPT level 2 | Internet service |
| 8. Communicating and Sharing | PPT level 3 | Desktop browsers | Excel level 3 | Growth of the Internet |
| 9. Networks and Communication | Excel level 3 | Cellular subscriptions | Word level 3 | Creating a secure password |
| 10. Security and Privacy | Word level 3 | Security certifications | PPT level 3 | Creating a user account |
| 11. Databases | Access level 1 | Course catalog | Word level 3 | Contact list |
| 12. Program Development | PPT level 3 | SDLC | Access level 2 | Project management |

| | WORD | POWERPOINT | EXCEL | ACCESS |
|---|---|---|---|---|
| **Level 1** | Enter and edit text<br><br>Format text<br><br>Insert and format graphics<br><br>Check spelling and grammar<br><br>Create headers and footers | Enter and edit text<br><br>Format text<br><br>Insert and format graphics<br><br>Check spelling and grammar<br><br>Create headers and footers<br><br>Apply slide transitions<br><br>Organize slides | Create and edit workbooks<br><br>Format workbooks (themes)<br><br>Format data (fonts, cell styles, number formats)<br><br>Use basic formulas and functions<br><br>Create headers and footers | Enter and edit table data<br><br>Create forms and reports |
| **Level 2** | Level 1 skills plus:<br><br>Format page and para-graphs (margins, line spacing, etc.)<br><br>Find and replace text<br><br>Use lists<br><br>Create footnotes | Level 1 skills plus:<br><br>Apply and modify themes<br><br>Format text<br><br>Use lists | Level 1 skills plus:<br><br>Use absolute cell references<br><br>Create column and pie charts | Level 1 skills plus:<br><br>Generate queries |
| **Level 3** | Level 1 and 2 skills plus:<br><br>Format graphics<br><br>Create tables<br><br>Use columns<br><br>Incorporate borders and shading<br><br>Create SmartArt | Level 1 and 2 skills plus:<br><br>Insert and format graphics<br><br>Use SmartArt<br><br>Create tables<br><br>Use charts<br><br>Create animations | Level 1 and 2 skills plus:<br><br>Use multiple sheets<br><br>Apply more complex functions<br><br>Use conditional formatting<br><br>Create sparklines<br><br>Sort and filter | N/A |

# Glossary

**AAC (advanced audio coding):** An audio file type that is compressed in a manner similar to MP3s and is the default file type supported by iTunes.

**acceptable use policy (AUP):** A policy that computer and network users in a business or school must abide by that forces users to practice safe computing.

**ad hoc network:** A network created when two wireless devices connect to each other directly.

**adaptive technology:** Software and hardware used by individuals with disabilities to interact with technology. Also called assistive technology.

**add-on:** An application that extends the functionality of a Web browser.

**adware:** A form of malware that shows ads in the form of pop-ups and banners.

**AGP (accelerated graphics port):** The standard analog video port on computers manufactured before 2009.

**algorithm:** A set of steps to solve a problem.

**all-in-one computer:** A compact desktop computer with an integrated monitor.

**Android:** A mobile Linux operating system found on many smartphones and tablets.

**antispyware software:** A form of security software necessary to prevent adware and spyware infections.

**antivirus program:** A form of security software that protects against viruses, Trojan horses, worms, and some spyware.

**application programming interface (API):** The feature of an operating system that allows an application to request services from the operating system, such as a request to print or save a file.

**ARPANET:** The network developed by the U.S. Department of the Defense in the 1960s that eventually became the Internet.

**arithmetic logic unit (ALU):** The part of a processor that performs arithmetic (addition and subtraction) and logic (AND, OR, and NOT) calculations.

**ASCII (American Standard Code for Information Interchange):** An 8-bit binary code set with 256 characters.

**artificial intelligence (AI):** The branch of science concerned with making computers behave like humans.

**assembly language:** A programming language that's written with statements closer than machine language to what humans speak and has to be converted into a machine language by an assembler before the computer can execute it.

**asynchronous online communication:** A form of online communication that does not require the participants to be online at the same time—for example, email.

**avatar:** A virtual body used online.

**back up:** The process of copying files to another location for protection.

**beta testing:** The process of testing a program under actual working conditions.

**beta version:** A prerelease version of software.

**binary code:** A code that represents digital data as a series of 0s and 1s that can be understood by a computer.

**binary number system (base 2):** The base 2 number system that has only two digits (0 and 1).

**bioinformatics:** A field of study in which information technology is applied to the field of biology.

**BIOS (Basic Input Output System):** A program stored on a chip on the motherboard that's used to start up the computer.

**bit:** A binary digit. It's the smallest unit of digital information.

**blog (weblog):** An online journal.

**blogosphere:** All the blogs on the Web and the connections among them.

**Bluetooth:** A technology designed to connect peripherals wirelessly at short ranges.

**Blu-ray disc (BD):** An optical disc with about five times the capacity of a DVD, which it was designed to replace. The single-layer disc capacity is 25 GB, and the double-layer disc capacity is 50 GB.

**Boolean operators:** Terms that define the relationships between words or groups of words and are used to create search filters: AND, OR, and NOT.

**botnet:** A network of computer zombies or bots controlled by a master. A botnet can be used to send out spam and viruses or to launch a denial-of-service attack.

**broadband:** Internet access that exceeds 200 Kbps. Examples include cable, DSL, fiber, and WiMAX.

**byte:** Equal to 8 bits and used to represent a single character in modern computer systems.

**cable Internet access:** Internet access provided by cable companies. Cable speeds range from 1 Mbps to 100 Mbps.

**cache memory:** A type of very fast memory that's used to store frequently accessed information close to the processor.

**campus area network (CAN):** A network that consists of multiple LANs located in the same location connected to each other using routers.

**captcha (Completely Automated Public Turing Test to Tell Computers and Humans Apart):** A series of letters and numbers that are distorted in some way. This makes them difficult for automated software to read but relatively easy for humans to read.

**CD (compact disc):** The oldest type of optical disc in use today, with a storage capacity of about 700 MB.

**cell:** The intersection of a row and a column in a spreadsheet.

**cellular network:** A network that uses cell towers to transmit voice and data over large distances.

**chat:** A real-time online conversation between multiple people at the same time in a chat room.

**ciphertext:** Plain text that has been encrypted.

**client:** The personal computers and other devices that connect to a server.

**client-server network:** A network that has at least one server at its center. Users log in to the network instead of their local computers and are granted access to resources based on that login.

**client-side program:** A program that runs on the client computer. The client must have the proper browser and plug-ins to execute scripts.

**clock speed:** The speed at which the processer executes the instruction cycle.

**cloud computing:** Moves the processing and storage off your desktop and business hardware and puts it in the cloud—on the Internet. Cloud computing consists of three parts: Infrastructure-as-a-Service (IaaS), Platform-as-a-Service (PaaS), and Software-as-a-Service (SaaS).

**cloud service provider:** A company that provides cloud (Internet-based) computing services: Infrastructure-as-a-Service (IaaS), Platform-as-a-Service (PaaS), and Software-as-a-Service (SaaS).

**CMOS (complementary metal oxide semiconductor):** A volatile form of memory that uses a small battery to provide it with power to keep the data in memory even when the computer is turned off. It stores settings that are used by the BIOS.

**CMYK:** The standard ink colors used by printers: cyan, magenta, yellow, and key (black).

**CODIS (Combined DNA Index System):** A system that searches across multiple local, state, and national DNA profile databases. CODIS consists of five indices: Forensic, Arrestee, Detainee, Offender, and Missing Persons.

**communication device:** A device that serves as both an input and output device and allows you to connect to other devices on a network or to the Internet. These include network adapters, modems, and fax devices.

**compact system camera (CSC):** An advanced point-and-shoot camera with interchangeable lenses and other D-SLR features.

**compiler:** A program that converts the programming code into machine language the computer can read and execute.

**compression:** The process of making files smaller to conserve disk space and make them easier to transfer.

**computer:** A programmable machine that converts raw data into useful information.

**computer fraud:** A scheme perpetrated over the Internet or by email that tricks a victim into voluntarily and knowingly giving money or property to a person.

**computer network:** Two or more computers that share resources including software, hardware, or files.

**computer program:** A sequence of instructions for a computer to follow, written in a language that the computer can understand and including any data the computer needs to perform the instructions.

**computer programming (coding):** The process of converting an algorithm into instructions the computer can understand.

**control structure:** The structures (sequence, selection, and loop) used in flowcharts and pseudocode to show logic and processing flow of an algorithm.

**control unit:** The part of the processor that manages the movement of data through the CPU.

**convergence:** The integration of technology on multifunction devices, such as smartphones, that has accustomed us to carrying technology with us.

**cookie:** A small text file placed on a computer when you visit a website. A cookie helps the website identify you when you return.

**CPU (central processing unit):** The brain of a computer; housed inside the system unit on the motherboard. It consists of two parts: the arithmetic logic unit and the control unit.

**crowd-sourcing:** Trusting the collective opinion of a crowd of people rather than that of an expert.

**CRT monitor:** A legacy technology that uses a cathode ray tube to excite phosphor particles coating a glass screen to light up the pixels.

**cyberbullying:** A form of computer harassment that happens between two minors.

**cybercrime:** Criminal activity on the Internet.

**cyberstalking:** A form of computer harassment that happens between two adults.

**cyberterrorism:** An unlawful attack against computers or networks that's done to intimidate a government or its people for a political or social agenda.

**data:** The unprocessed, or raw form, of information.

**database:** A collection of information that is organized in a useful way. Database records are organized into one or more tables.

**database administrator (DBA):** The person who manages existing database systems.

**database management system (DBMS):** The software used to create and manage the data in a database.

**data bus:** The wires on the motherboard over which information flows between the components of the computer.

**data center:** A facility designed to house a company's servers and other equipment in a secure and controlled environment; sometimes called a server farm.

**data dictionary:** The part of a database that defines all the fields and the type of data each field contains.

**data flow diagram (DFD):** A diagram that shows the flow of data through an information system.

**data normalization:** The process of reducing data redundancy in a database.

**data validation:** The rules designed to reduce data-entry errors by preventing invalid data from being entered. Rules may include data type, data length, acceptable values, and required fields.

**data warehouse:** A central repository for all the data that an enterprise uses: internal databases and external sources such as vendors and customers.

**debugging:** The process of detecting and fixing errors—or bugs—in a computer program.

**decision support system (DSS):** An information system designed to help make decisions in situations where there's uncertainty about the possible outcomes of those decisions.

**default program:** The program that's associated with a particular file type that automatically opens when a file of that type is double-clicked.

**defragmenter:** A disk utility that reorganizes fragmented files on a disk.

**desktop computer:** A personal computer that's designed to sit on a user's desk.

**denial-of-service attack:** An attack that sends out so much traffic that it could cripple a server or network.

**device driver:** A piece of software that acts as a translator, enhancing the capabilities of the operating system by enabling it to communicate with hardware.

**dial-up:** Internet access over ordinary telephone lines. The maximum speed of dial-up is 56 Kbps.

**digital footprint:** All the information that someone could find out about you by searching the Web, including social network sites.

**digital rights management (DRM):** A technology that is applied to digital media files, such as music, e-books, and videos, to impose restrictions on the use of these files.

**digital single lens reflex (D-SLR) camera:** A digital camera that uses interchangeable lenses, can be manually focused, and can cost thousands of dollars. D-SLR cameras give the user more control than point-and-shoot cameras.

**distributed computing:** The distribution of the processing of a task across a group of computers.

**DLP (digital light-processing) projector:** A projector that uses hundreds of thousands of tiny swiveling mirrors to create an image. They produce high-contrast images with deep blacks but are limited by having weaker reds and yellows.

**DNS (Domain Name System):** The service that allows you to use a friendly name, such as google.com, instead of an IP address, such as 74.125.224.72, to contact a website.

**document management system:** The ability to save, share, search, and audit electronic documents throughout their life cycle.

**domain:** A network composed of a group of clients and servers under the control of one central server.

**domain name:** The part of a URL that precedes the TLD and is sometimes called the second-level domain. The domain name represents a company or product name and makes it easy to remember the address.

**donationware:** A form of freeware where the developers accept donations, either for themselves or for a nonprofit organization.

**drive controller:** Located on the motherboard, it provides a drive interface, which connects disk drives to the processor.

**DSL (digital subscriber line):** Internet access over telephone lines designed to carry digital signals. DSL speeds range from 384 Kbps to 15 Mbps.

**DVD (digital video disc/digital versatile disc):** An optical disc that can hold about 4.7 GB of information (single-layer [SL]). Double-layer (DL) DVDs have a second layer to store data and can hold about 8.5 GB.

**dye-sublimation printer:** A printer that uses heat to turn solid dye into a gas that is then transferred to special paper.

**e-commerce:** Business on the Web; often broken into three categories: B2B, B2C, and C2C, where B stands for business and C stands for consumer.

**EIDE (enhanced integrated drive electronics):** A legacy drive interface found on the motherboard of older personal computers.

**email:** A system of sending electronic messages using store-and-forward technology.

**embedded computer:** A specialized computer found in ordinary devices, such as gasoline pumps, supermarket checkouts, traffic lights, and home appliances.

**embedded operating system:** A specialized operating system that runs on GPS devices, ATMs, smartphones, and other devices.

**encryption:** The process of converting unencrypted, plain text into code called ciphertext.

**ENIAC (Electronic Numerical Integrator and Computer):** The first working, digital, general-purpose computer.

**e-reader:** A tablet designed primarily for reading.

**Ethernet:** The most commonly used standard that defines the way data is transmitted over a local area network.

**e-waste:** Electronic waste, including old computers, cell phones, TVs, VCRs, and other electronic devices, some of which are considered hazardous.

**ergonomics:** The study of the relationship between workers and their workspaces.

**EULA (end-user license agreement):** License agreement between the software user and the software publisher.

**expansion card:** A card that plugs directly into an expansion slot on a motherboard and allows you to connect additional peripheral devices to a computer. Video cards, sound cards, network cards, TV tuners, and modems are common expansion cards. Also called adapter cards.

**expert system:** An information system programmed to make decisions in real-life situations (for example, diagnosing diseases based on symptoms).

**feasibility study:** The study created by a project team that includes the creation of the terms of reference or project charter, which states the objectives and scope of the project, the timeline for the project, risks, participants, deliverables, and budget. The four types of feasibility are economic, technical, operational, and political.

**fiber-to-the-home (FTTH):** Internet access over fiber optic cables. FTTH speed ranges up to 150 Mbps.

**field:** A single piece of information in a record in a database. For example, in a phone book record, the fields would be name, address, phone number.

**File Explorer:** The window you use to work with files, libraries, or folders on a Windows computer.

**file extension:** The second part of the file name. The extension is assigned by the program that is used to create the file and is used by the operating system to determine the type of file.

**fifth-generation language (5GL):** A system that allows the user to work with it without actually writing code. 5GLs are primarily used in artificial intelligence applications and in combination with Platform-as-a-Service (PaaS) application development.

**file fragmentation:** Unorganized files that are broken into small pieces that are stored in nonadjacent or noncontiguous clusters on the disk.

**file management:** The processes of opening, closing, saving, naming, deleting, and organizing digital files.

**file name:** The property of a file that's used to identify it using a name and file extension.

**file property:** Information about a file, such as authors, size, type, and date, which can be used to organize, sort, and find files more easily.

**file system:** Keeps track of what files are saved and where they're stored on the disk.

**Finder:** The tool you use to work with files and folders on a Mac computer.

**firewall:** A device that blocks unauthorized access to a network.

**FireWire:** A hot-swappable port that can connect up to 63 devices per port. It also allows for peer-to-peer communication between devices, such as two video cameras, without the use of a computer. Also known as IEEE 1394.

**first-generation language (1GL):** A machine language written in binary that can be understood by a computer.

**flash drive:** A small, portable, solid-state drive that can hold up to 128 GB of information. They have become the standard for transporting data. Also called key drives, thumb drives, pen drives, or jump drives.

**flash memory:** The technology used by solid-state storage devices, such as flash drives and memory cards, to store data. The data is stored on a chip.

**flat file database:** The simplest type of database that consists of a single list of items.

**flowchart:** A graphic view of an algorithm.

**folder:** A container used to store and organize files on a computer.

**folksonomy:** The social tagging of Web media.

**form:** A database object that makes it easier to enter data into a database and displays information in an easy-to-read layout.

**format:** The process of preparing a disk to store files by dividing it into tracks and sectors and setting up the file system.

**forum:** An online, asynchronous conversation, also known as a discussion board.

**fourth-generation language (4GL):** A computer language that's designed to be closer to natural language than 3GLs. Some programming knowledge is still needed to work effectively with 4GLs. Many 4GLs are used to access databases.

**freeware:** Software that can be used at no cost for an unlimited period of time.

**fuzzy logic:** A process used in artificial intelligence applications that recognizes that not everything can be broken down to true or false answers.

**game controller:** A type of input device that's used to interact with video games.

**gigahertz (GHz):** Used to measure the speed at which a processer executes the information cycle. A GHz is equal to one billion cycles per second.

**GIS (geographic information system):** An information system that combines layers—or datasets—of geographically referenced information about Earth's surface.

**GPS (global positioning system):** A system of 24 satellites that transmit signals that can be picked up by a receiver on the ground and used to determine the receiver's current location, time, and velocity through triangulation of the signals.

**graphical user interface (GUI):** The interface between a user and the computer. A GUI allows a user to point to and click on objects, such as icons and buttons, to initiate commands.

**green code:** Computer code written efficiently so the program runs on the hardware with minimal impact.

**green computing:** The efficient and eco-friendly use of computers and other electronics.

**grid computing:** Distributed computing using a few computers in one location.

**hacking:** The act of gaining unauthorized access to a computer system or network.

**hacktivism:** Gaining unauthorized access to a computer system or network to make a political statement.

**handheld:** *See* mobile device

**hard drive:** The main mass-storage device in a computer. A form of nonvolatile storage; when the computer is powered off, the data isn't lost. The primary hard drive holds the operating system, programs, and data files. Also called hard disk or hard disk drive.

**hardware:** The physical components of a computer.

**headphones:** An output device that converts digital signals into sound. They come in several different sizes and styles, ranging from tiny earbuds that fit inside your ear to full-size headphones that completely cover your outer ear. Headphones that also include a microphone are called headsets.

**hierarchy:** The folder structure created by Windows is a hierarchy. There are folders within folders, which are known as subfolders or children.

**homegroup:** A simple way to network a group of Windows computers that are all on the same home network.

**home page:** 1. The Web page that appears when you first open your browser. 2. The home page of a website is the main or starting page.

**hotspot:** A public wireless access point often available in public locations, such as airports, schools, hotels, and restaurants.

**hot-swappable:** A device that can be plugged and unplugged without turning off the computer.

**HTML (hypertext markup language):** The authoring language that defines the structure of a Web page.

**Human Genome Project (HGP):** A research project that determined the sequence of chemical base pairs that compose DNA and mapped the approximately 20,000–25,000 human genes.

**hyperlink:** A connection between pieces of information in documents written using hypertext.

**hypertext:** Text that contains links to other text and allows you to navigate through pieces of information by using the links that connect them.

**identity theft:** The form of cybercrime when someone uses your name, Social Security number, or bank or credit card number for financial gain.

**IAFIS (Integrated Automated Fingerprint Identification System):** A national fingerprint and criminal history system maintained by the FBI and used by local, state, and federal law enforcement. IAFIS is the largest biometric database in the world.

**IEEE 1394:** See FireWire.

**information:** The processed, useful form of data.

**information processing cycle (IPC):** The process a computer uses to convert data into information. The four steps of the IPC are input, processing, storage, and output.

**information system:** The people, hardware, and software that support data-intensive applications such as financial accounts, human resources, and other business transactions.

**Infrastructure-as-a-Service (IaaS):** Part of cloud computing. IaaS is the use of Internet-based servers.

**infrastructure wireless network:** A wireless network in which devices connect through a wireless access point.

**inkjet printer:** The most common personal printer, the inkjet works by spraying droplets of ink onto paper.

**input device:** A device that's used to get data into the computer system so it can be processed.

**instant messaging (IM):** A real-time online conversation between two people.

**instruction cycle:** The steps a CPU uses to process data: fetch, decode, execute, also store. Also known as the fetch-and-execute cycle or the machine cycle.

**integrated circuit:** A silicon chip that contains a large number of tiny transistors.

**integrated development environment (IDE):** A complete system for developing software, typically consisting of a code editor, one or more compilers, one or more SDKs, and a debugger.

**Internet (net):** The global network of computer networks.

**Internet backbone:** The high-speed connection point between networks that make up the Internet.

**Internet Crime Complaint Center (IC3):** The place for victims to report cybercrimes.

**Internet Exchange Points:** The backbone of the modern Internet.

**Internet2 (I2):** A second Internet designed for education, research, and collaboration.

**Internet service provider (ISP):** A company that offers Internet access.

**IP (Internet protocol):** The protocol responsible for addressing and routing packets to their destination.

**IP (Internet protocol) address:** A unique numeric address assigned to each node on a network.

**iOS:** A mobile operating system found on iPods, iPhones, and iPads.

**iOS device:** Devices that run the iOS mobile operating system: iPad, iPod, or iPhone.

**Joint Application Development (JAD):** A collaborative system development process that involves the end user throughout the design and development of the project through a series of JAD sessions.

**joystick:** An input device mounted on a base that consists of a stick, buttons, and sometimes a trigger. Typically used as a game controller, especially in flight-simulator games, a joystick may also be used for such tasks as controlling robotic machinery in a factory.

**keyboard:** An input device that consists of alphabet keys, numeric keys, and other specialized keys.

**keylogger:** A computer program that captures information a user enters on a keyboard.

**keypad:** A small keyboard that doesn't contain all the alphabet keys.

**laser printer:** The most common type of printers found in schools and businesses. They use a laser beam to draw an image on a drum. The image is electrostatically charged and attracts a dry ink called toner. The drum is then rolled over paper, and the toner is deposited on the paper. Finally, the paper is heated, bonding the ink to it.

**LCD (liquid crystal display):** The most common type of display found on desktop and notebook computers. They consist of two layers of glass that are glued together with a layer of liquid crystals between them. When electricity is passed through the individual crystals, it causes them to pass or block light to create an image.

**LCD projector:** A projector that passes light through a prism, which divides the light into three beams—red, green, and blue—which are then passed through an LCD screen.

**legacy technology:** Old technology that's still used alongside its more modern replacement, typically because it still works and is cost-effective.

**library:** Designed to help you organize your files on a Windows computer. There are four libraries: Documents, Music, Pictures, and Videos. You can use these folders to gather files that are located in different locations.

**Linux:** An open source operating system distribution that contains the Linux kernel and bundled utilities and applications.

**local area network (LAN):** A network that has all connected devices or nodes located in the same physical location.

**logic bomb:** An attack that occurs when certain conditions are met.

**logic error:** An error in programming logic that results in an unexpected outcome.

**lossless compression:** Uses a compression algorithm that looks for the redundancy in a file and creates an encoded file by removing the redundant information. When the file is decompressed, all the information from the original file is restored.

**lossy compression:** Uses a compression algorithm on files that contain more information than humans can typically discern (typically images, audio, and video files). That extra information is removed from the file. It's not possible to decompress this file, as the information has been removed from the file.

**LTE (Long Term Evolution):** A means of connecting to the Internet using cellular networks that provides 4G service.

**Mac:** A personal computer manufactured by Apple. Also referred to as a Macintosh.

**machine language:** A programming language written in binary that can be understood by a computer.

**macro:** A small program used to automate tasks in applications such as Word and Excel.

**malware:** Any computer program that's designed to be harmful or malicious.

**massively multiplayer online role-playing games (MMORPG):** An online game in which players interact with people in real time in a virtual world using an avatar, or virtual body.

**mainframe:** A large multiuser computer that can perform millions of transactions in a day.

**management information system (MIS):** An information system that includes software, hardware, data resources (such as databases), decision support systems, people, and project management applications.

**memory:** Temporary storage that's used by a computer to hold instructions and data.

**memory card:** A form of solid-state storage used to expand the storage of digital cameras, video games, and other devices.

**metropolitan area network (MAN):** A network that covers a single geographic area.

**microblogging:** A form of blogging where posts are limited to a small number of characters and users post updates frequently. Twitter is a microblog site.

**microphone:** An input device that converts sound into digital signals and is used to chat in real time or as part of voice-recognition applications used in video games and for dictating text.

**microprocessor:** A complex integrated circuit that contains the central processing unit (CPU) of a computer.

**Microsoft Windows:** The operating system found on most personal computers.

**minicomputer:** The smallest multiuser computer. Users connect to a minicomputer via dumb terminals, which have no processing capabilities of their own.

**mobile application (mobile app):** Downloadable application that extends the functionality of a mobile device.

**mobile browser (microbrowser):** A Web browser optimized for small screen devices, such as smartphones and tablets.

**mobile device:** A device such as a smartphone or tablet. A pocket-sized computer we carry with us wherever we go.

**mobile operating system:** An embedded operating system that runs on mobile devices such as smartphones and tablets and is more full-featured than other embedded OSs.

**modem:** A communication device used to connect a computer to a telephone line, modems are most often used for dial-up Internet access. Modem is short for modulator-demodulator. A modem modulates digital data into an analog signal that can be transmitted over a phone line and, on the receiving end, demodulates the analog signal back into a digital data.

**monitor:** A video output device that works by lighting up pixels on a screen. Each pixel contains three colors: red, green, and blue (RGB). From that base, all colors can be created by varying the intensities of the three colors.

**Moore's Law:** An observation made by Gordon Moore in 1965 that the number of transistors that can be placed on an integrated circuit had doubled roughly every 2 years. The current trend is closer to doubling every 18 months and is expected to continue for another 10 to 20 years.

**motherboard:** The main circuit board of a computer. It houses the CPU, drive controllers and interfaces, expansion slots, data buses, ports and connectors, BIOS, and memory and may also include integrated peripherals, such as video, sound, and network cards. It provides the way for devices to attach to your computer.

**mouse:** An input device that allows a user to interact with objects by moving a pointer, also called a cursor, on the computer screen. It may include one or more buttons and a scroll wheel and works by moving across a smooth surface to signal movement of the pointer.

**MP3:** MPEG-1 Audio Layer 3. A common audio file type used for music files. MP3 is a lossy form of compression that works by removing some of the detail. There is a trade-off between file size and quality.

**MP3 player:** A handheld device that allows you to carry with you thousands of songs and podcasts, so you can listen to them wherever you are. Also called portable media player if it supports photos and videos.

**multi-core processor:** A processor that consists of two or more processors integrated on a single chip. Multi-core processing increases the processing speed over single-core processors and reduces energy consumption over multiple separate processors.

**multidimensional database (MDB):** A type of database optimized for storing and utilizing data. It may be created using input from existing relational databases, but it structures the information into multidimensional data cubes.

**multifunction device:** A printer device with a built-in scanner and sometimes fax capabilities. Also known as an all-in-one printer.

**multimedia:** The integration of text, graphics, video, animation, and sound content.

**multitasking:** The ability to do more than one task at a time.

**multiuser computer:** A system that allows multiple, simultaneous users to connect to it, allowing for centralized resources and security. Multiuser computers are also more powerful than personal computers.

**municipal WiFi:** Wireless Internet access available in some cities and towns.

**netbook:** A lightweight, inexpensive notebook computer designed primarily for Internet access. Netbooks have built-in wireless capabilities but have small screens and offer limited computing power and storage.

**network adapter:** A communication device used to establish a connection with a network. The adapter may be onboard, an expansion card, or a USB device and may be wired or wireless.

**network address translation (NAT):** A security feature of a router that shields the devices on a private network from the public network (Internet).

**network operating system (NOS):** A specialized operating system found on servers in a client-server network that provides services requested by the client computers, such as file services, printing services, centralized security, and communication services.

**network resource:** The software, hardware, or files shared on a network.

**neural network:** A system that simulates human thinking by emulating the biological connections—or neurons—of the human brain.

**notebook:** A portable personal computer. Also referred to as a laptop.

**object-oriented database (OODB):** A type of database in which data is stored as objects, which are used by modern programming languages, such as C++ and Java. Often used to create databases that have more complicated types of data, such as images, audio, and video.

**object-oriented programming:** A programming model that defines objects and the actions that can be performed on them.

**office application suite:** A suite of productivity applications— such as a word processor, spreadsheet, presentation program, database, and personal information manager— integrated into a single package.

**office support system (OSS):** An information system that consists of the software and hardware that improve the productivity of employees by automating common tasks.

**OLED (organic light-emitting diode):** A new technology used in monitors that are composed of extremely thin panels of organic molecules sandwiched between two electrodes.

**open source:** Software that has its source code published and made available to the public, enabling anyone to copy, modify, and redistribute it without paying fees.

**online analytical processing (OLAP):** A system that enables a user to selectively extract and view data from different points of view and can be used for data mining or discovering relationships between data items.

**operating system (OS):** The system software that provides the user with the interface to communicate with the hardware and software on a computer. A computer can't run without an operating system installed.

**optical disc:** A form of removable storage. Data is stored on these discs using a laser to either melt the disc material or change the color of embedded dye. A laser can read the variations as binary data.

**optical network terminal (ONT):** The device that connects a LAN to a FTTH network.

**OS X:** The operating system installed on Macintosh computers.

**output device:** A device that returns information to the user.

**path:** The sequence of folders to a file or folder.

**payload:** The action or attack by a computer virus or other malware.

**PC:** A small microprocessor-based computer designed to be used by one person at a time.

**PCI (peripheral component interconnect):** The most common type of expansion slot on a motherboard that an expansion card plugs into.

**PCI express (PCIe):** A faster version of PCI that's typically used to connect a video card.

**peer-to-peer network (P2P):** A network in which each computer is considered equal. Each device can share its resources with every other device, and there's no centralized authority.

**peripheral device:** The components that serve the input, output, and storage functions of a computer system.

**personal area network (PAN):** A LAN that consists of devices connected by Bluetooth.

**personal computer:** *See* PC

**personal information manager (PIM):** A program used to manage email, calendar, and tasks and is often part of an office suite.

**pharming:** A form of cybercrime that redirects you to a phony website even if you type the right address into your browser.

**phishing:** A form of cybercrime that uses email messages and IMs that appear to be from those you do business with, such as your bank, credit card company, social network, auction site, online payment processor, or IT administrator. Messages are designed to trick you into revealing information.

**photo printer:** A printer designed to print high-quality photos on special photo paper. Photo printers can be inkjet printers that use special ink cartridges or dye-sublimation printers, which produce lab-quality prints.

**PictBridge:** An industry standard that allows a camera to connect directly to a printer, usually by a USB connection or special dock.

**piggybacking:** Using an open wireless network to access the Internet without permission.

**pipelining:** A method used by a single processor to improve performance. As soon as the first instruction has moved from the fetch to the decode stage, the processor fetches the next instruction.

**pixel:** A single point on a display screen. Short for picture elements. Each pixel contains three colors: red, green, and blue (RGB). From that base, all colors can be created by varying the intensities of the three colors.

**plasma monitor:** A large display type that works by passing an electric current through gas sealed in thousands of cells inside the screen. The current excites the gas, which in turn excites the phosphors that coat the screen to pass light through an image.

**Platform-as-a-Service (PaaS):** Part of cloud computing. PaaS is an online programming environment used to develop, deploy, and manage custom Web applications.

**plotter:** A printer that uses one or more pens to draw an image on a roll of paper.

**Plug and Play (PnP):** An operating system feature that allows you to easily add new hardware to a computer system. When you plug in a new piece of hardware, the OS detects it and helps you set it up.

**plug-in:** A third-party program that extends the functionality of a browser.

**podcast:** A prerecorded radio- and TV-like show that you can download and listen to or watch any time.

**podcast client:** A program used to locate, subscribe to, and play podcasts.

**point-and-shoot camera:** The simplest, least expensive digital camera type and has the fewest features.

**port:** A way to connect a peripheral device to a motherboard.

**portable apps:** Application software that can be run from a flash drive.

**portable media player:** A handheld device that allows you to carry with you thousands of songs and podcasts (and perhaps photos, videos, and games), so you can play them wherever you are. Also called MP3 player.

**primary key:** A field that uniquely identifies the record in the table.

**procedural programming:** A programming model that uses a step-by-step list of instructions.

**processor:** See CPU.

**Program Development Cycle:** A set of steps that a programmer follows to create a computer program.

**project manager (PM):** The leader of the project team who coordinates the project team and keeps the project on track.

**projector:** A video output device typically used when making a presentation or sharing media with a group in such places as classrooms, businesses, and home theaters because they can produce larger output than a monitor.

**project management software:** An application designed to help you to complete projects, keep within your budget, stay on schedule, and collaborate with others.

**protocol:** The rules for communication between devices that determine how data is formatted, transmitted, received, and acknowledged.

**pseudocode:** The expression of the steps of an algorithm using English-like statements that focus on logic, not syntax.

**Public folder:** The folder that is common to all users on a computer and provides an easy way to share files between them.

**query:** A database object that retrieves specific data from one or more tables to answer a question.

**QR code reader:** A program on a mobile device that can scan and decode the information found in a QR code such as a URL or more information about a product.

**RAM (random access memory):** A form of volatile memory that holds the operating systems, programs, and data the computer is currently using. Any information left in memory is lost when the power is turned off.

**Rapid Application Development (RAD):** An iterative development process that uses prototyping and user testing of the designs. RAD tools use object-oriented programming (OOP) and reusable code modules to speed the process.

**record:** A row of data in a database table that describes a particular entry in the database—for example, a customer or product.

**relational database:** The most common type of database, which consists of multiple tables or relations that are related by common information.

**report:** A database object that displays the data from a table or a query in an easy-to-read-and-print format.

**resolution:** The number of horizontal pixels by vertical pixels, for example 1280 × 1024 or 1024 × 768, on a display screen. The higher the resolution, the sharper the image.

**retail software:** The user pays a fee to use the software for an unlimited period of time.

**RFID tag:** A tag that can be read by an RFID (radio frequency identification) scanner. It contains a tiny antenna for receiving and sending a radio frequency signal.

**ROM (read-only memory):** A nonvolatile form of memory that doesn't need power to keep its data.

**rootkit:** A set of programs that allows someone to gain control over a computer system while hiding the fact that the computer has been compromised.

**router:** A device that connects two or more networks together. A router uses address information to route the data packets it receives to the correct locations.

**RSS (Really Simple Syndication):** A format used for distributing Web feeds that change frequently—for example, blogs, podcasts, and news—to subscribers.

**runtime error:** An error that occurs when a program is running and something entered causes it to crash.

**SATA (serial ATA):** The standard internal drive interface.

**satellite Internet access:** A means of connecting to the Internet using communication satellites.

**scanner:** An input device that can increase the speed and accuracy of data entry and convert information into a digital format that can be saved, copied, and manipulated.

**screen capture** —A software tool that allows you to create a video of what happens on your computer screen.

**search engine:** A database that indexes the Web.

**second-generation language (2GL):** An assembly language. This generation of languages has to be converted into a machine language by an assembler before the computer can execute it.

**security suite:** A package of security software that includes a combination of features such as antivirus, firewall, and privacy protection.

**serial and parallel ports:** Legacy ports used to connect peripheral devices to a computer.

**server:** A multiuser computer system that provides services, such as Internet access, email, or file and print services, to client systems.

**server-side program:** A program that runs on a Web server instead of the client computer. No special software is needed by the client.

**shareware:** Software offered in trial form or for a limited period that allows the user to try it out before purchasing a license.

**shutter lag:** The time between pressing the shutter button and the camera snapping the picture.

**smartphone:** A multifunction device that blends phone, PDA, and portable media player features. Popular in both the business and personal markets.

**social bookmarking site:** A site that allows you to save and share your bookmarks or favorites online.

**social media:** A collection of tools that enables users to create user-generated content, connect, network, and share.

**social media marketing (SMM):** The practice of using social media sites to sell products and services.

**social network:** An online community that combines many of the features of the other online tools.

**social news site:** An online news site that allows the community to submit content they discover on the Web and puts it in one place for everyone to see and to discuss.

**social review site:** A website where users review hotels, movies, games, books, and other products and services.

**Software-as-a-Service (SaaS):** Part of cloud computing. SaaS is the delivery of applications—or Web apps—over the Internet.

**software development kit (SDK):** A bundle of libraries and tools that are developed for a particular platform.

**solid-state drive:** A small drive often used in small electronic devices, such as media players and cell phones, as well as in notebooks and netbooks.

**solid-state storage:** A nonmechanical form of storage that uses flash memory to store data on a chip.

**sound card:** An expansion card that provides audio connections for both input devices (microphones and synthesizers) and output devices (speakers and headphones).

**spam:** The sending of mass, unsolicited emails.

**speakers:** An output device that converts digital signals from a computer or media player into sound.

**speech recognition:** A feature that allows users to use a computer without a keyboard by speaking commands. It can be used for such tasks as automatically providing customer service through a call center, dialing a cell phone, or even dictating a term paper.

**spreadsheet:** An application that creates electronic worksheets composed of rows and columns. Spreadsheets are used for mathematical applications, such as budgeting, grade books, and inventory. Spreadsheets are also good at organizing data so it can be sorted, filtered, and rearranged, making them useful for things that don't involve calculations, such as address lists and schedules.

**spyware:** A form of malware that secretly gathers personal information about you.

**SSID (service set identifier):** The name of a wireless network.

**stakeholder:** A person who has an interest in and will be affected by the successful completion of a project.

**storage area network (SAN):** A network between the data storage devices and the servers on a network that makes the data accessible to all servers in the SAN. Normal users are not part of the SAN but are able to access the information through the LAN servers.

**streaming:** Media, such as video or audio, begins to play immediately as it is being received and does not require the whole file to be downloaded to your computer first.

**Structured Query Language (SQL):** The most common query language used to create database queries.

**stylus:** A special pen-like input tool used by tablet computers, graphic design tablets, PDAs, and other handheld devices.

**supercomputer:** A very expensive computer system that's used to perform complex mathematical calculations, such as those used in weather forecasting and medical research.

**switch:** A device that connects multiple devices on a LAN and uses address information to send data packets only to the port that the appropriate device is connected to.

**synchronous online communication:** A form of online communication that requires the participants to be online at the same time—for example, chat and instant messaging.

**System Development Life Cycle (SDLC):** The traditional model for system development that consists of five phases: planning, analysis, design, implementation, and maintenance.

**system requirements:** The minimum hardware and software specifications required to run a software application.

**syntax error:** An error in the way code is written.

**syntax rules:** The rules that define the correct construction of commands in a programming language.

**system software:** The software that makes the computer run.

**system unit:** The case that encloses and protects the power supply, motherboard, CPU, and memory of a computer. It also has drive bays to hold the storage devices and openings for peripheral devices to connect to expansion cards on the motherboard.

**table:** A database object in which data is stored. It's arranged in rows and columns.

**tablet:** A handheld, mobile device somewhere between a computer and a smartphone that runs a mobile operating system.

**tablet PC:** A type of notebook computer that has a screen that can swivel to fold into what resembles a notepad or tablet. They include a special digital pen or stylus that allows the user to write directly on the screen.

**tagging:** Labeling images or files with keywords to make it easier to organize and search for them.

**TCP (transmission control protocol):** The protocol responsible for assuring that data packets are transmitted reliably on a network.

**TCP/IP protocol stack:** A suite of protocols that defines everything from how to transfer files (FTP) and Web pages (HTTP) to sending (SMTP) and receiving (POP) email. TCP/IP is the protocol stack that runs on the Internet, and because of this, it's also the protocol stack that runs on most LANs.

**thermal printer:** A printer that creates an image by heating specially coated heat-sensitive paper, which changes color where the heat is applied.

**third-generation language (3GL):** Most modern programming languages. Both procedural and object-oriented programming (OOP) languages fall in this category. A compiler is needed to convert the code into machine language the computer can understand and execute.

**time bomb:** A form of logic bomb where the attack is triggered by a specific time and date.

**top-level domain (TLD):** The suffix, such as .com or .edu, that follows the domain name in a URL.

**topology:** The physical layout of a computer network.

**touchpad:** An input device typically found on a notebook computer instead of a mouse. Motion is detected by moving your finger across the touch-sensitive surface.

**touchscreen:** An input device that can accept input from a finger or stylus.

**transaction-processing system (TPS):** An information system that links the multiple operations that make up a transaction together and ensures that all operations in a transaction are completed without error.

**transistor:** A tiny electric switch used in second-generation computers.

**ubiquitous computing (ubicomp):** Technology recedes into the background and becomes part of our environment.

**Trojan horse:** A program that appears to be a legitimate program but is actually something malicious instead.

**Unicode:** An extended ASCII set that has become the standard on the Internet and includes codes for most of the world's written languages, mathematical systems, and special characters. It has codes for more than 100,000 characters.

**URL (uniform resource locator):** An address, such as http://google.com, that consists of three main parts: protocol (http), domain name (google), and top-level domain (.com).

**USB (universal serial bus):** A standard port type that's used to connect many kinds of devices, including printers, mice, keyboards, digital cameras, cell phones, and external drives. Up to 127 devices can share a single USB port.

**USB hub:** A device used to connect multiple USB devices to a single USB port.

**User Account Control (UAC):** A Windows security feature that notifies you before allowing changes to be made on your computer.

**user-generated content:** Web content created by ordinary users.

**utility software:** A type of system software used to perform computer maintenance.

**vacuum tube:** A tube that resembles an incandescent lightbulb and was used in first-generation computers.

**video card:** An expansion card that provides the data signal and connection for a monitor or projector. It may also include input ports to connect a TV tuner or another video device to the system.

**video game system:** A computer that's designed primarily to play games.

**viral video:** A video that becomes extremely popular because of recommendations and social sharing.

**virtual private network (VPN):** A private network through the public network (Internet) that allows remote users to access a LAN securely. Such networks use encryption to ensure data security.

**virus:** A program that replicates itself and infects computers. A virus needs a host file to travel on, such as a game.

**VoIP (voice over IP):** A service that allows phone calls to be transmitted over the Internet instead of traditional phone lines.

**volunteer computing:** A form of distributed computing that relies on the processing power of hundreds or thousands of volunteers' personal computers.

**wardriving:** The practice of driving around and locating open wireless access points.

**wearable:** A computer designed to be worn on the body.

**Web 2.0:** New technologies used to communicate and collaborate on the Web. Web 2.0 tools rely on crowd-sourcing and enable users to create user-generated content, connect, and network. They are also called social media.

**Web browser:** A program that interprets HTML to display Web pages as you browse the Internet.

**webcam:** A specialized video camera that provides visual input for online communication, such as Web conferencing or chatting.

**webcasting:** Broadcasting on the Web.

**Web page:** Information on the Internet, written in HTML, that can be viewed with a Web browser.

**website:** One or more related Web pages that are all located in the same place.

**wide area network (WAN):** A network that spans multiple locations and connects multiple LANs over dedicated lines using routers.

**WiFi:** The type of wireless network found in homes and public hotspots.

**wiki:** A website that allows users to edit content, even if it was written by someone else.

**WiMAX Mobile Internet:** A means of connecting to the Internet using cellular networks that provides 4G service.

**Windows Experience Index:** A rating system that assesses the operating system version, processor type and speed, and amount of memory installed as well as your video card performance to determine the types of software that your computer can run.

**wireless access point (WAP):** A device that allows wireless devices to join a network much like a switch.

**wireless encryption:** Adds security to a wireless network by encrypting transmitted data.

**wireless LAN (WLAN):** A network that uses WiFi to transmit data.

**word processor:** An application that is used to create, edit, and format text documents. The documents can also contain images.

**workgroup:** The devices in a peer-to-peer network.

**workstation:** A high-end desktop computer or one that's attached to a network in a business setting.

**World Wide Web:** The hypertext system of information on the Internet that allows you to navigate through pieces of information by using hyperlinks that connect them.

**worm:** A form of self-replicating malware that doesn't need a host to travel. Worms travel over networks and spread over the network connections without any human intervention.

**zoom:** Making objects appear closer (telephoto) or farther (wide-angle) away.

# Index

# Photo Credits

Photo Credits

12-14a: djgis/ Shutterstock

12-14b: Ronen/ Shutterstock

12-15UN: Seregam/ Shutterstock

12-16UN: Ruslan Semichev/ Shutterstock

12-18UN: Tonis Pan/ Shutterstock

12-19UN: Danshutter/ Shutterstock

12-21UN: Perov Stanislav/ Shutterstock

12-22UN: Arlush/ Shutterstock

12-23UN: Lorelyn Medina/ Shutterstock

12-25UN: VikaSuh/ Shutterstock

12-26UN: artiomp/ Shutterstock

12-27UN: STILLFX/ Shutterstock

12-28UN: Andreas G Karelias/ Shutterstock

12-29UN:Simon Krzic/ Shutterstock

12-30UN:oknoart/ Shutterstock

k12-06UN:Levent Konuk/ Shutterstock

k12-12aSFC/ Shutterstock

k12-13-snowdrop/ Shutterstock

k12-17UN:Magnum Johansson/ Shutterstock

k12-20UN:DNY59/ iStockphoto.com

k12-24UN:Sergey Peterman/ Shutterstock